Streaming Media Architectures, Techniques, and Applications:
Recent Advances

Ce Zhu
Nanyang Technological University, Singapore

Yuenan Li
Tianjin University, China

Xiamu Niu
Harbin Institute of Technology, China

INFORMATION SCIENCE REFERENCE

Hershey · New York

Director of Editorial Content:	Kristin Klinger
Director of Book Publications:	Julia Mosemann
Acquisitions Editor:	Lindsay Johnston
Development Editor:	Michael Killian
Publishing Assistant:	Milan Vracarich Jr.
Typesetter:	Michael Brehm
Production Editor:	Jamie Snavely
Cover Design:	Lisa Tosheff

Published in the United States of America by
Information Science Reference (an imprint of IGI Global)
701 E. Chocolate Avenue
Hershey PA 17033
Tel: 717-533-8845
Fax: 717-533-8661
E-mail: cust@igi-global.com
Web site: http://www.igi-global.com

Copyright © 2011 by IGI Global. All rights reserved. No part of this publication may be reproduced, stored or distributed in any form or by any means, electronic or mechanical, including photocopying, without written permission from the publisher. Product or company names used in this set are for identification purposes only. Inclusion of the names of the products or companies does not indicate a claim of ownership by IGI Global of the trademark or registered trademark.

Library of Congress Cataloging-in-Publication Data

Streaming media architectures, techniques and applications : recent advances
/ Ce Zhu, Yuenan Li, and Xiamu Niu, editors.
     p. cm.
  Includes bibliographical references and index.
  Summary: "This book spans a number of interdependent and emerging topics in streaming media, offering a comprehensive collection of topics including media coding, wireless/mobile video, P2P media streaming, and applications of streaming media"--Provided by publisher.
  ISBN 978-1-61692-831-5 (hardcover) -- ISBN 978-1-61692-833-9 (ebook) 1. Streaming technology (Telecommunications) I. Zhu, Ce, 1969- II. Li, Yuenan, 1981- III. Niu, Xiamu, 1961-
  TK5105.386.S3746 2011
  006.7--dc22
                          2010016311

British Cataloguing in Publication Data
A Cataloguing in Publication record for this book is available from the British Library.

All work contributed to this book is new, previously-unpublished material. The views expressed in this book are those of the authors, but not necessarily of the publisher.

Editorial Advisory Board

Ton Kalker, *Hewlett-Packard Laboratories, USA*
Chia-Wen Lin, *National Tsing Hua University, Taiwan*
King-Ngi Ngan, *The Chinese University of Hong Kong, China*
David Taubman, *University of New South Wales, Australia*
Shuo-Zhong Wang, *Shanghai University, China*
Stephen Wolthusen, *University of London, UK*
Wen-Jun Zeng, *University of Missouri, USA*

List of Reviewers

Alain Renaud, *Bournemouth University, UK*
Alexander Carôt, *University of Lübeck, Germany*
Béatrice Pesquet-Popescu, *TELECOM ParisTech, France*
C. -C. Jay Kuo, *University of Southern California, USA*
Ce Zhu, *Nanyang Technological University, Singapore*
Diego Perino, *Orange Labs, France*
Dimitris N. Kanellopoulos, *University of Patras, Greece*
Elsa Macias, *Grupo de Arquitectura y Concurrencia (GAC), Spain*
Fabien Mathieu, *Orange Labs, France*
Fabio Pianese, *Alcatel-Lucent Bell Labs, Belgium*
Hermann Hellwagner, *Klagenfurt University, Austria*
Hyunggon Park, *Swiss Federal Institute of Technology, Switzerland*
Kok Keong (Jonathan) Loo, *Brunel University, UK*
Michael Ransburg, *Klagenfurt University , Austria*
Mihaela van der Schaar, *University of California, Los Angeles (UCLA), USA*
Nayef Mendahawi, *Research In Motion, Canada*
Riccardo Bernardini, *Università di Udine – DIEGM, Italy*
Sasan Adibi, *Research In Motion, Canada*
Song Guo, *Boston University, USA.*
Xuguang Lan, *Xi'an Jiao Tong University, P. R. China*
Yongjin Cho, *University of Southern California, USA*

Yuenan Li, *Tianjin University, P. R. China*
Zhen Li, *Nanyang Technological University, Singapore*
Zhenfeng Shi, *Harbin Institute of Technology, P. R. China*
Zhenzhong Chen, *Nanyang Technological University, Singapore*

Table of Contents

Section 1
Media Coding

> *Hermann Hellwagner, Klagenfurt University, Austria*
> *Ingo Kofler, Klagenfurt University, Austria*
> *Michael Eberhard, Klagenfurt University, Austria*
> *Robert Kuschnig, Klagenfurt University, Austria*
> *Michael Ransburg, Klagenfurt University, Austria*
> *Michael Sablatschan, Klagenfurt University, Austria*

> *Dimitris N. Kanellopoulos, University of Patras, Greece*

> *Wei Xiang, University of Southern Queensland, Australia*
> *Ce Zhu, Nanyang Technological University, Singapore*
> *Chee Kheong Siew, Nanyang Technological University, Singapore*
> *Yuanyuan Xu, Nanyang Technological University, Singapore*
> *Minglei Liu, Nanyang Technological University, Singapore*

> *Kok Keong (Jonathan) Loo, Middlesex University, UK*
> *Myo Tun, Dialogic Corporation, Canada*
> *Yoong Choon Chang, Multimedia University, Malaysia*

Detailed Table of Contents

Section 1
Media Coding

Chapter 1

Hermann Hellwagner, Klagenfurt University, Austria
Ingo Kofler, Klagenfurt University, Austria
Michael Eberhard, Klagenfurt University, Austria
Robert Kuschnig, Klagenfurt University, Austria
Michael Ransburg, Klagenfurt University, Austria
Michael Sablatschan, Klagenfurt University, Austria

This chapter covers the topic of making use of scalable video content in streaming frameworks and applications. Specifically, the recent standard H.264/SVC, i.e., the scalable extension of the widely used H.264/AVC coding scheme, and its deployment for adaptive streaming, the combined activities of content adaptation and streaming, are considered.

Chapter 2

Dimitris N. Kanellopoulos, University of Patras, Greece

This chapter focuses on the application layer techniques that adapt to the changes in network conditions, including layered encoding, rate shaping, adaptive error control, and smoothing. The chapter also discusses operating system methods to support adaptive multimedia.

This chapter investigates two popular techniques for error-resilient H.264/SVC video transmission over packet erasure networks, i.e., layered video coding (LVC) and scalable multiple description coding (SMDC). The authors compare the respective advantages and disadvantages of these two coding techniques. A comprehensive literature review on latest advancement on SMDC is provided. A two-dimensional scalable multiple description coding (2-D SMDC) scheme is presented.

This chapter presents the fundamental architecture of Dirac video encoder that is engineered by British Broadcasting Corporation (BBC) aiming at a wide range of applications from storage of video content to streaming video. The overall encoding structure is discussed followed by the detail description of each coding component. Finally, the block diagram of Dirac's bitstream syntax is presented.

This chapter addresses the coding and streaming issues of 3D model. This chapter first surveys the typical algorithms in static and dynamic 3D meshes coding where the coding and streaming of gigantic 3D models are specially introduced. Moreover, the MPEG4 3D mesh model coding standard is also briefed. This chapter concludes with a discussion providing an overall picture of the developments in mesh coding and the directions for future research.

Section 2
Wireless / Mobile Video

This chapter introduces a cross-layer approach to wireless/mobile video streaming system design. Beginning with the introduction to the motivation of the cross-layer design, this chapter covers fundamental issues, challenges and solutions of the cross-layer approach to video streaming systems for its practical employment.

Chapter 7

This chapter proposes a complete streaming framework for a wireless, in particular a 3G/UMTS, network environment. The authors describe choices one can make in terms of network architecture and then focus on the input parameters used to evaluate network conditions and to perform the adaptation. A particular attention is dedicated to the protocol information that can be exploited to infer the channel state. In addition, each implementation choice is a compromise between the industrial feasibility and the adaptation efficiency.

Chapter 8

This chapter studies the technical issues of video streaming over both Mobile Ad Hoc Networks (MANETs) and Vehicular Ad Hoc Networks (VANETs). This chapter shows how streaming can take place in those challenging environments. Error resilience and path diversity are presented as the key to robust streaming. As a form of management of streaming, distributed sourcing via peer-to-peer streaming over diverse paths is explored within VANETs.

This chapter presents a comprehensive study on the transmission of scalable video over wireless local area networks (WLAN). The authors give an analysis of the mechanisms and principles of the emerging scalable video coding (SVC) standard. Moreover, some studies of SVC over WLAN using cross-layer design techniques are presented. The aim of this chapter is to exploit the unique characteristics of SVC, to enhance personalized experience and to improve system performance in a wireless transmission system.

Chapter 10

S. Guo, Boston University, USA
T.D.C. Little, Boston University, USA

This chapter focuses on the analysis of the state of the art video delivery and data routing techniques for wireless video sensor networks. This chapter is intended to inspire additional efforts leading to video routing techniques optimized to different topologies, the physical medium, network channels, and energy constraints.

Section 3
P2P Media Streaming

Chapter 11

Hyunggon Park, Ewha Womans University, Korea
Rafit Izhak Ratzin, University of California, Los Angeles (UCLA), USA
Mihaela van der Schaar, University of California, Los Angeles (UCLA), USA

This chapter discusses P2P systems that have been deployed in file sharing and real-time media streaming. The authors discuss the limitations of the implementations for existing P2P-based file sharing and media streaming applications in detail. More advanced resource reciprocation strategies, where peers make foresighted decisions on their resource distribution in a way that maximizes their cumulative utilities are also discussed.

Chapter 12

Fabio Pianese, Alcatel-Lucent Bell Labs, Belgium

This chapter presents a survey of "data-driven" or "unstructured" peer-to-peer live media streaming techniques, which have been introduced in the recent years to overcome the limitation of classic application-layer tree overlays.

Chapter 13

Diego Perino, Orange Labs, France
Fabien Mathieu, Orange Labs, France

This chapter is intended as an introduction of epidemic live streaming. In this chapter, the authors propose some simple metrics to understand the behavior of a diffusion algorithm, and they use elementary diffusion schemes to understand the basics of the diffusion process, for both homogeneous and heterogeneous systems. The proposed approach mixes theoretical results, when available, with empirical observations in order to give the best possible insights.

This chapter describes a P2P transport protocol suited for multimedia streaming. The described protocol is characterized by the robustness to data losses and the low-start times. From the application point of view, the proposed protocol appears as a transport protocol similar to TCP or UDP.

Section 4
Applications of Streaming Media

This chapter covers the technical issues related to the subject of playing live music with musicians distributed over the Internet. In this chapter, the author first outlines purely human cognitive restrictions in context with the problem of latency. Based on these restrictions, a comprehensive technical overview is given, finally leading to a taxonomy of appropriate interaction approaches.

This chapter embodies the chronological advances of 3GPP-PSS, whose specifications define the framework for streaming capabilities for 3GPP mobile devices and networks. The discussions on the general specifications of different releases are also provided in this chapter with a focus on the Quality of Service (QoS) support.

This chapter analyses the application of video-streaming in video-lectures. An overview of several related research topics is presented in this chapter, including video-lecture summarization, automatic extraction of text from the audio track, lecture segmentation, search, semantic indexing and multimodal access, gesture analysis, and annotation of the videos.

Preface

The advances in computation and networking, as well as the prevalence of media sharing on the net have significantly increased the availability of multimedia resources. There have been profound changes in the ways of multimedia acquisition, distribution and consumption. Streaming media is one of the most exciting and active research topics with continuing significant progress in the multimedia area, where streaming media has been experiencing dramatic growth and stepped into mainstream media communications. Multimedia data including speech, audio, animation and video is transmitted as a continuous stream in streaming media. As a result, the end user can enjoy on-the-fly representation of multimedia content without downloading the entire file beforehand. Consequently, real-time, interactive and progressive access to multimedia becomes a reality with the advent of streaming media. In the past decade, we have witnessed the great success of streaming media in network broadcasting, distant learning, digital library, and video on demand (VOD) among others. Nowadays, streaming media based services are becoming the mainstream of multimedia consumption. Motivated by its wide-ranging application potential, great efforts have been as well as are being dedicated to the research on steaming media to attack technical challenges as discussed in the following.

Streaming media is inherently a cross-disciplinary subject that involves information theory, signal processing, communication and networking etc. Coding and transmission definitely lie in the core position in streaming media, and these research topics have been extremely active in recent years. The real-time, flexible and progressive natures of streaming media impose demanding requirements on media coding and transmission. It is challenging to maintain the quality-of-service (QoS) of streaming applications over bandwidth constrained, error prone and highly dynamic networks. Extensive research has been conducted to develop effective coding and transmission schemes for streaming media.

During the past decade, the media communication system has evolved from the conventional desktop computing and wired communication to mobile computing and wireless communication. With the excellent mobility, wireless streaming has turned the on-demand access of rich media content anywhere on any device into a reality. It is believed that mobile phones will turn out to be the fourth screen following cinema, television and PC. Apart from the entertainment industry, wireless streaming can also find extensive applications in military and disaster rescue where wireless sensors are widely deployed. However, as the communication paradigm evolves from the conventional point-to-point, wired and centralized communication to the current wireless, distributed, ad hoc, and massive communication, the system becomes more and more complex and challenging. As a result, the research on wireless streaming has drawn tremendous attentions by both academia and industry.

As the Internet is still undergoing unprecedented innovations and expansion, novel network architectures keep emerging, which also sheds new light on streaming media. The emergence of P2P network leads to an architecture shift from client-server streaming to P2P streaming. P2P streaming has become the most powerful and popular solution for large-scale streaming services due to its decentralization, self-organization, and flexibility. Given the initial success of P2P streaming, streaming media content over P2P networks is still fraught with great challenges. For instance, compared with P2P based file sharing applications, streaming over P2P networks imposes tighter timing requirements. Moreover, the limited and changing bandwidth of peers further complicate the problem of QoS control. Therefore, efficient protocol, coding and scheduling algorithms are desired to tackle the challenges in P2P streaming.

After more than a decade of development, substantial advances have been achieved in the diverse areas of streaming media, and a number of promising research directions are springing up. Following an open call for chapters and a few rounds of extensive peer-review, 17 chapters of good quality have been finally accepted, ranging from technical review and literature survey on a particular topic, solutions to some technical issues, to implementation of a practical streaming system, as well as perspectives of promising applications. According to the scope of those chapters, this book is organized into four sections, namely media coding, wireless/mobile video, P2P media streaming, and applications of streaming media. Below we briefly summarize the chapters in each section.

Section 1 (Chapter 1 to Chapter 5) focuses on media coding that is the key enabler for streaming media.

- Chapter 1 entitled "*Scalable Video Coding: Techniques and Applications for Adaptive Streaming*" covers the topic of making use of scalable video content in streaming frameworks and applications. Specifically, the recent standard H.264/SVC, i.e., the scalable extension of the widely used H.264/AVC coding scheme, and its deployment for adaptive streaming, the combined activities of content adaptation and streaming, are considered.
- Chapter 2 with the title "*Adapting Multimedia Streaming to Changing Network Conditions*" focuses on the application layer techniques that adapt to the changes in network conditions, including layered encoding, rate shaping, adaptive error control, and smoothing. The chapter also discusses operating system methods to support adaptive multimedia.
- Chapter 3 entitled "*2-D Scalable Multiple Description Coding for Robust H.264/SVC Video Communications*" investigates two popular techniques for error-resilient H.264/SVC video transmission over packet erasure networks, i.e., layered video coding (LVC) and scalable multiple description coding (SMDC). The authors compare the respective advantages and disadvantages of these two coding techniques. A comprehensive literature review on latest advancement on SMDC is provided. A two-dimensional scalable multiple description coding (2-D SMDC) scheme is presented.
- In Chapter 4 "*Dirac Video Codec: Introduction*", the authors present the fundamental architecture of the Dirac video encoder that is engineered by British Broadcasting Corporation (BBC) aiming at a wide range of applications from storage of video content to streaming video. The overall encoding structure is discussed followed by the detailed description of each coding component. Finally, the block diagram of Dirac's bitstream syntax is presented.
- Chapter 5 with the title "*3D Mesh Model Coding*" addresses the coding and streaming issues of 3D model. This chapter first surveys the typical algorithms in static and dynamic 3D meshes coding where the coding and streaming of gigantic 3D models are specially introduced. Moreover, the MPEG4 3D mesh model coding standard is also briefed. This chapter concludes with a discussion providing an overall picture of the developments in mesh coding and the directions for future research.

Section 2 (Chapter 6 to Chapter 10) addresses wireless and mobile video.

- Chapter 6 entitled "*A Cross-Layer Design to Wireless/Mobile video Streaming*" introduces a cross-layer approach to wireless/mobile video streaming system design. Beginning with the introduction to the motivation of the cross-layer design, this chapter covers fundamental issues, challenges and solutions of the cross-layer approach to video streaming systems for its practical employment.
- In Chapter 7 "*Bitrate Adaptation of Scalable Bitstreams in a UMTS Environment*", the authors propose a complete streaming framework for a wireless, in particular a 3G/UMTS, network environment. The authors also describe choices one can make in terms of network architecture and then focus on the input parameters used to evaluate network conditions and to perform the adaptation. A particular attention is dedicated to the protocol information that can be exploited to infer the channel state. In addition, each implementation choice is a compromise between the industrial feasibility and the adaptation efficiency.
- Chapter 8 entitled "*Robust Video Streaming over MANET and VANET*" studies the technical issues of video streaming over both Mobile Ad Hoc Networks (MANETs) and Vehicular Ad Hoc Networks (VANETs). This chapter shows how streaming can take place in those challenging environments. Error resilience and path diversity are presented as the key to robust streaming. As a form of management of streaming, distributed sourcing via peer-to-peer streaming over diverse paths is explored within VANETs.
- Chapter 9 with the title "*Scalable Video Delivery over Wireless LANs*" presents a comprehensive study on the transmission of scalable video over wireless local area networks (WLAN). The authors give an analysis of the mechanisms and principles of the emerging scalable video coding (SVC) standard. Moreover, some studies of SVC over WLAN using cross-layer design techniques are presented. The aim of this chapter is to exploit the unique characteristics of SVC, to enhance personalized experience and to improve system performance in a wireless transmission system.
- Chapter 10 entitled "*Video Delivery in Wireless Sensor Networks*" focuses on the analysis of the state of the art video delivery and data routing techniques for wireless video sensor networks. This chapter is intended to inspire additional efforts leading to video routing techniques optimized to different topologies, the physical medium, network channels, and energy constraints.

Section 3 (Chapter 11 to Chapter 14) deals with P2P media streaming.

- Chapter 11 entitled "*Peer-to-Peer Networks: Protocols, Cooperation and Competition*" discusses P2P systems that have been deployed in file sharing and real-time media streaming. The authors discuss the limitations of the implementations for existing P2P-based file sharing and media streaming applications in detail. More advanced resource reciprocation strategies, where peers make foresighted decisions on their resource distribution in a way that maximizes their cumulative utilities are also discussed.
- Chapter 12 with the title "*A Survey of P2P Data-Driven Live Streaming Systems*" presents a survey of "data-driven" or "unstructured" peer-to-peer live media streaming techniques, which have been introduced in the recent years to overcome the limitation of classic application-layer tree overlays.
- Chapter 13 entitled "*Epidemic Live Streaming*" is intended as an introduction of epidemic live streaming. In this chapter, the authors propose some simple metrics to understand the behavior of a diffusion algorithm, and they use elementary diffusion schemes to understand the basics of the

diffusion process, for both homogeneous and heterogeneous systems. The proposed approach mixes theoretical results, when available, with empirical observations in order to give the best possible insights.

- In Chapter 14 "*A Chunkless Peer-to-Peer Transport Protocol for Multimedia Streaming*", the authors describe a P2P transport protocol suited for multimedia streaming. The described protocol is characterized by the robustness to data losses and the low-start times. From the application point of view, the proposed protocol appears as a transport protocol similar to TCP or UDP.

Section 4 (Chapter 15 to Chapter 17) presents some application-driven research on streaming media.

- Chapter 15 with the title "*Low Latency Audio Streaming for Internet-Based Musical Interaction*" covers the technical issues related to the subject of playing live music with musicians distributed over the Internet. In this chapter, the author first outlines purely human cognitive restrictions in context with the problem of latency. Based on these restrictions, a comprehensive technical overview is given, finally leading to a taxonomy of appropriate interaction approaches.
- Chapter 16 entitled "*The 3rd Generation Partnership Project Packet-Switched Streaming (3GPP-PSS): Fundamentals and Applications*" embodies the chronological advances of 3GPP-PSS, whose specifications define the framework for streaming capabilities for 3GPP mobile devices and networks. The discussions on the general specifications of different releases are also provided in this chapter with a focus on the Quality of Service (QoS) support.
- In Chapter 17 "*Perspectives of the Application of Video Streaming to Education*", the author analyses the application of video-streaming in video-lectures. An overview of several related research topics is presented in this chapter, including video-lecture summarization, automatic extraction of text from the audio track, lecture segmentation, search, semantic indexing and multimodal access, gesture analysis, and annotation of the videos.

As can be seen from the above introductions, this book spans a number of interdependent and emerging topics in streaming media. In conclusion, we aim to acquaint the scholars and practitioners involved in the research and development of streaming media with such a most updated reference on a wide range of related topics. The target audience of this book would be those interested in various aspects of streaming media, such as coding, transmission, architecture and applications. This book is meant to be accessible to audiences including researchers, developers, engineers, and innovators working in the relevant areas. It can also serve as a solid advanced-level course supplement to media processing and communications for senior undergraduates and postgraduates.

Acknowledgment

On the occasion of the completion of this edited book, we would like to thank all the authors for contributing their high quality works. Without their expertise and contribution, this book will never come to fruition. We would also like to thank all the reviewers for their insightful and constructive comments, which helped to improve the quality of this book. We are grateful to the members of the Editorial Advisory Board (EAB) for their support. Our special thanks go to the editorial assistants of this book from IGI Global, Beth Ardner and Mike Killian, for their tremendous guidance and patience throughout the whole publication process. This project is supported in part by the National Science Foundation of China under Grant 60832010.

Ce Zhu
Nanyang Technological University, Singapore

Yuenan Li
Tianjin University, China

Xiamu Niu
Harbin Institute of Technology, China

Section 1
Media Coding

Chapter 1
Scalable Video Coding:
Techniques and Applications
for Adaptive Streaming

Hermann Hellwagner
Klagenfurt University, Austria

Ingo Kofler
Klagenfurt University, Austria

Michael Eberhard
Klagenfurt University, Austria

Robert Kuschnig
Klagenfurt University, Austria

Michael Ransburg
Klagenfurt University, Austria

Michael Sablatschan
Klagenfurt University, Austria

ABSTRACT

This chapter covers the topic of making use of scalable video content in streaming frameworks and applications. Specifically, the recent standard H.264/SVC, i.e., the scalable extension of the widely used H.264/AVC coding scheme, and its deployment for adaptive streaming, the combined activities of content adaptation and streaming, are considered. H.264/SVC is regarded as a promising candidate to enable applications to cope with bandwidth variations in networks and heterogeneous usage environments, mainly diverse end device capabilities and constraints. The relevant coding and transport principles of H.264/SVC are reviewed first. Subsequently, a general overview of H.264/SVC applications is given. The chapter then focuses on presenting architectural/implementation options and applications of H.264/SVC for adaptive streaming, emphasizing the aspect of where, i.e., on which network node and on which layer in the networking stack, in the video delivery path the content adaptation can take place; also, methods of content adaptation are covered. This pragmatic perspective is seen as complementing more general discussions of scalable video adaptation issues in the existing literature.

DOI: 10.4018/978-1-61692-831-5.ch001

Copyright © 2011, IGI Global. Copying or distributing in print or electronic forms without written permission of IGI Global is prohibited.

INTRODUCTION

Packet-switched, best-effort, mostly IP-based networks and the growing diversity of end devices represent significant challenges for video streaming. Such networks are subject to changing network conditions, specifically bandwidth variations, and non-negligible data losses, particularly when wireless networks are involved; end devices have widely different capabilities and constraints, e.g., computational power and display size. The major challenge is to deliver a video stream to potentially many users in the best quality possible for each user, irrespective of the networks being traversed and the devices being deployed.

Scalable Video Coding (SVC) and the use of SVC bit streams have been investigated as promising approaches to cope with these challenges. SVC has the potential to enable applications to adapt a video bit stream before or during streaming to the current network conditions and device characteristics. In this chapter, we refer to the combined tasks of streaming and adapting video content as *adaptive streaming*. There are stringent requirements on a scalable coding scheme and an adaptive streaming framework, including: support for low-complexity decoding; minimal real-time processing effort for adaptation/rate control; adaptability to unpredictable, potentially highly varying network conditions; support for unicast and multicast transmissions; and error resilience to data losses (Pesquet-Popescu, Li, & van der Schaar, 2007).

Driven by these requirements, scalable video coding has been devoted intense research efforts for many years. Several SVC schemes have been proposed. These include scalable extensions of the video coding standards H.263 and MPEG-2, fine-grain scalable (FGS) coding in the MPEG-4 Visual coding standard, and motion-compensated wavelet video coding structures (Pesquet-Popescu, Li, & van der Schaar, 2007). In many cases, the integration of scalability modes came at the cost of significant coding inefficiency. As a consequence,

these SVC approaches were not widely adopted in practical applications.

Yet, there has been considerable effort by the standardization communities in recent years to lay the basis for a more successful SVC scheme. The result is the Scalable Video Coding (SVC) extension of the widely adopted H.264/AVC standard (ITU-T Rec. H.264 | ISO/IEC 14496-10 Advanced Video Coding (Version 4), 2005), developed by the Joint Video Team (JVT) of the ITU-T Video Coding Experts Group (VCEG) and the ISO/IEC Moving Picture Experts Group (MPEG) and completed in late 2007. In this chapter, we refer to this new standard as *H.264/SVC*; it is documented in (ITU-T Rec. H.264 | ISO/IEC 14496-10 Advanced Video Coding / Amd. 3, 2007). The main design goals of the scalable extension were to provide scalability with coding efficiency and decoding complexity similar to single-layer coding, support of simple bit stream adaptation mechanisms, and an H.264/AVC backward compatible base layer. These goals were largely achieved and, at the time of writing, initial industrial applications are emerging.

Thus, this chapter will focus on two aspects. First, it will concentrate on the *H.264/SVC* coding scheme since this can currently be regarded as the most promising enabling technology for packet video transmission in heterogeneous, dynamically varying networking and media consumption environments. For other scalable video coding methods, the reader is referred to the literature pointed to in the sections on related work and additional reading. Second, a focus will be on the most interesting facet enabled by SVC, *adaptive streaming* of H.264/SVC content. More specifically, architectural options for adaptive streaming and application examples will be reviewed, mainly under the aspects of *on which node* in the delivery chain (on the server, client, or a mid-network device) and *on which layer* in the networking stack (on the application, transport, or network layer, if applicable) the content adaptation takes place. This discussion is seen as the major contribution of

Figure 1. Scalability dimensions offered by H.264/SVC

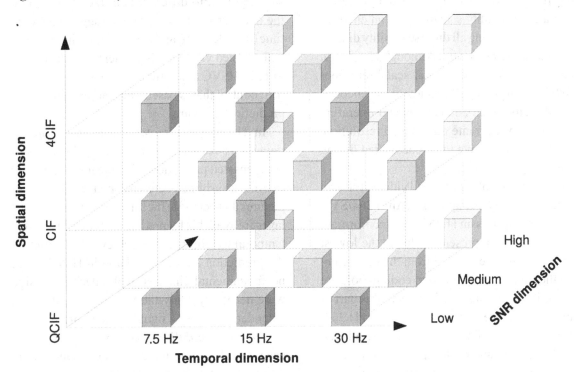

this chapter; many other issues of SVC adaptation have already been addressed in the literature, as will be briefly reviewed in the chapter. For related problems like rate control algorithms, the reader again is referred to the literature.

The remainder of this chapter is structured as follows. In the next section, the principal features of H.264/SVC video coding and transport will be reviewed. Then, a general overview of H.264/SVC applications will be presented. The main part focuses on adaptive video streaming applications and implementations on several layers, as supported by H.264/SVC. Several use case scenarios – representing the authors' as well as other researchers' work – will be described, in order to provide technical insight into how H.264/SVC can be used for flexible video delivery. Related work, current research activities, and concluding remarks will be given subsequently.

H.264/SVC CODING FUNDAMENTALS AND TRANSPORT INTERFACE

The H.264/SVC standard introduces scalability mechanisms in three different scalability dimensions. First, it offers *temporal scalability*, which refers to the extraction of the video content at different temporal resolutions (frame rate). Second, *spatial scalability* allows incorporating multiple spatial resolutions (e.g., HD, SD) of the same video in a single bit stream. Finally, *quality scalability* (or SNR scalability) refers to the possibility of extracting different quality variations of the same video from a single bit stream trading off visual distortion and required video bit rate. The three scalability dimensions of an encoded video bit stream are visualized in Figure 1. The corresponding coding tools that are specified in the standard allow combining the scalability dimensions depending on the targeted application or use case in a very flexible way. This ranges from providing only spatial or quality scalability of an encoded video up to combining all three scalability dimensions in a single bit stream. Although obvious, it should be explicitly noted that scalability does not imply an arbitrary adaptation of the encoded video. All envisaged adaptations and operating points (in terms of frame rate, spatial resolution, and video bit rate) have to be considered during the encoding of the video.

The scalability of the encoded video bit stream is achieved by a layered approach. An H.264/SVC bit stream comprises an H.264/AVC-conformant *base layer* which represents video at the lowest quality that can be extracted from the bit stream. Since the bit stream syntax and coding tools are backward-compatible to H.264/AVC, this part of the bit stream can be decoded by any legacy H.264/AVC decoder. Building on top of the base layer, the video quality and/or the spatial resolution of the video can be refined by *enhancement layers*. As a consequence, the adaptation of the scalable video bit stream is as simple as extracting certain parts of the bit stream or, putting it the other way round, truncating certain enhancement layers or parts thereof from the initial bit stream. Obviously, this mechanism can be implemented very efficiently and satisfies the intended design goal of a simple bit stream adaptation mechanism.

As H.264/SVC is based on the very successful H.264/AVC compression standard, it inherits many of its features and efficient coding tools. As with all modern *hybrid video coding* designs, the fundamental compression mechanism is based on motion-compensated temporal differential pulse code modulation (DPCM) combined with a spatial decorrelating transformation. This means that redundancy in the video signal is removed by using prediction between related video pictures and even within a single video picture. As a consequence, the encoder and decoder have to maintain a synchronous prediction loop in order to properly reconstruct the video sequence. However, adaptation or packet loss during transmis-

sion can lead to differences in the prediction at the decoder side. This behavior aggregates over time (decoder drift) and leads to annoying artifacts and reduced visual quality. Therefore, the design of H.264/SVC also offers means for an efficient drift control that is based on an adjustment of the prediction structure.

In H.264/SVC, *scalability in the temporal domain* is realized by restricting the motion-compensated prediction. This means that instead of using an arbitrary reference picture, only those pictures that belong to the same or a lower temporal layer are available for prediction. Since this kind of temporal scalability can be achieved by restricting the prediction already available in H.264/AVC, no fundamental changes of the decoder design were necessary. Only the bit stream syntax was extended in order to signal the temporal layers.

Spatial scalability is achieved by encoding each spatial resolution as a dedicated layer. Within each layer, the ordinary H.264/AVC prediction methods (intra-prediction, motion-compensated prediction) can be used. To increase the coding efficiency, the redundancy between the different resolutions can be exploited by inter-layer prediction. Basically, this prediction is based on an upsampled signal of a lower spatial layer or by combining the upsampled signal with temporal prediction. For better performance, the standard also allows to predict macroblock modes, motion information, and the residual signal from lower layers. The standard supports spatial scalability with arbitrary resolution ratios.

The prediction concepts introduced for spatial scalability are also used for a variant of quality scalability called *coarse-grain quality scalable coding (CGS)*. In fact, CGS is considered as an extreme case where two or more layers have identical spatial resolutions. Obviously some operations like upsampling can be omitted in that special case. This concept allows to encode a few different qualities (and corresponding bit rates) of the video in a single bit stream but has some encoding performance drawbacks when the bit rate difference between adjacent layers gets small. Furthermore, layer switching is only possible at pre-defined points within the bit stream. Therefore, H.264/SVC also offers coding tools for *medium-grain quality scalability (MGS)*, which can be used to encode video streams that cover a wider dynamic range of bit rates and allow switching the quality layers at any picture of the video stream.

For additional information on the coding fundamentals of H.264/SVC, the reader is referred to (Schwarz, Marpe, & Wiegand, 2007).

In order to transmit an H.264/SVC bit stream over a packet-switched network, the H.264/SVC bit stream needs to be divided into packets. Starting with H.264/AVC, the designers have taken this into consideration by introducing the *Network Abstraction Layer (NAL)*, which organizes coded media bits – the output of the *Video Coding Layer (VCL)* – into *NAL units (NALUs)*. Each NALU includes a number of macroblocks of a given picture and a given layer of the H.264/SVC bit stream. Other than these VCL NALUs, there are also NALUs which include meta-information, i.e., *Parameter Sets (PSs)* and *Supplemental Enhancement Information (SEI)*. PS NALUs contain header information which is needed for initializing the decoding, such as the spatial resolution of the video. SEI NALUs are not directly required for decoding of pictures but contain additional information to assist decoding or bit stream manipulation. An example of such an SEI NALU is the *scalability SEI message*, which contains a list of available layers in the bit stream and the corresponding bit rates, frame rates, and width/height values. This information may be used to decide whether to retain or discard a certain layer in case of insufficient network capacity.

As already specified in H.264/AVC, each NALU includes a NALU header which signals the type of the NALU. For backward-compatibility reasons, the new NALU types introduced in H.264/SVC extend this existing header by an extension header (depicted in Figure 2) that car-

Figure 2. Network abstraction layer unit (NALU) header

```
+---------------+---------------+---------------+
|0|1|2|3|4|5|6|7|0|1|2|3|4|5|6|7|0|1|2|3|4|5|6|7|
+-+-+-+-+-+-+-+-+-+-+-+-+-+-+-+-+-+-+-+-+-+-+-+-+
|R|I|   PRID    |N| DID |  QID  | TID |U|D|O| RR|
+---------------+---------------+---------------+
```

ries, amongst others, what we refer to as *decoding dependency information*. This information is used to signal which temporal, spatial, and quality layer a NALU belongs to (scalability hierarchy). The decoding dependency information consists of the dependency ID (DID), quality ID (QID), and temporal ID (TID) parameters. The *dependency ID* indicates the CGS or spatial scalability layer, the *quality ID* represents the MGS layer, and the *temporal ID* signals the temporal layer. Generally, layers of a higher ID predict from layers with a lower ID, but not vice versa. The actual adaptation of an H.264/SVC bit stream can be steered by specifying the desired layer combination as a triple of temporal ID, dependency ID and quality ID. The adaptation of a bit stream is then performed by simply discarding those NAL units that belong to a higher layer as specified by the triple. In addition to this layer signaling mechanism, the H.264/SVC standard also offers a simpler mechanism based on priorities. For that purpose, the NALU header also contains a *priority ID (PRID)* which signals the relative importance of a NALU within the bit stream. This priority indicator describes an adaptation path through the discardable NALUs, based on additional information (e.g., rate-distortion information) which may be available at encoding time.

For additional information on the transport interface of H.264/SVC, the reader is referred to (Wang, Hannuksela, Pateaux, Eleftheriadis, & Wenger, 2007).

The delivery of H.264/SVC is currently standardized for three content delivery protocols, each targeting a different area of application (Schierl, Stockhammer, & Wiegand, Mobile Video Transmission Using Scalable Video Coding, 2007):

Figure 3. Common RTP packetization modes for NALUs

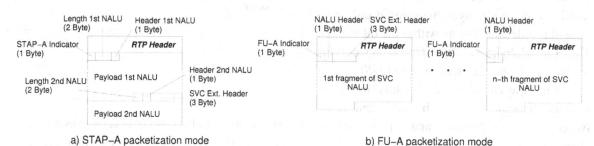

a) STAP–A packetization mode   b) FU–A packetization mode

- The *Real-time Transport Protocol (RTP)* (Schulzrinne, Casner, Frederick, & Jacobson, 2003) is meant to be deployed in packet-switched/IP networks.
- The *MPEG-2 Transport Stream (TS)* (ISO/IEC 13818-1:2000: Generic coding of moving pictures and associated audio information: Systems, 2000) is typically used in digital TV broadcast networks.
- The *H.264/SVC File Format* (ISO/IEC 14496-15:2004/Amd2: SVC File Format, 2008) was proposed for storage and non-real-time delivery of H.264/SVC.

In case of transmission via RTP, the NALUs of an H.264/SVC stream are packetized into RTP packets, as defined in (Wenger S., Wang, Schierl, & Eleftheriadis, 2009). For that purpose, the NALUs of the scalable video stream have to be packetized into RTP packets. The payload format defines modes for transmitting the NALUs in either decoding order or in an interleaved fashion. Depending on the size of a NALU, it has to be split up and transmitted in multiple RTP packets (fragmentation unit, FU) or multiple NALUs of the same video frame can be aggregated in a single RTP packet (single time aggregation packet, STAP). Both of these common packetization modes are illustrated in Figure 3. The packetization can be steered to either minimize the protocol overhead or to enhance the error resilience in case of packet loss (Wenger, Wang, & Schierl, 2007). Depending on the application, the scalable video can be transmitted in a single RTP session or distributed over multiple RTP sessions. Additionally, in conjunction with the RTP interface different extensions to the Session Description Protocol (SDP) (Handley, Jacobson, & Perkins, 2006)(Schierl & Wenger, 2009) are standardized that can be used to signal the scalability information (e.g., during session setup).

The packetization of H.264/SVC into an MPEG-2 TS (ISO/IEC 13818-1:2006/FPDAM 3.2: Transport of SVC Video (ISO/IEC 14496-10 Amd.3) over ISO/IEC 13818-1 Streams, 2008) is done in a more static way. In general, an Elementary Stream (ES) is packed into an MPEG-2 Packetized Elementary Stream (PES) and encapsulated into the 188-byte MPEG-2 TS packets. TS packets from different streams can then be multiplexed into a single MPEG-2 TS. An ES can either be a video or audio track or, in case of H.264/SVC, a single base or enhancement layer of the video. The multiplexed TS is transmitted over a network and received by the client, but in general no adaptation along the network path is specified. The client de-multiplexes the TS and reconstructs the ESs from the PES streams. Depending on the client capabilities, only the base layer or, additionally, all or parts of the enhancement layers of an H.264/SVC video may be reconstructed.

The H.264/SVC file format (ISO/IEC 14496-15:2004/Amd2: SVC File Format, 2008) is an extension of the H.264/AVC file format, which is based on the ISO base media file format (ISO/

IEC 14496-12:2005 Part 12: ISO Base Media File Format, 2005). Different media types like audio, video, and subtitles can be stored in the H.264/SVC file format. The media data is split into access units each comprising a specific size and decoding/display timestamp. The different media types are separated into so called tracks. Single H.264/SVC layers are also separated into tracks to enable easy extraction of the desired layers without the need of parsing the overall bit stream. The H.264/SVC file format additionally supports metadata to describe the media data more precisely. Apart from the typical layered approach, specific extraction paths can be defined in order to enable customized adaptation (Amon, Rathgen, & Singer, 2007).

OVERVIEW OF H.264/SVC APPLICATIONS

The layered approach of H.264/SVC that allows extracting video streams with different spatial resolutions and with different bit rates enables a variety of possible applications. The codec design, with an H.264/AVC backward compatible base layer and the backward compatible transport interfaces, allows the consumption of H.264/SVC content on legacy devices. This is an important facility since many handheld and mobile devices rely on hardware decoding chips which cannot be simply upgraded by software. Naturally, the layered encoding is suitable for applying different priority mechanisms like unequal error protection (Bakker, Comboom, Dams, & Munteanu, 2008), selective retransmissions or partial encryption (Stütz & Uhl, 2008)(Hellwagner, Kuschnig, Stütz, & Uhl, 2009) of parts of the encoded bit stream with different importance. Scalability support for legacy H.264/AVC devices is also possible by using a low-complex SVC-to-AVC rewriting technique (Segall & Zhao, 2008) which can be employed under certain circumstances.

In the case of a Video-on-Demand (VoD) streaming scenario, H.264/SVC allows to adapt the video stream according to the client's capabilities like decoding and display capabilities or network connectivity (Wien, Cazoulat, Graffunder, Hutter, & Amon, 2007) and congestion situations of the network (Xiaogang & Lei, 2007)(Gorkemli & Civanlar, 2006). A single pre-encoded H.264/SVC bit stream can be used to meet the requirements of different clients, leading to a more efficient storage at the server as well as smooth dynamic adaptation according to the network situation. For that purpose, the H.264/SVC design offers the MGS feature which gracefully supports bit rate adaptation in the SNR domain with a considerable dynamic range.

In multicast-enabled networks, the simultaneous transmission of the same content to a set of heterogeneous clients can be realized by using H.264/SVC. Typically, the RTP protocol is the preferred transport interface in multicast scenarios like IPTV services or videoconferencing solutions. The corresponding payload format (Wenger S., Wang, Schierl, & Eleftheriadis, 2009) specifies a packetization method to transmit the different layers or combinations thereof in separate RTP sessions. This operation mode is called Multi Session Transmission (MST) and provides means for synchronizing the layers among the different RTP sessions and for signaling their interdependencies. The RTP sessions are transmitted using different multicast addresses. As a consequence, each client can obtain an adapted version of the scalable video stream by subscribing to a set of multicast addresses based on the layer and scalability information provided. The layered transmission can be used in videoconferencing solutions as well. Typically the participants connect to a central component which is responsible for distributing the audio and video signals to all participants. In traditional systems this so called Multipoint Control Unit (MCU) is responsible to adapt the video and audio streams according to the participant's device capabilities and network connectivity.

As H.264/SVC offers computationally cheap video adaptation by bit stream extraction, future videoconferencing systems can leverage the load on the MCUs by taking advantage of the scalable coding and layered multicast transmission. Connectivity of legacy clients or through networks without multicast support can be achieved by H.264/SVC-aware middleboxes that perform the multicast-to-unicast conversion (Wenger, Wang, & Schierl, 2007).

The benefits of H.264/SVC are not at all limited to streaming applications but can be employed advantageously in the broadcasting domain as well. The content of mobile TV services (e.g., DVB-H) can be transmitted in different resolutions by using the spatial scalability of H.264/SVC (Hellge, Mirta, Schierl, & Wiegand, 2009). This allows broadcasting the same video to a heterogeneous spectrum of end devices. Without using scalable video coding, the same video content would have to be transmitted in different resolutions by simulcast, wasting the expensive wireless channel capacity. Therefore, H.264/SVC introduces new service features for broadcasting applications in a backward-compatible way while optimally utilizing the wireless channel. The scalability can be used both for live broadcast and for Near-VoD use cases (clipcasting) (Schierl, Stockhammer, & Wiegand, Mobile Video Transmission Using Scalable Video Coding, 2007) where the video content is served in a carousel fashion. Similar techniques for the live broadcast are also considered for satellite links to improve the transmission of different high-definition resolutions (720p/1080p). A further application in the case of broadcasting to mobile devices is to combine hierarchical modulation techniques with fidelity scalability (Hellge, Mirta, Schierl, & Wiegand, 2009). Certain wireless broadcasting systems offer methods to apply different modulation and error correction techniques to different parts of the transmitted bit stream. In combination with the layered concept of H.264/SVC, these methods can be exploited to protect the base layer at a higher degree than the enhancement layer(s). A more robust transmission of the base layer improves the service for standard quality when using highly mobile end devices or in areas with bad channel conditions. If the external conditions allow the reception of the weaker protected enhancement layer(s), the visual quality of the service is improved. In this scenario, the benefit of H.264/SVC is to have graceful degradation of the video quality when encountering bad channel conditions instead of experiencing a complete service outage.

In the context of mobile and wireless networks the deployment of H.264/SVC enables new approaches which were not considered feasible or scalable with traditional, non-scalable video coding techniques. In packet switched cellular networks the access to the scarce, shared wireless medium can be scheduled by taking into consideration the importance of the video packet. Another application is to adapt the video stream according to the available wireless network bandwidth of a wireless LAN. Evaluations have shown that the adaptation of H.264/SVC streams can be accomplished even with existing consumer networking hardware (Kofler, Prangl, Kuschnig, & Hellwagner, 2008). Such adaptive techniques that take into consideration different layers of the protocol stack are generally referred to as cross-layer approaches (van der Schaar & Shankar N, 2005) and benefit significantly from the cheap adaptation mechanisms offered by H.264/SVC.

In the field of video surveillance applications, the advent of H.264/SVC also raised significant interest. Such systems are typically composed of a large number of video cameras that provide video content that has to be made available to different users. Typically, the users can access the visual information either via large display walls in a control room or perform remote monitoring via a low-bandwidth connection on a mobile end device. Besides, the recorded material should also be available for long-term storage at a lower frame rate but in a resolution and fidelity that would allow an image analysis at a later date. All these use cases that are realized by transcoding and transrating in current surveillance systems can be implemented with lower complexity by using H.264/SVC.

Finally, the use of H.264/SVC is also investigated in peer-to-peer (P2P) systems where the video content is shared by a set of heterogeneous peers (Mushtaq & Ahmed, 2008). Similar techniques are also deployed beneficially in MANETs (Schierl, Johansen, Hellge, & Stockhammer, 2007) where H.264/SVC can be combined with distributed video streaming for rate-distortion optimal streaming.

ADAPTIVE STREAMING OF H.264/SVC CONTENT

The topic of adaptive streaming of video content, including H.264/SVC content, has been discussed in a general and systematic manner in several papers already. Examples include (Chang & Vetro, 2005)(Sun, Vetro, & Xin, 2007)(Ortega & Wang, 2007)(Wenger, Wang, & Schierl, 2007)(Thang, Kim, Kang, & Yoo, 2009); a complete, MPEG-21-based SVC adaptation platform is presented in (Wien, Cazoulat, Graffunder, Hutter, & Amon, 2007). The "big picture" of H.264/SVC adaptation was recently discussed in (Thang, Kim, Kang, & Yoo, 2009) along the following six questions:

- What are the adaptation goals?
- What are possible adaptation operators?
- How to acquire QoS data?
- How to represent QoS data?
- How to decide adaptation operator levels?
- How to truncate/adapt an SVC bitstream?

The papers give a fairly complete overview of these general issues of adaptive H.264/SVC streaming. Thus, we do not reiterate their findings here. Rather, architectural/implementation options and applications will be discussed mainly under the aspect of *where* content adaptation can take

place: *on which node* on the delivery path and, if applicable, e.g., on mid-network devices, *on which layer* of the networking stack. The first perspective, considering the node on which stream adaptation is performed (server, network node, client), is used to structure this section. Other aspects, including adaptation methods and communication settings (unicast, multicast, broadcast), will be covered in the course of the discussions. Representative use cases and implementations will be used to show which techniques can be combined reasonably and for which applications. These practical, implementation-oriented considerations are regarded as being complementary to the discussions of the earlier overview papers.

Server-Side Adaptation

Adaptation of the content at the server side has been a common solution for years. Server-side adaptation is based on unicast, i.e., content is streamed to each client in a separate streaming session. During a streaming session, the bit stream is adapted to suite the user's preferences and his/her terminal's capabilities. This unicast model allows each user to start a separate VoD session and to receive the content in a suitable quality and at a chosen time. The main advantages of this streaming model are that unicast is supported by all network providers and that only the layers that are actually required for the desired quality are streamed to the user, enabling the consumption of the content in the desired quality without any need for additional adaptation mechanisms.

To perform the adaptation of the content at the server, users need to provide their preferences, the capabilities of their terminals and possibly additional information about their usage environment to receive the content in a suitable quality. One possible solution to represent such context-related metadata is provided by *MPEG-21 Part 7, Digital Item Adaptation (DIA)* (Vetro, 2004). The DIA standard specifies two description formats that are highly useful when expressing context-related attributes. On the one hand, the *MPEG-21 DIA Usage Environment Description (UED)* (Vetro, 2004) allows expressing properties of the usage environment such as user and terminal characteristics, the capabilities and actual conditions of the network, and natural environment properties. On the other hand, *the MPEG-21 DIA Universal Constraint Description (UCD)* (Vetro, 2004) allows to specify constraints on the attributes described in the UED and hence enabling the user to specify his/her specific preferences. To match the information about the context of the user with the adaptation capabilities of the available content, MPEG-21 DIA also specifies the *Adaptation Quality of Service (AQoS)* (Vetro, 2004) description, which describes the layers of the scalable bit stream and allows to match them with the properties specified by the context-related metadata. More information on the context-related metadata specified by MPEG-21 DIA and their usage in different streaming applications can be found, e.g., in (Eberhard, Celetto, Timmerer, Quacchio, Hellwagner, & Rovati, 2008).

When server-side adaptation is performed, the H.264/SVC-specific adaptation indicated in the previous sections, i.e., discarding NALUs based on the decoding dependency information, provides one possibility to adapt the content to the quality desired by the receiving client. However, as the adaptation of scalable bit streams is performed in a simple way by discarding NALUs and potentially modifying bit stream header parameters, these operations can also be performed based on metadata describing the bit stream syntax. A solution for such metadata is provided by the *Bitstream Syntax Descriptions (BSDs)* of the MPEG-21 DIA standard (Vetro, 2004)(Panis, et al., 2003), which describe the syntax of the bit stream on a high level using XML. To perform an adaptation of the content based on BSDs, the BSD is firstly transformed based on the desired quality parameters, e.g., by using an *Extensible Stylesheet Language Transformation (XSLT)* library. Such a transformation process removes the metadata

descriptions of the parts of the bit stream that are not needed for the desired quality and modifies the corresponding parameters in the BSD accordingly. Based on the transformed BSD, the adapted bit stream can be simply generated by extracting the NALUs described by the transformed BSD and by modifying the parameters of the bit stream to the values provided by the transformed BSD. The main advantages of the metadata-driven adaptation approach in comparison to the H.264/SVC-specific adaptation approach are that the process is codec-independent and that it might offer better performance than the H.264/SVC-specific adaptation approach for some applications (Eberhard, Celetto, Timmerer, Quacchio, Hellwagner, & Rovati, 2008).

An example architecture for server-side adaptation in a single-client VoD scenario is depicted in Figure 4 and described as follows. Firstly, the user selects one of the video sequences available at the server and provides his/her preferences via the terminal (end device). The ID of the selected video, the preferences and the capabilities of the user's terminal are subsequently provided to the *Content Request Engine*. Before the transmission to the server, the capabilities and preferences need to be formatted for transmission, e.g., according to the format of the MPEG-21 DIA UED and UCD. After the transmission of the request data, the client receives an URL which can be used to start the VoD streaming session at a later point. The information is received at the server by the *Request Interface* and the context-related metadata is forwarded to an *Adaptation Decision-Taking Engine (ADTE)* (Kofler, Timmerer, Hellwagner, Hutter, & Sanahuja, 2007). The ADTE matches the context-related information with the information about the layers of the scalable bit stream. The information about the layers can be either extracted directly from the bit stream, i.e., by parsing PS and scalability SEI messages, or by accessing suitable metadata (e.g., the AQoS description) from the *Content Repository*. The ADTE subsequently matches the context information with the layer

Figure 4. Server-side adaptation

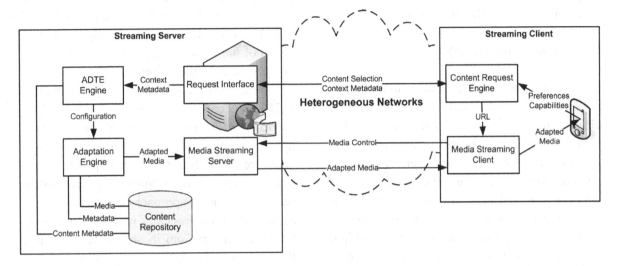

information and takes an adaptation decision, which is used to configure the *Adaptation Engine*.

When the client starts fetching the adapted content using the received URL, the Adaptation Engine performs the adaptation of the content from the Content Repository in a timed manner. The adaptation of the bit stream can be either performed by utilizing the H.264/SVC-specific approach or by performing the adaptation based on the BSD descriptions. If the timed adaptation is performed based on BDSs, the BSD needs to contain the MPEG-21 DIA *Streaming Instructions* (Ransburg, Devillers, Timmerer, & Hellwagner, 2007). On the one hand, the Streaming Instructions specify how the BSD needs to be fragmented and provide information about accessing the fragments in a timed manner. On the other hand, the Streaming Instructions describe how the access units within the bit stream can be localized and when they need to be accessed. The adapted parts of the bit stream are subsequently forwarded to the *Media Streaming Server* and are received at the client side by the *Media Streaming Client*. If the usage environment or the preferences of the user change during the streaming process, an update of the context-related metadata can be provided to the server at any time. As

the adaptation is performed in a timed manner, the new adaptation decision is utilized as soon as it is taken. The change of the adaptation decision is visible at the client as soon as the next access units are received and displayed.

The server-side adaptation architecture illustrated in Figure 4 has been implemented utilizing the VLC media player and streaming server as the basis for the client and the server (Eberhard, Celetto, Timmerer, Quacchio, Hellwagner, & Rovati, 2008). To implement the adaptation functionality at the client, the VLC GUI has been extended by the Content Request Engine, which allows the user to select a video sequence and provide the preferences for the streaming session. At the server side, two modules have been integrated. The Request Interface receives the user-selected values from the client and sets the adaptation parameters according to the user preferences, utilizing the ADTE to match the context-related metadata with the adaptation capabilities of the bit stream. The Adaptation Engine performs the adaptation of the access units during the streaming process based on these adaptation parameters. Together, the server and client implementations provide a fully interoperable streaming framework that supports adaptation of scalable video sequences based on MPEG-21 DIA metadata.

In-Network Adaptation

The advent of the scalable video coding technology enables computationally cheap adaptation of video content. This allows to deploy adaptation facilities directly in the network and to adapt the video stream as it is streamed over the network. Although similar ideas were already investigated with conventional video compression technologies, the main drawback of these approaches was the lack of scalability. In order to serve multiple simultaneous video sessions, significant computing power is required which is typically not available within the network because of practical and economical reasons.

The reasons for performing video adaptation in the network are diverse. In general, network nodes that perform video adaptation can use information that is not available at the server. This information can include knowledge about the network connectivity towards the client, possible congestion situations in the network, queue sizes, and simultaneous video streams or traffic flows to the client. In case of wireless networks, this information can further include the status of the wireless link, signal strengths, modulation, and loss statistics. Although parts of this information could potentially be transmitted upstream to an adaptive server, this is not always considered practicable, especially when dealing with fast changing conditions, e.g., on wireless links or when short-lived parallel traffic flows exist. A further case for performing in-network adaptation is adapting video streams in videoconferencing solutions where a single video stream of a participant has to be delivered to multiple receivers in different qualities.

In-network adaptation can be either performed on a dedicated proxy server that is deployed in the delivery chain between server and clients or even on network devices. In the latter case, the network devices have to be aware of the H.264/SVC transport layer. The layered video encoding of H.264/SVC can be used beneficially at different layers of the network stack, which is explained in more detail in the following.

The most straightforward way of adapting H.264/SVC content in the network is to perform adaptation *at the application layer*. In the literature, network components that act on the application layer are typically referred to as proxies. As a consequence, such techniques are also often called proxy-based approaches. Adaptation at the application layer basically works by retrieving the video stream from its source, reassembling the NAL units from the received packets, filtering the NAL units according to some adaptation parameters, re-packetizing the resulting bit stream and transmitting it to the client. Therefore, it is necessary that the adaptation component is aware of the transport interface that is used (e.g., RTP payload format, TS encapsulation). Additionally, it is required that the component is aware of the signaling between the video source and the client, which is accomplished by the RTSP protocol in most VoD deployments. The adaptation of the bit stream that consists of a consecutive sequence of NAL units can be performed in many different ways. The most obvious way is to perform H.264/SVC-specific adaptation by filtering the NALUs of the bit stream. However, as with the server-side adaptation, it is also possible to make use of a generic, metadata-based adaptation approach as illustrated in Figure 5. This requires that the metadata describing the video bit stream has to be transmitted to the adaptation node as well. The challenges with that approach are that the metadata has to be synchronized with the video stream (e.g., by using timestamps or, more sophisticated, MPEG-21 DIA Streaming Instructions) and that the metadata has to be compressed in order to reduce the metadata overhead. A detailed evaluation of different variations of this approach is provided in (Kuschnig, Kofler, Ransburg, & Hellwagner, 2008). One of the most important findings is that

Figure 5. In-network, metadata-driven adaptation

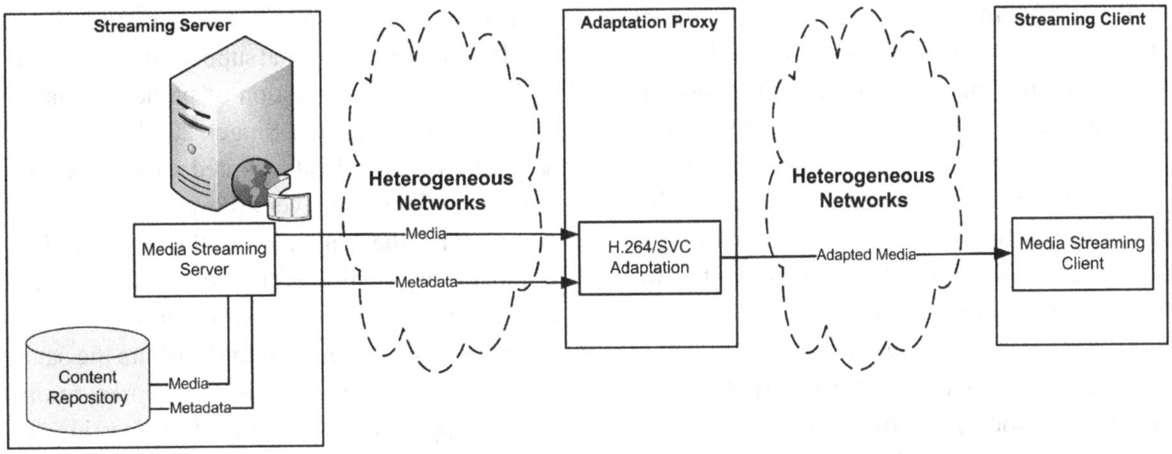

the metadata should be aggregated on a Group-of-Picture (GOP) basis in order to improve the compression efficiency but the adaptation itself should be done on a per-access-unit basis in order to improve the error resilience in case of packet loss. A further approach of performing H.264/SVC adaptation at the application layer is to utilize the RTP packetization and the included signaling information. By applying a stateful packet-based adaptation mechanism it is possible to adapt video streams without having to reconstruct complete access units. This leads to a very cheap adaptation implementation that entails a small memory footprint and is suitable for small network devices. In (Kofler, Prangl, Kuschnig, & Hellwagner, 2008) it was shown that by deploying this approach on an off-the-shelf wireless router with very limited computing resources (200 MHz RISC CPU, 16 MB of RAM), it is still possible to adapt up to five video streams in parallel. In the context of the IETF (Wenger S., Wang, Schierl, & Eleftheriadis, 2009), such middleboxes that perform, e.g., H.264/SVC adaptation are generally referred to as *Media-Aware Network Elements (MANE)*. By definition a MANE is signaling aware, relies on signaling information, and maintains a state.

The layered encoding of H.264/SVC can also be exploited beneficially *at the network layer* of

packet-switched networks. Naturally, packets that carry base layer NALUs of the scalable video stream should gain a higher transmission priority at the routers on the delivery path than those carrying enhancement layer data. At the network layer, different technologies and mechanisms which emerged in the last decades allow traffic shaping, priority management, or bandwidth sharing between different traffic flows. These mechanisms can be logically combined with the layered encoding of the bit stream. The main challenge is to signal the importance of the packets' content to lower layers. Since signaling information is necessary to properly decode the content of the flows, a router cannot simply determine the priority by inspecting the packets' payloads. A common practice for this problem is to use fields of the IP header (TOS field, DiffServ Code Point) to signal the priority and to rely on another component that performs the marking of the packet. In the simplest case, the marking can be done at the source of the video stream. A further approach is based on a hybrid mechanism where a proxy performs a priority marking of the packets and traffic shaping is performed at the network layer. Such an approach that allows sharing bandwidth between multiple scalable video streams and best-effort background traffic over a shared DSL link is introduced and evaluated in (Kofler, Kuschnig, & Hellwagner, Improving IPTV Services by H.264/SVC Adaptation and Traffic Control, 2009).

Finally, the same techniques can be used to perform scheduling *at the link layer*. Especially in wireless networks where different mobile stations share a single wireless medium, a scheduler has to assign transmission slots to each mobile station. The scheduler decides which packet in the radio link buffer has to be transmitted next or has to drop packets in case of congestion. Instead of dropping packets according to a fixed policy (e.g., tail drop or random), a media-aware link scheduler can make use of the different importance levels of the packets. In (Liebl, Schierl, Wiegand, & Stockhammer, 2006) such a system for a HSDPA base station is introduced and evaluated. Multiple users in the coverage area of a single base station are served with scalable video streams. The video streams are transmitted using RTP packets which are queued in the base station's radio link buffer. In case of congestion, the media-aware packet scheduler drops packets according to a priority that is calculated based on the layer information conveyed in the NALU header. The evaluations show that the overall quality of all video streams that are delivered to the mobile clients can be significantly improved by the media-aware scheduling policy.

It should be noted that these network and link layer approaches can be considered as adaptation in a broader sense, since adaptation happens implicitly in cases where packets carrying enhancement layers are discarded due to dropping and traffic shaping policies in case of congestion.

Receiver-Side Adaptation

For this kind of adaptation the initiative resides at the receiver side. The receiver triggers the adaptation based on client capabilities or network conditions, like the available bandwidth. The simplest form of receiver-side adaptation is

content selection. A client may choose to decode only a subset of layers of an H.264/SVC video. The H.264/SVC file format supports this operation and enables easy extraction of predefined layer sets (Amon, Rathgen, & Singer, 2007). In case of streaming over bandwidth limited networks, it may not be possible to deliver all layers to the client and perform the adaptation at the receiver-side. In the following, two receiver-driven approaches for adaptive content delivery are presented.

Broadcast systems aim to distribute the same content to multiple users. In IP networks, multicast is supposed to be used for broadcasting. To cope with the different bandwidth requirements of the clients, *Receiver-driven Layered Multicast (RLM)* (McCanne, Jacobson, & Vetterli, 1996) was introduced, which is based on layer subscriptions. A client can adjust the number of layers to meet its bandwidth requirements. Each layer of an H.264/SVC video is transmitted in a different RTP stream (Wenger S., Wang, Schierl, & Eleftheriadis, 2009). The receiver simply restricts the number of subscribed RTP streams (H.264/SVC layers). This streaming system is very efficient and simple, but the deployment requires a centrally administered network, because multicast routing has to be directly configured on the routers. So multicast is mainly deployed in provider networks, e.g., for IPTV.

Clipcasting (Schierl, Stockhammer, & Wiegand, Mobile Video Transmission Using Scalable Video Coding, 2007) was introduced for the distribution of popular content over unidirectional broadcast systems, especially for Mobile TV. The idea is to provide a Near-VoD service for popular video clips, which continuously broadcasts the clips at regular intervals (carousel). For the clip/file transmission mainly the File Delivery over the Unidirectional Transport (FLUTE) protocol (Paila, Luby, Lehtonen, Roca, & Walsh, 2004) is deployed. It is also possible to distribute H.264/SVC layers over different FLUTE sessions (Stockhammer, et al., 2007), where each session has different error protection on link level. The base layer gets the strongest protection, and protection decreases for each additional enhancement layer. This type of error protection is generally known as Unequal Error Protection (UEP). Similar to RLM, the client decides which FLUTE session(s) it wants to receive. In case of bad reception conditions only the FLUTE session with the strongest error protection, i.e., the H.264/SVC base layer, may be received properly. Thus, a graceful degradation of the video quality can be achieved.

RELATED WORK

Due to space restrictions, many important areas could not be covered in this chapter. Discussing the bulk of related research work comprehensively would also go beyond the scope of this section. For the sake of brevity, we restrict this presentation to list the most relevant related research areas and very active researchers in the areas. The readers are invited to consult the publications referenced in this chapter or listed as additional readings or on the Websites of the respective research groups:

- Scalable video coding, including MPEG-4 FGS and wavelet-based coding (Li, Pesquet-Popescu, Ohm, Sullivan, van der Schaar, Wiegand, Woods)
- Combined video coding and multimedia systems aspects, cross-layer considerations (van der Schaar, Radha)
- Rate-distortion optimization (Chou, Frossard, Girod, Ortega)
- Contention-distortion optimization, P2P (scalable) video streaming (Girod)
- MPEG-21 DIA, generic media adaptation in general (De Neve, Hellwagner, Ro, Timmerer, Thang, Van de Walle, Vetro)
- MPEG-21 DIA, bitstream syntax descriptions specifically (De Neve, Van de Walle)

FUTURE WORK

IPTV is still an important research topic today. IPTV services are already deployed by many telecommunication service providers. Many current IPTV installations are based on non-scalable video formats. However, scalable video fits the requirements of IPTV systems very well. Advantages of H.264/SVC in IPTV architectures cover the possibility to store and deliver multiple qualities within a single stream, unequal error protection, the applicability of RLM, and easy dynamic video adaptation. Consequently, the migration from current IPTV architectures to H.264/SVC is of interest for IPTV service providers, which raises issues concerning the backward compatibility of legacy devices (e.g., deployed set-top boxes) which typically do not support H.264/SVC. Although the base layer itself provides backward compatibility, it is often desirable to also present higher quality representations to legacy devices. One possible solution would be a complete transcoding from H.264/SVC to a more widespread format like H.264/AVC. However, this approach is computationally expensive and not suitable for real-time scenarios. With the *SVC-to-AVC rewriting* process (Segall & Zhao, 2008) such a conversion is possible without fully decoding and re-encoding the bit stream. Theoretically, an SVC-to-AVC rewriter module could be placed at the server, in the network (at a MANE), or even at the client. Practically, to the best of our knowledge, the applicability of such an SVC-to-AVC rewriter module has never been evaluated. A current cooperation with an IPTV service provider aims at the development of an innovative H.264/SVC-based IPTV architecture including application and evaluation of SVC-to-AVC rewriting. This project is part of a European project called *SCALNET* (Scalable Video Coding Impact on Networks) (SCALNET Project, 2009). SCALNET has the main objective to demonstrate the impact of the H.264/SVC technology on video streaming over various types of networks. In order to cope with QoS requirements of real-time video transmission on the one hand and the heterogeneity of receivers and networks on the other hand, SCALNET focuses on two key techniques: QoS management in a scalable video coding environment and control and adaptation of H.264/SVC streams within the networks.

Another current topic in today's research is the streaming of content over peer-to-peer (P2P) networks. The concept of streaming over P2P is well appreciated as it allows distributing the content to a great number of users while reducing the server costs for providing the content. However, the adaptation of content in P2P networks brings about new challenges. In P2P environments, not only the adaptation of H.264/SVC content but also the peer selection process presents a challenging problem. For the adaptation of H.264/SVC content, the pieces of those layers that are suitable for the given available bandwidth and the usage environment properties need to be selected. This problem is known as the piece selection problem and is very similar to the H.264/SVC adaptation problem described in the previous sections. The main issues for the piece selection part are to ensure that all the desired pieces are downloaded before their playback deadline and to make sure that the available bandwidth is utilized as fully as possible, i.e., the highest possible quality should be downloaded. Additionally, in P2P networks the peer selection process, which decides which pieces to download from which neighbor, needs to be performed. This process has to consider the priority of the pieces based on their deadline and layer and has to select a suitable peer based on the download bandwidth provided by the neighbor peers. The piece and peer selection problems are tightly connected and together present a challenging optimization problem. One of the major projects that addresses the streaming of scalable media content over P2P networks and works on solutions for the piece as well as the peer selection problem is the European project *P2P-Next* (P2P-Next Project, 2009).

CONCLUSION

The H.264/SVC standard and its use for adaptive streaming of scalable video content are timely topics. This chapter covered, from a systems point of view, architectural/implementation options, adaptation methods, and application cases of H.264/SVC adaptive streaming. It was attempted to show which techniques can be combined reasonably and for which applications. The large body of research work so far and initial adoption by industry indicate that H.264/SVC is indeed a promising enabling technology for delivering digital video over best-effort, unpredictable networks to diverse end devices in the best quality possible for each user. However, several challenges still lie ahead, among them the need for high-performance H.264/SVC encoder and decoder hardware and/or software, and the integration of H.264/SVC technology into today's multimedia systems that deploy legacy codecs.

ACKNOWLEDGMENT

This work was partially supported by the Austrian Science Fund (FWF) under project "Adaptive Streaming of Secure Scalable Wavelet-based Video (P19159)", by the Austrian Research Promotion Agency (FFG) under project "Scalable Video Based Provisioning of TV and VoD Services over the Internet (SCALIPTV)", and by the European Commission in the context of the projects ENTHRONE II (IST-1-507637) and P2P-Next (FP7-ICT-216217).

REFERENCES

P2P-Next (2009). *P2P-Next Project*. Retrieved August, 14, 2009 from http://www.p2p-next.org

Amon, P., Rathgen, T., & Singer, D. (2007). File Format for Scalable Video Coding. *IEEE Transactions on Circuits and Systems for Video Technology, 17*(9), 1174–1185. doi:10.1109/TCSVT.2007.905521

Bakker, D., Comboom, D., Dams, T., & Munteanu, A. (2008). Priority-based error protection for the scalable extension of H.264/AVC. *In Proc. SPIE, Optical and Digital Image Processing. Vol. 7000.*

Chang, S.-F., & Vetro, A. (2005). Video Adaptation: Concepts, Technologies, and Open Issues. *Proceedings of the IEEE, 93*(1), 148–158. doi:10.1109/JPROC.2004.839600

Eberhard, M., Celetto, L., Timmerer, C., Quacchio, E., Hellwagner, H., & Rovati, F. (2008). An Interoperable Streaming Framework for Scalable Video Coding based on MPEG-21. In *Proc. 5th IET Visual Information Engineering Conference (VIE'08)*, (pp. 723-728). Xi'an, China.

Gorkemli, B., & Civanlar, M. R. (2006). SVC Coded Video Streaming over DCCP. In *Proc. 8th IEEE International Symposium on Multimedia (ISM'06)*, (pp. 437-441). San Diego, CA.

Handley, M., Jacobson, V., & Perkins, C. (2006). SDP: Session Description Protocol. *RFC 4566.*

Hellge, C., Mirta, S., Schierl, T., & Wiegand, T. (2009). Mobile TV with SVC and hierarchical modulation for DVB-H broadcast. In *Proc. IEEE International Symposium on Broadband Multimedia Systems and Broadcasting (BMSB'09)*, (pp. 1-5). Bilbao, Spain.

Hellwagner, H., Kuschnig, R., Stütz, T., & Uhl, A. (2009). Efficient in-network adaptation of encrypted H.264/SVC content. *Signal Processing Image Communication, 24*, 740–758. doi:10.1016/j.image.2009.07.002

ISO/IEC 13818-1:2000 (2000). *Generic coding of moving pictures and associated audio information: Systems.* Geneva, Switzerland: International Organization for Standardization.

ISO/IEC 13818-1:2006/FPDAM 3.2 (2008). *Transport of SVC Video (ISO/IEC 14496-10 Amd.3) over ISO/IEC 13818-1 Streams.* Geneva, Switzerland: International Organization for Standardization.

ISO/IEC 14496-12:2005 Part 12 (2005). *ISO Base Media File Format.* Geneva, Switzerland: International Organization for Standardization.

ISO/IEC 14496-15:2004/Amd2 (2008). *SVC File Format.* Geneva, Switzerland: International Organization for Standardization.

Kofler, I., Kuschnig, R., & Hellwagner, H. (2009). Improving IPTV Services by H.264/SVC Adaptation and Traffic Control. In *Proc. IEEE International Symposium on Broadband Multimedia Systems and Broadcasting (BMSB'09)*, (pp. 1-6). Bilbao, Spain.

Kofler, I., Prangl, M., Kuschnig, R., & Hellwagner, H. (2008). An H.264/SVC-based adaptation proxy on a WiFi router. In *Proc. 18th International Workshop on Network and Operating Systems Support for Digital Audio and Video (NOSSDAV'08)*, (pp. 63-68). Braunschweig, Germany.

Kofler, I., Timmerer, C., Hellwagner, H., Hutter, A., & Sanahuja, F. (2007). Efficient MPEG-21-based Adaptation Decision-Taking for Scalable Multimedia Content. In *Proc. 14th SPIE Annual Electronic Imaging Conference - Multimedia Computing and Networking (MMCN 2007)*, (pp. 65040J-1 - 65040J-8). San Jose, CA.

Kuschnig, R., Kofler, I., Ransburg, M., & Hellwagner, H. (2008). Design options and comparison of in-network H.264/SVC adaptation. *Journal of Visual Communication and Image Representation, 19*, 529–542. doi:10.1016/j.jvcir.2008.07.004

Liebl, G., Schierl, T., Wiegand, T., & Stockhammer, T. (2006). Advanced Wireless Multiuser Video Streaming using the Scalable Video. In *Proc. IEEE International Conference on Multimedia and Expo (ICME'2006)*, (pp. 625-628). Toronto, Ontario.

McCanne, S., Jacobson, V., & Vetterli, M. (1996). Receiver-driven layered multicast. In *Conference Proceedings on Applications, Technologies, Architectures, and Protocols for Computer Communications (SIGCOMM'96)*, (pp. 117-130). Palo Alto, CA.

Mushtaq, M., & Ahmed, T. (2008). Smooth Video Delivery for SVC Based Media Streaming Over P2P Networks. In *Proc. 5th IEEE Conferenceon Consumer Communications and Networking (CCNC'08)*, (pp. 447-451). Las Vegas, NV.

Ortega, A., & Wang, H. (2007). Mechanisms for Adapting Compressed Multimedia to Varying Bandwidth Conditions. In van der Schaar, M., & Chou, P. (Eds.), *Multimedia over IP and Wireless Networks* (pp. 81–116). New York: Academic Press. doi:10.1016/B978-012088480-3/50005-9

Paila, T., Luby, M., Lehtonen, R., Roca, V., & Walsh, R. (2004). FLUTE - File Delivery over Unidirectional Transport. *RFC 3926*.

Panis, G., Hutter, A., Heuer, J., Hellwagner, H., Kosch, H., Timmerer, C., et al. (2003). Bitstream Syntax Description: A Tool for Multimedia Resource Adaptation within MPEG-21. *Signal Processing: Image Communication Journal - Special Issue on Multimedia Adaptation, 18*(8), 721-747.

Pesquet-Popescu, B., Li, S., & van der Schaar, M. (2007). Scalable Video Coding for Adaptive Streaming. In van der Schaar, M., & Chou, P. (Eds.), *Multimedia over IP and Wireless Networks* (pp. 117–158). New York: Academic Press. doi:10.1016/B978-012088480-3/50006-0

Ransburg, M., Devillers, S., Timmerer, C., & Hellwagner, H. (2007). Processing and Delivery of Multimedia Metadata for Multimedia Content Streaming. In *Proc. Datenbanksysteme in Business, Technologie und Web (BTW 2007)*, (pp. 117-138). Aachen, Germany.

ITU-T Rec. H.264 (2005). *ISO/IEC 14496-10 Advanced Video Coding (Version 4)*. Geneva, Switzerland: International Organization for Standardization.

ITU-T Rec. H.264 (2007). *ISO/IEC 14496-10 Advanced Video Coding / Amd. 3*. Geneva, Switzerland: International Organization for Standardization.

SCALNET Project. (2009). Retrieved August 27, 2009, from http://www.scalnet.info

Schierl, T., Johansen, S., Hellge, C., & Stockhammer, T. (2007). Distributed Rate-Distortion Optimization for Rateless Coded Scalable Scalable Video in Mobile Ad Hoc Networks. In *Proc. IEEE International Conference on Image Processing (ICIP 2007), 6*, pp. VI-497-VI-500. San Antonio, TX.

Schierl, T., Stockhammer, T., & Wiegand, T. (2007). Mobile Video Transmission Using Scalable Video Coding. *IEEE Transactions on Circuits and Systems for Video Technology, 17*(9), 1204–1217. doi:10.1109/TCSVT.2007.905528

Schierl, T., & Wenger, S. (2009). Signaling Media Decoding Dependency in the Session Description Protocol (SDP). *RFC 5583*.

Schulzrinne, H., Casner, S., Frederick, R., & Jacobson, V. (2003). RTP: A Transport Protocol for Real-Time Applications. *RFC 3550*.

Schwarz, H., Marpe, D., & Wiegand, T. (2007). Overview of the Scalable Video Coding Extension of the H.264/AVC Standard. *IEEE Transactions on Circuits and Systems for Video Technology, 17*(9), 1103–1107. doi:10.1109/TCSVT.2007.905532

Segall, A., & Zhao, J. (2008). Bit stream rewriting for SVC-to-AVC conversion. In *Proc. 15th IEEE International Conference on Image Processing (ICIP 2008)*, (pp. 2776-2779). San Diego, CA.

Stockhammer, T., Gasiba, T., Samad, W. A., Schierl, T., Jenkac, H., & Wiegand, T. (2007). Nested harmonic broadcasting for scalable video over mobile datacast channels. *Wireless Communications and Mobile Computing*, *7*(2), 235–256. doi:10.1002/wcm.476

Stütz, T., & Uhl, A. (2008). Format-Compliant Encryption of H.264/AVC and SVC. In *Proc. 10th IEEE International Symposium on Multimedia (ISM 2008)*, (pp. 446-451). Berkeley, CA.

Sun, H., Vetro, A., & Xin, J. (2007). An overview of scalable video streaming. *Wireless Communications and Mobile Computing*, *7*(2), 159–172. doi:10.1002/wcm.471

Thang, T. C., Kim, J.-G., Kang, J. W., & Yoo, J.-J. (2009). SVC adaptation: Standard tools and supporting methods. *Signal Processing Image Communication*, *24*, 214–228. doi:10.1016/j.image.2008.12.006

van der Schaar, M., & Shankar N, S. (2005). Cross-layer wireless multimedia transmission: challenges, principles, and new paradigms. *IEEE Wireless Communications Magazine*, *12*(4), 50-58.

Vetro, A. (2004). MPEG-21 Digital Item Adaptation: Enabling Universal Multimedia Access. *IEEE MultiMedia*, *11*(1), 84–87. doi:10.1109/MMUL.2004.1261111

Wang, Y., Hannuksela, M., Pateaux, S., Eleftheriadis, A., & Wenger, S. (2007). System and Transport Interface of SVC. *IEEE Transactions on Circuits and Systems for Video Technology*, *17*(9), 1149–1163. doi:10.1109/TCSVT.2007.906827

Wenger, S., Wang, Y., Schierl, T., & Eleftheriadis, A. (2009). RTP Payload Format for SVC Video. *Internet Draft (draft-ietf-avt-rtp-svc-18.txt)*.

Wenger, S., Wang, Y.-K., & Schierl, T. (2007). Transport and Signaling of SVC in IP Networks. *IEEE Transactions on Circuits and Systems for Video Technology*, *17*(9), 1164–1173. doi:10.1109/TCSVT.2007.905523

Wien, M., Cazoulat, R., Graffunder, A., Hutter, A., & Amon, P. (2007). Real-Time System for Adaptive Video Streaming Based on SVC. *IEEE Transactions on Circuits and Systems for Video Technology*, *17*(9), 1227–1237. doi:10.1109/TCSVT.2007.905519

Xiaogang, Y., & Lei, L. (2007). End-to-End Congestion Control for H.264/SVC. In *Proc. 6th International Conference on Networking (ICN'07)*, (pp. 84-89). Sainte-Luce, Martinique.

ADDITIONAL READING

Baccichet, P., Schierl, T., Wiegand, T., & Girod, B. (2007). Low-delay peer-to-peer streaming using scalable video coding. In *Proc. 16th International Packet Video Workshop (Packet Video 2007)*, (pp. 173-181). Lausanne, Switzerland.

Chakareski, J., & Frossard, P. (2005). Rate-Distortion Optimized Packet Scheduling Over Bottleneck Links. In *Proc. 2005 International Conference on Multimedia and Expo (ICME 2005)*, (pp. 1066-1069). Amsterdam.

Chakareski, J., & Frossard, P. (2005). Rate-Distortion Optimized Bandwidth Adaptation for Distributed Media Delivery. In *Proc. 2005 International Conference on Multimedia and Expo (ICME 2005)*, (pp. 763-766). Amsterdam.

Choi, S.-J., & Woods, J. W. (1999). Motion-compensated 3-D subband coding of video. *IEEE Transactions on Image Processing*, *8*(2), 155–167. doi:10.1109/83.743851

Chou, P. A., & Miao, Z. (2001). Rate-distortion optimized sender-driven streaming over best-effort networks. In *Proc. 2001 Workshop on Multimedia Signal Processing (MMSP 2001)*, (pp. 587-592). Cannes, France.

Chou, P. A., & Miao, Z. (2006). Rate-Distortion Optimized Streaming of Packetized Media. *IEEE Transactions on Multimedia, 8*(2), 390–404. doi:10.1109/TMM.2005.864313

Chou, P. A., & Sehgal, A. (2002). Rate-distortion optimized receiver-driven streaming over best-effort networks. In *Proc. 12th International Packet Video Workshop (Packet Video 2002)*. Pittsburgh, PA.

De Cock, J., Notebaert, S., Lambert, P., & Van de Walle, R. (2008). Advanced bitstream rewriting from H.264/AVC to SVC. In *Proc. IEEE International Conference on Image Processing (ICIP 2008)*, (pp. 2472-2475). San Diego, CA.

De Neve, W., Van Deursen, D., De Schrijver, D., Lerouge, S., De Wolf, K., & Van de Walle, R. (2006). BFlavor: A harmonized approach to media resource adaptation inspired by MPEG-21 BSDL and XFlavor. *Signal Processing Image Communication, 21*(10), 862–889. doi:10.1016/j.image.2006.08.005

De Schrijver, D., De Neve, W., De Wolf, K., De Sutter, R., & Van de Walle, R. (2007). An optimized MPEG-21 BSDL framework for the adaptation of scalable bitstreams. *Journal of Visual Communication and Image Representation, 18*(3), 217–239. doi:10.1016/j.jvcir.2007.02.003

De Schrijver, D., De Neve, W., De Wolf, K., Lambert, P., Van Deursen, D., & Van de Walle, R. (2007). XML-driven Exploitation of Combined Scalability in Scalable H.264/AVC Bitstreams. In *Proc. 2007 IEEE International Symposium on Circuits and Systems (ISCAS 2007)*, (pp. 1521-1524). New Orleans, LA.

De Schrijver, D., Poppe, C., Lerouge, S., De Neve, W., & Van de Walle, R. (2006). MPEG-21 bitstream syntax descriptions for scalable video codecs. *Multimedia Systems, 11*(5), 403–421. doi:10.1007/s00530-006-0021-5

Devillers, S., Timmerer, C., Heuer, J., & Hellwagner, H. (2005). Bitstream Syntax Description-Based Adaptation in Streaming and Constrained Environments. *IEEE Transactions on Multimedia, 7*(3), 463–470. doi:10.1109/TMM.2005.846794

Kalman, M., & Girod, B. (2004). Rate-distortion optimized video streaming using conditional packet delay distributions. In *Proc. 2004 Workshop on Multimedia Signal Processing (MMSP 2004)*, (pp. 514-517). Siena, Italy.

Kalman, M., & Girod, B. (2007). Network-Adaptive Media Transport. In van der Schaar, M., & Chou, P. (Eds.), *Multimedia over IP and Wireless Networks* (pp. 293–310). New York: Academic Press. doi:10.1016/B978-012088480-3/50011-4

Kantarci, A. (2008). Streaming of scalable H.264 videos over the Internet. *Multimedia Tools and Applications, 36*(3), 303–324. doi:10.1007/s11042-007-0147-2

Kim, J., Um, T.-W., Ryu, W., Lee, B. S., & Hahn, M. (2008). Heterogeneous Networks and Terminal-Aware QoS/QoE-Guaranteed Mobile IPTV Service. *IEEE Communications Magazine, 46*(5), 110–117. doi:10.1109/MCOM.2008.4557052

Lerouge, S., Lambert, P., & Van de Walle, R. (2003). Multi-criteria Optimization for Scalable Bitstreams. In *Proc. 8th International Workshop on Visual Content Processing and Representation*, (pp. 122-130). Madrid, Spain.

Li, W. (2001). Overview of fine granularity scalability in MPEG-4 video standard. *IEEE Transactions on Circuits and Systems for Video Technology, 11*(3), 301–317. doi:10.1109/76.911157

Mukherjee, D., Delfosse, E., Kim, J.-G., & Wang, Y. (2005). Optimal adaptation decision-taking for terminal and network quality-of-service. *IEEE Transactions on Multimedia, 7*(3), 454–462. doi:10.1109/TMM.2005.846798

Oelbaum, T., Schwarz, H., Wien, M., & Wiegand, T. (2008). Subjective performance evaluation of the SVC extension of H.264/AVC. In *Proc. 2008 IEEE International Conference on Image Processing (ICIP 2008)*, (pp. 2772-2775). San Diego, CA.

Ohm, J.-R. (1994). Three-dimensional subband coding with motion compensation. *IEEE Transactions on Image Processing*, *3*(5), 559–571. doi:10.1109/83.334985

Ohm, J.-R. (2005). Advances in Scalable Video Coding. *Proceedings of the IEEE*, *93*(1), 42–56. doi:10.1109/JPROC.2004.839611

Ohm, J.-R., van der Schaar, M., & Woods, J. (2004). Interframe Wavelet Coding: Motion Picture Representation for Universal Scalability. *Signal Processing Image Communication*, *19*(9), 877–908. doi:10.1016/j.image.2004.06.004

Radha, H., van der Schaar, M., & Chen, Y. (2001). The MPEG-4 fine-grained scalable video coding method for multimedia streaming over IP. *IEEE Transactions on Multimedia*, *3*(1), 53–68. doi:10.1109/6046.909594

Radha, H., van der Schaar, M., & Karande, S. (2004). Scalable video transcaling for the wireless Internet. *EURASIP Journal on Applied Signal Processing*, *24*(2), 265–279. doi:10.1155/S111086570430805X

Rajendran, R. K., & Rubenstein, D. (2006). Optimizing the quality of scalable video streams on P2P networks. *Computer Networks*, *50*(15), 2641–2658. doi:10.1016/j.comnet.2005.10.001

Segall, C., & Sullivan, G. (2007). Spatial Scalability within the H.264/AVC Scalable Video Coding Extension. *IEEE Transactions on Circuits and Systems for Video Technology*, *17*(9), 1121–1135. doi:10.1109/TCSVT.2007.906824

Setton, E., & Girod, B. (2004). Congestion-distortion optimized scheduling of video over a bottleneck link. In *Proc. 6th Workshop on Multimedia Signal Processing (MMSP 2004)*, (pp. 179-182). Siena, Italy.

Setton, E., Noh, J., & Girod, B. (2006). Congestion-Distortion Optimized Peer-to-Peer Video Streaming. In *Proc. 2006 IEEE International Conference on Image Processing (ICIP 2006)*, (pp. 721-724). Atlanta, GA.

Tappayuthpijarn, K., Liebl, G., Stockhammer, Th., & Steinbach, E. (2009). Adaptive video streaming over a mobile network with TCP-friendly rate control. In *Proc. 2009 International Conference on Wireless Communications and Mobile Computing (IWCMC'09)*, (pp. 1325-1329). Leipzig, Germany.

Thang, T. C., Kang, J. W., Yoo, J.-J., & Kim, J.-G. (2008). Multilayer Adaptation for MGS-based SVC Bitstream. In *Proc. 16th ACM International Conference on Multimedia (MM 2008)*, (pp. 689-692). Vancouver, British Columbia.

Thang, T. C., Kim, Y. S., Ro, Y. M., Kang, J. W., & Kim, J.-G. (2006). SVC bitstream adaptation in MPEG-21 multimedia framework. *Journal of Zhejiang University SCIENCE A*, *7*(5), 764–772. doi:10.1631/jzus.2006.A0764

Timmerer, C., Devillers, S., & Vetro, A. (2006). Digital Item Adaptation - Coding Format Independence. In Burnett, I., Pereira, F., Van de Walle, R., & Koenen, R. (Eds.), *The MPEG-21 Book* (pp. 282–331). New York: John Wiley and Sons Ltd. doi:10.1002/0470010134.ch8

Timmerer, C., & Hellwagner, H. (2005). Interoperable Adaptive Multimedia Communication. *IEEE Multimedia Magazine*, *12*(1), 74–79. doi:10.1109/MMUL.2005.7

van der Schaar, M., Andreopoulos, Y., & Hu, Z. (2006). Optimized scalable video streaming over IEEE 802.11 a/e HCCA wireless networks under delay constraints. *IEEE Transactions on Mobile Computing, 5*(6), 755–768. doi:10.1109/TMC.2006.81

van der Schaar, M., Krishnamachari, S., Choi, S., & Xu, X. (2003). Adaptive cross-layer protection strategies for robust scalable video transmission over 802.11 WLANs. *IEEE Journal on Selected Areas in Communications, 21*(10), 1752–1763. doi:10.1109/JSAC.2003.815231

van der Schaar, M., & Radha, H. (2001). A hybrid temporal-SNR fine-granular scalability for Internet video. *IEEE Transactions on Circuits and Systems for Video Technology, 11*(3), 318–331. doi:10.1109/76.911158

Van Deursen, D., De Neve, W., De Schrijver, D., & Van de Walle, R. (2007). Automatic generation of generic Bitstream Syntax Descriptions applied to H.264/AVC SVC encoded video streams. In *Proc. 14th International Conference on Image Analysis and Processing (ICIAP 2007)*, (pp. 382-387). Modena, Italy.

Van Deursen, D., De Neve, W., De Schrijver, D., & Van de Walle, R. (2008). gBFlavor: a new tool for fast and automatic generation of generic bitstream syntax descriptions. *Multimedia Tools and Applications*, (40): 453–494. doi:10.1007/s11042-008-0214-3

Van Deursen, D., De Schrijver, D., De Bruyne, S., & Van de Walle, R. (2007). Fully Format Agnostic Media Resource Adaptation Using an Abstract Model for Scalable Bitstreams. In *Proc. 2007 IEEE International Conference on Multimedia and Expo (ICME 2007)*, (pp. 240-243). Beijing, China.

Vetro, A., & Timmerer, C. (2005). Digital Item Adaptation: Overview of Standardization and Research Activities. *IEEE Transactions on Multimedia, 7*(3), 418–426. doi:10.1109/TMM.2005.846795

Vetro, A., Timmerer, C., & Devillers, S. (2006). Digital Item Adaptation - Tools for Universal Multimedia Access. In Burnett, I., Pereira, F., Van de Walle, R., & Koenen, R. (Eds.), *The MPEG-21 Book* (pp. 243–281). New York: John Wiley and Sons Ltd.doi:10.1002/0470010134.ch7

Wiegand, T., Sullivan, G. J., Bjøntegaard, G., & Luthra, A. (2003). Overview of the H.264/AVC Video Coding Standard. *IEEE Transactions on Circuits and Systems for Video Technology, 13*(7), 560–576. doi:10.1109/TCSVT.2003.815165

Wien, M., Schwarz, H., & Oelbaum, T. (2007). Performance Analysis of SVC. *IEEE Transactions on Circuits and Systems for Video Technology, 17*(9), 1194–1203. doi:10.1109/TCSVT.2007.905530

Xiao, S., Wu, C., Li, Y., Du, J., & Kuo, C. C. (2008). Priority Ordering Algorithm for Scalable Video Coding Transmission over Heterogeneous Network. In *Proc. 22nd International Conference on Advanced Information Networking and Applications (AINA'08)*, (pp. 896-903). Okinawa, Japan.

KEY TERMS AND DEFINITIONS

Adaptation: Adaptation refers to the transformation of multimedia content to a desired quality.

Decoding Dependency Information: The decoding dependency information, i.e., the parameters dependency ID, quality ID, and temporal ID, is included in the header of each H.264/SVC VCL NALU and indicates the layer the NALU belongs to.

H.264/SVC: H.264/SVC refers to the Scalable Video Coding extension of the H.264/AVC standard, which was standardized by the Joint Video Team of the ITU-T Video Coding Experts Group and the ISO/IEC Moving Picture Experts Group.

Metadata-Driven Adaptation: Metadata-driven adaptation refers to the adaptation of (scalable) content based on metadata, i.e., descriptions of the bit stream syntax. Specifications of such metadata-based bit stream syntax descriptions are part of MPEG-21 DIA.

MPEG-21 Digital Item Adaptation: MPEG-21 Digital Item Adaptation (DIA) specifies descriptions (metadata) for an interoperable adaptation framework that allows adapting scalable multimedia content independent of the coding format.

Scalability: In video coding, scalability refers to the provision of different qualities in possibly different dimensions embedded into a single bit stream; in H.264/SVC, scalability is provided in three dimensions: in the spatial domain (resolution), the fidelity domain (SNR quality), and the temporal domain (frame rate).

SVC-Specific Adaptation: SVC-specific adaptation refers to the adaptation of H.264/SVC content by parsing the bit stream syntax. When SVC-specific adaptation is performed, the decoding dependency information is utilized to decide which NALUs to discard to adapt the bit stream to the desired bit rate and quality.

Chapter 2
Adapting Multimedia Streaming to Changing Network Conditions

Dimitris N. Kanellopoulos
University of Patras, Greece

ABSTRACT

Providing a satisfactory multimedia service in networking environments requires an effective media delivery mechanism. However, the Internet does not provide a guaranteed network bandwidth to accommodate multimedia service in a reliable fashion. The Internet is a heterogeneous networking environment, in which resources available to multimedia applications are changing. In the last decade, the research community has proposed both networking techniques and application layer techniques, which adapt to the changes in network conditions. This chapter focuses on the application level techniques, including methods based on compression algorithm features, layered encoding, rate shaping, adaptive error control, and smoothing. The chapter also discusses operating system methods to support adaptive multimedia.

INTRODUCTION

Multimedia streaming over the Internet has received tremendous attention from academia and industry due to the increasing demand for multimedia information on the web. The current best-effort Internet does not offer any *quality of service* (QoS) guarantees to streaming video. Adaptive streaming applications have the capability to stream multimedia data over heterogeneous networks and adapt media transmission to network changes. Adaptation of multimedia applications can be done at several layers of the network protocol stack. This chapter presents techniques for adaptation based on compression methods. In particular the chapter discusses techniques for achieving adaptation at the application layer including layered encoding, receiver driven multicast, rate shaping, error control, adaptive synchronization, and smoothing. In addition, the chapter discusses operating system methods to support adaptive multimedia.

High-speed technologies such as ATM (asynchronous transfer mode), gigabit Ethernet, fast

DOI: 10.4018/978-1-61692-831-5.ch002

Copyright © 2011, IGI Global. Copying or distributing in print or electronic forms without written permission of IGI Global is prohibited.

Ethernet, and frame relay support real-time multimedia applications such as video-on-demand, video broadcasting and Internet telephony (Kanellopoulos, 2009). QoS refers to the capability of a networked system (e.g., a distributed multimedia system) to provide scalable service to selected network traffic. Various multimedia applications have different QoS requirements. For example, continuous media types such as audio and video require hard or soft bounds on the end-to-end delay, while discrete media such as text and images do not have any strict delay constrains. Multimedia streaming services impose new QoS requirements on the Internet (Li & Yin, 2007; Kanellopoulos *et al.*, 2008). Multimedia applications use application streaming for sending multimedia data streams. The *Real-time Streaming Protocol* (RTSP) (Schulzrinne *et al.*, 1998), the *Real-time Transport Protocol* (RTP) (Schulzrinne *et al.*, 1987) and the *Real-time Transport Control Protocol* (RTCP) were specifically designed to stream media over networks. The latter two are built on top of UDP. On the Internet, the available network resources provided to a multimedia application are changing dynamically. Network conditions may change due to difference in link speeds or variability in a wireless environment caused by interference and mobility (Kanellopoulos *et al.*, 2006). To provide end-to-end QoS guarantees, an intensive effort is necessary from all subsystems, including end-subsystems, network hardware, and communication protocols of a multimedia system. If multimedia applications are capable of adapting to changing network conditions, then network resources can be used efficiently. Adaptation of multimedia applications can be done at several layers of the network protocol stack (Vandalore *et al.*, 2001). At the physical layer, adaptive power control techniques can be used to alleviate variations in a wireless environment. At the data link layer, error control and adaptive reservation techniques can be used to protect against variation in error and available rate. At the network layer, dynamic re-routing mechanisms can be used to avoid congestion and mitigate variations in a mobile environment. At the transport layer, dynamic re-negotiation of connection parameters can be used for adaptation.

At the application layer, the multimedia application can adapt to changes in network conditions using several techniques including efficient compression, hierarchical encoding, smoothing of the video information transmitted, rate shaping, error control, and adaptive synchronization (Vandalore *et al.*, 2001). These methods can be classified into *reactive* and *passive* according to their approach towards adaptation. In reactive methods, the application modifies its traffic to suit the changes in the network. In passive methods, the application aims to optimize the usage of network resources. Smoothing of stored video and rate shaping are example applications of passive and reactive methods respectively.

This chapter presents techniques for adaptation based on compression methods. In addition, it discusses techniques for achieving adaptation at the application layer including layered encoding, receiver driven multicast, rate shaping, error control viz. forward error correction (FEC) techniques for Internet audio and video, adaptive synchronization, and smoothing.

- In *layered encoding*, the video information is encoded into several layers. The base layer carries important video and critical timing information. The higher layers improve the quality of video gradually. The receiver can get a reasonable quality with the base layer, and quality improves with reception of higher layers. The encoder allocates priorities to the encoded layers, with the base layer having the highest priority. When the network transmits layered video, it can drop lower priority (higher) layers in the event of congestion.
- The *Receiver driven Layered Multicast* (RLM) technique describes how layered video can be transmitted and controlled.

Receivers dynamically subscribe to the different layers of the video streams.

- In *rate shaping*, video encoder parameters (e.g., frame rate, quantization level) are changed to meet the changing network conditions.
- *Error control* techniques use FEC-based methods to provide protection against changing error conditions.
- *Adaptive synchronization* methods achieve intermedia and/or intramedia synchronization.
- *Smoothing techniques* attempt to reduce the variability in the resource requirements of multimedia applications.

Last but not least, multimedia applications require periodic access of CPU and other system resources. Techniques to achieve this include real-time upcall, adaptive scheduling and CPU management. These operating system techniques are discussed later.

Video Compression Algorithms

Humans are less sensitive to loss of video than audio, because audio is significant for comprehension. Besides, video requires larger bandwidth (100 kbps to 15Mbps) than audio (8 kbps - 128 kbps). Therefore, audio is given higher priority and as a result only the video can be used for adaptation. Video is always compressed before transmission because raw video would otherwise consume far too much bandwidth except in specialist photonic networks. The two main compression techniques used for video are: (1) discrete cosine transformation (DCT) based, and (2) wavelet transforms based. In the event of congestion in the network, video encoder can reduce its encoding rate by temporal scaling (reducing frame rate) or spatial scaling (reducing resolution). DCT is the compression method used in the popular MPEG (Moving Picture Experts Group) set of standards (ISO/IEC 13818-2, 1994). MPEG standards are used for both video and audio signals. Discrete cosine transformations are used in MPEG-2, MPEG-1 and JPEG. The transformed coefficients are quantized using scalar quantization and run length encoded before transmission. The transformed higher frequency coefficients of video are truncated given that the human eye is insensitive to these coefficients. The compression relies on two basic methods: *intra-frame DCT coding* for reduction of spatial redundancy, and *inter-frame motion compensation* for reduction of temporal redundancy. MPEG-2 video has three kinds of frames: *I*, *P*, and *B*.

- *I* frames are independent frames compressed using only intra-frame compression.
- *P* frames are predictive, which carry the signal difference between the previous frame and motion vectors.
- *B* frames are interpolated, i.e., encoded based on the previous and the next frame.

MPEG-2 video is transmitted in *group of pictures* (GoP) format, which specifies the distribution of *I*, *P*, and *B* frames in the video stream. The MPEG compression methods can be used for adaptation with two main schemes. First, the rate of the source can be changed by using different quantization levels and encoding rate (Duffield *et al.*, 1998; Bolot and Turletti, 1994). Second, DCT coefficients can be partitioned and transmitted in several layers with different priorities. The base layer carries the important video information and an additional layer improves the quality. In the event of congestion, the lower priority layer can be dropped to reduce the rate (Eleftheriadis and Batra, 2004; Pancha and Zakri, 1993). Lotfallah *et al.* (2006) present and evaluate adaptive streaming mechanisms, which are based on the visual content features for non-scalable (single-layer) encoded video, whereby the adaptation is achieved by selectively dropping B-frames.

MPEG-4 is an original collection of methods defining compression of audio and visual digital data. Uses of MPEG-4 include compression of audio and visual data for streaming media and CD distribution, voice (telephone, videophone) and broadcast television applications. MPEG-4 provides: (1) improved coding efficiency; (2) ability to encode mixed media data (video, audio, speech); (3) error resilience to enable robust transmission; (4) ability to interact with the audio-visual scene generated at the receiver.

H.264/MPEG-4 Advanced Video Coding (AVC) is a standard for video compression (Wiegand *et al.*, 2003). The ITU-T H.264 standard and the ISO/IEC MPEG-4 AVC standard (formally, ISO/IEC 14496-10 - MPEG-4 Part 10, AVC) are jointly maintained so that they have identical technical content. H.264/AVC/MPEG-4 Part 10 contains a number of features that allow it to compress video effectively and provide more flexibility for application to a wide variety of network environments. In particular, some such key features include: (1) multi-picture inter-picture prediction; (2) spatial prediction from the edges of neighboring blocks for "intra"coding; (3) lossless macroblock coding features; (4) flexible interlaced-scan video coding features; (5) a quantization design; (6) an in-loop deblocking filter which helps prevent the blocking artifacts common to other DCT-based image compression techniques, resulting in better visual appearance and compression efficiency; (7) an entropy coding; (8) loss resilience features. These techniques help H.264 to perform significantly under a wide variety of conditions in a wide variety of application environments. H.264 can often perform radically better than MPEG-2 video—typically obtaining the same quality at half of the bit rate or less, especially on high bit rate and high resolution situations.[REMOVED HYPERLINK FIELD] H.264/AVC has a reference software implementation that can be freely downloaded.

Wavelet Compression

Wavelet compression is frequently achieved by using a motion-compensated two-dimensional (2D) wavelet function (Tham *et al.*, 1998) or a 3D wavelet (Podilchuk *et al.*, 1995). In wavelet encoding, the image is separated into various sub-bands with increasing resolutions. In each sub-data, data is transformed using a wavelet function to get transformed coefficients. After that, the transformed coefficients are quantized and run length encoded before transmission. In wavelet compression, the whole image is used in encoding, instead of blocks, used in DCT based methods. Therefore, in wavelet compression scalability for image and video compression is supported. Continuous rate scalability is supported by wavelet transforms joined with encoding techniques. This requires that the video can be encoded at any desired rate within the scalable range (Taubman & Zakhor, 1996). Cheng *et al.* (1997) demonstrated that a wavelet encoder can benefit from network feedback (e.g., available bandwidth) to obtain scalability.

APPLICATION STREAMING

Multimedia applications use the application streaming technique for sending multimedia data streams (Wu, D. *et al.*, 2001). Typically, the architecture of a streaming system is shown in Figure 1. The system consists of three main components: a real-time streaming server, a corresponding real-time streaming client and a network which also serve for transmission of media data. The client requests are sent to the server via network connections. The buffers at the client end are used to provide some tolerance to variations in network delay as well as data consumption rates.

Fine granularity scalability (FGS) was defined to deliver multimedia applications in heterogeneous network environments with different bandwidth and loss behaviors (Radha *et al.*, 2001).

Figure 1. The scalable video streaming system

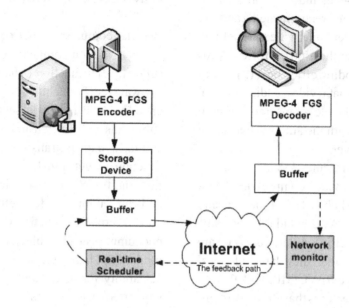

FGS is an evolution of the scalable hierarchical video encoding. An FGS stream has only two layers: a Base layer that must be received to make possible video decoding, and an enhancement layer (the FGS layer), which can be delivered optionally where bandwidth is available. FGS allows the source to adjust the relative sizes of both Base and FGS layers, therefore allowing the FGS layer to be broken up and allowing the decoder to decode any portion of the received FGS layer. The source or any intermediate node is responsible to do that. There are three types of scalability: (1) temporal (frame rate) scalability; (2) spatial (picture size) scalability; and (3) SNR (quality/fidelity) scalability. In all the three cases, the Base-layer pictures are encoded based on sub-sampling with either less frame rate (for temporal scalability), smaller picture size (for spatial scalability), or coarser picture quality (for SNR scalability). Full-quality video is obtained by the combination of both Base and FGS layers. FGS is provided by the MPEG-4 FGS coding scheme (Li, 2001). This scheme has become a part of the MPEG-4 as an amendment to the traditional non-scalable MC-DCT approach for

streaming video profile (MPEG-4, 2004). It consists of one base layer that is coded with an MPEG-4 compliant non-scalable coder, as well as one or more enhancement layers coded progressively with the embedded DCT coding scheme. Progressive fine granularity scalability (PFGS) coding (also called two-loop FGS coding) provides generally good compression efficiency as well as high flexibility in adapting the enhancement layer bit rate (Wu F. *et al.*, 2001). At the application streaming level, adaptation techniques include layered encoding, adaptive error control, adaptive synchronization and smoothing. As referred previously, these methods can be classified into reactive and passive according to their approach towards adaptation. In reactive methods, the application modifies its traffic to suit the changes in the network. In passive methods, the application aims to optimize the usage of network resources. Video streaming can effectively exploit the available network resources by adapting to the visual content variability as well as the variability of the available network bandwidth. Conventional techniques for network-aware video streaming optimize utility metrics that are based on the rates of the receivers (Liu *et al.* 2004).

Layered Encoding

Layered encoding is a passive method, in which the video information is encoded into several layers. The base layer carries important video (lower order coefficients of DCT) and critical timing information. The encoder allocates priorities to the encoded layers and the base layer has the highest priority while the higher layers improve the quality of video gradually. The receiver can get a reasonable quality with the base layer. When the network transmits layered video, it can drop lower priority (higher) layers in the event of congestion. Vickers *et al.* (1998) discussed adaptive transmission of multi-layered video. Their layered encoding method becomes reactive by adding or dropping layers based on network feedback. In particular, they discussed both credit-based and rate-based approaches for providing feedback. Eleftheriadis and Batra (2004) proposed an optimal data partitioning method for MPEG-2 encoded video. Data partitioning methods can benefit from network feedback. For example, if the network indicates that more bandwidth is available, more data can be sent in the base layer, and conversely data in the base layer can be reduced when bandwidth is limited.

Scalable Video Coding (SVC) is an extension of the H.264/MPEG-4 AVC standard. It serves different needs of different users with different displays connected through different network links by using a single bit stream, i.e., a single coded version of the video content. SVC can support: (1) appropriate resolution (spatial scalability); (2) convenient frame rate (temporal scalability); and (3) suitable data rate (quality scalability) by removing parts of the bit stream. The SVC extension is built on H.264/MPEG-4 AVC and re-uses most of its innovative components. As a distinctive feature, SVC generates an H.264/MPEG-4 AVC compliant, i.e., backwards-compatible base layer

and one or several enhancement layer(s). The base layer bit stream corresponds to a minimum quality, frame rate, and resolution (e.g., QCIF video), and the enhancement layer bit streams represent the same video at gradually increased quality and/or increased resolution (e.g., CIF) and/or increased frame rate. SVC conforming decoders can combine certain layers in a flexible way in order to adapt to different bit rates, frame rates or spatial resolutions of the video content:

- Spatial scalability within a wide range of resolutions.
- Temporal scalability within a wide range of frame rates.
- SNR (quality) scalability within a wide range of quality levels.

Coding efficiency of SVC depends on the application requirements but the goal is to achieve a rate-distortion performance that is comparable to non-scalable H.264 / MPEG-4 AVC. The benefits of SVC in terms of applications are the following:

- Ease of adaptation to different terminal capabilities.
- Resource conserving transmission, storage, and display of video, e.g., in surveillance applications.
- Higher transmission robustness, if combined with unequal error protection.
- Ease of Multicast Streaming through heterogeneous networks.

Rate Shaping

Rate shaping techniques adjust the rate of traffic generated by the video encoder according to the present network conditions. These techniques employ feedback mechanisms, which detect changes in the network and control the rate of the video encoder. The rate of the video sequence changes rapidly because of scene content and motion. The variable rate video is sent to a buffer, which is drained at a constant rate. Feedback information such as the *buffer occupancy level* can be used for controlling compression parameters of the video encoder. As a result, the video encoder can achieve constant rate. The rate shaping can be obtained by changing the *refresh rate, quantizer,* and *movement detection threshold.*

- *Refresh* (or frame) *rate* is the rate of frames, which are encoded by the video encoder. Decreasing the refresh rate entails the reduction of the output rate of the encoder, and thus quality will be reduced.
- *Quantizer* is the number of DCT coefficients that are encoded. Increasing the quantizer decreases the number of encoded coefficients and the image is coarser.
- *Movement detection threshold.* In interframe coding the movement detection threshold limits the number of blocks which are detected to be "sufficient different" from the previous frames. Increasing this threshold decreases the output rate of the video encoder and results in reduced video quality.

There are two modes for controlling the rate of the encoder:

- The *Privilege Quality mode* (PQ mode), in which only the refresh rate is changed.
- The *Privilege Rate mode* (PR mode), in which only the quantizer and movement detection threshold are changed.

The video encoder has power over its compression parameters based on the packet loss information. The receiver sends sporadically its current loss rate. In presence of congestion (indicated by loss), the rate is quickly decreased by the multiplicative factor 1/GAIN. Otherwise, the rate is slowly increased by the additive factor INC. This multiplicative decrease, additive increase mechanism adapts well to network changes. The following simple control algorithm is used to dynamically control the rate of the video encoder (Vandalore *et al.*, 2001):

```
If median loss > tolerable loss
THEN max_rate=max (max_rate/
GAIN, min_rate)
ELSE max_rate=max (max_rate+INC,
min_rate)
```

Bolot and Turletti (1994) presented rate shaping of the IVS video coder which uses the H.261 standard, while Bolot and Garcia (1996) considered control mechanisms for audio. Chou and Miao (2006) addressed the problem of streaming packetized media over a lossy packet network in a rate-distortion optimized way. They showed that although the data units in a media presentation generally depend on each other according to a directed acyclic graph, the problem of rate-distortion optimized streaming of an entire presentation can be reduced to the problem of error-cost optimized transmission of an isolated data unit. They showed how to solve the latter problem in a variety of scenarios, including the important common scenario of sender-driven streaming with feedback over a best-effort network, which they expressed in the framework of Markov decision processes. They derived a fast practical algorithm for nearly optimal streaming in this scenario, and they derived a general purpose iterative descent algorithm for locally optimal streaming in arbitrary scenarios. Experimental results showed that systems based on their algorithms have steady-state gains of 2–6 dB or more over systems that are not rate-distortion optimized. Furthermore, their systems essentially achieve the best possible performance: the operational distortion-rate function of the source at the capacity of the packet erasure channel.

Error Control

Multimedia applications need to adapt to changes in error and loss rates. In a wireless network, the error rate is variable due to interference. In the Internet, the loss rate is unpredictable due to congestion. Generally, error control methods include block erasure codes, convolutional codes, interleaving and multiple description codes.

Automatic Repeat Request (ARQ) and *Forward Error Correction* (FEC) are the main approaches to alleviate errors and losses. ARQ is a closed-loop and reactive mechanism in which the destination requests the source to retransmit the lost packets. ARQ increases the end-to-end delay dramatically in IP-based networks. Therefore, ARQ is unsuitable for error control of multimedia applications in the Internet. However, ARQ may be used in high-speed LANs where round trip latencies are small. FEC is an open-loop and passive method in which source sends redundant information, which can partly recover the original information in the event of packet loss. Bolot *et al.* (1999) proposed an adaptive FEC-based error control scheme (a reactive method) for interactive audio in the Internet. If we suppose that the audio packets are numbered 1, 2,...,n, the nth packet includes, in addition to its encoded signal samples, information about previous packet (n -1) which can be used to approximately reconstruct that packet if it is lost. The FEC-based scheme needs more bandwidth, so it should be coupled with a rate control scheme. The joint rate/FEC scheme can be used to adaptively control the rate and the amount of redundant information to be sent by the FEC method. Bolot and Turletti (1998) proposed an adaptive FEC for Internet video. The packet can carry redundant FEC information for up to four packets, i.e., packet n carries redundant information about packets n - 1, n - 2 and n - 3. Let $n - i$ indicates that packet n includes information about $n - i$. The different possible combinations of these methods are: (n), (n, n - 1), (n, n - 2), (n, n - 1, n - 2) and (n, n - 1, n - 2, n - 3). These are numbered as combination-1 through to combination-5. Different combinations can be used to adapt to network changes. The network changes are detected through packet loss, and a loss threshold (high loss) is used in the

algorithm for adaptation. The following simple adaptation algorithm was used:

```
If loss >= high loss
THEN Combination =
min(combination + 1, 4)
ELSE Combination =
max(combination - 1, 0)
```

This algorithm adds more error protection when there is more loss, and less protection when the losses are low. In this method, one way to use network feedback is to couple the rate available and the FEC combination used. For example, information about available rate and loss rate received as feedback from the network can be used to choose the FEC combination for error protection.

Error Resilience (ER) techniques can be used to make the coding scheme itself more robust against errors. In H.264/MPEG-4 AVC, the most striking resilience technique is *Flexible Macroblock Ordering* (FMO). One of the new characteristics of the H.264/AVC standard is the possibility of dividing an image in regions called '*slice groups*'. Each slice group can also be divided in several slices. Therefore, we need to define the word slice as a sequence of *macroblocks* that belong to the same slice group. These macroblocks are processed in a scan order (left to right and top to bottom). A slice can be decoded independently. FMO consists of deciding to which slice each macroblock of the image belongs. Each macroblock can be assigned freely to a slice group using an *MBAmap* (MacroBlock Allocation map). The MBAmap consists of an identification number for each macroblock of the image that specifies to which slice group that macroblock belongs. The number of slice groups is limited to 8 for each picture to prevent complex allocation schemes. If we deactivate the FMO, the images will be composed of a single slice with the macroblocks in a scan order. The use of FMO is totally compatible with any type of inter-frame prediction. With this technique, we can correct errors easily by exploiting the spatial redundancy of the images. It is a good idea to prefer the slice groups in a way that no macroblock and its neighbors belong to the same group. Therefore, if a slice is lost during transmission, it is simple to reconstruct the lost blocks with the information of the neighboring blocks. We have to consider the transmission characteristics of these slices: each slice is transmitted independently in separate units called packets. Each packet contains in its own header the information to decode itself without any other packet's information (if the images used as reference are the same in the encoder and the decoder side). The use of FMO together with advanced error resilience tools can keep the visual quality even with a packet loss rate of 10%.

Smoothing

Shaping or smoothing of the video information transmitted mitigates the rate variations of the multimedia application. For stored (pre-recorded) video, a priori video (frame) information can be utilized to smooth the video traffic at the source. Most smoothing techniques (Feng *et al*, 1997; Feng and Sechrest, 1995; Feng, 1997a; Feng, 1997b, Salehi *et al*., 1996) send ahead large frames, which needs to be displayed latter when there is enough buffer space at the client. These differ in the optimality condition achieved, and whether they assume that the rate is constrained or the client buffer size is limited. For live (non-interactive) video, a sliding window of buffers can be used and the buffer can be drained at the desired rate. Assume that a compressed video stream consists of n frames, where frame i requires f_i bytes of storage. To permit continuous playback, the server must always transmit video frames ahead to avoid buffer underflow at the client. This requirement can be stated as:

$$F_{under}(k) = \sum_{i=0}^{k} fi,$$

where *Funder(k)* indicates the amount of data consumed at the client when it is displaying frame k ($k = 0, 1,..., n - 1$). Likewise, the client should not receive more data than its buffer capacity. This requirement is stated as:

$$F_{over}(k) = b + \sum_{i=0}^{k} fi,$$

where b is client buffer size. Consequently, any valid transmission plan should stay within the limit outlined by these vertically equidistant functions. That is,

$$F_{under}(k) \leq \sum_{i=0}^{k} ci \leq F_{over}(k)$$

where c_i is the transmission rate during frame slot i of the smoothed video stream.

Cha *et al*. (2003) proposed a bandwidth-adaptive media smoothing technique, which smoothes the bandwidth requirement for media delivery at run time by considering the availability of network bandwidth. Their bandwidth smoothing technique still has the possibility of causing jitter because the policy runs on the application layer so that it cannot guarantee task completion in time. Thus, they proposed a task-scheduling algorithm optimized for the bandwidth adaptive smoothing. This scheduling technique handles the media data appropriately in order to minimize jitter. Simulation results with prerecorded MPEG videos show that the quality of delivered video is improved with the proposed bandwidth adaptive smoothing and task scheduling mechanisms.

Gao *et al*. (2005) proposed a real-time optimal smoothing scheduling algorithm for network adaptive video streaming with the variable network bandwidth and packet loss. Their algorithm adopts a rate-distortion optimized framework and real-time scheduling scheme to select and schedule the packets according to the network status. It attempts to minimize the quality variability at the client end while at the same time maximizing the utilization of the variable network bandwidth. Experiments show that, compared with frame-based scheduling algorithm, their proposed real-time smoothing algorithm improves and smoothes the quality in decoded video frames. Not to forget to mention that Feng and Rexford (1997) compared prior bandwidth smoothing algorithms.

Receiver Driven Multicast

McCanne *et al.* (1996) proposed the reactive method called "*Receiver driven Layered Multicast*" (RLM). RLM describes how layered video can be transmitted and controlled. In RLM, receivers dynamically subscribe to the different layers of the video streams. Using "probing" experiments, receivers decide when they can join a layer. If a receiver detects that extra bandwidth is available then it joins the next layer (adds a layer). Extra capacity is detected by join experiments. In a join experiment, the receiver measures the packet loss after joining. If a receiver detects congestion, the receiver quits the multicast group of the current highest layer, viz. it drops a layer. Li *et al.* (1999) presented another method that uses layered video, and it is called "*Layered Video Multicast with Retransmission*".

Adaptive Synchronization

Clock frequency drift, network delay, and jitter are some factors that generate problems for multimedia applications. Such problems can be solved using the adaptive synchronization technique, which provides the optimal delay and buffering for the given QoS requirement (Liu *et al.*, 1998). *Intramedia* (in a single stream) synchronization and *intermedia* (among multiple streams) synchronization can be achieved using this technique. Most synchronization algorithms divide the packets into three categories.

- *No wait* packets are displayed immediately.
- *Wait* packets are displayed after some time.
- *Discard* category packets are discarded.

The user specifies the acceptable synchronization error, maximum jitter and maximum loss ratio. This user information is required as input to the basic adaptive synchronization algorithm. And it is supposed that the sender puts a timestamp in the packets. At the receiver, the playback clock (PBC) and three counters for '*no wait*', '*wait*' and '*discard*' packets are maintained. When packets arrive early and enough wait packets have been received, the *PBC is incremented*. Similarly, when a threshold of '*no wait*' or '*discard*' packets are received, the *PBC is decremented*. This adaptive algorithm is shown to be resistant to clock drift. For synchronization among multiple streams, a group PBC is used which is incremented and decremented based on the slowest of the streams to be synchronized.

OPERATING SYSTEM SUPPORT

The end user perceives a continuous performance level for a real-time continuous media, if QoS guarantees are provided at all relevant subsystems (network, CPU, memory, I/O). Most operating systems (e.g., UNIX) are inherently inappropriate for the support of real-time continuous media. For example, continuous media require that latency and jitter be kept within stringent bound throughout a session. Multimedia applications running under conventional operating systems are at the mercy of unpredictable latency and jitter caused by non-deterministic scheduling, page swaps, high interrupt latency and multiplexed protocol stacks. In the CPU subsystem, the required QoS is expressed in terms of guaranteed CPU processing for those threads (real-time threads), which handle streams of real-time continuous media. Since continuous streams are handled by real-time threads, the kernel must deliver multimedia data directly to peripheral end-points with minimal or no interaction with the CPU. This is enforced by the real-time behavior of a continuous media stream, which implies a key requirement to the CPU scheduling of all processing threads related to this stream. *Threads associated with a continuous media stream should to be closely coordinated in such level such as to ensure that the temporal integrity of this media stream is not violated.*

Coulson *et al.* (1995) designed an application platform able to run distributed real-time and multimedia applications alongside conventional UNIX programs. The platform is embedded in a microkernel/PC environment and supported by an ATM-based, QoS-driven communication stack.

Coulson *et al.* focused on CPU scheduling, network resource-management aspects and memory management issues. Their architecture guarantees QoS levels of both communications and processing with varying degrees of commitment as specified by user-level QoS parameters. In addition, their proposed architecture uses admission tests to determine whether or not new activities can be accepted and includes modules to translate user-level QoS parameters into representations usable by the scheduling, network, and memory-management subsystems. In the same line, Kanellopoulos and Kotsiantis (2006) proposed a connection establishment protocol (C_MACSE protocol) for hard real-time multimedia communications. The C_MACSE protocol adopts a comprehensive approach for QoS as it incorporates resource management strategies for the CPU scheduling and the virtual memory of a multimedia system. The C_MACSE protocol provides services for the negotiation, renegotiation and monitoring of the comprehensive QoS. For supporting these functionalities, the C_MACSE protocol incorporates a QoS translator, a CPU scheduler, a virtual memory manager, and a flow manager. Lakshman *et al.* (1998) proposed an integrated QoS management system to manage CPU, network and I/O resources. This cooperative model and architecture, called AQUA (Adaptive Quality of service Architecture)

enables multimedia end-systems and operating system to cooperate dynamically for adaptively sharing end-system resources. In AQUA, the operating system allocates initial resources such as CPU time according to the user QoS specification. As the application executes, the operating system and the application cooperate to estimate the resource requirements and QoS received. By measuring QoS, resource changes are detected and the OS and the application renegotiate and adapt to provide predictable QoS with current resource constraints, the AQUA framework provides these functionalities as it includes a QoS manager, QoS negotiation library, and usage-estimation library. Yau and Lam (1997) proposed a framework called ARC (Adaptive Rate-Controlled) scheduling in order to be controlled the dynamic changes of the CPU requirement of a multimedia application. ARC consists of a rate-controlled online CPU scheduler, an admission control interface, a monitor, and a rate adaptation interface. ARC operates in an operating system which supports threads (Solaris 2.3). The threads can be of three types: RT (real-time), SYS (system) or TS (time-sharing). RT threads have the highest priority in accessing the CPU. The online CPU scheduler schedules the threads belonging to these classes based on their priorities.

FUTURE RESEARCH DIRECTIONS

- Current developed rate-adaptive video streaming methods are optimized for a single-sender single-receiver scenario. Further improvements should be done for scenarios where multiple wireless capable displays are actively streaming video from video gateways.

- Bandwidth smoothing algorithms take advantage of a priori information to reduce the burden on the network. However, these algorithms do not actively alter the video stream to make them network sensitive. More algorithms should be proposed that will combine the smoothing and rate changing technique. Such algorithms will solve the problem of finding the minimum number of frame discards for a sequence of frames. Dynamic programming and heuristics algorithms will be very promising for this.

- More adaptive rate-controlled scheduling algorithms should be proposed. Such algorithms will be enabled by monitoring network layer feedback (e.g., available bandwidth) and regulate CPU access rate accordingly.

CONCLUSION

Real-time streaming delivery over the Internet with bandwidth variation is a very challenging task. It is important to smooth the quality variability and improve the utilization of the available network bandwidth. A typical approach to assist multimedia delivery is via buffer management and task scheduling in end-systems. Buffer management techniques are classified into two categories; one is to adapt the changes in network load and the other is to smooth the bandwidth requirement. The former may cause a serious loss of service quality whereas the latter is unable to adapt to the dynamic network condition. This chapter surveys several techniques for achieving adaptation at the application layer to changing network conditions. These techniques are the following:

- *Compression methods*: We discussed DCT and wavelet compression methods as well as aspects of these methods that can be used for adaptation.
- *Application Streaming*: The application methods are broadly classified into reactive and passive methods. Passive methods reduce the network burden by optimization techniques, while reactive methods are

those where the application changes its behavior based on the environment.

- *Rate Shaping*: Video encoder parameters (e.g., frame rate, quantization level) are changed to meet the changing network conditions.
- *Error Control*: These techniques use FEC-based methods to provide defense against changing error conditions.
- *Adaptive Synchronization*: We discussed an adaptive synchronization technique for achieving intermedia and intramedia synchronization.
- *Smoothing*: Smoothing techniques attempt to reduce the variability in the resource requirements of multimedia applications.

Finally, multimedia applications need periodic access of CPU and other system resources. Operating systems have to to support such needs using various techniques such as real-time upcall, adaptive scheduling, and CPU management.

REFERENCES

Bolot, J., Fosse-Parisis, S., & Towsley, D. (1999). Adaptive FEC-based error control for interactive audio in the internet. *Proceedings - IEEE INFOCOM*, (March): 1999.

Bolot, J., & Garcia, A. (1996, November). Control mechanisms for packet audio in the internet. *Proceedings - IEEE INFOCOM, 1*, 232–239.

Bolot, J., & Turletti, T. (1994, November). A rate control mechanism for packet video in the internet. *Proceedings - IEEE INFOCOM, 3*, 1216–1223.

Bolot, J., & Turletti, T. (1998). Experience with rate control mechanisms for packet video in the Internet. *Computer Communication Review, 28*(1), 4–15. doi:10.1145/280549.280551

Cha, H., Kim, J., & Ha, R. (2003). Bandwidth constrained smoothing for multimedia streaming with scheduling support. *Journal of Systems Architecture, 48*(11-12), 353–366. doi:10.1016/S1383-7621(03)00022-5

Cheng, P., Li, J., & Kuo, C.-C. J. (1997). Rate control for an embedded wavelet video coder. *IEEE Transactions on Circuits and Systems for Video Technology, 7*(4), 696–702. doi:10.1109/76.611180

Chou, P. A., & Miao, Z. (2006, April). Rate-distortion optimized streaming of packetized media. *IEEE Transactions on Multimedia, 8*(2), 390–404. doi:10.1109/TMM.2005.864313

Coulson, G., Campbell, A., Rodin, P., Blair, G., Papathomas, M., & Shepherd, D. (1995). The design of a QoS-controlled ATM-based communications system in Chorus. *IEEE Journal on Selected Areas in Communications, 13*(4), 686–699. doi:10.1109/49.382159

Duffield, N.G., Ramakrishnan, K.K. & Reibman, A.R. (1998). SAVE: An algorithm for smoothed adaptive video over explicit rate networks. *IEEE/ACM Transactions on Networking, 6*(6), 717-728.

Eleftheriadis, A., & Batra, P. (2004). Optimal data partitioning of MPEG-2 coded video. *IEEE Transactions on Circuits and Systems for Video Technology, 14*(10), 1195–1209. doi:10.1109/TCSVT.2004.835149

Feng, W. (1997a). Rate-constrained bandwidth smoothing for the delivery of stored video. *In Proc. of SPIE Multimedia Networking and Computing*, November 1997, (pp. 316-327).

Feng, W. (1997b). Time constrained bandwidth smoothing for interactive video-on-demand. *In Proc. of ICCC*, November 1997, (pp.291-302).

Feng, W., Jahanian, F. & Sechrest, S. (1997) An optimal bandwidth allocation strategy for the delivery of compressed prerecorded video. *ACM/Springer-Verlag Multimedia Systems Journal, 5*(5), 297 – 309.

Feng, W., & Rexford, J. (1997). A comparison of bandwidth smoothing techniques for the transmission of prerecorded compressed video. *Proceedings - IEEE INFOCOM*, (April): 58–66.

Feng, W., & Sechrest, S. (1995). Critical bandwidth allocation for delivery of compressed video. *Computer Communications, 18*(10), 709–717. doi:10.1016/0140-3664(95)98484-M

Gao, K., Gao, W., He, S., & Zhang, Y. (2005). Real-time smoothing for network adaptive video streaming. *Journal of Visual Communication and Image Representation, 16*(4-5), 512–526. doi:10.1016/j.jvcir.2004.12.001

ISO/IEC 13818-2 (1994). *Generic coding of moving pictures and associated audio information.* Technical report, MPEG (Moving Pictures Expert Group), International Organization for Standardization, 1994.

Kanellopoulos, D. (2009). High-speed multimedia networks: Critical issues and trends. In Lee (Ed.) *Handbook of Research on Telecommunications Planning and Management for Business.* (pp.775-787). Western Illinois University, USA, PA: Information Science Reference.

Kanellopoulos, D., & Kotsiantis, S. (2006). C_MACSE: A novel ACSE protocol for hard real-time multimedia communications. *Int. J. of Computer Science and Network Security, 6*(3), 57–72.

Kanellopoulos, D., Kotsiantis, S., & Pintelas, P. (2008). Internet and multimedia communications. In Mehdi Khosrow-Pour (Ed.) *Encyclopedia of Information Science and Technology.* Second Edition (pp.2176-2182), Idea Group Inc (IGI).

Kanellopoulos, D., Pintelas, P., & Giannoulis, S. (2006). QoS in wireless multimedia networks. *Annals of Mathematics. Computing & TeleInformatics, 1*(4), 66–75.

Lakshman, K., Yavatkar, R., & Finkel, R. (1998). Integrated CPU and network-I/O QoS management in an end system. *Computer Communications, 21*(4), 325–333. doi:10.1016/S0140-3664(97)00166-7

Li, B., & Yin, H. (2007). Peer-to-peer live video streaming on the internet: issues, existing approaches, and challenges [peer-to-peer multimedia streaming]. *IEEE Communications Magazine, 45*(6), 94–99. doi:10.1109/MCOM.2007.374425

Li, W. (2001). Overview of fine granularity scalability in MPEG-4 video standard. *IEEE Transactions on Circuits and Systems for Video Technology, 11*(3), 301–317. doi:10.1109/76.911157

Li, X., Ammar, M., & Paul, S. (1999). Video multicast over the internet. *IEEE Network, 13*(2), 46–60. doi:10.1109/65.768488

Liu, C., Xie, Y., Lee, M. J., & Saadawi, T. N. (1998). Multipoint multimedia teleconference system with adaptive synchronization. *IEEE Journal on Selected Areas in Communications, 14*(7), 1422–1435.

Liu, J., Li, B., & Zhang, Y.-Q. (2004). An end-to-end adaptation protocol for layered video multicast using optimal rate allocation. *IEEE Transactions on Multimedia, 6*(1), 87–102. doi:10.1109/TMM.2003.819753

Lotfallah, O., Reisslein, M., & Panchanathan, S. (2006). Adaptive video transmission schemes using MPEG-7 motion intensity descriptor. *IEEE Transactions on Circuits and Systems for Video Technology, 16*(8), 929–946. doi:10.1109/TCSVT.2006.877387

McCanne, S., Jacobson, V., & Vetterli, M. (1996). Receiver-driven layered multicast. In *ACM SIGCOMM,* Stanford, CA, August 1996, (pp.117-130).

MPEG-4 (2004). *Coding of Audio-Visual Objects, Part-2 Visual, Amendment 4: Streaming Video Profile,* ISO/IEC 14496-2/FPDAM4, July 2000.

Pancha, P., & Zarki, M. (1993). Bandwidth-allocation schemes for variable-bit-rate MPEG sources in ATM networks. *IEEE Transactions on Circuits and Systems for Video Technology, 3*(3), 190–198. doi:10.1109/76.224229

Podilchuk, C. I., Jayant, N. S., & Farvardin, N. (1995). Three-dimensional sub-band coding of video. *IEEE Transactions on Image Processing, 4,* 125–139. doi:10.1109/83.342187

Radha, H., van der Schaar, M., & Chen, Y. (2001). The MPEG-4 fine-grained scalable video coding method for multimedia streaming over IP. *IEEE Transactions on Multimedia, 3*(1), 53–68. doi:10.1109/6046.909594

Salehi, J. D., Zhang, Z.-L., Kurose, J. F., & Towsley, D. (1996). Supporting stored video: Reducing rate variability and end-to-end resource requirements through optimal smoothing. In *ACM SIGMETRICS,* May 1996, (pp. 221-231).

Schulzrinne, H., Casner, S., Frederick, R., & Jacobson, V. (1987). *RTP: A Transport Protocol for real-time applications.* Audio-video transport working group. RFC 1889, Sept.1987.

Schulzrinne, H., Rao, A., & Lanphier, R. (1998). *Real Time Streaming Protocol (RTSP).* RFC 2326, April 1998.

Taubman, D., & Zakhor, A. (1996). A common framework for rate and distortion based scaling of highly scalable compressed video. *IEEE Transactions on Circuits and Systems for Video Technology, 6*(4), 329–354. doi:10.1109/76.510928

Tham, J., Ranganath, S., & Kassim, A. (1998). Highly scalable wavelet-based video codec for very low bit-rate environment. *IEEE Journal on Selected Areas in Communications, 16*(1), 12–27. doi:10.1109/49.650917

Vandalore, B., Feng, W.-C., Jain, R., & Fahmy, S. (2001). A survey of application layer techniques for adaptive streaming of multimedia. *Real-Time Imaging, 7*(3), 221–235. doi:10.1006/rtim.2001.0224

Vickers, B., Albuquerque, C., & Suda, T. (1998). Adaptive multicast of multi-layered video: rate-based and credit-based approaches. *In Proc. of IEEE INFOCOM*, San Francisco, Vol. 3, (pp. 1073–1083).

Wiegand, T., Sullivan, G., Bjøntegaard, G., & Luthra, A. (2003). Overview of the H.264/AVC Video Coding Standard. *IEEE Transactions on Circuits and Systems for Video Technology, 13*(7), 560–576. doi:10.1109/TCSVT.2003.815165

Wu, D., Hou, Y. T., Zhu, W., & Zhang, Y.-Q. (2001). Streaming video over the Internet: approaches and directions. *IEEE Transactions on Circuits and Systems for Video Technology, 11*(3), 282–300. doi:10.1109/76.911156

Wu, F., Li, S., & Zhang, Y.-Q. (2001). A framework for efficient progressive fine granularity scalable video coding. *IEEE Transactions on Circuits and Systems for Video Technology, 11*(3), 332–344. doi:10.1109/76.911159

Yau, D. K. Y., & Lam, S. S. (1997). Adaptive rate-controlled scheduling for multimedia applications. *IEEE/ACM Transactions on Networking, 5*(4), 475-488.

KEY TERMS AND DEFINITIONS

Bandwidth on Demand: It refers to data rate measured in bit/s (channel capacity or throughput-bandwidth consumption), which is required in order to transfer continuous media data (e.g., video).

Delay Variation (or Delay Jitter): It is a term used for the variation of end-to-end delay from one packet to the next packet within the same packet stream (connection/flow).

Network Congestion: It occurs when a link or node is carrying so much data that its QoS deteriorates. Typical effects include queueing delay, packet loss or the blocking of new connections.

Quality of Service (QoS): QoS functionality enables service providers to guarantee and enforce transmission quality parameters (e.g., bandwidth, jitter, delay, packet loss ratio) according to a specified service-level agreement (SLA) with the customer.

Real Time Streaming Protocol (RTSP): It is a network control protocol which is used to establish and control media sessions between end points. It is used in entertainment and communications systems to control streaming media servers. Clients of media servers issue commands, such as play and pause, to facilitate real-time control of playback of media files from the server.

Real-time Transport Protocol (RTP): It defines a standardized packet format for delivering audio and video over the Internet. It carries media streams controlled by H.323, MGCP, Megaco, SCCP, or Session Initiation Protocol (SIP) signaling protocols, making it one of the technical foundations of the voice over IP industry.

RTP Control Protocol (RTCP): It is a sister protocol of the RTP and is used to monitor transmission statistics and QoS information. RTCP provides feedback on the QoS in media distribution by periodically sending statistics information to participants in a streaming multimedia session.

Chapter 3
2–D Scalable Multiple Description Coding for Robust H.264/SVC Video Communications

Wei Xiang
University of Southern Queensland, Australia

Ce Zhu
Nanyang Technological University, Singapore

Chee Kheong Siew
Nanyang Technological University, Singapore

Yuanyuan Xu
Nanyang Technological University, Singapore

Minglei Liu
Nanyang Technological University, Singapore

ABSTRACT

In this chapter, we investigate two popular techniques for error-resilient H.264/SVC video transmission over packet erasure networks, i.e., layered video coding (LVC) and scalable multiple description coding (SMDC). We compare the respective advantages and disadvantages of these two coding techniques. A comprehensive literature review on latest advancement on SMDC is provided. Furthermore, we report new simulation results for the novel two-dimensional scalable multiple description coding (2-D SMDC) scheme proposed in our previous work (Xiang et al., 2009). The 2-D SMDC scheme allocates multiple description sub-bitstreams of a two-dimensionally scalable bitstream to two network paths with unequal loss rates. We formulate the two-dimensional scalable rate-distortion problem and derive the expected distortion for the proposed scheme. To minimize the end-to-end distortion given the total rate

DOI: 10.4018/978-1-61692-831-5.ch003

Copyright © 2011, IGI Global. Copying or distributing in print or electronic forms without written permission of IGI Global is prohibited.

budget and packet loss probabilities, we need to optimally allocate source and channel rates for each hierarchical sub-layer of the scalable bitstream. We consider the use of the Genetic Algorithm to solve the rate-distortion optimization problem. The simulation results verify that the proposed method is able to achieve significant performance gains as opposed to the conventional equal rate allocation method.

INTRODUCTION

In recent years, the increasing demand for mobile broadband access to multimedia applications and services has motivated enormous interest in media streaming over the Internet. Media streaming is characterized by high data transmission rate and low delay constraint. Therefore, its applications are highly susceptible to packet delay and delay jitter. However, packet erasure networks such as the Internet only offers best-effort service, and thus cannot guarantee bandwidth and delay. Conventional approaches for tackling packet loss such as retransmission is not effective for streaming media due to the real time nature of the service. Thus, additional mechanisms are needed to provide streaming media delivery over packet erasure networks.

Traditionally, layered video coding (LVC), which is also known as scalable video coding (SVC) with transport prioritization (Chakareski, 2005), is the most popular and effective approach for video transmission over error-prone networks. In LVC, a raw video sequence is coded into a base layer that provides a coarse level of visual quality and can be decoded independently, and multiple enhancement layers that refine the base-layer visual quality and are nevertheless useless alone. SVC has the advantage of enabling media providers to generate a single embedded bitstream from which appropriate subsets can be extracted to meet various requirements of a broad range of clients. SVC is thus essential for multicast applications, where a variety of end users with different capabilities such as bandwidth and processing power receive different presentations of the same media content. In general, temporal scalability, spatial scalability, and signal-to-noise-ratio (SNR) scal-

ability are among the most common scalability mechanisms for SVC. These mechanisms provide for frame rate, spatial resolution, and video quality adaptation to adjust the video source in accordance with device capability and channel bandwidth.

However, the fact that enhancement layers provide little refinement information if the base layer is not received or decoded correctly, is the root cause that scalable video bistreams are extremely vulnerable to transmission errors. Therefore, in an error-prone environment such as the Internet, providing error resilience against packet errors is as important as enabling scalability. LVC is usually used in conjunction with unequal loss protection (ULP) (Mohr *et al.*, 2000), which provides the base layer with the highest level of channel error protection through the use of forward error correction (FEC) coding.

The major weakness of LVC lies in its excessive reliance on the correct receipt and decoding of the base layer. As an alternative, multiple description coding (MDC) (Gamal & Cover, 1982), (Goyal, 2001) has recently emerged as a promising alternative technique for providing graceful degradation of performance in the presence of channel noise. The essential idea underlying MDC is to generate multiple (> 2) independent descriptions of a source such that each description independently describes the source with a certain desired fidelity. When more than one descriptions are received, they can be synergistically combined to enhance the quality. Therefore, the distortion in the reconstructed signal decreases upon the receipt of any additional descriptions, and is lower bounded by the distortion attained by single description coding.

In recent years, a plethora of different MDC methods have been proposed in the literature. The pioneering MDC scheme termed multiple description scalar quantization (MDSQ) (Vaishampayan, 1993) was proposed by Vaishampayan in 1993. The scheme minimizes the central distortion through jointly designing the quantization levels and the index assignment, subject to prescribed constraints on the side distortion and the rate. This principle has been generalized to multiple description trellis and lattice vector quantization in (Hafarkhani, 1999), (Vaishampayan, 2001), respectively. Multiple description transform coding (MDTC) is another popular class of MDC paradigms that employ pairwise correlating transforms (Goyal and Kovacevic, 2001).

Both LVC and MDC have their respective advantages and disadvantages. By combining the advantages of LVC and MDC, a hybrid approach, which is termed scalable MDC (SMDC), has the unique advantage of providing reliable video communication over a wider range of network scenarios and application requirements. It can simultaneously tackle the problem of heterogeneity of networks and reliability of transmission. SMDC improves upon LVC in that it introduces redundancy in each layer so that the chance of receiving at least one description of the base layer is greatly enhanced. In this chapter, we focus on the SMDC approach so as to exploit the benefits of both coding techniques. SMDC has received very limited attention to date, despite its advantages of providing simple rate adaptation and bandwidth savings for shared bottleneck links (Stankovic *et al.*, 2005). Chou *et al.* pioneered the idea of SMDC in (Chou *et al.*, 2003), where a video sequence is coded into multiple descriptions via combining layered video coding and FEC coding. The individual descriptions are then further split into multiple layers using ULP or an overlapping technique. In (Kondi, 2004), a video source is encoded into one base layer and two enhancement layers, but there is no hierarchy among the enhancement layers as in standard layered coding. Seeling and Reisslein presented a spatial scalable descriptor coding strategy that combines MDC with layered

spatial coding (Seeling & Reisslein, 2005). The approach creates two base layers each with one enhancement layer. Stankovic *et al.* (Stankovic *et al.*, 2005) proposed two fast heuristic algorithms for constructing optimal two-layer multiple description codes for multicast and broadcast applications, which offers a significantly better quality trade-off among clients.

In this chapter, we propose a novel two-dimensional, scalable, multiple description coding (2-D SMDC) for video transmission over noisy networks with path diversity. More explicitly, a video sequence is encoded into an embedded bitstream that is both temporally scalable and SNR scalable. The two-dimensionally scalable bitstream can be considered as being composed of multiple sub-bitstreams, each of which corresponds to one hierarchical sub-layer. Our approach allocates the sub-bitstreams to two paths with unequal loss rates so as to form a two-dimensional layered MDC configuration. We propose to use Genetic Algorithms to solve the rate-distortion optimization problem that may not be otherwise solved using the conventional Lagrangian multiplier method due to prohibitively overwhelming computational complexity. In contrast to other layered MDC schemes, our approach supports two-dimensional scalability in both the base and enhancement layers. The numbers of the temporal levels and SNR enhancement layers can be arbitrary. Another distinct feature of the proposed scheme centers around that it does not require the transmission of the base layer twice as opposed to the methods in (Chou *et al.*, 2003), (Kondi, 2004).

The remainder of this chapter is organized as follows. Section II compares the two coding paradigms for error-resilient video transmission, i.e., LVC and MDC, while Section III briefly reviews various approaches of SMDC proposed in the literature. In Section IV, the proposed 2-D SMDC scheme is described in detail, and the 2-D rate-distortion optimization problem of the scheme is formulated, followed by Section V presenting the genetic algorithm to solve the optimum rate allocation problem. Section VI is dedicated to simulation results, and Section VI draws concluding remarks.

COMPARATIVE STUDIES BETWEEN LVC AND MDC

LVC and MDC both are effective source coding techniques to overcome transmission errors introduced by imperfect channels, as opposed to the classic motion-compensation-based predictive video coding paradigm adopted by most existing international video coding standards such as the MPEG-x and H.26x family of standards.

LVC and MDC share similar characteristics in that both techniques encode a raw media source into a scalable bitstream that embeds two or more sub-bitstreams, in contrast to a conventional video coder that generates only a single non-scalable bitstream. For LVC, a raw video sequence is encoded into one base layer and several enhancement layers with different temporal, spatial, and quality scalabilities within a single embedded bitstream. The base-layer sub-bitstream can be decoded to provide a basic quality of the video, whereas the enhancement layer sub-bitstreams serve the purpose of refining the base-layer quality. However, the enhancement layers even if received perfectly become useless if the base layer is not decoded correctly. Therefore, the base layer is the most critical part of the scalable representation of the video bitstream, and usually protected by a stronger error-correcting code. If error-free transmission of the base-layer cannot be guaranteed, it will incur severe source distortion.

By contrast, a MDC encoder generates multiple sub-bitstreams (also called descriptions), which are completely independent, equally important, and mutually refining. Each description can be decoded independently to provide a basic level of reproduction quality of the original video source. The quality level can be gradually improved when the more number of descriptions are decoded

error-free and reconstructed in combination. In MDC, individual descriptions are expected to be routed over different transmission paths to reach the destination. This fact plus decoding independency between the descriptions is what makes MDC more robust to channel errors as opposed to LVC. Obviously, the added robustness of MDC comes at the expense of additional redundancy since MDC trades off coding efficiency for error resiliency.

In MDC, side distortion and central distortion are defined to measure the reconstruction quality of the source when part and all descriptions are received, respectively. In contrast with the traditional single description coding approach that aims to achieve the optimal rate-distortion performance, MDC design needs to take into account both side and central distortion given a total bit rate budget. However, the design criteria of minimizing both central and side distortion simultaneously are contradictive. The trade-off is controlled by redundancy among different descriptions. Generally speaking, more added redundancy will favour side distortion but result in less improvement of central distortion over side distortion. As a result, MDC attempts to strike a delicate balance between minimizing central and side distortion given a sum bit rate, which necessitates elegant design for redundancy control.

The fundamental difference between LVC and MDC lies in the fact that the sub-bitstreams for LVC have different levels of importance and inherent decoding dependency, while all sub-bitstreams for MDC are equally important and completely independent. Due to both similarities and differences in the two coding paradigms, several comparative studies between LVC and MDC have been undertaken in the literature. In (Reibman, 1999), the authors examined and compared the performance between LVC and MDC based upon forward error correction (FEC) codes over binary symmetric and erasure channels. It was concluded that MDC was more effective than LVC only for situations with very high channel error probabilities. Reibman *et al.* further compared LVC to MDC over enhanced general packet radio service (EGPRS) wireless networks (Reibman, 2000). The simulation results indicated that LVC and MDC performed equally well if the wireless channel assumed no prioritized transmission. However, it was shown that LVC outperformed MDC if transmission prioritization was enabled. In (Singh, 2000), the authors conducted experiments to compare the performance of LVC and MDC based upon networks simulations. Their experimental results showed that MDC outperformed LC over a broad range of scenarios, including no feedback support, networks with long round-trip-time (RTT), and applications with low latency requirements. Wang *et al.* considered the transportation of LVC and MDC coded video over wireless networks with multiple path routing (Wang, 2002). It was shown that MDC was better than LC when the underlying application had a very stringent delay constraint and the RTT on each path was relatively long. However, the converse is true when limited retransmission of the base-layer was acceptable.

More recently, Lee *et al.* conducted a comprehensive performance study of LVC and MDC for video streaming over error-prone networks (Lee, 2003). Their results confirmed most of the results reported earlier. The authors further investigated the error-resilience capabilities of these two encoding techniques over a wide range of network scenarios and packet loss rates in (Lee, 2003). The authors in (Nguyen, 2004) considered the application of MDC and LVC to Internet audio streaming. They concluded that LVC outperformed MDC if near-optimum rate allocation was achieved. In (Chakareski, 2005), the authors examined the performance of specific implementations of MDC and of LVC for video streaming over error-prone packet switched networks. It was shown that there was a large variation in relative performance between LVC and MDC depending on the employed transmission scheme. If the packet transmission schedules can be optimized in a rate-distortion sense, LVC provided a better

performance. Otherwise, MDC excelled if the condition was not satisfied.

In summary, we can conclude that MDC always has better performance than LVC if no error protection is applied to both LVC and MDC (Lee, 2003). This is true for applications that have very stringent delay constraints, e.g., video conferencing. In addition, MDC is more advantageous than LVC if the RTT between the server and client is relatively long or no feedback channel is available. If ARQ-based error protection is applied to both LVC and MDC, it can be said that LVC is preferred for low-to-medium loss rates. The gain is greater if the base layer data is protected using a stronger error protection method. If FEC-based error protection is applied to both LVC and MDC, both techniques have nearly equivalent performance. MDC performs slightly better than LVC when the channel condition is very poor, e.g., the packet loss rate is greater than 10%.

OVERVIEW OF SCALABLE MULTIPLED DESCRIPTION CODING

Recent Development of Scalable MDC

As mentioned in the previous section, LVC and MDC are both effective approaches for video streaming over error-prone packet switched networks. LVC is focused upon the problem of the heterogeneity of networks and end users, whereas MDC targets the problem of transmission reliability over imperfect channels. The complimentary advantages of LVC and MDC have served as a strong motivation for the integration of both coding techniques. As a result, scalable multiple description coding (SMDC) has most recently emerged as a new source coding paradigm for robust video streaming. In SMDC, each description is scalable coded and can be progressively decoded. Thus, descriptions can be efficiently adapted to the rate requirements of different transmission paths of the underlying packet-switching networks (Abanoz, 2009). The unique advantage of SMDC is that it is able to offer rate scalability and error resilience, simultaneously.

There are two primary means to create SMDC bistreams (Wang, 2005). The first one starts with generating MDC bistreams, which are then made scalable. On the contrary, the second method first generates a SVC bistream, where each layer is then mapped into a description with a different amount of redundancy. In the following, some popular SMDC schemes that have been proposed in the literature lately will be briefly reviewed.

Wang and Ortega (Wang, 2003) proposed a general approach for multiple description layered coding (MDLC) that uses an MDC encoder to generate two base layer descriptions BL1 and BL2. For each base layer description BLi, a corresponding enhancement layer Eli was created. The MDLC decoder selected which EL stream to decode given what base layer was received, and finally reproduced the signal by combining the base layer and enhancement layer information. The scheme provided the flexibility for the scheduling algorithm to choose the right base layer and enhancement layer descriptions based on the current network conditions and feedback information of previous transmission history.

Yu *et al.* proposed a new SMDC method based on macroblock splitting (MS) of the video sequence, which is termed multiple description layered coding with MS (MDLC-MS) (Yu, 2005). The proposed MDLC-MS method generated multiple descriptions using quincunx sub-sampling in the form of macroblock. Its performance was compared against three other MDLC schemes based up row, column, and frame decomposition. Experimental results showed that the proposed MDLC-MS scheme achieved higher coding efficiency and better reliability of transmission.

In (Zheng, 2005), a distributed multimedia delivery mobile network for video streaming in the third generation (3G) mobile communications was proposed. The system employed a new SMDC

framework compatible with the MPEG-4 standard codec, where LVC based on progressive fine granularity scalability (PFGS) and MDC based on multiple state recovery (MSR) were jointly designed to overcome the bandwidth fluctuation and packet loss problems in the wireless network and to further enhance the error resilience tools in MPEG-4.

An embedded (layered) MDC approach termed embedded multiple description scalar quantizers (EMDSQ) was proposed in (Verdicchio *et al.*, 2006). The proposed method for scalable erasure-resilient video coding coupled the compression efficiency of the open-loop architecture with the robustness provided by MDC. Numerical results demonstrated the advantage of the proposed approach.

Zhao *et al.* proposed a SMDC video coding scheme based on the standard MPEG-4 fine granularity scalability (FGS) video codec (Zhao, 2007). A pre-processor was employed to generate multiple descriptions with each description being fine grained scalable. A post-processor was then used to combine the descriptions to improve the quality of the reconstructed video. An optimal weighted combination of two descriptions was developed based on SNRs. It was reported that the proposed SMDC scheme achieved significant coding gains as opposed to simple average combination, especially when the quality difference between the two descriptions became large. However, it was noted that the gains were realized under the assumption of error-free decoding at the receiver.

Liu and Zhu proposed a very simple SMDC scheme based upon hierarchical B pictures in (Liu, 2007). Two descriptions were generated by encoding a video sequence using H.264/AVC. The difference between the descriptions lies in the selection of key pictures. Temporal scalability for each description was achieved by the hierarchical B picture structure. The scheme achieved a good central-side-distortion-rate trade-off. Experimental results demonstrated better rate-distortion performance over the odd/even frame splitting method.

Folli and Favalli proposed two new SMDC schemes in (Folli, 2008), i.e., the so-called inter layer prediction spatial multiple description scalable coding (ILPS-MDSC), and hierarchical B frame prediction spatial multiple description scalable coding (HBFPS-MDSC). The ILPS-MDSC scheme took advantage of the inter layer prediction method to generate spatial or coarse grain streams, whereas the HBFPS-MDSC scheme used dyadic B frame prediction, needed for temporal scalability, to predict one of the subsequences from another one. These schemes provided better performances than the popular polyphase spatial subsampling multiple description (PSS-MD) method (Vitali, 2005).

A SMDC scheme based upon odd and even frames was proposed for stereoscopic video (Karim, 2008). The method was very simple which extended the well-known multiple state video coding (MSVC) scheme proposed in (Apostolopoulos, 1999) to 3D video.

Stoufs *et al.* proposed a hybrid scalable MDC-JSCC (joint source-channel coding) approach for data transmission over error-prone packet-based channels (Stoufs, 2009). A comparative theoretical analysis was conducted and theoretical performance bounds for Gaussian sources assuming perfect source compression were derived, which revealed significant performance improvements of the hybrid MDC-JSCC approach over the scalable MDC equivalent. The authors further concluded that one can significantly improve the performance of an already existing MDC system by properly adding FEC codes.

In (Abanoz, 2009), the authors proposed a new SMDC generation methods based on various combinations of video segments coded at high and low rates. A multiple-objective optimization (MOO) framework was also proposed to select the best encoding configuration of the proposed SMDC schemes from a set of candidates in order to achieve the best trade-off between redundancy and reliability. Monte-Carlo simulation results for SMDC streaming with two descriptions over two paths with different packet losses were provided to demonstrate performance of the proposed methods.

FEC-Based Scalable MDC

In contrast to MDC, FEC is a traditional technique to add structured channel redundancy to compressed video signals for conveyance over lossy channels. In (Soldani, 2006), the authors conducted a performance comparison of using MDC and FEC codes for a scalable video coding system. It was shown that in matched channel conditions an FEC-based system yielded much better performance results than its MDC-based equivalent. There is a strong motivation to combine MDC with FEC to reap the benefits of both techniques. As a result, FEC-based SMDC techniques have been very popular in the literature (22-26).

The essential idea of FEC-based MDC methods is to apply unequal cross-packet FEC to different parts of a scalable bitstream. A classical MDC scheme based upon FEC coding and related to our proposed 2-D SMDC scheme is briefly described in this section. The idea was originated from the priority encoding transmission (PET) scheme proposed by Albanese (1996).

PET is essentially a packetization scheme that combines LC with ULP. The scheme encodes an image or video source into layers of different importance. Suppose an embedded bitstream is marked at N positions or layers. Denote by R_{n-1} and R_n in bits the boundary of the nth layer in the embedded bitstream such that:

$$0 = R_0 \leq R_1 \cdots \leq R_{n-1} \leq R_n \cdots \leq R_N.$$

Let $D(R_n)$ be the distortion if the first R_n bits of the bitstream are received. We have:

$$D(R_0) \geq D(R_1) \cdots \geq D(R_n) \cdots \geq D(R_N).$$

The nth layer is split equally into n partitions, and a $(N, n, N - n + 1)$ Reed-Solomon (RS) erasure code is applied, which is capable of correcting any $(N-n)$ erasures out of N codewords. Finally, the ith byte in each length-N RS codeword from all layers is packetized into the ith packet, $i = 1, \cdots N$. The PET packetisation strategy effectively removes the prioritization from layered coding. Therefore, this approach has the desirable property that the receipt of any $n(\leq N)$ packets allows the recovery of the initial n layers in the original progressive bitstream. The reconstruction quality of the source is only determined by the number of received packets, because all N packets are equally important. In this sense, the PET packetization scheme can be regarded as a type of balanced MDC with each packet being considered as an individual description in MDC.

Given N as the desired number of descriptions, p_n as the probability that n of the N descriptions are received, and the total rate budget as R_T, the optimisation problem of the PET-based MDC scheme aims to find a rate allocation vector $R = (R_0, R_1, \cdots, R_N)$ that minimises the expected distortion

$$D(R) = \sum_{n=0}^{N} p_n D(R_n), \tag{1}$$

where $p_n = \binom{N}{n}(1 - \varepsilon)^n \varepsilon^{(N-n)}$, and ε is the packet error loss probability. The rate in bits per packet is subject to the constraint of the total rate budget $R(\mathbf{R}) = \sum_{n=1}^{N} N(R_n - R_{n-1}) / n \leq R_T$.

The rate-distortion optimization problem can be solved by using the Lagrange multiplier via minimizing the unconstrained object function $D(\mathbf{R}) + \lambda R(\mathbf{R})$, where λ is a positive Lagrange multiplier. The bisection search algorithm can be used to find the appropriate λ.

TWO-DIMENSIONAL SCALABLE MDC

In view of the complimentary benefits of LVC and MDC, we discuss a new scheme dubbed two-dimensional scalable MDC (2-D SMDC) based upon our previous work (Xiang *et al.*, 2009). We consider scenarios where there are two paths between the transmitter and receiver, one with a lower packet loss probability and the other with a higher packet loss probability. Such assumptions are reasonable and typical of today's networks, where a main link and a secondary link exist for data transportation.

Architecture of the 2-D SMDC Scheme

The proposed 2-D SMDC scheme encodes group-of-pictures (GOPs) into a compressed video bitstream consisting of multiple substreams $\vec{b} = [\mathbf{b}_1, \mathbf{b}_2, \cdots, \mathbf{b}_{N_1 N_2}]$ using the scalable video coding (SVC) extension of the H.264/AVC standard (H.264/SVC) as illustrated in Figure 1, where each sub-bitstream $\mathbf{b}_i$ corresponds to one hierarchical sub-layer. As can be seen from the figure, the scalability in the proposed scheme is two-dimensional. Horizontally, bitstream $\vec{b}$ is temporally scalable, whereas the bitstream is signal-to-noise (SNR) scalable in the vertical direction. In Figure 1, N_1 is the number of hierarchical sub-layers in each SNR quality layer, whereas N_2 is the number of SNR quality layers. Each temporal sub-layer in the SNR base layer has the same number of N_2 SNR quality layers, which is independent of N_1.

In Figure 1, the gray level in each sub-layer implies the degree of importance of the corresponding sub-layer. The darker the grey colour, the more relative contribution it makes towards the overall video quality. It is apparent that the importance of sub-layers 1 to N_1 in the base layer (layer 1) gradually decreases. That is,

Figure 1. Illustration of compressed video bitstream with two-dimensional scalability. Dark gray colors imply the higher degree of importance of corresponding layers

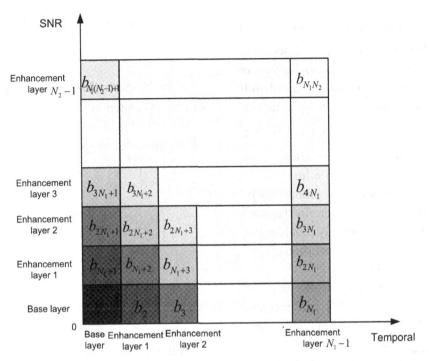

$D(R_1^{(1)}) \geq D(R_2^{1}) \cdots \geq D(R_{N_1}^{(1)})$, where the superscription (1) denotes the SNR base layer. As shown in Figure 1, there are N_1 temporal sub-layers in the base layer, whereas there are $N_1(N_2-1)$ sub-layers in enhancement layers 1 to N_2−1. Assuming that the temporal scalability takes priority over the SNR scalability, the relative importance of enhancement sub-layers increases with the increasing of the number. That is, $D(R_1^{(2)}) \geq D(R_2^{(2)}) \cdots \geq D(R_{N_1(N_2-1)}^{(2)})$, where the superscription (2) denotes enhancement layers.

The temporal scalability in the embedded bitstream is implemented by adopting the hierarchical B-picture structure in H.264/SVC. Hierarchical prediction structures are used to support multiple levels of temporal scalability in H.264/SVC. The coding structure is usually denoted as KBBB... KBB..., where K is referred to as a key picture that can be either an I or P picture. Two hierarchical B-picture modes are considered in this chapter,

i.e., KB3 and KB7. The number of temporal sublayers in each SNR layer is N_1=3 and the GOP size is P=4 for KB3, whereas N_1=4 and P = 8 for KB7.

We partition bitstream $\vec{b}$ into two independent portions, i.e., bitstreams $\vec{b}_1$ and $\vec{b}_2$. $\vec{b}_1$ consists of sub-bitstreams $b_1 b_2 \cdots b_{N_1}$ from the base layer or layer 1, whereas $\vec{b}_2$ is comprised of sub-bitstreams $b_{N_1+1} b_{N_1+2} \cdots b_{N_1 N_2}$ from enhancement layers of 2 to N_2. Without loss of generality and for the convenience of discussion, we assume decoding of a sub-layer only depends on the receipt of all its preceding sub-layers. The PET packetisation strategy will be applied to both $\vec{b}_1$ and $\vec{b}_2$ to generate two unbalanced descriptions (Albanese, 1996). Assume that $\mathbf{R}^{(1)} = (R_0^{(1)}, R_1^{(1)}, \cdots, R_{N_1}^{(1)})$ is the rate allocation vector in bitstream $\vec{b}_1$, and $\mathbf{R}^{(2)} = (R_0^{(2)}, R_1^{(2)}, \cdots, R_{N_1(N_2-1)}^{(2)})$ is rate allocation vector in bitstream $\vec{b}_2$ employing the PET scheme for the GOP.

The first x packets from $\vec{b}_1$ plus the first y packets from $\vec{b}_2$ will form the first description that is to be transmitted through a relatively more reliable channel with a lower packet loss probability p_1. On the other hand, the latter N_1-x packets from $\vec{b}_1$ plus the remaining $N_1(N_2-1)-y$ packets from $\vec{b}_2$ will form the second description that is to be transmitted through a less reliable channel with a higher packet loss probability p_2. The values of x and y will be determined assuming two paths having approximately equal loading so as to minimize the expected distortion given a total rate budget R_T, and p_1 and p_2.

It should be emphasised that the proposed scheme is not confined to SNR and temporal scalability. In effect, it can be applied to any scalability combinations including resolution scalability. However, it should be pointed out that the computational complexity of the optimization problem grows exponentially with the number of scalable dimensions. The two-dimensional rate-distortion optimization problem will be formulated in detail in the next subsection.

2-D SMDC Rate-Distortion Optimization

The combinatorial rate-distortion optimization problem for the proposed 2-D SMDC scheme can be formulated as follows. Given the total rate budget R_T, number of layers and sub-layers per layer N_1 and N_2, channel loss probabilities p_1 and p_2, we can derive the minimum expected distortion as (2), where $p_n^{(1)}$ and $p_n^{(2)}$ denote the probabilities of receiving n packets from bitstreams $\vec{b}_1$ and $\vec{b}_2$. The 2-D SMDC rate-distortion problem aims to find two rate-allocation vectors $\mathbf{R}^{(1)}$ and $\mathbf{R}^{(2)}$, and the values of x and y that minimize (2).

$$D(\mathbf{R}) = p_0^{(2)}\sum_{n=0}^{N_1} p_n^{(1)} D(R_n^{(1)}) + p_1^{(1)}\left(\sum_{n=0}^{N_2-2} p_{nN_1+1}^{(2)} D(R_{nN_1+1}^{(2)})\right) + \cdots$$
$$p_2^{(1)}\left(\sum_{n=0}^{N_2-2} p_{nN_1+2}^{(2)} D(R_{nN_1+2}^{(2)})\right) + p_{N_1}^{(1)}\left(\sum_{n=0}^{N_2-2} p_{(n+1)N_1}^{(2)} D(R_{(n+1)N}^{(2)})\right).$$

$$(2)$$

It can be shown that probabilities $p_n^{(1)}$ and $p_n^{(2)}$ can be calculated as

$$p_n^{(1)} = \binom{N_1}{n}(1-\overline{p_1})^n \overline{p_1}^{(N_1-n)},$$

$$(3)$$

$$p_n^{(2)} = \binom{N_1(N_2-1)}{n}(1-\overline{p_2})^n \overline{p_2}^{(N_1(N_2-1)-n)},$$

$$(4)$$

where $\overline{p_1}$ and $\overline{p_2}$ are the average packet loss rates for packets in $\vec{b}_1$ and $\vec{b}_2$. They can be inferred from the link loss rates p_1 and p_2

$$\overline{p_1} = \frac{xp_1 + (N_1-x)p_2}{N_1},$$

$$(5)$$

$$\overline{p_2} = \frac{yp_1 + (N_1(N_2-1)-y)p_2}{N_1(N_2-1)}.$$

$$(6)$$

The total rate R_t of the system, which is constrained by the rate budget R_T, can be shown as

$$R_t = \sum_{n=1}^{N_1} \alpha_n^{(1)} R_b^{(1)} + \sum_{n=1}^{N_1(N_2-1)} \alpha_n^{(2)} R_n^{(2)} \leq R_T,$$

$$(7)$$

where:

$\alpha_n^{(1)} = N_1/(n(n+1))$ for $n = 1,\cdots,N_1-1$, and $\alpha_n^{(2)} = N_1(N_2-1)/(n(n+1))$ for $n = 1,\cdots,N_1(N_2-1)-1$. Three other apparent rate constraints are:

$$0 = R_0^{(1)} \leq R_1^{(1)} \leq \cdots \leq R_{N_1}^{(1)}, \qquad (8)$$

$$R_{N_1}^{(1)} = R_0^{(2)} \leq R_1^{(2)} \leq \cdots \leq R_{N_1(N_2-1)}^{(2)}, \qquad (9)$$

$$0 \leq x \leq N_1, 0 \leq y \leq N_1(N_2 - 1). \qquad (10)$$

It is clear that the constrained rate-distortion optimization problem formulated by (2), (7), (8), (9), and (10) can be transformed into an unconstrained optimization problem using Lagrange multipliers (Everett, 1963) by minimizing

$$\min_{\mathbf{R}, x, y} \left(D(\mathbf{R}) + \lambda \left(\sum_{n=1}^{N_1} \alpha_n^{(1)} R_n^{(1)} + \sum_{n=1}^{N_1(N_2-1)} \alpha_n^{(2)} R_n^{(2)} - R_T \right) \right), \qquad (11)$$

where λ is the Lagrange multiplier, and x and y are defined in (5) and (6). To solve the minimization problem formulated by (11), the Lagrangian parameter λ needs to be eliminated, which can be achieved iteratively through using the bisection algorithm (Ramchandran, 1993). Although it may be possible to solve (11) using the method of Lagrangian multipliers, the computational complexity is prohibitively overwhelming. In the next subsection, we propose to solve this rate-distortion optimization problem using the Genetic Algorithm.

Genetic Algorithm for 2-D SMDC Rate-Distortion Optimization

Genetic algorithms (GAs) are an adaptive heuristic search algorithm used in computing to find exact or approximate solutions to optimization and search problems based upon the evolutionary ideas of natural selection, variation and inheritance. The basic concept of GAs is designed to simulate processes in natural system necessary for evolution, specifically those that follow the principles first laid down by Charles Darwin of survival of the fittest. As such they represent an intelligent exploitation of a random search within a defined search space to solve a problem.

A typical GA starts with definitions of an abstract representation of the solution domain and a fitness function to evaluate the solution domain. Binary encoding is the most popular representation and used in this chapter. The fitness function is defined to measure the quality of the represented solution, which is always problem dependent. GA proceeds to randomly generate an initial population of abstract representations of candidate solutions evolving toward better solutions iteratively. In each generation, the fitness of every individual in the population is evaluated, multiple individuals are stochastically selected from the current population based on their fitness, recombined and randomly mutated to form a new population. The new population is then used in the next iteration. The algorithm normally terminates when either a maximum number of generations has been reached, or a satisfactory fitness level has been found for the population.

In this section, we present the following GA algorithm to solve the combinatorial optimization problem governed by (11). The given GA algorithm is considerably faster than the Lagrangian multiplier method, and is able to achieve practical suboptimal solutions as demonstrated by our simulation results presented in the following section.

In Algorithm 1, there are altogether six phases, i.e., initialisation, fitness evaluation, reproduction, crossover, mutation, looping. Variables are initialised in Phase 1. Each candidate solution in the popular pool is generated randomly in this phase. The expected distortion given by (2) is computed for each solution in the population pool in the second phase. The most crucial phases 3-5 of the proposed GA update the population pool, and yield the next generation of candidate solutions through the mechanisms of reproduction, crossover, and mutation.

Algorithm 1. Genetic Algorithm for 2-D SMDC Rate-Distortion Optimization

---

1: **Phase 1 - Initialization**:

2: (1) initialise the number of bits for representing each candidate solution $\mathbf{S}^*$ to L

3: (2) initialise the population size of candidate solutions to N

4: (3) initialise the crossover probability to P_c

5: (4) initialise the mutation probability to P_m

6: (5) initialise a generation counter g to 0 and the total number of generation to G

7: (6) Randomly generate a population of candidate solutions $\mathbf{S}_0^*, \mathbf{S}_1^*, \cdots, \mathbf{S}_{N-1}^*$

8: **Phase 2 - Fitness evaluation**:

9: **for** $i \leftarrow 0$ to $N - 1$ **do**

10: Calculate $D(\mathbf{S}_i^*)$

11: **end for**

12: $n \leftarrow 0$ (population size counter)

13: **Phase 3 - Reproduction**:

14: (1) Select a father member from the population pool according to the roulette wheel method

15: (2) Select a mother member from the population pool according to the roulette wheel method

16: **Phase 4 - Crossover**:

17: $r_f \leftarrow$ a random float number $\in [0.0, 1.0]$

18: **if** $r_f > P_c$ or father $==$ mother **then**

19: offspring1 $\leftarrow$ father

20: offspring2 $\leftarrow$ mother

21: Return

22: **end if**

23: $r_d \leftarrow$ a random integer number $\in [0, N - 1]$

24: **for** $i \leftarrow 0$ to $r_d \leftarrow 1$ **do**

25: Offerspring1(i) $\leftarrow$ father(i)

26: Offerspring2(i) $\leftarrow$ mother(i)

27: **end for**

28: **for** $i \leftarrow r_d$ to $N - 1$ **do**

29: Offerspring1(i) $\leftarrow$ mother(i)

30: Offerspring2(i) $\leftarrow$ father(i)

---

continued on following page

Algorithm 1. continued

31: **end for**

32: **Phase 5 - Mutation**:

33: **for** $i = 0$ to $N - 1$ **do**

34: $r_f \leftarrow$ a random float number $\in [0.0, 1.0]$

35: **if** $r_f < P_m$ **then**

36: offspring1(i) $\leftarrow$ $\overline{\text{offerspring1}(i)}$

37: offspring2(i) $\leftarrow$ $\overline{\text{offerspring2}(i)}$

38: **end if**

39: **end for**

40: $n \leftarrow n + 2$

41: **Phase 6 - Looping**:

42: **if** $n < N$ **then**

43: goto **Phase 3**

44: **end if**

45: $g \leftarrow g + 1$

46: **if** $g < G$ **then**

47: goto **Phase 2**

48: **else if** $g \geq G$ **then**

49: Complete

50: **end if**

EXPERIMENTAL RESULTS

In this section, we present the simulation results to demonstrate the performance of the proposed 2-D SMDC scheme in Section 4.1, and optimum rate allocation results using the GA described in Section 4.3.

Two video test sequences *foreman.qcif* (300 frames, QCIF format 176 × 144) and *mobile.cif* (300 frames, CIF format 352_288) are encoded using the JSVM (Joint Scalable Video Model) codec software (Reichel, 2005) based upon the SVC extension of the H.264/AVC standard at 30 frames per second. The sequences are encoded into three SNR levels and three temporal levels, i.e., $N_1 = N_2 = 3$. Therefore, the scalable bitstream is made up of nine sub-bitstreams corresponding to nine hierarchical sub-layers. The temporal scalability is achieved via using the hierarchical B-picture mode of IBBBIBBB... as discussed previously. As a result, the corresponding frame rates for the three temporal levels are 7.5, 15 and 30 frames per second, respectively.

A two-path network configuration is considered. Each network path is characterized by a random independent and identically distributed (i.i.d.) packet loss probability. One path has a lower packet loss probability p_1, whereas the other has a higher packet loss probability p_2. The encoded video bitstream is FEC protected, packetized, and allocated to the two network paths according to the PET scheme discussed in Section 3.2. In our simulations, we use the packet loss probabilities

Figure 2. Rate allocation for foreman.qcif with $p_1 = 0.05$ and $p_2 = 0.1$, GOP = 4

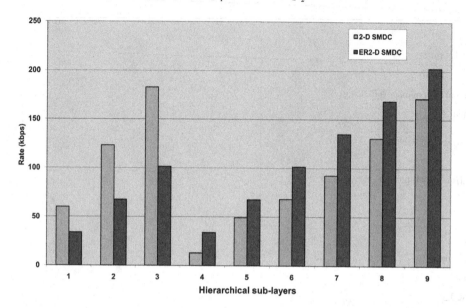

of $p_1 = 0.05$ and $p_2 = 0.1$ for each video sequence under each GOP size.

We compare our 2-D SMDS approach with a reference MDC system that allocates equal source encoding rates to all hierarchical sub-layers of the two-dimensionally scalable bit-stream, which is called the equal rate 2-D SMDC (ER2-D SMDC) system subsequently. Under the ER2-D SMDC scheme, it allocates MD packets to the two network paths exactly the same manner as the proposed 2-D SMDC scheme except that each sub-layer has the same source coding rate, which is not rate-distortion optimised as opposed to our approach. We would like to point out that we re-ran our simulation program to obtain a new set of results that match those reported in (Xiang *et al.*, 2009).

To achieve good suboptimal rate allocation, 1000 generations are used in the GA. Firstly, we use 12-bit binary coding for each rate, and therefore totally 108 bits representing each candidate solution using the KB3 hierarchical B-picture mode. The total rate budgets are set to around 700 kbps for *foreman.qcif*, and 6000 kbps for *mobile.cif*. Figure 2 presents the GA rate allocation results for the *foreman.qcif* sequence, whereas Figure 3

shows the results for the *mobile.cif* sequence. As can be observed from both figures, the 2-D SMDC approach allocates different rates to individual hierarchical sub-layers in a rate-distortion optimized manner, whilst the ER2-D SMDC allocates an equal rate to each hierarchical sub-layer. We further increase the GOP size to 8 through the use of the KB7 mode for the same sequences. Similar results are obtained as shown in Figures 4 and 5, respectively.

Finally, we present the peak-signal-to-noise-ratio (PSNR) comparison results for 2-D SMDC and ER2-D SMDC in Table 1. The numbers in the first column of Table 1 indicate the GOP sizes. The rate budgets for all the experimental configurations are indicated in the fifth column of Table 1. The last two columns of the table show the GA results of the numbers of base layer (BL) and enhancement layer (EL) packets allocated to path 1 as computed by the GA, under the assumptions that all BL packets are allocated to the better path and the two paths have approximately equal loading. Table 1 clearly demonstrates that the proposed 2-D SMDC scheme is able to achieve

Figure 3. Rate allocation for mobile.cif with $p_1 = 0.05$ and $p_2 = 0.1$, GOP = 4

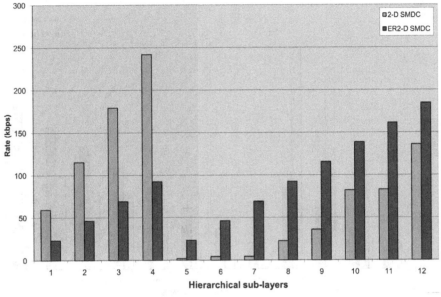

Figure 4. Rate allocation for foreman.qcif with $p_1 = 0.05$ and $p_2 = 0.1$, GOP = 8

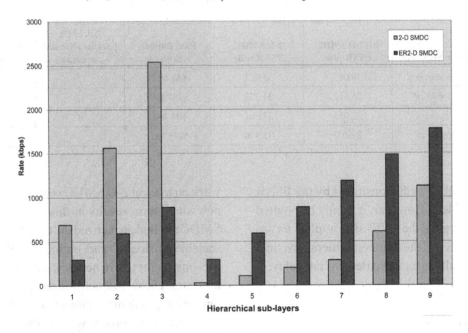

substantial coding gains in terms of PSNR compared to the conventional ER2-D SMDC scheme.

It is noted that the performance gains using GOP8 are slightly larger than those of GOP4. As reported in (Schwarz, 2006), the coding effi-ciency for hierarchical prediction structures increases with the size of the GOP because a larger GOP size improves rate-distortion performance. This coding efficiency improvement may be better exploited by our 2-D SMDC scheme relative

Figure 5. Rate allocation for mobile.cif with $p_1 = 0.05$ and $p_2 = 0.1$, GOP = 8

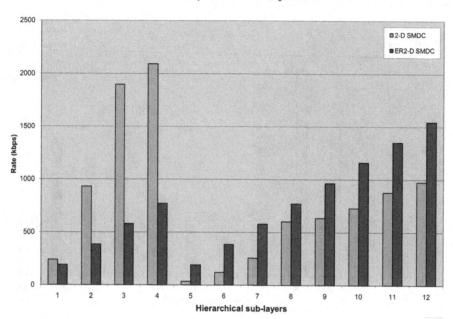

Table 1. Comparison of coding results by 2-D SMDC and ER2-D SMDC

GOP Size	Video Sequence	ER2-D SMDC PSNR (dB)	2-D SMDC PSNR (dB)	Rate Budget (kb/s)	No. of BL packets allocated to path1	No. of EL packets allocated to path1
4	*Foreman.qcif*	30.005	33.022	682.087	3	3
	Mobile.cif	26.813	34.333	5988.100	3	2
8	*Foreman.qcif*	32.075	37.561	694.450	4	1
	Mobile.cif	27.890	35.976	5945.717	4	1

to ER2-D SMDC as demonstrated by the PSNR results in Table 1. However, it should be pointed out that enlarging the GOP size implies an increased depth of the temporal hierarchy, and therefore results in an increased coding delay.

CONCLUSION

In this chapter, we discussed two popular techniques for error-resilient H.264/SVC video transmission over packet-erasure channels. A thorough literature review on layered video coding and SMDC was presented. Based upon our previous

work on a novel 2-D SMDC scheme, we reported new simulation results in this chapter. The 2-D SMDC method packetized the two-dimensionally scalable bitstream, and optimally allocated the sub-bitstreams to two network paths with unequal loss rates. The two-dimensional rate-distortion optimisation problem was formulated. To minimise the expected distortion, we considered the GA as a fast method to solve the optimization problem as opposed to the conventional Lagrangian multiplier method, which incurred overwhelmingly high computational complexity.

Experimental results were presented to demonstrate the superior performance of our method as opposed to the equal error rate allocation method. Two different types of video sequences and a range of packet loss probabilities were experimented. The results clearly demonstrated that our approach was able to achieve significant coding gains in terms of PSNR.

REFERENCES

Abanoz, T. B., & Tekalp, A. M. (2009). SVC-based scalable multiple description video coding and optimization of encoding configuration. *Signal Processing Image Communication, 24*, 691–701. doi:10.1016/j.image.2009.07.003

Albanese, A., Blomer, J., Edmonds, J., Luby, M., & Sudan, M. (1996). Priority encoding transmission. *IEEE Transactions on Information Theory, 42*(6), 1737–1744. doi:10.1109/18.556670

Apostolopoulos, A. G. (1999). Error-resilient video compression via multiple state streams, *Proc. International Workshop on Very Low Bit rate Video Coding (VLBV'99)*, Kyoto, Japan.

Chakareski, J., Han, S., & Girod, B. (2005). Layered coding vs. multiple descriptions for video streaming over multiple paths. *Multimedia Systems, 10*(4), 275–285. doi:10.1007/s00530-004-0162-3

Chou, P. A., Wang, H. J., & Padmanabhan, V. N. (2003). *Layered multiple description coding.* Proc. Packet Video Workshop.

Everett, H. (1963). Generalized Lagrange multiplier method for problems of optimum allocation of resources. *Operations Research, 11*, 399–417. doi:10.1287/opre.11.3.399

Folli, M., & Favalli, L. (2008). Scalable multiple description coding of video sequences. In *Proc. of the 2008 GTTI Annual Meeting*, Florence, Italy.

Gamal, A. E., & Cover, T. (1982, November). Achievable rates for multiple descriptions. *IEEE Transactions on Information Theory, 28*, 851–857. doi:10.1109/TIT.1982.1056588

Goyal, V. K. (2001). Multiple description coding: compression meets the network. *IEEE Signal Processing Magazine, 18*, 74–93. doi:10.1109/79.952806

Goyal, V. K., & Kovacevic, J. (2001, September). Generalized multiple description coding with correlating transforms. *IEEE Transactions on Information Theory, 47*(6), 2199–2224. doi:10.1109/18.945243

Hafarkhani, J., & Tarokh, V. (1999). Multiple description trellis-coded quantization. *IEEE Transactions on Communications, 47*(6), 799–803. doi:10.1109/26.771331

Karim, H. A., Hewage, C., Worrall, S., & Kondoz, A. M. (2008). Scalable multiple description video coding for stereoscopic 3D. *IEEE Transactions on Consumer Electronics, 54*(2), 745–752. doi:10.1109/TCE.2008.4560156

Kondi, L. P. (2004). A rate-distortion optimal hybrid scalable/multiple-description video codec," in *Proc. IEEE Int. Conf. Acoustics, Speech, and Signal Processing (ICASSP'04)*, Montreal, Canada, May 2004, pp. 269–272.

Lee, Y.-C., Kim, J., Altunbasak, Y., & Mersereau, R. M. (2003). Performance comparisons of layered and multiple description coded video streaming over error-prone networks. In *Proc. International Conference on Communications*, Anchorage, AK, pp. 35–39.

Lee, Y.-C., Kim, J., Altunbasak, Y., & Mersereau, R. M. (2003). Layered coding vs. multiple description coded video over error-prone networks. *Signal Processing Image Communication, 18*, 337–356. doi:10.1016/S0923-5965(02)00138-8

Liu, M., & Zhu, C. (2007). Multiple description video coding using hierarchical B pictures, *Proc. IEEE Conference on Multimedia and Expo*, Beijing, China, (pp. 1367-1370).

Mohr, A. E., Riskin, E. A., & Ladner, R. E. (2000). Unequal loss protection: Graceful degradation of image quality over packet erasure channels through forward error correction. *IEEE Journal on Selected Areas in Communications, 18*, 819–828. doi:10.1109/49.848236

Nguyen, V., Chang, E., & Ooi, W. (2004). Layered coding with good allocation outperforms multiple description coding over multiple paths. In *Proc. International Conference on Multimedia and Exhibition*, Taipei, Taiwan.

Ramchandran, K., & Vetterli, M. (1993). Best wavelet packet bases in a ratedistortion sense. *IEEE Transactions on Image Processing, 2*, 160–175. doi:10.1109/83.217221

Reibman, A. R., Jafarkhani, H., Orchard, M., & Wang, Y. (1999). Performance of multiple description coders on a real channel. In *Proc. International Conference on Acoustics, Speech, and Signal Processing*, Phoenix, AZ, (pp. 2415–2418).

Reibman, A. R., Wang, Y., Qiu, X., Jiang, Z., & Chawla, K. (2000). Transmission of multiple description and layered video over an EGPRS wireless network, *Proc. IEEE International Conference on Image Processing (ICIP'00)*, Vancouver, Canada, pp. 136–139.

Reichel, J. Schwarz, H., & Wien, M. (2005). Joint Scalable Video Model JSVM-4. ISO/IEC JTC1/SC29/WG11, Doc. JVT-Q202.

Schwarz, H., Marpe, D., & Wiegand, T. (2006). Analysis of hierarchical B pictures and MCTF, in *Proc. IEEE International Conference on Multimedia & Expo (ICME'06)*, Toronto, Canada, pp. 1929–1932.

Seeling, R., & Reisslein, M. (2005). Video coding with multiple descriptors and spatial scalability for device diversity in wireless multi-hop networks, in *Proc. IEEE Conference on Consumer Communications and Networking*, Las Vegas, Nevada, USA, Jan. 2005, pp. 278–283.

Singh, R., Ortega, A., Perret, L., & Jiang, W. (2000). Comparison of multiple description coding and layered coding based on network simulations, *Proc. SPIE Conference on Visual Communication Image Processing*.

Soldani, C., Leduc, G., Verdicchio, F., & Munteanu, A. (2006). Multiple description coding versus transport layer FEC for resilient video transmission. In *Proc. IEEE International Conference on Digital* Telecommunications, Cap Esterel, France, pp. 20-27.

Stankovic, V., Hamzaoui, R., & Xiong, Z. (2005). Robust layered multiple description coding of scalable media data for multicast. *IEEE Signal Processing Letters, 12*(2), 154–157. doi:10.1109/LSP.2004.840895

Stoufs, M. R., Munteanu, A., Barbarien, J., Cornelis, J., & Schelkens, P. (2009), Optimized scalable multiple-description coding and FEC-based joint source-channel coding: a performance comparison, *Proc. 10th Workshop on Image Analysis for Multimedia Interactive Services (WIAMIS'09)*, London, UK, pp. 73-76.

Vaishampayan, V. (1993). Design of multiple description scalar quantizers. *IEEE Transactions on Information Theory, 39*, 821–834. doi:10.1109/18.256491

Vaishampayan, V., Sloane, N. J. A., & Servetto, S. D. (2001). Multiple description vector quantization with lattice codebooks: Design and anaysis. *IEEE Transactions on Information Theory, 47*(5), 1718–1734. doi:10.1109/18.930913

Verdicchio, F., Munteanu, A., Gavrilescu, A. I., Cornelis, J., & Schelkens, P. (2006). Embedded multiple description coding of video. *IEEE Transactions on Image Processing*, *15*(10), 3114–3130. doi:10.1109/TIP.2006.877495

Vitali, A., Rovati, F., Rinaldo, R., Bernardini, R., & Durigon, M. (2005). Low-complexity standard-compatible robust and scalable video streaming over lossy/variable bandwidth networks, *IEEE International Conference on Consumer Electronics*, Las Vegas.

Wang, H., & Ortega, A. (2003). Robust video communication by combining scalability and multiple description coding techniques. In *Proceedings of the SPIE*, 111-124.

Wang, H., & Ortega, A. (2003). *Robust video communication by combining scalability and multiple description coding techniques.* Proc. Image and Video Communications and Processing.

Wang, Y., Panwar, S., Lin, S., & Mao, S. (2002, September). Wireless video transport using path diversity: multiple description vs. layered coding. In *Proc. IEEE International Conference on Image Processing (ICIP '02)*, New York (pp. 21-24).

Wang, Y., Reibman, A. R., & Lin, S. (2005). Multiple description coding for video delivery. *Proceedings of the IEEE*, *93*(1), 57–70. doi:10.1109/JPROC.2004.839618

Xiang, W., Zhu, C., Xu, Y., Siew, C. K., & Liu, M. (2009). Forward error correction-based 2-D layered multiple description coding for error-resilient H.264 SVC video transmission. *IEEE Transactions on Circuits and Systems for Video Technology*, *19*(12), 1730–1738. doi:10.1109/TCSVT.2009.2022787

Yu, M., Ye, X., Jiang, G., Wang, R., Xiao, F., & Kim, Y. (2005). New multiple description layered coding method for video communication, *Proc. 6th International Conference on Parallel and Distributed Computing, Applications and Technologies (PDCAT'05)*, Dalian, China, pp. 694-697.

Zhao, A., Wang, W., Chi, H., & Tang, K. (2007). Efficient multiple description scalable video coding scheme based on weighted signal combinations. *Journal of Tsinghua Science and Technology*, *12*(1), 86–90. doi:10.1016/S1007-0214(07)70013-5

Zheng, R., Zhuang, W., & Jiang, H. (2005). Scalable multiple description coding and distributed video streaming in 3G mobile communications. *Wireless Communications and Mobile Computing*, *5*, 95–111. doi:10.1002/wcm.279

Chapter 4
Dirac Video Codec:
Introduction

Kok Keong (Jonathan) Loo
Middlesex University, UK

Myo Tun
Dialogic Corporation, Canada

Yoong Choon Chang
Multimedia University, Malaysia

ABSTRACT

Dirac was started off by British Broadcasting Corp. (BBC) in 2003 as an experimental video coding system based on wavelet technology, which is different from that used in the main proprietary/standard video compression systems. Over the years, Dirac has grown out of its initial development and it is now on offer as an advanced royalty-free video coding system designed for a wide range of users, from delivering low-resolution web content to broadcasting high-definition (HD) and beyond, to near-lossless studio editing. The Dirac's video coding architecture and algorithms are designed with the "keep it simple" mindset. In spite of that the Dirac seems to give a two-fold reduction in bitrate over MPEG-2 for HD video and broadly competitive with state-of-the-art video codecs. This chapter introduces the architecture of Dirac video encoder. The overall encoding structure is discussed followed by the detail description of motion estimation, Overlapped Block-based Motion Compensation (OBMC), Discrete Wavelet Transform (DWT), Rate Distortion Optimization (RDO) quantization and entropy coding. The Dirac's bitstream syntax for compressed video data storage and streaming is described. Besides that, the coding performance of Dirac in terms of compression ratio, PSNR, SSIM and VQM in comparison with H.264 as a reference are discussed. Related issues such as transcoding and streaming over packat erasure channel are also discussed.

BACKGROUND

Nowadays, analogue video recording is a mature technology and has almost reached its limits.

Investments in enhancing the technology provide increasingly small returns. On the other hand, digital video technology has the potential to achieve much higher levels of quality and the technology is being improved at an increasing rate. It has a number of unique properties that make

DOI: 10.4018/978-1-61692-831-5.ch004

Copyright © 2011, IGI Global. Copying or distributing in print or electronic forms without written permission of IGI Global is prohibited.

possible applications that could not be realized using analogue video. Firstly, digital video can be manipulated more easily than analogue video. In addition to this, digital video can be stored on random access media, whereas analogue video is generally stored sequentially on magnetic tape. This random access allows for interactivity, since individual video frames are addressable and can be accessed quickly. Digital video can be duplicated without loss of quality which is important for editing applications.

The ability to easily store and transmit is by far its most important property. Video in digital form can be transmitted across channels where transmission of analogue video was almost impossible. Because compressed digital video can be transmitted using less bandwidth than analogue television, it is possible to provide many channels where before there were only a few or none. By exploiting the digital technology, cable TV systems can have enough capacity to provide hundreds of channels of digital video. Video-on-demand is currently available on trial basis. The video was delivered to the consumers homes via their copper telephone wire and normal telephone service was not disrupted. In future, video-on-demand services might eventually replace the trip to the video store.

In addition to the applications mentioned above, modern digital video applications also include storage on different media such as Video-CD, DVD, Blu-Ray Disc, broadcasting over wireless mobile channel, streaming over the internet, satellite and terrestrial digital TV, video-conferencing and video-telephony and many more. Wide development of the digital video applications has led the generation of the international standards for different types of applications under the auspices of the International Telecommunication Union Telecommunication Standardization Sector (ITU-T) and the International Organization for Standardization / International Electrotechnical Commission (ISO/IEC). The ITU-T's H.261 video coding standard is originally designed for

transmission over ISDN lines on which data rates are multiples of 64 Kbit/s and H.263 is designed as a low-bitrate compressed format for video conferencing. On the other hand, the Moving Pictures Expert Group (MPEG), established under the ISO/IEC, standardized MPEG-1 to compress Video Home System (VHS) quality raw digital video. Under the same group, another standard called MPEG-2 is widely used as the format of digital television signals that are broadcast by terrestrial (over-the-air), cable, and direct broadcast satellite TV systems. It also specifies the format of movies and other programs that are distributed on DVD. MPEG-4 is for compression of Audio Video data for web (streaming media) and CD distribution, voice (telephone, videophone) and broadcast television applications. It provides improved coding efficiency, ability to encode mixed media data (video, audio, speech) and error-resilience to enable robust transmission.

The latest standard, H.264 which is also called MPEG-4 Part 10 was developed by the ITU-T Video Coding Experts Group (VCEG) together with the ISO/IEC Moving Picture Experts Group (MPEG) as the product of a partnership effort known as the Joint Video Team (JVT). It is aimed to elaborate an open standard that is not application-specific and that perform significantly better than the existing standards in terms of compression, network adaptation and error robustness.

In the near future, H.264 will gain wide acceptance on many applications especially on Internet broadcasting. However, the usage of H.264 [License (2010)] incurs royalty fees which may not be cost effective for non-profit and public content owners such as public service broadcasters, archive institutes, etc., for deployment of Internet-based services. Whilst these costs are manageable initially, these could become prohibitive if the services scaling up to millions of users, or if new services are deployed which were not envisaged in the original license agreements.

As an alternative, a royalty-free general-purpose wavelet-based video codec called Dirac

[BBC-a (2010)BBC-b(2010)] is engineered by British Broadcasting Corporation (BBC) aiming at a wide range of applications from storage of video content to streaming video in view to address the above demands. Being "open technology", Dirac is an attractive option as it allows content owners to distribute compressed contents without royalty-fees in anyway.

This chapter presents the fundamental architecture of Dirac video encoder. The overall encoding structure is discussed followed by the detail description of motion estimation, Overlapped Block-based Motion Compensation (OBMC), Discrete Wavelet Transform (DWT), Rate Distortion Optimization (RDO) quantization and entropy coding. Finally, the block diagram of Dirac's bitstream syntax is presented.

DEVELOPMENT TIMELINE OF DIRAC VIDEO CODEC

Dirac has been undergoing major research and development works since it released in 2004. Even in its early development stage, the Dirac (release 0.54) performance is slightly less than the standards like, H.264 where the study was carried out by Onthriar, K., Loo, K.K., & Xue, Z. (2006) and very much better than MPEG2 (at least two folds). In Halbach, T. (2010), a more recent Dirac version, which came with the rate control mode, which was contributed by Tun, M., Loo, K.K., & Cosmas, J. (2008) has been tested against H.264 and Theora (another open-source wavelet-based video codec). The result revealed that H.264 is still superior to Dirac and Theora. However, Dirac is more comparable with H.264 but with superior subjective quality especially in High Definition (HD) format encoding. In this regard, Dirac is more desirable as it is a royalty-free video codec, and thus allows full exploitation by anyone.

Potential uses of Dirac codec include Internet distribution such as web clips, video on demand and IPTV. With industry plans for "On Demand"

TV and streaming over the Internet, open platforms technologies like Dirac have become even more significant. The way Dirac has been developed allows it to be used on any platform and without the payment of royalties. Dirac is the most prominent open source wavelet-based video codec to date. It is still continue to mature with improved performance both in terms of compression and implementation. Table 1 shows the development timeline of Dirac for some significant modification.

The specification was finalized on January 2008, and further developments are only the bug fixes and constraints. As part of the commitment to standardization, BBC has initiated process with the Society of Motion Picture and Television Engineers (SMPTE) to formulate Dirac Pro's specification under the name VC-2. Dirac Pro is an extension to the Dirac family of video compression tools optimized for professional production and archiving applications. It is designed for simplicity, efficiency, speeds and intended for high quality applications with lower compression ratios including transportation of signals between studios and production areas. In addition, it can be utilized for desktop production over IP networks, file storage and video editing. It provides wide range of bit rates from below 100Kbps to more than 1 Gbps but it is most suitable above 100 Mbps. In terms of architecture, Dirac Pro employs only I-Frame coding which means that each frame is coded independently, making editing and production easier and uses exp-Golomb coding which makes hardware and software implementation simple, efficient and low cost. Initial application of Dirac Pro (defined as Dirac Pro 1.5) was for use in transporting full HDTV (1080P50/60) giving 2:1 compression ratio with almost no loss in quality allowing full HDTV video to be carried on the same cables and infra structure used for conventional HDTV. A second application of Dirac Pro (defined as Dirac Pro 270) is to allow the transmission of HDTV signals using the cables and infrastructure formerly used

Table 1. Dirac development timeline

Initial Release of Dirac (Dirac 0.1.0) – March 2004
Added support for frame padding so that arbitrary block sizes and frame dimensions can be supported.
Added support for I-frame only coding by setting *num_L1* equal 0; *num_L1* negative gives a single initial I-frame ('infinitely' many L_1 frames)
Replaced zero-padding with edge-padding to eliminate colour fringing at low bitrates.
Added *QualityMonitor* class to do constant-quality encoding. Class looks at difference between locally decoded and original frames, and adjusts Lagrangian parameters or λ appropriately.
Added support for cut-detection and intra frame insertion.
Changed quality metric from PSNR to one based on 4th powers of errors, to give bigger weighting to large errors.
Changed structure to use a map for the different λ called λ map, which is encapsulated in the *MEData* structure. Limited size of MV costs to allow encoder to cope with motion transitions better.
Modified wavelet coefficient coding to code blocks of coefficients with skip flags if all coefficients are zero.
The arithmetic coding and decoding engines have been modified to improve speed and code organization.
Added classes to handle selecting of quantizers. These allow a single quantizer per subband to be chosen, or alternatively one for each code block.
Initial implementation of Global Motion. Allows for Global Motion Only switch for each frame. If this is set, only the Global Motion Parameters are coded - i.e. no block MVs are coded.
Speed-up to arithmetic coding and decoding, using probability range re-normalization to avoid unnecessary divides.
Added three new filter types with lifting implementations, all much faster than Daubechies (9,7).
Added support for multiple levels of MV precision - pixel, half pixel (1/2 pel), quarter pixel (1/4 pel) and eighth pixel (1/8 pel).
Changed default block height and width for motion compensation to 24 by 24 pixels from 20 by 20. Separation remains 16 by 16. The result is reduced blockiness in areas of poor motion prediction. Downside is slower encoder, but the block parameters are merely scaled-up versions of the SD parameters.
Reduced chroma weighting factors in order to increase chroma fidelity - chroma bit rates should increase from about 5% of total for 420 chroma format to 7.5% of total.
Changed default wavelet filters to fast filters, APPROX97 and FIVETHREE.
Removed constant quality encoding control mechanism, because it worked too poorly for varied sequences. Instead, *QualityMonitor* just monitors quality and encoder control reverts to constant Lagrangian parameters, λ.
Optimized 5_3 wavelet synthesis function, using MMX instructions resulting in 6 percent speed improvement in decoding SD.
Added support for lossless I-frame and long-GOP coding.
Inverse wavelet transform is now done for L_2 frames only if local decoding is required. This is because L_2 frames are (by definition) not used for reference and can be left in a partially reconstructed state if local decoding is not required.
Re-organized classes for doing SAD calculations at pixel and sub-pixel accuracy. These are present also in 'bailout' form so that the algorithm can leave the calculation as soon as it knows that the current SAD is not going to beat the best match so far. These modifications support speeding up motion estimation, and hence the encoder generally.
Search ranges restricted to improve motion estimation speed.
Modified motion compensation so that it takes MB splitting mode into consideration when compensating a row of blocks. Depending on the MB split mode, 1, 2 or 4 blocks of reference data are used to calculate the motion compensated data. This speed up the default quarter pixel block motion compensation routine by an average of 20-23% for a 2Mbps Dirac bitstream.
Optimized *WaveletTransform::VHFilter5_3::Split* using MMX instructions. Minor modification to *WaveletTransform::VHFilter5_3::Synth* function improve speed slightly.
Release of Dirac 0.5.4 (Interim Release) - December 2005
Modified calculation of quantization, inverse quantization and offset values so as to conform to specification. (This modifies the bitstream.)

continued on following page

Table 1. continued

Currently a frame is padded so that it has an integer number of whole MBs and is also a multiple of $2^{(\text{wavelet transform depth})}$. This has changed in the Dirac specification where a frame is padded so that its dimensions are a multiple of $2^{(\text{wavelet transform depth})}$ only. Also the luma and the chroma components can be padded differently. e.g. the luma dimensions may be a perfect multiple of $2^{(\text{wavelet transform depth})}$ so the luma component is not padded but the chroma component may need to be padded depending on the chroma format of the input. To take care of this, *FrameParams* class has been modified to accept both padded chroma and padded luma dimensions. (This modifies the bitstream.)
A linear function is used to calculate the OBMC weights instead of a raised cosine function to make it compliant with spec. Also motion compensation is performed only on true picture dimensions and not padded picture dimensions. (This modifies the bitstream.)
Modified arithmetic coding engine for speed and spec conformance. - Changed context statistics so that maximum weight is 256 - Changed look-up table so that inverse of weight is calculated to 16 instead of 31 bits. - Changed scaled count of zero *m_prob0* so that it's 16 bits instead of 10
Changing binarisation for arithmetic coding, and associated contexts. Binarisation for the magnitude values of wavelet coefficients, MV prediction residues and DC values has been changed from unary to interleaved exp-Golomb so that the number of symbols to be decoded in order to reconstruct a coefficient is reduced. Exp-Golomb binarisation takes a number $N \geq 0$ and codes it via the binary representation of $N+1$, 1*bbbbbb*. If there are K bits following the leading 1, the representation is K zeroes followed by the binary representation: 00...01*bbbb* Interleaved exp-Golomb is the same, except that the K bits are interleaved with the zeroes: 0*b*0*b* 0*b*1 so that a single decoding loop can be used. The zeroes here act as "follow bits" indicating that another bit is to be sent, with 1 as the terminator.
Changed quantization to give 2 bits of accuracy to quantization factors. This improves performance in high-quality applications, and reduces large steps in quality.
Max number of quantizers increased to 97 (0..96).
Computes PSNR instead of weighted 4th power metric; chroma PSNRs are also computed
Add support for Digital Cinema video formats.
Release of Dirac 0.6.0 (First major release complying with Dirac ByteStream Specification) – June 2006
Defined new Wavelet Filter class *VHFilterHaar* to include HAAR filter support in Dirac.
Non-overlapped blocks are now allowed and supported. The raised cosine macro has now been removed and only linear weights are supported.
- Changed Layer 1 frames with P frames and Layer 2 with B frames, rather than with Inter Ref and Inter Non-ref respectively. This is more efficient with the new GOP structure - Modified RDO framework to provide correction where there has been ME failure, i.e. lots of Intra blocks - Slightly increased ME search areas - Corrected the frame type parameter for the final B frame in a sequence
Changed quantizer offsets to be different for Intra and Inter frames, as per the latest draft of the spec. Having an offset of 0.5xquantizer for intra frames improves performance at high rate, especially iterated coding with Dirac Pro application.
Inserted intra frames are now given lower quality than other intra frames so as to match P and B frames more closely.
Changed spec. so that the size of the reference picture buffer is determined from the level and profile information rather than fixed as 5 pictures.
Added support for Constant Bitrate (CBR) encoding. This equalises bitrate over a GOP (I frame to I frame). It does not enforce bit rate, nor does it operate according to a buffer model. To apply CBR coding, add -targetrate N, where N is the target bit rate in Kb/s. Precedence: 1) if a QF is also set with -qf Q, then the value of Q is used as the initial value for the system, but CBR is still applied. 2) if -*lossless* is also set, then lossless coding is applied and CBR constraints are ignored.
Major re-factor of rate control algorithm. The algorithm has been revised so that a target buffer occupancy is aimed for, with the target bit rate set as equal to the mean bit rate plus an adjustment factor to steer back to target. A buffer size of 4xbit rate has been selected.
Updated quantisation factors so that they represent an integer approximation of $2^{((q/4)+2)}$ up to $q=128$.
Release of Dirac 0.7.0 (Major release complying with Dirac ByteStream Specification 1.0.0_pre4) – May 2007
Modified constant bit-rate operation, so that when a cut is detected, the long-term QF is used, instead of the current one in the rate model. This has the effect of reducing quality crashes and rate explosions.

continued on following page

Table 1. continued

Added supports for full-search block matching. This is controlled by using the flag *-full_search* [*xr*] [*yr*] to do an initial pixel-accurate search in the range [*-xr*, *xr*] x [*-yr*, *yr*]. Sub-pixel refinement is unaffected.
Added support for interlaced coding. Changes include refactoring of *PicIO* classes, *SequenceCompressor* class to handle interlaced coding. Modified GOP structure for interlaced coding to code interlaced material more efficiently.
Added support for using VLC codes for entropy coding of coefficient data.
Changed up conversion filter (used in subpel refine ME) to 8 taps with 6 signed bits per tap by approximating the original 10 tap, 9 bit filter. The intermediate calculations will now fit into 16 bits even for 10 bit input data. The new filter causes compression to be up to 0.1dB worse, in return for much speedier performance when optimized.
VC2 is now submitted to SMPTE (Dirac Pro)
Added support for various forms of pre-filtering. Pre-filtering using rectangular, diagonal or centre-weighted median filtering is now available as a command-line option.
Release of Dirac 0.10.0 – September 2008 Beta release complying with the latest Dirac Bytestream Specification Dirac 2.2.0. A stable version of the dirac-research codebase, Dirac 1.0.0, has been released.
- Adaptive GOP structure. - Improved constant bit-rate coding, motion estimation, pre-filtering. - Major code refactor of encoder classes. - Added conversion utility for horizontal 3/4 filtering. - Improved compression performance for small picture sizes, compression performance at low bit-rates. - Included macros to check the API version. - New 422 <-> 420 conversion utilities for interlaced video.
Release of Dirac 0.10.2 – February 2009 (Most current version)

for standard definition television. This requires more compression of HDTV signals than Dirac Pro 1.5 but Dirac Pro is sufficiently flexible to allow this to be achieved with little loss in quality.

OVERALL ENCODER ARCHITECTURE

Dirac is a general-purpose video codec. It is aimed at a wide range of applications, offering efficient coding at resolutions from QCIF (176x144) to HDTV (1920x1080). It is based on wavelet technology which is different from that used in the main standard video compression systems including H.264/MPEG-4 AVC and VC1. It aims to be competitive with the other state-of-the-art standard video codecs and its performance is very much better than MPEG-2 and slightly less than H.264. However, the performance was not the only factor driving its design. Achieving the

better subjective quality than any other blocked based video codecs including H264, is the main goal. The philosophy behind the Dirac codec is "keep it simple". This is an ambitious aim since video codecs, particularly those with state-of-the-art performance, tend to be fearsomely complex.

Figure 1 shows the structure of Dirac encoding architecture. The Dirac's design is that of a conventional hybrid motion-compensated architecture which based around fundamental coding algorithms. It uses hierarchical motion estimation and Overlapped Block based Motion Compensation (OBMC) to avoid block-edge artifacts. First the motion compensated residual frames are wavelet-transformed using separable wavelet filters and divided into subbands. Then, they are quantized using RDO quantizers. Finally, the quantized data is entropy coded using an Arithmetic encoder. Dirac offers facilities for both interlaced and progressive scan sources and common chroma formats (luma only, 4:4:4, 4:2:2, 4:2:0) by means of frame padding. The frame

Figure 1. Overall hybrid encoder architecture

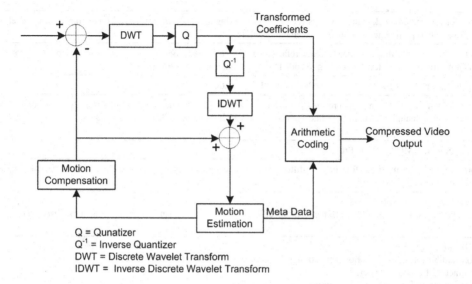

Q = Qunatizer
Q⁻¹ = Inverse Quantizer
DWT = Discrete Wavelet Transform
IDWT = Inverse Discrete Wavelet Transform

padding allows variable Macro Block (MB) size to be used for motion estimation and ensures that the wavelet transform to be made on irregular frame dimensions.

Most of the standard video codecs use block based transform coding technique to exploit spatial redundancy. As a consequence, the reconstructed images suffer from visually annoying effects known as blocking artifacts especially when using higher quantization step size at low bit rate encoding. Another source of blocking artifacts in video is motion compensated prediction. Motion compensated blocks are generated by copying the pixels pointed by the motion vector in the reference frame. This results in discontinuities on the edges of copied blocks due to the fact that there is almost never a perfect match for this data. In order to prevent this blocking artifacts, some standard video codecs use deblocking filters as optional non normative part of the standards. But in H264, the use of deblocking or loop filter is part of the standard and is used both in encoder and decoder in order to improve the subjective quality of motion compensated reference frame at the encoder and reconstructed frames at the decoder. Using loop filter in H264 removes the blocking artifacts significantly however, filtering increases the computational complexity of both encoder and decoder, and takes one third of the computational resources of the decoder according to an analysis of run-time profiles of decoder sub functions by Horowitz, M., Joch, A., Kossentini, F., & Hallapuro, A. (2003). In worst case, if the original image includes sharp edges (e.g. checker board), filtering these sharp edges which are at the boundary of a block could lose sharpness of the image.

But in Dirac, the application Wavelet Transform (WT), which applies over the whole frame instead of block by block basis in Discrete Cosine Transform (DCT) of most of the standard encoders, totally eliminates the blockiness of the image in removing the spatial redundancy. Wavelet transformed coefficients are quantized equally with the predefined set of quantizers for the different sub-bands, resulting smooth variation of image quality for different bit rate encoding. As for the motion compensation, OBMC is applied in order to compensate the artifacts that may arise because of the use of blocked based Motion Estimation (ME). These are the main differences in architecture of Dirac and H264 in achieving the better subjective

Figure 2. Prediction of L1 and L2 frame

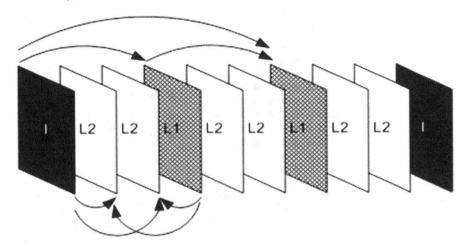

quality. With the use of WT and OBMC, Dirac can avoid the use of deblocking filter in its coding architecture which in turn, reduces the complexity significantly while maintaining good subjective quality in encoding of the smaller video formats (e.g. QCIF, CIF) and superior subjective quality compared with H264 in encoding of SD and HD video formats.

Dirac defines three frame types. Intra frames (*I* frames) are coded independently without reference to other frames in the sequence. Level 1 frames (*L1* frames) and Level 2 frames (*L2* frames) are both inter frames, which are coded with reference to other previously (and/or future) coded frames. The definition of the *L1* and *L2* frames are the same with *P* and *B* frames in H.264. The encoder operates with standard GOP modes whereby the number of *L1* frames between *I* frames, and the separation between *L1* frames, can be specified depending on the application. It can also be operated on *I* frame-only mode where all the frames are intra coded like in motion JPEG2000. A prediction method for frame coding using a standard GOP structure is shown in Figure 2. In this figure, the number of *L1* frames between *I* frames is 2 and the *L1* frame separation is 3.

The following sections will give the further explanation of each functional block shown in Figure 1.

Motion Estimation

In its hierarchical motion estimation, Dirac first down converts the size of the current and reference of all types of inter frames (both P and B) using the 12 taps down conversion filter. The number of down conversion levels depends upon the frame format (i.e. *width* and *height* or dimension of the frame) and can be calculated using Eq. (1) as follow.

$$level = \min\left[\log_2\left(\frac{width}{12}\right), \log_2\left(\frac{height}{12}\right)\right]$$

(1)

According to (1), the number of down conversion levels can be 4 or 6 depending upon the video formats whether it is CIF or HD (1920 ×1080). In the down conversion process, the dimension (both height and width) of the frames are reduced by the factor of two in each level. Motion estimation is performed first in the lowest resolution (smallest frame) level and gradually increased to the higher resolution levels until it reaches the original frame

Figure 3. Search patterns of dirac

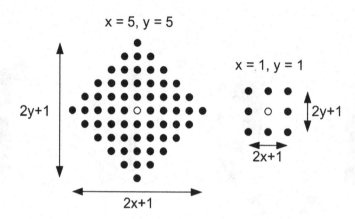

Figure 4. Spatially predicted MV of dirac, the current block is the block where ME is being performed

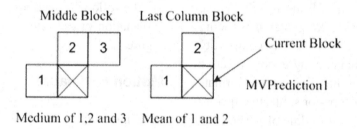

size. The search pattern used in the lowest level is Diamond shape with the search range 5 and all other levels except lowest use square shape search pattern with search range 1. Figure 3 shows both search patterns where there are altogether 61 search points in Diamond shape and 9 points in square shape.

First of all, candidate lists which are the lists to be searched are generated. A candidate list consists of a number of points to be searched, which follows a certain pattern either diamond or square as shown in Figure 3 and centered at a predicted MV. The predicted MV can be either zero, spatially predicted or guide MV. Spatially predicted MV is the medium vector of block number 1, 2 and 3 or mean vector of block 1 and 2 as shown in Figure 4, depending upon the location of the current block where motion estimation is carried out. Guide vector is the best MV at the corresponding block location of the adjacent

lower hierarchical level and it is not available for the lowest level.

In Figure 5, for lowest level search, two candidate lists are generated centered at zero MV and spatially predicted MV respectively with the Diamond Search (DS) pattern. Sum of the Absolute Difference (SAD) is used here as the cost function. At the initial search step, the SAD calculation is carried out only for the center point of diamond pattern in each list and finds the list which gives the minimum cost. The candidate lists to be searched are chosen by multiplying the minimum cost with 1.5 and choose all the lists which give the cost less than 1.5 times minimum costs. So, there can be at most two candidate lists and 122 search points can be involved in lowest level search if there is no overlapping between the two lists. In the refine step, SAD calculation is carried out for all chosen candidate lists on their corresponding search points and the coordinate

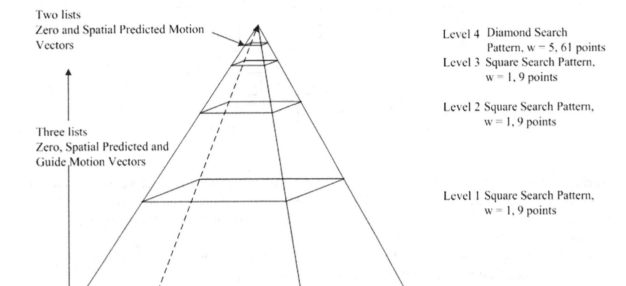

Figure 5. Dirac's four levels hierarchical motion estimation for CIF video format, where w is search range

Two lists
Zero and Spatial Predicted Motion
Vectors

Three lists
Zero, Spatial Predicted and
Guide Motion Vectors

Level 4 Diamond Search
Pattern, w = 5, 61 points
Level 3 Square Search Pattern,
w = 1, 9 points

Level 2 Square Search Pattern,
w = 1, 9 points

Level 1 Square Search Pattern,
w = 1, 9 points

Level 0 Square Search Pattern,
w = 1, 9 points

of the point which gives the minimum cost, is recorded as the best MV.

The search procedure is basically the same for all other levels except the addition of one more candidate list which is centered at the guide vector. So, there are three candidate lists in these levels with the square search pattern as shown in Figure 3 and the maximum number of search points can be at most 27 in each level if there is no overlapping between the lists.

After going through all these levels, the pixel accuracy MVs for each block are obtained. Dirac provides the option to find the MVs up to 1/8 pixel accuracy. In order to achieve this, motion estimation undergoes subpel refine process where the current and references pictures are up converted by 2, multiply the pixel accuracy MV by 2 and search around in order to get 1/2 pel accuracy MV. The above procedure is repeated until the required accuracy level is reached.

After getting the required accuracy MVs for each block, the last stage of motion estimation, mode decision is carried out by using RDO motion estimation metric. The metric consists of a basic block matching metric which is SAD plus the λ_{ME} multiplied by a measure of the local MV smoothness. The smoothness measure is based on the difference between the candidate MV and the median of the neighboring previously computed MVs. The total metric is a combination of the two metrics. Given a vector V with the components V_x and V_y in rectangular coordinates, which maps the current frame's block P to a block $R = V(P)$ in the reference frame, the metric is given by:

$$SAD\left(P, R\right) + \lambda_{ME} \times \max\left(\left|V_x - M_x\right| + \left|V_y - M_y\right|, 48\right)$$

(2)

Figure 6. MB splitting levels

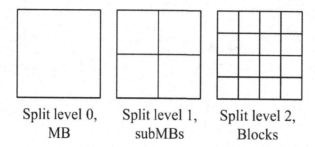

| Split level 0, MB | Split level 1, subMBs | Split level 2, Blocks |

where, M_x and M_y are the rectangular components of medium MV calculated from the MVs of left, top and top left blocks. λ_{ME} is the scaled version of Lagrangian multiplier (λ) and it is equal to two times the value of λ in Dirac 0.6. Dirac uses a parameter called Quality Factor (QF) to control the quality of the encoded frames. QF plays an important role since it is involved in the RDO processes of motion estimation and quantization as a Lagrangian multiplier (λ). In Dirac 0.6, the relation between λ and QF is defined as shown in (3).

$$\lambda = \left(10^{(10-QF)/2.5}\right)\Big/16 \qquad (3)$$

In mode decision, Dirac encoder considers the total of 12 modes which includes the combination of 3 MB splitting levels as shown in Figure 6 and 4 prediction modes. A MB consists of a 4x4 array of blocks, and there are three possible ways of splitting a MB:

- **Splitting level 0:** no split, a single MV per reference frame for the MB;
- **Splitting level 1:** split into four sub-macroblocks (sub-MBs), each a 2x2 array of blocks, one MV per reference frame per sub-MB;
- **Splitting level 2:** split into the 16 constituent blocks.

At the same time, the best prediction mode for each prediction unit (block, sub-MB or MB) is chosen. There are four prediction modes available:

- INTRA: intra coded, predicted by DC value;
- REF1_ONLY: only predict from the first reference;
- REF2_ONLY: only predict from the second reference (if one exists);
- REF1AND2: bi-directional prediction.

So, depending upon the MB splitting level and the prediction mode, there can be altogether 12 combination of mode which is decided by using the (2). Basically, mode decision process calculates the total cost using (2) for every combination of MB splitting level and prediction mode. And then, the best combination which yields the minimum cost is chosen as the best mode.

Overlapped Based-Based Motion Compensation (OBMC)

A large weakness in traditional Block Motion Compensation (BMC) used in many MPEG architectures is unwanted block-edge artifacts located around the block boundaries. For this reason, Dirac uses OBMC in order to avoid the block-edge artifacts which are sensitive to wavelet transforms and expansive to be coded. Dirac encoder can deal with any degree of overlapping with variable block sizes and this is configurable at the encoder. One

Figure 7. Overlapped block structure of dirac

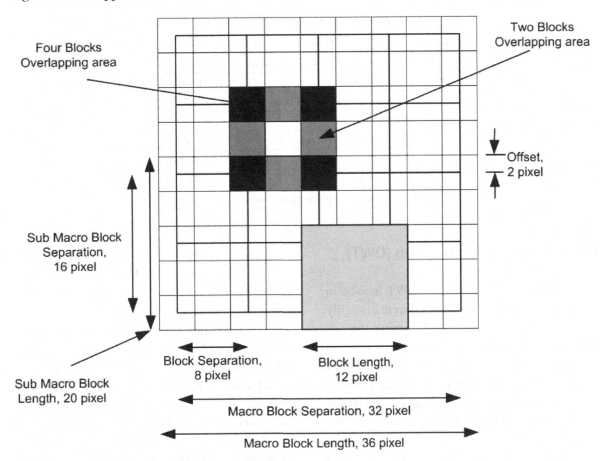

issue is that there should be an exact number of MB horizontally and vertically; otherwise it can also be achieved by padding the data.

Dirac's OBMC scheme is based on a separable Raised-Cosine mask. This acts as a weight function on the predicting block. Given a pixel $p(x,y,t)$ in frame t, p may fall within only one block or in up to four if it lies at the corner of a block as shown in Figure 7. The figure shows the overlapped block structure of a MB which includes 16 blocks with 12 pixel block length and 8 pixel block separation.

The predictor $\tilde{p}$ for p is the weight sum of all the corresponding pixels in the predicting blocks in reference frame, t'. The Raised-Cosine mask has the necessary property that the sum of the weights will always be 1. The predictor $\tilde{p}$ for MV set (V_i, W_i) for the frame t can be calculated as follow.

$$\tilde{p}\left(x,y,t\right) = \sum_{i=1}^{k} w_i p\left(x - V_i, y - W_i, t'\right) \qquad (4)$$

where, $\sum_i w_i = 1$, k is either 1, 2 or 4.

The value of k depends upon the physical location of the predicting pixel in the frame either within a single block, two overlapping blocks or four overlapping blocks.

Table 2. Wavelet filter presets of driac

Wavelet Index	Filter	Symbol
0	Approximate Daubechies (9, 7), default	DD9_7
1	LeGall (5, 3)	LEGALL5_3
2	Approximate Daubechies (13, 7)	DD13_7
3	Haar with no shift	HAAR0
4	Haar with single shift per level	HAAR1
5	Haar with double shift per level	HAAR2
6	Fidelity filter	FIDELITY
7	Daubechies (9, 7) integer approximation	DAUB9_7

Discrete Wavelet Transform (DWT)

As DCT is used in H.264, the DWT is used in Dirac in order to de-correlate the data in a roughly frequency-sensitive way, while having the advantage of preserving fine details better [BBC-c (2010)]. One of the weaknesses of DCT based encoder is that the picture goes all blocky when the encoder is applied under higher compression ratio because of the block based transformed method used in DCT. In contrast to DCT, DWT has been proven to be a more efficient technique where its transform can be applied to analyze the entire image without requiring block based transformation improving picture quality. This gives a wider coding spectrum and minimizes the block-edge effects. As a result, coding errors are spread out and artifacts found tend to be blended into the overall image. DWT is also used in the current JPEG2000 standard for image compression.

Once motion compensation has been performed, motion compensated residuals are treated almost identically to intra frame data. The only difference between intra picture coefficient coding and inter picture residual coefficient coding lies in the use of prediction within the DC wavelet sub-band of intra picture components. In both cases, there are three components (luminance and two chrominance) in the form of two-dimensional arrays of data values. So, a standard 2D DWT is employed to transform both intra and residue of the motion compensated inter frames up to N decomposition levels where N can be calculated using (1). Clearly, applying an N-level wavelet transform requires N levels of sub-samplings, and so for reversibility, it is necessary that 2^N divides all the dimensions of each component. The additional frame padding may be required in order to perform DWT for a given decomposition level if the dimension of the video frame is not divisible by 2^N. There are eight wavelet filter presets in Dirac encoder and the required transform filter for inter and intra frame can be chosen independently. The Table 2 shows the list of filters used in Dirac.

In wavelet coding, the band splitting is done by passing the image data through a bank of bandpass analysis filters. Since the bandwidth of each filtered version of the image is reduced, they can now in theory be down-sampled at a lower rate, according to the Nyquist criteria, giving a series of reduced size sub-images. At the receiver, they are restored to their original sizes by passing through a bank of synthesis filters, where they are interpolated and added to reconstruct the image. In the absence of quantization error, it is required that the reconstructed picture should be an exact replica of the input picture. This can only be achieved if the spatial frequency response of the analysis filter tiles the spectrum without overlapping, which requires infinitely sharp transition

Figure 8. A two-band analysis filter

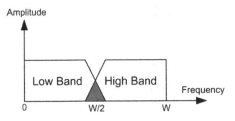

regions and cannot be realized practically. Instead, the analysis filter responses have finite transition regions and do overlap as shown in Figure 8, which means that the down-sampling/up-sampling process introduces aliasing distortion into the reconstructed picture [Ghanbari, M. (1999)].

In order to eliminate the aliasing distortion, the synthesis and analysis filters have to have certain relationships such that the aliased components in the transition regions cancel out each other [Ghanbari, M. (1999)]. The corresponding one dimension, two-band wavelet transform encoder/decoder is shown in Figure 9. In this figure, $H_0(f)$ and $H_1(f)$ represent the frequency domain transfer functions of the respective low pass and high pass analysis filters. Filters $G_0(f)$ and $G_1(f)$ are the corresponding synthesis filters. The down-sampling and up-sampling factors are 2.

At the encoder, down-sampling by 2 is carried out by discarding alternate samples, the remainder being compressed into half the distance occupied by the original sequence. This is equivalent to compressing the source image by a factor of 2, which doubles all the frequency components present. The frequency domain effect of this down-sampling is thus to double the width of all components in the sampled spectrum causing aliasing.

At the decoder, the up-sampling is a complementary procedure. It is achieved by inserting a zero-valued sample between each input sample, and is equivalent to a spatial expansion of the input sequence. In the frequency domain, the effect is as usual the reverse and all components are compressed towards zero frequency. Figure 10 shows this problem clearly and it is because of the impossibility of constructing ideal sharp-cut analysis filters.

Multi-dimensional and multi-band wavelet coding can be developed from the one-dimensional, two band low pass and high pass analysis/ synthesis filter structure of Figure 9. Wavelet coding of a two-dimensional image can be performed by carrying out a one-dimensional decomposition along the lines of the image and then down each column. A seven band wavelet transform coding of this type is illustrated in Figure 11, where band splitting is carried out alternately in the horizontal and vertical direction. In this figure, L and H represent the low pass and high pass filters with a 2:1 down-sampling.

As shown in Figure 11, a choice of wavelet filters is applied to each image component in both vertical and horizontal directions to produce four subbands termed Low-Low (LL), Low-High (LH), High-Low (HL) and High-High (HH) for each level. Only the LL band is iteratively decomposed to obtain the required decomposition level (in Figure 11, there is only two level) yielding a series

Figure 9. A two-band wavelet transform encoder and decoder [BBC-c (2010)]

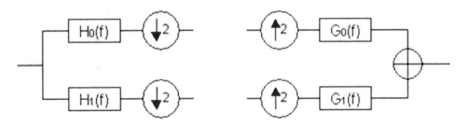

Figure 10. Low pass subband generation and recovery [Ghanbari, M. (1999)]

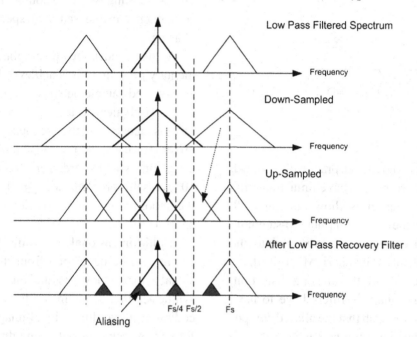

Figure 11. Two-dimensional, multi-band wavelet transform coding using repeated two-band splits [Ghanbari, M. (1999)]

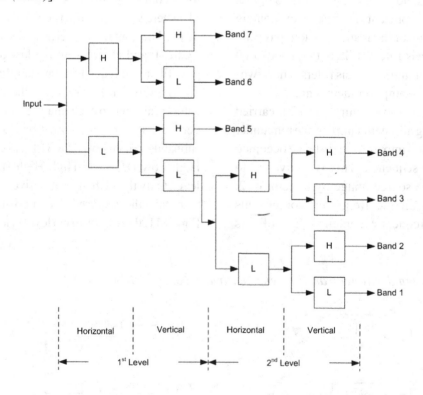

of sub bands. The subband decomposition of three level wavelet transform showing their corresponding subbands location on physical frame is shown in Figure 12.

Figure 13 shows original image and the resulting 10 subbands (3 levels) wavelet transform of Lena image. After decomposition, the number of samples in each resulting subband is one quarter of the samples of the input signal.

The choice of wavelet filters has an impact on compression performance. Filters need to have compact impulse response in order to reduce ringing artefacts. It also has an impact on encoding and decoding speed in software. There are numerous filters supported by Dirac as shown in Table 2 to allow a trade-off between complexity and performance. These are configurable in the reference software.

Since each subband represents a filtered and subsampled version of the frame component, coefficients within each subband correspond to specific areas of the underlying picture and hence those that relate to the same area can be related. There is also stronger relation between the coef-

ficients that have the same orientation (in terms of combination of high and low pass filters). The relationship is illustrated Figure 14, showing the situation for HL bands i.e. those that have been high pass filtered horizontally and low pass filtered vertically, LH bands and HH bands. Their relation can also be called as the horizontal orientation (i.e. LH bands), vertical orientation (i.e. HL bands) and diagonal orientation (i.e. HH bands).

In the diagram it is easy to see that a coefficient (the parent) in the lowest HL band corresponds spatially to a 2×2 block of coefficients (the children) in the next HL band, each coefficient of which itself has a 2×2 block of child coefficients in the next band, and so on. This relationship relates closely to spectral harmonics: when coding image features (edges, especially) significant coefficients are found distributed across subbands, in positions related by the parent and child structure. In particular, a coefficient is more likely to be significant if its parent is non zero and on the other hand, if a parent is zero, it is likely that its children in the higher bands are zero.

Figure 12. Two dimensional wavelet transform frequency decomposition (3 Levels) [BBC-c (2010)]

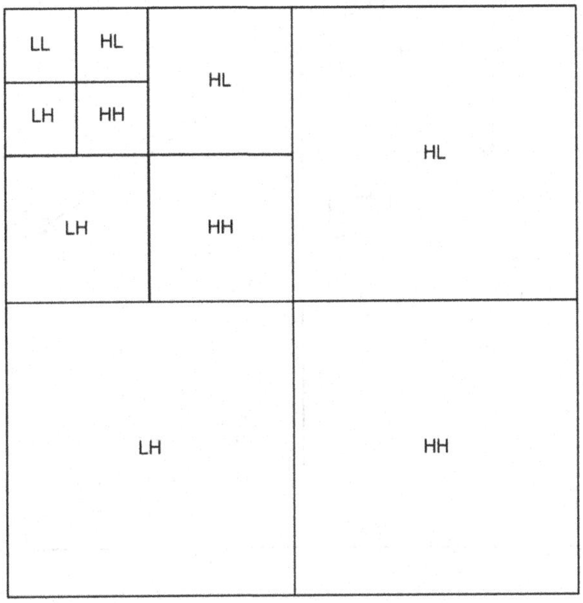

Figure 13. 3-level wavelet transform of Lena [BBC-c (2010)]

Figure 14. Parent and child relationship between subband coefficients

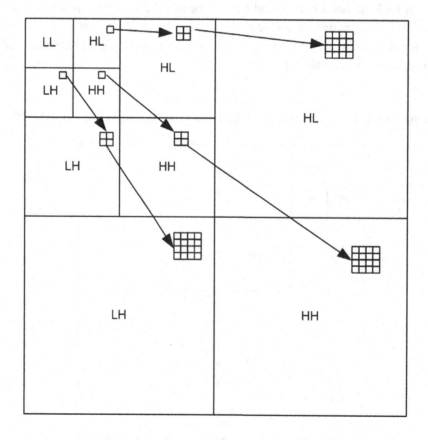

Figure 15. The architecture of wavelet coefficient coding

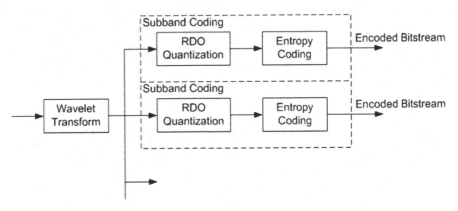

When entropy coding the wavelet transformed coefficients, these factors will be helpful to take the parents into account in predicting how likely their children to be say, a zero. By coding from low frequency subbands to high frequency ones, and hence by coding parent before child, parent and child dependencies can be exploited in these ways without additional signalling to the decoder.

After transforming a frame into multiple subbands, each wavelet subband's coefficients are coded in turn using RDO quantization and entropy coding. Figure 15 shows the architecture of wavelet coefficient coding in Dirac. The following sections will discuss these two functional blocks in details.

Rate Distortion Optimization Quantization

After having the image components treated by DWT, the resulting transform coefficients are quantized starting from lowest frequency to highest frequency subbands. There are 96 set of quantizers and the optimum Quantization Parameter (QP) index is chosen by RDO Quantization process. Dirac uses dead-zone quantizer in which the first region of the quantization steps is about twice wider than the uniform quantizer and so it applies more severe quantization of the smallest

values, which acts as a simple but effective denoising operation.

Figure 16 (a) and (b) show uniform quantizer and uniform dead zone quantizer, where the quantization factor is Δ with mid-point reconstruction values shown in bold marking. But in Dirac, the reconstruction value is calculated by offset value which is 0.375 from the margin instead of taking mid point where offset is 0.5. It is because the values of transformed coefficients in a wavelet subband have a distribution with mean very near zero and which decays pretty rapidly and uniformly for larger values. Values are therefore more likely to occur in the first half of the interval than in the second half and the smaller value of 0.375 reflects this bias and gives better performance in practice.

$$\Delta = \left\lfloor 2^{2+\frac{QP}{4}} + 0.5 \right\rfloor, \quad 0 \le QP \le 96 \qquad (5)$$

$$\text{offset} = (\Delta \times 0.375) + 0.5 \qquad (6)$$

The relation between QP and Quantization Factor (Δ) together with the calculation of their corresponding offset values for Dirac 0.6 is stated in (5) and (6).

The quantization process is carried out in three steps: firstly a quarter of coefficients are used to obtain bit-accuracy, a second quarter is used to

Figure 16. Uniform and dead-zone quantizers

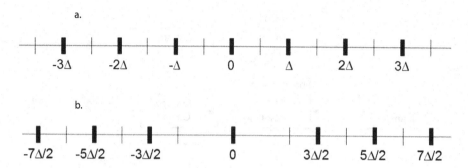

estimate half-bit accuracy and the remaining half is used to perform quarter-bit accuracy. In case of intra frame quantization, coefficient prediction is performed and is used to remove any residual interdependencies between coefficients in the subbands allowing for effective entropy encoding. A coefficient is predicted by the mean value of the surrounding pixels of the current pixel and the difference is quantized and sent.

The Dirac encoder uses an RDO technique to pick a quantizer by minimizing a Lagrangian combination of rate and distortion. Essentially, lots of quantizers are tried and the best is picked. Rate is estimated via an adaptively-corrected zero[th] order entropy measure, $Ent(\Delta)$ of the quantized symbols resulting from applying the quantization factor (Δ), calculated as a value of bits/pixel. Total entropy for estimating the rate is the combination of $Ent(\Delta)$ and sign entropy, $SignEnt(\Delta)$ and can be calculated as follow.

$$Total\_Ent\left(\Delta\right) = Ent\left(\Delta\right) + SignEnt\left(\Delta\right) \tag{7}$$

where, $Ent(\Delta)$ is measured in bit/pixel and can be found using Eq. (8) and (9) as follow.

$$Ent\left(\Delta\right) = -\left(P_0 \log_2\left(P_0\right) + P_1 \log_2\left(P_1\right)\right) \text{ bits} \tag{8}$$

$$Ent\left(\Delta\right) = \frac{Ent\left(\Delta\right) \times \left(num\_zero + num\_one\right)}{num\_coefficients} \text{ bits/pixel} \tag{9}$$

where, in (8), P_0 and P_1 are the probabilities of zeros and ones. The same idea applies for the calculation of $SignEnt(\Delta)$ where the calculation is based upon the probabilities of positive and negative coefficients.

Distortion, $D(\Delta)$ is measured in terms of the perceptually-weighted fourth-power (4th power) of the error resulting from the difference between the original and the quantized coefficients. For a coefficient, P_{ij} and its corresponding quantized value, Q_{ij}, where i and j are row and column indices of a subband, the distortion can be found using the (10) as follow.

$$D(\Delta) = \sqrt{\frac{\sum_{ij}\left|P_{ij} - Q_{ij}\right|^4}{num\_coeff \times w^2}} \tag{10}$$

where, w is the perceptual weight associated with the subband where higher frequencies will have a larger weighting factor. Finally, the optimization is carried out by minimizing the combination of total entropy measure, $Total\_Ent\left(\Delta\right)$ as the rate and distortion, $D(\Delta)$ as follow.

$$D\left(\Delta\right) + \lambda.C.Total\_Ent\left(\Delta\right) \tag{11}$$

where, C is the entropy correction factor which compensates any discrepancy between the measure of entropy and the actual cost in terms of bits, based on the actual bit rate produced by the corresponding elements of previous frames. It is necessary because the entropy measure does not take into account dependencies between coefficients that are taken into account in the actual coefficient entropy coding. In (11), λ is the Lagrangian multiplier and can be derived from the QF as given in (3). The QF plays an important role in controlling the quality of the encoded video sequence or the number of bits generated in the encoding process of Dirac video codec. At this point, it is worth to note that the RDO process described above is primarily meant to control constant quality rather than bitrate by using the QF, which is a user defined parameter, as a quality indicator to maintain the desired quality. Due to this reason, the early Dirac codec does not support rate control. Having said that, the latest Dirac codec does support rate control where the rate control algorithm proposed by Tun, M., Loo, K.K., & Cosmas, J. (2008) was adopted.

Entropy Coding

Wavelet Coefficient Coding

Dirac codes subbands from low-frequency to high frequency in a zig-zag order. Within each subband, the coefficients are further partitioned spatially divided into code blocks. Coefficients are scanned by coding the code blocks in normal raster order and coding the coefficients within each code block in raster order within that block. However, each code block can be skipped so a skip flag is included in the stream of symbols to be coded. The skip flag is interpreted in the decoder as setting all coefficients within the block to be zero.

The number of code blocks in a subband depends on the frame type and on the subband position. Intra frames have a single code block for the lowest-frequency subbands (i.e. the bottom 2 levels of the 4 levels wavelet transform) and a 4x3 array of code blocks for the remaining high frequencies bands. Predicted frames have more code blocks, as coefficients are more likely to be zero: only 1 block for the 4 lowest-level subbands; 8x6 for the next 3 subbands; 12x8 for the remaining subbands. There are two possible quantization modes made possible by the code block structure, which are a single quantizer for the whole subband or different quantizers for different blocks in a subband. The idea of multiple qunatizers for a subband is to allow the Region Of Interest (ROI) coding.

The entropy coding used by Dirac in wavelet subband coefficient coding is based on three stages: binarization, context modeling and adaptive arithmetic coding as shown in Fig. 17.

Binarization is the process of transforming the multi-valued coefficient symbols into bits. The resulting bitstream can then be arithmetic coded. The original symbol stream could have been coded directly, using a multi-symbol arithmetic coder, but this process is more likely to cause context dilution since most symbols occur very rarely and so only sparse statistics can be gathered, which reduces coding efficiency. To avoid this problem, binarization is applied to transform the multi-valued coefficient symbols into bitstream with easily analyzable statistic that can be coded by arithmetic coding. Binarization can be done by using one of the Variable Length Coding (VLC) formats. In Dirac, VLC are used in three ways, (i) for direct encoding of the header values into bit stream, (ii) for entropy coding of motion data and coefficients, where arithmetic decoding is not in use, and (ii) binarisation in the arithmetic encoding/decoding process. Unary code was used as VLC in which every non-negative number N is mapped to N zeros followed by a 1 and sign bit.

But, starting from Dirac 0.6.0 release, binarization for the magnitude values of wavelet coefficients, MV prediction residues and DC values has been changed from unary to interleaved

Figure 17. Entropy coding structure

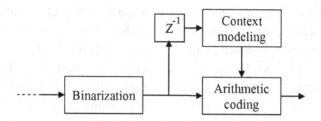

exp-Golomb in order to reduce the number of symbols to be decoded in reconstructing a coefficient. Exp-Golomb binarisation takes a number $N \geq 0$ and codes it via the binary representation of $N+1$, 1bbbbbb. If there are K bits following the leading 1, the representation is K zeroes followed by the binary representation, i.e. 00...01bbbbb. As explained, conventional exp-Golomb coding places all follow bits at the beginning as a prefix. This is easier to read, but requires a count of the prefix length and can only be decoded in two loops, the prefix followed by the data bits. Interleaved exp-Golomb is the same, except that the K bits are interleaved with the zeroes, i.e. 0b0b...0b1 so that a single decoding loop can be used without the need for a length count. The zeroes here act as "follow bits" indicating that another bit is to be sent, with 1 as the terminator. Contexts for coding these symbols are selected for the follow bits and other bits ("information bits") separately. Compression performance is hardly affected, nor is speed performance in software, but hardware performance is greatly facilitated [BBC-d (2010)]. Dirac actually uses unsigned interleaved exp-Golomb and singed interleaved exp-Golomb codes separately where the former one is for unsigned integer coding and the latter consists of unsigned interleaved exp-Golomb code for the magnitude, followed by a sign bit for non-zero values.

In order to use arithmetic coding to compress data, a statistical model for the data is needed. The model needs to be able to accurately predict the frequency/probability of symbols in the input data stream and at the same time, need to deviate from a uniform distribution.

The need to accurately predict the probability of symbols in the input data is inherent in the nature of arithmetic coding. The principal of this type of coding is to reduce the number of bits needed to encode a character as its probability of appearance increases. So if the letter "E" represents 25% of the input data, it would only take 2 bits to code. If the letter "Z" represents only 0.1% of the input data, it might take 10 bits to code. If the model is not generating probabilities accurately, it might take 10 bits to represent "e" and 2 bits to represent "Z", causing data expansion instead of compression.

The second condition is that the model needs to make predictions that deviate from a uniform distribution. The better the model is at making predictions that deviate from uniform, the better the compression ratios will be. For example, a model could be created that assigned all 256 possible symbols a uniform probability of 1/256. This model would create an output file that was exactly the same size as the input file, since every symbol would take exactly 8 bits to encode. The number of bits can be reduced only by correctly finding probabilities that deviate from a normal distribution, leading to compression.

The idea of context modelling in Dirac does exactly the job as explained above in getting the statistical information of the input symbols. According to the nature of wavelet transform, the value of transformed coefficient (either zero, small or large) can be predicted well by its neighbours and parents. The context modelling in Dirac is based upon this idea. The reason for doing this approach is that whereas the wavelet transform largely removes correlation between a coefficient and its neighbours, they may not be statistically independent even if they are uncorrelated. Small and especially zero coefficients in wavelet subbands tend to clump together, located at points corresponding to smooth areas in the image, and are grouped together across subbands in the parent-child relationship.

The value of "small" depends upon the subband since the wavelet transform implemented in Dirac has a gain of 2 for each level of decomposition. So a threshold is set individually based on the subband type.

For predicting through neighbours, neighbourhood sum is calculated at each point (x, y) of each subband. It is the sum of the two previously coded quantized neighbouring coefficients and can be calculated as follow.

$$nhood\_sum\left(x,y\right) = \left|c\left(x-1, y\right)\right| + \left|c\left(x, y-1\right)\right|$$

$$(12)$$

And then, determine whether the parent coefficient is zero or not though parent and child relationship in wavelet transform subbands. There are altogether 23 contexts used in transformed coefficients coding, which can be seen in appendix B.

After binarization, a context is selected and the probabilities for 0 and 1 that are maintained in the appropriate context will be fed to the arithmetic coding function along with the value itself to be coded. Contexts must be initialized with a count for both 0 and 1, which is used for encoding the first symbol in that context. An additional source of redundancy lies in the local nature of the statistics. If the contexts are not refreshed periodically then later data has less influence in shaping the statistics than earlier data, resulting in bias, and local statistics are not exploited. Dirac adopts a simple way of refreshing the contexts by halving

the counts of 0 and 1 for that context at regular intervals. The effect is to maintain the probabilities to a reasonable level of accuracy, but to keep the influence of all coefficients roughly constant [BBC-c (2010) and Borer, T., & Davies, T. (2005)].

Motion Vector Data Coding

MV data coding is important to the performance of video coding, especially for codecs with a high level of MV accuracy (1/4 or 1/8 pel). For this reason, MV coding and decoding is quite complicated, since significant gains in efficiency can be made by choosing a good prediction and entropy coding structure. The basic format of the MV coding module is similar to the coding of coefficient data: it consists of prediction, followed by binarization, context modelling and adaptive arithmetic coding as shown in Figure 18.

All the MV data is predicted from previously encoded data from adjacent blocks (i.e. left, top left and top blocks). In predicting the data, a number of conventions are observed. The first convention is that all the block data (prediction modes, MVs and/or any DC values) is actually associated with the top-left block of the prediction unit to which they refer. This allows for a consistent prediction and coding structure to be adopted.

Example: If splitting level=1 and then the prediction units in a MB are sub-MBs (refers to Figure 6). In this case, the prediction mode and any MVs are associated with the top-left block of each sub-MB and it is not required to encode other blocks' data in each sub-MB except top left.

The second convention is that all MB data is scanned in raster order for encoding purposes. All data is scanned first by MB in raster order, and then in raster order within each MB. That is, taking each MB in raster order and then each block value which needs to be coded within that MB is coded again in raster order as shown in Figure 19.

The third convention concerns the availability of values for prediction purposes. Since predic-

Figure 18. MV entropy encoding architecture

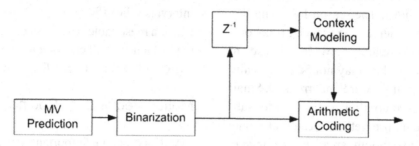

Figure 19. Block data scanning order

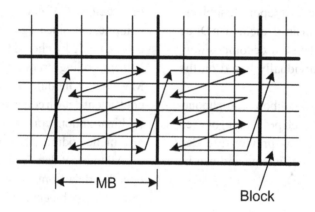

tion will be based on neighbouring values, it is necessary to propagate values for the purposes of prediction when the MV data has combined to ensure that values are not required for every block.

Example: Figure 20 shows the requirement of propagation of values. Suppose that only REF1_x is being encoded. In the first MB, splitting level = 0 and so at most only the top-left block requires a value, which can be predicted from values in previously coded MBs. After encoding this value (i.e. v) it is then required to be applied to every block inside this MB. In the next MB, splitting level = 1, so the unit of prediction is the sub-MB. In the top-left sub-MB, the prediction mode is, say, REF1AND2 and so a value x is coded for the top-left block of that sub-MB. It can be predicted from any available values in neighbouring blocks, and in particular the value v is available from the adjacent block.

The prediction used depends on the MV data being coded, but in all cases the aperture for the predictor is shown in Figure 21. This aperture is interpreted as blocks where block data is concerned and MBs where MB data is concerned. The splitting level is predicted as the mean of the levels of the three MBs in the aperture.

From among block data, the prediction mode is predicted for reference 1 and reference 2 separately. The prediction mode is interpreted as a two bit number encoding with four possibilities: IN-TRA = 0 (00), REF1_ONLY = 1 (01), REF2_ONLY = 2 (10) and REF1AND2 = 3 (11). In this way the first bit (bit 0, least significant bit) is a flag indicating presence of reference 1 and the second bit (bit 1, most significant bit) is indication the presence of reference 2. Bit 0 and Bit 1 are predicted separately: if most of the 3 predicting blocks use reference 1 (i.e. their mode is REF1_ONLY or REF1AND2) then it is predicted that

Figure 20. Propagation of data within MBs or sub-MBs

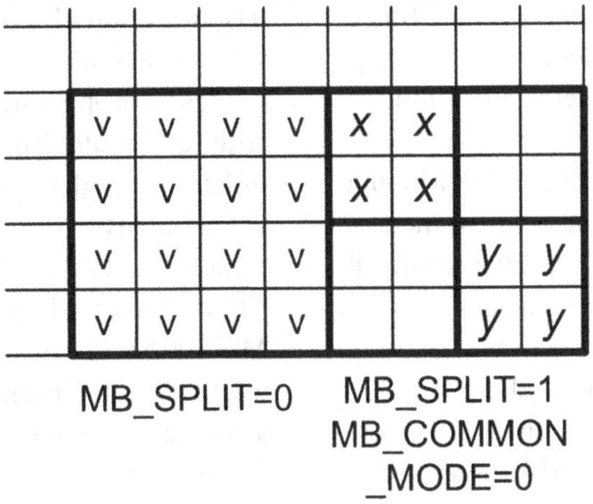

	v	v	v	v	x	x	
	v	v	v	v	x	x	
	v	v	v				y	y
	v	v	v				y	y

MB_SPLIT=0   MB_SPLIT=1
MB_COMMON
_MODE=0

bit 0 is set, and the same idea applies for bit 1 prediction.

The DC values are predicted by the average of the three values in the aperture. The MVs themselves are predicted by predicting the horizontal and vertical components separately. The predictor for MV components is the median of the three corresponding values in the prediction aperture for the block.

In many cases MV or DC values are not available from all blocks in the aperture, for example if the prediction mode is different. In this case, these blocks are excluded from consideration. Where only two values are available, the median MV predictor becomes a mean. Where only one value is available, it will be the predicted value. Where no value is available, no prediction is made, except for the DC values, where 0 is used by default.

PERFORMANCES OF DIRAC VIDEO CODEC

Objective tests were carried out to evaluate the performance of Dirac in four aspects: compression ratio, PSNR, Structural Similarity Index Metric (SSIM) and Video Quality Metric (VQM). H.264

Figure 21. Aperture for MV prediction

was simulated alongside the Dirac as a reference (or benchmark). The compression ratio results were produced by evaluating the file size of the compressed video produced by Dirac and H.264 at different constant bitrates (CRB), in comparison to the file size of the original video sequence. PSNR, SSIM and VQM are video quality metrics that differ in the perception of the quality of the video. The outcomes from these metrics were compared in order to analyze the quality of the video from an objective quality measurement perspective.

Four standard video sequences ranging from QCIF to HD frame sizes were used to perform the objective tests on the Dirac and H.264 under different video scenarios as described below:

- Carphone (QCIF, 176x144 pixels): It has slow motion with fast back ground movement.

- Football (CIF, 352x288 pixels): Quick motion scene, camera motion and frame changes through the video.
- Susie (SD, 704x480 pixels): Slow motion scene.
- Blue Sky (HD, 1920x1080 pixels): Moving camera, slow motion, the color of the sky gives transparency, with a touch of detail by the tree leaves and branches.

The Dirac codec version 0.8.0 from BBC-b(2010) and the H.264 codec version JM11.0 (most reliable version) from H.264 (2010) were used in the test. Main Profile of H.264 was used because it supports B-frame coding and that matches the coding profile of Dirac. Both Dirac and H.264 has the option of fixing the bitrate. This method was applied in all the tests as to ensure both the codecs were operating within the constraint of the required bitrate. The performance comparisons of both the codecs were quantified by using the video quality assessments such as PSNR, SSIM [Wang, Z., Lu, L., & Bovic, A.C. (2004) and VQM [Pinson, M., & Wolf, S. (2004)] offered by MSU [MSU (2010)]. Although PSNR is a widely used video quality assessment metric, it does not always correlate well with perceive quality. Thus, SSIM and VQM metrics were also considered in the assessment of the video quality produced by Dirac and H.264.

Figure 22. Compression ratio performance of dirac and H.264

a.

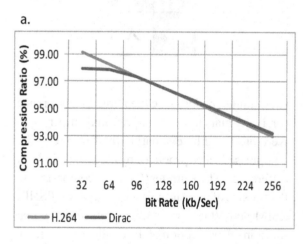

b.

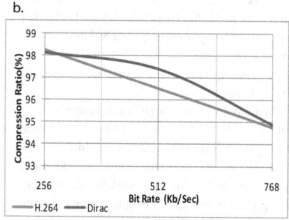

c.

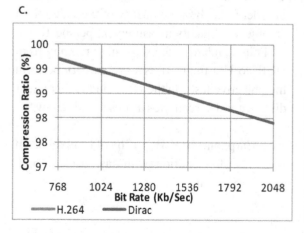

d.

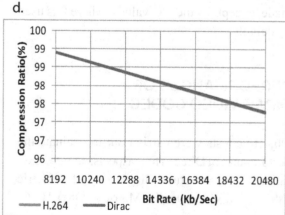

Figure 22 shows the compression ratio performance of Dirac and H.264. It shows that Dirac achieves a comparable compression ratio to that of H.264. However, Dirac has a slight deficiency when dealing with fast moving sequence namely the SD "Football" sequence. This deficiency is most likely the attribute of limited MB splitting mode where the picture area affected by fast moving MBs tend to be Intra coded. Nevertheless, Dirac's compression ratio is as stable as the H.264.

Figure 23 shows the average PSNR performance of Dirac and H.264. Generally, H.264 outperforms Dirac at low bitrates in all the test sequences. Dirac lags behind H.264 by ~3dB in the QCIF "Carphone" sequence at 256 Kbps. Dirac leads H.264 in HD "Blue Sky" at bitrate

beyond 10Mbps and continues to increase with the increase of bitrate. It is worth noting that for all the sequences tested, the PSNR values remain in the typical range between 25 dB and 42 dB as evident from the CIF "Football" and HD "Blue Sky", respectively. Although higher bitrate values may suggest improvement over 42 dB, after which the objective quality improvement is only few pixel per frame, thus it will not be useful to trade the bitrate with small PSNR increment. However, if the PSNR value is lower than 20 dB then it suggests that the video can be severely disrupted.

Figure 24 shows average SSIM index performance of Dirac and H.264. Generally, the SSIM results do follow the trend of PSNR which implies that H.264 produces slightly better quality than

Figure 23. Average PSNR performance of dirac and H.264

a.
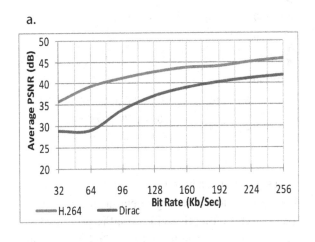

b.
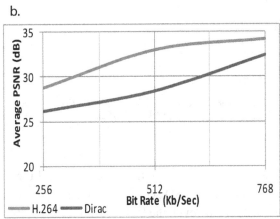

c.
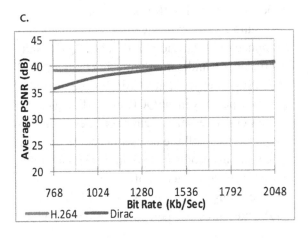

d.
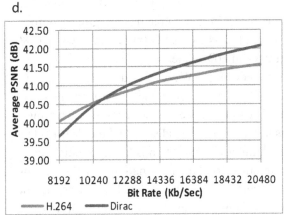

Figure 24. Average SSIM index performance of Dirac and H.264

a.

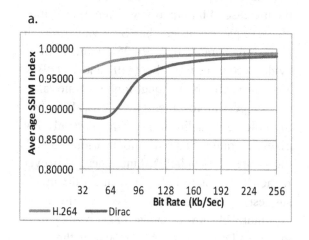

b.

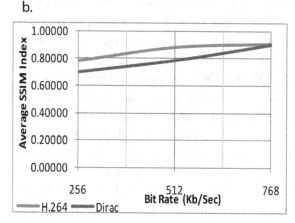

c.

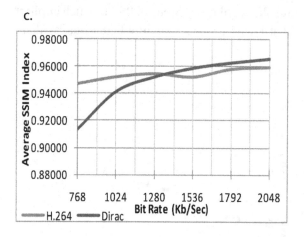

d.

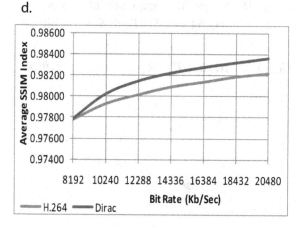

Dirac in the QCIF and CIF sequences at all the tested bitrate, and SD sequence at bitrate below 1280 kbps. However, the SSIM results show that Dirac has not performed badly as indicated by the PSNR results especially in the QCIF and CIF sequences. In fact, Dirac has marginally outperformed H.264 in the SD (at bitrate beyond 1280 kbps) and HD sequence.

According to Wang, Z., Lu, L., & Bovic, A.C. (2004), SSIM measures video quality using structural distortion instead of error based measurement as in the PSNR. The idea behind the SSIM is that the human vision system is highly specialized in extracting structural information from the viewing field and it is not specialized in extracting the errors. Thus, a measurement on structural distor-

tion should give a better correlation to the subjective impression. This argument does support the fact that the subjective video quality produced by Dirac is comparable to that of H.264 despite the deficiency in the PSNR assessment.

Figure 25 shows the average VQM index performance of Dirac and H.264. The VQM results overthrow the indication projected by the PSNR and SSIM metrics that H.264 has better video quality especially in the QCIF and CIF sequences. In the VQM assessment, Dirac confidently outperforms H.264 in all the test sequence. In fact, the video outputs produced by Dirac are comparable to that of H.264 in terms of perceived quality.

According to Pinson, M., & Wolf, S. (2004), VQM measures the perceptual effects of video

Figure 25. Average VQM index performance of dirac and H.264

a.
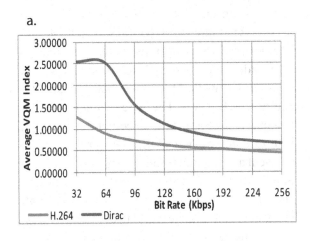

b.
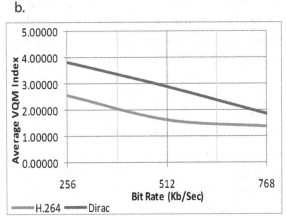

c.
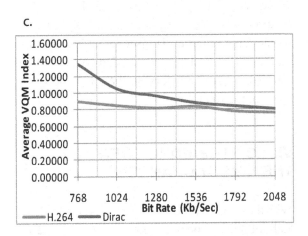

d.
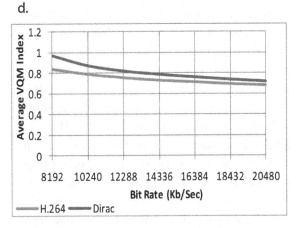

impairments including blurring, jerky/unnatural motion, global noise, block distortion and color distortion, and combines them into a single metric. In order words, VQM has a high correlation with subjective video quality assessment. This argument further explains the deficiency in the PSNR assessment does not correlate well with the actual perceived quality as in the case of Dirac.

In fact, according to Eq. (10), the internal distortion, $D(\Delta)$ used in the Dirac's RDO quantization operation, is measured in terms of the 4th power of the error resulting from the difference between the original and the quantized coefficients. This also means that Dirac is purposely distorting the video

quality to trade for more bitrate saving. In other words, Dirac is expected not performance well in the PSNR assessment as indicated by the PSNR results. Despite the harsh internal distortion, the perceived quality of the video produced by Dirac has not been affected mainly because human's eyes are less sensitive to high frequency pixels.

TRANSCODING

Video transcoding is to convert a video from one format into another format. As the number of networks, types of devices, and content representation formats increase, interoperability between different systems and different networks is becoming more important. Thus devices such as gateways, multipoint control units, and servers must be developed to provide a seamless interaction between content creation and consumption. Transcoding of video content is the key technology to make this possible Vetro, A., Christopoulos, C., & Sun, H. (2003).

A video transcoder is comprised of a decoding stage followed by an encoding stage. The decoding stage of a transcoder can perform full decoding to the pixel level or partial decoding to the coefficient level. Partial decoding is used in compressed domain transcoding where the transform coefficients in the input format are directly transcoded to the output format. This transformation is straightforward when the input and output formats of the transcoder use the same transform (e.g., MPEG-2 (DCT) to H264 (DCT) transcoding) [Kalva, H., Vetro, A., & Sun, H. (2003)]. But, when two video formats use different transform techniques e.g. H264 (DCT) to Dirac (DWT), pixel level transcoding would be the only option, in which transcoders will have a full decoding stage followed by a reduced complexity encoding stage. The complexity reduction is achieved by reusing the information gathered from the decoding stage as much as possible and it is considered as the efficient transcoding technique. It is assumed that the input video is encoded with reasonable R-D optimization (RDO).

In transcoding from H264 to Dirac, unfortunately, not much information can be re-used in intra frame (or MB) transcoding since directional intra prediction is not employed in intra MB encoding of Dirac. Instead, the whole frame is under gone DWT coding followed by RDO quantization and VLC coding. Quantization Parameter (QP) used in H264 will not be applicable as well because Dirac quantizes the coefficients in different sub-bands using different QPs (e.g. smaller QP for lower frequency sub-bands and higher QP for higher frequency sub-bands) instead of using constant QP for quantization of all the MBs in a particular frame in constant quality encoding of H264.

In inter frame (or MB) transcoding, Motion Vectors (MV) can be reused but may require slight adjustment since Dirac uses only square block shape while H264 uses both rectangular and square. But, it will be huge saving in terms of computational complexity since motion estimation is most complex part of the encoder. Until now, efficient transcoding solution for Dirac from most of the standard formats (e.g. MPEG-2, MPEG-4 and H264) is still missing and it is open to all researchers around the world to explore this area.

But there is one transcoding solution for Dirac from FFmpeg [FFmpeg (2010)], which requires fully decoding of the source format and re-encoding to Dirac. Transcoder called ffmpeg-2dirac, which can be downloaded from [BBC-e (2010)], converts any formats that can be decoded by FFmpeg to Dirac.

VIDEO STREAMING OVER THE NOISSY CHANNEL

With the rapid advances in computers and network technologies, especially with the emergence of Internet, audio/video steaming applications are becoming very popular. However, the challenges of video streaming due to the dependancy structure of compressed video, noisy channel condition and network properties, must be solved to maintain the Quality of Experience (QoE) of transmitted video. In the current application of real-time multimedia data streaming over the internet, routers drop packets randomly when output buffers are full without considering the relative importance of the packets. This may cause increased overall quality degradation in video communication because the important of the data in each packet varies. If the network is unable to transport all the data to the destination, one should guarantee that the most important part of the data is received to increase the reconstructed picture quality.

The most common way to protect data from packet losses is to request retransmission of any lost packets to the sender. However, unlike other application such as file transfer, real-time video applications may not benefit from retransmission-based error recovery because of the additional round-trip delay involved. Moreover, since packet losses often result from buffer overflow at the times of high network load, retransmitted packets make the network even more congested. Therefore, either source coding, channel coding (i.e. FEC) or combination of both (combined source and channel coding) is a more appropriate error control method for real-time Internet video applications.

However, current releases of Dirac have only been optimized for storage purposes and still there is no error-resilient encoding mechanism. Most of the error-resilient coding schemes in the literature were designed to work with DCT based encoders and some of the combined source and channel coding strategies were indented for either image transmission or 3D wavelet transform based video encoder. So, in this sub-section, we will discuss the overview of the error-resilient video streaming scheme which is suitable for two dimensional wavelet transform based Dirac video encoder. The detail description can be found in [Tun, M., Loo, K.K., & Cosmas, J. (2007)]. This scheme is based on the combined source and channel coding approach and designed mainly for the packet-erasure channel, i.e. targeted for the Internet broadcasting application. But it is also possible to extend the scheme in order to suit in other type of channels (e.g. wireless).

Overview of the Combined Source and Channel Coding Scheme

In the existing Dirac's encoding architecture [BBC-a (2010) and BBC-b(2010)], after DWT stage, the resulting coefficients of each subband are scanned in raster order from lowest to highest frequency in order to undergo quantization and entropy coding processes. Even though this method is ideal for storage purpose, there could be serious problem if the encoded bitstream is transmitted into the erroneous channel. Because of the nature of entropy encoding, any single bit error in the middle of the bitstream could create the remaining part of the bitstream which belongs to the entire frame to become useless to the decoder.

In order to prevent this, it is required to divide the main bitstream into a number of several smaller independent bitstreams so that they are completely isolated to each other and the decoder can decode them independently. So, the bit error in one bitstream does not affect the decoding of the others, resulting more uncorrupted information at the decoder. Dividing the bitstreams in order to limit the affect of channel error or resilient to the channel error is called error-resilient coding. It is based on the source coding which is modification to the encoder side and one of the error-resilient coding methods available in the literature. The method of bitstream division or coefficient partitioning method for wavelet transformed based image coding was reported by Creusere, C.D. (1997). Even though it is designed for image coding, it is possible to extend the idea to work as an error-resilient source coding for video encoder. But source coding only is not sufficient enough to protect the channel error in some case especially in the noisy channel where all the bitstreams are likely to be affected by the channel noise. So, it is required to add additional protection to the encoded bitstream in the form of channel coding. Combination of source and channel coding should protect the transmitted bitstream sufficiently from any kind of channel noises which normally occurs during the wireless or wired transmission.

Figure 26 shows the basic idea of the wavelet coefficient partitioning. It is to divide the wavelet coefficients at the output of the DWT process of the Dirac encoder into S groups and then quantize and code each of them independently so that S different bitstreams are generated [Creusere, C.D. (1997)]. By coding the wavelet coefficients with multiple independent bitstreams, any single bit error is

Figure 26. Wavelet coefficient partitioning for S = 4 with four levels wavelet transform

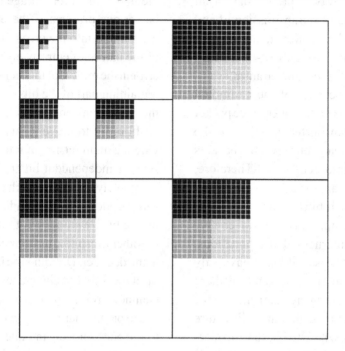

truncated only in one of the *S* bitstreams while the others are still correctly received. Therefore, the wavelet coefficients represented by a corrupted bitstream are reconstructed at reduced accuracy, while those represented by the error-free streams are reconstructed at the full encoder accuracy. The partitioning method used here is the extension of [Creusere, C.D. (1997)], in which the idea is applied to the *motion-compensated residual frames,* instead of the intra coded frames for the image transmission in [Creusere, C.D. (1997)] and 3D wavelet transformed frames in [Cho, S., & Pearlman, W.A. (2002)]. In this way, the quality of the reconstructed frames particularly at high packet loss rate becomes much better than the schemes by Creusere, C.D. (1997) and Cho, S., & Pearlman, W.A. (2002), especially when the MV data and reference frames are correctly received. It is because the corrupted data can still be replaced with the exact replica pointed by the MV in the reference frame. The quality of reconstructed frame at the corrupted area mainly depends upon the accuracy of the motion estimation at this par-

ticular location and the quality of the reference frame. Since the motion compensated residual data is completely lost, decoder has to rely only on the data from the reference frame and MV data in order to reconstruct the corrupted area. But the error-resilient scheme presented by Cho, S., & Pearlman, W.A. (2002) uses 3D wavelet transformed frames resulting total loss at the corrupted area since there is no way to compensate the loss data.

If the image is of size $X \times Y$ and L levels of wavelet decomposition are used, then the maximum number of independent bitstreams allowed can be calculated as shown below:

$$S = \left(X \times Y\right)\big/4^{L} \qquad (13)$$

For example,

$X = 352$, $Y = 288$, $L = 4$, i.e. CIF video format with 4 levels wavelet transform
$S = \left(X \times Y\right)\big/4^{L} = \left(352 \times 288\right)\big/4^{4} = 396$

Figure 27. Block diagram of error-resilient source encoding procedure using wavelet coefficient partitioning method

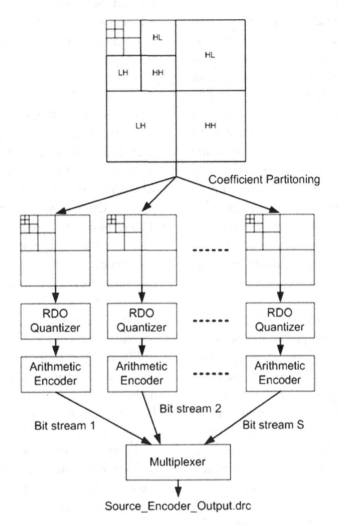

It is important to note that the maximum number of partitions depends also on the chroma format. For YUV 4:2:0, the maximum number of partitions is limited to $396/4 = 99$ since the dimensions of the U and V components are reduced by two times.

Figure 27 shows the block diagram of error resilient source encoding procedure of the Dirac Encoder. Output of the DWT process is divided into S sub-frames according to the wavelet coefficient partitioning method mentioned before. And then each of these sub-frames undergoes RDO quantization and arithmetic encoding independently so that S number of sub-bitstreams are generated. In the multiplexer, all the independent sub-bitstreams are combined together to get one serial bitstream and applied channel coding (either Rate-Compatible Punctured Convolutional (RCPC) Code or Turbo Code (TC)) before transmitting.

Channel is considered to be the packet erasure wired channel and generating no bit errors inside each packet except the loss of the whole packet because of network congestion. If a packet lost is occurred, all zero data packets are created at the receiver to replace the lost one and undergo channel decoding, de-multiplexing and Arithmetic decoding processes.

At the receiver, channel decoder, either Turbo or RCPC, normally tries to correct the errors. And then, CRC is used to detect the bit errors inside each packet. When the check bits indicate an error in the decoded packet, the error signal is sent to the Arithmetic decoder to stop decoding for that bitstream. So that the Arithmetic decoder at the receiver can skip the erroneous packet and jump directly to the beginning of another correctly received bitstream, preventing the possibility of Arithmetic decoder malfunctioning because of loosing synchronization in trying to decode erroneous bitstream and saving the decoding time. The decoding procedure continues until either the final packet has arrived or a decoding failure has occurred in all sub-bitstreams.

Error-Resilient decoding procedure is shown in Figure 28. The de-multiplexer separates the input bitstreams into S number of independent bitstreams. The arithmetic decoder is modified so that it stops decoding once the error symbol is found in the bitstream being decoded and simply jumps to the other bitstreams. The decoder continues to decode the packets of the other streams so that the receiver still has clean packets already decoded up to that point and loses only the remaining packets of the corrupted bitstream leaving the corresponding area in the entire frame to be reconstructed with the reduced quality.

In contrast, if a single bitstream is transmitted without partitioning, any single bit error in the middle of the bitstream will affect the whole remaining bitstream. Therefore, by coding the wavelet coefficients with multiple and independent bitstreams, any single bit error affects only one of the S bitstreams, while the others are received unaffected.

In Figure 28, once the arithmetic decoder finds the error symbol in the packet of the received bitstream, i.e. bitstream 2 packet number 10, it stops decoding of this packet and the remaining packets of this bitstream. After decoding, the un-partitioned format has only 9 clean packets while in the partitioned format still retain 14 clean packets. Obviously, the partitioned format could deliver more clean packets than un-partitioned since it just stops decoding at the step of first error occurrence. A better error resilient performance can be achieved by using maximum possible number of bitstreams which can be calculated by Eq. (13). Multiplexer in Figure 28 performs reverse process of coefficient partitioning shown in Figure 27 in order to reproduce the wavelet coefficient subbands. After that, Dirac decoder undergoes multiple processes including Inverse Discrete Wavelet Transform (IDWT) and motion compensation in order to reconstruct the frame.

Figure 29 shows the bitstream syntax structure of Dirac, where decoding can start from any Access Unit. A sequence is a concatenation of Access Units, comprised of Access Unit headers or Random Access Point (RAP) and a number of frame data units. A frame data unit includes frame header, frame prediction data and coefficient data of DWT. Again, coefficient data is composed of DWT transform parameters followed by transform

Figure 28. Error-resilient decoding process showing corrupted packet in bitstream [Tun, M., Loo, K.K., & Cosmas, J. (2007)]

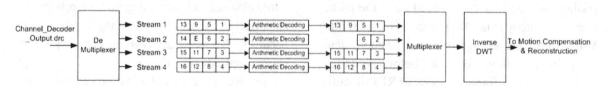

Figure 29. Bitstream syntax of dirac video encoder

coefficients of luminance (Y) and two chroma components (U and V). Each component will have 13 subband datas for 4 levels wavelet transform starting from lowest frequency subband to highest one. After source coding, because of the coefficient partition, the structure of the subband data arrangement is changed slightly as shown in

Figure 30. Transform data of each component will have S number of partitions where a partition in each component is made up of 13 subbands data for 4 levels wavelet transform. This changes is only at the encoder side and at the receiving end, all the partitions will be multiplexed again in order to have fully compatible Dirac bitstream.

Figure 30. Bitstream syntax of dirac video encoder after source coding

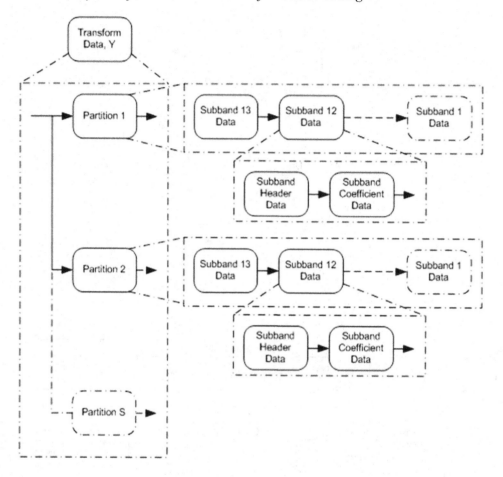

At the time of writing this chapter, the bytestream encoded with Dirac can be packaged in many of the existing transport streams, such as MPEG, MXF, IP, Ogg, etc [BBC-a (2010)] and hence it is able to use with a wide range of sound coding options, as well as easy access to all the other data transport systems required for production, broadcast metadata or streaming.

SUMMARY

The architecture of the Dirac encoder starting from development timeline has been presented followed by the detail description of motion estimation, Overlapped Block-based Motion Compensation, Discrete Wavelet Transform (DWT), RDO quantization and entropy coding. Besides that practical issues such as a transcoding from the standard encoder (e.g. H264) into Dirac and video streaming are also discussed.

REFERENCES

BBC-a. (2010). *The technology behind Dirac*. Retrieved February 2010, from http://www.bbc.co.uk/rd/projects/dirac/technology.shtml

BBC-b. (2010). *Dirac Video Codec Referencing Software*. Retrieved February 2010, from http://sourceforge.net/projects/dirac/

BBC-c. (2010). *Dirac algorithm*. Retrieved February 2010, from http://dirac.sourceforge.net/documentation/algorithm/algorithm/index.htm

BBC-d. (2010). *Dirac specification*. Retrieved February 2010, from http://diracvideo.org/download/specification/dirac-spec-latest.pdf

BBC-e. (2010). *Dirac Transcoder*. Retrieved February 2010, from http://diracvideo.org/download/ffmpeg2dirac/

Borer, T., & Davies, T. (2005). Dirac - video compression using open technology. *BBC R&D White Paper*. Retrieved February 2010, from http://downloads.bbc.co.uk/rd/pubs/whp/whp-pdf-files/WHP117.pdf

Cho, S., & Pearlman, W. A. (2002). A Full-Featured, Error-Resilient, Scalable Wavelet Video Codec Based on the Set Partitioning in Hierarchical Trees (SPIHT) Algorithm. *IEEE Transaction Circuits System Video Technology, 12*, 157–171. doi:10.1109/76.993437

Creusere, C. D. (1997). A new method of robust image compression based on the embedded zerotree wavelet algorithm. *IEEE Transactions on Image Processing, 6*, 1436–1442. doi:10.1109/83.624967

FFmpeg. (2010). *FFmpeg Project*. Retrieved February 2010, from http://ffmpeg.org/

Ghanbari, M. (1999). *Video Coding an introduction to standard codecs*. The Institute of Electrical Engineers.

H.264 (2010). *H.264 video codec referencing software*. Retrieved February 2010, from http://iphome.hhi.de/suehring/

Halbach, T. (2010). *A performance assessment of the royalty-free and open video compression specifications Dirac, Dirac Pro, and Theora and their open-source implementations*. Retrieved February 2010, from http://etill.net/projects/dirac_theora_evaluation/#intro

Horowitz, M., Joch, A., Kossentini, F., & Hallapuro, A. (2003). H264/AVC Baseline Profile Decoder Complexity Analysis. *IEEE Transactions on Circuits and Systems for Video Technology, 13*(7), 704–716. doi:10.1109/TCSVT.2003.814967

Kalva, H., Vetro, A., & Sun, H. (2003). Performance optimization of the MPEG-2 to MPEG-4 video transcoder. In proceeding, *SPIE Conference on VLSI Circuits and Systems* (pp. 341–350).

License (2010). *Summary of AVC/H.264 License Terms*. Retrieved February 2010, from http://www.mpegla.com/main/programs/avc/Documents/AVC_TermsSummary.pdf

MSU. (2010). *MSU Video Quality Measurement Tool*. Retrieved February 2010, from http://compression.ru/video/quality_measure/video_measurement_tool_en.html

Onthriar, K., Loo, K. K., & Xue, Z. (2006). *Performance Comparison of Emerging Dirac Video Codec with H.264/AVC*. In proceedings, *International Conference on Digital Telecommunications ICDT06* (pp. 22-26).

Pinson, M., & Wolf, S. (2004). A New Standardized Method for Objectively Measuring Video Quality. *IEEE Transactions on Broadcasting, 50*(3), 312–322. doi:10.1109/TBC.2004.834028

Tun, M., Loo, K. K., & Cosmas, J. (2007, Sept.). Error-Resilient Performance of Dirac Video Codec over Packet-Erasure Channel. *IEEE Transactions on Broadcasting, 53*(3), 649–659. doi:10.1109/LPT.2007.903636

Tun, M., Loo, K. K., & Cosmas, J. (2008). Rate Control Algorithm Based on Quality Factor Optimization for DIRAC Video Codec. *Elsevier Image Communication, 23*(9), 649–664.

Vetro, A., Christopoulos, C., & Sun, H. (2003). Video transcoding architectures and techniques: An overview. *IEEE Signal Processing Magazine, 20*(2), 18–29. doi:10.1109/MSP.2003.1184336

Wang, Z., Lu, L., & Bovic, A.C. (2004). Video quality assessment using structural distortion measurement. *Signal Processing: Image Communication special issue on Objective video quality metrics. 19*(2), 121-132.

Chapter 5
3D Mesh Model Coding

Zhen Li
Nanyang Technological University, Singapore

ABSTRACT

Application of 3D mesh model coding is first presented in this chapter. We then survey the typical existing algorithms in the area of compression of static and dynamic 3D meshes. In an introductory sub-section we introduce basic concepts of 3D mesh models, including data representations, model formats, data acquisitions and 3D display technologies. Furthermore, we introduce several typical 3D mesh formats and give an overview to coding principles of mesh compression algorithms in general, followed by describing the quantitative measures for 3D mesh compression. Then we describe some typical and state-of-the-art algorithms in 3D mesh compression. Compression and streaming of gigantic 3D models are specially introduced. At last, the MPEG4 3D mesh model coding standard is briefed. We conclude this chapter with a discussion providing an overall picture of developments in the mesh coding area and pointing out directions for future research.

INTRODUCTION

The development of compression algorithms for static meshes was mainly forced by the community of 3D graphics hardware accelerators. The goal is to reduce the amount of bytes that need to be transferred from the main memory to the graphics card. The compression of such huge static meshes not only increases the rendering

DOI: 10.4018/978-1-61692-831-5.ch005

performance but also decreases the storage cost at hard discs. Modern scanning devices are able to produce huge point clouds which are converted to extremely big triangle soups by surface reconstruction algorithms. For example, the biggest model consists of several 10^9 polygons, which can occupy a whole PC hard-disk. Furthermore, the transmission of static meshes over networks becomes important for applications like virtual shopping malls. In addition, efficient storage and broadcasting of dynamic 3D content gets crucial

Copyright © 2011, IGI Global. Copying or distributing in print or electronic forms without written permission of IGI Global is prohibited.

importance for commercial success of 3DTV technology. Dynamic 3D objects in their generic form represented as a sequence of static meshes require even multiple of times more storage than a single static mesh. As a result, a variety of algorithms have been proposed that work well for both static and dynamic meshes.

Interactive 3D graphics plays an important role in various fields such as entertainment, manufacturing and virtual reality. When combining the graphics technology with the Internet, the transmission delay for 3D graphics data and the high storage capacity requirement are becoming major performance bottlenecks, especially for the gigantic meshes consisting of tens of thousands of triangles. Thus reducing the amount of data is, go without saying, an effective solution. Consequently, interests in techniques for the 3D geometry data compression and streaming have surged in recent years.

Although many representation methods for 3D models exist, the triangle is the basic geometric primitive for standard 3D graphics applications, graphics rendering hardware and many simulation algorithms, while any other surface representations can be easily converted to triangle meshes. Triangle meshes are composed of two components: vertex data and connectivity data. Vertex data mainly include the positional coordinates of the vertices and, optionally, some other attributes. The connectivity data specify which vertices are connected.

By reading this chapter, the readers are expected to acquire the basic knowledge of 3D model, the basic concept of 3D mesh model codec, and the ideas of the state-of-the-art algorithms for 3D model coding and streaming.

BACKGROUND

In this section, we will introduce you some basic knowledge of 3D model, including 3D modeling, data representations, 3D model formats, 3D data

acquisition, 3D data display, 3D mesh model coding basics, and 3D mesh model quality assessment.

3D Modeling and Data Representations

What we call 3D modeling, is to use 3D data to reconstruct 3D objects or scenes of the real world in computers, and finally to simulate real 3D objects or scenes in computers. 3D data is sampled by various 3D data collectors, and include various physical parameters on discrete points on finite object surfaces. The basic information 3D data include are 3D coordinates of each discrete points of objects, and optionally colors, transparency, texture features, and etc. on surfaces of objects. 3D modeling play important roles in the fields of architecture, medical images, 3D graphic games, film trick design and so on. In the field of architecture, if we represent a building using common 2D pictures (e.g., photos), it is not convenient to observe some detailed parts or inside structures. Although blueprints of the building include abundant information, they are not easy to understand and not intuitional for nonprofessional clients. However, if we reconstruct the 3D model of this building using 3D modeling techniques, we can directly observe different aspects, whole structure and even interior structure of this building, which is convenient for the purposes of both architects evaluating the design effect and observation of clients. In the field of medicine, people always lay siege to 3D human-being vivisection drawing. Institute of medical mathematics and medical computer in Hamburg University in Germany have carried out a project of 3D visualization of vivisection named "Voxel-Man". Using the tools of "Voxel-Man", doctors can simulate the processes of surgical, solid location and punch. Virtual surgery is another example of application of 3D modeling in medicine. Biomedicine image processing resource center of the well-known proprietary hospital in USA have developed and designed a 3D interactive surgery assistant system for doctors to observe data of CT and MRI, resulting in more accuracy and security in real surgery by doctors. 3D modeling is also applicable in culture relic protection. Cultural relics and ancient architectures can be sampled by images, digital processed and data compressed to generate 3D models, so we can browse cultural relics and ancient architectures *ad arbitrium*. Meanwhile, it is a good method to protect and investigate cultural relics. At the present time, the industry of computer games has highly developed and 3D computer games have emerged as the times require. 3D animations have dominated the whole scenes of games at present, while they only partially emerged in games at the beginning. In regard to film tricks design, 3D modeling can also be utilized. In the real world, not all the scenes can be perfectly constructed, e.g., dangerous scenes. However, these scenes can be easily completed by clicking computer mouse rapidly and effectively.

The uppermost issue of 3D modeling is to use 3D data for rendering. This issue include how to depict a model in a satisfactory visual effect, i.e., solid and realistic, with smooth surfaces and without burrs or holes; at the same time, we should arrange the data properly to reduce the storage space for the purpose of data transmission and enable fast rendering. Acquisition, representation and rendering of 3D data will be briefly introduced as follows.

Two-dimensional graphics generated by computer has only horizontal and perpendicular coordinates along X and Y axes, but 3D graphics has an additional axis Z to represent the depth information. When applying lightening and texture to 3D object, the object seems more real than the two-dimensional object does. Besides, you can cut through or surround 3D models and graphics in the 3D space, which is similar to a tour in the virtual world. Establishing a 3D model involves tessellating it into simple and convex polygons. Tessellation is the process to convert mathematical representations of the object into many polygons. Simple polygon is defined that each edge only

intersects at the vertices of the polygon, and the intersection is at an end of an edge. One of characteristics of convex polygons is that there is no concave so the diagonal between any pair of vertices must locate in the interior of the polygon. The attribute of simpleness and convexity enables convex polygons by OpenGL (a display interface that will be elaborated later). Other polygon attributes, no matter how its shape is, produce complex problems in rendering, resulting in that OpenGL probably cannot perform satisfactorily. The most basic convex and polygon type in OpenGL is triangle. OpenGL divides irregular objects into triangles or some other regular shapes for the purpose of computer management. The adoption of triangles have some additional considerations: (1) The 3 vertices of a triangle can be represented as 3D coordinates along X/Y/Z axes in a 3D space; (2) The 3 vertices of a triangle always lie on a plane, so OpenGL can always render the triangle correctly when rotating the object in a 3D space. Otherwise, as the vertices are non-coplanar, complex and concave cases may occur when rotating and OpenGL cannot render it well; (3) In the search of computational geometry, a graph dual that spans triangular graphics can be represented by a bin-tree that is popular in computer science.

In the early years, 3D models are generally established manually based on triple views or pictures. This method is usually bounded with some software such as commonly used 3D Studio, Auto CAD, 3DS MAX and so on. The benefits of this method is that have strict mathematical representations in concept, precise representation of geometry shape, shape-controllable smoothness, and many advanced physics-based modeling tools. However, the cons are that it needs parameter representation of an object, discontinuity and inflexibility of topology structure. Some widely used methods of modeling and description are briefed below.

Polygonal Mesh Modeling

Polygon Modeling is the earliest used modeling technique. The idea is simple: approaching a surface with many small planes so that we can make a variety of 3D objects. The small planes can be triangles, rectangles or some other polygons, the former 2 types being the most popular in real applications. With polygon modeling, we can directly establish basic geometry shapes first, and then design works of virtual reality by adjusting shapes using modifying tools, or using reshaped sample, sculpt of curved surface or combined objects according to requirements. The main pros of polygon modeling are simpleness, convenience and speediness, while its con is that smooth surfaces are hard to design using this technique. As a result, polygon modeling is fit for construct objects with regular shapes, e.g., most man-made objects that can represented in different resolutions by only adjusting parameters of the model according to the displaying requirement in the virtual scenarios. Since 3D data acquired in different methods has different types and characteristics, rendering of polygon meshes corresponds to different tessellating strategies for different datasets. (1) Unorganized Data: there is no additional information other than sampled points. This is the most direct yet a representation of the highest computation complexity in the modeling process. (2) Contour Data: sample objects in the medical usage are usually cut into very thin slices, each of which is digitized into a contour. All the slices can be regarded as a set of overlapped closed polygons. (3) Volumetric Data: again in the medication, data acquired by MRI or CT is called volumetric data. They are 3D grids, from which, the surface of the model is expected to be extracted. Marching Cubes is a famous method to realize the surface extraction. However, it cannot produce the optimal results, because if the edge of a voxel grid is too long, mixture will occur on the model surface, resulting meshes with bad drawing. (4) Range Data: it is the data acquired by range scanning and normalized in the same coordinate system. This type of data usually contains depth information or 3D rectangular grids, so neighborhood information can be derived. The main difficulties includes establishing a unique mesh on range images from different scanning aspects, and large amount of data due to dense and uniform sampling when scanning. In terms of the above data of two structure, two types of approximating schemes can be adopted: one is interpolation, with which the vertices of the final mesh model is just the initial sample points; the other is approximation, which is more commonly used compared to interpolation especially for range data of extremely high resolution. Major approximation methods are briefed below: (1) Sculpting Based Methods. It belongs to the category of interpolating and is more common for unorganized data. With this method, a tetrahedron is established on the set of vertices, usually using the Delaunay triangulation, and then the whole shape of the object is acquired. The course shape is then gradually up-sampled and a proper subset of vertices is adopted to construct the final mesh. This method is fit for reconstructing surfaces from data with very sparse sampling, while both computation complexity and the memory required are large. (2) Volume Based Approximation. It is an approximating method available for both unorganized data and cloud model such as range data. A self-defined distance is estimated for each sample point and recorded in a structure of voxel or octree based on which a mesh can be established with the Marching Cubes method. A benefit of this method is that the computation complexity is controllable with the edge length of the voxel grid. (3) Incremental / Region-Growing methods: A seed is initialized followed by region growing until the whole input data is covered. The initial seed can be a triangle face, an edge, a range image, or a wireframe approximation. No matter what structure this method is based on, establishing a global polygon mesh is complex and hard to represent and, the computation complexity may increase in the exponent order. As a result, this method is unacceptable in network transmission and rendering in time.

Surface Based Modeling

1. NURBS Modeling. NURBS is the acronym of Non-Uniform Rational B-Splines, which is purely a concept in mathematical computer graphics. NURBS modeling technology is one of the most important modeling methods for 3D animation in recent years, which is particularly suited to the creation of smooth and complex model and, has incomparable advantages in the breadth of application and realistic details compared to other techniques. However, as NURBS modeling must use curved patches as its modeling primitives, so it also has the following limitations: NURBS patches have only a limited number of topology structures, so NURBS can hardly lead to the production of very complicated topology of objects (for example, objects with holes); The basic structure of NURBS patches is grid-like, so control points will increase dramatically and hard to control for more complicated models; Establishing complex models involves cutting surface, but decimation will lead to errors; NURBS technology cannot manage to construct objects "with branches".

2. Subdivision Surface Modeling. Subdivision surface technology can be trace back to the first subdivision surface work based on polygon mesh with Catmull-Clark and the work based on arbitrary topological mesh with Doo-Sabin in 1978. Subdivision scheme based on triangular mesh is first proposed by Charles Loop in his master thesis. Subdivision surfaces technology has resolved the difficulties in the establishment of surfaces with NURBS. This technique uses an arbitrary polyhedron as the control grid, and then automatically generates smooth surfaces according to the control grid. The mesh generated by subdivision surfaces grid technology can be an arbitrary shape, and can easily construct various topology structures while always maintaining the smoothness of the surface. Another important

feature of subdivision surfaces technology is the "subdivision" that is only partially increasing the details of objects, without having to increase the complexity of the objects, while maintaining the smoothness of the object with an increase of details. Subdivision modeling technology a new feature in 3D studio Max R4, and this technology can be used to create very complex model and animation.

Volumetric Modeling

In this kind of modeling, objects are represented by a volume of sampled data points, rather than by a list of surface polygons or spline patches. This allows us to represent object interiors as well as their surfaces. These applications are challenging because volumetric objects may consist of hundreds of thousands of volume elements. For real-time interaction, algorithms must make trade-offs between physical realism and speed. For academic research, this kind of representation is easy to be handled by mathematical theories due to its intrinsic nature of 3D function.

Formats of 3D Mesh Models

Polygon meshes can be represented by a variety of data storage formats including: 3DS, OBJ, ASE, MD2/MD3, MS3D, WRL, MAX, OFF and so on.

3DS Graphics file format is created by 3D computer animation software called 3D Studio that is developed by Autodesk. 3DS is a widely used data format, and a variety of 3Dgraphics CD-ROM material as well as content-rich Web site has various graphics 3DS model libraries. 3DS Max saves scenes to a proprietary binary format with the extension.MAX. The specification of the format is not public. The content of the file is heavily dependent on the plug-in data used to build the scene, thus parsing the file outside of 3ds Max makes little sense (although certain data fragments can be extracted). The file format supports certain Windows standards like storing a thumbnail (a snapshot of the active viewport at saving time) and user data in the header of the file which can be viewed in Windows Explorer and similar. The data portion of the.MAX file can be optionally compressed using built-in ZIP compression, leaving only the header, thumbnail and user data uncompressed. MAX scenes saved using the "Compress on Save" feature can be two to ten times smaller (depending on the type of objects) and cannot be effectively compressed much more using external tools.

WRL is the file format of VRML (Virtual Reality Modeling Language) for describing interactive 3D objects or "3D *worlds*". VRML can be used to create interactive 3D games, simulations of real or imagined devices and buildings or even cities for walk-throughs, interactive visualizations of scientific data, advertising banners, art, music, and many more. VRML is a system- and device-independent language, so one VRML world can be viewed on any VRML viewer of the correct vintage. A VRML file contains a file header, comments, and nodes. Nodes describe objects, and optionally names, fields and values. Comments and the file header begin with the pound sign, while the hierarchy of nodes and fields end with curly brackets. Named nodes may be reused elsewhere in the scene. It uses Cartesian, right-handed 3D coordinate system. By default, the viewer is positioned along the positive Z-axis so as to look along the -Z direction with +Y-axis up. VRML files measure distance in meters, angles in radians, time in seconds, and colors in normalized RGB triplets. VRML source is normally encoded in UTF-8, which is a superset of standard ASCII. In order to dramatically reduce the download time, GZIP can be used to compress the WRL files. The basic node for defining visible VRML objects is the *Shape*, which contains *Geometry* and *Appearance* nodes. So, for example, the following example defines a world containing one cylinder 3 meters high with a 2.1 meter radius with default material properties, meaning that the object will appear to be shining white:

```
#VRML V2.0 utf8
# A Cylinder
Shape {
    appearance Appearance {
        material Material { }
    }
    geometry Cylinder {
        height 3.0
        radius 2.1
    }
}
```

The available geometry nodes are:

Box. A type of geometric primitives.
Cone. A type of geometric primitives.
Cylinder. A type of geometric primitives.
Sphere. A type of geometric primitives.
ElevationGrid. This node creates surfaces and terrains.
Extrusion. This node creates solids by sweeping a 2D cross-section though a 3D spine.
IndexedFaceSet. This node uses Coordinate nodes to create solid faces.
IndexedLineSet. This node uses Coordinate nodes to create solid lines.
PointSet. This node uses Coordinate nodes to create solid points.
WorldInfo. This node holds the world's title and other information, such as author and copyright.
Text. This node displays a string with a specified font style.

These raw geometry nodes give you more flexibility than the geometric primitives, and can actually create more efficient VRML worlds.

You can control the diffuse (shading) color, emissive (glow) color, transparency, shininess, and the other optical properties of an object using its *Material* field in the *Appearance* node. These optical properties interact with the scene lighting to determine the image presented to the viewer. Shadows are not generated automatically, but you

Figure 1. (a) An example of OFF data format of 3D mesh model (b)The skeleton drawn according to the data in (a) (The number beside the vertex is the index)

```
OFF
8 12 0
0 0 0
0 1 0
0 0 1
0 1 1
1 1 1
1 0 1
1 0 0
1 1 0
3 0 1 3
3 0 3 2
3 1 7 4
3 1 3 4
3 4 7 6
3 4 6 5
3 0 6 5
3 0 2 5
3 3 4 5
3 3 2 5
3 1 7 6
3 0 1 6
```

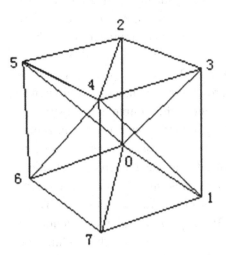

can fake them. Only some kinds of materials are well described by the optical properties specified in the *Material* field, such as metal and glass. You can override optical properties with *Color* nodes, or wrap textures, which is essentially two-dimensional images, around the 3D shapes. VRML supports three kinds of texture mapping fields: *ImageTexture* (from JPEG, PNG, and GIF files), *PixelTexture* (from raw image data), and *MovieTexture* (from MPEG files).

OFF file format defines the geometry object coordinates and topological relations explicitly in a very simple data format so that it is suitable for application to read or 3D file format conversion. The.off files in the Princeton Shape Benchmark conform to the following standard. OFF files are all ASCII files beginning with the keyword OFF. An example of OFF format of a 3D mesh model is shown in Figure 1 (a). Among them, "OFF" in line 1 is the keyword; the three numbers in line 2 represent the number of vertex, face and edge, respectively. Since the main concern is the number of vertex and the number of surface, the number of edges can be an arbitrary integer. The 8 lines beginning from line 3 represent the spatial

coordinates of eight vertices in the mesh, e.g. the coordinates for vertex 0 is (0, 0, 0), the coordinates for vertex 3 is (0, 1, 1), these coordinates can be either integers or floating-point numbers. Vertex color information is allowed to be added to the end of vertex coordinates at every vertex data line, but optionally, while texture data or other information is not provided in OFF file. Each line from line 11 to the last line represents a surface, in which the first component is the number of vertices (the surface are triangular in this example), the rest four components represent the indices of the vertices that comprise the triangle face, e.g. the first triangular surface is comprised of vertex 0, vertex 1 and vertex 0. The line skeleton of the mesh is depicted in Figure 1 (b).

3D Data Acquisition

Establishing 3D models of real 3D objects involves acquiring the related attributes of the sample object, e.g., geometry shape, surface texture, etc. The data representing these information is called 3D data, while the process of collecting sample object information and arrange them in the same representation of the sample is called acquisition of 3D data. The methods of collecting 3D data of a sample object mainly fall into 5 categories: (1) Design directly or by measurement: it is used widely in the early 3D modeling of architecture, in which the triple views of a model are acquired by charting or measurement. (2) Imaging: pictures in different aspects are acquired by imaging equipments, so the 3D model of the sample is reconstructed based on the geometrical and texture information. (3) Mechanical Probes: surface geometry data is sampled by physical touch of mechanical probes and the sample surface, with the assumption that the object is hard. (4) Volumetric Data: recover the 3D shape of the sample by acquiring the CT images of the sample. This technology is widely used in medical applications, and the available volumetric data includes X-ray image, CT image and MRI image. (5) Range Scanning: locate the geometry of surface points by measuring the distance between the sample surface and the apparatus. The measurements include optical triangulation and interferometry.

Along with the development of technology equipment and software support gradually improving universal, range scanning technology becomes a very important 3D data acquisition technology, and even caused innovation in 3D modeling and rendering technology. Now, range scanning process is first briefly explained. (1) Calibration. The coordinates of the system in the process of scanning is jointly decided by the hardware and the surroundings of the equipment, so a prior established unified coordinate system is necessary. (2) Scanning. Object surfaces are sampled in a perspective, and an intensive range image is generated. A number of scans are needed to cover the sampled images of the entire object. (3) Registration. Sample images from the scan are all in their respective local coordinate system, so they must be calibrated to the same global coordinate system. Two commonly used 3D laser scanner are *FastScan* and *Cyrax*. *FastScan* is a passive 3D handheld laser scanner, and popular for the acquisition of 3D data of small objects. *Cyrax* is an active 3D laser scanner, and need plank and drone for the acquisition of outdoor scenes and large-scale 3D data of buildings. It adopted the principle of radar range measurement. Point cloud data acquired by range scanning technology is dense and uniform. While displaying, we found that every pixel in the region will have at least one sampling point if we use a slight widening perspective, when 3-D model results can also be viewed without network building. Building a network directly on such a dense point cloud data will have a large overhead, while the last grid will be too-intensive for rendering. It is generally simplified, and then a grid with appropriate density can be acquired. However, the simplification is an exhaustive process of the calculation, especially for network building process of complex surface geometry models, while grid expression still needs local parameterized expression and the multi-resolution rendering, compression and transmission will also be very convenient.

3D Model Display Technology

A brief introduction to several popular 3D model rendering techniques will be described in this section.

OpenGL and Direct3D

A lot of excellent 3D graphics application development tools have emerged in the course of 3-D graphics technology development, in which, the 3D graphics library that SGI (Silicon Graphics Incorporated) designed for SGI workstation is the most prominent and has become numerous technical personnels' favorite and, finally developed into OpenGL. The goal of the formation of OpenGL is to make application procedures create high-level, high-quality color 3D images, and all this work is independent of the window system, operating systems and hardware platforms. Almost all successes of entities or image design that is

Figure 2. Examples of 3D mesh models (a) Skeleton mesh model of Rhinoceros (b) Rendered mesh model of Dragon (c) Rendered mesh model of Armadillo

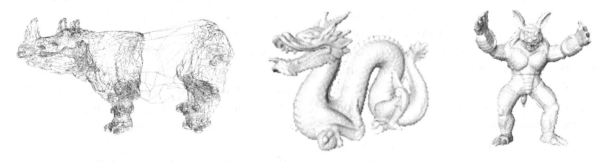

relying on 3D computer graphics are related to OpenGL. Now OpenGL is the *de facto* standard in 3D graphics processing industry. SGI has years of history in the design of cross-platform graphics software. SGI OpenGL is developed on the basis of the IRIS GL graphics that was launched in 1983. In 1992, OpenGL became 3D graphics application program interface (3D API) for use in a variety of computing environments. OpenGL not only conforms to industry standards, and easy to learn, convenient to use, and therefore becomes more and more popular for software developers. Not only can we quickly enter the world of 3D graphics by using OpenGL, but we can enjoy the fun. OpenGL can be extensively used in PCs, workstations and supercomputers. OpenGL is independent of hardware, window systems and operating systems, and can be integrated into the UNIX, Windows and X Windows. Its application procedures belong to the low-level graphics -oriented hardware interface, and are composed of a series of commands with *gl* and *GL* as the prefix. Programmers can use OpenGL commands to build interactive 3D color graphics procedures. OpenGL provides more than one hundred basic functions and many parameters so developers can use these functions for optical rendering of the entire color 3D graphics, thus a very realistic 3-D scene of the objective world can be rendered conveniently and rapidly. In addition, OpenGL can perform interactive and action simulation operations on 3D graphics. OpenGL is designed

to be independent of the hardware, independent of the window system, and can be run on various operating systems. It can work in client / server modes in network environment as a standard graphics library in many applications such as professional graphics processing and scientific computing. In the low-end applications its main competitor is MS-Direct3D. Since this graphics library is provided in the form of COM interfaces, it is extremely complicated. Besides, Microsoft owns the copyright, so it is currently only available in the Windows platform. D3D advantages in speed, but at present low-cost graphics hardware can also provide very good acceleration of OpenGL, it is not necessary to use Direct3D for professional high-end graphics applications. Some 3D meshes are depicted by OpenGL are rendered in Figure 2.

Image Based Rendering

Traditional graphics rendering technology are all scenery-geometry-oriented, thus rendering process involves complex modeling, occlusion culling, shadowing, blanking, and brightness calculation. Despite by the adoption of pre-computation of visibility and scene geometry reduction technology, the number of facets in the scenery to be processed can be greatly reduced, but for highly complex scenes, the existing computer hardware is still unable to realize the real-time rendering of the scene geometry. Thus we are faced with an important question that how a computer with ordinary computing power can realize the real-time rendering of realistic graphics. IBR technology is a brand-new graphics rendering mode for the realization of this goal. The technology is based on a number of pre-stored images (or the environment mapping) to generate scene images in different perspective and, compared with the traditional mapping technologies, it will have distinctive features: (1) Graphics rendering is independent of the complexity of the scene, only dependent on the resolution of the scene to be generated. (2) Pre-stored images (or the environment mapping) can be synthesized by computer, be practical shooting scenes, or can be mixed in use. (3) This rendering technique requires low computing resources, thus can achieve the real-time display of complex scenes in an ordinary personal computers or work-stations. IBR technology is a new research field, which will change people's understanding of the traditional computer graphics, making computer graphics more widely used. There are many other techniques and algorithms such as LOD which can be used to accelerate scene rendering. Real-time rendering is an attractive research field in computer graphics especially in the past ten years. Some researchers have proposed many various practical techniques and algorithms.

Point Rendering

In the situation that the 3D data acquisition technology and dense point cloud data becomes more and more popular while grid drawing cannot meet their development, point drawing aroused people's attention. The idea of point drawing originates in 1983, but it was not booming until 2000. Since point drawing does not need to deal with any over-all operations on point cloud data, and optionally needs consideration of the neighborhood information, so it has incomparable advantages over mesh rendering with respect to rendering speed and, can achieve real-time rendering requirements; While point drawing completely abandoned the

connectivity information, making its expression concise, storage capacity very small, transmission in network convenient. Meanwhile, we should also notice that the 3D model with point drawing only achieves surface continuity in visual effects, it is not as continuous as models rendered with mesh rendering, no matter considering the relationship of geometry or of topology, resulting in the inaccurate expression of the model.

3D Mesh Model Coding Principals

The compression algorithms for 3D meshes can be divided into two categories: single rate encoders and progressive encoders. Single rate encoders compress the mesh into a single bit stream which contains both the connectivity and the geometry information of the mesh. The decoder reads the bit stream and reconstructs all polygons and vertex positions. Progressive encoders first simplify the mesh by a sequence of simplification operations which results in a base mesh that contains fewer polygons than the original mesh. The encoder compresses the connectivity and the geometry information of this base mesh into a bit stream followed by a sequence of operations that enable to undo the simplification operations. The decoder first reconstructs the base mesh, second decodes the operations and applies the operations to the base mesh until the original mesh is reconstructed. Ideally, the compressed bit stream that is created by a progressive encoder is of the same size as the bit stream that a single rate encoder produces. Note that a progressive encoder does not construct a multi-resolution mesh but enables a streaming of the mesh whereby the quality of the mesh improves as more bits arrive. A well-designed progressive encoder optimizes the rate-distortion performance such that mesh is well approximated even if just a few bits have been arrived. Rate-distortion performances can be compared by curves as shown in Figure 3, in which the higher curve indicate better compression quality at the same bit rate.

Figure 3. Curves for comparison of bpv-PSNR (bit-per-vertex versus peak signal-noise ratio)

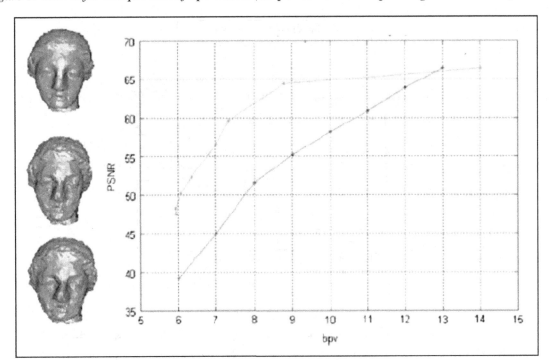

Single rate encoders often work by a traversal of the mesh to encode connectivity and predicting the subsequent vertices to encode geometry as shown in Figure 4. To encode the connectivity, the traversal of the mesh generates a symbol for each triangle which is entropy encoded. Often, the encoding of the geometry is steered by the traversal order of the mesh. Each time a new vertex is visited by the traversal, its coordinates are predicted from already visited vertices and the difference between the predicted location and the true location is encoded. In order to improve the encoding, a quantization step first maps the vertex locations onto a given quantized locations. Due to the quantization of the geometry information, the mesh cannot be recreated to its complete original quality. Whether or not the scheme is lossy or lossless depends on the tolerance of the user according to visual distortion.

Progressive encoders first simplify the mesh by a sequence of simplification operations. The resulting base mesh is compressed with a single rate encoder. The sequence of simplification operations is compressed afterwards by encoding a sequence of refinement operations that undo the simplification.

Basically, the encoded representation of the refinement operations must specify where and how the decoder can refine the mesh. Progressive encoders differ in how they specify this information, i.e. how they specify the location inside a mesh as well as the type of a refinement (and simplification) operation. A well designed progressive encoder improves the visual quality of the mesh very quickly as more bits of the model arrive and optimizes the rate distortion curve. Starting with a distorted base mesh, the distortion is tried to be decreased as soon as possible.

Quantitative Assessments for 3D Mesh Compression

For ease of data representation, basic nomenclatures are first introduced here. Denote a 3D mesh

Figure 4. Basic diagrams of 3D mesh codec. (a) Encoder (b) Decoder

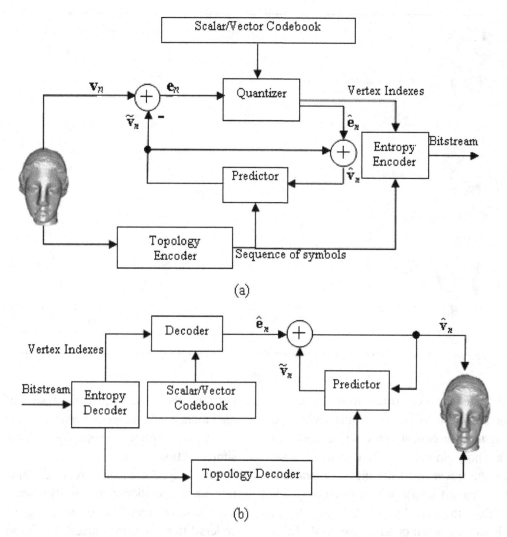

(a)

(b)

model $M=\{V, C\}$, consisting of the vertex set V and connectivity set C, in which set V contains N vertices v_i and the coordinates of each vertex are denoted by (x_i, y_i, z_i), i.e.

$$V = \{v_i\}, i = 0,1,\cdots,N-1, \quad v_i = (x_i,y_i,z_i) \tag{1}$$

and the connectivity set C is denoted as

$$C = \{\{i_k,j_k\}\}_{k=0,\cdots m-1}, \quad 0 \le i_k \le N-1, 0 \le j_k \le N-1 \tag{2}$$

where $\{i_k,j_k\}$ represent the k-th edge that is linked by the i_k-th vertex and the j_k-th vertex.

There are several methods of quantitative evaluations to measure the distortion caused by compression. In the following measures, N is the number of vertices, and v_i and v_i' denotes the original model and the compressed model respectively.

(1) Mean Square Error (MSE): The most straightforward method is to compare the difference between the predicted mesh coordinates with the true mesh coordinates that is defined as

$$\text{MSE} = \frac{1}{N} \sum_{i=1}^{N} \left\| \boldsymbol{v}_i - \boldsymbol{v}_i' \right\|^2 \tag{3}$$

(2) Peak Signal-noise ratio (PSNR):

$$\text{PSNR} = 10 \cdot \log_{10} \frac{N \cdot \left\| \boldsymbol{v} \right\|_{\max}^2}{\sum_i \left\| \boldsymbol{v}_i' - \boldsymbol{v}_i \right\|^2} \tag{4}$$

(3) Signal-noise ratio (SNR):

$$\text{SNR} = 10 \cdot \log_{10} \frac{\sum_i \left\| \boldsymbol{v}_i \right\|^2}{\sum_i \left\| \boldsymbol{v}_i' - \boldsymbol{v}_i \right\|^2} \tag{5}$$

(4) Hausdorff distance: Given two sets of points in R^n: $X = \{x_0, x_1, \cdots, x_n\}$ and $Y = \{y_0, y_1, \cdots, y_n\}$, the one-way Hausdorff distance from X to Y is defined as

$$d_E(X,Y) = \sup_{x \in X} d(x, Y) = \sup_{x \in X} \inf_{y \in Y} d(x, y) \tag{6}$$

where $d(x,y)$ is the Euclidean distance from the point x to point y.

The symmetric Hausdorff distance between X and Y is defined as

$$d_H(X,Y) = \max\left(d_E(X,Y), d_E(Y,X)\right) \tag{7}$$

(5) Face to face Hausdorff distance: Let $d(x,Y)$ be the Euclidean distance from a point x on X to its closest point on Y, then the distance from X to Y is defined as follows:

$$d(X,Y) = \sqrt{1 \big/ A(X) \cdot \int_{x \in X} d(x,Y)^2 \, dx} \tag{8}$$

where $A(X)$ is the area of X.

Since this distance is not symmetric so the distortion between X and Y is given as:

$$d = \max\left\{d(X,Y), d(Y,X)\right\} \tag{9}$$

This distance is called symmetric face to face Hausdorff distance and can be computed using the public available Mesh Tool (Aspert, Santa-Cruz & T. Ebrahimi, 2002). All the distortion errors reported in this work are in terms of percentage of the mesh bounding box. This distance is suitable for both mesh simplification and compression.

(6) Geometric Laplacian metric: MSE by itself is not sufficient, since it is possible that a model may be close geometrically, and yet provide a poor "visual" reconstruction. Karni & Gotsman (2000) introduced another metric, called the geometric Laplacian, defined as follows:

$$GL(\boldsymbol{v}) = \boldsymbol{v} - \frac{\sum_{j \in n(\boldsymbol{v})} l_j^{-1} \boldsymbol{v}_j}{\sum_{j \in n(\boldsymbol{v})} l_j^{-1}} \tag{10}$$

Where $n(v)$ is the set of the indices of the neighbors of vertex v, and l_j the Euclidean distance from v to v_j. This term intuitively measures the difference between the prediction made by simply averaging the coordinates of the neighbors of a vertex and the actual prediction. The final error in approximation is then defined as the sum of the normalized geometric Laplacian error and the geometric error:

$$d(X,Y) = \frac{1}{2N} \left(\left\| X - Y \right\| + \sum_{i=1}^{N} \left(GL(\boldsymbol{v}_i^x) - GL(\boldsymbol{v}_i^y) \right) \right) \tag{11}$$

where the two meshes X and Y share the same connectivity with N vertices, where $\boldsymbol{v}_i^x$ and $\boldsymbol{v}_i^y$ are the respective i-th vertices from X and Y. This distance is proper for 3D mesh compression evaluations.

(7) Discrete Differential Error Metric (DDEM): 3D *ad-hoc* metrics can be used to control mesh simplification algorithms, which consist in reducing the number of vertices while preserving the visual appearance. Kim & Kim & Kim (2002) stated that the human vision is sensitive to curvature changes and propose a Discrete Differential Error Metric (DDEM) between two vertices $\mathbf{v}_i$ and $\mathbf{v}_i'$ as follow

$$DDEM(\mathbf{v}_i, \mathbf{v}_i') = Q(\mathbf{v}_i, \mathbf{v}_i') + T(\mathbf{v}_i, \mathbf{v}_i') + C(\mathbf{v}_i, \mathbf{v}_i')$$
(12)

with Q a quadratic distance, T a normal vector difference and C a discrete curvature difference. This distance is used to control 3D mesh simplification algorithms.

(8) 3D mesh structural distortion measure (MSDM): Lavoue, Gelasca & Dupont (2006) proposed this metric which follows the concept of structural similarity for 2-D image quality assessment, and well reflects the perceptual distance between two 3-D objects. The local MSDM distance between two mesh local windows p and q (respectively in X and Y) is defined as follows:

$$d_{LMSDM}(p,q) = \left(0.4L(p,q)^3 + 0.4C(p,q)^3 + 0.2S(p,q)^3\right)^{1/3}$$
(13)

where L, C and S represent respectively curvature, contrast and structure comparison functions:

$$L(p,q) = \frac{\|\mu_p - \mu_q\|}{\max(\mu_p, \mu_q)}$$
(14)

$$C(p,q) = \frac{\|\sigma_p - \sigma_q\|}{\max(\sigma_p, \sigma_q)}$$
(15)

$$S(p,q) = \frac{\|\sigma_p \sigma_q - \sigma_{pq}\|}{\sigma_p \sigma_q}$$
(16)

With μ_p, σ_p and σ_{pq} respectively the mean, standard deviation and covariance of the curvature over the mesh local windows. The global MSDM measure between two meshes X and Y, is defined by a Minkowski summation of their n local window distances:

$$d_{MSDM}(X,Y) = \left(\frac{1}{n}\sum_{i=1}^{n} d_{LMSDM}(p_i, q_i)^3\right)^{1/3}$$
(17)

Its value tends toward 1 (theoretical limit) when the measured objects are visually very different and is equal to 0 for identical ones. The pros of this perceptual distortion metric are its strong robustness and its high correlation with the subjective evaluation results given by human beings.

TYPICAL AND STATE-OF-THE-ART ALGORITHMS

In this section, the typical and state-of-the-art algorithms are introduced in categories of connectivity coding, geometry coding, spectral coding, dynamic mesh coding, gigantic mesh coding and streaming, and MPEG-4 3D mesh coding standard.

Connectivity Coding

Beginning with the hardware-supported work of Deering (1995), we move on to methods that consider the mesh as a connected graph and encode spanning trees of the graph. We describe the first method that uses such a scheme, Edgebreaker by Rossignac (1999) and proceed with a description of methods that encode a traversal of mesh faces.

Connectivity data compression has been well studied. Rossignac (1999) proposed the popular Edgebreaker coder, which compressed the connectivity data to be 4 bits per vertex (in short, bpv) in the worst case. Since then, its derivatives (Cohen-Or, Levin & O. Remez, 1999; Gumhold,

2000; Isenburg & Snoeyink, 2000; King & J. Rossignac, 1999; Szymczak, King & J. Rossignac, 2001), and some other techniques (Bajaj, Pascucci & G. Zhuang, 1999; Gumhold & Straßer, 1998; Isenburg & Snoeyink, 1999; Touma & Gotsman, 1998) have also been proposed. Amongst them, depending on the type of the traversed mesh elements, we distinguish face-based methods like mesh elements transversal based spanning tree encoding (Deering, 1995), edge-based methods like FaceFixer (Isenburg, 1999) and vertex-based methods (Touma & Gotsman, 1998). A complete survey of these approaches is available (Cohen, Cohen-Or & T. Ironi, 2002). At present, connectivity compression has reached its limit of less than two bits per triangle for the connectivity portion of a mesh. On the other hand, compressing the geometry remains challenging, since the encoded geometry is much larger than the encoded connectivity. In addition, with hardware-oriented mesh representations such as triangle strips (Evans, Skiena & Varshney, 1996; Hoppe, 1999) or generalized triangle meshes (Chow, 1997; Deering, 1995), each vertex is often specified multiple times due to the storage constraints of hardware decoding. Therefore, it is crucial to develop effective compression techniques for the vertex data in order to further reduce the bit rate as well as the bandwidth requirement.

Inspired by Cut-Border Machine (Gumhold & Straßer, 1998), Rossignac (1999) proposed EdgeBreaker which is a simplified version of Cut-Border Machine. The triangle list is searched by region growing method beginning with a triangle face: the growing region contains all triangles that have already been encoded, and incorporate the adjacent triangles in the rest part of the mesh gradually. The border that partitions the encoded region and the remaining region to be encoded is called cut-border. A selected edge of the cut-border is called gate and defines the triangle that is encoded next. There are in total five possibilities for the next triangle to be encoded to indicate how it is positioned with respect to the gate and

the cut-border. Each possibility has a unique opcode assigned to it so that when encoding, the opcodes are added in the compressed bitstream in the order of the triangle list. Then a new gate is chosen and the encoder continues. The decoding process is simply the inverse process of the encoding process but is not easily implemented in hardware. Note that the special case comes when there is a *Split* operation. In such case, a new triangle is formed by the two vertices of the gate and another vertex on the cut-border. Through the process of symbol string operation from the *Split* to the *End*, the length of the cut-border is reduced. When the cut-border reaches zero after the *End* operation. Since the correct *Split* offset is obtained by counting the length of the cut-border in the decoding process, the EdgeBreaker decoder needs two runs over the bit stream. An example of triangulated boundary of a polyhedron that is cut into a flat triangulated polygon without interior vertices is shown in Figure 5.

Geometry Coding

Although the uncompressed geometry data is often given in precise IEEE 32-bit floating point representation for each vertex coordinate, the presentation of geometry data in a fewer number of bits is acceptable in some cases, e.g. the current Java3D geometry compression specification (Sun Microsystems, 1999). In this section, we briefly summarize several existing schemes for compressing geometry data. Since triangle mesh is the most popular representation of 3D mesh models, and 3D mesh models in representations other than triangle meshes can be easily converted to triangle meshes, we only focus on triangle mesh coding in this chapter.

The early works usually quantize, uniformly and separately, the vertex positions for each coordinate in the Cartesian space. Deering (1995) first proposed a vertex data compression scheme, where positions are first normalized within an axis-aligned bounding box. The coordinates are

Figure 5. The triangulated boundary of a polyhedron (left) may be cut into a flat triangulated polygon without interior vertices (right)

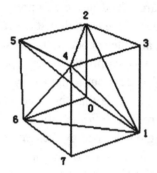 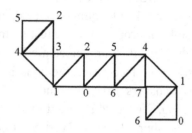

then uniformly quantized with entropy coding using a modified Huffman code. Since then, many variations of Deering (1995)'s scheme have also been proposed (Chou & Meng, 2002; Chow, 1997; Deering, 1995; Lee & Ko, 2000; Taubin, Horn & Rossignac, 1998; Taubin & Rossignac, 1998; Touma & Gotsman, 1998). Karni & Gotsman (2000) demonstrated the relevance of applying quantization in the space denoted by spectral coefficients. This algorithm is near optimal but needs large amounts of computation and memory for computing the eigenvalues and eigenvectors of a large sparse matrix derived from the mesh topology. Karni & Gotsman (2001) addressed this issue by using fixed spectral bases, while Sorkine, Cohen-Or & Toldeo (2003) addressed the issue on how to reduce the visual effect due to quantization errors.

An efficient progressive mesh compression algorithm was proposed based on a remeshing technique (Khodakovsky, Schroder & Sweldens, 2000). The basic idea is to convert an irregular mesh into a semi-regular one. An irregular mesh is first simplified to a base mesh. Then, the base mesh is refined by adding new vertices systematically. The geometry can also be effectively compressed by applying the wavelet transform to refinement vectors of vertex coordinates based on the semi-regular relation among vertices. Although remeshing techniques obtain better

compression ratios for geometric compression, it involves remeshing so the connectivity of the original mesh is somewhat changed.

While most mesh geometry compression techniques are guided by the underlying connectivity coding. Gandoin & Devillers (2002) proposed a fundamentally different strategy, where connectivity coding is guided by geometry coding. Their algorithm can encode arbitrary simplicial complexes without any topological constraint. Valette & Prost (2004) proposed a new lossy to lossless progressive compression scheme for triangular meshes, based on a wavelet multi-resolution theory for irregular 3D meshes. This approach is effective at mesh geometry compression when one wants to keep the connectivity completely unchanged.

As for the prediction scheme, the early work employed simple delta coding or linear prediction along the vertex order dictated by the coding of the connectivity data. Delta prediction was employed (Chow, 1997; Deering, 1995) and Taubin & Rossignac (1998) engaged linear prediction in his work. Touma & Gotsman (1998) used a more sophisticated parallelogram prediction scheme in which a lower bit rate was achieved by estimating the local surface curvature. Inspired by the TG parallelogram prediction scheme (Touma & Gotsman, 1998), Isenburg & Alliez (2002) completed the techniques by generalizing it to polygon mesh geometry compression (Isenburg, 2002; Khodakovsky, Alliez, Desbrun & Schroder, 2002). The coordinates of branching points are encoded directly while those of vertices along contours are encoded with a second-order prediction (Bajaj, Pascucci & Zhuang, 1999). Prediction trees are employed to improve the prediction where the geometry drives the traversal order instead of the connectivity as before (Kronrod & Gotsman, 2002). The optimization is significant especially in CAD models. Cohen, Cohen-Or & Ironi (2002) suggested a multi-way prediction technique, where each vertex position is predicted from all its neighboring vertices, as opposed to the one-way parallelogram prediction. Ahn, Kim & Ho (2006) proposed a new prediction method, in which redundancies in geometry data are eliminated by predicting each vertex position, exploiting the position and angle information in neighboring triangles. All these prediction schemes can be treated as a special case of the linear prediction scheme with carefully chosen coefficients.

Vector quantization (VQ) techniques exhibits many superiorities over scalar quantization methods, so VQ based schemes have also been proposed for 3D mesh compression since 2000 (Chou & Meng, 2002; Lee & Ko, 2000). Later, the Cartesian coordinates of a vertex are transformed into a model space vector using the three previous vertex positions and then quantized (Lee & Ko, 2000). Chou & Meng (2002) used several VQ techniques including the open loop VQ, the product code pyramid VQ and the asymptotic closed loop VQ that are applied for residual vector quantization.

Compressing the geometry of a mesh is mostly steered by the connectivity compression. The first issue in designing a scheme for compressing geometry data is how to map the source data into a discreet sequence. Many modern algorithms use prediction techniques in order to achieve high compression ratios. Firstly, the coordinates of the vertices are scalar/ vector quantized with a codebook. When the mesh traversal arrives at

a new vertex, its coordinates are predicted from already processed vertices. The difference between the predicted position and the real position is encoded. However, the prediction mode for 3D geometry data is different from the prediction of 2D image data that we are familiar with. For two-dimensional signals such as images, the vector sequence is commonly formed from blocks of neighboring pixels. The blocks can be directly used as the input vector for the quantizer. Since blocking neighboring samples in this manner enables the quantizer to exploit the intra-block correlation or the dependence that exists between neighboring samples, we can also employ the correlation or the dependence. In the case of triangle meshes, neighboring vertices are also likely to be correlated. However, blocking multiple vertices is not as straightforward as the case for images. The coordinate vector of a vertex cannot be directed regarded as an input vector to the quantizer because if multiple vertices are mapped into the same vertex, the distortion of the mesh will be unacceptable and the connectivity of the mesh will also disappear.

In order to exploit the correlation between vertices, it is necessary to use a scalar/vector quantizer with memory. A block diagram of the predictive encoder and decoder is shown in Figure 6. Let $\left\{ \mathbf{v}_i \right\}_{i=0}^{N}$ represent the sequence of vertices encountered as a mesh is being traversed and let $\mathbf{v}_n$ be the next vertex to be encoded. The encoder forms a prediction $\tilde{\mathbf{v}}_n$ of $\mathbf{v}_n$ based on observations of previously encoded vertices. The residual vector $\mathbf{e}_n$, representing the prediction error, is then computed as $\mathbf{e}_n = \mathbf{v}_n - \tilde{\mathbf{v}}_n$. This residual vector is then quantized by the vector quantizer, which generates a codevector $\hat{\mathbf{e}}_n$ that approximates $\mathbf{e}_n$. The index identifying this codevector is then stored or transmitted to the decoder.

However, the prediction error between $\mathbf{v}_n$ and $\tilde{\mathbf{v}}_n$ may be accumulated to the subsequent en-

Figure 6. Prediction $\tilde{\mathbf{v}}_n$ of the next vertex $\mathbf{v}_n$ using previously reconstructed vertices $\hat{\mathbf{v}}_{n-1}, \hat{\mathbf{v}}_{n-2}, \hat{\mathbf{v}}_{n-3}$

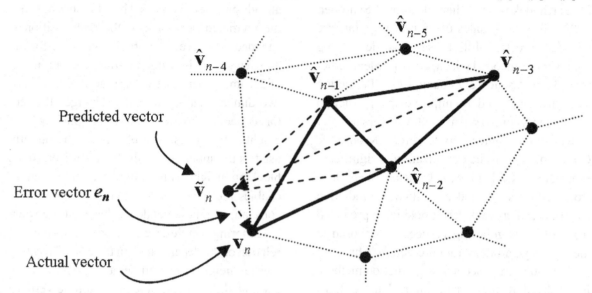

coded vertices. When the vertices number of a mesh is large enough, the accumulated error may be unacceptable. To permit reconstruction of the vertices by the decoder, the prediction must only be based on previous reconstructed vertices. Thus, the encoder also needs to update the constructed vertex to be the reconstructed vertex for computing prediction vectors for subsequent vertices.

The decoder receives the sequence of indices. Given an index, the decoder first performs a table lookup operation to obtain the residual codevector $\hat{\mathbf{e}}_n$. The decoder then adds $\hat{\mathbf{e}}_n$ and $\mathbf{e}_n$ to reconstruct the quantized vertex $\hat{\mathbf{v}}_n$. As in the case of the encoder, $\hat{\mathbf{v}}_n$ is fed back to the predictor for computing subsequent vertex predictions.

The most popular prediction scheme is the "parallelogram" prediction (Isenburg & Alliez, 2002), which is intuitively illustrated in Figure 6. A vertex can be predicted by its neighboring triangles, enabling exploitation of the tendency for neighboring triangles to be roughly coplanar and similar in size. This is particularly true for high-resolution, scanned models, which have little

variation in the triangle size. Suppose $\hat{\mathbf{v}}_{n-1}, \hat{\mathbf{v}}_{n-2}$ and $\hat{\mathbf{v}}_{n-3}$ in Figure 6 are the three vertices of a neighboring triangle buffered by the decoder. Then, an effective and computationally inexpensive way to compute the prediction $\tilde{\mathbf{v}}_n$ of the next vertex $\mathbf{v}_n$ is:

$$\tilde{\mathbf{v}}_n = \hat{\mathbf{v}}_{n-1} + \hat{\mathbf{v}}_{n-2} - \hat{\mathbf{v}}_{n-3} \qquad (18)$$

Touma & Gotsmann (1998) described an enhancement that also incorporates an estimate of the mesh curvature rather than assuming triangles are coplanar. This method increases prediction accuracy at the cost of greater complexity.

One of the most effective schemes is vector quantization (VQ) based scheme. The state-of-the-art VQ based method is dynamically restricted codebook based vector quantization (DRCVQ) (Lu & Li, 2007). In DRCVQ, a parameter is used to control the encoding quality to get the desired compression rate in a range with only one codebook, instead of using different levels of codebooks to get different compression rate. During the encoding process, the indices of the preceding encoded residual vectors which have high correlation with the current input vector are pre-stored in a FIFO so both the codevector searching range and bit rate are averagely reduced. The proposed scheme also incorporates a very effective Laplacian smooth operator. Simulation results show that, for various size of mesh models, DRCVQ can reduce PSNR degradation of about 2.5~6 dB at 10 bits per vertex comparative to the conventional vertex encoding method with stationary codebooks and, DRCVQ with arithmetic coding of codevector indices and Laplacian smoothener can outperform the state-of-the-art Wavemesh for non-smooth meshes while performs slightly worse for smooth meshes. In addition, a codevector search acceleration scheme is adopted so the compression is real-time. The most different point of this scheme from other VQ based schemes is that an effective mesh filtering that compensate for the high frequency noise caused by vector quantization.

The "parallelogram" prediction rule assumes that neighboring vertices are coplanar; however, since a universal codebook contains codevectors uniformly in all directions, when a vertex is reconstructed from its prediction vector and its quantized residual vector with a universal codebook, it deviates from the original plane. So vector quantization introduces high frequencies to the original mesh. In order to improve the visual quality of the decoded meshes, a Laplacian low frequency pass filter is designed (Lu & Li, 2007) which is derived from the mesh connectivity that has already been received and decoded before residual vectors are decoded.

Mesh Laplacian operator is defined as follows:

$$
L_{ij} = \begin{cases} 1 & \mathbf{v}_i = \mathbf{v}_j \\ -1/d_i & \mathbf{v}_i \text{ and } \mathbf{v}_j \text{ are neighbors} \\ 0 & \text{otherwise} \end{cases}
$$

$$(19)$$

where $\mathbf{v}_i$ is a vertex of the mesh and d_i is the valence of $\mathbf{v}_i$. Then the filtered vertex is defined as:

$$
\mathbf{v}_i' = \sum_j \left| L_{ij} \right| \cdot \mathbf{v}_j / 2 \tag{20}
$$

where $\mathbf{v}_i'$ is the filtered version of $\mathbf{v}_i$.

This filter can be operated iteratively. Based on the assumption that similar mesh models should have similar surface area, the criterion for terminating Laplacian filter is set to be:

$$
\left| \text{area}(M^{(i)}) - \text{area}(M) \right| \Big/ \text{area}(M) < \delta \tag{21}
$$

where $M^{(i)}$ is the i-th version of filtered original M, $\text{area}(M)$ is a 32 bit float value which can be transmitted along with the compressed mesh bit stream, and δ is a threshold. For more details, you can refer to Lu & Li (2007)'s work.

Spectral Coding

Karni & Gotsman (2000) proposed spectral geometry compression, where the geometry is projected on an orthogonal vector space, constructed with the eigenvectors of the mesh connectivity Laplacian matrix. The basic idea is to transform the 3Dgeometry into combination of basis functions weighted by basis coefficients, like 1D or 2D signal transformations such as discrete cosine transform in the JPEG image compression standard in order of importance. Low-frequency corresponds to important information while high-frequency corresponds to the details that we can ignore when compression. The signal can be a good approximation to consider only the most important basis functions.

For geometry, the eigenvectors of the Laplacian matrix correspond to the basis functions. The Laplacian **L** of a mesh is defined by the valences of its vertices and the connectivity graph as

$$L = V - A, \qquad (22)$$

where $\mathbf{V}$ is the diagonal valence matrix and $\mathbf{A}$ is the adjacency matrix of the mesh. So the elements of mesh Laplacian are as follows:

$$L_{ij} = \begin{cases} 1 & \mathbf{v}_i = \mathbf{v}_j \\ -1/d_i & \mathbf{v}_i \text{ and } \mathbf{v}_j \text{ are neighbors} \\ 0 & \text{otherwise} \end{cases}$$

$$(23)$$

where $\mathbf{v}_i$ is a vertex of the mesh and d_i is the valence of $\mathbf{v}_i$.

The next step is to perform eigenvalue decomposition on L as follow:

$$L = UDU^T, \qquad (24)$$

where $\mathbf{U}$ contains the eigenvectors of $\mathbf{L}$ sorted by their corresponding eigenvalues. Note that for reducing computation cost and circumventing the small eigenvalue problem, the 3D mesh is first partitioned into small patches according to some mesh segmentation algorithms, and then the Laplacian matrix is calculated and the eigenvalue decomposition is performed.

After obtaining the basis functions, we can quantize the eigenvalues and ignore the basis functions that correspond to low eigenvalues that are quantized to zeros, like the principal component analysis. The geometry, i.e. the coordinate matrix $\mathbf{P}$ of the mesh vertices are projected onto these basis functions by

$$Q = U^T P. \qquad (25)$$

The projected coordinate matrix $\mathbf{Q}$ is a sparse representation that can be encoded efficiently. The bonus benefit is that the spectral compression can be also used for a progressive transmission of the geometry information of the mesh since the geometry can be added with additional details

that correspond to less important eigenvectors. Figure 7 shows a sample mesh and two typical Laplacian stars.

Progressive Coding inspired by various single rate mesh coders abovementioned, Alliez & Desbrun (2001) introduced a progressive mesh encoding technique. In this scheme, the connectivity of the mesh is indicated by only the valence of the vertices and some supplementary codes called null-patch. A two-stage simplification scheme keeps the mesh connectivity as regular as possible, leading to an inverse subdivision for regular meshes. The vertices can also be removed according to a geometric criterion to improve the quality of the approximations. This approach compresses the mesh connectivity to an average of 3.69 bits per vertex.

Spectral geometry compression provides good mesh approximations even with few transmitted coefficients (Karni & Gotsman, 2000). However, this algorithm is not fully progressive as described above, i.e. the mesh connectivity remains the same, so only the geometry of the mesh changes with the resolution. Since the mesh itself is intended to approximate a surface in R^3 space, it is often beneficial to choose a different mesh that also approximates the surface but can be compressed much better. As a result, remeshing can be first performed, i.e. transforms from the original mesh into another mesh, followed by compressing the resulting mesh afterwards. Those encoders are lossy because the decoder reconstructs the modified mesh and not the original mesh. But because in most cases the error is not visible and thus can be ignored, such an encoding is still referred to as lossless encoding. Remeshing techniques have opened the door for wavelet analysis of meshes resulting in compact multi-resolution representation for meshes based on wavelets.

Valette & Prost (2000) proposed a new lossy to lossless progressive compression scheme for triangular meshes, named Wavemesh, which is based on a wavelet multi-resolution theory for

Figure 7. A sample mesh together with two typical Laplacian stars

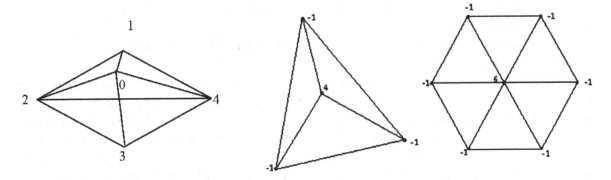

irregular 3D meshes. This approach can be very effective when one wants to keep the connectivity and geometry of the processed mesh completely unchanged. The simplification is based on the solving of an inverse problem. Optimization of both the connectivity and geometry of the processed mesh improves the approximation quality and the compression ratio of the scheme at each resolution level. This algorithm performs better than other previous published approaches for both lossless and progressive compression. The simplification is repeated until the resulting mesh cannot be simplified anymore. We obtain a hierarchy of meshes, from the simplest one $\mathbf{M^0}$ to the original mesh $\mathbf{M^J}$. In this scheme, the wavelet decomposition is applied to the geometrical properties by the following matrix relations:

$$\mathbf{C}^{j-1}=\mathbf{A}^j\,\mathbf{C}^j \qquad (26)$$

$$\mathbf{D}^{j-1}=\mathbf{B}^j\,\mathbf{C}^j \qquad (27)$$

$$\mathbf{C}^j=\mathbf{P}^j\,\mathbf{C}^{j-1}+\mathbf{Q}^j\,\mathbf{D}^{j-1} \qquad (28)$$

where $\mathbf{C}^j$ is the matrix representing the coordinates of the vertices of $\mathbf{M^J}$. $\mathbf{D}^{j-1}$ is the matrix of the wavelet coefficients at level j. $\mathbf{A}^j$ and $\mathbf{B}^j$ are the analysis filters, $\mathbf{P}^j$ and $\mathbf{Q}^j$ are the synthesis filters. The connectivity simplification is inversed to 1:4 subdivisions as much as possible.

Dynamic Mesh Coding

Up to now, only single meshes have been discussed. But modern animation frameworks are able to create a series of meshes that together form an animation. Such animated meshes are often called dynamic meshes. In order to visualize dynamic scenery the 3D representation of objects and scenes must be dynamic as well, and the modern animation techniques can also create 3D animation meshes such as 3D cartoons. Dynamic 3D objects and scenes are widely used in computer graphics for games, web-sites, movie and TV production, etc. These 3D animations can be either created by sophisticated artists virtually or automatically captured and reconstructed by multiple synchronized cameras.

Coming from either source dynamic 3D geometry can be conveniently represented using 3D meshes. The simplest approach is just to use completely independent meshes for every time instant, i.e. a succession of static meshes. But obviously this is not the most efficient approach. Instead the geometry of moving 3D objects may be represented by a constant part and a dynamic part. The constant part reflects the part of the object that contains the constant properties while the dynamic part reflects the changing properties. Intuitively, the shape or connectivity of the skeleton and some statistics of the mesh geometry can be regarded as constant attributes, while motion and shape deformation can be regarded as changing properties that will be constrained by a certain model with a limited number of parameters. The simplest case of the changing property model is the temporal displacement of vertices.

Ibarria & Rossignac (2003) introduced Dynapack that compresses the first frame mesh using a spatial predictor and the subsequent mesh frames using spatial and temporal predictors. First, the connectivity of the first mesh frame is encoded by one of the existing connectivity coding techniques. Then we can encode the geometry using a spatial predictor, of which the most popular one is the parallelogram predictor. The first mesh frame is now encoded, followed by the subsequent mesh frames compressed using a temporal predictor for encoding the first triangle and several predictors for encoding the remaining triangles. The rest triangles can be encoded by one of the following four predictors which are examined by Rossignac:

1. Parallelogram Spatial Predictor

$$\text{prediction }(\mathbf{v}_f) = \mathbf{n}_f + \mathbf{p}_f - \mathbf{o}_f. \tag{29}$$

2. Temporal Predictor

$$\text{prediction}(\mathbf{v}_f) = \mathbf{n}_{f-1}. \tag{30}$$

3. Extended Parallelogram Spatial and Temporal Predictor

$$\text{prediction }(\mathbf{v}_f) = \mathbf{n}_f + \mathbf{p}_f - \mathbf{o}_f + \mathbf{v}_{f-1} - \mathbf{n}_{f-1} - \mathbf{p}_{f-1} + \mathbf{o}_{f-1} \tag{31}$$

4. Replica Spatial and Temporal Predictor (This predictor perfectly predicts rigid-body motions and uniform scaling transformations)

$$\text{prediction }(\mathbf{v}_f) = \mathbf{o}_f + a\mathbf{A}_f + b\mathbf{B}_f + c\mathbf{C}_f \tag{32}$$

where $\mathbf{A}_f = \mathbf{p}_f - \mathbf{o}_f$, $\mathbf{B}_f = \mathbf{n}_f - \mathbf{o}_f$, $\mathbf{C}_f = \mathbf{A}_f \times \mathbf{B}_f / \sqrt{\|\mathbf{A}_f \times \mathbf{B}_f\|^3}$, and the constants

a, b, and c are estimated from the geometry information of the previous frame.

Gigantic Mesh Compression

The standard representation of a polygon mesh uses an array of floats to specify the vertex positions and an array of integers containing indices into the vertex array to specify the polygons. For large and detailed models this representation results in files of gigantic size that consume large amount of storage space. The need for more compact representations has motivated research on mesh compression and a number of efficient schemes have been proposed as mentioned in the previous subsections. However, few of these schemes are capable to dealing with meshes of the GB size on common desktop PCs that would benefit from compression the most.

Current compression algorithms and some of the corresponding decompression algorithms can only be used when connectivity and geometry of the mesh are small enough to be totally stored in the main memory. Realizing this limitation, Ho, Lee & Kriegman (2001) proposed to cut gigantic meshes into manageable pieces and encode each piece separately using existing techniques. However, partitioning the mesh introduces artificial discontinuities, which will cause damage to the rate-distortion performance of the algorithm as well as significantly reduce decompression speeds.

Up to a certain mesh size, the memory requirements of the compression process could be satisfied using a 64-bit super-computer with vast amounts of main memory. Research labs and industries that create GB sized meshes often have access to such equipment. But to decompress on common desktop PCs, at least the memory footprint of the decompression process needs to be small. In particular, it must not have memory requirements in the size of the decompressed mesh. This eliminates a number of popular multi-pass schemes that either need to store the entire mesh for connectivity decompression (Taubin &

Rossignac, 1998) or that decompress connectivity and geometry in separate passes (Isenburg & Alliez, 2002).

Isenburg & Gumhold (2003) introduced a recent out-of-core technique that achieved several improvements upon the previous work (Ho, Lee & Kriegman, 2001) by (i) avoiding the need to explicitly break up the model into several pieces, (ii) decoding the entire model in a single pass without any restarts, and (iii) streaming the entire mesh through main memory with a small memory foot-print. The core technique underlying this compression method consists of building a new external memory data structure – the out-of-core mesh – in several stages, all of them being restricted to clusters and active traversal fronts which fit in-core. The latter traversal order, consisting of a reordering of the mesh primitives, is computed in order to minimize the number of memory cache misses, similar inspirit to the notion of a "rendering sequence" (Bogomjakov & Gotsman, 2002) developed for improving performance of modern graphics cards, but at a much larger scale. The resulting compressed mesh format can stream very large meshes through the main memory by providing the compressor transparent access to a so-called processing sequence that represents a mesh as a fixed, yet seamless interleaved ordering of indexed triangles and vertices. At any point in time, the remaining part of the mesh data is kept on disk.

Gigantic 3D Mesh Streaming

Now a gigantic mesh model can be encoded using the out-of-core technology, and it is natural to consider the issue of decoding a gigantic mesh model in real time. One can imagine that there is a huge virtual 3D world consisting of a large amount of 3D mesh models. It may have a size of 30 GB (of decoded models). First he/she downloads one part and can walk inside this part, but while going forward, he/she would like to download the next models, so first he/she only needs 1 MB, but

after downloading the rest dynamically and he/she can walk around of the 3D world. How can he/she do this?

This is can be addressed by streaming the 3D models. Streaming 3D models is the critical issue in multimedia applications such as online gaming and virtual reality. However, a gap exists between the zero-loss-tolerance of the existing compression schemes and the lossy network transmissions. A generic 3D middleware between the 3D application layer and the transport layer is proposed for streaming 3D models (Li, Li & Prabhakaran, 2006). It can be used for the transmission of triangle-based progressively compressed 3D models. In this middleware, a half-edge data structure (Mantyla, 1988) is used as foundation for the out-of-core data structure, which offers the functionality needed by the compression algorithm at minimal storage space consumption.

First, based on the observation that the structural data affects the quality of the decoded mesh more than the geometric data does, without any changes to the encoder/decoder, Li, Li & Prabhakaran (2006) identified and separated the structural data from the geometric data for a given 3D data stream irrespective of its format. Then the geometric data is further decomposed into sub-layers based on the significant bit, and the distortion of the rendered 3D mesh due to the loss of a sub-layer is calculated. Next, a subset of the 3D data stream is selected for the transmission based on the user's quality requirement. In order to maintain the same mesh connectivity, the base mesh and the selected structural sub-layers are transmitted over reliable channel. For geometric sub-layers, Li, Li & Prabhakaran (2006) choose reliable/unreliable channel for the transmission depending on the relative importance to minimize the delay and distortion simultaneously. Finally, Li, Li & Prabhakaran (2006) handle packet loss and out of sequence packets by inserting additional fields into packets and synchronize the reliable and unreliable channels by sending an "END" marker on the reliable channel to indicate the end of a refinement.

Specifically, a static data structure with an array **V** of vertices and an array of half-edges **H** is basically sufficient. After clustering vertices and half-edges they are re-indexed into so-called *index-pairs*. Given the input mesh in an indexed format, the out-of-core mesh is built in six stages (Isenburg & Gumhold, 2003), all of which restricted to the memory limit:

1. The first vertex pass that determines the bounding box. Each of the three vertex passes reads and processes the vertex array one time sequentially.
2. The second vertex pass that determines a spatial clustering. A balanced spatial clustering of the vertices is computed: the bounding box is partitioned into a regular grid of cubical cells and for each cell the number of vertices falling into it is counted; then the non-empty cells are partitioned into compact clusters of balanced vertex counts using a graph partitioning package.
3. The third vertex pass that quantizes and sorts the vertices into the clusters: The vertices are sorted into clusters and transformed into corresponding index-pairs using the cell partitioning.
4. Face pass that creates the half-edges and sorts them into the clusters: Given a face, its vertex indices are mapped to vertex index-pairs according to the map file. Then one half-edge for each of its edges is created, a suitable cluster is determined, and then stored clusters.
5. Matching of incident half-edges: With the target vertex index-pairs, a sorting strategy is used again for matching inverse half-edges.
6. Linking and shortening of borders and non-manifold vertices detection.

Significant features of this middleware include:

1. Handling 3D compressed data streams from multiple progressive compression techniques.
2. Considering end user hardware capabilities for effectively saving the data size for network delivery.
3. A minimum cost dynamic reliable set selector to choose the transport protocol for each sub-layer based on the real-time network traffic.

Extensive simulations with TCP/UDP and SCTP show that the proposed 3D middleware can achieve the dual objectives of maintaining low transmission delay and small distortion, and thus supporting high quality 3D streaming with high flexibility. Simulation results also show that this scheme can effectively reduce the delay and distortion experienced at the receiver.

There already exist several software for streaming 3D models, amongst which the most popular ones in the field of scientific visualization include VRML97 and Java3D. VRML97 can be operated on stand-alone players, web browser, and Java virtual machines. It provides universal interchange format for integrating any geometry and behavior. However, its scope of scene graph architecture limits real-time performances for many web applications. Java 3D provides a lower-level platform API that is suitable for developing new authoring applications. Higher level (e.g. VRML) languages can be layered on top of Java 3D.

MPEG-4 3D Mesh Coding Standard

MPEG-4 is an ISO multimedia standard which includes most of the VRML scene graph structure, with a more efficient binary encoding called Binary Encoding for Scenes (BIFS). Polygonal models are represented in VRML by *IndexedFaceSet* nodes, which can be encoded with the simple BIFS quantization scheme. Major components in *IndexedFaceSet* are connectivity, geometry, and other optional properties such as colors, normals, and texture coordinates.

As one of the well-known conventional algorithms, three-dimensional mesh coding (3DMC) was introduced in MPEG-4 Version 2. 3DMC provides a representation and compression tool for *IndexedFaceSet* node of 3D objects onto which images and video may be mapped. 3D mesh coding is to compress static mesh models. The animation of 3D mesh models is possible by using key-frame animation (with Interpolators). 3DMC provides additional functionalities—such as high compression, incremental rendering, and error resilience—that are useful to many applications. 3D mesh compression is one of the very first attempts to address compression of 3D objects. 3DMC can be efficiently used and applied with AFX tools, where 3DMC can be utilized to represent static models as well as some animated 3D models. The MPEG-4 3D mesh object is a compressed bitstream of the *IndexedFaceSet* VRML/BIFS node.

The major concept of 3DMC is called topological surgery (Sun Microsystems, 1999), which decomposes a 3D mesh model into the 2D mesh structure composed of a dual graph pair of vertex graph and simple polygon. The simple polygon is a 2D mesh torn down from the 3D mesh. The vertex graph is connectivity information necessary to stitch the 2D mesh together to restore the original 3D mesh model (Walsh & Sevenier, 2002). Using topological surgery, 3DMC can compress the connectivity of a 3D mesh model with a cost of around 2 bits per triangles in a lossless manner. 3DMC comprises three major coding blocks: topological surgery (data transformation); differential quantization of connectivity, geometry and other properties (quantization), and entropy coding. A high level block diagram of a general 3DMC encoder is shown in Figure 8 (a), while the 3DMC decoder architecture is presented in Figure 8 (b).

Although in MPEG-4 Version 2 the *IndexedFaceSet* nodes can be encoded using the more

efficient 3DMC tools. But in MPEG-4 Version 2 there is a new node called *Hierarchical3DMesh*, which supports the full functionality of the 3DMC tools, including the streaming of polygonal data into the scene graph through a separate thread. The BIFS syntax, including the *Hierarchical3D-Mesh* node, is described in the System part of the standard, while the 3D Mesh Coding toolkit is described in the part Coding of Visual Objects of the standard.

3DMC provides 30:1 to 40:1 compression ratio without noticeable visual degradation based on the VRML compressed binary format. However, lossless compression is not the only advantage to using 3DMC. The following functionalities are supported by 3DMC:

1. Incremental single resolution mode: With 3DMC, there is no need to wait until the complete bitstream is received to start rendering it. With the incremental rendering capability, the decoder can begin building the model with just a fraction of the entire bitstream. This functionality is important when the latency is a critical issue, such as for home shopping. This mode is based on Topological Surgery (IBM/EPFL).

2. Support for non-manifold coding: Because of the compression characteristic using 3DMC topological surgery, only orientable and manifold[REMOVED HYPERLINK FIELD] models are supported. For non-orientable or non-manifold models, a dedicated operation based on Cutting and Stitching (IBM) is performed to support these models.

3. Support for error resilience: With a built-in error-resilience capability, 3DMC can suffer less from network errors, as the decoder can build a model from the partitions that are not corrupted by the errors. This technique is based on Component Based Data Partitioning (Samsung).

4. Progressive levels of detail for transmission: 3D mesh models can be quite complex,

Figure 8. (a) Block diagram of 3DMC encoder (b) Block diagram of 3DMC decoder (Adapted from Chang, Hur & Jang, 2008)

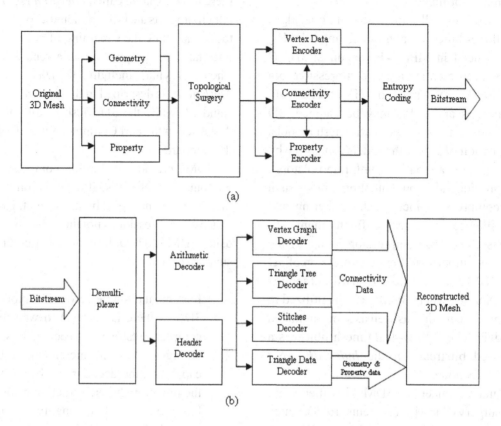

(a)

(b)

with millions of polygons. Depending on the viewing distance, the user may not need million-triangle accuracy, but may be satisfied with hundreds of triangles. A scalable bitstream similar to LOD (level of detail) representation allows building 3D models with different resolutions to serve such a case. This technique is based on Progressive Forest Split (IBM).

5. Near-lossless to lossy compression of 3D models is supported.

FUTURE RESEARCH DIRECTIONS

For single-rate geometry compression algorithms, wavelet based schemes provide good trade-offs between compression rate and quality distortion. However, vector quantization based geometry coding is also rather effective and easy implementing but is undervalued by the current research community. The key benefits of the VQ-based techniques include superior rate-distortion performance, efficient decompression that is amenable to hardware implementation, compatibility with existing connectivity compression schemes as well as some geometry compression schemes, low computation complexity, and suitability for incorporating low-pass filters to reduce distortion. One of the future directions is that combining the vector quantization and wavelet based methods that seem to be able to provide better performances. For progressive coders, the spectral coding is rather effective with only few coefficients. However, the connectivity is kept unchanged in this scheme. In contrast, wavelet based methods such as Meshwave can offer the capability of changing both the connectivity and geometry in the progressive manner. To achieve a better performance, another future direction seems to be incorporating the spectral analysis in the manner of progressive connectivity based on wavelet analysis. For the dynamic mesh coding, the compression framework should be similar to 2D image sequence compression standards. However, in the current stage, the 3DMC standard is still immature compared to image and video coding in MPEG4. For real time 3D model rendering and browsing, the streaming technology for gigantic models is a very promising direction.

CONCLUSION

Connectivity compression has been thoroughly studied, and the compression performance has nearly reached to the limit of entropy. So nowadays, geometry compression is essential for dealing with the growing complexity and bandwidth requirements resulting from the increasing geometric complexity of 3D mesh models. We summarize some of the most successful approaches for single rate encoders for 3D static mesh by categories of connectivity information compression, geometry compression and spectral coding. VQ-based geometry coding is described especially. Progressive coding techniques of 3D static mesh coding are also given, followed by brief introduction to 3D dynamic mesh coding that is a new area. Compression and streaming of gigantic 3D models are specially introduced for the purpose of storing and real time rendering, respectively. At last, the MPEG-4 3D mesh model coding standard is briefed.

REFERENCES

Ahn, J. H., Kim, C. S., & Ho, Y. S. (2006). Predictive Compression of Geometry, Color and Normal Data of 3-D Mesh Models. *IEEE Trans. on Circuits and Systems for Video Technology, 16*(2), 291–299. doi:10.1109/TCSVT.2005.861945

Alliez, P., & Desbrun, M. (2001). Valence-driven connectivity encoding of 3D meshes. *Computer Graphics Forum, 20*, 480–489. doi:10.1111/1467-8659.00541

Aspert, N., Santa-Cruz, D., & Ebrahimi, T. (2002). MESH: Measuring Error between Surfaces using the Hausdorff Distance. In. *Proceedings of the IEEE International Conference on Multimedia and Expo, I*, 705–708.

Bajaj, C. L., Pascucci, V., & Zhuang, G. (1999). Single resolution compression of arbitrary triangular meshes with properties. *Computational Geometry Theory and Application, 14*, 167–186.

Bogomjakov, A., & Gotsman, C. (2002). Universal Rendering Sequences for Transparent Vertex Caching of Progressive Meshes. *Computer Graphics Forum, 21*(2), 137–148. doi:10.1111/1467-8659.00573

Chang, E. Y., Hur, N., & Jang, E. S. (2008). 3D model compression in MPEG, *International Conference on Image Processing.* (pp. 2692-2695).

Chou, P. H., & Meng, T. H. (2002). Vertex Data Compression through Vector Quantization. *IEEE Transactions on Visualization and Computer Graphics, 8*(4), 373–382. doi:10.1109/TVCG.2002.1044522

Chow, M. M. (1997). *Optimized geometry compression for real-time rendering* (pp. 346–354). IEEE Visualization.

Cohen, R., Cohen-Or, D., & Ironi, T. (2002). *Multi-way geometry encoding, (Technical report).* Tel-Aviv University.

Cohen-Or, D., Levin, D., & Remez, O. (1999). Progressive compression of arbitrary triangular meshes, *Proc. IEEE Visualization* (pp. 67-72).

Deering, M. F. (1995). Geometry compression, *Proc. ACM SIGGRAPH.* (pp. 13-20).

Evans, F., Skiena, S., & Varshney, A. (1996). *Optimizing triangle strips for fast rendering* (pp. 319–326). IEEE Visualization.

Gandoin, P. M., & Devillers, O. (2002). Progressive Lossless Compression of Arbitrary Simplicial Complexes. *ACM Transactions on Graphics, 21*(3), 372–379.

Gumhold, S. (2000). *New bounds on the encoding of planar triangulations*, (Technical Report WSI-2000-1), Univ. of Tubingen.

Gumhold, S., & Straßer, W. (1998, July). Real time compression of triangle mesh connectivity, *Proc. ACM SIGGRAPH.* (pp. 133-140).

Ho, J., Lee, K. C., & Kriegman, D. (2001). Compressing Large Polygonal Models. *IEEE Visualization Conference Proceedings.* (pp. 357–362).

Hoppe, H. (1999). *Optimization of mesh locality for transparent vertex caching* (pp. 269–276). ACM SIGGRAPH.

Ibarria, L., & Rossignac, J. (2003). Dynapack: Space-time compression of the 3d animations of triangle meshes with fixed connectivity. *Proceedings of the ACM SIGGRAPH/Eurographics Symposium on Computer Animation.* (pp. 126-135).

Isenburg, M. (2002). Compressing polygon mesh connectivity with degree duality prediction, *Graphics Interface Conference Proceedings.* (pp. 161-170).

Isenburg, M., & Alliez, P. (2002). Compressing polygon mesh geometry with parallelogram prediction, *IEEE Visualization Conference Proceedings.* (pp. 141-146).

Isenburg, M., & Gumhold, S. (2003, July). Out-of-Core Compression for Gigantic Polygon Meshes, *Proceedings of SIGGRAPH.* (pp. 935-942).

Isenburg, M., & Snoeyink, J. (1999). Mesh collapse compression, *Proceedings of SIBGRAPI,* (pp. 27-28). Campinas, Brazil.

Isenburg, M., & Snoeyink, J. (2000). Spirale reversi: reverse decoding of the edgebreaker encoding, In *Proceedings of 12th Canadian Conference on Computational Geometry.* (pp. 247-256).

Karni, Z., & Gotsman, C. (2000). Spectral Compression of Mesh Geometry. *ACM SIGGRAPH Conference Proceedings.* (pp. 279-286).

Karni, Z., & Gotsman, C. (2001, June). 3D Mesh Compression Using Fixed Spectral Bases, *Proceedings of Graphics Interface.* (pp. 1-8). Ottawa.

Khodakovsky, A., Alliez, P., Desbrun, M., & Schroder, P. (2002). Near-optimal connectivity encoding of 2-manifold polygon meshes, *Graphical Models,* special issue, *64*(3-4), 147-168.

Khodakovsky, A., Schroder, P., & Sweldens, W. (2000). Progressive Geometry Compression. *Proc. SIGGRAPH.* (pp. 271-278).

Kim, S., Kim, S., & Kim, C. (2002). *Discrete differential error metric for surface simplification* (pp. 276–283). Pacific Graphics.

King, D., & Rossignac, J. (1999). Guaranteed 3.67V bit encoding of planar triangle graphs, *11th Canadian Conference on Computational Geometry.* (pp. 146-149).

Kronrod, B., & Gotsman, C. (2002). Optimized compression of triangle mesh geometry using prediction trees, *Proceedings of 1st International Symposium on 3D Data Processing, Visualization and Transmission.* (pp. 602-608).

Lavoue, G., Gelasca, E. D., Dupont, F., Baskurt, A., & Ebrahimi, T. (2006). Perceptually driven 3D distance metrics with application to watermarking, *Proc. of the SPIE Electronic Imaging: Vol. 6312.* (pp. 63120L.1–63120L.12).

Lee, E., & Ko, H. (2000). Vertex data compression for triangular meshes. In *Proceedings of Pacific Graphics.* (pp. 225-234).

Li, H., Li, M., & Prabhakaran, B. (2006). Middleware for streaming 3D progressive meshes over lossy networks. *ACM Transactions on Multimedia Computing, Communications, and Applications, 2*(4), 282–317. doi:10.1145/1201730.1201733

Lu, Z. M., & Li, Z. (2007). Dynamically Restricted Codebook Based Vector Quantisation Scheme for Mesh Geometry Compression. *Springer Journal of Signal. Image and Video Processing, 2*(3), 251–260. doi:10.1007/s11760-008-0053-8

Mantyla, M. (Ed.). (1988). *An Introduction to Solid Modeling*. New York: Computer Science Press.

Rossignac, J. (1999). Edgebreaker: Connectivity compression for triangle meshes. *IEEE Transactions on Visualization and Computer Graphics, 5*(1), 47–61. doi:10.1109/2945.764870

Sorkine, O., Cohen-Or, D., & Toldeo, S. (2003). High-pass quantization for mesh encoding. In *Proceedings of Eurographics Symposium on Geometry Processing*. (pp. 42-51).

Sun Microsystems. (1999), *The Java3D API Specification*. Retrieved November 30, 2009, from http://java.sun.com/javase/technologies/desktop/java3d/forDevelopers/j3dguide/j3dTOC.doc.html

Szymczak, A., King, D., & Rossignac, J. (2001). An edgebreaker-based efficient compression scheme for regular meshes. *Computational Geometry, 20*(1-2), 53–68. doi:10.1016/S0925-7721(01)00035-9

Taubin, G., Horn, W., Rossignac, J., & Lazarus, F. (1998). Geometry coding and VRML. *Proceedings of the IEEE, 86*(6), 1228–1243. doi:10.1109/5.687837

Taubin, G., & Rossignac, J. (1998). Geometric compression through topological surgery. *ACM Transactions on Graphics, 17*(2), 84–115. doi:10.1145/274363.274365

Touman, C., & Gotsman, C. (1998). Triangle mesh compression. In *Proceedings of Graphics Interface 98 Conference* (pp. 26-34).

Valette, S., & Prost, R. (2004). Wavelet-Based Progressive Compression Scheme for Triangle Meshes: Wavemesh. *IEEE Transactions on Visualization and Computer Graphics, 10*(2), 123–129. doi:10.1109/TVCG.2004.1260764

Walsh, A. E., & Bourges-Sevenier, M. (Eds.), (n.d.). *MPEG-4 Jump Start*. Upper Saddle River, NJ: Prentice-Hall.

KEY TERMS AND DEFINITIONS

Manifold: If each edge is incident to only one or two faces and the faces incident to a vertex form a closed or an open fan. Non-manifold meshes can be cut into manifold meshes by replicating vertices with more than one fan and edges incident to more than two faces.

Orientable: If there exists a choice of face orientations that makes all pairs of adjacent faces compatible. The orientation of two adjacent faces is compatible, i.i.f the two vertices of the common incident edge are in opposite order.

Section 2
Wireless / Mobile Video

Chapter 6
A Cross–Layer Design to Wireless/Mobile Video Streaming

Yongjin Cho
University of Southern California, USA

C. -C. Jay Kuo
University of Southern California, USA

ABSTRACT

This chapter introduces a cross-layer approach to wireless/mobile video streaming system design to meet its flexibility and adaptability requirements. On one hand, with the rapid development of wireless/mobile communication infrastructure, wireless video applications are gaining more popularity. On the other hand, there exist many new challenges due to the inherent characteristics of wireless networks and communication systems. This is especially true for video delivery under a stringent time constraint. To address these issues, flexibility and adaptability of communication systems, which are the objectives of cross-layer design, have been extensively studied for performance enhancement. In this chapter, we begin with the motivation of the cross-layer approach, which is needed in response to several challenges of efficient wireless/mobile video streaming. Then, some fundamental issues of the cross-layer design are introduced followed by video-specific system requirements. Furthermore, we examine a couple of cross-layer design ideas proposed in the past. Finally, we consider issues associated with the practical employment along with software simulations, and demonstrate the benefit of the cross-layer approach.

1. INTRODUCTION

The access to digitized video contents over wireless/mobile networks has drawn a lot of attention from the academia and industry due to its potential as a killer application as witnessed in the wired Internet environment. Although the wireless Internet technologies, such as the IEEE 802.11 and 802.16 standards, have provided an access means, it is restricted to a static environment with limited receiver mobility. Wireless video streaming with mobile receivers is still under development due to several technical barriers. That is, video services over wireless network are characterized by burst noise, dependence in the compressed bit stream, and the time constraint in data delivery. Besides,

DOI: 10.4018/978-1-61692-831-5.ch006

Copyright © 2011, IGI Global. Copying or distributing in print or electronic forms without written permission of IGI Global is prohibited.

video applications consume a huge amount of radio resource and a careful system design is needed to avoid unnecessary waste of the limited radio resource.

In a conventional wired network, the potential performance gain by inter-layer interaction is traded for conceptual simplicity and convenience of layer-independent design and optimization. In fact, the success of the Internet is contributed by the well-structured definition of each network layer, where the inter-layer communication is strictly disallowed. However, the layered approach to mobile wireless data communication system design does not offer satisfactory performance. For this reason, researchers have re-visited the cross-layer approach, which is the major concern of this chapter. In principle, the cross-layer design paradigm provides a large degree of freedom and, as a consequence, we have observed numerous cross-layer proposals addressing various aspects of the system design to deliver better performance. Although the benefit of the cross-layer approach has been evidenced by rich research activities in the academia and industry, it is important to address various aspects of the cross-layer design in terms of its advantages and disadvantages.

The rest of this chapter is organized as follows. In Section 2, we discuss major challenges of a wireless/mobile video streaming system to motivate the cross-layer approach. In Section 3, we examine system requirements and describe several representative examples of cross-layer video streaming systems. In Section 4, we consider practical issues with the cross-layer design based on the characteristics of video streaming applications. Finally, concluding remarks are given in Section 5.

2. BACKGROUND

This section provides the motivation of the cross-layer design approach to wireless/mobile video streaming system design. We first discuss the major

challenges of the wireless/mobile communication environment by considering each functional unit of the system. Then, we describe the potential benefits of adopting the cross-layer design to overcome these challenges.

2.1 Challenges in Wireless/Mobile Video Streaming System Design

We show the functional blocks of a source coding unit and a transmission unit along with their corresponding network layers in a wireless video streaming system in Figure 1. In this figure, a compressed bit stream travels through a heterogeneous network to arrive its destination. There are three sub-systems involved: (1) a video codec, (2) a packet-switching backbone network, and 3) a wireless/mobile communication system. For the conventional layered network architecture, the distinction of these sub-systems provides great abstraction and simplicity in system design. However, their clear partition may not be proper in the development of an efficient wireless streaming system as explained below.

2.1.1 Wireless/Mobile Radio Channel

The wireless/mobile radio channel is the physical path in the digital communication with the radio frequency (RF) microwave as the transmission medium. Two major issues arise due to the characteristics of the radio channel.

First, the condition of a wireless/mobile channel is determined by the physical environment between the transmitter and the receiver, where the quality of the received signal is determined mainly by the propagation path and receiver mobility. The wireless/mobile channel is often characterized by a multi-path propagation model with multiple reflectors, where each propagation path is associated with its own attenuation factor, phase shift and propagation delay. Combined with the multi-path fading, receiver mobility further complicates the characteristics of received

Figure 1. The functional diagram of a wireless video streaming system

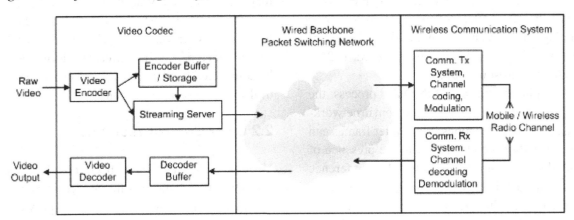

signals, which is known as the Doppler fading. As a result of independent multi-path and Doppler fading effects, we have four fading channel models (*i.e.,* frequency selective/non-selective or fast/slow fading). The frequency-selective fast fading channel is most challenging to reliable digital communication.

While the BER drops exponentially with the additive Gaussian noise radio channel (AWGN) without fading, Cavers (2000) reported that the average bit error rate (BER) decreases only inversely with the increase of SNR as a consequence of the fading effect. This implies that the increase of the transmission power may not be very effective in reducing the average BER for a fading radio channel. Moreover, Cavers (2000) had another important observation about the fading channel, where errors occur in bursts and the performance of data communication systems can be significantly degraded accordingly.

Another problem can be found in a multi-user scenario. Since the radio channel is a shared medium, participating users have to compete for limited radio resource using various multi-access schemes. For this reason, radio resource management such as call admission control (CAC), scheduling, and power control have to be carefully designed in a multi-user communication environment.

2.1.2 Application Characteristics

Digital video is composed by a sequence of highly correlated digital images. The high coding efficiency of modern hybrid video coders is contributed by the successful removal of spatial and temporal redundancy in video signals. Generally speaking, two types of frames are defined in video compression standards. The intra (I) frames are obtained using the spatial predictor in an image so that they are independent of other images in a video clip. The inter frames are encoded by exploiting the temporal correlation in a sequence of images with temporal predictors. The frames that provide the temporal predictor are called reference frames. There are two types of inter-coded frames, called the P- and B-frames, depending on the position of the predictor.

Generally, inter frames have better coding efficiency than intra frames. The motion compensated prediction (MCP) process for inter frames is the major contributor to the high coding gain of the modern video codec. When digital video is compressed by the MCP process, a sequence of input images form a dependence chain, whose length is determined by the period of independent intra frames. Typically, the dependence chain is determined by the structure of a group-of-pictures (GOP), which is defined by a number of inter frames followed by one intra frame. For example, IPPP... and IBBP... are two common GOP structures. Detailed explanations of video coding process can be found in the overview of the most recent video coding standard, H.264/AVC (Richardson, 2003).

Despite the success of the MCP process, the dependence chain provides a problem in network-based video applications. Since inter frames can be correctly decoded only with the presence of its reference frames, failure to deliver reference frames results in error propagation in subsequent inter frames. The error in a video frame is often measured by the pixel-wise mean squared error (MSE) in comparison with the original raw video input. Girod & Fäber (2001) proposed an error propagation model that is approximately inversely proportional to the elapsed time (t) after the occurrence of transmission error. The model can be expressed mathematically by

$$MSE_d(t) = MSE_e + \frac{MSE_0}{1 + \gamma \cdot t},\qquad (1)$$

where γ is a parameter that represents the effectiveness of the loop filter for error removal, MSE_d and MSE_e are MSE values at the decoder and the encoder, respectively, and MSE_0 is the initial MSE caused by the transmission error at $t=0$. The error propagation model implies the natural prioritization of video data in a dependence chain. Intuitively, video frames at the head of a dependence chain are more important than those located at the tail.

In video streaming applications, a stream of compressed video data is packetized and delivered through a data service network with a time constraint to guarantee continuous and smooth play-back. Considering the hostility of the transmission environment, the time constraint and the massive amount of video data, it is often that only a portion of all video packets can be delivered on time in a realistic video streaming scenario. Then, even at the same packet loss rate, Eq. (1) suggests

that the video quality at the receiver end could be different depending on which video packet is lost. For this reason, the service differentiation among video packets of different priority has to be considered for the performance enhancement of the video streaming system.

2.2 Error Control Techniques

Various techniques have been developed to overcome the challenges introduced in Section 2.1 at each layer. In this section, we provide a brief introduction to major efforts in performance improvement at the physical, link and application layers.

2.2.1 Physical and Link Layer

We have two relatively independent methods to cope with error-prone radio channels. They are *error control* and *diversity* techniques. While error control techniques try to minimize the affect of bad channel condition, the goal of diversity techniques is to avoid poor channel conditions by exploiting the co-existence of various independent channels.

Two basic error control methods in digital communications are: forward error correction (FEC) and automatic repeat request (ARQ). FEC techniques cope with transmission errors by adding redundant bits (error correcting codes) to the original data such that transmission errors can be detected and corrected. With the ARQ method, erroneous data are retransmitted and the retransmission request is often made indirectly by the acknowledgement (ACK) message from the receiver. Generally speaking, FEC is preferred in time-constrained applications such as voice communication and ARQ is better in applications with a loose delay constraint. In practical systems, hybrid ARQ (H-ARQ) is often used to compensate for the shortcomings of FEC and ARQ. We refer interested readers to the book by Lin and Costello (1995) that covers details of error correcting systems.

Diversity techniques exploit multiple independently fading channels from a transmitter to a receiver. For a modern multi-carrier communication system, there exist multiple channels of different quality between a transmitter and a receiver that can be specified by frequency bands and/or antenna positions, *i.e.*, *frequency* and *spatial* diversity. Diversity techniques can effectively overcome the fading effects of the radio channel by utilizing diverse channels. For example, the transmitter may send the same information through multiple carriers in different frequency bands, or multiple antennas can be employed to increase the probability of having good channel quality (Proakis, pp. 821-839).

The multi-user diversity is another diversity technique that utilizes multiple radio channels among receivers. It is often implemented by different scheduling algorithms, which are directly related to resource allocation in a multi-user communication environment. Different scheduling algorithms have various optimization objectives depending on the utility function of scheduling algorithms. For example, an user with the best channel condition is always selected with the maximum throughput scheduling algorithm and users are assigned channels periodically regardless of their channel condition with the round robin algorithm. More information on scheduling algorithms can be found in the articles by Fattah & Leung (2002) and Ajib & Haccoun (2005) and the references therein.

2.2.2 Application Layer

With the proliferation of network-based video applications, modern video coding standards employ various tools to overcome the transmission error in the video data delivery process. In general, we have two types of error resilient techniques to be performed at the encoder or the decoder.

Error resilient tools at the encoder are standardized so that its output bit stream is compliant with video coding standards. For example, the most recent video coding standard, H.264/AVC, provides the following tools to overcome transmission errors (Stockhammer *et al.*, 2003 and 2005), (Sulivan & Wiegand, 2005) and (Wenger, 2003):

- Slice based video coding
- Flexible macroblock ordering (FMO)
- Arbitrary slice ordering (ASO)
- Data partitioning
- Redundant slices
- Switching (SI/SP) pictures

However, they cannot fully overcome the limitation of single layer video coding; namely, parts of decoded frames are still subject to errors or the cost of the rate overhead could be prohibitive. The rate overhead becomes even more costly, when error resilient techniques are employed without any consideration on the underlying radio channel condition.

Error concealment techniques target at the restoration of corrupted video frames and they are performed at the decoder as a post processing step. Most of error concealment techniques restore corrupted portions in video frames based on the information in error-free regions. For this reason, the performance of error concealment techniques is often unsatisfactory since the decoded frames still contain erroneous portions. The work of Wang *et al.* (2000 and 2005) provided a comprehensive overview of error resilient techniques for wireless/mobile video delivery.

To overcome the limitation of error resilient techniques in the single layer video coding, the joint video team (JVT) has standardized a scalable extension of H.264/AVC, which will be briefly reviewed in Section 4.1.

2.3 Cross-Layer Design

Discussion in Section 2.1 suggests that the dynamic service environment caused by the random time-varying radio channel and the unequal importance of video data imposes main challenges on the development of an efficient wireless/mobile video streaming system. Moreover, if error control techniques introduced in Section 2.2 are employed without considering other layers, their performance is limited and the end-user quality cannot be guaranteed. To address these challenges, we may consider an adaptive network that is responsive to the dynamic environment. Since the rigid layered architecture of the conventional network systems does not offer a good solution, a recent trend in network design is to consider the cooperation among different network layers, called a cross-layer design approach. This will be detailed in this subsection.

2.3.1 Concepts and Definitions

The cross-layer design allows the interaction among layers of a network system. Although the term "cross-layer" only appeared recently, its basic concept can be found in the context of Internet-based Quality-of-Service (QoS) architectures (Braden & Clark, 1994; Blake, Black, Carlson, Davies, Wang & Weiss, 1998; and Xiao & Ni, 1999), where QoS classes are defined by time sensitivity of certain applications. The QoS architectures attempt to overcome the limitation of the best effort service and offer the primitive form of cross-layer design.

In the beginning, cross-layer design research has concentrated on the modification and extension of the conventional network architecture to overcome the shortcomings of the Internet. For example, the addition of Explicit Congestion Notification (ECN) to TCP/IP (Ramakrishnan, Floyd & Black, 2001) addressed the issue of wireless TCP/IP networks that misinterprets packet errors as network congestion. More recently, Shakkotai *et al.* (2003) initiated the cross-layer design as the overall network system design. Srivastave and Motani (2005) viewed the cross-layer design as a protocol design by the violation of a reference layered communication architecture. A more comprehensive definition of cross-layer design was given by Jurdak (2005) that embraces a wider range of system design aspects.

Regardless of the definition, inter-layer interaction that enables the adaptation of network layers is at the core of the cross-layer design principle. It is not a coincidence that the cross-layer design proposals are more prevalent in wireless networks than wired ones. The requirement for channel adaptation to maximize capacity in wireless networks has naturally led to information passing between the physical layer and upper layers. For this reason, many of early cross-layer proposals have concentrated on the PHY-MAC interactions, which resulted in Adaptive Modulation and Coding (AMC), Hybrid Automatic Repeat reQuest (H-ARQ), channel adaptive scheduling, etc.

2.3.2 Classifications of Cross-Layer Approaches

Cross-layer approaches are classified to provide further insights and a structured view on the cross-layer design principles.

First, we consider the classification by Zhang *et al.* (2005, pp. 124-131) below:

- **End-system centric approach:** The system parameters are controlled by the end-system application, where the end-system refers to a video application system such as the media streaming server. That is, the end-system is responsible for congestion control, error control and power control to maximize the application layer performance (*e.g.*, the quality of streamed *vid*eos at the receiver). This approach has two advantages. First, the cost involved in the construction of a cross-layer system could be low since an extensive modification of the network infrastructure can be avoided. Second, end-user quality maximization can be easily achieved since this approach operates at the application layer. However, it may suffer from a relatively longer system response time because the round trip time (RTT) between a sender and a receiver is longer than that between lower-layer communications. Moreover, the overall system efficiency may degrade significantly because of granularity mismatch in the processing unit (PDU) under a highly dynamic wireless video streaming environment. For example, a video frame may not be decoded properly because of a single bit error at the physical layer.

- **Network-centric approach:** Cross-layer optimization is performed in lower layers of the transmission system. As compared with the end-system centric approach, its advantages lie in faster response time, proper data granularity and easier access to transmission parameters such as the channel coding rate, power level control, etc. However, discrepancy between quality metrics at different layers imposes major issues on this approach. For example, the video application quality metric, the MSE or the peak-signal-to-noise-ratio (PSNR), requires a proper interpretation in terms of lower layer quality metrics such as data throughput, the bit error rate and delay requirements.

Another classification for the cross-layer design was suggested by Van der Schaar & Sai Shankar (2005) as follows.

- **Application-centric approach:** The optimization is performed by application layer protocols. Because of the slower time-scale and the coarser data granularity of the application layer, this approach does not always provide efficient solutions.
- **MAC-centric approach:** The MAC layer determines the optimal transmission strat-

egy based on the information from the application and the physical layers. Since this approach does not involve source coding, it can be disadvantageous for adaptive source channel coding in time varying channel conditions.

- **Integrated approach:** This approach considers strategies of participating layers jointly. However, it may not be practical due to the computational complexity if all possible combinations of each layer's strategies and parameters have to be examined for the optimal solution.

Another classification based on the direction of information flow was also considered by Van der Schaar & Sai Shankar (2005).

- **Top-down approach:** Higher layer protocols serve as the controller of lower layer parameters. For example, the MAC layer parameters and strategies are controlled by the application layer protocols, and the MAC layer protocols determines the physical layer parameters such as channel coding rate, modulation, etc. This approach is most prevalent among cross-layer designs since QoS enabled communication systems can employ this approach and determine lower layer parameters by the QoS class of application data.
- **Bottom-up approach:** Lower layers are insulated from higher layers in losses and bandwidth variations. However, this approach tends to result in delay and unnecessary throughput reduction.

The above categorization schemes may not be mutually exclusive. For example, an application-centric approach may take either a top-down or a bottom-up approach.

3. CROSS-LAYER WIRELESS/ MOBILE VIDEO STREAMING

Due to its capability to deliver better QoS, the cross-layer approach has gained its popularity in the design of wireless service networks as evidenced by a massive number of proposals in the literature. In this section, we begin with the requirements of a cross-layer system and provide a review of representative wireless/mobile video streaming systems based on the cross-layer design.

3.1 Requirements of Cross-Layer Video Streaming Systems

3.1.1 Preliminary Issues

Although the cross-layer approach seems to offer a right choice for the design of wireless/mobile video streaming systems, its success still depends on careful design considerations. Kawadia & Kumar (2005) pointed out the following cautionary aspects of a cross-layer design.

- **Architecture for technology proliferation:** The Internet is a set of interconnected computer networks operating on the standardized common protocol – TCP/IP. Although the World Wide Web (WWW) service has facilitated its commercial success, its technical success is fundamentally rooted on well defined protocols and network architectures. For this reason, it is important for the cross-layer design to have a well defined structure and architecture.

- **Tractability of cross-layer design:** The divide-and-conquer approach offers one of the most effective approaches in deriving solutions to various problems. The component-wise development of a system is advantageous in its maintenance and extension since only the corresponding components have to be considered. In contrast, the cross-layer design demands simultane-

ous consideration of system parameters. For this reason, system maintenance and extension could be problematic with recklessly designed cross-layer systems.

- **Establishment of stability:** Due to its adaptive characteristics, cross-layer systems are necessarily a closed-loop system, which always brings up the system stability issue. To develop a successful cross-layer system, every consequence of cross-layer interaction must be well understood to avoid system instability.

3.1.2 System Requirements

Due to the concerns stated in the above subsection, we discuss requirements for the development of a well-structured cross-layer wireless/mobile video streaming system. Major technical obstacles in the practical deployment of cross-layer systems include: (1) discrepancy between layer parameters, (2) cross-layer information exchange and (3) flexibility of application data. They are detailed below.

3.1.2.1 Abstraction of System Parameters

Inter-layer interaction involves the passing of numerous system parameters. To realize well-structured interaction, it is important to extract representative parameters from each layer and define their proper abstractions. For example, discussion in Section 2.1.2 suggests the prioritization of a video packet based on its contribution to the end quality according to the error propagation model. Thus, we can define the priority index of a video packet based on its MSE profile according to Eq. (1) to enable more efficient information exchange than using the actual MSE value of the video packet directly.

3.1.2.2 Interface for Information Exchange – Cross-layer Signaling

Inter-layer information exchange is not common in the conventional layered architecture. It is however one of the fundamental elements in a cross-layer network architecture. Protocols may be defined or extended from the conventional protocols. Srivastava & Motani (2005) considered three cross-layer information exchanging methods: (1) direct communication between layers, (2) a shared database across layers, and (3) completely new abstraction. To realize efficient information exchange, a new network element that is capable of understanding the cross-layer information is essential while maintaining the conventional network architecture for backward compatibility. The media aware network element (MANE) proposed by Wenger *et al.* (2004) may serve this purpose well since it is acknowledged by the H.264 video payload in RTP packets.

Given the information exchange path, the simplicity of cross-layer operations is also an important issue. The cross-layer design may demand complicated overhead to control the network operation. For example, complex cross-layer algorithms may fail to provide a prompt response to the time-stringent video streaming application. Moreover, complex cross-layer operations may hurt the system stability due to its intractability and unintended consequences.

3.1.2.3 Flexibility of Compressed Videos

To be adaptive to a dynamic communication environment, the flexibility of compressed video data is essential. However, most video coding standards do not provide a sufficient amount of flexibility for network-based video applications as explained in Section 2.2.2. As a consequence, compressed video streams still suffer from error vulnerability due to transmission errors.

Recently, the video coding community has made efforts in increasing flexibility in compressed video data, by adding scalability and/or multiple descriptions of compressed video. In the last two decades, practical deployment of scalable video does not happen in the industry due to the reduction of the coding gain and the additional complexity overhead. More recently, H.264/SVC has been standardized as a scalable extension of

the H.264/AVC standard. With its great flexibility and excellent coding performance inherited from H.264/AVC, H.264/SVC is expected to provide a practical network-based video solution in the near future.

3.2 Cross-layer Wireless/Mobile Video Streaming System

The goal of designing a good video streaming system is to maximize the quality of streamed video at the receive end. Adaptation is at the core of a cross-layer design to overcome the hostile wireless/mobile radio channel. Thus, it is important to understand how *channel adaptation* is performed to overcome the physical obstacle. In this section, we provide a review on cross-layer solutions from a practical point of view by considering the system requirements stated in Section 3.1.2. We first discuss the cross-layer architecture for service differentiation and then adaptive error control algorithms.

3.2.1 Network-Centric Approach - MAC-Centric QoS Control

The network-centric approach is the choice of today's industry, which has been developed based on a well-established conventional QoS architecture. The QoS control unit is often implemented at the MAC layer of a digital communication system. As the middle layer between the application and the physical layers, the MAC layer has a positional advantage in the cross-layer design due to its proximity to the fast varying radio channel.

Figure 2 demonstrates a general QoS support architecture for video applications, where the QoS support is realized by an adaptive QoS mapping unit, a radio channel estimator and a prioritized transmission unit. First, the adaptive QoS mapping unit classifies the application data into a number of MAC-layer QoS classes based on the estimated available channel rate. Then, the prioritized transmission unit realizes differentiated services

Figure 2. QoS support architecture for video applications

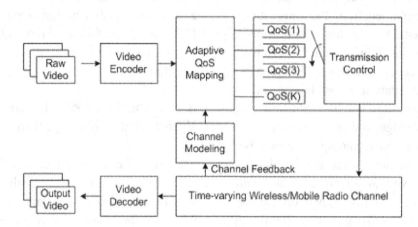

to MAC-layer PDUs of different QoS classes. Although the operation is conceptually simple as the description of the QoS control procedure, the implementation of each component has a number of technical issues.

The fundamental technical issue arises from the requirement of translating different layers' characteristics to the MAC-layer parameters. QoS metrics in the MAC layer includes the data rate, the packet loss rate (PLR), the delay, the delay violation probability etc. On the other hand, the quality of a streamed video is measured by distortion and uninterrupted play-back at the receive end. Since the radio channel condition represented by SNR or SINR does not have direct correspondence to QoS metrics in the MAC layer, the development of efficient cross-layer information exchange is one of the major challenges with the network-centric cross-layer design.

3.2.1.1 End-to-End Cross-Layer QoS Architecture for Wireless Video Delivery

Kumwilaisak *et al.* (2003) proposed an end-to-end cross-layer QoS architecture for wireless video delivery. They concentrated mainly on the wireless last hop such as the wireless connection between a base station (BS) and a mobile station (MS). The proposed architecture embraces system components for end-to-end video delivery, which

include the video codec module, the cross-layer QoS mapping and adaptation module, the link layer packet transmission module, the time varying wireless channel and the adaptive wireless channel modeling module. Main considerations in the design of each module are described in the following.

- **Video encoder/decoder:** Video streams were prepared using MPEG-4 PFGS (Progressive Fine Granular Scalable) video codec to provide flexible compressed video.

- **Wireless channel model:** Since the QoS control unit was implemented at the link layer, a link-layer wireless channel model that assumes the fading, time-variant and non-stationary wireless radio channel was adopted. To reflect the randomness of the radio channel, they employed a discrete-time Markov model, where each state in a Markov chain was combined with the available transmission rate under the current channel condition. In the proposed system, the wireless channel condition was modeled in the adaptive channel modeling module based on the feedback from the physical layer radio channel.

- **Link-layer transmission control module:** Service differentiation among application data of various QoS classes was implemented by the transmission control module. It is implemented by a class-based buffering and scheduling mechanism that employs a strict priority scheduling. Based on effective capacity (EC) theory by Wu & Negi (2003), they computed the rate constraint of each QoS class, which specified the maximum data rate to be transmitted reliably with certain statistical QoS guarantee. The video stream classification and the transmission bandwidth allocation of each QoS class were determined by the rate constraints.

- **Cross-layer QoS mapping and adaptation module:** This QoS control module was the key component of the proposed system that performs the optimal application-to-link layer QoS mapping to the estimated channel condition adaptively. At the application layer, each video packet is labeled by its loss and delay properties and the GOP based optimal QoS mapping is performed based on the rate constraint of each QoS class to maximize video quality at the receive end.

Now, we recall the system requirements in Section 3.1.2 for practical feasibility of the proposed cross-layer QoS architecture. The employment of the MPEG-4 PFGS video codec for video stream preparation resolves the issue of application data flexibility. However, the system parameter abstraction and the cross-layer information exchange could be partially addressed by the proposed QoS architecture only. That is, the delivery of the application layer information to the adaptive QoS mapping module is not clearly presented although a lot of application layer information such as the loss and the delay characteristics, the packet size and the GOP number is used for the video packet classification and in the solution framework.

3.2.1.2 QoS Support of Mobile WiMax

It is important to note that any QoS support architecture must not concentrate on a specific type of application such as video streaming. Since different types of application traffic should coexist in realistic application scenarios, fairness among mixed traffics has to be established. To examine this issue, we provide the QoS support architecture of the IEEE 802.16e standard as an example, which is known as Mobile WiMax.

Mobile WiMax implements service-flow-based QoS support that combines a unidirectional packet flow with particular QoS parameters. The QoS parameters determine the transmission order and scheduling on the air interface such that the connection-oriented QoS support can provide accurate control over the air interface. Specifically, the radio channel state information (CSI) is passed to the scheduler through a Channel Quality Information Channel (CQICH) from user terminals. Moreover, dynamic resource allocation is realized by having the resource allocation information at the beginning of each MAC-layer frame, which is delivered by the Media Access Protocol (MAP). The QoS support in Mobile WiMax is performed by two system components of the classifier and the scheduler, which are responsible for the application packet-to-QoS class mapping and prioritized transmission, respectively.

Mobile WiMax defines five QoS classes based on different application types and their requirements. They are summarized below (Huang *et al.*, 2007).

- **Unsolicited Grant Service (UGS):** This service is designed to support real-time applications that generate constant bit-rate data packets periodically. To reduce the latency, this class of services is granted the radio channel periodically. The QoS of this class is specified by the maximum sustained rate, maximum latency tolerance and jitter tolerance.

- **Real-Time Polling Service (rtPS):** This service is for real-time service flows that generate variable-size data packets periodically. Although this service incurs more request overhead and latency than UGS, it can support the variable-bit-rate (VBR) traffic such as video streaming applications. The QoS of this class is specified by the minimum reserved rate, the maximum sustained rate, maximum latency tolerance, and traffic priority.

- **Extended Real-Time Polling Service (ertPS):** The ertPS supports real-time VBR applications. It is different from rtPS in that it is granted unicast at the BS as the UGS to reduce the latency caused by the bandwidth request. VoIP is the target application of this service, and the QoS is specified by the minimum reserved rate, the maximum sustained rate, maximum latency tolerance, jitter tolerance and traffic priority.

- **Non-Real-Time Polling Service (nrtPS):** The nrtPS is designed to support delay-tolerant applications such as FTP and HTTP. The QoS specification parameters of this service include the minimum reserved rate, the maximum sustained rate and traffic priority.

- **Best Effort Service (BE):** The BE service supports applications with no minimum service requirements and, thus, the service of applications of this class is subject to resource availability. Data transfer applications such as the email service belong to this class, and the QoS are specified by the maximum sustained rate and traffic priority.

Although the cross-layer information can be effectively delivered in a well structured manner with the QoS support architecture of Mobile WiMax, the generic issues with the network-centric cross-layer design still remain. For example, because

Mobile WiMax defines the MAC and the PHY layers only, the resource allocation conveyed in the MAP messages is still subject to the higher layer abstraction of the application traffic that determines the video quality at the receive end.

3.2.2 Application-Centric Approach – Adaptive Error Control

The unequal importance of video packets has naturally brought up a lot of adaptive error control proposals termed unequal error protection (UEP). The basic idea of UEP algorithms is to provide more protection to video packets with higher priority to maximize the quality at the receive end. Forward Error Correction (FEC) and Automatic Repeat request (ARQ) are common techniques to combat transmission errors in the digital communication system, whose preference is dependent on the application data characteristics. Generally, ARQ demonstrates better performance in terms of error protection at the cost of delay. For this reason, the employment of ARQ has to be carefully determined with real-time applications such as video streaming. Modern digital communication systems such as Mobile WiMax and cdma2000 1x EV-DO employ the two techniques in a combined manner, which is termed Hybrid-ARQ (H-ARQ).

3.2.2.1 Communication Channels for Adaptive Error Control

Figure 3 shows the communication channel, where error control techniques may take place. The physical layer is divided into a number of controllable sub-layers, including channel-coding, modulation and power-control sub-layers. Similarly to the network-centric approach, the feedback information (CSI) from the radio channel plays a major role in the adaptive error control. In general, FEC may be applied to PDUs of any layer from the APP layer to the channel coding sub-layer, where the communication delay decreases following the same order. ARQ algorithms are often

Figure 3. Communication channels for adaptive error control

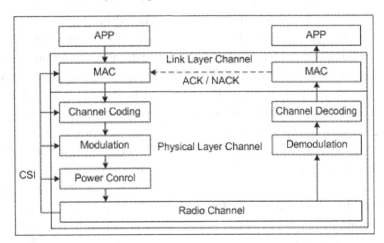

implemented at the link layer based on the link layer feedback message.

In digital communications, the transmission power is a resource regulated by the Federal Communications Commissions (FCC). For the efficient use of the limited resource, Adaptive Modulation and Coding (AMC) techniques are common in the modern communication systems, whose objective is to achieve a pre-specified target bit error rate (BER) at the radio channel adaptively to the channel condition. Moreover, in advanced system design proposals, power control is also considered to provide unequal protection with prioritized data.

3.2.2.2 Joint Source Coding and Optimal Energy Allocation

Katsaggelos *et al.* (2005) presented an overview on a number of energy efficient wireless video techniques considering the energy limited environment of mobile communication. They formulated a distortion optimization problem with source coding (S) and the channel parameters (C) as the variables:

$$\min_{\{S,C\}} D_{tot}(S,C), \text{ subject to } E_{tot}(S,C) \le E_0 \text{ and } T_{tot}(S,C) \le T_0,$$

$$(2)$$

where D, E and T are the distortion at the receiver, consumed energy and the end-to-end delay, respectively, E_0 and T_0 are the maximum allowable energy consumption and end-to-end delay constraint imposed by the application .

Based on the problem formulation in Eq. (2), they introduced three optimization problems (*i.e.,* joint source coding and power adaptation, joint source-channel coding and power adaptation, and joint source coding and data rate adaptation) and used the power level and the transmission rate as part of a UEP mechanism. More specifically, they have employed the distortion and the channel model to determine the solution to the optimization problem. First, the radio channel is modeled by the packet loss rate that is expressed as a function of transmission power, the channel status information and the transmission rate assigned to a packet. Then, the end-to-end distortion is modeled by the packet loss rate in the solution framework. They have assumed flexible source coding parameters for video preparation and error concealment techniques as a post processing.

This chapter and the references therein provide detailed analysis on the problem and the solution framework, which have demonstrated great potential and presented important theoretical fundamentals of the joint source coding and channel optimization (JSCC) techniques. However, they are still subject to several practical issues. First, the cross-layer information exchange is implicitly assumed in the solution framework, which is one of the most important issues in the practical employment of cross-layer solutions. Second, although the wireless channel is modeled as a packet loss network, the connection between the packet loss probability and the physical layer parameters such as the fading effect is not clearly identified.

3.2.2.3 Systematic Cross-layer Approach to Wireless Video Streaming

Shan (2005) has proposed a systematic approach to the wireless video streaming application. The cross-layer wireless video streaming system was implemented by three schemes of (1) application layer packetization, (2) class-based UEP and (3) priority-based ARQ (P-ARQ). The UDP-Lite employed in the proposed system overcomes the inefficiency caused by the TCP based service implementation. Moreover, the proposed system implements the application-to-link layer retransmission request by the property of UDP-Lite that allows the delivery of corrupted packets to the application layer.

The system description is detailed below.

- **Application layer packetization:** The application layer packetization performs the decomposition of the application layer packets into an integer number of equal-sized RLP packets. The identification of corrupted RLP packets can be easily performed at the application layer of the receiver because the integer number of RLP payload blocks is combined with corresponding 4 bit sequence number. Then, the receiver side application layer determines the retransmission request based on the knowledge of the FEC level for that class of application data. Another important system feature achieved by this application layer packetization is the operational es-

timation of the wireless channel condition based on the loss statistics of RLP packets. The channel estimation is then used to determine the optimal FEC level for each class of application data at the sender side.

- **Class-based UEP:** MPEG-4 video coding standard is employed for the application data preparation in the proposed work, where different parts of a compressed bit stream are classified into 4 classes according to their importance and dependency of frames:
  - **Class 0:** Header information;
  - **Class 1:** I and P frames with scene change;
  - **Class 2:** Shape and motion information of P frames;
  - **Class 3:** Texture information of P frames.

  Then, a block-based Reed-Solomon (RS) code is applied for the error protection of different classes, where the protection level is adaptively determined by the application data class and the estimated channel condition.

- **P-ARQ:** With the P-ARQ scheme, application data with different classes are assigned of different number of retransmission request limits. That is, once an application packet is identified to be erroneous, the retransmission request for the corresponding RLP packet is determined by the expected decoding time of the application data and the remaining number of retransmission requests. The expected decoding time is determined by the round trip time (RTT) and the current decoder buffer status in terms of play-back time and its consideration provides the minimal play-back interrupt given the system parameters such as the round trip time (RTT).

The major advantage of the proposed system comes from its realistic design that provides compatibility with conventional data communication systems. Because only the application layer is subject to the complex implementation, the burden of re-designing underlying data communication network could be kept at a reasonably low level. In the proposed system, the cross-layer information exchange is implicitly enabled by the application packetization scheme. Moreover, they developed a simple cross-layer operation, *i.e.*, the prioritized application-to-link layer retransmission request based on the expected decoding time, which does not incur huge complexity overhead in the system operation. Although the video format in the proposal is not flexible, the basic idea of video packet prioritization should be applicable to other flexible video formats with slight modification. Another important feature is channel adaptation of the proposed system. That is, channel estimation is performed at the receiver end to adaptively determine the proper FEC rate for different classes of video packets, which tends to be incapable of catching fast channel fluctuations. Besides, the application layer channel estimation is employed without proper justification, and its performance and validity were simply demonstrated by simulation results.

We will show in the next section that the application channel estimation may suffice for wireless video streaming applications, which should relieve video streaming systems from tracing a wireless radio channel of fast fluctuation.

4. TOWARD PRACTICAL CROSS-LAYER VIDEO STREAMING SYSTEM

In this section, we consider the development of a practical cross-layer video streaming system for wireless/mobile networks. We employ H.264/SVC as the video codec and assume a MANE at the proximity of the BS for cross-layer information exchange. By analyzing the video streaming characteristics and its sensitivity to channel fluctuation, we propose an efficient and effective cross-layer video streaming system.

4.1 H.264/SVC for Wireless/Mobile Video Streaming

For the practical employment of a cross-layer video streaming system, it is essential to have a standardized infrastructure that enables the cross-layer system design. In this section, we describe efforts of the standardization bodies to establish such an infrastructure. Specifically, we consider H.264/SVC for the video stream preparation and the RTP/UDP/IP protocol stack for video delivery in a packet-based network environment.

H.264/SVC is a recently standardized scalable video codec based on the state-of-the-art H.264/AVC standard. It provides great flexibility of compressed video by its temporal (T), spatial (D), and quality/SNR (Q) scalability. A scalable bit stream is generated in such a way that a global bit stream carries embedded bit streams of combined scalable layers (T, D and Q) and the scaling operation is performed simply by discarding higher scalable layer bit streams from the global bit stream to produce a sub-bit stream composed of lower scalable layer bit streams. In a global bit stream, lower scalable layer bit streams are used as references for the encoding of higher scalable layers and, thus, the dependence chain is naturally formed following the scalability structure. The scaling operation always corresponds to the temporal/spatial down sampling or quality degradation of a global scalable bit stream, and it is important to consider inter-dependency of each scalable layer when discarding higher scalable layer bit streams.

The H.264/AVC standard assumes network-based video applications in its design. It defines a Network Abstraction Layer (NAL) unit as its basic processing unit. There are two types of NAL units: (1) Video Coding Layer (VCL) NAL units and (2) non-VCL NAL units. Compressed video data are stored in VCL NAL units, and non-VCL NAL units contain supplemental enhancement information (SEI), parameter sets, picture delimiter, or filler data. Each NAL unit is combined with 1 byte NAL unit header that contains the abstraction

Figure 4. The NAL unit header of H.264/SVC

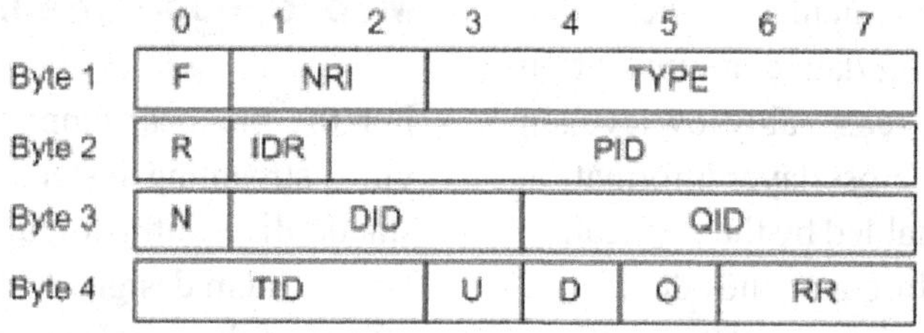

	0	1	2	3	4	5	6	7
Byte 1	F	NRI		TYPE				
Byte 2	R	IDR		PID				
Byte 3	N	DID			QID			
Byte 4	TID				U	D	O	RR

of the NAL unit payload such as the NAL unit type and the non-reference indicator. An extension of the NALU header is defined for H.264/SVC video, which contains various identifier flags to signal the priority and the scalable layers (D, T and Q) of the corresponding NALU payload as shown in Figure 4. Among different identifiers, the 6-bit PID does not have any influence on the decoding of H.264/SVC video. Instead, it is defined to store the operator/user defined priority of the corresponding NAL unit.

Given the flexibility and abstraction of compressed video, the next step is to establish the information interface between the application layer and the underlying network layers. For packet based wireless video streaming, the RTP/UDP/IP protocol stack is a common choice as an alternative to the conventional TCP/IP protocol stack. In RFC 3984, the RTP payload format for H.264 video is used to allow packetization of one or more NAL units in each RTP payload. RFC 3984 also introduces an important network interface element called the media aware network element (MANE), which is capable of parsing the NAL unit header information of H.264/SVC video. With the existence of the MANE, the abstraction of application layer data (H.264/SVC video) can be successfully passed to the lower network layer protocol stacks to enable the cross-layer operation for system performance enhancement.

4.2 Characteristics of Wireless/Mobile Video Streaming Application

In this section, we examine the operational characteristics of scalable video streaming in a wireless/mobile environment. We assume that video streams are pre-encoded so that adaptive source encoding is not considered in the following discussion. First, we discuss two idealistic video streaming application scenarios based on a non-scalable video and a scalable video, where the channel rates are fully known. Figure 4 shows the application scenarios characterized by a number of characteristics curves. In Figure 5(a), $s(t)$, $r(t)$ and $p(t)$ are the cumulative source rate, the channel rate, and the play-back characteristic curves, respectively, and subscripts in Figure 4(b) indicates scalable layers.

We determine the initial delay (d_{init}) that guarantees uninterrupted play-back of a streamed video given the source and the channel rate. That is, in Figure 4(a), uninterrupted play-back can be guaranteed if the play-back curve, $p(t)$, is always less or equal to the channel rate, $r(t)$. Mathematically, we have

$$p(t) = s(t - d_{init}) \leq r(t), \text{ for } d_{init} \leq t \leq d_{init} + T_{src},$$
(3)

where T_{src} is the length of the video source. There are two issues with this scenario in a practical video streaming system. First, it is not realistic to assume the full channel knowledge so that d_{init} cannot be determined based on the channel con-

Figure 5. Operational application characteristics

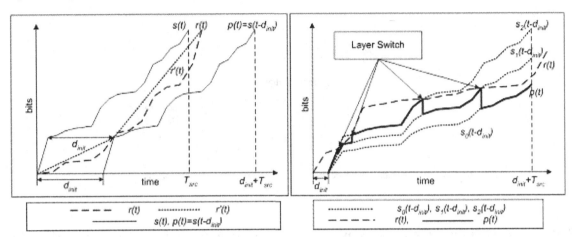

(a) Non-scalable video streaming   (b) Scalable video streaming

dition. Second, the video streaming application is not sensitive to fast radio channel fluctuation. For example, the piece-wise linear channel rate characterized by $r'(t)$ in Figure 4(a) should lead to the same decision of d_{init}. The second observation suggests an important implication for the design of a wireless/mobile video streaming system that the only required channel information for video streaming is the average rate of an interval and, as a result, communication systems can be relieved from the burden of tracking the fast fluctuation of radio channels. This also justifies the validity of the application layer channel estimation introduced in Section 3.2.2.3 that the time granularity of the application channel estimation does not degrade the performance of the video streaming system.

Now, we consider a more realistic scenario, where the play-back begins without an assumption of the full channel knowledge. Then, the condition in Eq. (3) may be violated causing the intermediate play-back interruptions with non-scalable video streams. Under this setting, the scalability of compressed video data can be beneficial. Figure 4(b) illustrates such a scenario with a scalable video of 3 layers represented by $s_0(t)$, $s_1(t)$ and

$s_2(t)$, respectively. In the figure, the play-back begins at d_{init} without considering the future channel condition. Then, the layer switch occurs to avoid the play-back interrupt (low channel rate) or to provide higher video quality (high channel rate). The layer switching operation can be formulated mathematically by

$$p(t) = \arg\max_{i=1,\dots,N_L-1} s_i(t) \;\; \text{subject to } p(t) \le r(t), \;\; \text{for } d_{init} \le t \le d_{init}+T_{src},$$

(4)

where N_L is the number of layers in a scalable video stream. The problem in Eq. (4) is a quality maximization problem under the constraint of resources such as transmission rate and time, since the presence of higher layers corresponds to higher quality of a scalable video.

The streaming scenario in Figure 4(b) is still idealistic in that the layer switch occurs exactly at the intersections between $r(t)$ and $s_i(t - d_{init})$. However, it is clear from the discussion that an efficient layer switching algorithm should realize a good video streaming system in a more realistic environment.

Figure 6. Scalable video streaming system architecture

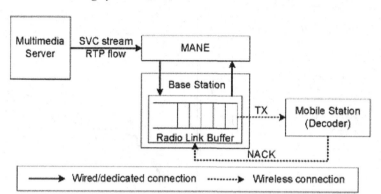

4.3 H.264/SVC Based Cross-Layer Wireless/Mobile Video Streaming

We examine a wireless video streaming system in Figure 6 based on previous discussion. Once the video streaming service is initiated, the H.264/SVC bit stream is encapsulated into RTP payloads and delivered to a MANE through a packet switching network. Then, the MANE performs the RTP-to-RLP packetization while keeping the RTP-to-RLP mapping information for the cross-layer operation. Under this setting, we need an efficient packet selection algorithm that finds an optimal subset of scalable video for an uninterrupted play-back at the receive end.

Consider a GOP as the basic optimization unit so that the system is responsive to the average channel condition. The GOP-based priority information of each video packet is conveyed in the NAL unit header to enable prioritized the RLP packet transmission. The priority identifier (PID_{RLP}) of an RLP packet maintained in the RTP-to-RLP mapping table at the MANE is determined by

$$PID_{RLP} = PID \cdot 2^{10} + DID \cdot 2^7 + QID \cdot 2^3 + TID, \quad (5)$$

where DID, QID, and TID are the scalable layer identifiers. The GOP number of the video packet is stored in PID to enable the GOP based priori-

tized packet transmission. Given the prioritized RLP packets, two mechanisms of the GOP-based prioritized packet and the wireless congestion control are implemented at the radio link layer to guarantee continuous play-back at the receive end. The radio link buffer management mechanism performs post-channel adaptation based on the decoder buffer status, which eliminates the estimation of the future channel condition.

With the prioritized transmission control algorithm, the head-of-line (HOL) packet in the radio link buffer is transmitted only when the decoder buffer contains an enough amount of data to play for a GOP duration. Here, we assumed that RLP packets are stored in the radio link buffer in the order of priority. The priority transmission mechanism tries to maintain the decoder buffer at a constant level in terms of play-back time. The congestion control mechanism is triggered when the decoder buffer level drops below a GOP duration to avoid the decoder buffer underflow. It performs a GOP-based packet drop such that all RLP packets belonging to the current GOP are discarded in the radio link buffer at the transmitter in case of wireless congestion. The decoder buffer status is inferred from the highest RLP packet number with NACK by assuming continuous retransmission of failed packets.

Figure 7 demonstrates the simulation result of the cross-layer radio link buffer management mechanism, where the channel rate variation for

Figure 7. Simulation results

a. Channel rate

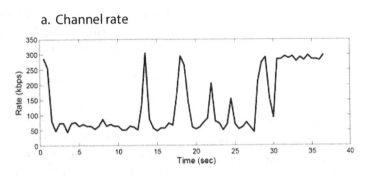

b. Video quality at the streaming client (Δ: initial delay)

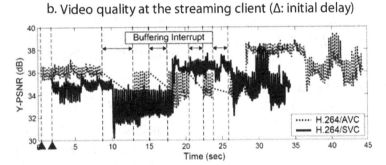

the simulation duration is plotted in Figure 7(a) at every 0.5 sec. For the performance comparison, the input video is encoded into a non-scalable H.264/AVC and a scalable H.264/SVC formats in the simulation. The source rates of the non-scalable and the scalable bit streams are 132.7 kbps and 137.2 kbps, respectively. The streaming results of the two video formats are shown in Figure 7(b), where play-back of the non-scalable video is frequently corrupted by the buffering interrupt due to the decoder underflow. In contrast, the scalable video streaming enables smooth play-back at the receiver without any interrupt. The simulation results clearly show the benefit of the cross-layer design for wireless video streaming.

5. CONCLUSION

In this chapter, we examined a cross-layer approach to wireless/mobile video streaming system design. We specified the time-varying random radio channel, the unequal importance of video data and the time constraint of the streaming applications as the major challenges to overcome. We also introduced the cautionary perspective of cross-layer design along with the system requirements. Representative proposals have been reviewed along with comments on their advantages and possible enhancements. Finally, we examined the design of a realistic video streaming system based on a cross-layer approach.

Cross-layer design of a video streaming is a challenging task since every aspect of the system components has to be carefully considered. It is a huge topic that embraces three major research fields; namely, video coding, computer networks, and digital communications. Hence, discussion in this chapter may be neither sufficient nor complete. However, the important aspects of the cross-layer approach to the design of wireless/mobile video streaming system have been mostly covered in this chapter. We encourage more interested readers to follow the additional readings provided at the end of this chapter.

REFERENCES

Ajib, W., & Haccoun, D. (2005). An overview of scheduling algorithms in MIMO-based fourth-generation wireless systems. *IEEE Network*, *19*(5), 43–48. doi:10.1109/MNET.2005.1509951

Blake, S., Black, D., Carlson, M., Davies, E., Wang, Z., & Weiss, W. (1998). *An architecture for differentiated services, RFC-2475. Internet Engineering Task Force.* IETF.

Braden, R., Clark, D., & Shenker, S. (1994). *Integrated services in the Internet architecture: An overview, RFC-1633. Internet Engineering Task Force.* IETF.

Cavers, J. K. (2000). *Mobile Channel Characteristics*. Hingham, MA: Kluwer Academic Publishers.

Fattah, H., & Leung, C. (2002). An overview of scheduling algorithms in wireless multimedia networks. *IEEE Wireless Communications*, *9*(5), 76–83. doi:10.1109/MWC.2002.1043857

Girod, B., & Fäber, N. (2001). Wireless Video. In Sun, M.-T., & Reibman, A. R. (Eds.), *Compressed Video over Networks* (pp. 465–511). New York: Marcel Dekker.

Huang, C., Juan, H.-H., Lin, M.-S., & Chang, C.-J. (2007). Radio resource management of heterogeneous services in Mobile WiMax systems. *IEEE Wireless Communications*, *14*(1), 20–26. doi:10.1109/MWC.2007.314547

Jurdak, R. (2007). *Wireless ad hoc and sensor networks: A cross-layer design perspective*. New York: Springer-Verlag.

Katsaggelos, A. K., Zhai, F., Eisenberg, Y., & Berry, R. (2005). Energy efficient wireless video coding and delivery. *IEEE Wireless Communications*, *12*(4), 24–30. doi:10.1109/MWC.2005.1497855

Kawadia, V., & Kumar, P. R. (2005). A cautionary perspective of cross-layer design. *IEEE Wireless Communications*, *12*(1), 3–11. doi:10.1109/MWC.2005.1404568

Kumwilaisak, W., Hou, Y. T., Zhang, Q., Zhu, W., Kuo, C.-C. J., & Zhang, Y.-Q. (2003). A cross-layer Quality-of-Service mapping architecture for video delivery in wireless networks. *IEEE Journal on Selected Areas in Communications*, *21*(10), 1685–1698. doi:10.1109/JSAC.2003.816445

Lin, S., & Costello, D. J. (1995). *Error Control Coding: Fundamentals and Applications*. Englewood Cliffs, NJ: Prentice Hall.

Proakis, J. G. (2001). *Digital Communications* (4th ed.). New York: McGraw Hill.

Ramakrishnan, K., Floyd, S., & Black, D. (2001). *The addition of Explicit Congestion Notification (ECN) to IP, RFC-3168, Internet Engineering Task Force.* IETF.

Richardson, I. E. (2003). *H.264 and MPEG-4 video compression*. New York: John Wiley & Sons. doi:10.1002/0470869615

Shakkottai, S., Rappaport, T. S., & Karlsson, P. S. (2003). Cross-layer design for wireless networks. *IEEE Communications Magazine*, *41*(10), 74–80. doi:10.1109/MCOM.2003.1235598

Shan, Y. (2005). Cross-layer techniques for adaptive video streaming over wireless networks. *EURASIP Journal on Applied Signal Processing*, (2): 220–228. doi:10.1155/ASP.2005.220

Srivastava, V., & Motani, M. (2005). Cross-layer design: A survey and the road ahead. *IEEE Communications Magazine*, *43*(12), 112–119. doi:10.1109/MCOM.2005.1561928

Stockhammer, T., & Hannuksela, M. M. (2005). H.264/AVC video for wireless transmission. *IEEE Wireless Communication*, *12*(4), 6–13. doi:10.1109/MWC.2005.1497853

Stockhammer, T., Hannuksela, M. M., & Wiegand, T. (2003). H.264/AVC in wireless environments. *IEEE Transactions on Circuits and Systems for Video Technology, 13*(7), 657–673. doi:10.1109/TCSVT.2003.815167

Sullivan, G. J., & Wiegand, T. (2005). Video compression – from concepts to the H.264/AVC standard. *Proceedings of the IEEE, 93*(1), 18–31. doi:10.1109/JPROC.2004.839617

Van der Schaar, M., & Sai Shanker, N. (2005). Cross-layer wireless multimedia transmission: Challenges, principles, and new paradigms. *IEEE Wireless Communications, 12*(4), 50–58. doi:10.1109/MWC.2005.1497858

Wang, Y., Wenger, S., Wen, J., & Katsaggelos, K. (2000). Error resilient video coding tecnniques. *IEEE Signal Processing Magazine*, 61–82. doi:10.1109/79.855913

Wang, Y., & Zhu, Q.-F. (2005). Error control and concealment for video communication: A review. *Proceedings of the IEEE, 86*(5), 974–997. doi:10.1109/5.664283

Wenger, S. (2003). H.264/AVC over IP. *IEEE Transactions on Circuits and Systems for Video Technology, 13*(7), 645–656. doi:10.1109/TCSVT.2003.814966

Wenger, S., Hanuksela, M., Stockhammer, T., Westerlund, M., & Singer, D. (2004). *RTP payload format for H.264 Video, RFC-3984, Internet Engineering Task Force*. IETF.

Wu, D., & Negi, R. (2003). Effective capacity: A wireless link model for support of Quality of Service. *IEEE Transactions on Wireless Communications, 2*(4), 630–643.

Xiao, X., & Ni, M. L. (1999). Internet QoS: A Big Picture. *IEEE Network, 13*(2), 8–18. doi:10.1109/65.768484

Zhang, Q., Zhu, W., & Zhang, Y. (2005). End-to-end QoS for video delivery over wireless Internet. *Proceedings of the IEEE, 93*(1), 123–134. doi:10.1109/JPROC.2004.839603

ADDITIONAL READING

Albanese, A., Blomer, J., Edmonds, J., & Luby, M. (1996). Priority Encoding Transmission. *IEEE Transactions on Information Theory, 42*(6), 1737–1744. doi:10.1109/18.556670

Chou, P. A., & Miao, Z. (2006). Rate-distortion optimized streaming of packetized media. *IEEE Transactions on Multimedia, 8*(2), 390–404. doi:10.1109/TMM.2005.864313

Girod, B., & Fäber, N. (1999). Feedback-based error control for mobile video transmission. *Proceedings of the IEEE, 87*(10), 1707–1723. doi:10.1109/5.790632

Goldsmith, A. (2005). *Wireless Communications*. New York: Cambridge University Press.

He, Z., Cai, J., & Chen, C. W. (2002). Joint source-channel rate-distortion analysis for adaptive mode selection and rate control in wireless video coding. *IEEE Transactions on Circuits and Systems for Video Technology, 12*(6), 511–523. doi:10.1109/TCSVT.2002.800313

Le Boudec, J. Y., & Thiran, P. (2001). *Network calculus: a theory of deterministic queueing systems for the Internet*. New York: Springer.

Li, Q., & Van Der Schaar, M. (2004). Providing adaptive QoS to layered video over wireless local area networks through real-time retry limit adaptation. *IEEE Transactions on Multimedia, 6*(2), 278–290. doi:10.1109/TMM.2003.822792

Liu, Q., Zhou, S., & Giannakis, G. B. (2004). Cross-layer combining of adaptive modulation and coding with truncated ARQ over wireless links. *IEEE Transactions on Wireless Communications, 3*(5), 1746–1755. doi:10.1109/TWC.2004.833474

Liu, Q., Zhou, S., & Giannakis, G. B. (2005). Queueing with adaptive modulation and coding over wireless links: Cross-layer analysis and design. *IEEE Transactions on Wireless Communications, 4*(2), 1141–1153.

Naghshineh, M., & Willebeek-LeMair, M. (1997). End to end QoS provisioning multimedia wireless/mobile network using an adaptive framework. *IEEE Communications Magazine, 35*(11), 72–81. doi:10.1109/35.634764

Rappaport, T. S. (1996). *Wireless Communications: principles and practice.* Englewood Cliffs, NJ: Prentice Hall.

Schwarz, H., Marpe, D., & Wiegand, T. (2006). Overview of the scalable video coding extension of H.264/AVC standard. *IEEE Transactions on Circuits and Systems for Video Technology, 17*(9), 1102–1120.

Shin, J., Kim, J., Kim, J. W., & Kuo, C.-C. J. (2001). Dynamic QoS mapping control for streaming video in relative service differentiation networks. *European Transactions on Telecommunications, 12*(3), 217–230. doi:10.1002/ett.4460120309

Shin, J., Kim, J., & Kuo, C.-C. J. (2001). Quality-of-service mapping mechanism for packet video in differentiated services network. *IEEE Transactions on Multimedia, 3*(2), 219–231. doi:10.1109/6046.923821

Stockhammer, T., Jeankač, H., & Kuhn, G. (2004). Streaming video over variable bit-rate wireless channels. *IEEE Transactions on Multimedia, 6*(2), 268–277. doi:10.1109/TMM.2003.822795

Sun, M.-T., & Reibman, A. R. (Eds.). (2001). *Compressed Video over Networks.* Hingham, MA: Kluwer Academic Publishers.

Van der Schaar, Krishnamachari, M. S., Choi, S., & Xu, X. (2003). Adaptive cross-layer protection strategies for robust scalable video transmission over 802.11 WLANs. *IEEE Journal on Selected Areas in Communications, 21*(10), 1752–1763. doi:10.1109/JSAC.2003.815231

Wang, H. S., & Moayeri, N. (1995). Finite-state Markov channel – a useful model for radio communication channels. *IEEE Transactions on Vehicular Technology, 44*(1), 163–171. doi:10.1109/25.350282

Wiegand, T., Sullivan, G. J., Bitengaard, G., & Luthra, A. (2003). Overview of the H.264/AVC video coding standard. *IEEE Transactions on Circuits and Systems for Video Technology, 13*(7), 560–576. doi:10.1109/TCSVT.2003.815165

Wu, D., Hou, Y. T., & Zhange, Y. Q. (2001). Streaming video over the Internet: approaches and directions. *IEEE Transactions on Circuits and Systems for Video Technology, 11*(3), 282–300. doi:10.1109/76.911156

Chapter 7
Bitrate Adaptation of Scalable Bitstreams in a UMTS Environment

Nicolas Tizon
TELECOM ParisTech, France

Béatrice Pesquet-Popescu
TELECOM ParisTech, France

ABSTRACT

In this chapter, we propose a complete streaming framework for a wireless, in particular a 3G/UMTS, network environment. We describe choices one can make in terms of network architecture and then focus on the input parameters used to evaluate network conditions and to perform the adaptation. A particular attention is dedicated to the protocol information one can exploit in order to infer the channel state. In addition, each implementation choice is a compromise between the industrial feasibility and the adaptation efficiency.

INTRODUCTION

Bitrate adaptation is a key issue when considering streaming applications involving throughput limited networks with error prone channels, as wireless networks (Girod, Kalman, Liang & Zhang, 2004). Concerning the availability of real time values of the network parameters like resource allocation among users or channel error rate, it is worth noticing that today, in a majority of practical cases, the media server is far away from the bottleneck links, thus preventing real time adaptation. Classically, only long term feedbacks

DOI: 10.4018/978-1-61692-831-5.ch007

like RTCP reports can be used to perform estimations. In the same time, the emergence of recent source coding standards like the scalable extension of H.264/AVC (Wiegand, Sullivan, Bjontegaard & Luthra, 2003; ISO/IEC & ITU-T Rec., 2003), namely Scalable Video Coding (SVC) (Schwarz, Marpe & Wiegand, 2006; Reichel, Schwarz & Wien, 2007), that allows to encode in the same bitstream a wide range of spatio-temporal and quality layers, offers new adaptation facilities (Wang, Hannuksela & Pateux, 2007; Amonou, Cammas, Kervadec & Pateux, 2007). Standardized scalability domains (spatial, temporal and SNR) can also be completed by a Region Of Interest (ROI) approach (Tizon & Pesquet-Popescu,

Copyright © 2011, IGI Global. Copying or distributing in print or electronic forms without written permission of IGI Global is prohibited.

2007; Tizon & Pesquet-Popescu, 2008) in order to improve the perceived quality. The concept of scalability, when exploited for dynamic channel adaptation purposes, raises at least two kinds of issues: how to measure network conditions and how to differentiate transmitted data in terms of distortion contribution?

Firstly, in order to select the appropriate subset of scalable layers, a specific network entity must be able to parse the SVC high level syntax and to derive the transmission conditions from the specific protocol feedbacks. Hence, we need to define an architecture to specify the localization of adaptation operations and which protocols are used to infer the channel characteristics. In this chapter, we propose and compare two different approaches in terms of network architecture in order to comply with different practical requirements. The first approach consists in not modifying the existing network infrastructure and keeping the adaptation operations in the server that exploits long term feedbacks, like RTCP reports (Wenger, Sato, Burmeister & Rey, 2006), from the client. To our knowledge, the framework proposed by Baldo, Horn, Kampmann and Hartung (2004) is one of the most developed solutions, that allows to control the sent data rate and to infer network and client parameters based on RTCP feedbacks. The main purpose of the described algorithm is to avoid packet congestion in the network and client buffer starvation. This first solution can be integrated very easily in an existing video streaming framework, but its adaptation abilities are quite low.

On the other hand, the second approach consists in a video streaming system that uses SVC coding in order to adapt the input stream at the radio link layer as a function of the available bandwidth, thanks to a Media Aware Network Element (MANE) (Wenger, Wang & Schierl, 2009) that assigns priority labels to video packets. In this way, a generic wireless multi-user video streaming system with a MANE that assigns priority labels to video packets was proposed by Liebl,

Schierl, Wiegand and Stockhammer (2006). In the proposed approach, a drop priority based (DPB) radio link buffer management strategy (Liebl, Jenkac, Stockhammer & Buchner, 2005) is used to keep a finite queue before the bottleneck link. The main drawback of this method is that the efficiency of the source bitrate adaptation depends on buffer dimensioning and with this approach, video packets are transmitted without considering their reception deadlines. In this chapter, we will discuss where to introduce the MANE in order to enable both network condition estimation and SVC bitstream parsing. This approach is no longer compliant with the OSI model but provides finer adaptation capabilities.

In the scope of packetized media streaming over best-effort networks and more precisely channel adaptive video streaming, Chou and Miao (2001) described a rate-distortion optimized (RaDiO) scheduling algorithm that has been extended in many recent works (Setton, 2003; Chakareski & Apostolopoulos, 2005; Chakareski & Frossard, 2006; Chakareski & Chou, 2006). The use of scalable coded streams brings new perspectives and also raises new problems in the field of content aware adaptive video streaming algorithms. In the SVC standard, the high level syntax (Wiegand, Sullivan, Reichel, Schwarz & Wien, 2007) permits to parse the bitstream and to assign priorities to packets based on their dependencies to others packets for the decoding process. These syntax elements provide interesting information to differentiate packets following their importance and without adding complexity to the scheduling algorithm. However, this approach does not take into account the content of the video packets and does not use distortion measurements. Hence, in this chapter, we present a recursive distortion model, which is used to dynamically calculate the contribution of each packet to the final distortion. Coupled with channel capacity information obtained from client feedbacks, this distortion information is used to perform an adaptive packet scheduling algorithm which aims at maximizing the perceived quality at the decoder side.

NETWORK ARCHITECTURE AND PROTOCOLS

Video Streaming Issues

As described in Figure 1, when congestion is measured on the network, is crucial to precisely evaluate the reception deadline of each packet in order to optimize resource utilization. When designing a streaming system one of the key configuration parameter is the maximum end-to-end delay from which one can calculate these reception deadlines. In the illustrated example, the client is composed of a client buffer preceding a decoder and a display stage. Actually a second buffer must be positioned between the decoder and the monitor in order to synchronize the display. Here for simplicity, we assume that encoding and decoding delays are null. Packets are regularly sent following the video frame rate $1/T_e$ (e.g. $T_e = 33\,\text{ms}$) in the display order and they are decoded/displayed with the same frequency at client buffer output. We assume also that packets are received in the same order they have been transmitted by the server. Let us denote D_i the transmission delay of the packet conveying the $(i+1)^{th}$ frame which timestamp is given by $i \times T_e$. The length of the represented client buffer can be seen as the cumulated lengths of pre-decoding and post-decoding buffers. Let us denote T_{buf} the time interval equivalent to this buffer length. This value is fixed by the server at the beginning of the session in response to a "RTSP PLAY" request, through the appropriated header fields (3GPP, TS 26.234, 2009):

- x-initpredecbufperiod:<initial pred-decoder buffering period>

- x-initpostdecbufperiod:<initial post-decoder buffering period>

These two fields represent the buffering delay respectively before and after the decoder. The value of T_{buf} is obtained by adding the values of these two fields. In the given example, $T_{buf} = 4 \times T_e$.

In Figure 1, a transmission scenario with congestion and late delivery of video packets is illustrated:

a. The first picture is sent by the server ($t=0$).
b. Packets are accumulated in the client buffer and the first picture is displayed after an initial buffering delay T_0.
c. The network becomes congested and the client buffer is empty.
d. After the congestion period, packets reach the client and can be discarded if the reception deadline is past.

The initial delay T_0 is the time spent by the network to fill the reception buffer. In the given example, $T_0 = 4 \times T_e + D_4 = T_{buf} + D_4$. At time $T_0 + 5 \times T_e$, due to congestion, there are no longer decoded pictures available to be displayed, which typically causes image frozen. Then, the network transmits the accumulated packets to the client. The packet with index 5 arrives to the decoder after its reception deadlines and is discarded. For a given picture with index i, a necessary condition to be decoded at time is:

$$i \times T_e + D_i < T_0 + i \times T_e \Leftrightarrow D_i < T_0 \qquad (1)$$

When packets are sent with the video refresh cadence by the server, their transmission delays need to be inferior to the initial buffering delay in order to be received at time. This condition can also be written $D_i > T_{buf} + D_j$ where $j+1$ is the number of pictures stored in the client buffer during the initial buffering period (j=4 in the

Figure 1. Transmission scenario with congestion and late delivery of video packets

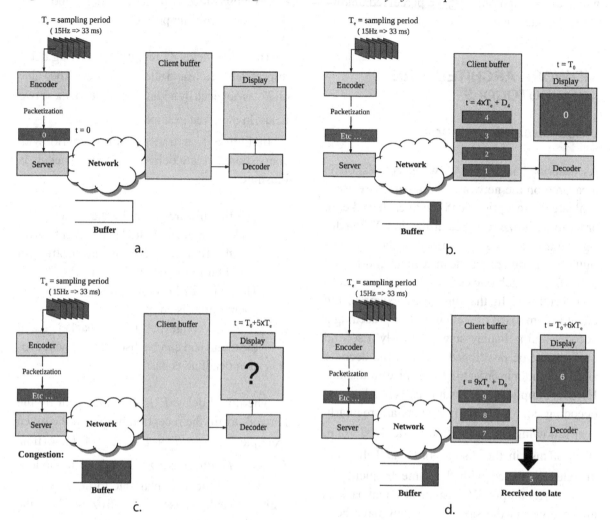

example). Typically, one can neglect the transmission delay D_j and the maximum end-to-end delay is equal to T_{buf}.

Long Term Feedbacks

The main idea of this approach is to maintain the video playout continuity at the client side, preventing network **congestion** thanks to well established network protocols and complying with the OSI model. Hence, jointly with the history of sent data, the RTCP Receiver Report (RTCP-RR) (Schulzrinne, Casner, Frederick & Jacobson,

2003; Wenger, Sato, Burmeister & Rey, 2006) packets transmitted by the client to the server provide an efficient tool in order to estimate the network congestion. As illustrated in Figure 2, we consider a classical client-server architecture in which a bottleneck link, like a wireless channel, accumulates data at its entry point. This entry point is modeled as a buffer containing RTP packets and packets life is governed by a time-out policy. For simplicity, we also consider that the delay for a packet to reach the bottleneck queue from the video server is null.

Figure 2. Network architecture

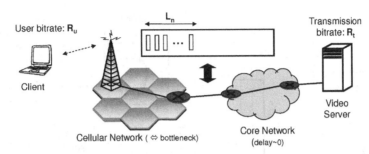

In terms of memory requirements, we assume that the server stores the size of each transmitted RTP packet together with its corresponding time-stamp and sequence number. In RTCP-RR, the field "fraction lost" indicates the fraction of RTP data packets lost since the previous RR packet was sent. A classical method to compute the number of lost packets is to make the difference between the expected number of packets, calculated using the sequence number of the last received packet, and the number of received packets. In our algorithm, to evaluate precisely the effective video bitrate received by the user and denoted by R_u in the sequel, we only take into account packets that are received before their deadline by the client. Moreover, the server keeps in memory the value of the "extended highest sequence number received" field of the last received RTCP-RR. Thus, receiving the next RTCP-RR and using the history of sent packets, the server is able to calculate the bitrate R_u of data arrived at the user decoder.

As illustrated in Figure 2, let us denote by L_n the total size of packets accumulated in the network and waiting to be transmitted through the network channel. This variable can be evaluated thanks to the knowledge of the sequence number of the last transmitted packet and the sequence number of the last received packet, given the history of previously scheduled packets. From the estimation of the two parameters R_u and L_n, the latency of the network can be computed as follows:

$$t_{latency} = L_n / R_u. \qquad (2)$$

This latency is then compared with a threshold value $T_{congest}$ empirically fixed. Depending on the result of this test, the scheduling algorithm will operate in one of the two following modes:

- Not congested ($t_{latency} < T_{congest}$): the capacity of the channel is not efficiently exploited and the algorithm takes the decision to increase the transmission bitrate using the following rule: $R_t = R_u(1 + \alpha)$.
- Congested ($t_{latency} \geq T_{congest}$): the maximum capacity is reached and the network is going to accumulate data. The server transmission rate is $R_t = R_u$.

In the non congested case, the α coefficient allows to gradually increase the transmission bitrate. The value of this coefficient depends on the congestion level, measured by the ratio between the latency and the threshold value as follows:

$$\alpha = \alpha_{max}(1 - t_{latency} / T_{congest}), \qquad (3)$$

where α_{max} determines the increasing rate of the transmission bitrate before reaching the congested state. This increasing rate is adapted according to the network conditions. When the congestion level is low, the bitrate is signifi-

Figure 3. Packet scheduling principle with a MANE based architecture

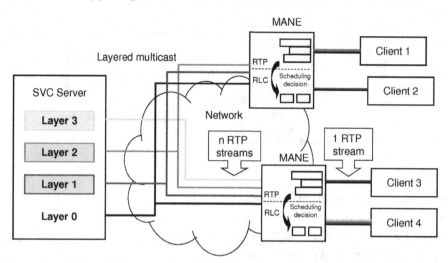

cantly increased and when the congestion limit is reached, the increase is slowed in order to avoid saturating the channel with the consequence of undesirable packet loss.

Media Aware Network Element (MANE)

From a conceptual point of view, a MANE is in charge of cross-layering operations. The key idea is to allow the network to take advantage at the radio layer of the adaptation properties of SVC in order to better react to the channel state variations (Tizon & Pesquet-Popescu, 2008). Here, we adopt an adaptation framework in which the streaming server sends scalable layers as multiple RTP substreams that are combined into a single RTP stream, adapted to each client transmission conditions in the MANE, as described in Figure 3.

On the one hand, in a cellular network, in order to be aware of the channel state in real time conditions, it is preferable to be close to the Node B which performs the radio packet scheduling operations (Ameigeiras, 2003; Holma & Toskala, 2004). On the other hand, in order to deal with application based information in agreement with the OSI protocol model, it is better to operate

close to the streaming server. More precisely, a MANE integrated to the node B will be profitable because:

- Radio measurements and channel feedbacks (see next section) are available in real time conditions, allowing adaptation with better reactivity.
- Scheduling functionalities of the MAC layer, which consists in a hierarchical transmission of streams or user substreams with different priorities, are very similar to the adaptation mechanisms of the MANE. This aspect suggests a reuse of the existing architecture.

However, some restrictions can be formulated concerning a MANE localization into the Node B. At the MAC layer, the application related information is no longer available and it is not really conceivable to retrieve it from the MAC segmented and formatted data for wireless transmissions (Stockhammer, 2006). Packet dropping (adaptation) below RTP layer would be inefficient, as an RTP packet would be ignored by the application layer if underlying radio segments are not present. In a general manner, solutions which involve node

Figure 4. MANE localisation in the RNC

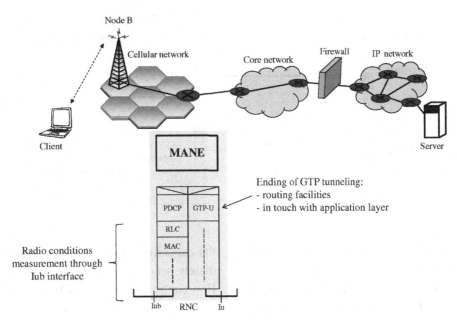

B scheduling implementations do not seem to be achievable, due to the high number of concerned elements and to the difficulty of dealing with MAC (and below) protocol layers.

Whereas it is easier to comply with an existing architecture when integrating adaptation mechanisms in the server, this approach raises some problems:

• In order to finely estimate the transmission conditions, a feedback protocol must be implemented in order to transmit channel based information from radio entities to the server.

• The temporal scale of bitrate variations that must be taken into account is about ten milliseconds. However, round trip delays between the server and network elements that manage physical and data link layers are close to this value, leading to a system with poor performances caused by a too high response time.

From these observations, the best compromise for the MANE localization seems to be close to the Radio Network Controller (RNC), as described in Figure 4. Indeed, thanks to its intermediate position, the RNC has the ability to be aware of the channel conditions in real time. Thus:

• Information concerning radio conditions transits from the node B to the RNC through Iub interface.

• The periodicity of channel measurements is close to the time transmission interval, in order to allow radio resource management and retransmissions of ARQ protocol.

The main difficulty concerning the implementation is to analyze the GTP datagrams in order to identify video streaming based data and to route them after bitrate adaptation at the application level. In order to allow bitrate adaptation, the MANE must be aware of the instantaneous channel capacity. Then, as presented in Figure 4, this kind of information is available through the Iub interface.

Figure 5. Flow control between RNC and MAC-hs

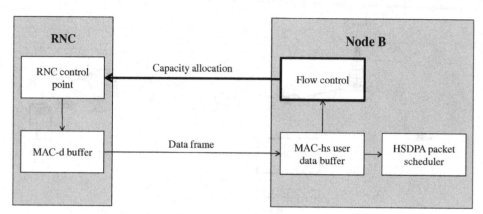

The way to infer the instantaneous channel capacity will be specific to the nature of the channel: dedicated or shared (HSDPA, for High Speed Downlink Packet Access). In the case of a dedicated channel, the channel configuration is statically fixed throughout the duration of the session and the RNC is in charge of this configuration. The concerned parameters are:

- The TTI (Time Transmission Interval), typically fixed to 10 ms.
- The RLC (Radio Link Control) (3GPP & Siemens, 2005) bloc size, typically fixed to 80 bytes.

Given these two parameters, the MANE is able to compute the channel bitrate. To infer the effective channel capacity, the MANE needs to take into account of the bit error rate. Actually, the channel capacity decrease due to packet errors on the wireless link can be measured thanks to the ARQ protocol in acknowledged mode (AM) and handled by the RNC.

With **HSDPA** (3GPP, TS 25.308, 2009), the **Frame** Protocol (FP) (Soldani, Man & Renaud, 2004) is responsible for the transmission of user data between the RNC and the Node B. When a new HSDPA connection is set up, the RNC can ask for the user capacity. If the RNC has data in its MAC-d buffers and the Node B has granted

the capacity, a data frame is transmitted immediately according to the allocated capacity. The flow control interactions between the Node B and RNC are illustrated in Figure 5.

In the Node B, the MAC-hs flow control (FC) algorithm monitors the content of the MAC-hs user data buffer and also the rate at which data are removed from the buffer. This is done using two thresholds, high and low. Comparing the buffer content with the thresholds, the MAC-hs FC algorithm allocates credits (CRs) to the user, so that the RNC knows how many PDUs belonging to that user it is allowed to forward to the Node B in every download channel (HS-DSCH) interval.

In this section, we developed two network condition estimation approaches in order to perform SVC bitrate adaptation. In a first time, SVC standard provide interesting tools to truncate a scalable bitstream to match with a given target bitrate. Then, in order to provide a finer discriminating factor, one can expect that good distortion measurements are necessary. Indeed, inside one scalable layer, the high level syntax of SVC does not distinguish the impact of a packet. In the next section, in order to provide this finer differentiation tool, we propose a distortion model that allows to recursively estimate the expected distortion decrease when sending a packet carrying SNR refinement information.

Figure 6. GOP structure in SVC

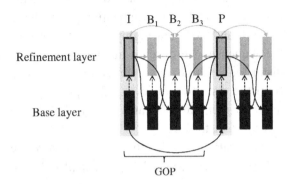

A DISTORTION MODEL

Calculation of Distortion Contributions

In this section, we develop a distortion model which is used further in order to differentiate queuing packets according to their contribution to the global distortion. In the sequel, we focus on an SVC stream encoded with a FGS (Fine Grain Scalability) quality refinement layer, as represented in Figure 6.

Let us denote by D_I^q, D_{B1}^q, D_{B2}^q, D_{B3}^q the measured distortions between original and encoded pictures: $q=0$ indicates the low quality picture and $q=1$ refers to the image decoded with its refinement layer. The distortion of a picture X can be expressed as follows:

$$D_X^q = \alpha_X \sigma_X^2 2^{-2R_X^q},$$ (4)

where α_X is a constant depending on the source distribution, σ_X is the variance of the picture, and R_X^q is the data bitrate. Maugey, André, Pesquet-Popescu and Farah (2008) used this relation to recursively calculate the distortion of bi-predicted pictures (B type) after decorrelation hypothesis. Hence, for $B2$:

$$
\begin{aligned}
D_{B2}^q &= \alpha_{B2} \sigma_{B2}^2 2^{-2R_{B2}^q} \\
&= \alpha_{B2} \left(M_{2,2} + \frac{1}{4} D_I + \frac{1}{4} D_P \right) 2^{-2R_{B2}^q},
\end{aligned}
$$ (5)

where $M_{2,2}$ is the prediction error obtained from non-quantized pictures. Next, we assume that each packet of the base layer ($q=0$) is correctly received by the decoder and that a packet is sent only if all packets necessary for its decoding have already been sent. From this equation, one can calculate the expected distortion decrease when a packet is sent to the client. For example, with a GOP size of 2, for the I picture we have:

$$\Delta D_I = D_I^1 - D_I^0 + \frac{1}{4} \alpha_{B2} (D_I^1 - D_I^0) 2^{-2R_{B2}^q}.$$ (6)

where $q=1$ if the refinement layer of the $B2$ picture that has been already sent and $q=0$ otherwise.

In Eq. (6), the terms indexed by P, corresponding to the first frame of the GOP, do not appear. Indeed, the implemented coding scheme uses the concept of key pictures (gray background in the figure). These pictures are encoded in a prediction loop which only uses decoded frames at the lowest quality. Hence, the distortion of these pictures only depends on the reception (or loss) of their refinement layer. Eq. (6) can be generalized for other packets and with other GOP sizes. In addition, with FGS based SNR scalability, motion information used for the base layer prediction is also used to encode the higher layers. Thus, the relation between distortion values of a picture decoded with and without the refinement layer is given by:

$$D_X^1 = D_X^0 2^{-2R_X^q}.$$ (7)

In a general manner, the distortion of a bi-predicted picture can be simply expressed as a linear function of the two distortions. D_{ref0}. et D_{ref1} of its reference pictures:

$$D_B^0 = a_B^0(D_{ref0} + D_{ref1}) + b_B^0, \qquad (8)$$

where a_B^0 and b_B^0 are two constants empirically fixed. Additionally, from the relation $D_B^1 = D_B^0 2^{-2R_B^1}$, we can define the constants a_B^1 and b_B^1 as follows: $a_B^1 = a_B^0 2^{-2R_B^1}$ and $b_B^1 = b_B^0 2^{-2R_B^1}$. Given these relations, we can formulate the distortion decrease, associated to each kind of picture, key picture (K index) and bi-predicted (B indices), when the packet of the refinement layer is received by the decoder:

$$\Delta D_K = \left(D_K^0 - D_K^1\right)\left(1 + \sum a_{B_i}^{q_i}\right),$$

$$\Delta D_B = D_B^0\left(1 - 2^{-2R_B^1}\right)\left(1 + \sum a_{B_i}^{q_i}\right),$$

$$(9)$$

where $a_{B_i}^{q_i}$ are the constants, introduced in Eq. (8), corresponding to bi-predicted pictures for which the considered picture is used as a reference. The value of q_i is 1 when the refinement layer has been sent and 0 otherwise. The distortion decrease ΔD estimated thanks to Eq. (9) can be used by the scheduling algorithm in order to evaluate the packet importance, as we will see further.

Model Validation and Parameter Values

In the sequel we encode a QCIF video of 75s at 15Hz, which is in fact a concatenation of some well known sequences: COASTGUARD, HALL MONITOR, MOBILE, STEFAN, BUS, CITY, CONTAINER and FOREMAN. In a first time, this video has been encoded with one FGS refinement layer and a GOP size of 2 in order to validate the distortion model. The quantization parameter is constant and the bitrate highly fluctuates through the sequence. We observe in Figure 7 that the distortion of high quality pictures, calculated from the distortion of low quality pictures and the refinement layer bitrates is very close to the measured distortion.

In addition, we determined empirically the a_B^0 and b_B^0 values used in D_B^0 calculated as in Eq. (8). To obtain these two values, we perform a linear regression from the measured distortions over the whole sequence, in the two cases: reference pictures decoded with and without the refinement layer. We observe a good adequacy of the model when we set $a_B^0 = 0.5$ and $b_B^0 = 0$ for all bi-predicted pictures of the sequence. Figure 8 represents the distortion evolution given by the model and the distortion measured on the decoded pictures. We observe that the calculated values are very close to the measured ones, more particularly when the reference picture is decoded without the refinement layer.

In the same way as in Figure 7, the model keeps away from real values with STEFAN sequence in which camera displacements are very important. Nevertheless, the distance between the two curves is relatively constant. Locally, picture priorities inferred from the estimated distortion would be very close to the priorities inferred from measured distortions.

In this section, we described a distortion model, which can be used to recursively calculate the expected distortion decrease when transmitting a packet. In the next section, we present two scheduling algorithms that perform bitrate adaptation from network measurements by exploiting SVC features. The first one is based on the MANE approach and only differentiates queued packets thanks to SVC standard layer definitions. The second solution utilizes the long term feedbacks approach, already described, in order to infer transmission conditions and the algorithm dif-

Figure 7. Estimation of the distortion D_B^1 (mean square error) of bi-predicted pictures from the distortion D_B^0 and the bitrate R_B^1, with a GOP size of 2 (top: $D_K = D_K^1$, bottom: $D_K = D_K^0$)

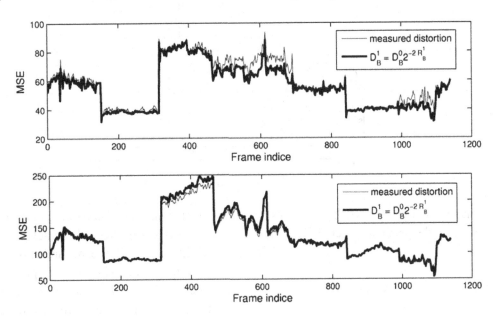

Figure 8. Estimation of the distortion D_B^1 (mean square error) of bi-predicted pictures from the distortion D_{ref0} and D_{ref1} of the reference frames (top: $D_K = D_K^1$, bottom: $D_K = D_K^0$)

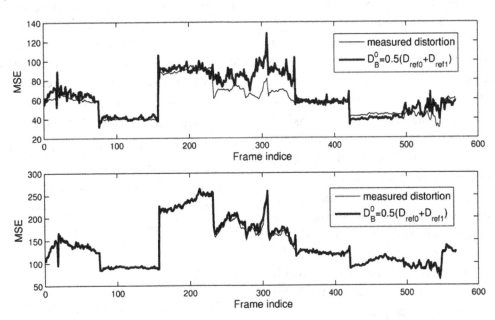

Figure 9. Scalable scheduling principle with three substreams

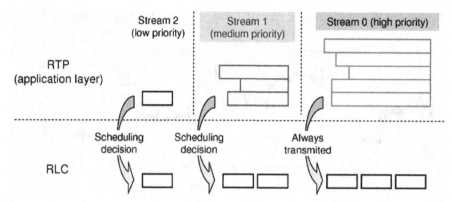

ferentiates packets of a given SNR layer thanks to the distortion model previously detailed.

SCHEDULING ALGORITHMS

A MANE Approach with SVC

In the remaining, we consider that the MANE sees the RLC layer as the bottleneck link and performs packet scheduling from the IP layer to the RLC layer as described in Figure 9. Moreover, we neglect transmission delay variations between the server and the MANE. Then, each RTP packet (Wenger, Wang & Schierl, 2009) is received by the MANE at $t = ts + t_0$, where ts is the sampling instant of the data and t0 the constant delay between the MANE and the server. Next, to simplify, we put $t_0 = 0$ knowing that this time only impacts the initial playout delay.

Moreover, inside each scalable stream, packets are received in their decoding order, which can be different from the sampling order due to the hierarchical B pictures structure. Hence, the timestamp of the Head-Of-Line (HOL) data unit of a stream queue is different from the minimum sampling instant of queued packets: ts_{min}.

Input RTP streams are processed successively. When scheduling an RTP packet, the algorithm examines the transmission queues of the most important streams and, according to the network state, the current packet will be delayed or sent to the RLC layer. All streams are next transmitted over the same wireless transport channel and when an RTP packet reaches the RLC layer, all the necessary time slots are used to send the whole packet. Therefore the general principle of the algorithm is to allow sending a packet only if the packet queues with higher priorities are not congested and if the expected bandwidth is sufficient to transmit the packet before its deadline.

In order to detail the algorithm, we are considering that the bitstream is transmitted as a set of K substreams and the scheduler is up to send the HOL packets of the kth stream at time t ($k = 0..K - 1$). Let us denote by $ts_k(t)$ the sampling instant of this packet, $L_k(t)$ its size, $d_k(t)$ its transmission time and Δ_{max} the maximum end to end delay for all packets of the streaming session. Scheduling opportunities for this packet will be inspected only if its reception deadline is not past:

$$(t - ts_k(t)) < \Delta_{max}. \tag{10}$$

If this condition is not verified, the packet is discarded. Then, a second condition is tested in order to ensure that the packet can be received before its deadline:

$$(t - ts_k(t)) < \Delta_{max} - d_k(t). \qquad (11)$$

If this condition is not verified, the algorithm lets the packet on the top of the queue and examines the $(k+1)^{th}$ stream. Otherwise, queuing packets of higher priority streams indexed by j ($0 \le j < k$) are considered as a single packet with the timestamp $ts_{min}(t)$. Then we define $d_{ag}(k,t)$, the transmission time for this aggregated packet and we fix $t' = t + d_k(t)$. The last condition which must be verified before sending the packet is:

$$(t' - ts_{min}(t')) < \Delta_{max} - d_{ag}(k,t'). \qquad (12)$$

With this condition, the algorithm ensures that the network is able to send the packet without causing future packets loss from streams with higher priorities. If this condition is not verified, the packet is put on the top of the kth stream queue and the algorithm examines the $(k+1)^{th}$ stream. The processing loop of stream queues at time t is summarized in the algorithm 1.

The three defined functions: *transmit_packet*, *delay_packet* and *discard_packet* correspond to the action that occurs on the top of the stream which is currently inspected.

In addition, packet dependency can exist between packets from the same stream, in the case of a combined scalability based stream definition, or between packets from different streams. Therefore, in order to provide an efficient transmission of scalable layers, the algorithm delays packets sending until decoding dependencies are satisfied.

Given the two conditions (10) and (11), the main difficulty is to evaluate the 5 variables that are defined as a function of time and need to be calculated in the future. Firstly, $ts_{min}(t)$ is easily obtained scanning packets in the queues. After the transmission of the current packet (stream

Algorithm 1. Processing loop of queued packets in the MANE at time t

```
for k = 0 to K − 1 do
    if (t − ts_k(t)) < Δ_max then
        if (t − ts_k(t)) < Δ_max − d_k(t) then
            if (t' − ts_min(t')) < Δ_max − d_ag(k,t') then
                transmit_packet(k)
                break
            else
                delay_packet(k)
            end if
        else
            delay_packet(k)
        end if
    else
        discard_packet(k)
    end if
end for
```

indexed by k), the oldest packet of other streams remains unchanged, hence: $ts_{min}(t) = ts_{min}(t')$.

Next, we calculate the $d_k(t)$ value, which amounts to perform a channel delay estimation. In order to do this, we are considering that the channel state is governed by a 2-state Markov chain. Therefore, thanks to this model, the network is simply considered to be in "GOOD" or "BAD" state, as depicted in Figure 10. The transition probabilities of this model, λ and μ, are considered as a function of time variables in order to take into account possible channel state evolutions. In order to complete the network model, we define

Figure 10. A 2-state Markov channel model

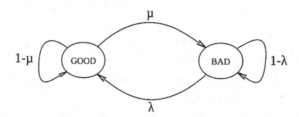

tti and rfs the variables that represent the Transmission Time Interval (TTI) and the Radio Frame Size (RFS) constant values. A radio frame is actually an RLC-PDU (RLC Protocol Data Unit). Before reaching the RLC layer, an RTP packet is segmented into radio frames and an RLC-PDU is sent every TTI. In fact, if *tti* and *rfs* are constant, we implicitly assume that we are dealing with a dedicated channel with constant bitrate. Nevertheless, in our simulations, the *tti* value can be modified in order to simulate a radio resource management based decision of the network which can perform bandwidth allocation on the long run. Additionally, channel state transitions occur every TTI, so we can write the current time as a discrete variable: $t = n \times tti$. Finally, the transition probabilities, λ and μ are dynamically calculated every TTI by performing a state transition count over a sliding time window $T = N \times tti$.

Let us define the random process TT(t) (Transmission Time) which represents the time spent by the network (including RLC retransmissions) to send a radio frame whose first sending instant is t. Actually, TT is a discrete time process and we have: $TT(t) = TT(n \times tti) = TT(n)$. As *rfs* is constant, $I = \left\lceil \dfrac{L_k(t)}{rfs} \right\rceil$ is the number of RLC-PDUs involved in the transmission of the current HOL RTP packet of the kth stream. With these notations, let us denote by $tti \times \{n_0, n_1, .., n_I\}$ with $n_0 = n$, the sequence of sending instants corresponding to the first transmission of the related RLC-PDUs. So, we can express the overall transmission time of an RTP packet as:

$$d_k(t) = \sum_{i=n}^{I} TT(n_i) \tag{13}$$

In order to evaluate TT(n), we use past observations thanks to the RLC AM (Radio Link Control Acknowledged Mode) error feedback information sent by the receiver. This information is received by the transmitter after a certain feedback delay: r×tti and r is a fixed integer value which depends on the RLC configuration. Moreover, we estimate the average value of TT over the RTP packet transmission duration by the average value of $TT(n-r)$. In other words, we consider that the average channel state is constant through the RTP packet transmission duration. So, we have the following estimated parameter:

$$\widehat{d_k}(t) = E\{TT(n-r)\} \times \left\lceil \dfrac{L_k(t)}{rfs} \right\rceil \tag{14}$$

When the channel is in "GOOD" state, $TT(n) = tti$ and when the channel state is "BAD" state we approximate $TT(n)$ by the average TT value of previously retransmitted RLC-PDU (one time at least) over the previously defined time window T. Let us denote by tt_{bad} this average value. We have:

$$tt_{bad}(n) = \dfrac{\displaystyle\sum_{\substack{i=n-N \\ TT(i)>tti}}^{n} TT(i)}{\displaystyle\sum_{\substack{i=n-N \\ TT(i)>tti}}^{n} i} \tag{15}$$

Then, the mean value of $TT(n)$ can be expressed as:

$$
\begin{aligned}
E\{TT(n)\} = \quad & tt_{bad}(n) \times P(TT(n) > tti \mid TT(n-1)) \\
+ \quad & tti \times P(TT(n) = tti \mid TT(n-1))
\end{aligned}
$$
(16)

In order to provide the estimation of $d_{ag}(k,t')$ involved in the scheduling condition defined by Eq. (11), we define $L_{ag}(k,t')$ as the size of the aggregated RTP packets of the streams with higher priorities. In addition, let us define $r(k,t)$ as the cumulated source bitrate of these streams, calculated over the previously defined time window T. Thus, in the sequel, we will use the following approximation:

$$
L_{ag}(k,t') = L_{ag}(k,t) + r(k,t) \times d_k(t).
$$
(17)

Next, we estimate the transmission time of this aggregated packet assuming that the transmission time estimation, given by Eq. (16), will be useful over the time interval: $[t, d_{ag}(k,t')]$. Therefore, similarly to Eq. (14), we can write:

$$
\widehat{d_{ag}}(k,t') = E\{TT(n-r)\} \times \left\lceil \frac{L_{ag}(k,t')}{rfs} \right\rceil.
$$
(18)

To evaluate the efficiency of the proposed scheduling algorithms, some experiments have been conducted using a network simulator provided by the 3GPP video ad-hoc group (3GPP & Siemens, 2005). This software is an offline simulator for an RTP streaming session over 3GPP networks (GPRS, EDGE and UMTS). Packet errors are simulated using error masks generated from link level simulations at various bearer rates and block error rate (BLER) values. Moreover, this simulator offers the possibility to simulate time events (delays) using the timestamp field of the RTP header. The provided network parameters are nearly constant throughout the session.

For simulating radio channel conditions two possible input interfaces are provided: bit-error patterns in binary format, as well as RLC-PDU losses in ASCII format. Error masks are used to inject errors at the physical layer. If the RLC-PDU is corrupted or lost, it is discarded (i.e. not given to the receiver/video decoder) or retransmitted if the RLC protocol is in acknowledged mode (AM). The available bit-error patterns determine the bitrates and error ratios that can be simulated. Two bit-error patterns with binary format are used in the experiment. These patterns are characterized by a relatively high BER ($BER = 9.3e-3$ and $BER = 2.9e-3$) and are suited to be used in streaming applications, where RLC layer retransmissions can correct many of the frame losses. All bearers are configured with persistent mode for RLC retransmissions and their bitrates are adjusted using the RLC block size and the TTI parameters provided by the simulator. An erroneous RLC packet is retransmitted until it is correctly received. If the maximum transfer delay due to retransmission is reached, the corresponding RTP packet is discarded. Therefore, the residual BER is always null, only missing RTP packets may occur, as depicted in Figure 11. In order to validate a strategy, results must be provided over a large set of simulations varying the error mask statistics. Therefore, for a simulation, the error pattern is read with an offset varying from 0 at the first run and incremented by 1 for each run and finally the results are evaluated over a set of 64 runs, as recommended in (3GPP & BenQmobile, 2006).

In addition, the RTP packetization modality is Single Network Abstraction Layer (NAL) unit mode (one NAL unit/RTP payload), the division of original stream into many RTP substreams leads to an increase of the number of RTP headers. To limit the multiplications of header information, the interleaved RTP packetization mode allows multi-time aggregation packets (NAL units with

Figure 11. Simulation model

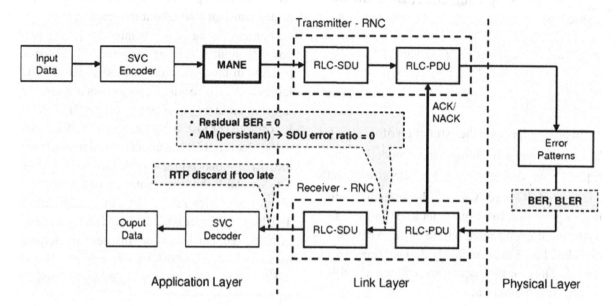

different timestamps) in the same RTP payload. In our case, we make the assumption that RoHC mechanisms provide RTP/UDP/IP header compression from 40 to 4 bytes in average, which is negligible compared to RTP packet sizes, and we still packetize one NAL unit per RTP payload.

To evaluate the proposed approach, we present some simulation results obtained with the three test sequences (15fps, QCIF): MOTHER AND DAUGHTER (M&D), PARIS and STEFAN. The prediction mode scheme for frame sequencing is the classical IPPP... pattern, in order to evaluate the robustness of the proposed approach and its capacity to limit the distortion due to error propagation. Concerning the scalability features, SVC bitstreams are encoded with a group of pictures (GOP) size of 8 (4 temporal levels) and one SNR refinement layer, which corresponds to a quantization factor difference of 6 from the base to the refinement quality layer. Then, each RTP packet can be either the quality base layer of a slice group or its enhanced quality layer at a given temporal level. The constants defined previously are used with the following values:

$\Delta_{max} = 1.5$ s, $rfs = 80$ bytes, $tti = 10$ ms by default and $r=2$.

Table 1 presents the simulation results obtained by configuring each channel with a BLER of 10.8% ($BER = 9.3e - 3$). For PARIS and MOTHER AND DAUGHTER sequences the bitrate provided at the RLC layer is 64 kbps and then by removing 4 bytes/packet of RLC header information, the maximum bitrate available at the application level (above RTP layer) is approximately 60.8 kbps. Moreover, for these two sequences, in the case of H.264/AVC non-scalable coding, a bitrate constrained algorithm at source coding (Wiegand, Schwarz, Joch, Kossentini & Sullivan, 2003; Tourapis, Leontaris, Sühring & Sullivan, 2009) was used in order to match an average target bitrate of 60 kbps. Concerning STEFAN sequence, the motion activity is much more significant and in order to obtain an acceptable quality, we encode the video with an average target bitrate of 120kbps. Thus, the corresponding channel used to transmit this sequence is configured with a TTI of 5ms, leading to a maximum available bitrate of 121.6kbps.

Table 1. Performance comparison between H.264/ AVC (one RTP stream) and SVC (2 RTP streams: base layer and SNR refinement)

	M&D	PARIS	STEFAN
H.264/AVC	27.58 dB	26.43 dB	18.6 dB
SVC	34.2 dB	29.74 dB	27.73 dB

In the case of SVC coding, the video is encoded without a bitrate control algorithm and streamed through two RTP streams. The first one corresponds to the base layer transmitted with the highest priority and the second one corresponds to the enhanced quality layer transmitted with lower priority. For this set of simulations no other scalability features, temporal or SNR, are used to differentiate the RTP streams. PSNR values are measured over the whole sequence and the proposed method allows to gain from 3.3dB to 9.13dB.

Next, new simulations are conducted in order to study the combined effects of channel errors and bandwidth decrease. Indeed, the implementation of a dedicated channel with a purely constant bitrate is not really efficient in terms of radio resource utilization between all users. Then, a more advanced resource allocation strategy would decrease the available bandwidth of the user when its conditions become too bad, in order to better serve other users with better experienced conditions. This allocation strategy, which aims at maximizing the overall network throughput or the sum of the data rates that are delivered to all the users in the network, corresponds to an ideal functioning mode of the system but it is not really compatible with a QoS based approach.

Actually, with a classical video streaming system, it is not really conceivable to adjust the initially allocated channel bitrate without sending feedbacks to the application server, which is generally the only entity able to adapt the streamed bitrate. Moreover, when these feedbacks are implemented, adaptation capabilities

of the server are often quite limited in the case of a non scalable codec: transcoding, bitstream switching... Then, in our proposed framework, with the MANE located close to the wireless interface, it is possible to limit the bitrate at the entrance of the RLC layer if a resource management decision (e.g. bandwidth decrease) has been reported. In this case, as illustrated in Figure 12, our adaptive packet transmission method allows to maintain a good level of quality while facing a high error rate and a channel capacity decrease. In the presented simulation results, after 15ms, a quality decrease of 1.7dB in average and 4dB in the worst case is measured, whereas the available user bitrate is reduced by more than 30% because of the combined effects of allocated bandwidth decrease (30%) and BLER increase.

Distortion Based Policy and Long Term Feedbacks

In the sequel, we propose and evaluate a scheduling algorithm which differentiates packets of a given SNR layer thanks to the distortion model previously detailed. The developed approach uses the long term feedbacks framework in order to infer transmission conditions.

Queued packets of the refinement layer are periodically examined by the server in order to be transmitted, delayed or discarded. This decision is taken periodically at the maximum video frame rate frequency. Before considering a possible transmission of a packet, the algorithm ensures that its reception deadline is not past. Let us denote by ts the timestamp of the packet, t the current time and Δ_{max} the end to end delay. This first condition is given by:

$$t < ts + \Delta_{max}. \tag{19}$$

If this condition is not verified, the packet is discarded and we examine the next packet in the queue following the chronological order given by

Figure 12. Bitrate adaptation with two RTP streams: base layer and SNR refinement layer (PARIS)

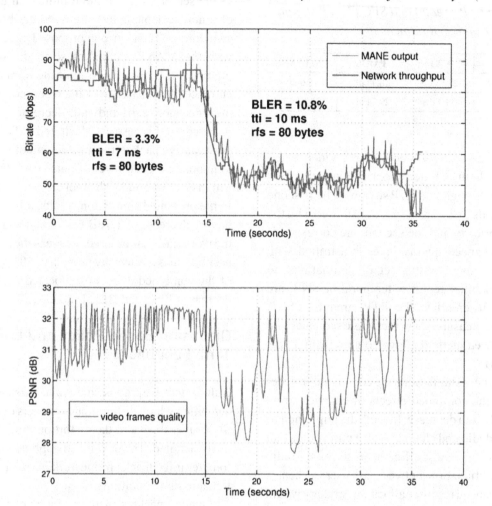

the timestamps. If the condition is not verified, the server ensures that the packet can be received before its deadline. Let us denote by L_p the size of the packet. A second condition can be written as:

$$t + L_n / R_t + L_p / R_t < ts + \Delta_{max}, \qquad (20)$$

where L_n and R_t have been defined when considering network architecture with long term feedbacks. Through this condition, we estimate the arrival time of the packet: $t + L_n / R_t + L_p / R_t$ and we ensure that it does not exceed the reception deadline $ts + \Delta_{max}$. If this condition is not true,

the algorithm lets the packet on the top of the queue and examines the next packet in the increasing timestamp order. Let us denote by n the index of the picture with the oldest timestamp and for which the two conditions (19) and (20) are verified. Let us denote by $\Delta D(n)$ the distortion value, computed from the previously defined distortion model, associated with this packet. Then, we build a packet concatenating queued packets that belong to pictures with indices: $n_0,...,n_N$ and such that: $\forall k = n_0,..,n_N$, $\Delta D(k) > \Delta D(n)$. Let us denote by $L_{p'}$ the size of this new packet. The reception deadline of this packet is given by the reception

Algorithm 2. Processing loop of queued packets in the server at time t

$b\_process\_packet = true$

repeat

if $t < ts + \Delta_{max}$ **then**

if $t + L_n / R_t + L_p / R_t < ts + \Delta_{max}$ **then**

if $t + L_n / R_t + L_p / R_t + L_{p'} / R_t < ts_{min} + \Delta_{max}$ **then**

$transmit\_packet(k)$

else

$delay\_packet(k)$

end if

else

$delay\_packet(k)$

end if

else

$discard\_packet(k)$

end if

until $b\_process\_packet$

deadline of the packet with the oldest timestamp, denoted by ts_{min} in the sequel. Finally, the packet containing the refinement layer of the picture indexed by n is sent if the following condition is true:

$$t + L_n / R_t + L_p / R_t + L_{p'} / R_t < ts_{min} + \Delta_{max}. \quad (21)$$

From the RTCP-RR and the transmission history, the server estimates at every transmission time slot the size L_n of data in the input buffer of the wireless link. Given this value and the estimation of the channel capacity R_t, the server ensures that the packet transmission of the

packet indexed by n does not prevent a successful reception of the concatenated data with higher priorities. If the condition is true, the packet is sent. Otherwise, the packet is delayed and the algorithm examines the next packet. The distortion values ΔD associated with each packet are updated according to already sent packets.

The transmission loop of queued packets at time t is summarized in algorithm 2. The three functions: *transmit_packet*, *delay_packet* and *discard_packet* correspond to the action that occurs on the inspected packet (indexed by n). The waiting queue in the server is scanned in chronological order, from the oldest to the most recent packets and when all the packets have been ex-

Figure 13. PSNR evolution along the time (QCIF@15Hz)

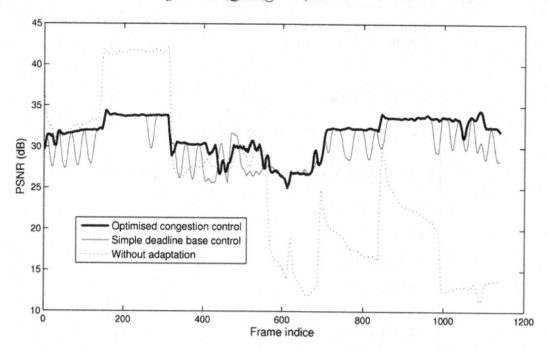

amined, the boolean *b_process_packet* becomes false.

To evaluate the relevance of our approach, we simulate streaming sessions in a scenario where network conditions become more and more difficult along the time. At the beginning of the session, the channel is set with a bandwidth of 128kbps and a Block Error Rate (BLER) of 3.3% Around the $_{30}$th second, the BLER reaches 10% and the bandwidth falls to 100kbps. During the second part of the session, the BLER remains stable at 10% and the bandwidth reaches a minimum value of 80kbps. In addition, we encode a QCIF video of 75s at 15Hz, which is in fact a concatenation of 8 sequences, as previously described in the MANE based approach. We use one quality refinement layer (FGS) and a GOP size of 8. The encoder is configured with constant quantization steps through the video and therefore the bitrate highly depends on the content of the underlying sequence. Here we compare the PSNR evolution of the decoded video with three different transmission strategies: without adaptation, with a simple deadline based control and the optimized congestion control previously described.

Figure 13 illustrates the ability of our long term feedback driven scheduling algorithm to face a drastic deterioration of network conditions. Moreover, during the transition states, the coupling introduced between packet transmission decision allows to use the available resource more efficiently. The average PSNR gain over the whole sequence compared to the simple deadline based control method is 1.13.dB.

SUMMARY

In this chapter, we have proposed a complete streaming framework for a wireless, and more particularly a 3G/UMTS, network environment. Firstly we described the different choices one can make in terms of network architecture. More precisely, we focused on the input parameters used to evaluate network conditions and to perform the adaptation. In addition, we paid a particular attention to the protocol information one can exploit in order to infer the channel state. In addition, each implementation choice is a compromise between the industrial feasibility and the adaptation efficiency.

We focused on the case where the media server only receives RTCP-RR as network feedback information. Considering a report period of about one second, we estimated the reception conditions of the user by distinguishing between two functioning modes: congested and not congested. In addition, we detailed a recursive distortion model and how we use it in the packet scheduling algorithm. Experimental results validated our approach, showing the efficiency of the algorithm to face network conditions deterioration.

Next, in order to multiplex scalable layers, we adopted a MANE approach. In our system, the MANE is close to the wireless interface and it manages RTP packets transmission to the RLC layer following priority rules. In order to do this, a bitrate adaptation algorithm performs packet scheduling based on a channel state estimation. This algorithm considers the delay at the RLC layer and the packet deadlines in order to maximize the video quality, avoiding network congestion. Our simulations show that the proposed method outperforms classical non scalable streaming approaches and the adaptation capabilities can be used to optimize the resource utilization.

REFERENCES

Ameigeiras, P. (2003). *Packet Scheduling And Quality of Service in HSDPA*. (PhD thesis), Institute of Electronic Systems, Aalborg University.

Amonou, I., Cammas, N., Kervadec, S., & Pateux, S. (2007). Optimized rate-distortion extraction with quality layers in the scalable extension of H.264/AVC. *IEEE Transactions on Circuits and Systems for Video Technology, 17*(9), 1186–1193. doi:10.1109/TCSVT.2007.906870

Baldo, N., Horn, U., Kampmann, M., & Hartung, F. (2004). RTCP feedback based transmission rate control for 3G wireless multimedia streaming. *IEEE Int. Symp. Personal, Indoor and Mobile Radio Com., 3*, 1817–1821.

Chakareski, J., Apostolopoulos, J. G., Wee, S., Tan, W., & Girod, B. (2005). Rate-distortion hint tracks for adaptive video streaming. *IEEE Transactions on Circuits and Systems for Video Technology, 15*(10), 1257–1269. doi:10.1109/TCSVT.2005.854227

Chakareski, J., & Chou, P.A. (2006). Radio edge: Rate-distortion optimized proxy-driven streaming from the network edge. *IEEE/ACM Transactions on Networking, 14*(6), 1302–1312.

Chakareski, J., & Frossard, P. (2006). Rate-distortion optimized distributed packet scheduling of multiple video streams over shared communication resources. *IEEE Transactions on Multimedia, 8*(2), 207–218. doi:10.1109/TMM.2005.864284

Chou, P. A., & Miao, Z. (2001). Rate-distortion optimized streaming of packetized media. *Microsoft Corporation, Tech. Rep. MSR-TR-2001-35*.

Girod, B., Kalman, M., Liang, Y., & Zhang, R. (2002). Advances in channel adaptive video streaming. *Wireless Communications and Mobile Computing, 2*, 549–552. doi:10.1002/wcm.87

3GPP & BenQmobile. (2006). *Components for TR on video minimum performance requirements. Doc. for decision*. TSG Services and System Aspects.

3GPP & Siemens. (2005). *Software simulator for MBMS streaming over UTRAN and GERAN. Doc. for proposal*. TSG Services and System Aspects.

3GPP (2009). Radio Link Control (RLC) protocol specification. *Technical Specification TS 25.222*.

3GPP (2009). Technical High Speed Downlink Packet Access (HSDPA); Overall description; Stage 2. *Technical Specification TS 25.308.*

3GPP. Transparent end-to-end Packet-switched Streaming Service (PSS); Protocols and codecs. *Technical Specification TS 26.234.*

Holma, H., & Toskala, A. (2004). *WCDMA for UMTS, Radio Access for Third Generation Mobile Communications.* New York: Wiley.

ISO/IEC & ITU-T Rec. (2003). *H.264: Advanced Video Coding for Generic Audio-visual Services. Technical report, Joint Video Team (JVT) of ISO-IEC MPEG&ITU-T VCEG, Int.* Standard.

Liebl, G., Jenkac, H., Stockhammer, T., & Buchner, C. (2005). *Radio Link Buffer Management and Scheduling for Wireless Video Streaming.* New York: Springer Science & Business Media.

Liebl, G., Schierl, T., Wiegand, T., & Stockhammer, T. (2006). Advanced wireless multiuser video streaming using the scalable video coding extensions of H.264/MPEG4-AVC. *IEEE Int. Conf. on Multimedia and Expo.*, 325–328.

Maugey, T., André, T., Pesquet-Popescu, B., & Farah, J. (2008). *Analysis of error propagation due to frame losses in a distributed video coding system.* Paper presented at the conference EUSIPCO2008, Lausanne, Switzerland.

Reichel, J., Schwarz, H., & Wien, M. (2007). Joint Scalable Video Model JSVM-12 text. *JVT_Y202, Output document of the 25th JVT meeting.*

Schulzrinne, H., Casner, S., Frederick, R., & Jacobson, V. (2003). RTP: A Transport Protocol for Real-Time Application. *RFC3550.*

Schwarz, H., Marpe, D., & Wiegand, T. (2006). Overview of the scalable H.264/MPEG4-AVC extension. *IEEE Int. Conf. on Image Proc.*, 161–164.

Setton, E. (2003). *Congestion-aware video streaming over peer-to-peer networks.* (PhD thesis), Information Systems Laboratory, Department of Electrical Engineering, Stanford University, Stanford,USA, 2003.

Soldani, D. Man, Li., & Renaud, C. (2004). *QoS and QoE Management in UMTS Cellular Systems.* New York: Wiley.

Stockhammer, T. (2006). *Robust System and Cross-Layer Design for H.264/AVC-Based Wireless Video Applications.* EURASIP Journal on Applied Signal Processing.

Tizon, N., & Pesquet-Popescu, B. (2007). *Content based QoS differentiation for video streaming in a wireless environment.* Paper presented at the conference EUSIPCO 2007, Poznan, Poland.

Tizon, N., & Pesquet-Popescu, B. (2008). *Scalable and media aware adaptive video streaming over wireless networks.* EURASIP Journal on Advances in Signal Processing.

Tourapis, A., Leontaris, A., Sühring, K., & Sullivan, G. (2009). H.264/MPEG-4 AVC Reference Software Manual. *JVT_AD010, Output document of the 30th JVT meeting.*

Wang, Y.-K., Hannuksela, M. M., Pateux, S., Eleftheriadis, A., & Wenger, S. (2007). System and transport interface of SVC. *IEEE Trans. on Circuits and Systems for Video Technology, 17*(9), 1149–1163. doi:10.1109/TCSVT.2007.906827

Wenger, S., Sato, N., Burmeister, C., & Rey, J. (2006). Extended RTP profile for real-time transport control protocol (RTCP)-based feedback. *RFC4585.*

Wenger, S., Wang, Y.-K, & Schierl, T. (2009). RTP payload format for SVC video. *IETF draft.*

Wiegand, T., Schwarz, H., Joch, A., Kossentini, F., & Sullivan, G. J. (2003). Rate-constrained coder control and comparison of video coding standards. *IEEE Transactions on Circuits and Systems for Video Technology*, *13*(7), 688–703. doi:10.1109/TCSVT.2003.815168

Wiegand, T., Sullivan, G., Reichel, J., Schwarz, H., & Wien, M. (2007). Joint Draft ITU-T Rec. H.264 | ISO/IEC 14496-10 / Amd.3 Scalable video coding. *JVT_X201, Output document of the 24th JVT* meeting.

Wiegand, T., Sullivan, G. J., Bjontegaard, G., & Luthra, A. (2003). Overview of the H.264/AVC video coding standard. *IEEE Trans. on Circuits and Systems for Video Technology*, *13*(7), 560–576. doi:10.1109/TCSVT.2003.815165

Chapter 8
Robust Video Streaming over MANET and VANET

Martin Fleury
University of Essex, UK

Nadia N. Qadri
University of Essex, UK

Muhammad Altaf
University of Essex, UK

Mohammed Ghanbari
University of Essex, UK

ABSTRACT

Mobile Ad Hoc Networks (MANETs) are a further step towards wireless networks with no or limited infrastructure and Vehicular Ad Hoc Networks (VANETs) extend this concept, introducing diverse mobility patterns but removing the need for battery power conservation. Video streaming and multimedia applications in general have become an engine of growth in wireless networking and this Chapter shows how video streaming can take place in this challenging environment. Error resilience and path diversity are presented as the key to robust streaming. The Chapter shows that simplified forms of multiple description coding are a practical route to take, with redundant frames in the temporal domain or Flexible Macroblock Ordering in the spatial domain offering preferred solutions. As a form of management of streaming, distributed sourcing via peer-to-peer streaming is experimented within VANET simulations. Error resilience methods, peer-to-peer streaming, and multi-path routing are reviewed. The Chapter considers the exploitation of path diversity over a MANET and a VANET. Path diversity allows the merging of the peer-to-peer concept with ad hoc networks. Future research directions are reviewed.

INTRODUCTION

We consider video streaming over a wireless Mobile Ad Hoc Network (MANET) and over an extension of the MANET concept, an automotive Vehicular Ad Hoc Network (VANET). Both involve multi-hop routing across infrastructure-less wireless networks. That is wireless communication takes place from node-to-node in the

DOI: 10.4018/978-1-61692-831-5.ch008

Copyright © 2011, IGI Global. Copying or distributing in print or electronic forms without written permission of IGI Global is prohibited.

case of a MANET and from vehicle-to-vehicle within a VANET, without routing via a network access point. Multi-hop routing is necessary due to the limited range of wireless communication. Therefore, ad hoc networks are networks in which wireless nodes communicate with each other without any established infrastructure or network core (Manoj & Siva Ram Murthy, 2004). Nodes act as both terminals (i.e. source and destination of the message) and relays for routed messages. In ad hoc networks, messages hop from node to node until they reach their destination, which requires each node to be more intelligent than the conventional terminals found in other wireless networks such as cellular networks. At the same time, their flexibility allows both MANET and VANET to extend cellular networks to where there are coverage gaps or to where there is temporary excessive demand. Therefore, whatever multimedia applications are planned for 3G cellular networks such as 3GPP's Multimedia Broadcast and Multicast Service (MBMS) (Luby et al., 2007) will be enhanced by extensions to ad hoc networks. In particular, projected applications of MBMS within sport stadiums and airports (Luby et al., 2007), which include multimedia streaming as well as download, may be better delivered by an ad hoc extension to the cellular system to reduce congestion at base stations.

Node mobility causes an ad hoc network's topology to be in a constant state of flux. Route changes and link failures are the most common problems in communication over ad hoc networks, causing an increase in delay, delay variation (jitter) and packet loss. In these networks, in the absence of a central scheduling node, the nodes must be always available to receive and forward packets even when they are not the origin or destination of transmission. Power management becomes an important issue in MANETs, when appropriate schemes for energy consumption can reduce the effect on and increase the lifetime of battery-powered devices. The energy consumption problem becomes even more severe in multimedia

communication, as it has been reported) (Chen et al., 1998) that one third of total energy consumption in a mobile device is due to transmission and video play back together with transmission amounts to about 80% of total power consumption in a receiver. In MANETs, per-packet routing overhead is a metric of power efficiency that helps judge the efficiency of the streaming process.

A MANET will typically be formed by a group of people moving on foot or on vehicles at relatively slow speeds with random patterns of motion. A scenario explored is that of a team of emergency workers coping with a natural disaster, when the existing communication infrastructure has been removed. Real-time video communication will significantly help to describe an emergency scene to other members of the response group. Military applications of ad hoc networks share some similarities with this scenario and equally a video link between members of a platoon will be of value. In addition in a military setting, an ad hoc network is not as easily disrupted as other types of network. The mobility of the group members in a MANET is often described with a random waypoint model (Broch et al., 1998).

Unlike MANETs, VANETs are not faced with power limitations. Consequently, they are able to maintain large receiver buffers without worries over their energy consumption, though clearly larger buffers will lead to start-up delay if this is an issue for an application. A VANET also differs from a MANET because on a highway there are high speeds but linear motion. In urban and suburban settings, mobility is not as restricted. For example, in inner city areas, a Manhattan grid of roads is commonly assumed in generic modeling (Bai et al., 2003). However, there remain 'obstacles' such as road junctions and traffic control lights. 'Intelligent' driver mobility models (Fiore et al., 2007) describe the way vehicles cluster at road junctions, overtake using lanes, and behave in the presence of other vehicles. Buildings, roadside foliage, road signs and other vehicles all restrict signal propagation in differing ways, leading to packet loss. In both MANET and VANET, wireless path loss through diffraction and multipath is a serious threat, which the research illustrated aims to model accurately. Choice of routing algorithm is also important. In VANETs, it is possible to select position-aware algorithms, as GPS devices are already available as navigation aids. However, routing algorithms and, indeed, medium-access-control algorithms (Murthy & Manoj, 2004) remain the source of a major research investigation.

These circumstances impede compressed video streaming, causing packet loss and subsequent degradation of delivered video quality through error propagation due to the fragile nature of a compressed video stream. Of course, a compressed video stream is vulnerable to: temporal error propagation through the inability of a decoder to reconstruct a frame if it only receives residual, motion-estimated data and spatial error propagation through the loss of entropic decode synchronization arising from corrupted data.

Within a VANET too, video communication is of value in an urban emergency, which, in the scenario analyzed, takes place between early responders' vehicles (fire-engines, police cars, and so on) converging upon the scene. A novel aspect of this situation is that the multicast group formed by the emergency vehicles must take advantage of other vehicles (typically cars in the vicinity) to relay the video streams. Vehicle-to-vehicle streaming has also been suggested as a way of reporting forward traffic conditions through forward triggering of roadside cameras (Guo et al., 2005). Other 'infotainment' VANET applications exist (Kosch et al., 2009) such as travel information, location-based services, and trip planning, which could be enhanced with video. Thus, both MANETs and VANETs offer potential challenging and novel applications of video streaming which will be analyzed through detailed simulations. Because of the number of different parameters, such as node density, node speed, mobility patterns and propagation conditions, it is unrealistic to expect

to test video streaming algorithms through live testing. Therefore, simulation is the predominant method of investigation (Liu et al., 2009), and recently a number of fine-grained VANET simulators (Tonguz et al., 2009) have been constructed through the agency of car manufacturers. IEEE 802.11 networks with distributed medium access control are usually assumed. For VANETs, the IEEE 802.11p variant (Stibor et al., 2007) is in the process of ratification to support Dedicated Short Range Communication (DSRC) between vehicles and to roadside stations.

We are mainly interested in to what extent video error resilience measures can protect video streaming across these networks. The H.264/Advanced Video Codec (AVC) codec has introduced a number of such measures, some of which such as Flexible Macroblock Ordering (FMO) (Lambert et al., 2006) are new to this codec. We analyze the response of the error resilience measures to isolated errors, burst errors caused by fading, and typical wireless error patterns. In addition, multipath routing of video through layered coding or Multiple Description Coding (MDC) (Wang et al., 2005) are a potential resource within such networks. Combining multi-path MDC and error resilience can significantly improve delivered video quality. By using multiple path routing algorithms (Wei & Zakhor, 2004) instead of single-path ones, there is greater utilization of network resources. Moreover, communication becomes more reliable, especially when communicating over highly loaded networks with a higher density of nodes. The research described will examine practical temporal and spatial MDC schemes that can be implemented on mobile devices without customized codecs or excessive complexity. Specifically, temporal MDC is tested using either redundant frames or Video Redundancy Coding, and spatial MDC with FMO slicing and error concealment. An error resilience strategy adopts FMO for high packet loss regimes but includes Gradual Intra-Refresh (GDR) or intra-macroblock refresh to reduce the overhead from frequent intra-frames.

For mobile applications of video streaming, a Peak-Signal-to-Noise Ratio (PSNR) range of 25 dB to 30 dB inclusive is tolerated by viewers. This is approximately equivalent to an ITU-R Mean Opinion Score (MOS) of 3 or 'fair'. The general experience of our research is that packet loss rates of above around 10% lead to 'poor' quality on the ITU-R ranking. However, error resilience can return the quality range to 'fair' for packet loss rates of up to 20%. Beyond 20% packet loss rates, it is no longer possible to improve the quality to an acceptable level by this means. Though we have used practical versions of MDC, MDC still adds complexity to the sending and receiving devices. For some applications, especially over MANETs the added complexity may still present a challenge. Jitter levels may also be increased if path diversity is employed.

There is a synergy between mesh peer-to-peer (P2P) streaming and MANET networks. Both MANETs and P2P networks are decentralized, autonomous and highly dynamic in a fairly similar way. In both cases, network nodes contribute to the overall system performance in an intermittent and unpredictably manner but nonetheless the network as a whole exhibits a high level of resilience and availability. Moreover, several decentralized P2P streaming systems such as mesh-P2P streaming have been deployed to provide live and on-demand video streaming services on the Internet and the same ideas may be useful in providing real-time video streaming in ad hoc networks. Therefore, we will develop the concept of mesh-P2P streaming, building upon earlier discussion of general-purpose streaming without a P2P structure. P2P streaming differs in that a set of overlay video source nodes must be dynamically selected to supply the needs of a destination. These nodes stream on the basis of 'chunks' of video data. The chunks subsequently are reordered at the destination (in a reorder buffer) to form a continuous stream. Because of the multi-hop wireless environment, MDC or layering is again important to reduce the impact of packet loss.

BACKGROUND

Error Resilience Techniques

Error resilience is a form of error protection through source coding. Due to the growing importance of multimedia communication over wireless the range of these techniques has been expanded in the H.264 codec (Wenger, 2003). Error resilience introduces limited delay and as such is suitable for real-time, interactive video streaming, especially video-telephony, and video conferencing. It is also suitable for one-way streaming over cellular wireless networks and broadband wireless access networks to the home. As physical-layer Forward Error Correction (FEC) is normally already present at the wireless physical layer, application-layer FEC may duplicate its role. The exception is if application-layer FEC can be designed to act as an outer code after inner coding at the physical layer, in the manner of concatenated channel coding. Various forms of Automatic Repeat ReQuest (ARQ) are possible but, in general, their use has been limited in ad hoc networks, because the mobility of the nodes and multi-hop nature of routing tends to introduce more delay. For example, in (Mao et al., 2001) if packets from the base layer of a layered video stream (sent over multiple paths) failed to arrive then only a single ARQ is permitted.

Compressed frame data is often split into a number of slices, each consisting of a set of macroblocks, Figure 1. Prior to FMO in H.264/AVC, slice structuring was possible but without breaching the raster-scan order of macroblock formation. This scheme maintains the syntactic and semantic resynchronization information in slice headers but without any macroblock assignment mapping overhead from FMO. Typically, in the MPEG-2 codec, slicing is restricted to a row-by-row basis. Slice resynchronization markers ensure that if a slice is lost then the decoder is still able to continue with entropic decoding (Huffman or Arithmetic). Therefore, a slice is a unit of error

Figure 1. Typical data layout of two macroblock (MB) slice with macroblock headers, motion vectors (MVs), and DCT transform residuals (after motion compensation). For simplicity only two MBs are shown

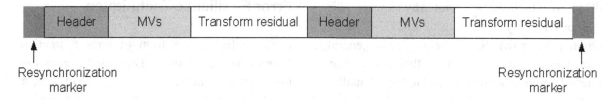

Resynchronization
marker

Resynchronization
marker

Figure 2. Example FMO slice groups and types (after (Lambert et al., 2006) a) Continuing row (type 0) b) geometrical selection (type 2) c) checkerboard selection (type 1)

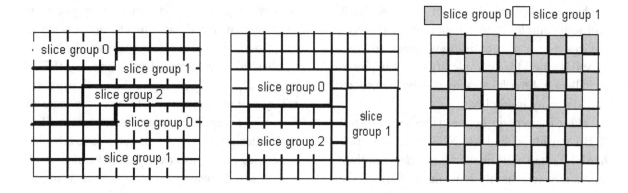

resilience and it is normally assumed that one slice forms a packet. Consequently, for a given frame, the more slices the smaller the packet size and, in error-prone wireless networks, the less risk of packet loss. In the H.264/AVC, data from the Video Coding Layer (VCL) are packetized into a Network Abstraction Layer unit (NALU). Each NALU is encapsulated in an RTP packet, with subsequent addition of UDP/IP headers.

In H.264/AVC, by varying the way in which the macroblocks are assigned to a slice (or rather group of slices), FMO gives a way of reconstructing a frame even if one or more slices are lost. Within a frame up to eight slice groups are possible. A simple FMO method is to continue a row of macroblocks to a second row, Figure 2a, but allow disjoint slice groups (Lambert et al., 2006). Regions of interest are supported, Figure 2b. Checkerboard slice group selection, Figure 2c allows one slice group to aid in the reconstruction

of the other slice group (if its packet is lost) by temporal (using motion vector averaging) or spatial interpolation. Assignment of macroblocks to a slice group can be general (type 6) but the other six types pre-define an assignment formula, thus reducing the coding overhead from providing a full assignment map. The checkerboard type stands apart from other types, as it does not employ adjacent macroblocks as coding references, which decreases its compression efficiency and the relative video quality after decode. However, if there are safely decoded macroblocks in the vicinity of a lost packet error concealment can be applied. Consequently, the rate of decrease in video quality with an increase in loss rate is lower than for the other pre-set types.

A motion-vector-based error concealment method, Figure 3, performs best except when there is high motion activity or frequent scene changes. Alternatively, the intra-coded frame

Figure 3. (a) The missing central macroblock can be reconstructed by means of the vertically or horizontally adjacent macroblocks L, R, T, and B (or an average of their MVs). When a macroblock is formed by a different mode (16 x 8 for R), then the average of the MVs is used. (b) When a candidate match is found, boundary matching can establish its suitability

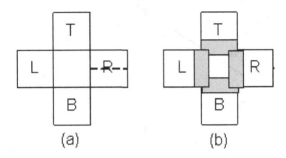

(a)   (b)

Figure 4. H264/AVC data-partitioning in which a single slice is split into three NAL units (types 2 to 4). The relative size of the C partition will depend on the quantization parameter (QP), with a lower QP leading to higher quality and a larger C partition

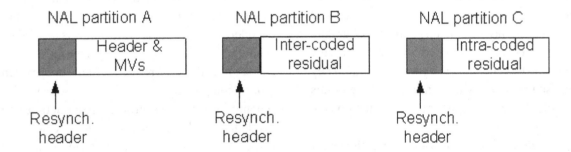

method of spatial interpolation can provide smooth and consistent edges. In practice, either one or the other method of error concealment should be selected or the choice could be made dynamically, based on the continuity at macroblock boundaries.

Data partitioning in H.264/AVC, Figure 4, separates the compressed bitstream into: A) configuration data and motion vectors; B) intracoded transform coefficients; and C) inter-coded coefficients. This data form A, B, and C partitions which are packetized as separate NALUs. The arrangement allows a frame to be reconstructed even if the inter-coded macroblocks in partition C. are lost, provided the motion vectors in partition A survive. Partition A is normally strongly

FEC-protected at the application layer or physical layer protection may be provided such as the hierarchical modulation scheme in (Barmada et al., 2005) for broadcast TV. Notice that in codecs prior to H.264/AVC, data partitioning was also applied but no separation into NALUs occurred. The advantage of integral partitioning is that additional resynchronization markers are available that reset entropic encoding. This mode of data partitioning is still available in H.264/AVC and is applied to I-frames.

The insertion of intra-coded macroblocks into frames normally encoded through motion-compensated prediction allows temporal error propagation to be arrested if matching macroblocks in a previous frame are lost. Intra-refresh through

Figure 5. Multi-hop routing over an ad hoc network, utilizing dual paths. Video streams may either be split as in MDC, or via layered coding with base and enhancement layers

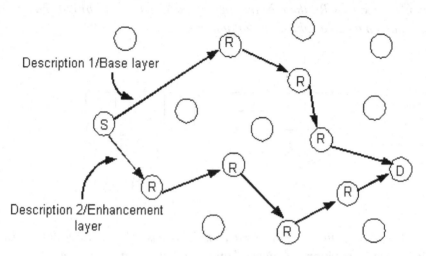

periodic insertion of I-frames with all macroblocks encoded through spatial reference (intra-coded) is the usual way of catching error propagation. However, I-frames cause periodic increases in the datarate when encoding at a variable bitrate. They are also unnecessary if channel switching points or Video Cassette Recorder (VCR) functions are not required.

This review by no means exhausts the error-resilience facilities in H.264/AVC, with switching frames and flexible reference frames considered in (Stockhammer and Zia, 2007).

Path Diversity in Video Streaming

A number of alternative ways of taking advantage of path diversity have been investigated in the research literature. In a general context, the research in (Chakereseki, J. et al., 2005) concluded that layered video is competitive if the rate is modified according to the distortion. Rate-distortion analysis is now a built-in facility of the H.264 codec and can be simplified to reduce the computational overhead. In (Mao et al., 2003), two further multi-path schemes, Figure 5, were compared with layering combined with ARQ, namely: 1) feedback requesting reference frames; and 2) a

variant of MDC with motion compensation. In the first of these approaches, the problem of loss of decoder-encoder synchronization was tackled by sending a negative ARQ to indicate the most recent successfully received reference frame upon which motion compensation can be based. Therefore, this scheme also assumed sufficient playout time and bandwidth to allow ACKs. Sending ACKs will also cause more control packet overhead, which can be high. In the variant of MDC tested, no ARQs were sent but a correction method at the decoder was necessary to counter drift between decoder and encoder. The CSMA/CA MAC was assumed with a multipath variant of the reactive Dynamic Source Routing (DSR). The authors concluded (Mao et al., 2003) that acceptable video quality is possible but which scheme is selected is dependent on the ad hoc scenario.

To overcome the problem of FEC complexity, rateless coding with linear decoder complexity was employed in (Schierl et al., 2008) to protect the video layers. Unequal layer protection allows the receiver to control the number of layers and protection level it receives. Though the scheme is formally described as multi-source, it is close to P2P distribution. Unfortunately, the extent of

Figure 6. P2P overlay over VANET with (a) Tree-based multicast topology (b) Mesh-based multicast topology. Arrowed lines represent logical connections, which may be over multiple wireless hops

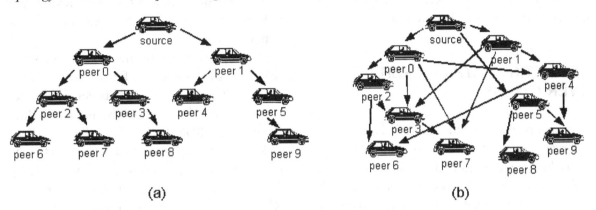

(a)   (b)

physical layer modeling is unclear and, therefore, so is the effectiveness.

Peer-to-Peer Video Streaming

The P2P streaming concept has nowadays been developed into several trial P2P streaming systems, such as Joost (Fu et al., 2007), Sopcast, Zattoo, PPlive, and Coolstream (Zhang et al., 2005). The online broadcasting arena is evolving in response to the clear commercial interest for these new technologies in support of IPTV (TV over IP-framed networks). P2P streaming architectures can be categorized according to their distribution mechanisms. The various approaches to P2P streaming have been surveyed by (Liu et al., 2008). Two main topologies have emerged, Figure 6, i.e. tree-based (Padmanabhan et al., 2003) and mesh-based P2P (for a comparison see (Sentinelli et al., 2007)). In a MANET, the network topology changes randomly and unpredictably over time. Hence, an application that can easily adapt to the dynamic behavior of the ad hoc network will be an effective solution. Mesh-P2P streaming is flexible and can be managed easily in comparison to a tree-based topology. Moreover, it is not affected by the churn of peers or the effects of handoff. A mesh-based topology can also overcome the bandwidth heterogeneity present in

a MANET. Mesh-based distribution is becoming more widespread than tree-based distribution and has been adopted by most successful P2P streaming systems (Fu et al., 2007; Zhang et al., 2005; Rejaie, R. 2006).

The very successful BitTorrent P2P file distribution protocol (Shah and Paris, 2007) has been the inspiration behind mesh-P2P streaming. In the all-to-all connectivity of a mesh, the overlay network supporting the stream distribution incorporates the swarm-like content delivery introduced by BitTorrent. To deliver a video stream, the video is divided into chunks or blocks in such a way that allows a peer to receive portions of the stream from different peers and assemble them locally, leading to the delivery of good quality streams to a large number of users. The original video stream from a source is distributed among different peers (Jurca et al., 2007). A peer joining the mesh retrieves video chunks from one or more source peers. The peer also receives information about the other receiver peers from the same sources that serve the video chunks. Each peer periodically reports its newly available video chunks to all its neighbors. The chunks requested by each peer from a neighbor are determined by a packet scheduling algorithm based on available content and bandwidth from its neighbors (Jurca et al., 2007). This approach is more robust than the tree-based architecture, since when a stream comes from various sources communication does not break when only a subset of peers disconnect.

EXPLOITING PATH DIVERSITY OVER A MANET

In a man-made or natural crisis, it is vital that emergency workers in a team can readily communicate between each other (Dilmaghani and Rao, 2007) as they move across a disaster scenario. A MANET becomes part of the solution, allowing small teams (10-20 people in (Karlsson et al., 2005) to move through the area on foot or possibly on some form of vehicle. Because of the display resolution and processing power of hand-held or wearable devices Quarter Common Intermediate Format (QCIF) (176×144 pixel/frame) at a frame rate possibly as low as 10 fps is likely (Karlsson et al., 2005). This is convenient as supportable data rates across multi-hop paths could be low.

Exploiting the path diversity available in an ad hoc network through MDC is attractive. However, in general, MDC is difficult to organize and computationally complex (Wang et al., 2005) because it requires synchronization between encoders and decoders to reduce motion estimation error drift. Therefore, in the general case, specialist MDC codec software is required, which is a barrier to the deployment of MDC. Various forms of splitting between the descriptions can occur including in the spatial (Franchi et al., 2004) and the frequency domain (Reibman et al., 2001), but we consider temporal splitting in which a number of practical solutions are proposed. In mobile devices with a limitation in battery power and/or processor computation power, simplicity is advisable.

A practical scheme is VRC (Wenger et al., 1998) in which two independent streams are formed from encoding odd and even frame sequences and sent over different paths. By insertion of intra-coded I-frames (spatially coded with no removal of temporal redundancy through motion

compensation) either sequence can be resynchronized at the decoder, at a cost in increased data redundancy compared to sending a single stream with I-frames.

To improve error resilience in both paths, redundant frames intended for error resilience in H.264/AVC, can also serve to better reconstruct frames received in error. Redundant frames (Baccichet et al., 2006) (or strictly redundant slices making up a frame) are coarsely quantized frames that can avoid sudden drops in quality marked by freeze frame effects if a complete frame (or slice) is lost. The main weakness of the redundant frame solution is that these frames are discarded if not required but the redundancy is still likely to be less than including extra I-frame synchronization, as redundant frames are predictively coded. A subsidiary weakness of this scheme is the delay in encoding and transmitting redundant frames, making it more suitable for one-way communication. If the redundant frame/slice is substituted for the loss of the original frame/slice there will be some mismatch between encoder and decoder. This is because the encoder will assume the original frame/slice was used. However, the effect will be much less than if no substitution took place. We have investigated redundant frames as this is a new feature of the H.264 codec that has had comparatively little attention.

As an alternative way to avoid the need for I-frame synchronization lost frames in one description are reconstructed (Apostopoulos, 2001) from temporally adjacent frames in the other description. In this solution, all frames apart from the first I-frame in each description are predictively coded (P-frames) from previous frames, though reconstruction may occur with the aid of past and future P-frames. However, reconstruction with P-frames from a different description reintroduces the risk of picture drift from lack of synchronization between encoder and decoder. To overcome this problem, redundant pictures intended for error resilience in H.264/AVC, can serve to better reconstruct P-frames received in error (Radulovic et al., 2007).

Figure 7 illustrates the schemes tested. The frame numbers indicate the raw video frame from which a coded frame is constructed. (Frames are arranged is display order though the transmission order may differ to ensure that references frames arrive before the frames that are predicted from them.) Frames are decoded with motion compensation from reference frames in the same stream. By separately decoding from each stream, the problem of MDC decoder complexity is avoided. In Figure 7a, a single stream or description is sent as an I-frame, followed by a series of P-frames in the Baseline Profile of H.264/AVC. In the latter Profile, Context Adaptive Variable Length Codes (CAVLC) (dynamic Huffman entropic coding) is employed for simplicity, with some reduction in latency for interactive applications. In Figure 7b, for VRC the skip frame(s) facility of the H.264/AVC Main Profile has been exploited. This profile allows bi-predictive B-frames with greater coding efficiency than if only P-frames were to be employed. The GOP size was again 15 frames with the usual repeating pattern of two B- and one P-frame until the next I-frame. B-frames may be dropped with no impact on later frames. In the Main Profile, Context-Adaptive Binary Arithmetic Coding (CABAC) results in a 9-14% bit saving at a small cost in computational complexity (Marpe et al., 2003). In Figure 7c, redundant frames are sent in each stream, at a cost in latency but a potential gain in delivered video quality. There is only one initial I-frame, as, upon loss of the first I-frame or a subsequent P-frame, its matching redundant frame (if not lost) is available as a substitute.

The QCIF video clip Foreman, intended as an illustration of communication between mobile devices, exhibits the typical features of a hand-held camera and, because of scene motion and a scene change, exhibits a significant coding complexity. CBR-encoded data rates of around 51 kbps were employed in simulations. The frame rate of the video stream was set to be 15 fps. As

Figure 7. Different path diversity schemes: a) Single stream b) VRC with odd and even descriptions, c) Two streams with redundant frames

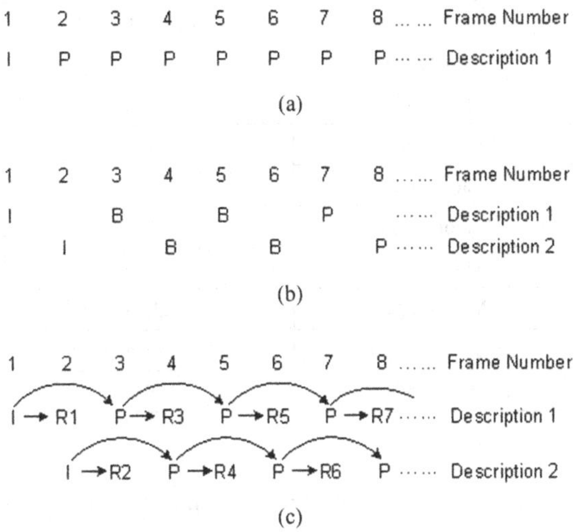

buffer memory significantly contributes to energy consumption, actively during access, and passively due to the need for refresh of DRAM, the size was set to three frames (with buffer sharing for two stream schemes). This implies that the delay deadline is 198 ms, which is actually larger than that in (Wei and Zakhor, 2004).

MANET Simulation

The Global Mobile System Simulator (Glo-MoSim) (Zeng et al., 1998) simulation library was employed to generate our results. GloMoSim was developed based on a layered approach similar to the OSI seven-layer network architecture. IP framing was employed with UDP transport, as TCP transport can introduce unbounded delay, which is not suitable for delay-intolerant video streaming. The well-known Ad-hoc On demand Distance Vector (AODV) routing protocol (Perkins & Royer, 1999) was selected as it does not transmit periodic routing messages, which, for table-driven protocols, can result in greater control overhead, unless network traffic is high.

Table 1. Parameters for multi-path streaming experiments

Parameter	Value
Wireless technology	IEEE 802.11
Channel model	Two-ray
Max. range	250 m
Roaming area	1000 m^2
Pause time	5 s
No. of nodes	20
Min. speed	0 m/s
Max. speed	1 – 35 m/s
Mobility model	Random waypoint
Routing protocol	AODV

The parameters for the simulations are summarized in Table 1. GloMoSim provides a two-ray ground propagation channel model with antenna height hardwired at 1.5 m, and with a Friss free-space model with parameters (exponent, sigma) = (2.0, 0.0) for near line-of-sight and plane earth path loss (4.0, 0.0) for far line-of-sight. The radio range was 250 m with 1 Mbps shared maximum data-rate. Setting the bandwidth capacity to the latter value in the simulation allows modeling of a limited available bandwidth. The two-ray model is adequate for line-of-sight modeling (Oda et al., 2000) and for modeling in rural areas, provided the terrain is flat. This is because, in these circumstances. these two rays dominate other paths. Otherwise, reflections and diffractions around obstacles such as building become important.

For the video source, each frame was placed in a single packet, unless it was an I-frame. In which case, two packets were employed. An I-frame may occupy as much as 1 kB, whereas a B-frame will commonly be encoded in less than 100 B. This implies that, though encoder CBR mode is selected, an encoder output is never completely CBR. In fact, the H.264/AVC codec in CBR mode also smoothes quality transitions to avoid disturbing the end user by sudden transitions in quality. In line with the practice in (Wei

& Zakhor, 2004), if one of the I-frame packets arrives before the playout deadline but the other does not, this is counted as 'acceptable', as partial decoding can still take place while the other packet arrives. Two cross-traffic sources were set up sending 100 packets each at intermittent intervals over the simulation period. It is certainly true that cross-traffic will be present, yet such sources can generate large control packet overheads which interfere with the traffic of interest.

Both streams are coded at 15 fps in the two description schemes and played out at 15 fps. This allows for substitution of frames within the final merged sequence, should a frame(s) be lost. Of course, substitution of frames can only take place if the appropriate reference frame or redundant frame (if needed) is available. As is normal to reduce computation overhead (Kalman et al., 2003), previous or 'freeze frame' error concealment was turned on at the decoder, rather than more complex concealment.

The results from VRC streaming over dual paths are represented in Figures 8–10. From Figure 8 it is apparent that when one stream suffers excessive bad frames another can compensate. Moreover, the lower level of frame loss is below 10%. From detailed inspection, the major cause of bad frames occurring is packet loss rather than missed arrival deadlines. This is the reverse of the single stream situation, when, in most cases, bad frames occur through late arrivals. The result is consistent with low levels of jitter in the VRC case. However, from Figure 9, delay is high, again making interactive video unfeasible. Delay also varies considerably, depending on node speed. Jitter levels, Figure 10, may be increased over single path streaming.

From Figure 11, reporting dual path streaming with redundant frames, it will be apparent there is again a compensatory pattern of bad frames occurring, so that the weakness of one path can be balanced by the strength of the other. The number of frames dropped through late arrival is generally higher than in VRC streaming, but this

Figure 8. Bad frame ratio with variation in node speed for VRC dual stream transfer

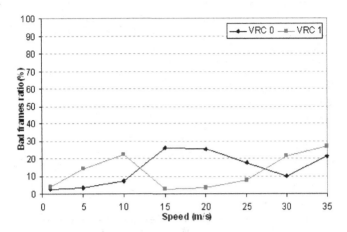

Figure 9. Delay with variation in node speed for VRC dual stream transfer

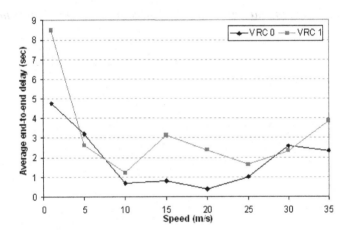

Figure 10. Jitter with variation in node speed for VRC dual stream transfer

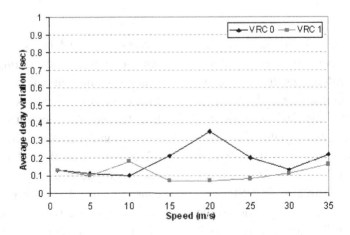

Figure 11. Bad frame ratio with variation in node speed for dual stream with redundant frames transfer

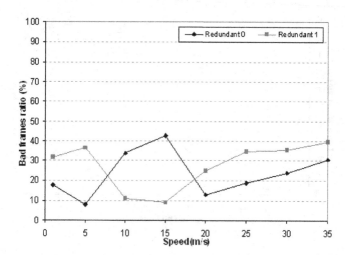

Figure 12. Delay with variation in node speed for dual stream with redundant frames transfer

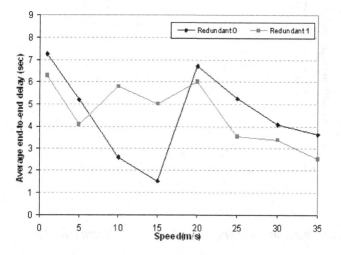

should not be surprising as additional redundant frames are now being sent. However in general, sending redundant frames results in greater packet loss and consequently more bad frames than in VRC streaming. This is not necessarily a problem for the resulting video quality if a majority of redundant frames are lost, as these frames do not contribute to the decoded video sequence except when they are used to replace lost P-frames. End-to-end delay, Figure 12, is high and erratic according to node speed. Therefore, a viewer will be subject to a start-up delay before a video stream

arrives. Start-up delay is obviously less of a problem in an emergency setting, as unlike conventional streaming in which a video is selected and then there is a wait before it arrives in this situation, the receiver does not know when the stream was originally started. Thus, there would be no effect noticed by the video viewer. Once again end-to-end delay is high and it is unlikely that changes could be made to reduce the delay to allow an interactive application. Jitter levels, Figure 13, for redundant frame streaming are

Figure 13. Jitter with variation in node speed for dual stream with redundant frames transfer

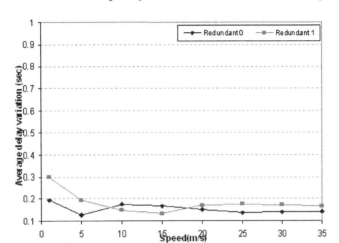

Figure 14. Overhead from all control packets for the three schemes

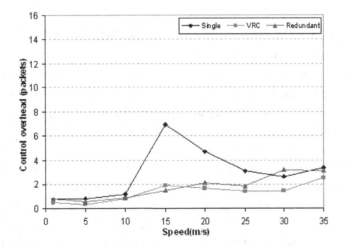

consistent across the speeds, implying that the playout buffer size can be conveniently set.

Control packets consist of route requests, replies, and error messages. Figure 14 shows the overhead from all control packets including cross-traffic control packets during the video streaming sessions. The overhead is the number of control packets over the number of data packets received. There are normally considerably more short control packets than data packets. It can be seen that at a speed of 15 m/s the set-up of the simulation results in more control packets from the cross-traffic sources during the single stream session. This was traced to the need for the cross-traffic to take long multi-hop routes at that speed. Interference between cross traffic and video stream can consequently lead to lost packets within the video stream. This is a general rule, as no firm conclusions can be made about which speed to avoid so as to reduce the impact of overhead. However, there is a rising trend in overhead from control packets with speed, implying a rising trend in energy consumption.

Figure 15. Delivered video comparison for Foreman between the three tested schemes

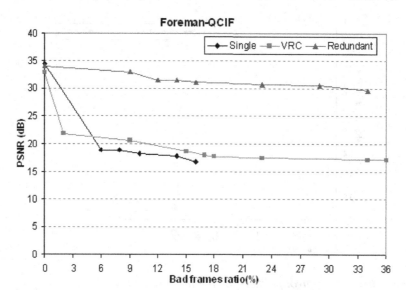

In Figure 15, the resulting delivered video quality is compared for the Foreman clip. Perhaps surprisingly, given the number of bad frames is higher, inserting redundant frames allows lost or dropped predictive frames to be reconstructed, resulting in a considerable improvement in delivered video quality over single path transfer.

In general, jitter levels were also low, leading to a smaller energy conserving playout buffer. All multi-path schemes suffer from high start-up delay and could not be used for interactive video. Node speed may have a considerable impact on the number of bad frames, as can the presence of cross traffic. It is probably the case that video communication will be erratic and dependent on the ad hoc scenario. The redundant frame multi-path scheme discussed in this Section shows that video transfer is possible and is practical, whereas previous research had resulted in rather complex schemes to implement, which, however attractive to researchers, would stretch the wireless node capability.

COMBINING AD HOC AND P2P

Both ad hoc and P2P networks are decentralized, autonomous and highly dynamic in a fairly similar way. In both cases, network nodes contribute to the overall system performance in an intermittent and unpredictably manner but nonetheless exhibit a high level of resilience and availability. Figure 16 illustrates a P2P application overlay over an ad hoc network, in which an overlay network is placed over the network layer. It is important to note that the overlay node placement is logically different to that of the physical placement of the nodes. A mesh-based topology can also overcome the bandwidth heterogeneity present in an ad hoc network. Consequently, a mesh-P2P could be an effective solution for an ad hoc network.

A mesh-P2P overlay is shown in Figure 17. In this example, seven nodes form a mesh within which two nodes are the original source nodes for the same video. Likely ways that two nodes in a VANET could acquire the same video clip is that both could have passed a roadside unit offering informational/advertising video clips. How-

Figure 16. An example of a P2P application overlay over an ad hoc network

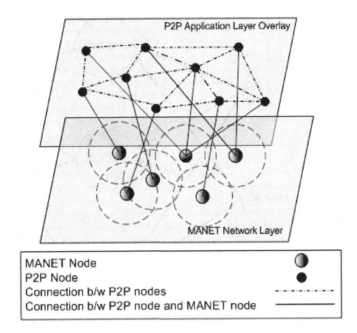

ever, it is also possible that these two nodes previously could have acquired the same video from a single node, prior to the distribution process illustrated in Figure 17. Three nodes (node C, node D and node E) receive video from these two source nodes. The three nodes in turn also act as sources to two further nodes (node F and node G). Hence, nodes C, D and E download and upload at the same time i.e. act as receivers and sources at the same time. All receiving nodes, C to G, are served by multiple sources. Moreover, in Figure 17, nodes F and G originally receive the two MDC streams from two other nodes in the overlay network. They then receive a stream from another node when the stream from one of the sending nodes is interrupted.

Peer selection for streaming purposes can either be achieved in one of three ways. Firstly, it is achieved in a hybrid fashion, by including some server nodes in the manner of commercial P2P streaming. Secondly, a structured overlay can be organized that allows quicker discovery of source peers than in an unstructured overlay. However, structured overlays require the source

data to be placed in particular nodes, which may not be practical in a VANET. Therefore, we assume an unstructured and decentralized overlay such as Gnutella, KaZaa, or GIA (Chawathe et al., 2003).

VIDEO DISTRIBUTION IN A VANET

In this Section, we introduce spatial decomposition rather than temporal decomposition of a video frames into slices, through checkerboard FMO in the H.264/AVC, which allows lost chunks from one description to be reconstructed from another. As the same frame structure is preserved, no extra frames are required and error drift is actively prevented by the decomposition. When chunks are reordered in the cache or buffer-map of the destination prior to decode and playback, if there are still missing chunks or chunks lacking some slices, checkerboard FMO can aid decoding through the mechanism of error concealment. Video error resilience through GDR was also applied. These measures are necessary, despite the

Figure 17. Mesh-based P2P topology sending data streams from sources to receivers

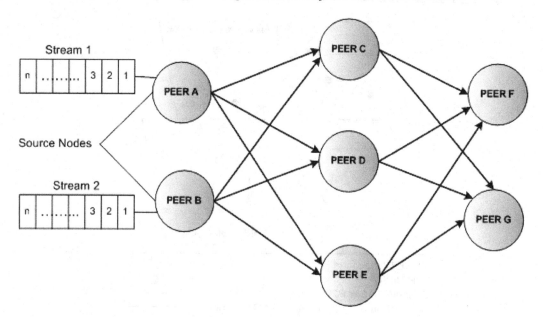

3–27 Mbps supported by IEEE 802.11p, because vehicle mobility still causes broken links and traffic congestion results in wireless interference. In fact, the extra capacity is not required for the efficient H.264/AVC, resulting in delivery at a faster rate than is required at a cost in the need to protect against packet loss.

Figure 18 is an example of a P2P slice compensation scheme for MDC with FMO, assuming the receiver lacks all of the video sequence. Within the stream before decomposition into descriptions, an initial intra-coded I-frame is followed by predictive-coded P-frames, supported by GDR. Recall that B-frames do not occur in the less complex Baseline profile of H.264/AVC. The *same* video stream is available from two sets of peers (MDC 1 and 2). That is MDC 1 and 2 are duplicates of each other. Each frame with a video stream is further split into two slices (slices 0 and 1) to form two descriptions, resulting in four sender streams in all. The associated slice numbers in Figure 18 do not refer to a decoding sequence but to the original display frame order, as produced by the encoder. Suppose P_{4S1} and P_{6S1} from MDC

1 and P_{2S1}, P_{4S1}, P_{6S0} and P_{6S1} from MDC description 2 are lost. P_{2S1} of MDC 2 can be replaced by P_{2S1} of MDC 1. P_{4S1} of both the descriptions can be decoded from P_{4S0} of any description and similarly P_{6S1} can be decoded from P_{6S0} of MDC 1, both using the properties of checkerboard FMO. However if only one stream (MDC 1 or 2) and no error resilience were used then it would not be possible to recover the lost frames. Furthermore, one row of macroblocks per slice in turn is coded in intra-mode (rather than inter-mode) in order to increase error resiliency, as that portion of the P-frame can readily be decoded without any prior reference frame. Thus, GDR further helps restore frames reconstructed through FMO.

Figure 19 is a logical representation of the scheme, in which after distribution of video chunks by roadside units acting as sources to passing vehicles, these vehicles act as peers within the P2P network. These peers may upload or download at the same time. As soon as a sender receives chunks it can send them to other peers. A single receiver vehicle must receive at least two descriptions and each description must be delivered from

Figure 18. An example of the slice compensation scheme with MDC and FMO, with arrows indicating the relationship "can be reconstructed from"

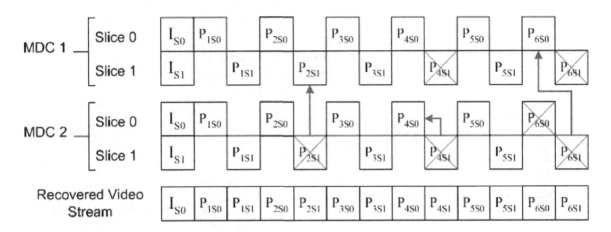

multiple peers. However, a receiver may well try to connect to other sending peers in a process called handover. A handover generally occurs due to two reasons: 1) the receiver is receiving few or no chunks from its current senders or 2) for load-balancing purposes. The receiver stores the received chunks from different peers into its buffer-map. Having buffered a certain number of contiguous chunks, it then sends them correctly ordered to its playback buffer. The decoder renders the video from its playback buffer, taking advantage of the slice compensation scheme to reconstruct missing data.

VANET Simulation

We again employed the GloMoSim simulator for simulating VANETs. IP framing was utilized with UDP transport. There was one video clip and one destination vehicle with four senders at any one time. Data points are the average (arithmetic mean) of 50 runs with 95% confidence intervals established for each data point. For these generic simulations, a two-ray propagation model with an omni-directional antenna height of 1.5 m at receiver and transmitter was selected for which the reflection coefficient was -0.7, which is the

same as that of asphalt. The plane earth path loss exponent was set to 4.0 for an urban environment, with the direct path exponent set for free space propagation (2.0). The IEEE 802.11p transmission power was set to 23 dBm (0.2 W) with a range of 300m, to reduce interference as much as possible within the city. Receiver sensitivity was set to -93 dBm. The MAC modeled was CSMA/CA with Request-to-Send/Clear-to-Send (RTS/CTS) turned on. IEEE 802.11p's robust Binary Phase Shift Keying (BPSK) modulation mode at 1/2 coding rate was simulated. The resulting bitrate is at the lower end of IEEE 802.11p's range at 3 Mbps. Bit Error Rate (BER) modeling within the simulator introduced a packet length error dependency. Total simulation time was 900 s. To simulate handover, new sending peers were selected by the destination approximately every 7.5 s. As GloMoSim does not conveniently allow automatic selection of peers, choice of new sending peers was hard-wired into the simulations.

The downtown topology of VanetMobiSim (Fiore et al., 2007) was selected. In the simulations, a 1000 m² area was defined and vehicles were initially randomly placed within the area. Other settings to do with road cluster density, intersection density, lanes (2) and speeds are given in

Figure 19. Mesh-based P2P topology sending video chunks from roadside sources to peers within the VANET, from which the chunks are distributed over multiple paths

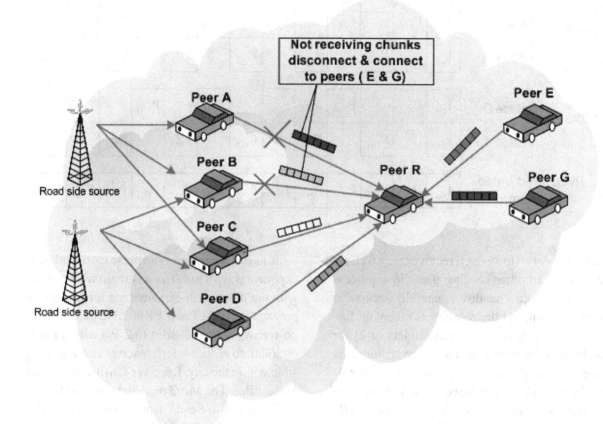

Table 2 to allow reproduction of the experiments. The number of traffic lights (at intersections) and time interval between changes was also defined.

The Intelligent Driver Model (IDM), accords with car following model developed elsewhere (Treiber et al, 2000) and based on live observations. In car-following models of which the IMD is an improved version, a driver does not approach a vehicle arbitrarily closely as can occur in some mobility models but will de-accelerate if another car is ahead or overtake in another lane. Vanet-MobiSim adds to this with modeling of intersection management (IDM-IM). The IDM-IM is extended to include lane change behavior in the IDM-LC model, which was used in our simula-

tions. The micro-mobility models presented by VanetMobiSim are of increased sophistication in driver behavior, which increase the realism and reduce optimistic assessments of what can be achieved in a VANET. Unfortunately, when driver behavior is introduced into simulations it is no longer possible to easily examine node speed dependencies, as the vehicles will have a range of speeds depending on local conditions, though the minimum and maximum speeds are not exceeded.

We compared the slice compensation scheme to a very simple form of MDC. In the simplified MDC, there were just two senders and a duplicate set of chunks was sent from each sender, i.e. no

Table 2. Settings for road layouts and mobility models

Global Parameters	
Simulation Time	900 s
Terrain Dimension	1000 x1000 m^2
Graph type	Space graph (Downtown model)
Road Clusters	4
Intersection Density	2e^{-5}
Max. traffic lights	10
Time interval between traffic lights change	10000 ms
Number of Lanes	2
Min. Stay	10 s
Max. Stay	100 s
Nodes (vehicles)	20, 60, 100
Min. Speed	3.2 m/s (7 mph)
Max. Speed	13.5 m/s (30 mph)
IDM-LC Model	
Length of vehicle	5 m
Max. acceleration	0.6 m/s^2
Normal deceleration	0.5 m/s^2
Traffic jam distance	2 m
Node's safe time headway	1.5 s
Recalculation of movement parameters time	0.1 s
Safe deceleration	4 m/s^2
Politeness factor of drivers when changing lane	0.5
Threshold acceleration for lane change	0.2 m/s^2

slicing occurred and consequently just one set of chunks over one path was sent from each of two senders. Obviously, if packets from one chunk are lost then these can be replaced by those from the other but if the same packet is lost from both senders then reconstruction is no longer possible. In that case, previous frame replacement only is available, causing freeze frame effects. Handover of senders occurs periodically.

In the case of the slice compensation scheme, the chunk size was set to 30 RTP packets, each bearing one H.264/AVC NAL unit, implying 15 frames per chunk or 1 s of video at 15 fps. The FMO NAL unit size was approximately half that of the size before slicing, i.e. RTP packet size was around 260 B. In the simplified scheme, the RTP packets without FMO slicing were not exactly the same as two single slice RTP packets because of the need to accommodate FMO mapping information (Lambert et al., 2006) in the NAL unit.

In terms of network performance, Figure 20 shows that, for both variants of MDC, as the density of the network increases then the packet loss ratio (number of lost packets to total sent) decreases. The bars reflect average (arithmetic means). Because of path diversity the number of packets lost is much reduced compared to what one would normally expect. Moreover, the packet loss ratios for the slice compensation scheme (labeled MDC with E. Res) are consistently below those of the simplified MDC scheme. Therefore, there is a gain from increasing the number of paths from two to four. In fact, the ratios are also stable as the number of vehicles is increased from 60 to 100, implying an efficient solution once a certain network density has been reached. However, a problem now arises at the sparse density of 20 vehicles. This is because in some of the fifty test runs it was likely that the vehicles were widely separated and road obstacles reduced the chance of the vehicles approaching close enough to facilitate chunk exchange. In these runs, the packet loss ratio was as high as 40%, which explains the large 95% confidence intervals. Therefore, because of the overlap in the confidence intervals these results need to be treated with caution, though the trend across the tests is apparent.

Mean per packet overhead (measured in terms of additional packets required to route each packet) increases with the number of vehicles in the network, Figure 21, reflecting the extra hops traversed. This effect is a consequence of the extra congestion and interference introduced by more dense networks in an urban VANET. As a result the routing protocol has to 'work harder' to maintain the low packet loss routes. As is clear

Figure 20. Mean packet loss ratio by VANET size with and without error resilience (R. Res) showing 95% confidence intervals

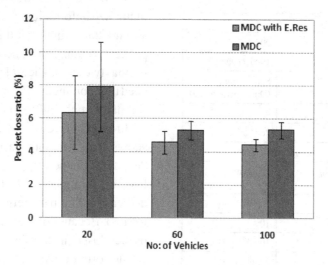

Figure 21. MDC per packet overhead by VANET size with and without error resilience (E. Res) showing 95% confidence intervals

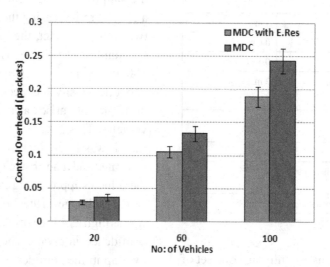

from Figure 21, the multi-routing protocol when used with more senders (four rather than two) becomes progressively better, presumably because it has a better chance to find some of its routes more efficiently than others, increasing the over-all efficiency. Notice, however, that the impact of extra control overhead upon battery usage in a VANET can be neglected as there is a readily available power source in the vehicle's alternator.

Figure 22 shows the resulting video quality for one of the fifty simulation runs. The run was selected so that the indicators were within the confidence intervals of Figures 20 and 21. Also included in Figure 22 is the PSNR for zero packet loss. This shows that there is a considerable penalty from using FMO because the extra bits taken up in macroblock mapping, for a given fixed target CBR, are no longer available to improve

Figure 22. Example MDC video quality with and without error resilience

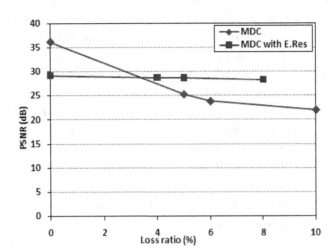

the video quality. Nevertheless H.264/AVC has achieved good QCIF quality at the low datarate for both schemes. However, when the packet loss ratio increases due to FMO with error concealment the slice compensation scheme is able to almost completely maintain video quality, while the simple MDC scheme results in deteriorating quality. Below 25 dB, quality is barely acceptable even for a mobile application.

RESEARCH DIRECTIONS

Pioneering work examined the feasibility of video streaming over MANETs but the pace of this research has slackened off in recent years. This is unfortunate, as MANETs are now being actively pursued as a way of extending the coverage and flexibility of existing cellular networks (Wu et al., 2001; Lu et al., 2002). This may be a reflection of the increased specialization that has been introduced into MANET research, which makes it difficult to keep abreast of both video streaming and ad hoc networking research.

The research in (Setton et al., 2004) examined point-to-point CBR video streaming in a 15-node network in a 1000 m² area. The reference 'Foreman' QCIF video clip at 30 fps was simulated

at rates ranging from around 50 kbps up to 350 kbps. GOP sizes were varied with playout buffer settings equivalent to 350 ms and 500 ms of video. The research paper reported that as the number of multi-path routes increased to six, the delivered video quality increased. Unfortunately, (Setton et al., 2004) did not report on node mobility or radio range. However, the paper did show that optimal regimes exist but that simple formulas require perfect network traffic knowledge by each node, which is impractical.

A denser node distribution (60 nodes in a 1200 × 800 m² area) was chosen in (Wei & Zakhor, 2004) with the random waypoint mobility model and with maximum speeds varying from 2.5 m/s to 15 m/s. The playout buffer size was 100 ms of video storage with video streamed at a rate of 192 kbps for 12 fps. Radio range was 250 m for an IEEE 802.11 wireless LAN in ad hoc mode but the node pause period was not given in the paper. Because of the node density, the effects of mobility were not strongly felt, because it is not possible for nodes to quickly loose radio contact with surrounding nodes (resulting in broken wireless links). Though Reed-Solomon (RS) FEC was employed in simulations, it should be borne in mind that this RS FEC has quadratic computational complexity which may overwhelm battery powered devices. The paper showed the advantage of the authors' multiple tree algorithm for video multicast. Another paper by the same authors (Wei & Zakhor, 2006) amongst other results showed that, provided the paths were disjoint, IEEE 802.11's CSMA/CA is unlikely to lead to traffic interference. This line of research was continued in the authors' most recent contribution at the time of writing (Wei & Zakhor, 2009), in which the robustness of the paths is estimated in advance. For example, the received signal strength could be reported along with the level of contending cross-traffic. This work's strength is that physical tests have now confirmed the findings.

In (Fiandrotti et al., 2008), the term ad hoc is used in the sense that there is direct wireless communication between nodes, rather than via a network access point. The authors consider the Scalable Video Coding (SVC) extension of H.264 and reduce the number of small packets generated by means of packet aggregation. In (Adlakha et al., 2007), the network capacity, flow and rate allocation are jointly optimized across the wireless protocol stack in such as way that the network traffic as a whole benefits. A distinct average improvement in video quality was demonstrated compared to a non-cross-layer approach. Another route to improvement (Liao & Gibson, 2007) is to improve MDC error concealment at the decoder by combining the predictions from both streams in spatial (intra-) decoding. However, any improvement in video quality reported in (Chow & Ishii, 2007) could not be applied to the emergency scenario unless there is a way to copy the same video to multiple sources. An interesting suggestion is contained in (Arce et al, 2008), that hierarchical routing may improve the performance of ad hoc network video streaming. Finally, in this examination of recent work on video over ad hoc networks, in (Sheltami, 2008) a restriction on the number of hops and an increase in the data-rate to 5.5 Mbps was advocated for comfortable transfer of H.264/AVC video over an ad hoc network.

It is the transience of the video sources in a VANET on a highway that poses a problem to video communication on a highway (Guo et al., 2005), as the sources can quickly be isolated by a network partition (Wu et al., 2004). On the other hand, even at fast car speeds (up to 65 mph) it is possible (Bucciol et al., 2008) to achieve a 1 Mbps data rate with an IEEE 802.11b system operating with a range of 250 m. In (Guo et al., 2005), multiple video sources were modeled traveling on a 4-5 lane highway in Atlanta. Video was collected by sending from a car approaching a destination a request trigger to a camera on a remote vehicle passing a destination region. Video transport back to the requestor was by a store-carry-and-forward sub-system, though the method was not detailed in (Guo et al., 2005). The main analysis in (Guo et al., 2005) was of delay characteristics, whereas, in fact, delay can be absorbed by a large on-board buffer.

In (Xie et al., 2007), a similar scenario to (Guo et al., 2005) was simulated but video quality was now considered. It was observed that the delivered video quality was good (30 dB PSNR at medium traffic density with sufficient buffer size (300 packets and above)) but deteriorated at lower densities. In the event of buffer overflow, an early drop policy was better than the normal drop-tail policy but the buffer drop test was only conducted for a relatively small buffer size of 100 packets, which was already known to result in poorer quality delivered video. Wireless range was 400 m with a data-rate of 6 Mbps to approximate IEEE 802.11p at 5.9 GHz but the propagation model was not given and may have been free space.

Research in (Park et al., 2006), extending the work in (Guo et al., 2005), simulated a two-ray wireless propagation model and imposed a FEC-based solution through network coding. In fact, research in (Park et al., 2006) seems to have first introduced channel error control for video over a VANET. Unfortunately, though network coding of FEC and in particular rateless error coding is an effective means of limiting the impact of packet erasures upon streamed video, it depends on action by intervening nodes. When these nodes are not possible destinations and consequently may not be expected to make special provision for video data, then network coding is not feasible.

Increased detail in VANET simulation has not only encompassed mobility modeling but also takes channel modeling (Matolak, 2008) into account. The emerging IEEE 802.11p introduces rapid connection of ad hoc nodes (vehicles), higher transmitter powers (33 dBm for emergency vehicles on a highway), a channel structure that includes safety and application channels, and IEEE 802.11e traffic prioritization. However, in an urban environment node interference may restrict high transmitter powers and urban canyons confine the wireless signal. Therefore, multi-path modeling through the Rayleigh, Rician (for line-of-sight), Nakagami, and Lognormal models may well need to be introduced into detailed simulations. Alternatively, multi-ray models (Sun et al., 2005) represent a means of estimating path loss with lower computational complexity.

CONCLUSION

Video streaming applications at the high-resolution end of the market are a core part of future business plans (Cisco, 2009), which see tele-presence in the business and the home becoming ubiquitous through optical network. However, such views should be tempered by the results of psychological studies on computer-mediated communication, which show that, for some purposes, the need for individuals *not* to have to present themselves visually may improve communication. However, clearly these findings depend on the application. There is another dimension to this vision in which video streaming is extended from wireless broadband to the more challenging environments of MANET and VANET. This is one further step towards providing multimedia coverage to those

who move from home to office or who are mobile because of their job. There is no doubt that video streaming in a MANET is challenging because of limited battery power and mobility. In a VANET, restricted mobility and hostile channel conditions increase the difficulties. However, this Chapter has sought to show the feasibility of video streaming within a VANET. Streaming can be achieved provided path diversity and error resilience are combined in a suitable robust mix.

REFERENCES

Adlakha, S., Zhu, X., Girod, B., & Goldsmith, A. J. (2007, September). Joint capacity, flow and rate adaptation for multiuser video streaming over wireless networks. *IEEE International Conference on Communications*, (pp. 69-72).

Apostolopoulos, J. G. (2001, January). Reliable video communication over lossy packet networks using multiple state encoding and path diversity. *Visual Communications and Image Processing*, (pp. 392-409).

Arce, P., Guerri, J. C., Pajares, A., & Lázaro, O. (2008). Performance evaluation of video streaming over ad hoc networks using flat and hierarchical routing protocols. *Mobile Networks and Applications*, *30*, 324–336.

Baccichet, P., Rane, S., & Girod, B. (2006, May). Systematic lossy error protection based on H.264/AVC redundant slices and Flexible Macroblock Ordering. *Journal of Zheijang University. Scientific American*, *7*(5), 727–736.

Bai, F., Adagopan, N., & Helmy, A. (2003, April). IMPORTANT: A framework to systematically analyze the Impact of Mobility on Performance of routing protocols over Adhoc NeTworks. *IEEE INFOCOM*, 825-835.

Barmada, B., Ghandi, M. M., Jones, E., & Ghanbari, M. (2005, Aug.). Prioritized transmission of data partitioned H.264 video with hierarchical QAM. *IEEE Signal Processing Letters, 12*(8), 577–580. doi:10.1109/LSP.2005.851261

Broch, J., Maltz, D. A., Johnson, D. B., et al. (1998). A performance comparison of multi-hop wireless ad hoc network routing protocols. *ACM Mobicom Conference*, 85-97.

Bucciol, P., Ridolfo, F., & de Martin, J. C. (2008, April). Multicast voice transmission over vehicular ad hoc networks: Issues and challenges", *7th International Conference. on Networking*, (pp. 746-751).

Chakereseki, J., Han, S. & Girod, B. (2005). Layered coding vs. multiple descriptions for video streaming over multiple paths. *Multimedia Systems*, online journal.

Chen, K. M. Sivalingam, Agrawal, P., & Kishore, S. (1998). A comparison of MAC protocols for wireless local networks based on battery power consumption. *IEEE INFOCOM*, (pp. 150-157).

Chow, C.-O., & Ishii, H., H. (2007). Enhancing real-time video streaming over mobile ad hoc networks using multipoint-to-point communication. *Computer Communications, 30*, 1754–1764. doi:10.1016/j.comcom.2007.02.004

Cisco (Sept. 2009). Reshaping Cisco: The world according to Chambers. *The Economist*, 54-56.

Dilmaghani, R. B., & Rao, R. R. (2007, June). Future wireless communication infrastructure with application to emergency services. *IEEE International Symposium on the World of Wireless, Mobile and Multimedia Networks*, (pp. 1-7).

Fiandrotti, A., Gallucci, D., Masala, E., & De Martin, J. C. (2008, December). High-performance H.264/SVC video communications in 80211e ad hoc networks. *International Workshop on Traffic Management and Engineering for the Future Internet*.

Fiore, M., Härri, J., Filali, F., & Bonnet, C. (2007, March). Vehicular mobility simulation for VANETs. *40th Annual Simulation Symposium*, (pp. 301-307).

Franchi, N., Fumagalli, M., Lancini, R., & Tubaro, S. (2004). Multiple description video coding for scalable and robust transmission over IP. *IEEE Transactions on Circuits and Systems for Video Technology, 15*(3), 321–334. doi:10.1109/TC-SVT.2004.842606

Fu, X., Lei, J., & Shi, L. (2007). *An experimental analysis of Joost peer-to-peer VoD service*. Germany: Technical Report, Institute of Computer Science, University of Göttingen.

Guo, M., Ammar, M. H., & Zegura, E. W. (March 2005). V3: A vehicle-to-vehicle live video streaming architecture. *3rd IEEE International Conference on Pervasive Computing and Communications*, (pp. 171-180).

Jurca, D., Chakareski, J., Wagner, J., & Frossard, P. (2007). Enabling adaptive video streaming in P2P systems. *IEEE Communications Magazine, 45*(6), 108–114. doi:10.1109/MCOM.2007.374427

Kalman, M., Ramanathan, P., & Girod, B. (September 2003). Rate-Distortion optimized video streaming with multiple deadlines. *International Conference on Image Processing*, (pp. 662-664).

Karlsson, J., Li, H., & Erikson, J. (October 2005). Real-time video over wireless ad-hoc networks. *14th International Conference on Computer Communications and Networks*, (pp. 596-607).

Kosch, T., Kulp, I., Bechler, M., Strassberger, M., Weyl, B., & Laswoski, R. (2009, May). Communication architecture for cooperative systems in Europe. *IEEE Communications Magazine, 47*(5), 116–125. doi:10.1109/MCOM.2009.4939287

Lambert, P., de Neve, W., Dhondt, Y., & van de Walle, R. (2006). Flexible macroblock ordering in H.264/AVC. *Journal of Visual Communication, 17*, 358–375.

Liao, Y., & Gibson, J. D. (October 2008). Refined error concealment for multiple state video coding over ad hoc networks. *Asilomar Conference Conference Signals, Systems,& Computers.*

Liu, B., Khorashadi, B., Du, H., Ghosal, D., Chuah, C.-N., & Zhang, M. (2009, May). VGSim: An integrated networking and microscopic vehicular mobility simulation platform. *IEEE Communications Magazine, 47*(5), 134–141. doi:10.1109/MCOM.2009.5277467

Liu, Y., Guo, Y., & Liang, C. (2008). A survey on peer-to-peer video streaming systems. *Journal of P2P Networking and Applications, 1*(1), 18-28.

Lu, W.-F., & Wu, M. (2002). MADF: Mobile-Assisted data forwarding for wireless data networks. *Journal of Communications and Networks, 6*(3), 216–233.

Luby, M., Gasiba, T., Stockhammer, T., & Watson, M. (2007). Reliable multimedia download delivery in cellular broadcast networks. *IEEE Transactions on Broadcasting, 53*(1), 235–246. doi:10.1109/TBC.2007.891703

Manoj, B. S., & Siva Ram Murthy, C. (2004). *Ad Hoc Wireless Networks*. New Jersey: Prentice Hall.

Mao, S., Lin, S., Panwar, S. S., Wang, Y., & Celebi, E. (2003). Video transport over ad hoc networks: multistream coding with multipath transport. *IEEE Journal on Selected Areas in Communications, 21*(4), 1721–1737.

Mao, S., Lin, S. S. S., Panwar, S. S., & Wang, Y. (2001). Reliable transmission of video over ad-hoc networks using automatic repeat request and multi-path transport. *IEEE Vehicular Technology Conference*, (pp. 615-619).

Marpe, D., Schwarz, H., & Wiegand, T. (2003). Context-based adaptive binary arithmetic coding in the H.264/AVC video compression standard. *IEEE Transactions on Circuits and Systems for Video Technology, 13*(7), 620–636. doi:10.1109/TCSVT.2003.815173

Matolak, D. W. (2008, May). Channel modeling for vehicle-to-vehicle communications. *IEEE Communications Magazine, 46*(5), 76–83. doi:10.1109/MCOM.2008.4511653

Oda, Y., Tasunekawa, K., & Hata, M. (2000, November). Advanced LOS path-loss model in microcellular mobile communications. *IEEE Transactions on Vehicular Technology, 49*(6), 2121–2125. doi:10.1109/25.901884

Padmanabhan, V. N., Wang, H. J., & Chou, P. A. (2003). Resilient Peer-to-Peer streaming. *IEEE International Conference on Network Protocols,* (pp. 16-27).

Park, J.-S., Lee, U., Oh, S. Y., Gerla, M., & Lun, D. (2006). Emergency related video streaming in VANETs using network coding. UCLA CSD Technical Report, TR-070016.

Perkins, C. E., & Royer, E. M. (1999). Ad hoc on-demand distance vector routing (AODV). *2nd IEEE Workshop on Mobile Computing Systems and Applications*, (pp. 90-100).

Radulovic, I., Wang, Y.-K., Wenger, S., Hallapuro, A., Hannuksela, M. N., & Frossard, P. (September 2007). Multiple description H.264 video coding with redundant pictures", *International. Workshop on Mobile Video*, (pp. 37-42).

Reibman, A. R., Jafarkhani, H., Orchard, M. T., & Wang, Y. (October 2001). Multiple description video using rate-distortion splitting. *IEEE International Conference on Image Processing*, (pp. 971-981).

Rejaie, R. (2006). Anyone can broadcast video over the Internet. *Communications of the ACM, 49*, 55–57. doi:10.1145/1167838.1167863

Schierl, T., Jhansen, S., Perkis, A., & Wiegand, T. (2008). Rateless scalable video coding for overlay multisource streaming in MANETs. *Journal of Visual Communication and Image Representation, 19*, 500–507. doi:10.1016/j.jvcir.2008.06.004

Sentinelli, L., Marfia, G., Gerla, M., Kleinrock, L., & Tewari, L. (2007, June). Will IPTV ride the P2P storm? *IEEE Communications Magazine, 45*(6), 86–92. doi:10.1109/MCOM.2007.374424

Setton, E., Zhu, X., & Girod, B. (June 2004). Congestion-optimized multipath streaming of video over ad hoc wireless network. *IEEE International. Conference on Multimedia and Expo,* 1619-1622.

Shah, P., & Paris, J.-F. (April 2007). Peer-to-peer multimedia streaming using BitTorrent. *IEEE International Performance Computing and Communication Conference,* (pp. 340-347).

Sheltami, T. R. (2008). Performance evaluation of H.264 protocol in ad hoc networks. *Journal of Mobile Multimedia, 4*(1), 59–70.

Stibor, L., Zhang, Y., & Reumann, H.-J. (2007, March). Evaluation of communication distance in a vehicular ad hoc network using IEEE 802.11p. *Wireless Communication and Networking Conference,* (pp. 254-257).

Stockhammer, T., & Zia, W. (2007). Error-resilient coding and decoding strategies for video communication. In Chou, P. A., & van der Schaar, M. (Eds.), *Multimedia in IP and Wireless Networks* (pp. 13–58). Burlington, MA: Academic Press. doi:10.1016/B978-012088480-3/50003-5

Sun, Q., Tan, S. Y., & Tan, K. C. (2005, July). Analytical formulae for path loss prediction in urban street grid microcellular environments. *IEEE Transactions on Vehicular Technology, 54*(4), 1251–1258. doi:10.1109/TVT.2005.851298

Tonguz, O. K., Viriyasitavat, W., & Bai, F. (2009, May). Modeling urban traffic: a cellular automata approach. *IEEE Communications Magazine, 47*(5), 142–150. doi:10.1109/MCOM.2009.4939290

Treiber, M., Henneke, A., & Helbing, D. (2000, August). Congested traffic states in empirical observations and microscopic simulations. *Physical Review E: Statistical Physics, Plasmas, Fluids, and Related Interdisciplinary Topics, 62*(2), 1805–1824. doi:10.1103/PhysRevE.62.1805

Wang, Y., Reibman, A. R., & Lee, S. (2005). Multiple description coding for video delivery. *Proceedings of the IEEE, 93*(1), 57–70. doi:10.1109/JPROC.2004.839618

Wei, W., & Zakhor, A. (2004, October). Multipath unicast and multicast video communication over wireless ad hoc networks. *International Conference on Broadband Networks,* (pp. 494-505).

Wei, W., & Zakhor, A. (2006, October). Path selection for multi-path streaming in wireless ad hoc networks. *International Conference on Image Processing,* (pp. 3045-3048).

Wei, W., & Zakhor, A. (2009). Interference aware multipath selection for video streaming in wireless ad hoc networks. *IEEE Transactions on Circuits and Systems for Video Technology, 19*(2), 165–178. doi:10.1109/TCSVT.2008.2009242

Wenger, S. (2003, July). H264/AVC over IP. *IEEE Transactions on Circuits and Systems for Video Technology, 13*(7), 645–656. doi:10.1109/TCSVT.2003.814966

Wenger, S., Knorr, G. D., Ou, J., & Kossentini, F. (1998). Error resilience support in H.263+. *IEEE Transactions on Circuits and Systems for Video Technology, 8*(7), 867–877. doi:10.1109/76.735382

Wu, H. R., Fujimoto, R. M., & Riley, G. (2004, September). Analytical models for information propagation in vehicle-to-vehicle networks. *Vehicular Technology Conference,* (pp. 4548-4552).

Wu, H., Qiao, C., De, S., & Tonguz, O. (2001). Integrated cellular and ad hoc relaying service: iCAR. *IEEE Journal on Selected Areas in Communications, 19*(10), 2105–2113. doi:10.1109/49.957326

Xie, F., Hua, K. A., Wang, W., & Ho, Y. H. (2007, October). Performance study of live video streaming over highway vehicular ad hoc networks. *Vehicular Technology Conference*, (pp. 2121-2125).

Zeng, X., Bagrodia, R., & Gerla, M. (1998, May). GloMoSim: A library for parallel simulation of large-scale wireless networks. 12th *Workshop on Parallel and Distributed Simulations*, (pp. 154-161).

Zhang, X., Liu, J., Li, B., & Yum, Y.-S. P. (March 2005). CoolStreaming/DONet: a data-driven overlay network for peer-to-peer live media streaming. *IEEE INFOCOM*, (pp. 2102-2111).

ADDITIONAL READING

Agboma, F., & Liotta, A. (2008). Quality of Experience for mobile TV services. Ahmad, A. H. A. and Ibrahim, I. K. (eds.) *Multimedia Transcoding for Mobile and Wireless Networks*, (pp. 178-197). Hershey, PA: Information Science Reference.

ASTM E2213-03 (2003, July). Standard Specification for Telecommunications and Information Exchange Between Roadside and Vehicle Systems – 5.9 GHz Band Dedicated Short-Range Communications (DSRC) Medium Access Control (MAC) and Physical Layer (PHY) Specifications. *ASTM International*.

Blum, J. J., Eskandarian, A., & Hoffman, L. J. (2004). Challenges of inter-vehicle ad hoc networks. *IEEE Transactions on Intelligent Transportation Systems, 5*(4), 347–351. doi:10.1109/TITS.2004.838218

Chawathe, Y., Ratnasamy, S., Breslau, L., Lanham, N., & Shenker, S. (Aug. 2003). Making Gnutella-like P2P systems scalable. *ACM SIGCOMM*, (pp. 407–418)

Chen, J., Chan, S.-H. G., & Li, V. O. K. (2004). Multipath routing for video delivery over bandwidth-limited networks. *IEEE Journal on Selected Areas in Communications, 22*(10), 1920–1932. doi:10.1109/JSAC.2004.836000

Chou, P. A., & van der Schaar, M. (Eds.). (2007). *Multimedia in IP and Wireless Networks*. Burlington, MA: Academic Press.

Frossard, P., de Martin, J. C., & Civanlar, M. R. (2008, January). Media streaming with network diversity. *Proceedings of the IEEE, 96*(1), 39–53. doi:10.1109/JPROC.2007.909876

Giordano, E., Ghosh, A., Pau, G., & Gerla, M. (July 2008). Experimental evaluation of peer-to-peer applications in vehicular ad-hoc networks. *First Annual International Symposium on Vehicular Computing Systems*.

Gürses, E., & Kim, A. N. (November 2008). Maximum utility peer selection for P2P streaming in wireless ad hoc networks. *IEEE GLOBECOM*, (pp. 1-15).

Jiang, D., & Delgrossi, L. (May, 2008). IEEE 802.11p: Towards an international standard for wireless access in vehicular environments. *IEEE Vehicular Technology Conference*, (pp. 2036-2040).

Katz, B., Greenberg, S., Yarkoni, N., Blaunstein, N., & Giladi, R. (2007). New error-resilient scheme based on FMO and dynamic redundant slices allocation for wireless video transmission. *IEEE Transactions on Broadcasting, 53*(1), 308–319. doi:10.1109/TBC.2006.889694

Lee, S.-J., & Gerla, M. (June 2001). Split multipath routing with maximally disjoint paths in ad hoc networks," *IEEE International Conference on Communication*, (pp. 3201-3205).

Leung, M.-F., Chan, S. H., & Au, O. (2006). COSMOS: Peer-to-peer collaborative streaming among mobiles. *IEEE International Conference on Multimedia and Expo*, (pp. 865-868).

Liang, Y. J., Setton, E., & Girod, B. (2002). Channel-adaptive video streaming using packet path diversity and rate-distortion optimized reference picture selection. *IEEE 5th Workshop on Multimedia Signal Processing*, (pp. 420-423).

Lin, L., Ye, X.-Z., Zhang, S.-Y., & Zhang, Y. (2005). H.264/AVC error resilience tools suitable for 3G mobile video services. *Journal of Zhejiang University*, *6A*(Suppl. I), 41–46.

Manoj, B. S., & Siva Ram Murthy, C. (2004). *Ad Hoc Wireless Networks*. Upper Saddle River, NJ: Prentice Hall.

Oda, Y., Tsunekawa, K., & Hata, M. (2000, November). Advanced LOS path-loss model in microcellular mobile communications. *IEEE Transactions on Vehicular Technology*, *49*(6), 2121–2125. doi:10.1109/25.901884

Oliveira, L. B., Siqueira, I. G., & Loureiro, A. F. (2005). On the performance of ad hoc routing protocols under a peer-to-peer application. *Journal of Parallel and Distributed Computing*, *65*(11), 1337–1347. doi:10.1016/j.jpdc.2005.05.023

Puri, P., & Ramchandran, K. (1999). Multiple description source coding using forward error correction codes. *33rd Asilomar Conference Signals, Systems, & Computers*, (pp. 342–346).

Stockhammer, T., Hannuksela, M. M., & Wiegand, T. (2003). H264/AVC in wireless environments. *IEEE Transactions on Circuits and Systems for Video Technology*, *13*(7), 657–673. doi:10.1109/TCSVT.2003.815167

Takai, M., Martin, J., & Bagrodia, R. (2001). Effects of wireless physical layer modeling in mobile ad hoc networks. *International Symposium on Mobile Ad Hoc Networking and Computing*, (pp. 87-94).

Tamai, M., Sun, T., Yasumoto, K., Shibata, N., & Ito, M. (April 2004). Energy-aware video streaming with QoS control for portable computing devices. *14th International Workshop on Network and Operating System Support for Digital Audio and Video*, (pp. 68-74).

Vars, V., & Hannuksela, M. N. (2001). *Non-normative error concealment algorithms*, ITU-T SGI6 Document, VCEG-N62.

Wang, Y., Wenger, S., Wen, J., & Katsagellos, A. K. (2000). Error resilient video coding techniques. *IEEE Signal Processing*, *17*(4), 61–82. doi:10.1109/79.855913

Wang, Y., & Zou, Q. F. (1998). Error control and concealment for video communication: A review. *Proceedings of the IEEE*, *86*(5), 974–997. doi:10.1109/5.664283

Yan, L. (2005). Can P2P benefit from MANET? Performance evaluation from users' perspective. *International Conference on Mobile Sensor Networks*, (pp. 1026-1035).

Yousefi, S., Mousavi, M. S., & Fathy, M. (January 2006). Vehicular ad hoc networks (VANETS): Challenges and perspectives, *6th International Conference on ITS Telecommunications*, (pp. 761-766).

Zhengye, L., Shen, Y., Panwar, S. S., Ross, K. W., & Wang, Y. (2007). P2P video live streaming with MDC: Providing incentives for redistribution. *IEEE International Conference on Multimedia and Expo*, (pp. 48-51).

KEY TERMS AND DEFINITIONS

Error propagation: Because of the predictive nature of video coding, errors may propagate if data is lost in its journey across the network. Assuming a packet-switched network, then packets may be lost or partially reconstructed through channel error on a wireless network or buffer overflow as a result of self-congestion (the sending rate is too rapid) or cross-congestion (other traffic intervenes at buffers). Packets may also be lost if display deadlines are missed. Two basic forms or error propagation exist: 1) at the slice level if the variable length decoder is unable to interpret the symbols because of missing or corrupt symbols; and 2) at the frame/picture level if slices or the entire reference frame has been dropped. Reference frames are required to base motion compensated prediction on (as only the residual is encoded to reduce the dynamic range of the encoded data). Anchor frames are spatially coded to provide an anchor for subsequent predictively-coded frames, and their loss is particularly damaging. Error propagation can be halted by the arrival of an anchor frame, usually after half a second. Related to error propagation is error drift in which the encoder's view of the data received at the decoder drifts from the decoder's view.

Error Resilience: Is a form of error protection through source coding (compression of the raw vido data). As Forward Error Correction or channel coding is provided at the physical layer for wireless communication, error resilience measures are a way of bolstering that protection for fragile data streams such as video (see error propagation). In the H.264 advanced video codec many measures were newly added to cater for the increased presence of multimedia over wireless networks. These measures include: Flexible Macroblock Ordering, allowing regions of interest to be given special protection or interleaving of slices within the frame such that if one or more slices are lost others can assist error concealment at the decoder; data partitioning, that is separation of the compressed data by importance, again allowing extra protection to more important data; and gradual macroblock refresh in which spatially coded macroblocks are dispersed amongst predictively-coded macroblock.

MANET: Is a highly dynamic, self-configuring network that can operate autonomously, without the need for a connection to a network infrastructure. The term Mobile Ad hoc Network (MANET) appears to have originated with the Internet Engineering Task Force (IETF), which set up various work groups on this topic. The term 'ad hoc' from the Latin for 'for the moment' or literally 'at this' implies that these networks can be formed spontaneously. Such networks are normally wireless and apart from underway ad hoc networks, which use acoustic waves, communicate at radio frequencies. The main networking implication of being ad hoc is that routing is hop-by-hop, because of the restrictions of range with wireless routing. MANETs may be characterized by a high degree of mobility which may cause nodes to go out of range. Nodes may also leave or join the network at frequent intervals. If radio transceivers are reliant on battery power, then energy consumption in communication is a primary concern, implying a need to reduce control packets to a minimum.

Multiple Description Coding (MDC): Is a form of **error resilience** in which in which a raw video stream is coded as two or more descriptions. Each description forms a separate stream that can exploit path diversity. Unlike layered coding, it is not necessary for a base layer to be successfully decoded if enhancement layers are to be decoded (thus improving the video quality beyond its basic quality). One or more descriptions are sufficient for reconstruction. MDC decomposition can take place in the temporal, spatial and transform domains. An interesting example is matching pursuits MDC. In part because of the specialized codecs that may be required, various simplified versions of MDC have arisen such as Video Redundancy Coding.

Path Diversity: is the ability to route data over more than one path within a network. In a wired network, path diversity is usually provided as a protection against link outages. However, in an ad hoc network then the use of multiple paths brings many potential benefits. If the network devices are battery-powered then transmitting a decomposed video stream over more than one path allows load balancing. Conversely, bandwidth aggregation becomes possible if there is restricted bandwidth over any one link. Wireless channel conditions can be localized and volatile and therefore path diversity spreads the risk. In a MANET/VANET the movement of nodes leads to link breakages as nodes go out of range, again an argument for path diversity. Multiple paths can also provide a way of selecting for the shortest path and, normally, the path with least end-to-end delay, which is important to maintain video rates. Security can also be enhanced if network coding is used.

Peer-to-Peer Streaming: peer-to-peer (P2P) overlay networks are those that have no central server for distribution of content (though in hybrid networks, a server acts as a contact point to distribute the location of files held by nodes). An overlay network is one that is superimposed on the physical network, providing a topological set of connections. In P2P streaming, unlike file download, a continuous stream of data is supplied to a destination. For video streaming there are clearly display deadlines that should be met in order to meet the decoded frame-rate. By making use of multiple nodes as the data sources, bottlenecks are avoided and the streaming session reduces the risk of a source failure. Normally data are distributed in 'chunks' and re-ordered in a buffer at the destination.

VANET: is a variation on a MANET (see previous definition) in which the nodes within the network are vehicles bearing radio transceivers, hence Vehicular Ad hoc Network (VANET). Alternative names exist such as vehicle-to-vehicle networks. VANETs are distinguished from MANETs in that they exhibit higher speeds on highways, though in an urban setting speeds maybe similar. They may also not be affected by battery energy consumption concerns. For automotive networks, mobility will be restricted by road layouts and road obstacles such as intersections, traffic lights, ramps, and accidents. Roadside units may act as short term servers and data sinks.

Chapter 9
Scalable Video Delivery over Wireless LANs

Maodong Li
Nanyang Technological University, Singapore

Seong-Ping Chuah
Nanyang Technological University, Singapore

Zhenzhong Chen
Nanyang Technological University, Singapore

Yap-Peng Tan
Nanyang Technological University, Singapore

ABSTRACT

Recent advances in wireless broadband networks and video coding techniques have led the rapid growth of wireless video services. In this chapter, we present a comprehensive study on the transmission of scalable video over wireless local area networks (WLAN). We analyze first the mechanisms and principles of the emerging scalable video coding (SVC) standard. We then introduce the IEEE 802.11 standards for WLAN and related quality of service (QoS) issues. We present some studies of SVC over WLAN using cross-layer design techniques. We aim to exploit the unique characteristics of the scalable video coding technology to enhance personalized experience and to improve system performance in a wireless transmission system. Examples and analyses are given to demonstrate system performances.

1. INTRODUCTION

The past decade has witnessed the success of wireless video applications which led to the remarkable progress in the research and development of video coding technologies and wireless communication standardizations. Nowadays, wireless networking technologies, such as wireless personal area network WPAN (IEEE Std 802.15), wireless local area network WLAN (IEEE Std 802.11, IEEE Std 801.11a, IEEE Std 802.11b, IEEE Std 802.11g, IEEE Std 802.11e, IEEE Std 802.11n), wireless metropolitan area network WMAN (IEEE Std 802.16), and cellular networks make people to communicate easier and more efficient. The improvement in long-life battery, low-cost mobile CPU, and small-size storage device enable the

DOI: 10.4018/978-1-61692-831-5.ch009

Copyright © 2011, IGI Global. Copying or distributing in print or electronic forms without written permission of IGI Global is prohibited.

multimedia-rich applications in mobile devices. Moreover, the advanced of video coding technologies such as standardization of MPEG-2 (ISO 1994), MPEG-4 (ISO 1999), H.264 (JVT 2003) have provided efficient solutions with high compression performance, robust error resilience, and flexible functionalities for wireless video service. In addition, extensive research and development activities have been conducted to provide intelligent resource allocation and efficient power management to further enhance the seamless mobile multimedia experience.

Video delivery over wireless medium faces a multitude of challenges. Wireless networks are well-known for their volatile variation in channel conditions due to multipath propagation, fading, co-channel interferences and noise. As for the medium access, competition for channel access and bandwidth among users further complicate the networking design for bursty multimedia traffics. User mobility in mobile networks always leads to the varying network topology, which necessitates a frequent reformulation of optimal routing protocol. The negative effects caused by different factors always interweave between each other and complicate the system design. As mobile users always seek personalized experiences, an efficient multimedia transmission strategy should therefore be adaptive and content-aware. Unlike the data communication, multimedia communication over wireless networks is often characterized as bandwidth intensive, delay sensitive, but loss-tolerant. Provision of Quality of Service (QoS) for different users poses great challenges to the design of efficient algorithms and comprehensive strategies to effectively design the transmission strategy and provide trade-offs among multimedia quality, resource utilization, and implementation complexity.

A variety of video coding and streaming techniques have been developed. Among these comprehensively investigated techniques, the emerging scalable video coding technique shows distinctive advantages in coding efficiency and

bitstream manipulation. Although different video applications provide different constraints and degrees of freedom in the system design, the main challenges are time-varying bandwidth, delay jitter, and packet loss. Scalable video coding is competent to provide solutions to these problems by its scalability and efficiency.

Scalable video coding (SVC) (H. Schwarz, D. & Marpeand et al. 2007) encodes video into base and enhance layers. The base layer contains the lowest level spatial and temporal resolutions and the coarsest quality representation. Enhance layers increase the quality and/or resolutions of the video. For example, the base layer of a stream might be encoded at 15 frames per second, in a QCIF resolution, and at a data rate of 100Kbps for viewing on mobile phone through cellular network. Additional layers could expand that stream to CIF video at 500Kbps for a larger display screen on PDA. If video is downloaded through Internet, more enhancement layers could be sent out concurrently. The highest supportable resolution and quality could go up to a relative high-quality streaming over the WLAN, say at 1280×720×60 with 4Mbps datarate to support viewing on TV screen. All the layers are incorporated into a single file, reducing the administrative expense of linking and encoding. Compared to H.264/AVC, SVC is very efficient, as the SVC-encoded bitstream is only about 10% larger than the H.264/AVC non-scalable video bitstream at the same quality (Schwarz & Wien 2008). In addition, the SVC base layer is compatible with existing H.264/AVC encoding standard. With existing hardware encoders, content producers can convert their current formats to SVC compatible streams on the fly. Therefore video publishers will not need to convert their existing library to leverage the new technology. The most distinctive feature comes from the easy adaptation of the encoded bitstreams to accommodate heterogeneous users. For a scalable encoded video, the base layer video at resolution 174×144 and frame rate 15fps could be provided to handheld users when channel bandwidth is low. For broadband users with larger display size, an enhanced quality at resolution 352×288 and frame rate 30fps with more quality enhancement bitstreams would be favorable. If the encoded video is transmitted to high definition TV, the whole encoded video which supports full HD resolution could be delivered to support the most favorable user experience. On the other hand, the reduction on resolutions and quality could also be reached instantaneously once bursty network congestion happens.

Among various types of wireless access approaches, WLAN attracts a lot of attention. SVC streaming over WLAN shows great prospect in applications. The access points could be placed in offices, living quarters, campuses and even vehicles because of the low cost and easy deployment. The flexibility and convenience offered by WLAN are incomparable due to these reasons. As far as wireless video is concerned, video transmission over WLANs advances in robustness and high datarate efficiently addresses the issue of bandwidth variations, transmission delays and network congestion. Advance in rate and coverage area is the major motivation to the improvement of the IEEE 802.11 standards (IEEE Std 801.11a, IEEE Std 802.11b, IEEE Std 802.11g, IEEE Std 802.11e, IEEE Std 802.11n). An enhanced QoS scheme for multimedia application has been completed in the IEEE 802.11e standard (IEEE Std 802.11e). Finalized in September 2009, IEEE 802.11n (IEEE Std 802.11n) deploys multiple input multiple output (MIMO) technology and smart antenna techniques to extend the datarate up to 100Mbps. Such high datarate is achieved by transmitting data through multiple spatial channels which could achieve better spectral efficiency.

To ensure Quality of Service (QoS) for video over wireless networks, a multitude of protection and adaptation strategies have been proposed in different layers of Open Systems Interconnection (OSI) stack. Among the single layer adaptation strategies are scalable video coding, transcoding,

at the application layer, multipath and multihop adaptive routing at the network layer, priority queuing and adaptive medium access control protocol at the Medium Access Control (MAC) layer and adaptive modulation and coding techniques, power control and link adaptation at the physical layer. However, single layer based solutions cannot efficiently improve the system performance. The resource management and adaptation strategies at the lower Physical (PHY) layer, MAC layer, Network layer, and Transport layer could be optimized by the interactions with the specific characteristics of videos from the Application (APP) layer. On the other hand, the video and streaming strategies could be optimized by considering the scheduling and protection schemes at the lower network layers. In such a case, the notion of cross-layer design (M. van der Shaar & Shankar 2005) is widely employed to address challenges in wireless video. We show in this chapter how the cross-layer strategies could optimize the end-to-end video quality within resource constraints.

This chapter presents challenges and approaches for scalable video transmission over WLAN. Considerations at different OSI layers and at the encoder side are listed for the purpose of designing high performance wireless streaming system. Section 2 starts by illustrating the encoding mechanisms in SVC and a summary of the IEEE 802.11 WLAN standard's key features and functionalities that could be employed to enhance performance for a video streaming system. It should be stressed that these mechanisms and strategies can be easily applied to other wireless networks as well, thank to the widely modeled OSI layers in any wireless networks. Section 3 starts with an illustration of the cross-layer paradigm. Some cross-layer designs are formalized and analyzed, where optimization frameworks are discussed. In Section 3, we show how to enhance the cross-layer performance by providing some efficient solutions. Section 4 concludes this chapter.

2. BACKGROUND OF SCALABLE VIDEO CODING AND IEEE 802.11 WLAN

2.1 Scalable Extension of H.264/ AVC Video Coding Standard

Wireless video transmission system is typically characterized by time-varying channel conditions and heterogeneities of clients. Scalable Video Coding (SVC), the scalable extension of H.264/ AVC, is a highly attractive solution to the problems posed by the characteristics of modern video transmission systems.

2.1.1 Overview of Scalable Video Coding

Video coding standards since 1994 including MPEG-2/H.262 (ISO 1994), H.263 (ISO 1995), and MPEG-4 part 2 (ISO 1999), all present temporal, spatial, and quality scalabilities. However, in these previous scalable video coding methods, the spatial and quality scalability features come along with a significant loss in coding efficiency as well as a large increase in decoder complexity, when compared to corresponding non-scalable profiles. The scalable extension of H.264/AVC, SVC, is the latest scalable video coding standard which adopts the hierarchical B picture structure due to its efficiency (H. Schwarz & T.Wiegand, 2006) and is mainly developed based on key features of H.264/AVC. Providing some key concepts of H.264/AVC is helpful for understanding the mechanism of SVC. Conceptually, the design of H.264/AVC covers a Video Coding Layer (VCL) and a Network Abstraction Layer (NAL). While the VCL creates a coded representation of the source content, the NAL formats these data and provides header information in a way that enables simple and effective customization of the use of VCL data for various applications.

- The VCL of H.264/AVC follows the so-called block-based hybrid video coding approach. Its basic design is similar to that of prior video coding standards, but AVC also includes new features that enable it to achieve a significant improvement in compression efficiency. Each picture is partitioned into macroblocks that each covers a rectangular picture area of 16×16 luminance samples. The samples of a macroblock are either spatially or temporally predicted, and the resulting prediction residual signal is represented using transform coding. The macroblocks of a picture are organized in slices, each of which can be parsed independently of other slices in a picture. Depending on the degree of freedom for generating the prediction signal, H.264/AVC supports three basic slice coding types. I-slice indicates those are predicted from neighboring regions. P-slice is from intra-picture predictive coding and inter-picture predictive coding with one prediction signal for each predicted region. B-slice is from intra-picture predictive coding, inter-picture predictive coding, and inter-picture bipredictive coding with two prediction signals that are combined with a weighted average to form the region prediction. For transform coding, H.264/AVC specifies a set of integer transforms of different block sizes. It supports two methods of entropy coding; both use context-based adaptivity to improve performance relative to prior standards. Context-based adaptive variable length coding (CAVLC) uses variable-length codes and its adaptivity is restricted to the coding of transform coefficient levels, context-based adaptive binary arithmetic coding (CABAC) utilizes arithmetic coding and a more sophisticated mechanism for employing statistical dependencies. H.264/AVC also allows much

Figure 1. SVC NAL unit structure

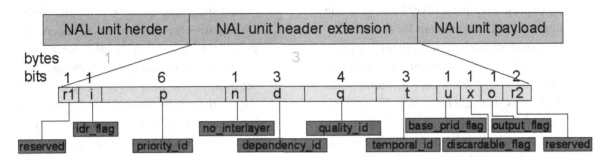

more encoding flexibility with the adoption of reference picture memory control and slice group. The former presents more options for choosing reference pictures and the later facilitates that a picture can be arbitrarily partitioned into slice groups via a slice group map.

- The coded video data are organized into NAL units. An NAL unit starts with a one-byte header, which signals the type of the contained data. The remaining bytes are payload data. NAL units are classified into VCL NAL units and non-VCL NAL units. The former ones contain coded slices or coded slice data partitions, whereas the later ones are for associated additional information. The most important non-VCL NAL units are parameter sets and Supplemental Enhancement Information (SEI). Among them the sequence and picture parameter sets contain infrequently changing information for a video sequence, the SEI messages provide additional information which can assist the decoding process or related processes like bit stream manipulation or display. SEI messages are not required for decoding the samples of a video sequence. A set of consecutive NAL units with specific properties form an access unit. The decoding of an access unit generates one decoded picture. A set of consecutive access units with certain prop-

erties constitute a coded video sequence. A coded video sequence represents an independently decodable part of a NAL unit bit stream. It always starts with an instantaneous decoding refresh (IDR) access unit, which signals that the IDR access unit and all following access units can be decoded without decoding any previous pictures of the bit stream (H. Schwarz, D. Marpeand et al. 2007). For SVC, the NAL unit is expanded to cover more information that is related to scalability realization. The most important ones contain scalability IDs, discardable and truncatable flags, priority ID, etc. An illustration of NAL unit structure for SVC is plotted in Figure 1.

2.1.2 Basic Concepts of SVC

SVC has been developed by extending the well-designed core coding tools from H.264/AVC supporting the required types of scalability.

- **Temporal Scalability.** A bit stream provides temporal scalability when the set of corresponding access units can be partitioned into a temporal base layer and one or more temporal enhancement layers. Temporal layer ID starts from 0 for the base layer and is increased by 1 from one temporal layer to the next. The bit stream can be truncated by removing all temporal layers with temporal layer IDs greater than the expected temporal layer ID to generate a new and valid bit stream for the decoder. Temporal scalability with dyadic temporal enhancement layers can be efficiently provided with the concept of hierarchical B-pictures, as could be seen in *Figure 2*(a). Other two types of temporal scalability are in *Figure 2*(b) and (c). Generally, different prediction relations introduce different types of delay and memory requirements.

- **Spatial scalability.** To support spatial scalable coding, SVC follows the conventional approach of multilayer coding as in previous video coding standards. Each layer corresponds to a supported spatial resolution and is referred to by a spatial layer ID. The

ID increases from 0 for base layer to the largest supported spatial resolution. Within each spatial level, adoption of general hierarchical structure is helpful for combination of spatial scalability with temporal scalability. The inter layer prediction is to enable the usage lower layer information for improving rate-distortion efficiency of the enhancement layers. The reconstructed lower layer pictures are upsampled for motion compensation. A competing alternative of inter layer prediction is temporal prediction within single layer, which may be more applicable especially for low motion segments. Three inter-layer prediction modes: inter-layer motion prediction, inter-layer residual prediction and inter-layer

Figure 2. Structure for temporal scalability. (a) Dyadic (b) Nondyadic (c) Zero delay

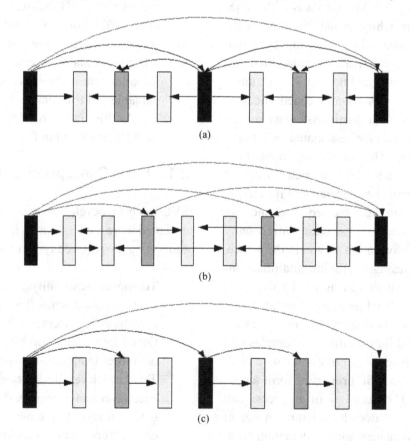

intra-prediction, are used to implement spatial scalability. An inter layer prediction structure of spatial scalability is shown in Figure 3.

- **Quality scalability.** SVC uses a key-picture concept (H. Schwarz, T. Hinz et al. 2004) for medium-grain quality scalability (MGS). The modified high level signaling allows a switching between different MGS layers in any access unit. A quality enhancement bitstream can be truncated to provide quality scalability. The key picture concept allows the adjustment of a suitable trade-off between drift and en-

hancement layer coding efficiency for hierarchical prediction structures. For each picture a flag is transmitted, which signals whether the base quality reconstruction or the enhancement layer reconstruction of the reference pictures is employed for motion-compensated prediction. So the pictures can be decoded within a single loop. *Figure 4* illustrates the combination of hierarchical prediction structures and the key-picture concept.

- **Bit-depth scalability.** Modern multimedia interfaces allow transmitting digital video data with up to 16 bits per sample. It is de-

Figure 3. Prediction structure for spatial scalable coding

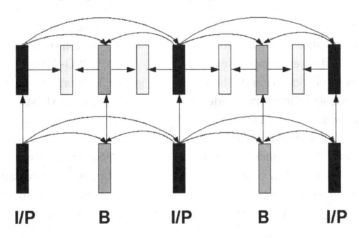

I/P   B   I/P   B   I/P

Figure 4. Prediction structure for quality scalable coding

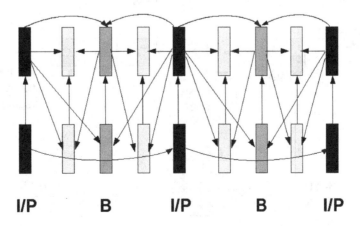

I/P   B   I/P   B   I/P

sirable to provide two or more bit-depths in different scalable layers. Such as video applications with high dynamic range scenes and mixed display environment could benefit from a design where base layer is encoded by conventional 8 bits and enhancement layer uses more bits. High compression efficiency could be acquired with bit-depths greater than 8 bits per pixel. Combined scalability could be realized, inverse tone mapping is employed to achieve inter-layer prediction (Winken, Marpe et al. 2007). A reference scheme for bit-depth scalability is illustrated in *Figure 5*. More work should be done to comply with the other scalabilities and applications.

A generic SVC encoder structure can be seen in Figure 6, which combines spatial, temporal, and quality scalabilities together. SVC is organized based on spatial layers. Within each spatial level, temporal scalability is implemented in the hierarchical structure and quality refinement is added on. To obtain a substream at a reduced resolution and/or bit rate, parameters like the spatial ID, the quality ID, the temporal ID, and other auxiliary coding parameters are presented in coded slice NAL unit. Layers not required for decoding can be removed accordingly with the reference to these parameters. SVC also specifies additional

SEI messages, which contain information like spatial resolution or bit rate of the layers that are included in an SVC bit stream. This information can further assist the bit stream adaptation process. Details on the system interface of SVC are provided in (S. Pateux, Y.-K. Wang et al. 2007).

2.1.3 Profiles & Levels of SVC

SVC contains three profiles: Scalable Baseline, Scalable High, and Scalable High Intra. These profiles are defined as a combination of the H.264/MPEG-4 AVC profiles that achieve the scalable extension:

- **Scalable Baseline Profile:** Mainly proposed for conversational, mobile, and surveillance applications.
  - Base layer conforms to restricted version of Baseline profile of H.264/MPEG-4 AVC.
  - Supports B slices, weighted prediction, CABAC entropy coding, and 8×8 luma transform in enhancement layers.
  - Supports spatial factors: 1, 1.5 and 2 between successive spatial layers in both horizontal and vertical directions and macroblock-aligned cropping.

Figure 5. Prediction structure for bit-depth scalable coding

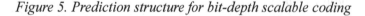
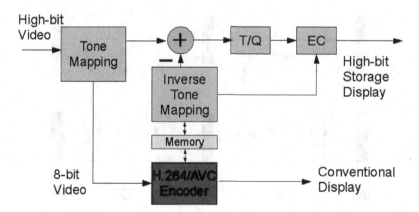

○ Supports quality and temporal scalable coding.

- **Scalable High Profile:** Primarily designed for broadcast, streaming, storage and videoconferencing applications.
  - ○ Base layer conforms to High profile of H.264/MPEG-4 AVC
  - ○ Supports all tools specified in the Scalable Video Coding extension.
  - ○ Supports all spatial factors,
  - ○ Supports quality and temporal scalable coding.
- **Scalable High Intra Profile:** Mainly designed for professional applications.
  - ○ Uses Instantaneous Decoder Refresh (IDR) pictures only.
  - ○ Base layer conforms to High profile of H.264/MPEG-4 AVC with only IDR pictures allowed.

○ Supports all scalability tools as in Scalable High profile but only adopts IDR pictures in any layer.

The illustrated mechanisms make SVC a favorable choice for wireless streaming. In the wireless environment, capacities of different types of links can be significantly different. In addition, QoS requirements can be different for different applications and different network environments.

2.2 IEEE 802.11 WLAN

The IEEE 802.11 series for wireless local area network (WLAN) are the wireless versions of Ethernet. It focuses on the medium access control (MAC) layer and physical (PHY) layer. The first standard was adopted in 1997 and many improvement versions have been established subsequently to include more features, such as QoS provision, higher data rate, increased mobility support and

Figure 6. SVC encoding structure

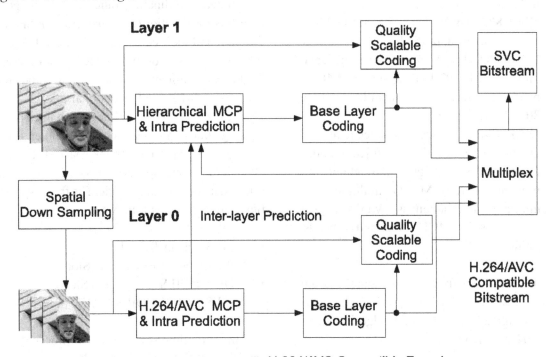

Figure 7. IEEE 802.11 MAC architecture

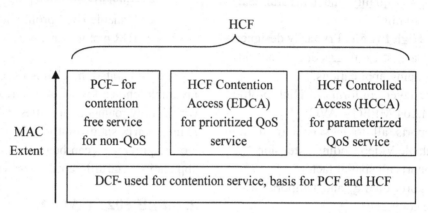

2.2.1 MAC Layer

security. A summary of the key features in various IEEE 802.11 standards is given in the following:

- **IEEE 802.11:** Carrier Sense Multiple Access with Collision Avoidance (CSMA/CA) Medium Access Control (MAC), and 1 and 2 Mbps for DSSS, FHSS in 2.4 GHz band, and Infrared, ratified in 1997;
- **IEEE 802.11a:** Works at 6, 9, 12, 18, 24, 36, 48 and 54 Mbps in 5GHz band, ratified in 1999;
- **IEEE 802.11b:** Works at 5.5 and 11 Mbps in 2.4 GHz band, ratified in 1999;
- **IEEE 802.11g:** Works at the same data-rate as IEEE 802.11a, meant for 2.4GHz band and is backward compatible to IEEE 802.11b, ratified in 2003;
- **IEEE 802.11e:** MAC enhancements for Quality of Service (QoS), ratified in 2005;
- **IEEE 802.11n:** Higher throughput improvements using MIMO (multiple input multiple output antennas). Works at over 100 Mbps in 2.4GHz and 5GHz bands, ratified in 2009;

This section briefly describes some relevant features of MAC and PHY layers in the standards for the design of video streaming algorithm over IEEE 802.11 WLAN.

Medium Access Control (MAC) layer controls the access of packet transmission to the wireless medium. The MAC layer is responsible for channel access procedure, protocol data unit (PDU) frame formatting, error checking and fragmentation and reassembly. The MAC architecture is as illustrated in Figure 7. In the IEEE 802.11 MAC, several operation modes have been specified, namely the distributed coordination function (DCF), point coordination function (PCF), hybrid coordination function and their coexistence in the WLAN. In non-QoS user station (STA), HCF is not present. In QoS STA implementation, both DCF and HCF are present, while PCF is optional.

IEEE 802.11 MAC defines some inter frame spacing times. Among them, short inter frame space (SIFS), PCF inter frame space (PIFS) and DCF inter frame space (DIFS) are commonly referred in the operation mode. The frame spacing times are defined as follows:

- SIFS = as in Table 1
- PIFS = SIFS + one Time Slot
- DIFS = PIFS + one Time Slot
- EIFS = SIFS + DIFS + ACK time

Time of a time slot and SIFS differ in different IEEE 802.11 standards. The time spacing

Table 1. Time spacing for various IEEE 802.11 standard

PHY	Time Slot (µs)	SIFS(µs)	PISF(µs)	DISF(µs)
802.11a	9	16	25	34
802.11b/g	20	10	30	50

parameters for the well-known standards are given in Table 1.

2.2.1.1 Distributed Coordination Function (DCF)

The DCF is the fundamental access method based on the carrier-sense multiple access with collision avoidance (CSMA/CA) mechanism. CSMA/CA is designed to reduce the probability of collision between STAs in wireless medium. In the DCF mode, each STA in the wireless network contends for the channel access to transmit data and relinquishes control after the transmission. The DCF channel contention diagram is shown in the Figure 8.

When a STA wants to transmit data, it must sense if the channel is idle. If the channel is idle, the STA waits for a DIFS period and samples the channel again. If the channel is still idle, the STA proceeds to transmit an MPDU. The receiving STA calculates the checksum and determines whether the packet is received correctly. Upon finish receiving the correct packet, the receiving STA wait a SIFS interval and transmit a positive ACK, signaling a successful transmission. If the STA senses the channel to be busy initially, it will wait for the channel to be idle for DIFS period, and then sets a random backoff timer. The random backoff time slot is the contention window (CW) with uniform distribution within the range $CWmin \leq CW \leq CWmax$. The backoff timer is computed as: *Backoff timer = Random CW × a SlotTime.*

The backoff timer decrements until the channel becomes busy again or the timer reaches zero. If the channel becomes busy again, the backoff timer freezes. Otherwise, the STA transmits its frame when the timer reaches zero. If two or more STAs timers decrement to zero simultaneously, collision occurs and all STAs involved will have to generate new backoff timers in another CW range. Each retransmission attempt after collision will use different ranges of CW, which is exponential.

2.2.1.2 Point Coordination Function (PCF)

The PCF is an optional channel access mode in the IEEE 802.11 standard which provides contention free access to wireless medium. It is useful for delay-sensitive applications such as multimedia streaming. The PCF relies on the point coordinator (PC), which is usually the AP, to perform polling and to enable the polled STA to transmit without contending for the channel.

The PCF coexists with the DCF and logically based on top of the DCF. Contention free period (CFP) repetition interval determines the frequency with which the PCF occurs, as illustrated in Figure 9. The CFP period is initiated by a beacon frame which is transmitted by the access point (AP). The primary function of the beacon is for synchronization and timing.

Figure 8. IEEE 802.11 DCF access method

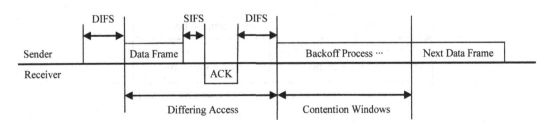

During CFP, a STA can only transmit in response to a poll from the PC, or for the transmission of ACK a SIFS interval after receipt of an MPDU. The CFP operation is illustrated in Figure 10. At the beginning of CFP, all STAs update their NAV to the maximum length of the CFP. PC senses the wireless medium. If the medium is idle for PIFS interval, the PC transmits a beacon frame to initiate the CFP. After a SIFS period, the PC transmits a CF-Poll (no data), Data or CF-Poll+Data frame. A CF-aware STA receives CF-Poll frame from the PC, the STA responds after a SIFS period with a CF-ACK (no data) or CF-ACK+Data frame. If the PC receives a CF-ACK+Data, the PC can send a CF-ACK+CF-Poll+Data frame to different STAs, where the CF-ACK part is used to acknowledge receipt of the previous data frame. The piggybacking of ACK frame is designed to improve efficiency. If the PC transmits a CF-Poll frame and the STA has no data frame to send, it sends a Null Function (no data) frame back to PC. If PC fails to receive an ACK for a transmitted data frame, it waits a PIFS interval and continues transmitting to the next STA in the polling list. The PC can terminate the CFP by transmitting a CF-End frame.

2.2.1.3 Enhanced Distributed Channel Access (EDCA)

DCF adopted in conventional IEEE 802.11 a/b/g standards can only provide the best-effort service which restricts the quality of service for multimedia applications. EDCA is a superset of DCF protocol that is adopted by the 802.11e standard (IEEE Std 802.11e) to provide quality of service (QoS).

QoS support is realized by providing differentiated traffic prioritization by means of MAC layer access categories (ACs). Each station supports eight user priorities (UPs) which are mapped into four ACs. Each AC works as an enhanced variant of DCF station, contending for transmission opportunity with a certain set of access parameters specified. The parameters include arbitration interframe space (*AIFS*), *CWmin*, *CWmax*, retry limit (*RL*) and *TXOP* which are set on a per-class basis for each AC. Most of parameters are explained the same as in DCF, the exception is AIFS which is differentiated by arbitration interframe space number (*AIFSN*) among different ACs. Smaller *AIFS*, larger *CWmin*, *CWmax*, *RL* and *TXOP* are designated to high priority ACs to increase the probability of gaining medium access for more important data flows. Once internal collision happens, a virtual collision handler will grant transmission opportunity to the AC with higher priority, whereas the lower priority AC needs to start new process of sensing and backoff. Figure 11 illustrates the EDCA architecture.

The parameters for all ACs are defined by stations and can be regulated by QoS AP (QAP). The regulation enables the station to adjust to changing conditions and give QAP the ability to manage overall QoS performance. Stations and APs use the same access mechanism. A station that wins the transmission opportunity can transmit multiple frames within an AC. This design ensures that more important packets could be continuously transmitted which guarantee the quality for multimedia applications.

Figure 9. Coexistence of DCF and PCF

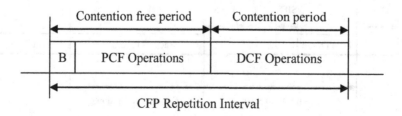

Under overloaded condition, there may be severe performance degradation, and more time is spent on backoff procedure rather than sending data. Admission control is employed in EDCA to regulate the amount of data contending for the medium. Stations claim their medium requirement and QAP calculates the existing load to decide whether new requests should be accepted or denied. If denied, higher priority AC is forced to use lower priority parameters. In addition, access category index (ACI) mapping scheme is suggested as in Table 2 for reference.

2.2.1.4 HCF Controlled Channel Access (HCCA)

The HCCA mechanism employs hybrid coordinator (HC) to manage medium access. It inherits some of the rules of the legacy PCF. All stations

Figure 10. PC to STA transmission in PCF mode

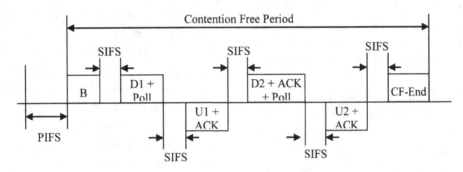

Figure 11. EDCA architecture

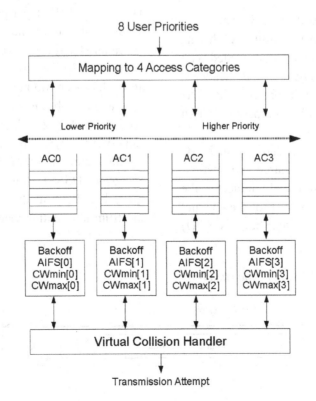

Table 2. ACI-to-AC coding

ACI	AC Abbreviation	AC Name
00	AC_BE	Best effort
01	AC_BK	Background
10	AC_VI	Video
11	AC_VO	Voice

are polled to acquire the medium for a period of time. But HCCA provides different polling access scheme compared to PCF, as polling operation may also take place during CP and packet scheduling is based on admitted traffic specification (TSPECs). Frames exchanges can be maintained with short delay whilst the delay does not increase with increased traffic. This shows advantage compared to EDCA as collision is avoided. These mechanisms provide parameterized QoS for HCCA, where bitstreams from application layer could be regulated to have user-specific QoS parameters and tighter latency control. Therefore, short delay can be maintained.

2.2.1.5 MAC Protocol Data Unit Format

In the MAC layer of the transmitter, each data payload from the upper layer is prepended with a MAC header. Conversely, the MAC header is removed from a MPDU at the receiver side. The standard IEEE 802.11 MAC protocol data unit (MPDU) is illustrated in

Figure 12. The IEEE standard 48-bit MAC address is used to identify source and destination stations. The duration field indicates the time (in microsecond) allocated for the channel to transmit the MPDU. The frame body (MSDU)

is a variable-length field consisting of the data payload. A 32-bit cyclic redundancy check (CRC) is used for error detection.

2.2.2 Physical Layer

Physical (PHY) layer acts as an interface between MAC layer and wireless medium shared by other users. The PHY layer consists of two sublayers, namely the physical layer convergence procedure (PLCP) sublayer and the physical medium dependent (PMD) sublayer. There are three major functionalities of the PHY layer. First, it provides frame interface between MAC and PHY under the PLCP sublayer. The PLCP sublayer provides frame exchange between the MPDU from MAC layer and the PLCP protocol data unit (PPDU) in PHY layer. Secondly, the PMD sublayer transmits the PPDU to the wireless medium by transforming it into radio frequency signal using a spread spectrum modulation technique. Conversely, it also receives and demodulates radio frequency signal from the wireless medium to obtain the binary PPDU. Thirdly, the PHY layer provides information of the state of wireless medium to the MAC layer via channel and carrier sense mechanism.

Several spread spectrum modulation techniques has been adopted in the IEEE 802.11 PHY layer and its subsequent variation standards. The original IEEE 802.11 legacy had two variations, namely the *Frequency Hopping Spread Spectrum* (FHSS) technique and the *Direct Sequence Spread Spectrum* (DSSS). Both of them offer the same speed but differ in the radio frequency spread spectrum modulation technique. For both FHSS

Figure 12. IEEE 802.11 MPDU frame structure

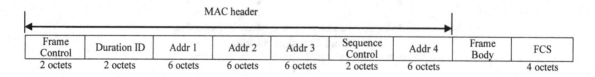

MAC header								
Frame Control	Duration ID	Addr 1	Addr 2	Addr 3	Sequence Control	Addr 4	Frame Body	FCS
2 octets	2 octets	6 octets	6 octets	6 octets	2 octets	6 octets		4 octets

and DSSS, spread spectrum techniques operate at 2.4 GHz band and 1Mbps or 2Mbps data rate. The IEEE 802.11a extension adopts the Orthogonal Frequency Division Multiplexing (OFDM) technique which operates at 5GHz band with data rate up to 54Mbps.

2.2.2.1 The Frequency Hopping Spread Spectrum (FHSS) PHY

In this sublayer, MPDU from MAC layer is packetized into a PPDU which is unique to the PHY layer while the received PPDU is de-packetized into MPDU. Each PPDU consists of a PCLP preamble, PCLP header, and whitened PSDU, as shown in Figure 13. The PCLP preamble provides a period of time for several receiver functions, including the antenna activity, clock and data recovery, and field delineation of the PCLP header and the PSDU. The PCLP header is used to specify the length of the whitened PSDU field and support any PCLP management information. Data whitening is applied to the PSDU to minimize DC bias on the data if long string of 1s or 0s are contained in the PSDU.

FHSS PHY operates in the 2.4GHz ISM band. PMD sublayer at the transmitter transmits PPDU by using FHSS modulation technique. At the receiver side, it receives and demodulates the radio frequency signal accordingly to recover the PPDU.

The IEEE 802.11 legacy uses two-level Gaussian frequency shift key (GFSK) in FHSS PMD to transmit the PCLP preamble and PCLP header at the basic rate of 1Mbps. In addition, four-level GFSK is an optional modulation defined in the standard that enables data packets to be transmitted at a higher rate. GFSK is a modulation technique where signal frequency deviates from the carrier frequency depending on the binary data of which the signal carries. For two-level GFSK modulation, the carrier frequency deviation is defined as

$$\text{Binary } 1 = f_c + f_d$$

$$\text{Binary } 0 = f_c - f_d$$

where f_c and f_d are the carrier frequency and frequency deviation respectively. Four-level GFSK is similar to two-level GFSK, where four symbol pairs {00, 01, 10, 11} are defined. Each symbol pair represents a frequency deviation from the carrier frequency. The resulting enhanced data rate is 2Mbps.

FHSS PHY defines a set of hop sequences in the operating band. The channels are equally spaced across a bandwidth of 83.5 MHz. The centers of hopping channel are spaced uniformly across the 2.4 GHz band occupying a bandwidth of 1 MHz. The operating range of the channel bandwidths differs in different regions. In North America and Europe (excluding France and Spain), the number of hopping channels is 79, operating from 2.402 GHz to 2.480 GHz. The FHSS PMD transmits the PSDU by hopping from channel to channel in a pseudorandom fashion using one of the hopping sequences. The hoping sequences are used to co-locate multiple PMD entities in the similar networks within the same geographic area to enhance overall efficiency and the throughput capacity of each network.

Figure 13. A PCLP frame format for FHSS PHY

PCLP Preamble		PCLP Header			Whitened PSDU
Sync	SFD	PLW	PSF	HEC	
80 bits	16 bits	12 bits	4 bits	16 bits	Variable octets

Figure 14. A PCLP frame format for DSSS PHY

PCLP Preamble		PCLP Header				MPDU
Sync	SFD	Signal	Service	Length	CRC	
128 bits	16 bits	8 bits	8 bits	16 bits	16 bits	Variable octets

2.2.2.2 The Direct Sequence Spread Spectrum (DSSS) PHY

The DSSS PCLP sublayer is similar to the FHSS PCLP sublayer. An MPDU is prepended with a PCLP preamble and header to create the PPDU in the transmitter's PCLP sublayer. At the receiver, the PCLP sublayer preprocesses the PCLP over-head for the demodulation and delivery of MPDU to MAC layer. The PCLP frame format is shown in Figure 14.

The PCLP preamble is for synchronization purpose while the PCLP header carries information to aid reception, demodulation and error correction.

DSSS PHY operates at 2.4GHz ISM band too. PMD sublayer at the transmitter transmits PPDU by using FHSS modulation technique. At the receiver side, it receives and demodulates the radio frequency signal accordingly to recover the PPDU.

All binary bits transmitted by DSSS PMD are scrambled using a self-synchronizing 7-bit polynomial. The scrambling polynomial for DSSS PMD is $G(z) = z^{-7} + z^{-4} + 1$ where z is delay operator. It randomizes the data in SYNC field of the PCLP and data pattern that contains long string of ones or zeros. The receiver can descramble the bits without prior knowledge from the sender.

DSSS PMD adopts differential phase shift keying (DPSK) as the modulation technique. The PCLP preamble and PCLP header are always transmitted at the rate of 1 Mbps using differential binary phase shift keying (DBPSK). The MPDU can be sent by differential quadrature phase shift keying (DQFSK) at 2Mbps.

In DPSK modulation, carrier signal is phase modulated and carries symbols mapped from the binary bits in PPDU. The mapping of carrier phase

Table 3. 1Mbps DBPSK mapping

Symbol bit	Phase Change ($j\omega$)
0	0
1	π

Table 4. 2Mbps DQPSK mapping

Symbol bit	Phase Change ($j\omega$)
00	0
01	$\pi/2$
10	π
11	$-\pi/2$

and binary bits for both DBPSK and DQPSK are shown in Table 3 and Table 4,[REMOVED REF FIELD] respectively. Note that in DQPSK, the distances between symbols are closer to each other. Therefore, higher transmission rate is subject to higher erroneous transmission when the symbols are corrupted by noise and decoded by wrong detection and demodulation.

In DSSS PHY, each channel has a bandwidth of 22MHz with the spectral shape of a filtered *sinc* function. The standard requires that the spectral products be attenuated to −30dB from the center frequency and −50dB for all other products. This allows for three non-interfering channels spaced 25MHz apart in the 2.4GHz band. Besides, 14 center frequency channels are defined with 5MHz channel spacing for operations. However, attention must be given to ensure there is proper spacing and distance between STAs and APs to prevent adjacent channel interference. The number of DSSS channels varies from regions to

Table 5. Maximum allowable transmit power worldwide

Region	Max. Transmit Power
North America	1000mW
Europe	100mW
Japan	10mW/MHz

regions. For example, in North America, 11 channels from 2.412GHz to 2.462GHz are allowed whereas in Europe (excluding France and Spain), 13 channels are allowed, ranging from 2.412GHz to 2.472GHz. (IEEE Std 802.11 1999)

The transmit power regulation for DSSS PHY varies from regions to regions. The maximum allowable transmit power for DSSS PHY for different regions is shown in Table 5. In fact, many of the IEEE 802.11 DSSS PHY products on the market select 100mW as the nominal RF transmit level.

2.2.2.3 IEEE 802.11a Orthogonal Frequency Division Multiplexing (OFDM) PHY

The IEEE 802.11a PHY is one of the PHY extensions of IEEE 802.11 which adopts OFDM modulation. The OFDM PHY offers multiple data rates up to 54Mbps in the 5GHz frequency band for dense deployment, less interference and considerations of multimedia contents. OFDM modulation technique divides a high-speed binary signal into a number of low data rate orthogonal subcarriers for transmission. In IEEE 802.11a OFDM, 48 data subcarriers and 4 pilot subcarriers are defined. Intersymbol interference (ISI) is generally not a concern for lower speed carriers. But the subchannels may be subjected to frequency selective fading. Thus, bit interleaving and convolutional encoding are used to improve performance. Prior to transmission, each PPDU is encoded using convolutional coding rate R = ½, followed by reordering and interleaving. Each bit is then mapped into a complex number according to the modulation mode and subdivided into 48 data carriers and 4 pilot carriers before transmitting to the wireless medium.

The PPDU is unique to the OFDM PHY. The frame structure of a PPDU for OFDM PHY is shown in Figure 15.

The PCLP preamble is for acquisition of incoming signal and the synchronization of demodulator. It consists of 10 short training symbols (0.8µs per symbol) and 2 long training symbols (4µs per symbol). PCLP header contains information of the PSDU from the sender. As in the legacy, the PCLP preamble and PCLP header are always transmitted at the basic rate which will be

Figure 15. Structure of a PPDU for OFDM PHY

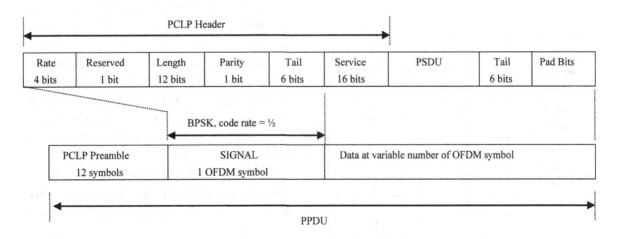

introduced in the following subsection. The Service, PSDU, Tail and Pad Bits are transmitted in a certain modulation mode by a number of OFDM symbols whose duration is 4µs.

IEEE 802.11a OFDM PHY adopts several modulation modes to provide multiple data rates. The modulation modes are differentiated by the constellation sizes of phase shift keying (PSK) and the coding rates. The modulation modes with corresponding data rate are shown in Table 6. The 6Mbps mode is the basic rate in which the PCLP overheads and MAC layer handshaking packets are transmitted. Modulation modes adapt to the channel condition to provide robust transmission.

Convolutional encoding is a type of forward error correction coding. All information contained in Service field, PSDU, tail bits and pad bits are encoded in one of the code rate stated in the Table 6. Convolutional encoding is generated using the polynomial: $g_0 = 1338$ and $g_1 = 171$ of coding rate $R = \frac{1}{2}$. Puncture codes are used for the higher data rates. While lower code rate leads to extra transmission overhead, it is more robust for transmission.

The 5 GHz frequency band is segmented into four bands for worldwide operation, namely lower U-NII bands, middle U-NII bands, additional U-NII bands and upper U-NII bands. Each band has a fixed number of channels and limits on the transmit power. The channel center frequencies are spaced 20MHz apart. The channel frequencies

and the numbers are defined in 5 MHz increments starting at 5GHz. Each channel occupies 20MHz of bandwidth and conforms to the spectral mask which specifies attenuation to −40dB at 30MHz from the center frequency. The spectral mask specification allows operation of overlapping channel with minimal adjacent channel interference. In addition, four transmit power level: 40mW, 200mW, 800mW, and 1000mW, are specified for the four bands, respectively. Besides, the IEEE 802.11a must comply with the local geographical regulatory domain.

2.2.2.4 IEEE 802.11b High-Rate DSSS (HR/DSSS) PHY

IEEE 802.11b HR/DSSS PHY is an extension of IEEE 802.11 DSSS PHY. It operates at 2.4GHz and extends the data rates to 5.5Mbps and 11Mbps using an enhanced modulation techniques. The HR/DSSS PHY also provides a rate shift mechanism which allows the enhanced rates to fall back to 1Mbps and 2Mbps to interoperate with the legacy IEEE 802.11 DSSS PHY. The PCLP sublayer and the PMD sublayer for HR/DSSS are similar to the existing IEEE 802.11 DSSS PHY legacy.

Four modulation modes are defined in IEEE 802.11b. The basic rates of 1Mbps and 2Mbps are archived via DPSK technique discussed in Section 2.2.2.2. The enhanced rates of 5.5Mbps and 11Mbps are archived by using complementary code keying (CCK) modulation and packet binary convolutional code (PBCC). CCK is a variation on *M*-ary Orthogonal Keying modulation and is based on an in-phase and quadrature architecture using complex symbols. CCK allows for multichannel operation by using the existing 1Mbps and 2Mbps DSSS channelization scheme. PBCC is an optional coding scheme defined in IEEE 802.11b. The coding option uses a 64-state binary convolutional code (BCC), code rate $R = 1/2$, and a cover sequence. To ensure that the PPDU frame is properly decoded at the receiver, the BCC encoder's memory is cleared at the end of a frame.

Table 6. IEEE 802.11a modulation modes

Modulation	Code Rate	Data Rate (Mbps)
BPSK	1/2	6
BPSK	3/4	9
QPSK	1/2	12
QPSK	3/4	18
16-QAM	1/2	24
16-QAM	3/4	36
64-QAM	2/3	48
64-QAM	3/4	54

2.2.2.5 IEEE 802.11g PHY

IEEE 802.11g is a new PHY extension that incorporates features from both IEEE 802.11a and IEEE 802.11b. It provides multiple data rate from 1Mbps up to 54Mbps operating in the 2.4GHz frequency band. IEEE 802.11g specifies CCK from IEEE 802.11b and OFDM from IEEE 802.11a as mandatory modulations for the PHY. The standard is designed to support three types of WLANs:

- IEEE 802.11b CCK
- Mixed mode of IEEE 802.11b CCK and IEEE 802.11g OFDM
- IEEE 802.11g OFDM

The mandatory and optional data rates are shown in Table 7. As for PPDU frame format, it is mandatory to include CCK short and long preamble. All IEEE 802.11g STA must support PLCP headers and three types of preamble as follows:

- Long preamble
- Short preamble
- OFDM preamble

The spectral mask for IEEE 802.11g in the 2.4GHz frequency utilizes the mask defined for IEEE 802.11b CCK and IEEE 802.11a OFDM. It allows three noninterfering channels spaced 25MHz apart over the frequency band. This feature enables CCK and OFDM STAs and APs to coexist spectrally with legacy IEEE 802.11b and provides a seamless upgrade path to employ IEEE 802.11g.

3 CROSS-LAYER DESIGNS FOR SVC OVER WLAN

The rapid progress in video coding technology and hardware production technique along with the pervasive deployment of wireless communication access points are bringing wireless multimedia applications into daily life. The wireless video faces great challenges such as rapid network variations, high packet error rate, limited battery life, severe interferences, and so on. In existing network protocols, video communication in WLAN attracts more and more attentions because the easy deployment and affordable cost of local access point could meet the intensive requirements in offices and living quarters. To provide certain degree of QoS support, various approaches have been proposed (Y. Pei and Modestino 2001; A. Majumda, D. G. Sachs et al. 2002; Shan and Zakhor 2002; M. van der Shaar and Shankar 2005). These methods aim to combat network fluctuation and packet loss by so called cross-layer design, in which involved network layers in Open System Interconnection (OSI) stack are considered together to maximize video quality for the end users. Many important concepts such as link adaptation, buffer control, unequal power allocation, have been proposed to maximize the end-to-end video quality. Their specific principles and details on implementation will be shown and analyzed in later of this chapter.

Among various video coding standards, SVC is regarded as a good solution for wireless video

Table 7. Various IEEE 802.11g data rates

Modulation	Data Rate (Mbps)	Mandatory/ Optional
BPSK (DSSS)	1	Mandatory
QPSK (DSSS)	2	Mandatory
CCK	5.5	Mandatory
BPSK 1/2	6	Mandatory
BPSK 3/4	9	Optional
CCK	11	Mandatory
QPSK 1/2	12	Mandatory
QPSK 3/4	18	Optional
PBCC	22	Optional
16-QAM 1/2	24	Mandatory
PBCC	33	Optional
16-QAM 1/2	36	Optional
64-QAM 2/3	48	Optional
64-QAM 3/4	54	Optional

applications. SVC has full compatibility of base layer which can be decoded independently by H.264/AVC decoders. In addition, SVC offers temporal, spatial, and quality scalabilities. For an SVC bitstream comprises of a base layer and one or more enhancement layers, the enhancement layers can be truncated to match the channel conditions or client requirements. In a favorable network condition, more transmitted enhancement layer packets could increase the resolution and/or quality of the received video. The primal problem lies in how to exploit the characteristics of SVC bitstream so to achieve an ideal truncation or manipulation such that the reserved bitstream could well match the specific needs and retain the best quality. The second question is how to allocate and schedule the reserved bitstreams into network layers to achieve a certain goal such as maximal quality, economical power consumption, fairness among multiple clients, lowest delay, etc.

3.1 Cross-Layer Paradigms for Scalable Video over WLAN

In this part, we present an illustration on the general cross-layer design that could be employed to facilitate the scalable video over WLAN. We present the advantages of cross-layer design that could greatly improve the end-to-end performance and provide useful references that could be adopted to enhance the video communication in wireless environment.

The conventional layered paradigm has greatly simplified network design and led to the robust scalable protocols in the wired network such as Internet. This conventional layered optimization leads to a simple independent implementation, but results in suboptimal multimedia performance. Especially when the application has high bandwidth needs and stringent delay constraints, the isolation between layers leads to significant performance degradation. Cross-layer design breaks away from traditional network design where each layer of the protocol stack operates

independently. A cross-layer approach seeks to enhance the performance of a system by jointly designing multiple protocol layers. The flexibility helps to provide better QoS support given network dynamics and limited resources. Such a design introduces additional functions to link different protocol layers of individual responsibilities with a single goal of achieving optimized multimedia delivery. In (M. van der Shaar and Shankar 2005), the authors discussed various possible approaches to achieve cross-layer QoS design and classified it into five categories as follows.

- **Top-down approach:** The higher-layer protocols optimize their parameters and the lower layer operates the strategies accordingly. After the APP layer decides scheduling and adaptation strategies, the PHY layer optimally chooses the corresponding modulation scheme.

- **Bottom-up approach:** The lower layers try to insulate the higher layers from losses and bandwidth variations. This solution can respond to network fluctuation timely as the lower layer can sense network variation in time.

- **Application-centric approach:** The APP layer optimizes the layer parameters either in a bottom-up or top-down manner, based on its requirements. However, this approach is not always efficient, as the APP operates at slower timescales and coarser data granularities than the lower layers. Hence, it is not able to instantaneously adapt their performance to achieve an optimal performance.

- **MAC-centric approach:** In this approach, the APP layer passes its traffic information and requirements to the MAC, which decides which APP layer packets/flows should be transmitted and at what QoS level. The MAC also decides the PHY layer parameters based on the available channel information. The disadvantages of this approach reside in the inability of the MAC layer to perform adaptive source channel coding trade-offs given the time-varying channel conditions and multimedia service requirements.

- **Integrated approach:** Strategies are determined jointly by mixing and matching the above approaches. As exhaustively trying all the possible strategies and their parameters in order to choose the composite strategy leading to the best quality performance is impractical, so the use of cross-layer information should be carefully considered.

The abovementioned cross-layer approaches exhibit different merits and limitations for wireless multimedia transmission, Deciding the optimal solution depends on the application requirements, used protocols, algorithms at the various layers, complexity and optimization goals, and so on. We will illustrate several cross-layer optimization examples that dedicate to enhance the end-to-end performance of video streaming over WLAN. We show in the first design how the APP, MAC, and PHY layers can cooperate in determining the optimal scheduling and allocation strategies to achieve the optimized delivery of multi-videos to heterogeneous mobile clients. Then we illustrate the interactions and trade-offs between various strategies deployed APP, MAC and PHY layers to archive energy-efficient transmission.

3.2 Cross-Layer Design for Multiple Video Streaming to Heterogeneous Mobile Clients

This section illustrates how cross-layer design could be employed to optimally deliver multiple SVC videos to heterogeneous mobile clients through the IEEE 802.11e wireless networks. This design jointly makes use of packet priority information collected from APP layer, throughput differentiation of access categories at MAC layer

and link layer queue control to acquire the maximal overall quality for heterogeneous mobile clients.

We consider a video downlink scenario where bitstreams from several pre-encoded SVC videos are stored in a source node. These videos are all encoded with the maximal supportable scalabilities. Various end users with different display devices request different videos at different resolutions simultaneously. In this case some clients may need only part of the bitstreams to obtain pictures with corresponding quality and resolution. Considering the time-varying network conditions for mobile clients in WLAN and severe competence among end users, we assume a scenario in which the total needed datarate is larger than the available bandwidth. We aim to design a optimal packet scheduling strategy such that the system performance could be maximized. Figure 16 shows the network structure where all users communicate with the source node through one-hop transmission.

Assume there are N clients requiring videos from the source node at the same time. We characterize the QoS of a user n by a utility function $U_n(R_n)$, which is an increasing and strictly concave function of the communication resource R_n allocated to user n. This models various commonly used video quality measures where $U_n(R_n)$ could be defined as PSNR, minus MSE, or others. R_n could be defined as datarate, power, timing or other resources being allocated to user n. In our setting, we want to allocate datarate R_n to user n such that the overall quality of all users could be maximized. Let R_T denote the total available datarate, the resource allocation scheme could be formulated as:

$$\max \sum_{n=0}^{N-1} U_n(R_n) \quad \text{s.t.} \quad \sum_{n=0}^{N-1} R_n \leq R_T \qquad (1)$$

Traditional way of solving this problem requires a centralized computation due to the coupling resource constraint. However, since the

Figure 16. Multiple scalable videos to heterogeneous mobile clients

BUS
QCIF 15 fps

Tennis
4CIF 30 fps

Tennis
HD 60 fps

Akiyo
CIF 15 fps

base station typically does not know the utility functions of individual video users and encoded stream may need to be further truncated to obtain a lower resolution or worse quality pictures, an alternative solution that could greatly reduce the computational complexity should be favorable, specially for mobile devices that usually have limited battery life and computation capability.

3.2.1 Cross-Layer Optimization

To distributively tackle the aforementioned problem, we want to match the rate constraint into several different formulations that could be handled at each layer. Then based on the cross-layer interaction, the optimal parameters and scheduling scheme could be considered jointly at different layers to promote the overall performance.

3.2.1.1 APP Layer Packet Prioritization

The distinctive characteristic of SVC packets lies in that they are entitled with different priorities in the realization of scalability. This is quite useful in deciding which packet should be scheduled first in an insufficient wireless networks. Whereas how to

decide packet priority is not easy task. As discussed in section 2.1, every encoded packet is assigned spatial, temporal and quality IDs in its encoded NAL unit. This information is important since it conveys packet position information in encoding structure thus could be employed to decide packet priority. However, when more enhancement layers are considered, the interlaced prediction relations for different scalabilities complicate the priority analysis. We do not bother to employ the R-D model of a particular video to acquire the linkage between allocated data and the utility measure, since it is expensive to build the model for every substream for heterogeneous clients. Instead, a packet prioritization scheme based on packet layer information that is easy to implement and is efficient for prioritizing packet from multiple videos. In section 2, we illustrate the NAL unit header structure in which each packet is specified with a set of parameters. These parameters characterize a packet by giving scalability ID and reference information in encoding. Since GOP is the basic unit that is employed to encode multiple frames, we want to conduct the packet prioritization GOP by GOP. For each packet, its priority index is derived by following procedure:

- If the packet is employed for decode the higher spatial layer, it is put into the highest class. Otherwise it is put into the middle class.
- If the packet is from base quality layer and the highest spatial layer, it is put into the highest class.
- If the packet is from the key frame, it is put into the highest class.
- If the packet is from the enhancement quality layer and the highest spatial layer, it is put into the lower class.

In each class, packets are prioritized by following the temporal layer ID (TID). Packets with the same TID belong to one priority level. Suppose some videos having the most priority levels C_{max}^H in the highest class and the most levels C_{max}^M in the middle class. A priority index is given to packets in the highest class from 0 onwards, in the middle class form C_{max}^H onwards, in the lower class from $C_{max}^H + C_{max}^M$ onwards.

We up to now acquire the individual packet priority information. The formulated problem (1) thus can be interpreted as to select a set of packets for each video such that the summation of utility functions for all videos could be maximized. If the utility is defined as the video quality, then the objective is to find the optimal set of video packets for each sequence such that the overall quality for all sequences could be maximized.

$$\max \sum_{n=0}^{N-1} U_n(\mathbb{C}_n) \ \text{s.t.} \ \sum_{n=0}^{N-1} R_n \leq R_T \qquad (2)$$

where $\mathbb{C}_n$ stands for a collection of packets for user n which has total rate R_n. With packets from every sequence are entitled with a priority index, a straightforward solution is to select more im-

portant packets first until the rate constraint is violated. The remaining packets could be discarded to avoid congestions.

3.2.1.2 MAC Layer Packet Scheduling

As has been mentioned in previous section, IEEE 802.11 a/b/g employs contention-based channel access function DCF and an optional centrally controlled channel access function PCF. To support MAC level QoS, HCF including contention-based EDCF and centrally controlled HCCA are adopted in IEEE 802.11e standard to support differentiated service for multimedia applications. Contention based schemes are widely used because the polling based strategies are inefficient for normal data transmission and complex for implementation. We concentrate on the analysis of MAC performance for video streaming. A backoff-based priority scheme for EDCF (Y. Xiao 2005) is introduced in this part. The polling based schemes will be explained in the later subsection.

For reserved packets that meet the rate constraint, we aim to maximize the opportunity that they can be mostly received by end users and will not influence the transmission of other traffics. IEEE 802.11e MAC recommends the use of $AC2$ for video traffics. We can schedule more important packets into $AC2$, which is designed for video traffic, and the others into $AC1$, which serves in a best-effort fashion. We describe a Markov model that analyzes the performance of EDCF mechanism and acquires normalized throughput of each AC. Based on the model, the packets are optimally distributed.

In EDCA, different ACs are entitled with differentiated priorities to access the wireless medium. For a given AC in priority class i ($i = 0, 1, 2, 3$), $b(i, t)$ is defined as a random process representing the value of the backoff counter at time t, and $s(i, t)$ is defined as the random process representing the backoff stage j ($j = 0, 1, ..., L_{i,retry}$), where $L_{i,retry}$ is the retry limit. The value of the backoff counter is uniformly chosen in the range $(0, 1, ..., W_{i,j} - 1)$, where $W_{i,j} = \sigma^j W_{i,0}$ denotes the contention windows size in j^{th} retransmission. σ is persistent factor which is fixed once its value reaches the maximum contention window size. Let p_i denote the probability that one AC encounters collision. As in (G. Bianchi 2000), the bidimensional random process $\{s(i, t), b(i, t)\}$ is a discrete-time chain. The state of each station in the priority class i is described by $\{i, j, k\}$, where j stands for the backoff stage taking values from $(0, 1, ..., L_{i,retry})$ and k stands for the backoff delay taking values from $(0, 1, ..., W_{i,j} - 1)$ in timeslots.

Let $b_{i,j,k} = \lim_{t\to\infty} P[s(i,t) = j, b(i,t) = k]$ be the stationary distribution of the Markov chain. In the steady state, the initial value could be derived as (Y. Xiao 2005):

$$b_{i,0,0} = \frac{1}{\sum_{j=0}^{L_{i,retry}}[1 + \frac{1}{1-p_i} \sum_{k=1}^{W_{i,j}-1} \frac{W_{i,j} - k}{W_{i,j}}]p_i^k} \tag{3}$$

Let τ_i be the probability that an AC in the priority i class transmits during a generic slot time.

$$\tau_i = \sum_{j=0}^{L_{i,retry}} b_{i,j,0} = b_{i,0,0} \frac{1 - p_i^{L_{i,retry}+1}}{1 - p_i} \tag{4}$$

Suppose there are $n_i (i = 0, 1, ..., N - 1)$ ACs in priority class i, the probability p_i that AC in the backoff stage senses the channel busy is:

$$p_i = 1 - \left[\prod_{h=0}^{i-1}(1 - \tau_h)^{n_h}\right](1 - \tau_i)^{n_i-1}\left[\prod_{h=i+1}^{N-1}(1 - \tau_h)^{n_h}\right] \tag{5}$$

When at least one AC transmits during a slot time, the channel has a probability being busy:

$$p_b = 1 - \prod_{h=0}^{N-1}(1 - \tau_h)^{n_h} \tag{6}$$

Let $p_{s,i}$ denote the probability that a successful transmission occurs in a slot time for the prior-

ity i class and p_s the probability that a successful transmission occurs in a slot time. We have

$$p_{s,i} = n_i\tau_i(1 - \tau_i)^{n_i-1}\prod_{h=0, h\neq i}^{N-1}(1 - \tau_h)^{n_h} \tag{7}$$

$$p_s = (1-p_b)\sum_{h=0}^{N-1} \frac{n_h\tau_h}{1 - \tau_h} \tag{8}$$

Let δ, $T_{E(L)}$, T_s, and T_c denote the duration of an empty slot time, the time to transmit the average payload, the average time that the channel is sensed busy because of a successful transmission, and the average time that the channel has a collision, respectively. Normalized throughput for AC in priority class i is:

$$S_i = \frac{p_{s,i}T_{E(L)}}{(1-p_b)\delta + p_sT_s + [p_b - p_s]T_c} \tag{9}$$

When the retransmission limit is reached, the packet will be discarded directly, the packet dropping probability is:

$$p_{i,drop} = p_i^{L_{i,retry}+1} \tag{10}$$

Correspondingly, the frame successful probability should be:

$$p_{i,suc} = 1 - p_i^{L_{i,retry}+1} \tag{11}$$

The saturation delay based on this is:

$$E(D_i) = E(X_i)\delta + E(B_i)[\frac{p_s}{p_b}T_s + \frac{(p_b - p_s)}{p_b}T_c] + E(N_{i,retry})(T_c + T_o) + T_s \tag{12}$$

where $E(X_i)$ and $E(B_i)$ are the total number of idle and busy slots that a frame encounters during backoff stages, respectively. $E(N_{i,retry})$ is the average number of retries. As for parameters and definition involved in the deduction, please refer to (Y. Xiao 2005) and (G. Bianchi 2000) for details.

We have acquired up to now the EDCF model that illustrates the contention based access mechanism. With availability of a series parameters like channel busy probability, packet dropping probability, normalized throughput, and expected delay, etc., the packet allocation strategy could be interpreted as: How to schedule video packets into two different ACs, *AC*2 and *AC*1, to attain the minimum overall packet dropping probability and keep the ratio of the scheduled packet approximate to S_2/S_1.

The solution of this problem lies in an analysis in mathematical programming. The problem is similar to a classic knapsack problem; we resort to a heuristic way to solve it with limited computations. A packet scheduling solution is to allocate the more important packets into *AC*2 and the remaining ones into *AC*1 and keep the length ratio allocated approximate to S_2/S_1 in an allocation time slot. Here we conduct the calculation and reallocation in every GOP so to combat the network fluctuations.

3.2.1.3 Interface Queue Control

Although the least important packets have already been discarded beforehand to meet the rate constraint, the reserved packets do not enjoy the full credibility that they can be successfully delivered. The time-varying wireless channel and the mobility of nodes may lead to packet loss.

If MAC layer is occupied for a long time, the accumulation of packets in Interface Queue (IFQ) will face overflow.

An adaptive regulation scheme should be presented to minimize this kind of packet loss.

Let IFQ keeps watch on the packets departed from the queue in the last time unit that sending the previous GOP. Departure rate is calculated on the number of UDP packets that have been successfully sent down to MAC layer. According to this rate, the admissible packet number could be

derived at the same rate under the consumption that the network fluctuation goes in a stationary way. Packets are filtrated first based on their priority index. Excessive packets are only the least important ones which are blocked out without entering the queue. Since SVC packets vary greatly in their packet length, larger video packets result in bursty UDP packets and will massively enter the queue simultaneously. To reduce IFQ overflow in such a case, each packet should be scheduled for transmission after waiting a time interval. Denote L_k the length of packet k, the waiting interval is:

$$T_k = \frac{T^{total} L_k}{L_{ACi}} \qquad (13)$$

where T^{total} is the total time allocated to current GOP for transmission, and L_{ACi} is total length of packets scheduled in *ACi* for transmission. Two ACs are handled independently.

3.2.2 Performance Validation

To validate the performance, two videos encoded with JSVM 9.8 (J. Reichel, H. Schwarz et al. 2007) are transmitted under Network Simulator (NS-2.33) with the following encoding settings:

- Bus: 1800 frames (repeated from its original shorter sequence), 30 frames per second, CIF size, supports temporal, spatial and quality scalabilities.
- Foreman: 900 frames (repeated from its original shorter sequence), 15 frames per second, QCIF size, supports temporal and quality scalabilities.

The experimental results are shown in Figure 17. The proposed scheme achieves superior results as compared to the reference strategy in which no packet prioritization and scheduling schemes are employed. The packet prioritization based on packet layer IDs introduces negligible extra

Figure 17. Validation of the proposed scheme with reference to the scheme proposed in (A. Fiandrotti, D. Gallucci et al. 2008), (a): Bus, (b): Foreman

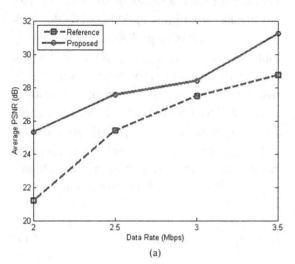

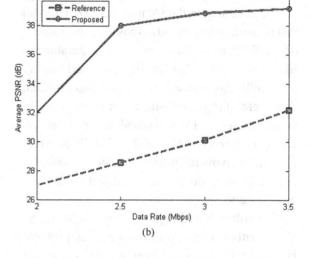

computations and is effective for videos with different resolution and quality characteristics.

The main conclusions of the aforementioned cross-layer optimization case study are threefold. First, the analysis based on NAL unit header renders useful information on prediction relations. A design based on this is easy for implementation in handheld devices as the involved computation is negligible. Meanwhile, it can best accommodate to multiple videos with different resolution and contents. Second, the scheduling at MAC layer fully exploits the transmission capacity and ensures the largest possibility that the reserved packets could be sent out. Finally, the IFQ queue control can timely follow the network variations and keep the overall performance maintain at higher level. The overall design decomposes the centralized problem and presents a simple and efficient solution. The cross-layer interactions add to the controllability on the problem and can greatly enhance the system performance.

3.3 Cross-Layer Design for Energy Efficient Scalable Video Multicast over WLANs

Energy efficiency has been one of the critical issues in video streaming over wireless networks. High data rate of video traffic and computationally expensive coding algorithm consume significant portion of energy over the energy-limited mobile devices. While the silicon fabrication technology and IC design strives to increase the energy efficiency of CPU for mobile platform, the overall energy performance can only be optimal if wireless transmission algorithm is energy-efficient.

3.3.1 Cross-Layer Methodology for Energy-Efficient Resource Allocation

Conventional energy efficient solutions focus on PHY to minimize scalable transmission energy by leveraging modulation, code-rate, and transmit power. The fixed energy consumptions by the hardware circuit of transceivers during sleep, idle, transmit, and receive modes, are not taken into consideration. While lowering the modulation rate and transmit power minimizes the transmission energy, it however shortens the sleep and idle duration, thereby increasing the fixed energy consumptions.

(S. Pollin, R. Mangharam et al. 2008) introduced MEERA algorithm on their cross-layer design for energy efficient video transmission. They formulated the cross-layer design problem as a resource allocation problem. A network is assumed to include n flows of video traffic F_i, $1 \leq i \leq n$. Network parameters are defined as the following:

1.   Cost function C_i: the expected energy to complete a job for flow F_i.
2.   QoS function Q_i: the minimum QoS to satisfy the user in flow F_i, defined as job failure rate JFR.
3.   Rate function $R_{i,l}$, $1 \leq i \leq n$, $1 \leq l \leq r$: fraction of channel access time by flow F_i.
4.   Control dimensions $K_{i,j}$, $1 \leq i \leq n$, $1 \leq j \leq k$: the control parameters such as modulation, code rate, and transmit power, etc, to control the cost, QoS and rate. A combination of all control dimensions $K_{i,j}$ for node i is defined as configuration point K_i.
5.   System state $S_{i,m}$, $1 \leq i \leq n$, $1 \leq m \leq s$: the channel conditions which are independent of control parameters.

Each flow F_i is associated with a set of possible system state $S_{i,m}$ which determines the profile mapping of the control dimensions $K_{i,j}$ to the cost, QoS, and rate functions. The resource allocation problem is formulated as the following:

$$\min_{C} \sum_{i=1}^{n} w_i C_i$$
$$\text{s.t. } JFR_i \leq JFR_i^* \qquad \text{QoS Constraint}$$
$$\sum_{i=1}^{n} R_{i,l} \leq R_l^{\max} \qquad \text{Rate Constraint}$$
$$K_i, S_{i,m} \rightarrow \{R_{i,l}, C_i, Q_i\} \qquad \text{Profile Mapping}$$
$$1 \leq i \leq n, 1 \leq m \leq s, 1 \leq l \leq r, 1 \leq j \leq k$$
$$(14)$$

A two-phase solution approach is introduced by (S. Pollin, R. Mangharam et al. 2008) to solve the above optimization problem. Design-time phase is carried out first followed by the run-time phase. In the design-time phase, only the configuration of the control dimensions that satisfies the quality constraint and achieves the minimal cost for that resource unit is adopted. For each system state, a subset of point is determined by pruning the Cost-Rate-Quality curve to yield minimum cost configurations. The convex minorant of these pruned curves along the Cost, Rate and Quality dimensions is calculated to determine the deviation of solution from the optimum. The calibration function for every state $S_{i,m}$ is given by

$$p_i(R_i, Q_i) = \min \left\{ C_i \mid \left(K_i, S_{i,m} \rightarrow \{R_{i,l}, C_i, Q_i\} \right) \cap K_i \right\}$$
$$(15)$$

In the run-time phase, system configuration is assigned to each user based on the system state to deploy the greedy algorithm. The greedy algorithm first constructs the optimal local Cost-Rate trade-off curve by taking the optimal points in both dimensions that meet the run-time average quality constraints. The scheduler traverses all flows' two-dimensional Cost-Rate curves and consumes resources corresponding to the maximum negative slope at every step.. It ensures for every additional unit of resource consumed, the corresponding cost saving is the maximum across all flows. The complexity of run-time algorithm is $O(L.n.log(n))$ for n nodes and L configuration points per curve.

The proposed algorithm is evaluated by experiments of streaming MPEG-4 over IEEE802.11a WLAN (IEEE Std 802.11a). Numerical results demonstrate that MEERA outperforms other techniques such as PHY-layer- and MAC-layer-driven designs and other scheme without adaptation. MEERA primarily takes the advantage of the energy saved in both sleeping and scaling of the network.

3.3.2 Cross-Layer Design for Energy-Efficient Scalable Video Multicast

We consider another cross-layer design problem for energy-efficient scalable video streaming. We assume that a scalable video multicast system built over wireless ad hoc/mesh networks. A mobile node is to stream a multiple layered video to heterogeneous mobile clients. Practically, the mobile nodes have limited battery lifespan while other data traffic may compete for the limited bandwidth. The scalable video multicast is therefore channel access constrained and energy-constrained.

In this scenario, we formulate a cross-layer multicast strategy such that the overall visual quality of heterogeneous clients is maximized under the energy and channel access constraints. This cross-layer algorithm is jointly optimized with SVC layer prioritization, packet scheduling, channel access control, channel quality and transmit power control. We assume there are n scalable video bitstreams to be transmitted to heterogeneous clients. Each video packet belongs to a spatial layer s, temporal layer t, and quality layer q. Due to the inter-layer prediction and motion-compensated temporal prediction, dependency exists among packets from different layers in the same scalable bitstream. We group the heterogeneous clients into multicast group $\Phi_{n,r}$ according to their requested video n and display resolution r.

The channel SNR between a transmitter i and a receiver j is given by

$$\gamma_{ij} = \frac{G_{ij}P_t}{\sum_{k \neq i} G_{kj}P_k + B\eta_{ij}} \tag{16}$$

where G_{ij} is path gain between node i and node j, P_t is the transmit power, B is channel bandwidth and η_{ij} is the power spectral density of noise floor over the link. When there is no concurrent transmission during the multicast, $G_{kj}P = 0$ for all $k \neq i$. A wireless link quality is defined as

$$\xi_{ij} \triangleq \frac{B\eta_{ij}}{G_{ij}} \tag{17}$$

In wireless multicast, packets are transmitted from one sender to multiple receivers. Different receivers may experience different channel condition leading to different link qualities. To ensure successful transmission for all clients, we take the worst link quality as the channel representation for our subsequent algorithm formulation. The worst link condition is characterized with highest path loss or noise level. For a multicast group $\Phi_{n,r}$, the worst link condition and the highest path loss are respectively defined as

$$\bar{\xi}_{\Phi_{n,r}} = \max\{\xi_{ij} \mid j \in \Phi_{n,r}\}, \hat{G}_{\Phi_{n,r}} = \min\{G_{ij} \mid j \in \Phi_{n,r}\} \tag{18}$$

Next, the packet transmission time is determined. Time overhead due to packet headers and network protocol should be taken into account for accurate channel access allocation. Media delivery usually adopts UDP/RTP packetization whose header length is 20 octets. In the MAC layer, each MPDU consists of the UDP and an additional overhead of MAC header and FCS which are 28 octets in total. In the PHY layer, a PLCP preamble and a PLCP header are further added to MPDU to create a PPDU. The sender waits for an SIFS time interval between two video packet transmissions. As presented in Section 2.2.2.3, several transmission modes with different speeds are defined in IEEE802.11a. The transmission duration, $t(L, \pi)$ and the effective channel access time, $t\square(L, \pi)$ for a video packet of L-octet long are given by

$$t(L, \pi) = t\text{PLCPPreamble} + t\text{PLCP\_SIG} + \left\lceil \frac{2.75 + \text{MAC}_{header} + \text{UDP/RTP}_{header} + L}{BpS(\pi)} \right\rceil \cdot t\text{Symbol} \tag{19}$$

$$\overline{t}(L,\pi) = t(L,\pi) + t\text{SIFS} \qquad (20)$$

Parameters are summarized as in Table 8.

For each GOP interval, video multicast of all multicast groups are bounded by a limited channel access time, t_{max} and a transmit energy budget E_{max}:

$$\sum_{\{n,r\}} \overline{t}(L,\pi) \leq t_{max} \leq t\text{GOP} \quad , \quad \sum_{\{n,r\}} t(L,\pi)P_t \leq E_{max} \qquad (21)$$

where tGOP is the display time of a GOP. The transmission time allocation problem is transformed to the IEEE 802.11 mode selection problem. Whereas given the worst channel statistics of a multicast group and a desired network QoS, the transmit power allocation is equivalent to seeking the optimal SNR allocation. It has been shown that for a given packet success rate, a wireless transmission could achieve higher speed at the expense of higher energy consumption and vice versa. However, due to the limited channel access for each node, practical network protocols do not permit arbitrary long transmission time. Similarly, arbitrary high transmit power is usually limited by hardware constraint.

We further consider the packet success rate (PSR) of the wireless link. In IEEE 802.11a, if the M-ary QAM modulation technique is used to transmit a packet of L payload length in bit over an AWGN channel with SNR per symbol γ_s, the symbol error rate (SER) is given by

$$p_{SER}(\gamma_s, M) = 4\left(1 - \frac{1}{M}\right)Q\left(\sqrt{\frac{3\gamma_s}{M-1}}\right) \qquad (22)$$

where γ_s is the SINR per symbol. The Q function is the complementary error function defined as

$$Q(x) \triangleq \frac{1}{2\pi}\int_x^\infty e^{-\frac{y^2}{2}}\,dy \qquad (23)$$

Table 8. IEEE 802.11a PHY Parameters

Notation	Value	Description
π	$\{1,\ldots,8\}$	802.11a PHY Mode
tPLCPPreamble	16µs	PLCP Preamble duration
tPLCP_SIG	4µs	PLCP SIGNAL duration
tSymbol	4µs	OFDM symbol duration
tSIFS	16µs	Short inter-frame spacing
BpS(π)	$\{3,4.5,\ldots,27\}$	Byte per OFDM symbol

With Gray coding, the bit error rate (BER) is approximated by

$$p_{BER}(\gamma_s, M) \approx \frac{p_{SER}(\gamma_s, M)}{\log_2 M} \qquad (24)$$

Note that for BPSK modulation, the BER is the same as SER, given by $p_{BER} = p_{SER} = Q\left(\sqrt{\gamma_s}\right)$. In IEEE 802.11a, the binary convolutional coding with hard decision Viterbi decoding is applied. The probability that an incorrect path at distance d from the correct path being chosen by the Viterbi decoder is given by

$$p_d(\gamma_s, M) = \begin{cases} \sum_{k=(d+1)/2}^{d} \binom{d}{k} p_{BER}^k (1-p_{BER})^{d-k} & , d \text{ is odd} \\ \frac{1}{2}\binom{d}{d/2} p_{BER}^{d/2}(1-p_{BER})^{d/2} + \sum_{k=(d+1)/2}^{d}\binom{d}{k}p_{BER}^k(1-p_{BER})^{d-k} & , d \text{ is even} \end{cases} \qquad (25)$$

The union bound for the BER using the channel coding is

$$p_c(\gamma_s, M) = \sum_{d=d_{free}}^{\infty} a_d p_d(\gamma_s, M) \qquad (26)$$

Finally, the upper bound of packet error rate (PER) is given by

$$p_{PER}(L, \gamma_s, M) \leq 1 - \left(1 - p_c(\gamma_s, M)\right)^L \qquad (27)$$

The analytical expression of PSR function is complex and determined by many factors, such as packet length, modulation mode, link SNR, and channel coding. Nevertheless, for a packet of length $L\square$ being transmitted via IEEE 802.11a PHY mode π, the function can be approximated as

$$p(\pi, \overline{L}, \gamma^{dB}) = 1 - a(\pi, \overline{L})\exp\{b(\pi, \overline{L})\gamma^{dB}\}$$

(28)

where γ^{dB} is the link SNR in dB. $a(\pi, L\square)$ and $b(\pi, L\square)$ can be determined via experiments. As SVC packet size varies significantly with possible truncation to multiple MPDUs, the probability of a video packet being successfully received by a receiver is formulated as:

$$p(\pi, \gamma^{dB}, L) = \left[1 - a(\pi, \overline{L})\exp\{b(\pi, \overline{L})\gamma^{dB}\}\right]^{(k+L_{pkt\_hdr})/l}$$

(29)

$$l = \left\lceil \frac{L}{\overline{L} - L_{pkt\_hdr}} \right\rceil, \quad k = \frac{L}{l}$$

Since multicast timing is precisely controlled by the sender, no delay issue and buffer overflow on both the sender and receivers are assumed. As a result, video quality of a receiver is solely affected by the PSR. Thus, video quality of a receiver is reflected via the PSR of video packets. Due to the layered coding of SVC, a video packet from different spatial layer s, temporal layer t and quality layer q has different quality impacts on the reconstructed video n. We therefore describe the utility function for the multicast of video sequence n as the weighted sum of PSR of all layers:

$$U_n(\pi_{n,s,t,q}, \gamma^{dB}_{n,s,t,q}) = \sum_{s,t,q} w_{n,s,t,q} p(\pi_{n,s,t,q}, \gamma^{dB}_{n,s,t,q})$$

(30)

where $w_{n,s,t,q}$ serves as an index of priority for a SVC layer. It can be determined as in the packet

prioritization scheme presented in Section 3.2.1.1. A larger value of $w_{n,s,t,q}$ hints a higher quality impact of the corresponding SVC layer.

Following the derivations, we seek the optimal PHY mode $\pi_{n,s,t,q}$ and SNR $\gamma^{dB}_{n,s,t,q}$ for the multicast of all video packets for video n, spatial layer s, temporal layer t, and quality layer q. The resource allocation problem is formulated as

$$\max_{\pi_{n,s,t,q}, \gamma^{dB}_{n,s,t,q}} \sum_n U_n(\pi_{n,s,t,q}, \gamma^{dB}_{n,s,t,q})$$

$$\text{s.t.} \quad \sum_{n,s,t,q} t_{n,s,t,q}(\pi_{n,s,t,q}, \gamma^{dB}_{n,s,t,q}) \leq t_{max}$$

$$\sum_{n,s,t,q} t_{n,s,t,q}(\pi_{n,s,t,q}, \gamma^{dB}_{n,s,t,q})\hat{\xi}_\Phi 10^{\frac{\gamma^{dB}_{n,s,t,q}}{10}} \leq E_{max}$$

$$\hat{G}_\Phi \bar{\xi}_\Phi 10^{\frac{\gamma^{dB}_{n,s,t,q}}{10}} \geq CS_{Threshold}$$

$$\gamma^{dB}_{lb} \leq \gamma^{dB}_{n,s,t,q} \leq \gamma^{dB}_{ub}, \quad \pi_{n,s,t,q} \in \{1,...,8\}$$

(31)

We aim to maximize the utility of video streaming for all multicast groups, while satisfying the channel access and transmit energy constraint. It is a mixed integer problem which is not readily solvable. We propose to break the joint optimization problem into two sub-problems. The PHY mode for each SVC layers is first selected, and followed by the SNR allocation.

The PHY modes for each SVC layer are selected such that t_{max} is fully utilized:

$$\pi^*_{n,s,t,q} = \arg\min\left\{\sum \pi_{n,s,t,q}\right\}$$

$$\text{s.t.} \quad \pi^i_{n,s,t,q} \leq \pi^{i+1}_{n,s,t,q}$$

$$\sum_{n,s,t,q} t_{n,s,t,q}(\pi_{n,s,t,q}) \leq t_{max}$$

(32)

where i denotes priority order based on $w_{n,s,t,q}$. PHY modes are iteratively selected for SVC layers according to i. Layers with higher priorities are assigned to lower mode (for instance, BPSK ½ code rate) for higher robustness and lower energy consumption. The priority ordering ensures less important layers are discarded when time constraints are exceeded. Having selected PHY modes, joint-optimization problem is reduced to a nonlinear constrained maximization problem. Although the solution is tractable, it is however too computationally intensive. Since the quality impacts of all SVC layers are known and only a single energy constraint remains, we iteratively allocate the transmit energy such that the allocated energy is fully utilized.

$$\gamma_{n,s,t,q}^{dB*} = \arg\min\left\{E_{\max} - \sum_{n,s,t,q} t_{n,s,t,q}(\pi_{n,s,t,q}^*, \gamma_{n,s,t,q}^{dB})\hat{\varepsilon}_{\Phi} 10^{\frac{\gamma_{n,s,t,q}^{dB}}{10}}\right\}$$
(33)

$$p_{n,s,t,q}(\pi_{n,s,t,q}, \gamma_{n,s,t,q}^{dB*}, L) \geq \bar{p}_{s,t,q}$$
(34)

Packets of different priorities are guaranteed with different PSR levels $\bar{p}_{s,t,q}$. The priority ordering is based on $w_{n,s,t,q}$. It ensures only least important layers are discarded when the energy budget exhausts.

NS-2 simulation is conducted to verify the cross-layer design of scalable video multicast. A sender multicasts the Foreman and Bus videos to eight receivers surrounding it. Each video is of 300 frames and compressed at CIF/30pfs and QCIF/15fps. Eight receivers are equally distributed to the subscription of two videos with two display resolutions. IEEE 802.11a is adopted as the wireless network standard. The cross-layer design is compared to a multicast algorithm without prioritized allocation and scheduling, under the same channel access and energy constraint. The average PSNR performances of video sequences for all receivers are provided in Table 9 and Table 10.

The PSNR performances illustrate superior performance of cross-layer design over the reference algorithm. In summary, the case study demonstrates the advantage of cross layer design for energy-efficient scalable video multicast over wireless network. The proposed algorithm formulates efficient transmission strategies by exploiting the knowledge on wireless channel conditions, video packet length, and SVC layers of different priority. The priority ordering and efficient energy allocation algorithm improve PSR of high priority layers and also increase the op-

Table 9. Average PSNR of the foreman sequence

Node	QCIF 15fps		CIF 30fps	
	Reference	Cross-layer	Reference	Cross-layer
1	33.66	34.33	-	-
5	33.66	34.33	-	-
2	-	-	29.80	34.53
6	-	-	30.99	34.89

Table 10. Average PSNR of the bus sequence

Node	QCIF 15fps		CIF 30fps	
	Reference	Cross-layer	Reference	Cross-layer
3	30.91	31.47	-	-
7	30.91	31.52	-	-
4	-	-	24.70	31.39
8	-	-	25.89	31.52

portunity of transmission for low priority layers. Lower loss rate of high impact video packets and higher transmission opportunity for all packets lead to significant performance improvement of efficiency in the resource-constrained wireless networks.

3.4 Enhanced Cross-Layer Design

Besides the cross-layer design covered in former sections, there are other considerations and starting points in different layers that could be employed to enhance the overall performance for SVC over WLAN. In this section, we describe the characteristics of single network layer to exploit the possible manipulations that could be employed to improve the cross-layer design. Generally, in WLAN, MAC and PHY layers are core mechanisms. The operation on encoded bitstreams can be carried on at APP layer. Moreover, if multi-hop network is considered, the network layer should also be considered by routing algorithms.

3.4.1 Cross-Layer Design at Encoder and Application Layer

Application layer is important because it always operates interactively with other layers. Besides the layer ID based prioritization scheme described in former example, there are other existing methods focusing on this problem in the literature which is computationally complex but more accurate. They can be used when offline calculation is allowed or the computation is not a main concern in applications. The first intuitive consideration is distortion based ranking, where those leading larger distortion are considered to be more important. That is, loss of a given packet k will give rise to normalized distortion, measured by Mean Square Error (MSE) as

$$D_k = \frac{1}{F \times W \times H} \sum_{n=0}^{F-1} \sum_{x=0}^{W-1} \sum_{y=0}^{H-1} |p(x,y) - \hat{p}(x,y)|^2$$

(35)

Where F, W and H are frame number, frame width and frame height respectively. $p(x, y)$ is pixel value of original sequence, $\hat{p}(x, y)$ is from reconstructed sequence when packet k is discarded. It is accurate but involves high computations, even though the distortion could be acquired offline. Computation reduction could be achieved by considering only frames from current Group of Pictures (GOPs) to the next intra coded frame, since error propagation is confined between two intra coded pictures.

An alternative is the default bitstream extractor adopted in Joint Scalable Video Model (JSVM) (J. Reichel, H. Schwarz et al. 2007), the official software module to implement scalable video coding. It prioritizes packet first according to temporal layer ID, the lower temporal layer packet (much closer to base layer) are ranked before those from higher layer. This design follows the bitstream quickly, but its accuracy depends on the resolution and hierarchical prediction order. Within the same temporal level, packets are ranked first by the spatial layer ID then by quality layer ID. This method is easy for implementation and can acquire truncated quality levels for end users based on their needs. Another prioritization scheme is the quality based bit extraction. From the highest resolution layer to the lowest one, the bit stream is arranged first by the quality layer ID, then the temporal layer ID and finally the spatial layer ID. Generally, this method outperforms the default truncation scheme adopted in JSVM if the higher supportable resolution and quality are expected.

Another bitstream extraction scheme using distortion model is proposed in (E. Maani and Katsaggelos 2009). The total distortion D_n^t of frame n is considered to be brought by both factors: D_n^d by drift $D_n^e(q)$ due to truncation. The distortion $D_n^e(q)$ due to enhancement layer truncation could be computed at the encoder when performing the quantization of the transform coefficients. The deduction of D_n^d will resort to a prediction from parent frames by the second order Taylor expansion. The coefficients in the expansion are first and second order coefficients and could be obtained by fitting a 2-dimensional quadratic surface to the data points acquired by decoding frames with various qualities. With distortion for each frame deduced, bitstream extraction will add packets gradually based on the global distortion gradient until the rate constraint is met. A selection function $\Box(n)$ is increased from 1 for the key frame. The next packet n* is selected by

$$n^* = \arg\ \max\ \left| \frac{\partial D(\phi) \,/\, \partial \phi(n)}{\partial R(\phi) \,/\, \partial \phi(n)} \right| \qquad (36)$$

Here, $R(\Box)$ represents the source rate associated with the current selection function. This process continues until the rate constraint is reached. For details, please refers to (E. Maani and Katsaggelos 2009).

3.4.2 Network Layer Optimization for SVC Packet Delivery

The network layer is responsible for source to destination packet delivery via certain routing protocols. It provides functional and procedural means of transferring variable length data packets from source to destination via one or more networks. It should be differentiated from the data link layer which is only concerned about hop-to-hop frame delivery on the routing path.

The network layer plays a very important part in the cross-layer design of ad hoc and mesh networks which are distributed in nature with dynamic topology. While there are some well known routing protocols such as Ad hoc On-Demand Distance Vector (AODV) routing (Perkins, Royer et al. 2001), Dynamic Source Routing (DSR) (Johnson 1994), Destination-Sequenced Distance-Vector (DSDV) (C. E. Perkins and Bhagwat 1994) routing, they may not be optimal for the video traffic. Routing algorithm design for video streaming

over wireless ad hoc/mesh networks should take different considerations from the data traffic routing as below:

- Delay-sensitive nature of each video packet,
- Unequal priority among video packets, depending on source coding architecture,
- Higher tolerance to certain packet loss,
- Higher data rate.

Several cross-layer algorithms related to multipath routing have been investigated. (Kompella, Shiweri et al. 2007) proposed the multipath routing algorithm for multiple description coding (MDC) based video in wireless networks. The wireless link states are modeled by a two-state Markov model. The routing algorithm is formulated to minimize the expected video distortion over the wireless links. A branch-and-bound framework and Reformulation-Linearization technique are developed to solve the optimization problem which is otherwise NP-hard. Multihop routing of a video packet in wireless mesh networks runs some risk of not meeting the playout deadline due to long queues in the buffer of intermediate nodes. Finally, another promising technique in network layer is the network coding. While the traditional routing algorithm assume that the intermediate nodes only play a passive role of receive-and-forward to the packet, (R. Ahlswede, N. Cai et al. 2000) in their seminal work showed that the network throughput can be enhanced via simple processing by the intermediate nodes. It is intuitively demonstrated by the following simple example in Figure 18. Traditional routing requires 4 transmissions to relay message a and b between nodes at both end. By mixing the message a and b together, network coding technique manages to relay the messages in 3 transmissions.

(H. Seferoglu and Markopoulou 2007) further demonstrates the application of network coding in the video streaming over wireless networks. Networks throughput is enhanced by mixing

Figure 18. Traditional passive routing and the network coding

Traditional routing   Network coding

packets from different video flows into a single packet, as shown in Figure 19. The video-aware opportunistic network coding schemes takes into account of decodability by several receivers as well as distortion and playout deadline of the video packets. Network codes with the highest decodability to receivers are selected to maximize the network throughput.

3.4.3 MAC and PHY Layers Optimization

MAC layer provides the medium access and re-transmission mechanisms, which play a decisive role in handling packet loss and packet delay for multimedia applications. With the packet information obtained from APP layer and network condition information acquired from PHY layer, MAC

layer bears the responsibility of coordination to decide medium access strategy for each packet and combat potential factors of packet loss. The analysis for EDCA mechanism has been given in previous section. Here we present the scheduling and access mechanism in the polling based multiple access strategy. HCCA that is defined in IEEE 802.11e is illustrated as an example.

IEEE 802.11e introduces the concept of Traffic Stream (TS) which can be thought of as a set of data units (MSDU) that have to be delivered conforming to a corresponding Traffic Specification (TSPEC). The TSPEC parameters which are considered during the negotiation include nominal MSDU size in octets, mean data rate, Maximum Service Interval (MaxSI) which is the maximum interval in between two successive polls for the stream, minimum PHY rate, and delay bound.

Figure 19. Example of network coding for video by (H. Seferoglu and Markopoulou 2007)

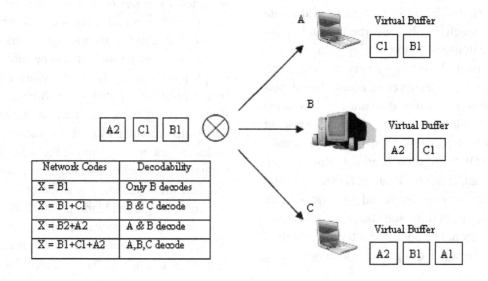

Network Codes	Decodability
X = B1	Only B decodes
X = B1+C1	B & C decode
X = B2+A2	A & B decode
X = B1+C1+A2	A,B,C decode

These crucial parameters are determined through the HCCA scheduler that strives to make sure that the performance experienced by the admitted TSs conforms to the QoS guarantees. The scheduler determines the TXOP duration needed for each stream by considering the number of packets that may arrive within an SI. The TXOP for admitted TS i in a QSTA is (M. M. Rashid, E. Hossain et al. 2007):

$$TXOP_i = \max(\frac{G_i \times S_i}{R} + X, \frac{Z}{R} + X) \qquad (37)$$

where G_i is the number of MSDUs arrived in the QSTA, S_i is the nominal MSDU size, R is the physical transmission rate, Z is the maximum allowable size, and X denotes the overhead.

The admission controller (AC) works as follows. If there are m streams admitted by the AC and the newly arrived stream is TS_{m+1}. When this new stream initiates TSPEC negotiation, the AC determines the SI for all the streams from TS_1 to TS_{m+1}. The AC also determines the required $TXOP_{m+1}$ for the new stream. The stream is admitted if the following are satisfied:

$$\frac{TXOP_{m+1}}{SI} + \sum_{i=1}^{m} \frac{TXOP_{m+1}}{SI} \leq \frac{T_B - T_{CP}}{T_B} \qquad (38)$$

$$\sum_{i=1}^{m+1} TXOP_i \leq CAPlim \qquad (39)$$

where T_B is the beacon interval, T_{CP} is the time for EDCA traffic and *CAPlim* is the maximum allowed duration of a Controlled Access Periods. Having the knowledge how HCCA implements admission control and scheduling, the corresponding algorithms could be designed to regulate retransmission limitation and control delay. An example could be found in (van der Schaar, Andreopoulos et al. 2006).

Physical layer (PHY) acts as an interface of the wireless terminal to the wireless medium. It defines the way to transmit and receive the raw binary bits over the wireless medium. PHY listens to the wireless medium and forwards the channel state information to the MAC layer. It accesses the wireless medium according to the instruction of MAC layer. For packet transmission, it modulates the digital data packets from the MAC layer and transmits them to the wireless medium via antenna. In a reverse fashion, the PHY layer receives radio frequency signal via the antenna and performs demodulation to obtain the digital data packets. It then forwards the digital data packets to the MAC layer for further processing.

QoS factors of a wireless link, such as the transmission speed, bit error rate, link throughput and energy consumption, are determined by the PHY layer based on modulation technique, channel coding, power allocation and symbol rate. Owing to the different priority and importance of each layer in SVC, transmission of video packet over a wireless link can be more efficient by differentiated QoS assignments to each SVC layer with proper configurations of those PHY parameters.

Throughput of a wireless link is defined as the datarate of the successful data transmission over a wireless link. It is one of the key measurements of QoS and determines the rate of the effective data transmission over the link. The throughput of a wireless link in IEEE 802.11a standard is

$$C(L, \gamma_s, M) = \frac{L-h}{L} \cdot (1 - p_{PER}(L, \gamma_s, M)) \cdot \log_2 M \cdot R_s \cdot CR \cdot ChanNum \qquad (40)$$

where h is the packet header overhead, M is the constellation size, γ_s is SNR per symbol, $R_S = 250kHz$ is the symbol rate, $CR \in \{1/2, 2/3, 3/4\}$ is the convolution code rate, and $ChanNum = 48$ is the number of OFDM channel used in the transmission.

The cross-layer design for link's throughput adaptation is always associated to the minimization of PER via transmission mode selection and the optimal payload length. The impact of payload length and rate adaptation for multimedia communication in WLANs have been studied in (S. Choudhury and Gibson 2007). Throughput and PER of wireless link have been examined in Nakagami-*m* fading channels. The optimal payload length at a given SNR and transmission mode is derived as:

$$L^* = -\frac{h}{2} + \frac{1}{2}\sqrt{h^2 - \frac{4h}{\log\left(1 - p_c(\gamma_s, M)\right)}} \quad (41)$$

where $p_c(\gamma_s, M)$ is the union bound of the first event error probability given in (26). Joint adaptation of payload length and transmission rate is demonstrated to achieve maximum throughput. Simulations have showed that higher SNR ranges are required for each transmission mode with the maximum PER constraint given a fixed payload length.

In the work by (Y. P. Fallah, H. Mansour et al. 2008), a link adaptation mechanism based on a transmission mode selection algorithm has been proposed to deliver scalable video over WLANs. They have presented temporal fairness constraints for channel access and formulated an optimization problem for assigning different PHY modes to different video layers. The proposed algorithm reduces PER for more important layers. Unequal error protection in joint source-channel coding (JSCC) is another cross-layer design for scalable video transmission over WLAN. Video packets of different priorities are allocated with different source and channel coding rates such that the end-to-end video distortion is maximized. In (M. Stoufs, A. Munteanu et al. 2008), the authors have proposed a novel JSCC for the scalable extension of H.264/AVC and low-density parity-check (LDPC) code. It relies on Lagrangian-based optimization technique to derive the appropriate protection level for each SVC layer.

4. SUMMARY

The increasing demands in wireless video applications call for enhanced video coding technology and reliable video transmission. SVC serves great flexibility to accommodate the special needs to provide QoS assurance in a time-varying wireless environment. Moreover, WLAN exhibits overwhelming advantages which could provide QoS support and higher transmission capacity. In this chapter, we present the cross-layer designs for SVC over WLAN and show the advantages of cooperation among different network layers.

ACKNOWLEDGMENT

This work is supported in part by a research grant awarded by The Agency for Science, Technology and Research (A*STAR), Singapore, under the Mobile Media Thematic Strategic Research Programme of the Science and Engineering Research Council.

REFERENCES

Ahlswede, R., & Cai, N. (2000). Network Information Flow. *IEEE Transactions on Information Theory, 46*(4), 1204–1216. doi:10.1109/18.850663

Bianchi, G. (2000). Performance analysis of the IEEE 802.11 distributed coordination function. *IEEE Journal on Selected Areas in Communications, 18*(3), 535–547. doi:10.1109/49.840210

Choudhury, S., & Gibson, J. D. (2007). Payload length and rate adaptation for multimedia communications in wireless LANs. *IEEE Journal on Selected Areas in Communications, 25*(4), 796–807. doi:10.1109/JSAC.2007.070515

Fallah, Y. P., & Mansour, H. (2008). A link adaptation scheme for efficient transmission of H.264 scalable video over multirate WLANs. *IEEE Transactions on Circuits and Systems for Video Technology, 18*(7), 875–887. doi:10.1109/TCSVT.2008.920745

Fiandrotti, A. Gallucci, D., et al. (2008). Traffic Prioritization of H.264/SVC Video over 802.11e Ad Hoc Wireless Networks. *17th International Conference on Computer Communications and Networks*, St. Thomas, US Virgin Islands.

Johnson, D. B. (1994). Routing in ad hoc networks of mobile hosts. In *Proceedings of The Workshop on Mobile Computing Systems and Applications, 1994*.

JVT. (2003). *Advanced Video Coding for Generic Audiovisual Services, ITU-T Rec.* H.264 and ISO/IEC 14496-10 (MPEG-4 AVC), ITU-T and ISO/IEC JTC 1.

Kompella, S., & Shiweri, M. (2007). Cross-Layer Optimized Multipath Routing for Video Communications in Wireless Networks. *IEEE Journal on Selected Areas in Communications, 25*(4), 831–840. doi:10.1109/JSAC.2007.070518

Maani, E., & Katsaggelos, A. K. (2009). Optimized Bit Extraction Using Distortion Modeling in the Scalable Extension of H.264/AVC. *IEEE Transactions on Image Processing, 18*(9), 2022–2029. doi:10.1109/TIP.2009.2023152

Majumda, A., & Sachs, D. G. (2002). Multicast and unicast real-time video streaming over wireless LANs. *IEEE Transactions on Circuits and Systems for Video Technology, 12*(6), 524–534. doi:10.1109/TCSVT.2002.800315

Network Simulator. (n.d.). *The Network Simulator*. Retrieved from http://www.isi.edu/nsnam/ns/

Pateux, S., & Wang, Y.-K. (2007). System and transport interface of the emerging SVC standard. *IEEE Transactions on Circuits and Systems for Video Technology, 17*(9), 1149–1163.

Pei, Y., & Modestino, J. W. (2001). Multi-layered video transmission over wireless channels using an adaptive modulation and coding scheme. In *Proceedings of the International Conference on Image Processing*.

Perkins, C. E., & Bhagwat, P. (1994). *Highly Dynamic Destination-Sequenced Distance-Vector Routing (DSDV) for Mobile Computers. SIGCOMM*. London: ACM.

Perkins, C. E., & Royer, E. M. (2001). Performance comparison of two on-demand routing protocols for ad hoc networks. *Personal Communications, IEEE, 8*(1), 16–28. doi:10.1109/98.904895

Pollin, S., & Mangharam, S. (2008). MEERA: Cross-Layer Methodology for Energy Efficient Resource Allocation in Wireless Networks. *IEEE Transactions on Wireless Communications, 7*(1), 98–109. doi:10.1109/TWC.2008.05356

Rashid, M. M., Hossain, E., et al. (2007). HCCA Scheduler Design for Guaranteed QoS in IEEE 802.11e Based WLANs. In *Proceedings of the Wireless Communications and Networking Conference*, IEEE: 1538-1543.

Reichel, J., Schwarz, H., et al. (2007). *JSVM 9.8 Software*, Joint Video Team of ISO/IEC MPEG and ITU-T VCEG N9212.

Schwarz, D. M. (2007). Overview of the Scalable Video Coding Extension of the H.264/AVC Standard. *IEEE Transactions on Circuits and Systems for Video Technology, 17*(9), 1103–1120. doi:10.1109/TCSVT.2007.905532

Schwarz, H., Hinz, T., et al. (2004). *Technical Description of the HHI Proposal for SVC CE1*. (ISO/IEC JTC 1/SC 29/WG 11, Doc. M11244).

Schwarz, H., & Wiegand, T. (2006). Analysis of Hierarchical B Pictures and MCTF. *Multimedia and Expo, IEEE International Conference on*: 1929-1932.

Schwarz, H., & Wien, M. (2008). The Scalable Video Coding Extension of the H.264/AVC Standard [Standards in a Nutshell]. *IEEE Signal Processing Magazine*, *25*(2), 135–141. doi:10.1109/MSP.2007.914712

Seferoglu, H., & Markopoulou, A. (2007). Opportunistic network coding for video streaming over wireless. *Packet Video*, *2007*, 191–200.

Shan, Y., & Zakhor, A. (2002). Cross layer techniques for adaptive video streaming over wireless networks. *Multimedia and Expo. IEEE International Conference on,* 1: 277-280.

Stoufs, M., & Munteanu, A. (2008). Scalable Joint Source-Channel Coding for the Scalable Extension of H.264/AVC. *IEEE Transactions on Circuits and Systems for Video Technology*, *18*(12), 1657–1670. doi:10.1109/TCSVT.2008.2004922

Van der Schaar, M., & Andreopoulos, Y. (2006). Optimized scalable video streaming over IEEE 802.11 a/e HCCA wireless networks under delay constraints. *IEEE Transactions on Mobile Computing*, *5*(6), 755–768. doi:10.1109/TMC.2006.81

van der Shaar, M., & Shankar, S. (2005). Cross-layer wireless multimedia transmission: challenges, principles, and new paradigms. *IEEE Transactions on Wireless Communications*, *12*(4), 50–58. doi:10.1109/MWC.2005.1497858

Winken, M., & Marpe, D. (2007). Bit-Depth Scalable Video Coding. In. *Proceedings of the IEEE International Conference on Image Processing*, *1*, 5–8.

Xiao, Y. (2005). Performance analysis of priority schemes for IEEE 802.11 and IEEE 802.11e wireless LANs. *IEEE Transactions on Wireless Communications*, *5*(4), 1506–1515. doi:10.1109/TWC.2005.850328

KEY TERMS AND DEFINITIONS

Cross-Layer Design: A network design concept that allows inter-layer information exchange so that parameters of each layer could adapt accordingly to optimize the overall performance of the system.

Joint Source-Channel Coding: Video streaming technique that jointly determines the source and channel coding rates such that, under error-prone wireless link, the overall video quality at receiver is optimal.

Resource Allocation: Distribution of network resources, such as bandwidth, power, channel access, channel coding rate among network users.

Scalable Video Coding: A video coding technique that allows scalability in decoding partial bitstream to provide lower resolution or graceful degradation of a video display.

Scheduling: Transmission order that determines which packet to be transmitted at what time such that some QoS are met.

Unequal Error Protection: A technique that allocates different level of protection to different flows or packets which are supposed to be different in priority or importance.

WLANs: Wireless Local Area Networks (LANs), where mobile users can connect to a LAN through wireless connection within a geographical area.

Chapter 10
Video Delivery in Wireless Sensor Networks

S. Guo
Boston University, USA

T.D.C. Little
Boston University, USA

ABSTRACT

Recent advances in wireless communications technology and low-power, low-cost CMOS imaging sensors stimulate research on the analysis and design of ubiquitous video sensing and delivery in wireless sensor networks. However, scalable deployments remain limited or impractical. Critical challenges such as radio interference, limited channel capacity, and constrained energy resources are still barriers to large-scale deployment of these wireless video sensor networks. The solution space can be explored in several dimensions including data compression, video image analysis and extraction, and intelligent data routing. In this chapter we focus on the analysis of video delivery and data routing techniques for wireless video sensor networks. Our work is intended to inspire additional efforts leading to video routing techniques optimized to different topologies, the physical medium, network channels, and energy constraints.

1. INTRODUCTION

Advances in computer and network technology have led to wireless sensor networks – networks comprised of many small, low-power embedded processors capable of sensing and communicating using short-range networking. Today, sensor networking has emerged as a frontier interconnecting the Internet to the physical world. For example,

DOI: 10.4018/978-1-61692-831-5.ch010

one can deploy a series of moisture sensors to monitor soil moisture on a farm, for water management, or in smart grid applications to monitor and control lighting in a home or business. Among the many sensor modalities supported by the sensor devices (or motes—sensor nodes), we concentrate our focus on ones that produce single or multiple images in a video stream. With the development of low-power, low-cost CMOS imaging sensors, scientists envision great potential for multimedia streaming applications of wireless sensor networks

Copyright © 2011, IGI Global. Copying or distributing in print or electronic forms without written permission of IGI Global is prohibited.

in the areas of homeland security, habitat monitoring, and image-based monitoring and control.

For these applications a sensor node can capture images, audio and/or video information, and send them in a compressed form to a consumer elsewhere on the network. A user need not wait for the download of the entire video sequence but instead can playback the content immediately once data begin to arrive at the receiver. The flexibility of wireless sensor networks coupled with this sensing modality makes video observation very promising to enable humans to observe phenomena or locations that are otherwise difficult or dangerous to access. For instance, ornithologists might deploy such a system in a bird habitat and watch bird behavior without any human disturbance. This kind of network also exhibits value in the areas of military detection and security surveillance. Broadly speaking, the technology is a variant of sensor networking called wireless video sensor networking (WVSN).

Challenges in providing WVSN have to do with resource limitations. The data intensity of video creates several problems: (1) capturing and compressing continuous video is expensive in terms of energy costs at a sensor node, (2) data transmission over multiple hops from a video node to an arbitrarily-located consumer uses a communication channel that is prone to contention, (3) nodes comprising intermediate hops have limited data buffering capacity, and (4) the existence of multiple video sources and video consumers creates resource management complexity.

Much research has been conducted in the field of sensor networking; considerable effort has also been applied to delivering video in networks. Examples include monitoring near-shore environments (Holman et al. 2003), assisted living for elders (Teixeira et al. 2006), deploying large scale surveillance video sensor networks (Chu et al. 2004), people counting and indoor localization (Teixeira et al. 2007), multi-target tracking (Kulkarni et al. 2005) and other uses of vision sensing (Rowe et al. 2007).

Many of the WVSN applications above are an integration of Internet video streaming solutions to the domain of wireless sensor networks. Some applications rely on conventional wired video cameras. Others assume wireless communications but do not address scale-up to large numbers of video cameras nor the support of many streams. Two distinguished applications among the above are SensEye (Kulkarni et al. 2005) and FireFly (Rowe et al. 2007). SensEye uses a multi-tier video solution for pervasive video sensing. The low tier network cooperates with the higher tier network to perform the video sensing task. Experiments demonstrate that this network decomposition can result in energy-efficient field sensing. However, the requirement of inter-tier communication and cooperation introduces heterogeneity problems to the network and also increases the complexity and cost of the hardware. FireFly presents an image processing framework with operating system, network and image processing primitives that assist in the development of distributed vision sensing tasks. The success for this application is attributed to the utilization of collision-free TDMA link layer for wireless video streaming. However, the required network-wide synchronization scheme for TDMA link restricts the scalability of the network deployment.

The main obstacle for the scalability here is the lack of mechanisms to manage contention among multiple source-to-destination video streams in the context of sensor network energy and communication constraints. The remainder of the chapter surveys the state-of-the-art of video routing schemes applicable to a WVSN with the intent of guiding the development of new video routing protocols for WVSNs.

The remainder of this chapter is as follows: Section 2 provides a background on video streaming over wireless sensor networks. Section 3 introduces the challenges and characteristics of routing algorithms for WVSN. Section 4 focuses on the survey of the state-of-the-art data routing techniques for video streaming application over

Figure 1. WVSN application deployment scenario

Figure 2. WVSN decomposition

WSNs. Section 5 explains performance evaluation criteria for different data routing techniques on WVSNs and proposes design metrics for their characterization. Section 6 presents a methodology to justify the performance of different video data routing techniques. Section 7 concludes the chapter.

2. PRELIMINARIES FOR WVSN

Video streaming in a WSN can be conceptualized as three cascaded components: video generation, video delivery, and video playback as shown in figure 2.

In the following, we list critical design elements with their definitions and roles in each of the components.

Video Generation

- **In-Network Processing:** Closely-positioned video cameras record highly correlated video content. In-network processing acts as a filter at the beginning of video recording to remove content redundancy. Localized information is shared by neighboring video nodes to coordinate video recording for a targeted area.
- **Video Processing/Data Compression:** To save energy for data transmission, video processing is used to extract relevant features of interest prior to transmission to minimize the total data transmission energy cost.
- **Video Coding:** Video coding is critical for success of video streaming. Many coding techniques have been developed support-

ing a variety of goals. For example, network coding is introduced to achieve high data transmission efficiency, multiple description coding (MDC) is used to achieve reliable data transmission and provide QoS guarantees.

Video Delivery

- **Bandwidth:** Generally speaking, bandwidth is a resource that a link obtains to deliver the data over a communication link measured in bits per second. Bandwidth is also used as an indicator of link capacity. Congestion occurs if the potential load is larger than the link bandwidth. However, in wireless video networks, link capacity can only be viewed as a relaxed link load upper bound due to radio collisions; real link throughput is far less than the available capacity.

- **Multihop Routing:** Multihop routing refers to the use of intermediate nodes to propagate data from source to destination. Multihop routing reduces the cost deployment by eliminating wired infrastructure, but is practically limited by progressive degradation as hops increase.

- **Multipath Routing:** A path is a series of cascaded links between a source and a destination. Multipath routing defines the use of multiple paths between the same source and destination pair to deliver data. Multiple paths provide an option for increasing the capacity to deliver data to a destination if congestion at the source and destination can be managed and the interference among different paths can be controlled.

- **Energy Efficient Routing:** WSNs assume battery-powered operation perhaps with energy replenishment via harvesting technology. The depletion of battery power at individual node can result in broken

links in the established network topology and influence the continuity of video data transmission. Energy-aware routing is necessary to achieve policies for managing energy depletion that can disrupt network connectivity and the video dissemination mission.

- **Latency:** Latency describes the delay of a data packet from source to destination. Streaming data is affected by both delay and delay jitter. The packets consisting of a video frame must all be correctly received at the destination before the playback of the frame. If the packet cannot be delivered within the deadline, this packet would be obsolete and useless. The data routing component has a goal of delivering packets on time while real time streaming is a requirement.

- **Data Dissemination Pattern:** Many practical sensor networks funnel data from leaf nodes in a tree structure to a single data sink. This model creates congestion and energy depletion in the region of the sink, especially for wireless nodes. Video sensing exacerbates this problem due to its data density. For more general-purpose design of video data routing, the data dissemination model is on demand to support multiple sources and multiple sinks.

Video Playback

- **Playback Gap:** This gap is defined as the period between initiating video download and the start of playback. Video streaming technology enables users begin playback prior to completing the full download. A local buffer is used to cache downloaded video, and successive frames are fetched from the buffer for playback. The larger the buffer, the more able the playback can accommodate delay variations (jitter) in the video transmission.

- **Video Distortion:** Video distortion defines the visual quality degradation due to the lost data.

Video delivery is a critical component for achieving video streaming over WSNs. The performance as quantified as quality of service (QoS) for video playback is highly depended on the video delivery techniques. Although video generation and playback are relevant topics, they are not the focus of this chapter. In the following section we introduce the characteristics and challenges for achieving routing in a WVSN.

3. CHARACTERISTICS AND CHALLENGES FOR ROUTING IN A WVSN

Routing is an essential component for video streaming in WVSNs. Routing deals with three basic issues: where to route the video data, how to satisfy the end-to-end delay requirement of the video streaming application and how to keep the network functional as long as possible under energy depletion. We label these three challenges as: Addressing, Resources, and QoS as described next.

Addressing Challenge

Unlike IP (Internet Protocol) addressing which is hierarchical, sensor networks are typically configured with flat addressing that leverages locality. Assigning global IDs for each sensor node is not always a requirement. Moreover, a hierarchical model can introduce excessive overhead when most communications are neighbor-based. And in some cases, based on the characteristic and function of wireless video sensor network, there can be no need to distinguish one node from another by ID (e.g., Intanagonwiwat et al., 2000). Thus, the development of routing protocols based on IP address is not a requirement for a WVSN.

Resource Constraint Challenge

A typical wireless sensor network consists of a large number of autonomous, inexpensive and simple sensor nodes that are powered by batteries. Although advances of circuit design have made substantial improvements for battery life in recent years, compared to desktops in wired networks, sensor nodes are still strictly constrained by energy. Such limitations have a great impact on communication ability and routing protocol design.

QoS Requirement Challenge

Designing a routing protocol to ensure the sensed video data to be delivered reliably and timely while traversing a series of unpredictable wireless links is an ongoing research challenge.

Understanding the above challenges leads us to the creation of quantitative metrics for evaluating the success of existing approaches, which we describe next.

4. STATE OF THE ART VIDEO ROUTING TECHINIQUES

In this section we review the recent works focused on routing algorithm design for supporting video transmission in WVSN applications.

4.1. Addressing Techniques

4.1.1. Content-Based Addressing

As previously indicated, for many wireless sensor network applications, it is not practical nor a requirement to assign global IDs such as an IP address to each sensor node. Many investigators have recognized that the data flow within a sensor network can be characterized by the content of the data itself. A mapping between the sensor node's functionality and data content can be established during data transmission. By summarizing the data interests of participating sensor nodes, content-based routing is achieved (Intanagonwiwat et al., 2000; Guo et al., 2008; Carzaniga et al., 2004). In such a routing scheme, data-receiving nodes propagate data interests across the network in a publish-subscribe or push-pull model. Guo et al. (2008) provide an example of the 'push' method with the use of an application-specific property to distinguish different nodes. A node address is represented by a set node attributes defining its function in the application (e.g., 'with a light sensor,' 'measure rate,' etc.). Each data stream is prefixed by a structured description using typed language which defines a set of criteria for the destination node of the stream called predicates, such as 'nodes inside certain area,' 'node with certain brand.' The protocol establishes a hierarchical property-interest tree rooted at source node. The source node pushes the data stream onto the tree and thus the stream will flow to the node with the corresponding interest. Directed diffusion (Intanagonwiwat et al., 2000) is an example of content-based routing using the 'pull' method. Directed diffusion aims at diffusing data through sensor nodes by using a naming scheme for the data. A significant advantage of directed diffusion is the simplification of the programming abstraction and routing mechanism for propagating data to a data sink. Direct Diffusion suggests the use of attribute-value pairs for the data and queries the sensors in an on demand basis by using those pairs. In order to create a query, an interest is defined using a list of attribute-value pairs such as name, interval, duration, geographical area, etc. A sink broadcasts an interest through its neighbors. Each node receiving the interest broadcast caches the interest for later use. The nodes also have the ability to perform in-network data aggregation to merge similar interests. The cached interests are then used to compare the received data with the values in the interests. The interest entry also contains several gradient fields. A gradient is a reply link to a neighbor from which the interest was received and is characterized by a data rate,

duration and expiration time derived from the received interest fields. Hence, by utilizing interest and gradients, paths are established between sink and sources. Several paths can be established so that one of them is selected by reinforcement. The sink resends the original interest message through the selected path with a smaller interval hence reinforces the source node on that path to send data more frequently. There are many variations proposed for efficient wireless sensor network data routing based on Directed Diffusion.

GEBR (Li et al., 2007) expand the concept of Directed Diffusion to provide global energy balancing and real-time routing for video data transmission. Their path formation process is nearly identical to that of directed diffusion; however, they introduce node energy as a criterion for data transmission and path reinforcement.

Wang et al. (2007) propose synchronized pipelined transmission for video data streaming. Unlike Directed Diffusion which floods interest message to explore the optimal path, the route discovery process in uses a probabilistic method. The source node periodically sends out route probing packets. The probing packets are randomly relayed to a neighbor of the current hop until they reach the subscriber node. When the predefined route-probing timer expires, the subscriber node calculates the optimal path based on all received probing packets. Although this process can largely eliminate the data load created by the path exploration stage, it performs poorly when the network is relatively large and the source and destination nodes are scarce and far from each other.

Li et al. (2008) provide a multipath data delivery solution to deal with the challenge of delay control in video transmission applications with another expansion of directed diffusion. Instead of using the metric of transmission time, the scheme uses a weighted metric that captures delay, interference and throughput. A timestamp is given to both interest message and exploration data. The sink station chooses exploration data whose timestamp is within a predefined threshold to satisfy the delay constraint as compared to the interest message's timestamp. The sink tags the senders of these qualified exploration data messages into the reinforcement path candidate pool. The reinforcement scheme in this solution supports the set-up of multiple disjoint paths. However, the length of the path set-up period is largely dependent on the compound metric it adopts and subject to variable delay. Furthermore, the data supporting the adopted metric is difficult to obtain. For example, the measurement of SNR needs the power level of three terms: noise, interference, and signal strength. The author does not provide the method to measure such terms. A simpler metric that can be directly obtained or estimated by the network layer is more preferable and flexible.

From the above exploration, we find that there are three major problems existing in the current content-based video routing technique for wireless sensor networks. First, all of the current techniques are application-dependant addressing schemes. It is difficult to port data interest from one application to another unless the two applications are similar. Second, the content-based routing schemes utilize a route exploration stage using route exploration data. The motivation for this approach is to simulate data transmission and thus select what might be an optimal route. However, in video streaming applications, the prevailing conditions during route exploration can be substantially different from when video data are in transmission. In other words, a good route obtained during a data exploration stage will not necessarily be the good route during a data transmission stage. Thus, a specially designed exploration stage is required to find a good video streaming route for WVSNs. Third, we lack the control of path selection involving overused nodes. It is very likely that multiple data paths will share common nodes since these paths become reinforced. These nodes soon become overloaded and compromise the video data transmission.

4.1.2. Location-Based Addressing Techniques

The second group of addressing schemes is location-based. A number of proposed routing schemes fall into this category. Since most WSNs are comprised of nodes deployed in a known area, they have proper coordinates established that can be used to assist routing. The distance between the source node and sink node in real world can be used as a proxy for the energy cost for data delivery. There are two kinds of location-based routing strategies. The first one we call real coordinate routing. GPSR (Karp & Kung, 2000) is one such example. In real coordinate routing, each node uses geometric distance as the routing metric. This strategy establishes coordinates for each node based on its absolute (Cartesian) location. By obtaining the location information of a destination node and its neighbor nodes, senders always forward a packet to a neighbor with a shorter distance to the destination (a greedy technique). Real coordinate routing suffers from well-known dead-end problem especially in a sparse network or one with physical obstructions. The second strategy is called virtual coordinate routing (Rao et al., 2003; Newsome & Song, 2003; Zhao et al., 2007). This routing strategy applies routing metrics to reflect the relative location of the sensor nodes within the network instead of using absolute coordinates. Zhao et al. (2007) propose a method in which individual node constructs a vector with elements corresponding to the hop distance to the set of pre-established landmarks. This vector is exactly the virtual coordinate of the node. The routing process is identical to GPSR (a greedy formula) except that it uses a more elaborate distance function instead of the geographic distance. Virtual coordinate routing performs well for the dead-end problem in sparse scenarios and it reduces the hardware requirements of sensor nodes. However, the virtual coordinate setup process is not easy and is energy consuming.

Thus most recent works in location-based routing continue to use real coordinates.

Cosma et al. (2006) have an interesting application of location-based routing for video streaming. This paper is not a complete solution for video transmission over wireless sensor networks but introduces a topology extraction protocol using video cameras equipped on each sensor node. There are two steps to achieve the topology extraction. First, a central node/server or gateway floods routing messages over the network and every node records routing information. After a path set-up phase, every node in the network captures an image using its video camera, and passes the image through to the central node/server. This node then performs image registration to extract the topology and location of each sensor node. The result is analogous to a bird's-eye view of the global topology of the system. The authors further suggest that the global topology can be optimized for path routing and energy conservation. This scheme is creative but impractical at present. Image registration of a large number of disparate images is complex, time consuming, and potentially performed with sparseness of view. It is also likely that the extracted topology has significant error due to the limited camera resolutions, focal lengths, and fields of view.

DGR (Chen et al., 2007) is a mechanism proposed to transmit real-time video. The idea of DGR is to construct an application-specific number of multiple disjointed paths for a video node to transmit parallel FEC-protected H.26L real-time video streams over a bandwidth-limited, unreliable networking environment. Unlike traditional location-based routing algorithms using greedy routing schemes (Karp & Kung, 2000; Yu et al., 2001) the author introduces a concept of "deviation angle" to spread the paths in all directions by the side of the line-proximity of the source and sink nodes. It implies that packets along some paths are likely to be forwarded to a neighbor that is a greater distance from the sink. To deal with problems with route coupling (Pearlman et al., 2000) caused by interference between packets transmitted over different paths, the authors separate physical paths as far as possible. When a node receives a path set-up packet, it calculates its virtual coordinate based on the location of the upstream message sender, destination, and itself. The origin of the virtual coordinate is the upstream node's location and a reference line (x-axis) is between upstream node and sink node. The angle between the x-axis and the line segment of the receiving node and the upstream node is then obtained. The upstream node then chooses the node whose angle is least different from the "deviation angle" as the next hop. Deviation angle is controlled by a function with respect to hop count to ensure the path will definitely go back to the sink. DGR uses node location to identify different sensor nodes. Instead of using pure location for routing decision, DGR introduces deviation angle-controlled routing to find detours. This idea is efficient for establishing multiply separated paths from source to sink. The video data can then be subdivided into multiple streams and transmitted through multiple disjoint paths to the sink.

The TPGF routing protocol (Shu et al. 2008) is another example of a greedy location-based scheme. In order to solve the hole-bypassing problem (Fang et al, 2004; Yu et al., 2007; Jia et al., 2007), TPGF proposes "step back and mark" process to explore possible paths to the base station and guarantees to find a route to the destination as if one exists. This protocol is designed to execute multiple times to find multiple disjoint paths from source node to sink node. However, unlike the scheme adopted by Chen et al. (2007) which introduces a way to separate paths as far as possible, on the contrary, this scheme put these paths as close as possible to the centerline which can cause very severe path coupling problems.

According to the above analysis, location-based routing schemes are application independent. Moreover, the information required for data routing is simple and localized without necessary knowledge of the global network topology. But some variants are not entirely practical. For example, most location-based routing exploits GPS data that is often unavailable due to cost or indoor locations. Another problem for location-based routing is to deal with network holes. An efficient hole-bypassing algorithm is very important for location-based data routing over WVSNs.

4.1.3. Hierarchical Addressing Techniques

Yet another routing scheme is based on hierarchical addressing. The basic idea of hierarchical addressing and routing is to group sensor nodes into multiple clusters based on some assignment criteria. A cluster "head" is selected to coordinate communications within the cluster and to any nodes corresponding to other clusters. LEACH (Heinzelman et al., 2000) is a milestone protocol in this area and it inspires a large number of hierarchical routing protocols for wireless sensor network. The idea of LEACH is to form clusters based on radio signal strength and to use local cluster heads as routers to the sink. This scheme saves energy by simplifying routing in a locality and managing the propagation of data that must traverse multiple clusters. The optimal number of clusterheads is estimated to be 5% of the total number of nodes. All the data processing such as data fusion and aggregation is local to the cluster. The assignment of clusterhead is rotated in order to share the energy burden of this function.

Akkaya and Younis (2003) provide a three tier network architecture to route data as illustrated in Figure 3. Before network operation is established, sensor nodes are grouped into clusters. Each cluster has a gateway node. Sensor nodes only route data to the gateway nodes, and gateway nodes are responsible for routing data to the central command node. The sensor nodes do not require globally unique IDs. The path setup process is a centralized scheme. The cluster's gateway node is assumed to know the cluster's topology and link state between any two nodes inside cluster.

Figure 3. Three tier network (Adapted from Akkaya & Younis, 2003)

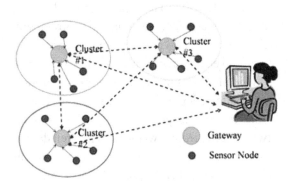

The idea proposed is to find a detour path to the gateway instead of transmitting data directly. However, the authors neglect to consider that all the sensor nodes of a cluster are within the radio range of the cluster head and are thus potential interferers. Changing the route without changing the radio range can cause severe interference.

Politis et al. (2008) describe another hierarchical video data routing scheme. The network architecture setup is a slight modification of architecture of LEACH. Instead of using a direct link between a cluster head and base station for data collection, cluster heads are allowed to establish links to each other. Hence, a video sensor node can select a number of available paths through other cluster heads in order to transmit its data to the base station. This modification decreases the transmission power of a clusterhead for shorter-range communication and saves energy. This paper can be viewed as a complementary work of Akkaya and Younis (2003). Instead of addressing routing inside a cluster, Politis et al. propose a scheme to address routing from clusterhead to a base station. The algorithm is adapted from the work of Chen et al. (2004) and it uses a centralized algorithm based on the knowledge of the network topology, link capacity and link delay. Unfortunately, the scalability of such routing algorithm is not sufficiently addressed.

Besides the communication management benefit, another inspiration to use hierarchical network architecture for video data transmission is that such architecture is efficient for redundant data removal. High data rates of a video stream inevitably will cause rapid energy consumption by sensor nodes. To avoid node failure and network disruption due to battery depletion, an aggregation-driven routing scheme is proposed. In a hierarchical network, nodes from lower level send their data to higher-level nodes for data aggregation. Nodes at a higher level are then responsible for comparing and removing redundant data from each stream and compressing the data before sending them to their upper-level controllers. Navda et al. (2006) propose one such routing scheme. The basic idea is to merge multiple flows at early stage of data transmission and form spatially separated paths to minimize inter-path radio interference. The root node first floods a message to setup a spanning tree. Source nodes attempt to send data to the neighbors of the root through nodes which are not carrying any flows and do not have contending transmitters in their radio range. If the node cannot find such path, it will route to the nearest node that carries the fewest flows. Unlike traditional schemes which route data through disjoint paths, this scheme tries to merge data at an early stage of the data transmission and form spatially independent routing paths.

From the above analysis, the main advantage for building a hierarchical network topology is for data fusion and data transmission management. However, the data fusion costs for video are not very carefully studied in this prior work. According to Liu & Das (2006), the fusion cost of video can be equivalent to that of transmission. The shortcoming of hierarchical network organization is the imbalanced network load distribution across participating nodes. Such a network would result in unfair resource consumption for different nodes in different layers.

4.1.4. Global ID Routing Attempts

The absence of globally unique IDs hinders the integration of WSNs and IP-based networks. In order to solve this problem, schemes have been investigated to assign unique network-wide IDs (Ould-Ahmed-Vall et al. 2005). However, these ideas face the risk of incompatibility with the established standards of the Internet. Another approach is via IPv6; a sensor can concatenate its cluster ID with its own MAC address to create a full IPv6 address. However the 16 byte address field of IPv6 potentially introduces excessive overhead in each sensor data packet, but in this way, the existing Internet solution for video transmission can be adapted to achieve video transmission over a wireless sensor network.

4.2. Energy-Efficient Routing Techniques

As stated at the beginning of this chapter, energy consumption is always the primary concern of wireless sensor network application design. This section considers recent efforts in energy-efficient routing.

The energy saving idea from GEBR (Li et al., 2007) is to send data through the path of fewest hops and most longevity. The longevity of a path is measured with something called Minimum-Path-Energy (MPE), which is the minimum energy of all the nodes along a path. The interest message generated by a sink destination contains hop count requirement, MPE value, and path length. When a source node receives a set of interest messages, it calculates the maximum value of the MPE from different paths whose path length is smaller than the hop count requirement. The hop count requirement is a proxy for a real-time streaming requirement. The authors assume that a path with fewer hops will yield the lowest data transmission delay. Afterwards, the source station sends exploration data that contains the maximum MPE value (BMPE value). The node only

Figure 4. BMPE generation (Adapted fromLi et al., 2007)

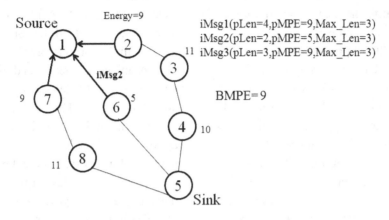

Figure 5. Optimal path selection (Adapted from Li et al., 2007)

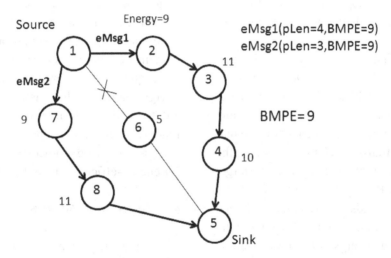

forwards the exploration data to its upper stream node if the neighbor's energy is larger than the BMPE value. This process ensures that exploration data only goes through the most survivable path and balances the traffic load. However, the pure BMPE-based routing does not consider problems with packet collision. If multiple source and sink nodes exist, it is very likely that the BMPE path will be heavily loaded or even be badly interfered with by other BMPE paths resulting in significant packet losses, delay, and energy waste. Figures 4 and 5 illustrate examples of BMPE generation and optimal path selection:

Wang et al. (2007) consider energy conservation through the reduction of packet retransmissions in the presence of node failures. A synchronized and pipelined transmission scheme is proposed with flow control. They use a secondary buffer to ensure the maximum retransmission distance is not more than the equivalent of twice the size of the failed node's buffer. However, it is not clear how well this scheme scales under their synchronization requirement. The flooding of synchronization messages will not be efficient for large networks. Instead, synchronizing node for a particular route seems more feasible and efficient. Also, buffering packets at the neighboring nodes is a good idea; however, to the means to update these secondary buffer data according to the update of the primary buffer data is not described.

Cosma et al. (2006) propose that every node maintains a record of their neighbors' energy level and hop count to the server. Any node with a relatively high energy (>20%) will be in the candidate set for next hop during routing. The candidate with smallest hop count will be chosen as the next hop. This solution, although more conformal to energy fairness on a per hop basis, does not prevent instantaneous overuse of a path. Moreover, for long-lived video streams, there can be significant change in energy levels for nodes participating in multihop routing. How to adapt to short-term energy change and contention for shared paths is not considered.

Based on the first-order radio model (Heinzelman et al., 2000; Shin et al., 2006; Fang et al., 2004), Shu et al. (2008) derive the node energy consumption rate as a function of data rate and radio transmission range. The goal here is to manipulate the radio transmission range to satisfy the energy consumption constraint to achieve a target network lifetime. Results indicate that a greater transmission range leads to lower latency. A node will prefer to use the maximum radio range if the corresponding node energy consumption rate is lower than the expected rate. The radio range and energy consumption rate are computed based on two critical terms: the energy cost to power the transmitter circuitry to send one bit, and the energy cost for transmitter amplifier to send one bit. These two terms are difficult to measure; inaccuracies will interfere with the success of the routing algorithm.

Politis et al. (2008) introduce the clusterhead energy consumption model. The authors propose a packet-scheduling algorithm that allows a source node to drop packets queued for transmission in order to avoid downstream congestion. This is achieved considering the residual energy of the clusterheads on the path to the destination.

Akkaya & Younis (2003) address energy efficient routing in the context of a single cluster. They assume that all sensor nodes in a cluster are within the radio range of its associated gateway. A link cost function is defined based on the consideration of delay, residual energy, distance, and other factors. The gateway node is assumed to know all link states; Dijkstra's algorithm is applied to find the least cost path between sensor nodes and gateways. The gateway continuously monitors the available energy level of every sensor node active in data processing, sensing, or relaying. Rerouting is triggered by the depletion of energy of an active node. But the details of node residue energy monitoring and energy metrics are not disclosed in this paper.

In summary, we find some practical limitations of many of the exiting energy-constrained routing techniques. Either there is no clearly established energy metrics or the existing metrics are difficult to obtain robust measurements. Designing a practical energy consumption model and residual energy monitoring protocol would be very helpful for energy-efficient video data routing.

4.3. QoS Techniques

Video and audio data transmission requires certain quality of service (QoS) achievement in a WVSN, especially when streamed continuously. For example, a streamed video must deliver each frame to the user on-time to achieve continuous playback. Unfortunately, there are many uncertainties in WVSNs that can cause significant delay that diminish video playback quality. In the following we discuss techniques that have been adopted to deal with such challenges.

Li et al. (2008) propose to deliver MDC-coded data through multiple selected paths to overcome packet loss due to network congestion and transmission delay. Cross-layer design and disjoint routing path selection are considered to provide better QoS. During the path exploration period, the algorithm tags identified paths into a pool and

Figure 6. Node A is the bottleneck (Adapted from Li et al., 2008)

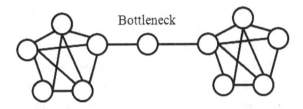

sorts them in an ascending order according to the path length. The first N shortest paths that satisfy the data delivery cost constraint are chosen to be candidate routing path. In order to find multiple reliable paths from the source to sink, the sink chooses the first N shortest paths based on cost. N is chosen to be a slight larger than the required number of paths for the transmission, since some candidate paths may not be reinforced if disjoint nodes cannot be found or the delay exceeds the playback deadline. During the path reinforcement stage, if two nodes happen to reinforce a same node, the second reinforcement will be invalid to guarantee disjoint path selection and avoiding loop generation. To deal with bottleneck problem shown in Figure 6, Li et al. (2008) eliminate the existence of bottleneck links through a deployment density control.

DGR (Chen et al., 2007) uses multipath transmission to achieve low latency. A FEC coding scheme is used to recover data due to packet loss or data corruption. Although multiple path transmission can expand available bandwidth, it is not clear how data path merging is achieved which can result in severe data contention at the destination.

Base on TPGF (Shu et al., 2008), L. Zhang et al. (2008) uses a multi-priority multipath selection scheme for video streaming for WSNs. In this technique, a priority index is assigned to different paths based on end-to-end delay. Streams are identified and prioritized based on their ability to monitor an event. Streams are also split into audio and video components. A mapping scheme

is implemented to assign a higher priority path to a higher priority stream. A shortcoming of this scheme is that it relies on direct paths from source to sink and does not fully address the path interference problem.

Akkaya and Younis (2003) propose a link cost function that considers link delay. The idea is to adjust the bandwidth split ratio r to let the average end-to-end delay satisfy the delay requirement. The average delay estimation is based on an implied assumption that each packet could be delivered to the destination through multiple hops without any corruption or loss. If we consider packet collision or loss, we expect that the average delay of each packet will increase beyond their model's prediction and the bandwidth split ratio value r.

Politis et al. (2008) propose to transmit the most important video packets through multiple paths to the destination to achieve a QoS target. A video distortion model presented by Politis et al. (2007) is applied to estimate the importance of different encoded video packets of the H.264/AVC stream. The algorithm developed by Fang et al. (2004) is used to find multiple paths from source to destination that can satisfy the video bandwidth requirement. A baseline packet-scheduling algorithm is introduced to manage the transmission by dropping excessive video traffic based on the packet importance. For further improvement, the authors developed an packet-scheduling scheme that factors the residual energy of cluster heads in the algorithm. This approach can reduce the distortion of the decoded video sequence by deciding which and how many packets will be dropped according to transmission rate limitations and power failure of the nodes prior to transmission. Politis et al. (2008) borrow the multipath formation scheme developed by Chen et al. (2004). The path formation algorithm considers two factors: end-to-end delay and aggregate bandwidth. This scheme guarantees to find multiple paths from source to destination that satisfy the bandwidth and delay requirements. However, due to uncertainty of wireless channels, the actual throughput of the multipath is usually much less than the aggregate value. A limitation of this idea is that it is only applicable to single source-destination pairs., An additional limitation is the reliance of the distortion-reduction algorithm on a specific video encoding scheme.

A rate-based flow control algorithm called doubling and reducing-by-half is proposed by Navada et al. (2006). By monitoring the throughput of per flow at the root, the source is allowed to double the load of the flow until the throughput of other flows is influenced and dropped under a threshold. Thereafter, the source node reduces load in the next step to half of the previous incremental load until throughputs per flow match again. Packet scheduling based on packet delay requirements and flow priority is proposed to promote performance. Also, early dropping of packets is used to deal with anticipated congestion. Unfortunately, these schemes are not fully analyzed to demonstrate their practical applicability.

Chai and Ye (2007) adapt Internet streaming models the wireless mesh context. Each node is assumed to have a unique IP address. Data consumers contact a central server for authorization and channel setup. The central server coordinates different video servers to stream video data to the corresponding users. A media transfer server working at background is responsible for converting the various multimedia file formats to the internal streaming file format suitable for reading and indexing by the delivery server and uploading data to the distributed file systems or data storage center. The authors adapt RTSP/RTP protocols used in Internet video streaming to stream the video data over wireless mesh network. The only difference is that the underlying transmission mode of RTP packet is replaced by TCP connection to overcome the high error rate and bandwidth fluctuation of the wireless channel. Authorization process and packet scheduling algorithm for multi-users is introduced to solve the challenge brought by RTP-on-TCP transmission such as robust and se-

curity connection problems, delay jitter problems and system blocking problems. Non-important packets can be dropped before transmission to avoid potential network congestion and improve network performance.

In reviewing recent QoS management techniques for video delivery in WSNs, three main techniques emerge as best candidates for adoption:

1. **Multipath Transmission:** This technique is used to expand the available network capacity through multiple links. Existing proposals can benefit by additional models for path interference and wireless data transmission.
2. **Controlled Packet Scheduling:** This technique is used to predict and reduce data congestion within a network. Priority-based packet scheduling is favored to achieve required QoS.
3. **Coding:** Video coding is used to overcome the corruption of data during transmission and to mitigate the frequency of retransmissions, thus reducing data volume and associated energy consumption due to transmission.

5. METRICS AND PERFORMANCE EVALUATION CRITERIA

We seek a good design for video data routing. A design must consider WSN video application requirements and yield a reasonable tradeoff of performance based on current technologies limitations (e.g., battery capacity, video encoding, and radios). In this section we propose a canonical set of metrics on which we can base design decisions and performance evaluation for future designs.

Resource Conservation Performance

As we know, WVSNs are resource-constrained. Applications built on WVSNs are limited by bandwidth, battery energy, available channels, etc. Performance evaluation in this dimension will indicate that how good the routing technique will perform to save limited network resources. The following metrics define resource conservation performance and are adopted from a survey of prior work:

- *Number of Channels:* Number of channels utilized for wireless communication.
- *Residual Energy:* Instantaneous battery energy at a sensor node (Joules)
- *Circuit Power:* Instantaneous energy consumption at a sensor node.

Path Formation Performance

There are two metrics related to routing: path setup delay and path setup flexibility. The former indicates how quickly an algorithm will respond to a request to send data and the latter indicate the reusability of a path setup by the algorithm. The two metrics are defined as follows:

- *Path Setup Delay:* The time period for a data path to be found and ready for data transmission.
- *Path Setup Flexibility:* Assessment of the adaptability of the path instance especially for related data transmission requirements.

Data Delivery Performance

Data delivery performance is one of the most important characterizations of WVSN routing designs. This performance indicates how well the data will be transmitted along the data path. Two critical terms are evaluated:

1. *End-to-End Delay:* The time to send one packet from a source to a destination
   - **Metrics:**
     - **Hop Count:** Total number of hops from source to destination, generally speaking, a larger hop count corresponds to a larger delay.
     - **Propagation Time:** Time for a packet transmission from source to destination.
     - **ETX (Expected data transmission time):** The expected number of transmissions for a successful packet transit. Generally speaking, the larger the value the higher the delay.
     - **Data Path Capacity:** The maximum data rate can be achieved in the absence of any cross traffic. This capacity is equivalent to the capacity of bottleneck link along the path
     - **Packet Queuing Delay:** The average queuing delay of a packet on a path.
     - **Throughput:** Average number of packets traversing a path per unit time.
2. *Transmission Interference:* Interference caused by data transmission on adjacent links.
   - **Metrics:**
     - **Link Failure Probability:** the likelihood of a link to fail.
     - **SNR:** signal to noise ratio
     - **BER:** bit error rate

Network Performance

Network performance defines aggregate performance of all data paths in a network. In much of the related work we find that performance evaluation focuses on single path performance rather than aggregate performance. Network performance evaluation considers interactions among different data paths and indicates the global performance of the routing protocol. We propose the following metrics for network performance measurement:

- *Number of active paths*: How many video streams can be active simultaneously in the network. This metric reflects the capability of the routing algorithm. A good routing algorithm will support as many video streams as possible with relatively low overhead and energy cost.
- *Average throughput per path*: This defines the expected number of packets that are delivered per unit time for a path. This metric is a key benchmark of performance for a routing algorithm. If the average path throughput is higher than the threshold requirement of the WVSN application, then the algorithm is expected to perform well in practical application.
- *Data Transmission Cost*: The inverse of throughput. This metric can also involve energy costs.
- *Data Collection Cost*: Due to the data path throughput requirement, an upper bound for the path length will exist that makes the network base station unreachable with a certain probability. One possible solution is to deploy mobile gateways to gather data for the base station with certain deployment cost. Data collection cost is the total of the mobile gateway deployment costs.
- *Data Transmission Cost:* This term is defined as the total energy consumption for carrying a video stream on a certain path. It can be measured using the total active time of the sensor nodes along the path.
- *Network Operation Cost*: This is a measurement of total cost for delivering video data from sources to their destinations from the view of the network. This metric is usually a weighted combination of data transmission cost and data collection cost.

6. RECENT RESEARCH RESULTS

We have developed a performance evaluation framework for assessing the performance of video delivery in WVSN, which is described next.

We measure the performance of the video delivery based upon the network operation cost and the achieved QoS. Network operation cost is an abstract term that captures the cost of data transmission and data gathering. Designers using our following performance evaluation framework can adapt this metric to local conditions. We select throughput as our QoS metric. We select the throughput as our QoS metric due to that we believe many existing video delivery QoS requirements could be projected to this metric. Moreover, there are two basic QoS requirements for video delivery applications, timeliness and reliability. Timeliness requires that packets be delivered as promptly as possible. This requirement can be implemented by designing a routing algorithm with prioritized packet scheduling scheme to provide a lower bound of throughput satisfying the delay constraint of the application. The higher the video delivery throughput the more likely the application will deliver data on time. As a result, a timeliness requirement can be projected to our throughput requirement. A reliability algorithm leverages channel diversity to overcome packet loss while increasing the data redundancy by exploiting multi-path transmission. The data loss constraint in this kind of application can also be translated to throughput constraint. We can maximize the data redundancy to recover lost packets by designing a routing algorithm that achieves the maximum aggregate throughput at the destination. Such conversion enables us to measure the performance of these applications with our QoS metric.

Although achieving high QoS with less cost is an implied objective for many video delivery applications, most existing efforts focus on the optimization of either the cost or the QoS. A balanced consideration on both sides is not well presented. We find that the two design factors are indeed closely related to each other. Let us consider the network operation cost unit; it can be expressed as "cost/second". We can rewrite this unit as follows:

cost/second = (cost/packet)*(packet/second)

The first term on the right side is the average data delivery cost for each packet, the second term on the right side is the throughput of the whole network, which can be used as a QoS indicator. If we fix the network operation cost, we can plot the data delivery cost and network throughput as shown in Figure 7:

The different protocols will achieve different performance nodes along the black curve. These curves correspond to different network operation costs. Given a location of the performance node for a base protocol as shown above, we can divide the graph into four quadrants. If a new protocol performance node lies in the upper left quadrant, we can immediately conclude that such protocol is even worse than the base protocol since the performance in this quadrant requires higher packet delivery cost but achieves lower network throughput. If the protocol performance node is in the upper right or lower left quadrant, we say that the new protocol is at least as good as the base protocol since these protocols achieve high throughput at high cost or low throughput at low cost. If the protocol performance node is in the lower right quadrant, we can tell that this protocol is better than the base protocol. The new protocol achieves higher throughput with lower packet delivery cost. Figure 7 is called constellation graph of video data routing protocol. No matter how many routing techniques you would like to compare for the application, as long as you have the values of the two metrics of each routing technique and plot its constellations, a simple glance of such graph will assess the performance of each technique.

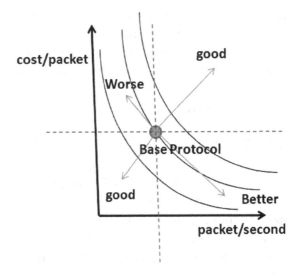

Figure 7. Video data routing algorithm performance evaluation

7. CONCLUSION

Based on the above analysis of the pros and cons of the state-of-the-art in video data routing in WVSN, we envision a series of design requirements for improved video routing protocol to deal with the proposed three basic challenges. These are:

Addressing Challenge

The addressing scheme is better to be application independent. For example, content-based routing is a good idea to solve node identity problem but it is difficult to port data interest for one application to another unless the two applications are similar. Application-specific interest messages limited the commonality of these routing protocols. A better solution is to design an adaptive architecture for various applications. However, such interest generalization task requires extensive effort to explore the similarity among different potential applications.

Energy Challenge

Energy conservation is a critical design challenge for video data routing. A path formation algorithm needs to consider energy use as a control parameter. Unfortunately support for accurate network-wise energy status measurement and consumption models are not well defined.

QoS Challenge

QoS is an important design factor for video routing over wireless sensor networks. The design in this space focuses on transmitting data on-time using multipath and packet scheduling schemes to avoid network congestion and data loss. However, most of the previous work focuses on simple scenarios, a comprehensive study of multi-source multi-destination with unsynchronized data transmission must be conducted to understand the efficiency of any protocol. Furthermore, in wireless sensor networks, bandwidth and channel resources are limited. A simple addition of bandwidth of multiple paths is only the relaxed upper bound of the end-end throughput. Due to the severe inter-path and intra-path interference and network congestion, the actual delay and throughput can be quite different that one is found in an isolated path. Most previous works suggest the establishment of disjoint paths to ease the problem. The relationship of the packet collision probability, the path length, path number and path positions needs to be carefully studied to guide the path formation design. The use of path hop count as a reflection of potential packet delay is insufficient. A new path metric, which considers the path length, traffic load and queuing delay, would have strong potential for path formation.

Based on the suggestions above, we are exploring routing protocols to balance the outlined design requirements. We believe the new routing protocol must have a practical dynamic source-to-sink path formation scheme to isolate video streams, preventing intersection and collision,

such a scheme could achieve full-capability live video streaming within a WSN while balancing the need for energy conservation via load balancing, in-network localized computation and path selection collaboration. New practical wireless data delivery models need to be introduced and with the help of such models, the protocol can derive the path formation elements, including number of stream per destination/video, network wide stream support capacity, and path length bound based on general requirement of video transmission QoS. These design elements/constraints could be computed at runtime during the video transmission in order to achieve a dynamic video data routing and scheduling.

So far, the routing protocol design we have discussed above is focused on traditional wireless sensor network where the wireless channel can only have limited bandwidth and can be easily interfered by other radio radiations. However, with the development of wireless technology we believe that this design bottleneck can be well addressed in the near future. Some researchers have attempted to incorporate CDMA/FDMA technology to address the interference problems. Some references in this area can be found in (Sohrabi et al. 2000; Caccamo et al. 2002; Liu et al. 2003).

REFERENCES

Akkaya, K., & Younis, M. (2003, May). *An energy-aware QoS routing protocol for wireless sensor networks*. Paper presented at the IEEE Workshop on Mobile and Wireless Networks, Providence, RI.

Akkaya, K., & Younis, M. (2005). A Survey of Routing Protocols in Wireless Sensor Networks. *Elsevier Ad Hoc Network Journal, 1*(3), 325–349.

Caccamo, M., & Zhang, Y. L., & Sha, L., & Buttazzo, G. (2002). An Implicit Prioitized Access Protocol for Wireless Sensor Networks. In *Proceedings of 23rd IEEE Real-Time Systems Symposium*, 39–48.

Carzaniga, A., Rutherford, M., & Wolf, A. (2004). A Routing Scheme for Content-Based Networking. *Proceedings of IEEE 2004 International Conference on Computer Communications, HK, 2,*918-928.

Chai, Y., & Ye, D. (2007). The Design and Implementation of a Scalable Wireless Video Streaming System Adopting TCP Transmission Mode. In *Proceedings of the 7th IEEE International Conference on Computer and Information Technology, Fukushima,* 534-538.

Chen, J., Chan, S., & Li, V. (2004). Multipath routing for video delivery over bandwidth-limited networks. *IEEE Journal on Selected Areas in Communications, 22*(10), 1920–1932. doi:10.1109/JSAC.2004.836000

Chen, M., Leung, V., Mao, S., & Yuan, Y. (2007). Directional Geographical Routing for Real-Time Video Communications in Wireless Sensor Networks. *Elsevier Computer Communications, 30*(17), 3368–3383.

Chu, M., Reich, J., & Zhao, F. (2004). Distributed Attention in Large Scale Video Sensor Networks. In *Proceedings of IEEE Intelligent Distributed Surveillliance Systems,* 61-65.

Cosma, M., Pescaru, D., Ciubotaru, B., & Todinca, D. (2006, May). *Routing and Topology Extraction Protocol for a Wireless Sensor Network using Video Information.* Paper presented at 3rd Romanian-Hungarian Joint Symposium on Applied Computational Intelligence, Timisoara, Romania.

Fang, Q., Gao, J., & Guibas, L. (2004). Locating and bypassing routing holes in sensor networks. In *Proceedings of the 23rd Conference of the IEEE Communications Society, China, 4,* 2458-2468.

Guo, S., Fan, C., & Little, T. (2008, July). Supporting Concurrent Task Deployment in Wireless Sensor Networks. *Symposium on Network Computing and Applications* (pp. 111-118). Los Alamitos, CA: IEEE Computer Society.

Heinzelman, W., Chandrakasan, A., & Balakrishnan, H. (2000). Energy-efficient Communication Protocol for Wireless Microsensor Networks. In *Proceedings of Hawaii International Conference System Sciences.*

Heinzelman, W., Chandrakasan, A., & Balakrishnan, H. (2002). An application-specific protocol architecture for wireless microsensor networks. *IEEE Transactions on Wireless Communications, 1*(4), 660–670. doi:10.1109/TWC.2002.804190

Holman, R., Stanley, J., & Ozkan-Haller, T. (2003). Applying Video Sensor Networks to Nearshore Enviroment Monitoring. *IEEE Persave computing,* 14-21.

Intanagonwiwat, C., Govindan, R., & Estrin, D. (2000, August). *Directed diffusion: a scalable and robust communication paradigm for sensor networks.* Paper presented at the 6th Annual ACM/IEEE International Conference on Mobile Computing and Networking, Boston, MA.

Jia, W., Wang, T., Wang, G., & Guo, M. (2007). Hole avoiding in advance routing in wireless sensor networks. In *Proceedings of the IEEE Wireless Communication & Networking Conference, USA,* 3519-3523.

Karp, B., & Kung, H. (2000, August). *GPSR: Greedy Perimeter Stateless Routing for Wireless Networks.* Paper presented at the 6th Annual International Conference on Mobile Computing and Networking, Boston, MA.

Kulkarni, P., Ganesan, D., Shenoy, P., & Lu, Q. (2005). SensEye: A Multi-tier Camera Sensor Network. In *Proceedings of the 13th annual ACM international conference on Multimedia,* 229-238.

Li, P., Gu, Y., & Zhao, B. (2007, December). *A Global-Energy-Balancing Real-time Routing in Wireless Sensor Networks.* Paper presented at the 2nd IEEE Asia-Pacific Service Computing Conference, Tsukuba Science City, Japan.

Li, S., Neelisetti, R., Liu, C., & Lim, A. (2008, June). Delay-Constrained High Throughput Protocol for Multi-Path Transmission over Wireless Multimedia Sensor Networks. *IEEE 2008 International Symposium on a World of Wireless, Mobile and Multimedia Networks* (PP.1-8). Los Alamitos, CA: IEEE Computer Society.

Little, T., Dib, P., Shah, K., Barraford, N., & Gallagher, B. (2008). Using LED Lighting for Ubiquitous Indoor Wireless Networking. In *Proceedings of the 4th IEEE Intl. Conf. on Wirless and Mobile Computing, Networking and Communications, Avignon, France*

Little, T., Ishwar, P., & Konrad, J. (2007). A Wireless Video Sensor Network for Autonomous Coastal Sensing. In *Proceedings of Conference on Coastal Environmental Sensing Networks.*

Liu, X., Wang, Q., Sha, L., & He, W. (2003). Optimal QoS Sampling Frequency Assignment for Real-Time Wireless Sensor Networks. In *Proceedings of 24th IEEE Real-Time Systems Symposium,* 308–319.

Liu, Y., & Das, S. (2006, November). Information-Intensive Wireless Sensor Networks: Potential and Challenges. *IEEE Communications Magazine, 44*(11), 142–147. doi:10.1109/MCOM.2006.248177

Navda, V., Kashyap, A., & Ganguly, S. (2006). Real-time video stream aggregation in wireless mesh network. In *Proceedings of 17th International Symposium on Personal, Indoor and Mobile Radio Communications, Finland,* 1-7

Newsome, J., & Song, D. (2003). GEM: Graph Embedding for Routing and Data-Centric Storage in Sensor Networks without Geographic Information. *Proceedings of the First ACM Conf.: Embedded Networked Sensor Systems, USA,* 76-88.

Ould-Ahmed-Vall, E., Blough, D., Heck, B., & Riley, G. (2005). Distributed global identification for sensor networks. In *Proceedings of 2nd IEEE International Conference on Mobile Ad-hoc and Sensor Systems, Washington, DC.*

Pearlman, M., Haas, Z., Sholander, P., & Tabrizi, S. (2000). On the Impact of Alternate Path Routing for Load Balancing in Mobile Ad Hoc Networks. In *Proceedings of the 1st ACM International Symposium on Mobile Ad hoc Networking and Computing, Boston, MA,* 3-10.

Politis, I., Tsagkaropoulos, M., Dagiuklas, T., & Kotsopoulos, S. (2007). Intelligent Packet Scheduling for Optimized Video Transmission over Wireless Networks. In *Proceedings of the 3rd International Mobile Multimedia Communications Conference, Nafpaktos, Greece, 329*

Politis, I., Tsagkaropoulos, M., Dagiuklas, T., & Kotsopoulos, S. (2008). Power Efficient Video Multipath Transmission over Wireless Multimedia Sensor Networks. *Mobile Networks and Applications, 13*(3-4), 274–284.

Rao, A., Ratnasamy, S., Papadimitriou, C., Shenker, S., & Stoica, I. (2003). Geographic Routing without Location Information. In *Proceedings of the 9th Annual International Conference on Mobile Computing and Networking, San Diego, CA.*

Rowe, A., Goel, D., & Rajkumar, R. (2007). FireFly Mosaic: A Vision-Enabled Wireless Sensor Networking System. In *Proceedings of the 28th IEEE International Real-Time Systems Symposium,* 459-468.

Shin, J., Chin, M., & Kim, C. (2006). Optimal Transmission Range for Topology Management Wireless Sensor Networks. In *Proceedings of International Conference on Information Networking, Japan, 3961,* 177-185.

Shu, L., Zhang, Y., Zhou, Z., Hauswirth, M., Yu, Z., & Hyns, G. (2008). Transmitting and Gathering Streaming Data in Wireless Multimedia Sensor Networks within Expected Network Lifetime. *Mobile Networks and Applications, 13*(3-4), 306–323.

Sohrabi, K., Gao, J., Allawadhi, V., & Pottie, G. (2000). Protocols for Self-organization of a Wireless Sensor Network. *IEEE Personal Communications, 7*(5), 16–27. doi:10.1109/98.878532

Teixeira, T., Lymberopoulos, D., Culurciello, E., Aloimonos, Y., & Savvides, A. (2006). A Lightweight Camera Sensor Network Operating on Symbolic Information. In *Proceedings of the first Workshop on Distributed Smart Cameras, Boulder, CO, USA.*

Teixeira, T., & Savvides, A. (2007). Lightweight People Counting and Localizing in Indoor Spaces Using Camera Sensor Nodes. In *Proceedings of the first ACM/IEEE International Conference,* 36-43.

Wang, J., Masilela, M., & Liu, J. (2007, December). Supporting Video Data in Wireless Sensor Networks. In *Proceedings of the 9th IEEE International Symposium on Multimedia* (pp. 310-317). Los Alamitos, CA

Wu, X., Cho, J., d'Auriol, B., & Lee, S. (2007). Energy-aware routing for wireless sensor networks by AHP. In *Proceedings of IFIP Workshop on Software Technologies for Future Embedded & Ubiquitous Systems, Greece,* 446-455.

Yu, F., Lee, E., Choi, Y., Park, S., Lee, D., & Tian, Y. (2007). A modeling for hole problem in wireless sensor networks. In *Proceedings of the International Wireless Communications and Mobile Computing Conference, USA,* 370-375.

Yu, Y., Govindan, R., & Estrin, D. (2001, May). *Geographical and energy aware routing: a recursive data dissemination protocol for wireless sensor networks.* Unpublished UCLA Computer Science Department Technical Report UCLA/CSD-TR-01-0023, UCLA, CA.

Zhang, L., Hauswirth, M., Shu, L., Zhou, Z., Reynolds, V., & Han, G. (2008, June). *Multi-priority Multi-Path Selection for Video Streaming in Wireless Multimedia Sensor Networks.* Paper presented at the fifth International conference on Ubiquitous Intelligence and Computing, Oslo, Norway.

Zhao, Y., Chen, Y., Li, B., & Zhang, Q. (2007). Hop ID: A Virtual Coordinate-Based Routing for Sparse Mobile Ad Hoc Networks. *IEEE Transactions on Mobile Computing, 6*(9), 1075–1089. doi:10.1109/TMC.2007.1042

KEY TERMS AND DEFINITIONS

Bandwidth: Generally speaking, bandwidth is a resource that a link obtains to deliver the data over a communication link measured in bits per second. Bandwidth is also used as an indicator of link capacity. Congestion occurs if the potential load is larger than the link bandwidth. However, in wireless video networks, link capacity can only be viewed as a relaxed link load upper bound due to radio collisions; real link throughput is far less than the available capacity.

Data Delivery Performance: This performance indicates how well the data will be transmitted along the data path. Two critical terms are evaluated, End to End Delay and Transmission Interference.

Data Dissemination Pattern: Many practical sensor networks funnel data from leaf nodes in a tree structure to a single data sink. This model creates congestion and energy depletion in the region of the sink, especially for wireless nodes. Video sensing exacerbates this problem due to its data density. For more general-purpose design of video data routing, the data dissemination model is on demand to support multiple sources and multiple sinks.

Energy Efficient Routing: WSNs assume battery-powered operation perhaps with energy replenishment via harvesting technology. The depletion of battery power at individual node can result in broken links in the established network topology and influence the continuity of video data transmission. Energy-aware routing is necessary to achieve policies for managing energy depletion that can disrupt network connectivity and the video dissemination mission.

Latency: Latency describes the delay of a data packet from source to destination. Streaming data is affected by both delay and delay jitter. The packets consisting of a video frame must all be correctly received at the destination before the playback of the frame. If the packet cannot be delivered within the deadline, this packet would be obsolete and useless. The data routing component has a goal of delivering packets on time while real time streaming is a requirement.

Multihop Routing: Multihop routing refers to the use of intermediate nodes to propagate data from source to destination. Multihop routing reduces the cost deployment by eliminating wired infrastructure, but is practically limited by progressive degradation as hops increase.

Multipath Routing: A path is a series of cascaded links between a source and a destination. Multipath routing defines the use of multiple paths between the same source and destination pair to deliver data. Multiple paths provide an option for increasing the capacity to deliver data to a destination if congestion at the source and destination can be managed and the interference among different paths can be controlled.

Network Performance: Network performance defines aggregate performance of all data paths in a network. Network performance evaluation considers interactions among different data paths and indicates the global performance of the routing protocol.

Path Formation Performance: This performance includes measurement of path setup delay and path setup flexibility. The former indicates how quickly an algorithm will respond to a request to send data and the latter indicate the reusability of a path setup by the algorithm.

Resource Conservation Performance: How good the routing technique will perform to save limited network resources.

Section 3
P2P Media Streaming

Chapter 11
Peer–to–Peer Networks:
Protocols, Cooperation and Competition

Hyunggon Park
Ewha Womans University, Korea

Rafit Izhak Ratzin
University of California, Los Angeles (UCLA), USA

Mihaela van der Schaar
University of California, Los Angeles (UCLA), USA

ABSTRACT

P2P applications have become enormously popular and currently take into account a large majority of the traffic transmitted over the Internet. A unique characteristic of P2P networks is their flexible and robust operation, which is enabled by the peers' ability to serve as both servers and clients. Thus, P2P networks are able to provide a cost effective and easily deployable solution for sharing large files among participating peers with no significant help from a de facto, centralized infrastructure. Due to these advantages, P2P networks have also recently become popular for multimedia streaming. The requirements for general file sharing and real-time media streaming are very different and thus, we discuss in this chapter solutions for both these applications. We begin the chapter with an overview of various P2P network structures and their advantages and disadvantages. We then present in detail the BitTorrent system, which is one of the most popular file sharing protocols. We then overview existing P2P-based media streaming applications, and discuss mechanisms that have been developed to support such applications. We also discuss state-of-the-art research in P2P networks which is based on several game theoretic approaches.

1. INTRODUCTION

Peer-to-peer (P2P) networks connect many end-hosts (also referred to as peers) in an ad-hoc manner. P2P networks have been typically used for file sharing applications, which enable peers to share digitized content such as general documents, audio, video, electronic books, etc. Recently, more advanced applications such as real-time conferences, online gaming, and media streaming have also been deployed over such networks. Unlike traditional client-server networks, where servers only provide content, and clients only consume

DOI: 10.4018/978-1-61692-831-5.ch011

Copyright © 2011, IGI Global. Copying or distributing in print or electronic forms without written permission of IGI Global is prohibited.

content, in P2P networks, each peer is both a client and a server.

It has been observed that P2P file sharing applications dominate Internet traffic usage. In fact, a wide range of measurements, which were performed in 8 different geographic regions during the years of 2008-2009, show that P2P networks generated most of the traffic in all monitored regions, ranging from 43% in Northern Africa to 70% in Eastern Europe (http://www.ipoque. com/). The same study also identified that BitTorrent (Cohen, 2003) is the most popular protocol on the Internet, generating most of the traffic in 7 out of 8 regions ranging from 32% in South Africa to 57% in Eastern Europe. The details of the BitTorrent protocol will be discussed in Section 3. Recently, media delivery and streaming services over the Internet such as YouTube (http:// www.youtube.com/), PPLive (http://www.pplive. com), and Internet video broadcasting (e.g., AOL broadcast, MSNBC, CBS, etc.) have emerged. These services have become very popular, as they can deliver video to a large number of receivers simultaneously at any given time. In order to reduce infrastructure, maintenance, and service costs, and provide more reliable services, the content providers often implement their services using P2P network.

While several designs for P2P systems have been successfully deployed for file sharing and real-time media streaming, key challenges such as the design of optimal resource reciprocation strategies among self-interested peers still remain largely unaddressed. For example, pull-based techniques (Cohen, 2003., Pai et al., 2005., Zhang et al., 2005) are designed assuming that peers are altruistic and are willing to provide their available data chunks (pieces) whenever requested. However, such assumptions may be undesirable from the perspective of a self-interested peer, which aims to maximize its own utility. Thus, efficient resource reciprocation strategies need to be deployed, which can also provide incentives to the peers for their contributions.

In BitTorrent systems, incentive strategies are based on the so-called tit-for-tat (TFT) strategy, where a peer selects some of its associated peers (i.e., leechers), which are currently uploading at the highest rates, and provides them its content for downloading (Cohen, 2003). This simple strategy is currently implemented in BitTorrent systems, and provides good performance. However, a key disadvantage of this resource reciprocation strategy is that peers decide how to determine their resource reciprocation based on only the *current* upload rates that it receives from its associated peers, and does not consider how this reciprocation will impact their upload rates in the future. In other words, the resource reciprocation based on the TFT is *myopic*. Since peers in P2P networks are generally involved in repeated and long-term interactions, such myopic resource reciprocation strategy can result in a suboptimal performance for the involved peers.

More advanced resource reciprocation strategies have been recently proposed in (Park & van der Schaar, 2009), where the resource reciprocation among the interested peers is modeled as a stochastic game (Fudenberg & Tirole, 1991). In this framework, peers determine their resource distributions by explicitly considering the probabilistic behaviors (reciprocation) of their associated peers. Unlike existing resource reciprocation strategies, which focus on myopic decisions, it formalizes the resource reciprocation game as a Markov Decision Process (MDP) (Bertsekas, 1976) to enable peers to make foresighted decisions on their resource distribution in a way that maximizes their cumulative utilities, i.e., the sum of their immediate and future utilities. Thus, this strategy can improve the performance of the peers, which are generally involved in long-term and repeated interactions. When the foresighted strategies are deployed in practice, the peers' *bounded rationality* should be considered, because perfectly rational decisions are often infeasible in practice due to their memory and computational constraints. Peers can only have limited knowledge of the other players' behavior and limited ability to analyze their environment. Therefore, it is essential to study the impact of the peers' bounded rationality on (1) the performance degradation of the proposed resource reciprocation strategy and (2) their repeated interactions (resource reciprocation).

This chapter is organized as follows. In Section 2, we overview various P2P network structures and discuss their advantages and disadvantages. In Section 3, we discuss the BitTorrent system, which is one of the most popular file sharing protocols. We also discuss the limitations of BitTorrent systems. In Section 4, we overview existing P2P-based media streaming applications, and discuss how several mechanisms have been developed to support real-time media streaming requirements. In Section 5, we show the recently proposed foresighted resource reciprocation strategies, which can improve the performance of P2P-based applications. In Section 6, we discuss new directions for game-theoretic approaches to incentive design in P2P networks. Conclusions of this chapter are drawn in Section 7.

2. OVERVIEW OF P2P SYSTEM STRUCTURES

P2P systems can be classified into two different classes: *structured* P2P systems and *unstructured* P2P systems. In structured P2P systems, connections among peers in the network are fixed, and peers maintain information about the resources (e.g., shared content) that their neighbor peers possess. Hence, the data queries can be efficiently directed to the neighbor peers that have the desired data, even if the data is extremely rare. Structured P2P systems impose constraints both on node (peer) graph and on data placement to enable efficient discovery of data. The most common indexing that is used to structure P2P systems is the Distributed Hash Tables (DHTs) indexing. Similar to a hash table, a DHT provides a lookup service with (*key, value*) pairs that are stored in

the DHT. Any participating peers can efficiently retrieve the value associated with a given unique key. However, this may result in higher overhead compared to unstructured P2P networks. Different DHT-based systems such as Chord (Stoica et al., 2001), Pastry (Rowstron & Druschel, 2001), Tapestry (Zhao et al., 2004), CAN (Ratnasamy et al., 2001) are different in their routing strategies and their organization schemes for the data objects and keys.

Unlike structured P2P systems, in unstructured P2P systems, connections among peers in the network are formed arbitrarily in flat or hierarchical manners. In order to find as many peers that have the desired content as possible, peers in unstructured P2P systems query data based on several techniques such as flooding (e.g., among the super-peers in KaZaA (http://www.kazaa.com/)), random walking (Gkantsidis et al., 2004), and expanding-ring (e.g., Time-To-Live counter in Gnutella (http://wiki.limewire.org/)). Three different designs of unstructured P2P systems exist: centralized unstructured P2P systems, hybrid unstructured P2P systems, and decentralized (or pure) unstructured P2P systems.

In a centralized unstructured P2P system, a central entity is used for indexing and bootstrapping the entire system. In contrast to the structured approach, the connection between peers in the centralized unstructured approach is not determined by the central entity. A BitTorrent network discussed in Section 3 is an example of a centralized unstructured P2P network. Napster (http://www.napster.com/), the network that pioneered the idea of P2P file sharing, is another example of a centralized design. In Napster, a server (or server farm) is used to provide a central directory. A peer in the network informs the directory server of its IP address and the names of the contents that it makes available for sharing. Thus, the directory server knows which objects each peer in the network have, and then, creates a centralized and dynamic database that maps content name into a list of IPs. The main drawback of Napster's design is that the directory server is a single point of failure. Hence, if the directory server crashes, then the entire network will also collapse. Moreover, increasing the size of the network may cause a bottleneck in the directory server, due to the need of responding to many queries and maintaining a large database for this meta-data information. The bottleneck can only be resolved by adding more infrastructure (e.g., more servers), which may be expensive.

The decentralized (or pure) unstructured P2P network is an overlay network. An overlay network is a logical network. An edge in this network exists between any pair of peers that maintain a TCP connection. The decentralized unstructured overlay network is flat, meaning that all peers act as equals. There is neither a central server that manages the network, nor are there preferred peers with a special infrastructure function. The network has a single routing layer. Gnutella (http://wiki.limewire.org/) is an example of a decentralized unstructured P2P network. In order to join the Gnutella network, a user initially connects to one of several known-bootstrapping peers. The bootstrapped peers then respond with the information about one or more existing peers in the overlay network. This information includes the IP address and port of each peer. The peers in Gnutella are aware only of their neighbor peers. Peers that are connected with each other in the overlay network have a common virtual edge in the overlay network. In Gnutella, queries are distributed among the peers using a variation of a flooding mechanism. A peer that is interested in specific content sends a query to its neighbors in the overlay network. Every neighbor then forwards the query to all of its neighbor peers. The procedure continues until the query reaches a specific depth of search limit (counted by Time-To-Live counter). Upon receiving a flood query, a peer that has a copy of the desired content sends a 'query hit response' to the peer that originated the query, which is an indication of having the content. The response is sent on the reverse path

of the query, using pre-existing TCP connections. The peer that originated the query then selects one peer from the responded peers, and downloads the desired content through a direct TCP connection from the selected peer. Although Gnutella design is simple, highly decentralized, and does not require peers to maintain information related to location of contents, it is often criticized for its non-scalability. This is because query traffic can grow linearly with the total number of queries, which in turn grows with the system size. In addition, another drawback of the protocol is that a peer that originated the query may not find the desired content especially if the content is rare.

A hybrid unstructured P2P network allows the existence of infrastructure nodes, often referred to as *super-peers* (or *super-nodes* or *overlay nodes*). This creates a hierarchical overlay network that addresses the scaling problems on pure unstructured P2P networks such as Gnutella. A peer in such network can typically change roles over time. For example, a regular peer can become a super-peer that takes part in coordinating the P2P network structure. KaZaA (http://www.kazaa.com/), which is based on the FastTrack (http://www.fasttrack.nu/) protocol, is an example of a hybrid unstructured P2P network. This network uses specially designated super-peers with high bandwidth, disk space and processing power. When a peer joins the network, it is assigned to a super-peer. The peer then informs its super-peer about the content that it will share. The super-peer facilitates the search by maintaining a database that maps content to peers, and tracks only the content of its assigned peers. Similar to the centralized design, the super-peer plays the role of a directory server, although only to its assigned peers. The super-peers together create a structured overlay of super-peers, which makes search for content more efficient. A query in this network is routed to a super-peer. Then, as in the decentralized design, the query is flooded in the overlay super-peer network. The super-peer then responds to the peer that originated the query with a list of peers having the content. The hybrid networks are no longer dedicated to a single server, since the database is distributed among the super-peers. Moreover, the size of the database is relatively small, since each super-peer tracks only the contents of its assigned peers. However, the drawback of this approach is that it is considerably complicated, and requires non-trivial maintenance of the overlay network. Moreover, the fact that super-peers may have more responsibilities than ordinary peers can result in a bottleneck.

3. P2P-BASED FILE SHARING: BITTORRENT SYSTEMS

BitTorrent is a popular peer-to-peer file sharing protocol that was created by Cohen (2003). Bit-Torrent has been shown to scale well with large number of participating end hosts. Ipoque (http://www.ipoque.com/) measurements for years 2008-2009 show that BitTorrent is the dominant protocol in the Internet, and that it accounted for approximately 20-57% of all Internet traffic depending on the geographical location.

3.1 System Description

BitTorrent is a centralized unstructured system, which consists of two interacting units:

1. A "control" level describes control methods such as the required file sharing prepara-tion, which takes place prior to sharing the actual content, and the coordination among end hosts, which is performed by a central entity during the downloading process.
2. A "reciprocation" level describes the actual data exchange among the end hosts.

These two design levels are described in detail next.

3.1.1 The BitTorrent System Design: Control Level

The BitTorrent content distribution system con-sists of the following components:

*   Data content
*   An original content provider
*   The metainfo file
*   The tracker
*   The end hosts or peers or clients

A *torrent*, or *swarm*, is a collection of end hosts (or peers) participating in the download of *content*, where content may refer to one (e.g. the Linux operating system) or multiple (e.g. several video or audio) files. *The tracker* is a server that coordinates and assists the peers in the swarm. It maintains the list of peers that are currently in the swarm, as well as statistics about the peers. The tracker listens on a BitTorrent TCP port for coming client requests. While the default BitTor-rent port is port 6969, several trackers may use different ports.

Prior to the content distribution, *a content provider* divides the content into multiple *pieces*, where each piece is typically 256KB. Each piece is further divided into multiple *subpieces* with a typical size of 16KB. The content provider then creates *a metainfo file*. The metainfo file contains information that is necessary for initiating and maintaining the download process. For example, the metainfo file contains the URL of the tracker, the name of the data file (files), the length of the data file (files), and the length of a piece. The metainfo file may also contain information related to multiple data files, and optional information such as creation date, author's comments, name and version of the.torrent creator, etc. The me-tainfo file also contains a special string, which is a concatenation of 20-byte encoded hash values. Each value is a SHA-1 hash of a piece at the cor-responding data content, which is used for data integrity.

Figure 1. BitTorrent system: Prior to file sharing

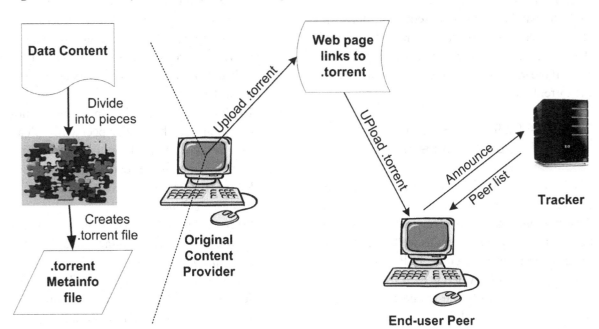

The metainfo file is usually uploaded to a website, thereby making it accessible to peers that are willing to download content by joining the swarm.

A peer that is willing to join the swarm first retrieves the out-of-band metainfo file. Then, this peer contacts the tracker by sending an "announce" HTTP GET request. The request in general may include necessary information such as the total amount uploaded, the total amount downloaded, the number of bytes the peer still has to download, an event description such as *started* – if it is the first request to the tracker, *completed* — if the peer shut down gracefully, *stopped* – if the download completed. This information helps the tracker keep overall statistics about the torrent (e.g., number of seeds, number of leechers, life time of a seed, etc). The tracker responds back with a "text/plain" document, which includes a randomly selected set of peers that are currently online. A typical size of a peer set is 50. The random peer set may include both *seeds* and *leechers*. Seeds are the peers who already have the entire content and

are sharing it with others. Leechers are the peers who are still in the process of downloading (i.e. they do not possess the entire file). The new peer can then initiate new connections with the peers in the swarm and start to exchange data content pieces. The maximum number of connections that a peer can open is limited in BitTorrent to 80 in order to avoid performance degradation due to competition among concurrent TCP flows. In addition, the new peer is also limited to establish a fixed number of outgoing connections, typically 40, in order to ensure that some connection slots are kept available for new peers that will join at a later time. Figure 1 portrays the preliminary steps that need to be performed before starting to distribute the data content.

A peer that has already begun downloading may contact the tracker and ask for more peers if its peer set falls below a given threshold, which is typically set to 20 peers. Moreover, usually there is a minimum interval between two consecutive peer requests to avoid overwhelming the tracker. In addition, peers contact the tracker periodically, typically once every 30 minutes, to indicate that they are still present in the network. If a peer does not contact the tracker for more than 45 minutes, the tracker assumes that the peer has left the system and will remove the peer from the torrent list.

3.1.2 The BitTorrent System Design: Reciprocation Level

The connection between two peers starts with a handshake message followed by control and data message exchanges. The control messages between peers in the swarm as well as data messages are transferred over the TCP protocol. The range of TCP ports, which is used by BitTorrent clients is 6881-6999. The connection between peers is symmetric and the control messages in both directions have the same format. The data can flow in either direction. The messages that are used in a connection between two peers are:

- **Handshake:** the "handshake" message is a required message that ensures connections from both sides and must be the first message that is sent by the peer.
- **Bitfield:** the "bitfield" message is an optional message and may only be sent after the handshaking sequence is completed, and before any other messages are sent. A peer can choose not to send this message if it has no pieces. Using a single bit for every piece, bits that are set indicate valid and available pieces, which can be shared with other peers, and bits that are cleared indicate missing pieces, which must be downloaded from other peers.
- **Interested:** an "interested" message is a notification that the sender is interested in some of the receiver's data pieces.
- **Not-interested:** a "not-interested" message is a notification that the sender is not interested in any of the receiver's data pieces.

- **Choke:** the term *choke* is commonly used in BitTorrent as a verb that describes a temporary refusal to upload. A "choke" message is a notification that the sender will not upload data to the receiver until *unchoking* happens.
- **Unchoke:** An "unchoke" message is a notification that the sender peer will upload data to the receiver if the receiver is interested in some of the sender's data pieces.
- **Request:** a "request" message is used to request a subpiece.
- **Piece:** a "piece" message is sent in response to a request message, and contains the requested subpiece.
- **Have:** a "have" message describes the index of a piece that has been downloaded and verified via the SHA-1 hash function.
- **Keep-alive:** Peers may close the TCP connection if they have not received any messages for a given period of time, generally 2 minutes. Thus, the "keep-alive" message is sent to keep the connection between two peers alive, if no message has been sent in a given period of time.
- **Cancel:** a "cancel" message is used to cancel subpiece requests. It is mostly sent towards the end of the download process (see more details in Section 3.3.3).

A peer *A* in the swarm maintains a 2-bits connection state for every associated peer *B* that it is connected to. The first bit is the choking/unchoking bit. The second bit is the interested/not-interested bit. The connection state is initialized to choked and not interested. Peer *B* transfers data to peer *A* only if the state of the connection with *A* is unchoked and interested. Peer *B* responds to peer *A*'s "request" messages with encapsulated subpieces in "piece" messages. After peer *A* finishes downloading a piece, it verifies that the piece is uncorrupted. It calculates the SHA-1 value of the downloaded piece and compares this value with the encrypted reference value of the piece that is

Figure 2. An illustrative example for a message flow among peers

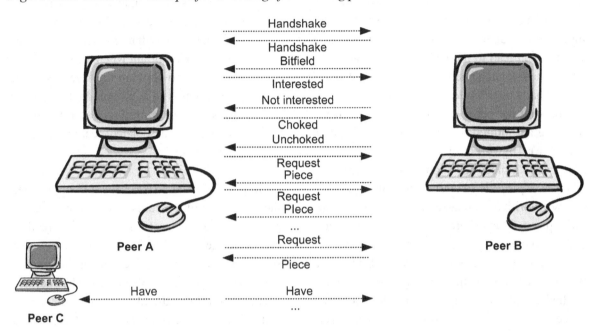

given in the metainfo file. Since the SHA-1 value is assumed to be unique, a corrupted piece's hash would not match the reference hash value. After verifying that the piece is uncorrupted, peer A announces that it has the piece to all of its associated peers using the "have" message.

Figure 2 shows an example of a possible message flow among peers that have an active connection in a BitTorrent overlay network. In the example, the connection is established after peer *A* sends a "handshake" message, and *B* responses with one as well. Then, peer *B* sends a "bitfield" message but peer *A* does not. Such a scenario might happen if *A* has no piece ready to be shared. Peer *B* sends a "not interested" message to *A*, and *A* sends a "choke" message to *B*. Thus, data will not flow from peer *A* to peer *B* until both messages are replaced. On the other hand, data does flow from peer *B* to peer *A* because peer *A* sends an "interested" message to peer *B* and peer *B* sends an "unchoked" message to peer *A*. Then, peer *A* requests subpieces of a particular piece and *B* responds with "piece" messages, uploading the requested subpieces. Once peer *A* obtains the

entire piece and confirms the validity of the piece, it sends "have" messages to all the peers that it is connected to in the BitTorrent overlay network.

3.2 Piece Selection Mechanisms

In the BitTorrent system, peers download the data content in a random order, unlike other protocols such as http or ftp, where an end host downloads a file from beginning to end. In order to facilitate such a downloading process, when a BitTorrent application is activated in a peer, the peer first allocates space for the entire content. Then, the peer tracks the pieces that each of its associated peers possess. A peer is able to identify what pieces its associated peers have by exchanging "bitfield" messages upon establishing new connections and by tracking the "have" messages that its associated peers send after downloading and verifying pieces. In this way, a peer is able to select a particular piece to download from a particular associated peer.

The piece selection mechanism is fundamental in achieving efficient P2P networks. A poor selection strategy can lead to an inability to download, e.g., when a peer is not interested in any of the pieces its associated peers have to offer, and vice versa, it can lead to the inability to upload, e.g., when all associated peers are not interested in the pieces that a peer has to offer. More generally, it can prevent the peer selection mechanism from reaching an optimal system capacity (Legout et al., 2006). BitTorrent applies the strict priority policy for subpiece selection. Once the first subpiece of a piece is requested, the strict priority policy prioritizes subpieces that are part of the same piece. This ensures that a complete piece is downloaded as quickly as possible.

The piece selection mechanism in BitTorrent is composed of three different algorithms that are applied in different stages of the downloading process. The three algorithms are Random Piece First, Rarest Piece First, and End Game.

3.2.1 Rarest Piece First Selection

The rarest piece is the piece that has the least amount of copies in the peer set. For every piece, the peer maintains a counter of the number of copies that exists in its peer set. A peer, which runs the rarest piece first selection algorithm, selects the rarest missing piece as the next piece to download. If there are multiple equally-rare missing pieces, then the peer chooses at random to download one of the rarest pieces. A leecher that uses the rarest piece first algorithm will:

1. Upload pieces that many of the associated peers are interested in, such that uploading can be performed when needed.
2. Increase the likelihood that peers will offer pieces through the entire downloading process by leaving pieces that are more common to a later download.
3. When downloading from a seed, a leecher downloads new pieces first, where new pieces are those pieces that no leecher has. This is crucial, especially when the system

has a single seed that may eventually be taken down, since this can lead to the risk that a particular piece will no longer be available. This is also important when the seeds in the system are slower than the leechers in the system. In this case, a redundant download wastes the opportunity of a seed to upload new pieces to associated peers with faster uploader speeds.

In (Legout et al., 2006), the authors studied the efficiency of the rarest piece first selection algorithm in BitTorrent. More specifically, they evaluated the efficiency of the rarest piece first selection strategy by characterizing the entropy of the system, with peer availability. They defined peer availability as the ratio of time that a peer is interested in its associated peer. They showed that the rarest piece first strategy can achieve a close to ideal entropy, when each leecher is almost always interested in all other leechers.

3.2.2 Random Piece First Selection

The download time of a random piece will be shorter on average than the download time of the rarest piece. A piece that is chosen at random is likely to be more replicated than the rarest piece, and thus, its download time will be shorter on average by downloading simultaneously from more peers. Despite this, the download time of complete piece may not affect the performance of a peer that uses the rarest-first piece selection strategy if the peer has other complete pieces to share. However at the beginning of the downloading process, a leecher has no pieces to share, and thus, the leecher should download pieces faster than in the rarest-first piece selection strategy, as it is important for a new peer to obtain some complete pieces and to start reciprocate pieces. Hence, at the beginning of the process the peer selects a piece to download at random, while applying the random piece first selection algorithm. Once the peer downloads C pieces that are ready to be shared (C is a constant that may vary in different BitTorrent client implementations), the leecher switches to the rarest piece first selection algorithm.

3.2.3 End Game Piece Selection

The end game piece selection algorithm is performed after a peer has requested all the subpieces of the content. In this phase, a peer sends a request to all of its associated peers for all of the pending subpieces (i.e., those subpieces that have not been received yet). This step is performed in order to avoid potential delays at the end of the content download, which can occur if a request has been sent to a peer having a very slow upload rate instead of a peer having a fast upload rate. Since multiple requests for the same subpieces are sent out, once a subpiece is downloaded in the end game phase, the peer sends "cancel" messages to its associated peers so they do not waste upload bandwidth by sending redundant data. The end game is performed at the very end of the process, and thus, it may have only a small impact on the downloading process.

3.3 Peer Selection Mechanisms

In BitTorrent, peers download from whom they can, and upload simultaneously to a constant number of peers. The number of associated peers, which a peer uploads to, is limited in order to avoid sending data over many connections at once, which may result in poor TCP congestion control behavior. Thus, peers need to make decisions on which peers to unchoke. The default number of peers to unchoke (*unchoke slots*) is four. However, this number may increase unless a peer's upload bandwidth is saturated. A peer independently makes the decision regarding whom to unchoke and whom to choke, in every *unchoke period* which is typically ten seconds. The peer uploads to unchoked peers for the duration of the unchoke period.

The peer selection mechanism, which is also referred to as the choking mechanism, can affect the performance of the system. A good choking mechanism should:

1. Motivate peers to contribute and upload data to the network,
2. Utilize all available resources,
3. Be robust against free-riding behaviors where peers only download and do not upload.

In BitTorrent, the peer selection (choking) mechanism is applied differently to peers that are leechers and those that are seeds.

3.3.1 Leecher's Peer Selection Mechanism

The leecher's peer selection mechanism has two parts: The TFT mechanism and the optimistic unchoke mechanism.

3.3.1.1 The TFT Mechanism
In the TFT peer selection mechanism, a leecher decides to unchoke peers from which it currently downloads data. It chooses the peers who have the highest upload rate. The idea of TFT is to have several connections that actively transfer data in both directions at any time. In order to avoid wasting of resources due to rapidly choking and unchoking peers, the designer of the protocol sets the rechoke period to 10 seconds, claiming that "Ten seconds is a long enough period of time for TCP to ramp up new transfers to their full capacity" (Cohen, 2003).

3.3.1.2 The Optimistic Unchoke Mechanism
BitTorrent applies the optimistic unchoke mechanism in parallel with the TFT mechanism. The goals of the optimistic unchoke mechanism are: (1) to enable a continuous discovery of better peers to reciprocate with, (2) to bootstrap new leechers that do not have any content pieces to

download some data and start reciprocate pieces with others. The optimistic unchoke mechanism chooses to unchoke a peer randomly regardless of its current upload rate. Optimistic unchoke is rotated every optimistic unchoke period, when an optimistically unchoked peer is unchoked for the entire optimistic unchoke period. The designer of the protocol chose the optimistic unchoke duration to be 30 seconds, because 30 seconds is enough time for the upload to get to full capacity, for the download to reciprocate, and finally for the download to get to full capacity. Optimistic unchoke is typically applied on a single unchoke slot while TFT is applied on the rest of the unchoke slots.

3.3.1.3 Anti-Snubbing

If a peer has received no data from a particular peer for a certain period of time, typically 60 seconds, it marks the particular peer's connection as snubbed. A peer does not upload to an associated snubbed peer through the TFT peer selection mechanism. This may result in more than one simultaneous optimistic unchoke, when the peer is choked by many of its associated peers. In such a case, the peer may experience poor download rates until the optimistic unchoke finds better peers. Thus, increasing number of optimistic unchokes in this scenario is important.

3.3.2 Seed's Peer Selection Mechanism

Seeds, which do not need to download any pieces, follow a different choking mechanism than the leechers. The most common mechanism is based on a round-robin mechanism, which strives to distribute data uniformly.

3.3.3 Modeling the Peer Selection Mechanism

Many researchers studied the choking mechanism in BitTorrent by suggesting mathematical and game theoretical models. Qiu & Srikant (2004) studied a fluid analytical model of BitTorrent

systems. They analytically studied the choking mechanism and investigated how it affects the peer performance. They showed that the optimistic unchoke mechanism may allow free-riding. Fan et al. (2006) characterized the design space of Bit-Torrent-like protocols capturing the fundamental tradeoff between performance and fairness. Other works such as (Izhak-Ratzin, 2009., Izhak-Ratzin et al., 2009., Neglia et al., 2007) model the choking mechanisms in BitTorrent as games with strategic peers. Massoulié & Vojnoviċ (2005) introduced a probabilistic model of coupon replication systems, and they argued that performance of file sharing system such as BitTorrent does not depend critically on altruistic behavior or on piece selection strategy (e.g., the rarest first algorithm). Levin et al. (2008) presented an auction based model of the peer selection mechanism. They claimed that the insight behind their model is that BitTorrent uses an auction model to decide which peers to unchoke and not to tit-for-tat as widely believed.

3.4 Limitations of BitTorrent Systems

In addition to the analytical models of BitTorrent, some measurement studies have been performed (Guo et al, 2005., Izal et al., 2004., Pouwelse et al., 2005., Piatek et al., 2007., Piatek et al., 2008). Most of these studies were performed on peers that were connected to public torrents. These studies provide interesting results about the overall behavior of deployed BitTorrent systems. The studies also pinpoint several limitations of the BitTorrent protocol. In this section, we discuss two of the limitations of BitTorrent protocol that were shown in these studies:

1. The feasibility of free-riding,
2. The lack of fairness.

3.4.1 Free-Riding in BitTorrent Systems

Free riders are the peers who attempt to circumvent the protocol mechanism and download data without uploading data to other peers in the network. Researchers have argued that free-riding in BitTorrent is feasible through the optimistic unchoke mechanism and through seeds.

The first to pinpoint that effective free-riding in BitTorrent is feasible was Shneidman et al. (2004). They briefly described a scenario in which peers can attack the tracker while they exploit involved leechers by lying about the pieces they have. Jun et al. (2005) also argued that free-riding is feasible in BitTorrent by investigating the incentives in BitTorrent choking mechanism. Liogkas et al. (2006) showed that free-riding in BitTorrent is feasible by implementing three selfish BitTorrent exploits that allow free-riders to achieve high download rates and evaluate their effectiveness under specific circumstances. Locher et al. (2006) extended these results and presented the BitThief, a free-riding client that combines several attacks. They demonstrated that free-riding is feasible even in the absence of seeds. More recently, Sirivianos et al. (2007) evaluated an exploit based on maintaining a larger-than-normal view of the system, which affords free-riders a much higher probability of receiving data from seeds and optimistic unchokes. They argued that the large view exploit is effective and has the potential for wide adoption. Wide adoption of free-riding strategy can result in a "tragedy of the commons", where overall performance in the system will decrease.

Several works have attacked the ability of free-riders to download data from seeds without uploading in return, intending to considerably hurt free-riders' performance. Locher et al. (2007) proposed a source-coding scheme. Seeds in this scheme only upload a fixed number of content pieces to each leecher they connect to, thereby placing a hard limit on the data that free-riders can obtain in this manner. Chow et al. (2008) presented an alternative modified seed unchoking algorithm that gives preference to leechers that are either at the beginning or the end of their download.

Complementary to these approaches that modify the seed strategy, other works suggested to replace or limit the optimistic unchokes. Izhak-Ratzin et al. (2009) suggested a team mechanism that limits the optimistic unchokes as the collaboration with peers having similar upload rate increases. A foresighted resource reciprocation mechanism was suggested in (Izhak-Ratzin et al., 2009b) to replace the choking mechanism in BitTorrent. Finally, reputation systems such as (Buchegger & Le Boudec, 2004, Xiong & Liu, 2004, Yang et al., 2005) that use a peers' reputation history to make the choking decision were also suggested in order to help limit the ability to free-ride.

3.4.2 Lack of Fairness in BitTorrent Systems

Fairness in BitTorrent is commonly defined as "receive as much as they give." Fairness among peers participating in content distribution encourages peers to actively collaborate in disseminating content. Thus, fairness is an important factor, which can lead to improved system performance. However, research studies, such as (Guo et al., 2005., Piatek et al., 2007., Bharambe et al., 2006., Legout et al., 2007), show that BitTorrent does not provide fair resource reciprocation, especially in node populations with heterogeneous upload bandwidths. Two of the mechanisms that contribute to the lack of fairness are the TFT and optimistic unchoke mechanisms, which are used for peer selection in BitTorrent.

The TFT mechanism is based on a short-term history, i.e., upload decisions are made based on the most recent observations of resource reciprocation. Thus, a peer can follow the TFT policy only if it continuously uploads pieces of a particular file and as long as it receives pieces of interest in return. However, this is not always possible because peers may not have any pieces that other peers are interested in, regardless of their willingness to cooperate (Piatek et al., 2008). This behavior is still perceived as a lack of cooperation.

Figure 3. Upload and download in BitTorrent network

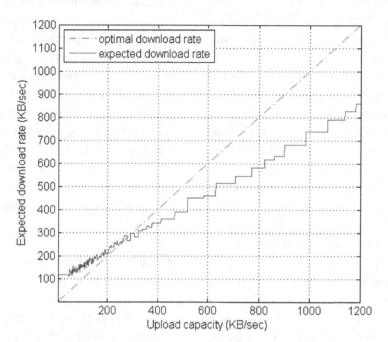

The impact of optimistic unchokes on fairness in the BitTorrent system is shown in Figure 3 [the Figure is taken from (Izhak-Ratzin, 2009)], which shows the impact of optimistic unchokes on the expected download rate as a function of the peer's upload rate. The peer upload rate distribution is based on observed bandwidth distribution given in (Piatek et al., 2007). It is assumed that one unchoke slot is used by the optimistic unchoke mechanism, and that the regular unchoke mechanism works perfectly in terms of fairness, i.e., the download rate and the upload rate through TFT unchokes are equal. Clearly, we can see that the sub-linear behavior of the expected download rate leads to unfairness for high capacity leechers that are forced to interact with low-capacity peers, and low-capacity leechers that benefit from this unfairness. Note that in the observed bandwidth distribution, the majority of the leechers are low-capacity leechers with 88% of the leechers having less than 300KB/s upload capacity.

Finally, the number of unchoke slots may also lead to a lack of fairness in BitTorrent. The number of unchoke slots that a leecher uses for regular unchoke is a function of the leecher's ability to fully utilize its upload capacity. This again may lead to unfairness, since typically, in real torrents, the download capacity of a leecher may be greater than the upload capacity. Thus, high capacity leechers may upload in full capacity, but not be able to download as much, due to upload constraints of the downloading leechers and limited number of unchoke slots.

Fairness in BitTorrent systems has been largely discussed in the literature. Guo et.al. (2005) performed extensive measurements of real torrents and pinpointed several BitTorrent limitations including lack of fairness. Bharambe et al. (2006) utilized a discrete event simulator to evaluate the impact of BitTorrent's mechanisms such as the peer selection mechanism, and observed that rate-based TFT incentives cannot guarantee fairness. They suggested a block-based TFT policy to improve fairness. Legout et al. (2007) studied clustering of peers having similar upload bandwidth. They observed that when the seed is underprovisioned, all peers tend to complete their downloads approximately at the same time, regardless of their upload rates. Moreover, high-capacity peers assist the seed to disseminate data to low-capacity peers. Piatek et al. (2007), observed through extensive measurement on real torrents the presence of significant altruism, where peers make contributions that do not directly improve their performance. They proposed the BitTyrant client, which adopts a new peer selection mechanism that reallocates upload bandwidth to maximize peers' download rates. Izhak-Ratzin (2009) identified the potential of there being a significant difference between a leecher's upload and download rates and proposed the Buddy protocol that matches peers with similar bandwidth. Other researchers acknowledged the importance of cooperation incentives through additional reputation mechanism. Anagnostakis & Greenwald (2004) extended BitTorrent's incentives to $n - way$ exchange among rings of peers, providing incentive to cooperate. Later, Lian et al., (2006) proposed multi-level TFT incentives as a hybrid between private and shared history schemes. More recently, Piatek et al., (2008) proposed a one-hop reputation system, in which peers that are not interested in the current available content perform data exchanges for the assurance of future payback.

4. P2P-BASED MEDIA STREAMING

4.1 Challenges and Requirements for Media Streaming

As discussed in Section 3, several protocols and incentive mechanisms have been developed for efficient data dissemination over P2P networks. However, they may only provide a limited performance for media streaming, because media streaming needs much more consideration such as real-time and high bandwidth requirements than general data dissemination. Extensive studies on video transmission over IP multicast have

discussed in the literature (e.g., Liu et al., 2003., van der Schar & Chou, 2007), and various P2P based overlay multicast systems have also been recently proposed (e.g., Zhang et al., 2005., Liang et al., 2009., Lin et al., 2009). Unlike proxy-assisted overlay multicast systems, where several proxies are coordinated and placed such that an efficient overlay can be constructed (Zhuang et al., 2001., Guo et al., 2004., Hefeeda et al, 2004., Shi & Turner, 2002), the P2P based systems do not need such dedicated nodes and coordination. Rather, these systems consist of autonomous and often self-interested nodes that self-organize into groups, exchange information, and share their data.

Designing efficient protocols and mechanisms for the media streaming applications over P2P networks is challenging, because:

- the real-time and continuous delivery of content to a large number of participants should be supported in dynamically changing network conditions and groups of interacting peers, and
- a higher bandwidth is required in general.

Therefore, the media streaming applications require different design rules and approaches that consider such requirements. For example, the objective of the file sharing applications such as BitTorrent is to *completely* download the content data as fast as possible. Therefore, the timely downloading of data objects is not critical. Rather, downloading data objects that can be rarely found is more important. However, media streaming applications should consider stringent real-time constraints. Thus, a mechanism that enables peers to download data objects that meet the playback deadline is required, such that media streaming is uninterrupted. Second, each data object has an equal importance for file sharing P2P applications, as all the data objects should be completely downloaded. However, for media streaming applications, each data object has different importance based on the coding structure, playback deadline, etc. Thus, data objects that have higher quality impact or that have stringent playback deadline can have higher priority. Therefore, packet prioritization and scheduling mechanisms should be developed in the media streaming applications over P2P networks. Finally, a mechanism that provides graceful quality degradation also needs to be implemented, which enables adaptive and flexible media streaming in dynamic networks where heterogeneous peers having different bandwidth interact with each other.

In order to address these challenges, several solutions for media streaming have been proposed in the literature (see e.g., Vlavianos et al., 2006., Zhang et al., 2006., Banerjee et al., 2002., Castro et al., 2003., Deshpande et al., 2001., Trans et al., 2004., Heffeeda et al., 2003., Kostic et al., 2003., Pai et al., 2005., Padmanabhan et al., 2003., Tian et al., 2005., Venkataraman et al., 2006., Zhang et al., 2005b). The implementation of these solutions varies depending on their focuses, which can be broadly classified as (1) peer clustering strategies, (2) overlay constructions and (3) incentive strategies on resource reciprocations.

4.2 Peer Clustering Strategies

Several approaches for efficient and reliable delivery of media streams over P2P networks have focused on developing peer clustering strategies. As discussed, the media content is directly shared by peers interacting with each other. Hence, it is important to select good peers and form clusters (or groups) with them. For example, Purandare & Guha (2007) proposed that peers can form groups based on alliance formation process, where this process considers the time and resource constraints. In (Venkataraman et al., 2006), the participating nodes form a graph, where the degree of the graph is determined proportionally to its desired transmission load. In addition, several other strategies such as SpreadIt (Deshpande et al., 2001), NICE (Banerjee et al., 2002), and ZIG-ZAG (Banerjee et al., 2002) have been proposed,

where these algorithms perform hierarchically from clusters such that a minimized transmission delay can be achieved.

In order to enhance the efficiency and robustness of the media delivery, various coding structures and packetizing strategies can also be implemented in conjunction with the abovementioned clustering strategies. For instance, Multiple Description Coding, or MDC (Goyal, 2001), is an illustrative example of coding structure for P2P based media delivery, and its deployment for media delivery has been studied in e.g., Padmanabhan et al., 2003., Padmanabhan et al., 2002b., Chu et al., 2004., Li et al., 2004. Alternatively, network coding techniques are also deployed for efficient media delivery (e.g., Nguyen et al., 2007., Wang & Li, 2007., Wang & Li, 2007b., Gkantsidis & Rodriguez, 2005).

4.3 Overlay Constructions: Tree-Based and Data-Briven Approaches

4.3.1 Tree-Based Approach: Description

One of design approaches of data dissemination over P2P networks is based on tree structure. In this approach, peers are organized into tree structure, where each peer is participating in disseminating data. In general, peers (or nodes) in the tree are hierarchically organized (i.e., parent – children node relationship) and data is disseminated by typically push-based approach, where the data is forwarded from parent nodes to children nodes. Because the data is disseminated in a structured way, it is important to

1. design optimal tree constructions that provide an efficient performance to each peer,
2. develop approaches for tree construction that are robust to nodes' (unexpected) joining and leaving trees and provide easy tree repair, and
3. construct non-cyclic trees, i.e., trees that have no loops.

Note that one of the major concerns in this approach is the failure of nodes. If a node cannot appropriately perform forwarding data due to node crash or node malfunction, its children nodes in the tree receive no data packets, resulting in significantly poor performance. Moreover, since a significantly large number of nodes are located in the end of the trees, an efficient utilization of outgoing bandwidth of them is challenging. In order to address these issues, several approaches have been proposed (e.g., Chu et al., 2000., Deshpande et al., 2001., Padmanabhan & Sripanidkulchai, 2002., Padmanabhan et al., 2002b., Padmanabhan et al., 2003., Li et al., 2004). In order to successfully implement the tree-based approaches, the following mechanisms have been proposed.

4.3.1.1 Group Management Mechanism

To maintain a robust and efficient tree, each peer (or node) may need the information about a set of other nodes and the path from a source. Peers in a tree keep exchanging the information that they have, which may include the group member information, and thus, they can have updated information about the tree. The information exchange can be implemented based on gossip-like protocols (e.g., End System Multicast, ESM, (Chu et al., 2000)). Peers already participating in a tree can switch their parent nodes if the performance (e.g., download rates) achieved in a current position is not satisfied. If a peer newly joins the network (i.e., a tree), it contacts the server, and obtains the (partial) information about the existing peers and the corresponding paths. Then, the peer can determine its parent nodes. Finally, the records of peers that left the tree are simply removed from the group member list.

4.3.1.2 Parent Selection Algorithm

As discussed, the way of selecting parents is important for both peers in a tree and newly joining peers. In order to select the parent nodes, a peer can contact a node that is randomly chosen from its group member list. Then, it retrieves the

information that includes the currently achieved performance, the number of children nodes, etc. from the contacted node, while estimating the round-trip time. The peer evaluates the contacted node only if the contacted node is not included in its children nodes, and the contacted node has not exceeded its children nodes limit. The evaluation of the contacted node can include the achievable performance and induced delay. Several criteria can be deployed in order to evaluate the node based on goals of applications. For file sharing applications, the performance (i.e., bandwidth) can be one of the most important criteria. For media streaming applications, however, the delay may be the most important criterion for parent selection. Alternatively, the obtained media quality can also be a criterion for parent selection (Park and van der Schaar, 2009d).

4.3.2 Data-Driven Approach

Alternative approaches for data dissemination over P2P networks are based on data-driven structures (Pai et al., 2005, Zhang et al., 2005). Unlike the tree-based structures, where well-designed trees need to be constructed and continuously maintained for efficient data dissemination in dynamically changing networks, data-driven approaches focus on

1. how to efficiently exchange information about the data availability,
2. how to form groups of peers and share their data, and
3. how to develop group management algorithms and scheduling algorithms.

In data-driven approaches, a newly generated data of a peer can be forwarded to its randomly selected neighbor nodes, and the neighbor nodes also forward the data to their neighbor nodes, which can be continued. Finally, the messages can be distributed to all the nodes. This approach can be implemented based on gossip algorithms

(Eugster et al., 2004). While such random *push* approaches enable the P2P systems to be robust to the random node failures, which is one of challenges for tree-based approach, these approaches may result in significant redundancy for receiving nodes (Gkantsidis et al., 2004).

In order to reduce the redundancy, *pull-based* techniques are proposed (Cohen, 2003., Pai et al., 2005., Zhang et al., 2005). In pull-based techniques, peers self-organize into groups and each peer requests necessary data packets from other peers in its group. Thus, each peer can avoid receiving redundant packets from its neighbor peers. The metadata that may include information about the peers can be downloaded from a server (e.g., trackers in BitTorrent systems), and then, each peer forms a group (e.g., swarm) with the other randomly selected peers or joins an existing group. The groups can be maintained by periodically exchanging the information about data availability with the group members. This approach has been actually implemented in BitTorrent (Cohen, 2003), and has shown efficient performance for general file sharing. In this example, a source distributes its content to peer A and peer B, and then, they exchange the content with their group members. Note that peer C also has its own group (which is not shown in this example), which also includes peer A.

However, this approach cannot be directly deployed for media streaming applications that require explicit playback deadlines, unless appropriate scheduling algorithms are implemented. Thus, for efficient media streaming over P2P networks based on data-driven approaches, several approaches have been proposed in (Pai et al., 2005., Zhang et al., 2005), where they explicitly implement scheduling algorithms. These mechanisms that support the data-driven approaches are discussed next.

4.3.2.1 Group Management Mechanism

One of the key mechanisms required for data-driven approaches is the *group management mechanism*, which enables peers to maintain their groups, such that they can continuously exchange necessary data packets among the peers. For newly joining peers, they can contact a server to obtain an initial set of group member candidates (e.g., End System Multicast (Chu et al., 2000), BitTorrent, CoolStreaming (Zhang et al., 2005)). Based on the initial information, each peer can form a group with partial set of peers or join an existing group. Then, each peer maintains its group by exchanging the information about the data availability. For example, CoolStreaming deploys an existing gossip membership protocol for exchanging the information about the data availability, which is referred to as membership message. The information is generated based on a Buffer Map (BM) that represents active data segments. More details about the BM are discussed next.

4.3.2.2 Prioritization and Scheduling Mechanisms

Unlike file sharing applications, it is critical for media streaming applications to deliver data segments timely and continuously. Thus, piece selection mechanism (i.e., the rarest first mechanism) implemented in BitTorrent systems can only provide limited performance, as it does not consider the priority of each data segment when it is downloaded. In order to explicitly consider the priority of data segments, scheduling mechanisms can be deployed. For example, in

CoolStreaming, a sliding window (see Figure 4), or BM, is used, which consists of 120 segments that correspond to 120 seconds of media data (i.e., 1 segment includes media data of 1 second). In this illustration shown in Figure 4, the peer is focusing on downloading the segment that is not in the window (empty segment) with the highest priority at this playback point.

Thus, the scheduling algorithms should be designed while taking into account the playback deadline (i.e., priority) for each segment, and the available upload bandwidth of associated peers. This is because peers in a P2P system may be

Figure 4. Sliding window in scheduling mechanisms

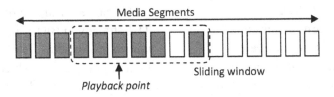

heterogeneous, having different upload bandwidth, etc. In CoolStreaming, a simple and heuristic algorithm has been proposed.

4.3.2.3 Group Update Mechanism

In general P2P systems, peers can leave the systems, and thus, leave their groups, at any time, which changes the groups that the peers have been associated. Thus, an efficient group update mechanism needs to be deployed, such that peers can easily capture the group changes and efficiently respond to the changes. This may include an efficient rescheduling algorithm for data segment request, and the exchanged information about data availability that can be used. For instance, in CoolStreaming, the groups are periodically updated by randomly contacting peers in local membership list, and the rescheduling algorithms are performed based on exchanged BM information.

4.4 Incentives for Resource Reciprocation

While several approaches discussed in the previous sections provide efficient solutions to media streaming over P2P networks, they are designed based on an implicit assumption that peers are unconditionally cooperative and collaborative – they are willing to provide correct and true information, exchange and share their resource actively, by honestly following the pre-designed protocols. However, in reality, this is not always true. Rather, peers are often self-interested and are trying to maximize their own benefits (e.g., download rates, media quality, etc.) by deviating

from the pre-determined rules in the systems. One of the representative examples for self-interested behaviors of peers is the *free-riding*, which is discussed in Section 3. The free-riders may not contribute their resources while downloading content from the other peers (data-driven approach), or they try to become leaf nodes by intentionally announcing that their upload bandwidth is poor. Moreover, it has been observed from several P2P based systems that the majority of uploading requests are concentrated on a small set of peers (Ali et al., 2006., Adar & Huberman, 2000), which may prevent potentially cooperative peers from actively contributing their resources.

One of the reasons why such behaviors that can result in significant degradation of both the system and individual peers' performance are allowed is the lack of well-designed *incentive mechanisms*. In order to provide incentives for each peer's contribution, simple incentive mechanisms have been developed based on TFT strategy for a general file sharing in BitTorrent-like protocols (e.g., Cohen, 2003., Legout et al., 2006., Piatek et al., 2007) or for a media streaming in BiToS (Vlavianos et al., 2006). Incentives can also be provided based on each peer's reputations, which can be managed in various ways (e.g., Credence (Walsh & Sirer, 2006), DARWIN (Jaramillo & Srikant, 2007), EigenTrust (Kamvar et al., 2003), PeerTrust (Xiong & Liu, 2004), DCRC and CORC (Gupta et al., 2003), Despotovic & Aberer, 2005). Finally, several game theoretic approaches have been adopted for providing incentives (see e.g., Chen et al., 2007., Fan et al., 2006., Zhang et al., 2007., Buragohain et al., 2003., Jun & Ahamad, 2005., Lai et al., 2003., Golle et al., 2001., Feldman et al., 2004., Park & van der Schaar, 2009., Park & van der Schaar, 2009c).

While simple incentive mechanisms have been developed and deployed in practice (e.g., TFT strategy in practical BitTorrent systems), it is still reported that existing incentive mechanisms do not efficiently prevent such self-interested behaviors in P2P systems. In the next section, we will discuss recently proposed game theoretic approaches for incentive mechanisms in detail, which model the resource reciprocation among self-interested peers as a stochastic game and find an optimal strategy that maximizes each peer's long term benefit in P2P systems

5. FORESIGHTED RESOURCE RECIPROCATION STRATEGIES

5.1 Challenges of Incentive Design: Cooperation and Competition

As discussed in Section 4, one possible solution for providing cooperation incentives is the TFT strategy, which has been actually implemented in practical file sharing P2P systems such as BitTorrent. The TFT strategy is deployed in BitTorrent as a choking algorithm, which effectively encourages peers' cooperation and penalizes peers' selfish behaviors (see Section 3.1.2 for more detail). While it has been shown that this strategy performs effectively in various P2P network scenarios, it may not completely eliminate selfish behaviors such as free-riding (Liogkas et al., 2007., Locher et al., 2006., Sirivianos et al., 2007). Moreover, the resource reciprocation based on TFT is *myopic*, because a peer unchokes some of its associated peers (i.e., leechers) that are *currently* uploading at the highest rates. Thus, the resource reciprocation decisions based on TFT may not provide optimal solutions that maximize the long-term rewards. Since peers in P2P networks are generally involved in repeated and long-term interactions, such myopic decisions on peer selection and

bandwidth allocation can result in a sub-optimal performance for the involved peers. Finally, the TFT strategy in BitTorrent is based on the *equal* upload bandwidth distribution (Cohen, 2003., Legout et al., 2007) which is neither a fair nor an optimal resource allocation for heterogeneous content and diverse peers with different upload/download requirements (Park & van der Schaar, 2007).

To address these challenges, a foresighted resource reciprocation strategy has been recently proposed, which enables the peers to determine their resource reciprocation decisions that maximize a long-term utility. The interactions among the peers are modeled as a stochastic game, where they determine their resource distributions by considering the probabilistically changing future behaviors of their associated peers. The resource reciprocation process of a peer is modeled as a Markov Decision Process (MDP), and the foresighted resource reciprocation strategy is obtained by solving the MDP. It has been shown that the foresighted strategy provides improved performance compared to existing incentive mechanisms in BitTorrent or heuristic algorithms in several media streaming approaches (e.g., Lee et al., 2009).

5.2 Formalization of Resource Reciprocation as Stochastic Games

5.2.1 Group-Based Resource Reciprocation

Resource reciprocation games in P2P networks are played by the peers interested in each other's media content. A resource reciprocation game is played in a *group*, where a group consists of a peer and its associated peers. The group-based resource reciprocation has been discussed in the literature, where a group could be formed of swarms (Cohen, 2003., Legout et al., 2006), partnerships (Zhang et al., 2005), or neighbors (Pai et al., 2005).

Figure 5. Block diagram for group-based resource reciprocation

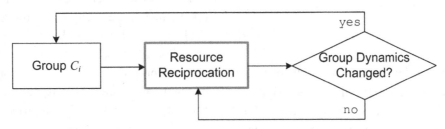

The group members associated with a peer i is denoted by C_i, where a peer $k \in C_i$ also has its own group C_k which includes peer i. Due to the dynamics introduced by peers joining, leaving, or switching P2P networks, the information about groups needs to be regularly (periodically) updated or it needs to be updated when group dynamics change (Cohen, 2003., Legout et al., 2006). This process is shown in Figure 5. In this diagram, the group dynamics change when group members are changed or their behavior are changed, etc. Moreover, resource reciprocation in Figure 5 may include several modules for its actual implementation, such as an estimation of the state transition probability and a level of accuracy for behavior estimation. These will be discussed in the following sections.

5.2.2 Modeling Resource Reciprocations as Stochastic Games

The resource reciprocation game in a group C_i consists of

- a finite set of players (i.e., peers): $C_i \cup \{i\}$
- for each peer $l \in C_i \cup \{i\}$, a nonempty set of actions: $\mathbf{A}_l$
- for each peer $l \in C_i \cup \{i\}$, a preference relation (i.e., utility function) of peer l: $U_l(\cdot)$.

To play the resource reciprocation game, a peer can deploy an MDP, defined as follows.

For a peer i, an MDP is a tuple $\langle \mathbf{S}_i, \mathbf{A}_i, P_i, R_i \rangle$, where $\mathbf{S}_i$ is the state space, $\mathbf{A}_i$ is the action space,

$P_i: \mathbf{S}_i \times \mathbf{A}_i \times \mathbf{S}_i \rightarrow [0,1]$ is a state transition probability function that maps the state $s_i \in \mathbf{S}_i$ at time t, corresponding action $\mathbf{a}_i \in \mathbf{A}_i$ and the next state $s_{i'} \in \mathbf{S}_i$ at time $t + 1$ to a real number between 0 and 1, and $R_i: \mathbf{S}_i \rightarrow \mathrm{R}$ is a reward function, where $R_i(s_i)$ is a reward derived in state $s_i \in \mathbf{S}_i$. This MDP-based resource reciprocation model and its variations in P2P networks have been discussed in (Park & van der Schaar, 2009., Park & van der Schaar, 2009b., Park & van der Schaar, 2009c). We review the details in the following.

5.2.1.1 State Space

A state of peer i represents the set of received resources from the peers in C_i, which is expressed as

$$\left\{ (x_{1i}, \ldots, x_{N_{C_i}i}) \,\middle|\, 0 \leq x_{ki} \leq L_k, \forall k \in C_i \right\} \quad (1)$$

where x_{ki} denotes the provided resources (i.e., rate) by peer k in C_i and L_k represents the available maximum upload bandwidth of peer k. The total received rates of peer i in C_i is thus $\sum_{k \in C_i} x_{ki}$. Due to the continuity of $x$ki, the cardinality of the set defined in (1) can be infinite. Hence, we assume that peer i has a function ψ_{ik} for peer k, which maps the received resource $x$ki into one of n_{ik} discrete values, i.e., $\psi_{ik}(x_{ki}) = s_{ik} \in \{s_{ik}^1, \ldots, s_{ik}^{n_{ik}}\}$. These values are referred to as *state descriptions* in this chapter. Hence, the state space can be considered to be finite. The state space of peer i can be expressed as

$$\mathbf{S}_i = \left\{ s_i = (s_{i1}, \ldots, s_{iN_{C_i}}) \middle| s_{ik} = \psi_{ik}(x_{ki}), k \in C_i \right\}, \quad (2)$$

where s_{ik}^l denotes the lth segment among n_{ki} segments that corresponds to the lth state description of peer i. For simplicity, we assume that each segment represents the uniformly divided total bandwidth, i.e., $\psi_{ik}(x_{ki}) = s_{ik}^l$ if $(l-1)\dfrac{L_k}{n_{ik}} \le x_{ki} < l\dfrac{L_k}{n_{ik}}$ for $1 \le l \le n_{ik}$.

5.2.1.2 Action Space

An action of peer i is its resource allocation to the peers in C_i. Hence, the action space of peer i can be expressed as

$$\mathbf{A}_i = \{ \mathbf{a}_i = (a_{i1}, \ldots, a_{iN_{C_i}}) \middle| 0 \le a_{ik} \le L_i, 1 \le k \le N_{C_i}, \sum_{k \in C_i} a_{ik} \le L_i \}, \quad (3)$$

where $a_{ik} \in A_i$ denotes the allocated resources to peer k by peer i in C_i. Hence, peer i's action a_{ik} to peer k becomes peer k's received resources from peer i, i.e., $a_{ik} = x_{ik}$. To consider a finite action space, we assume that the available resources (i.e., upload bandwidth) of peers are decomposed into *unit*s of bandwidth (Jain et al., 2007). Thus, the actions represent the number of allocated units of bandwidth to the associated peers in their groups. We define the *resource reciprocation* as a pair $(\mathbf{a}_i, s_i) = \left((a_{i1}, \ldots, a_{iN_{C_i}}), (s_{i1}, \ldots, s_{iN_{C_i}}) \right)$ comprising the peer i's action, a_{ik}, and the corresponding modeled resource reciprocation s_{ik}, which is determine as $s_{ik} = \psi_{ik}(x_{ki})$ for all $k \in C_i$.

Note that various scheduling schemes can be used in conjunction with the resource allocation (i.e., actions) deployed by peers in order to consider the different priorities of the different data segments (chunks). We assume that the chunks that have higher quality impact on average media quality have higher priority and are transmitted

first when each peer takes its actions. However, other scheduling algorithms, such as the rarest first (Cohen, 2003., Legout et al., 2007) method for general file sharing applications or several scheduling methods proposed in e.g., (Zhang et al., 2005) for media streaming applications, can also be adopted. It is important to note that appropriate scheduling schemes need to be deployed in conjunction with our proposed resource reciprocation strategies, depending on the objectives of multimedia applications (e.g. maximizing achieved quality, minimizing the playback delay etc.).

5.2.1.3 State Transition Probability

A state transition probability represents the probability that by taking an action, a peer will transit into a new state. We assume that the state transition probability depends on the current state and the action taken by the peer, as peers decide their actions based on their currently received resources (i.e., state). Hence, given a state $s_i \in \mathbf{S}_i$ at time t, an action $\mathbf{a}_i \in \mathbf{A}_i$ of peer i can lead to another state $s_i^{'} \in \mathbf{S}_i$ at $t^{'} (t^{'} > t)$ with probability $P_{\mathbf{a}_i}(s_i, s_i^{'}) = \Pr(s_i^{'} \mid s_i, \mathbf{a}_i)$. Hence, for a state $s_i = (s_{i1}, \ldots, s_{iN_{C_i}})$ of peer i in C_i, the probability that an action $\mathbf{a}_i$ leads the state transition from s_i to $s_i^{'}$ can be expressed as

$$P_{\mathbf{a}_i}(s_i, s_i^{'}) = \prod_{l=1}^{N_{C_i}} P_{a_{il}}(s_{il}, s_{il}^{'}) \quad (4)$$

The state transition probabilities of peers are identified based on the histories of past resource reciprocation. One approach that efficiently builds the state transition probability functions is discussed in (Park & van der Schaar, 2009).

5.2.1.4 Reward

Reward of a peer i represents the derived utility from its state s_i. The utility of peer i can be differently defined depending on the goals of applications. For example, in (Park & van der Schaar, 2009., Park & van der Schaar, 2009b), the reward $R_i(s_i)$ for a peer i in state s_i is the total received resources in C_i, defined as

$$R_i(s_i) = R_i(s_{i1}, \ldots, s_{iN_{C_i}}) = \sum_{k \in C_i} r_i(s_{ik}) \qquad (5)$$

where $r_i(s_{ik})$ is a random variable that represents the received resource in state s_{ik}. If the media quality is the ultimate goal of the application, the utility that corresponds to reward $R_i(s_i)$ of peer i in state s_i is $U_i\left(\sum_{k \in C_i} r_i(s_{ik})\right)$. Utility function $U_i(\cdot)$ of peer i downloading a demanded content from its peers at rate x_i is defined as

$$U_i(x_i) = \begin{cases} 0, & \text{if } x_i < R_i^{req}, \\ \rho_i \cdot Q_i(x_i), & \text{otherwise} \end{cases} \qquad (6)$$

where R_i^{req} is the minimum rates to successfully decode the downloaded content and ρ_i is a constant representing the preference of peer i for the downloading content. The derived quality $Q_i(x_i)$ with downloading rate x_i is represented by a widely used quality measure, Peak Signal to Noise Ratio (PSNR), which is a non-decreasing and concave function of x_i for multimedia applications (van der Schaar & Chou, 2007). Alternatively, in (Park & van der Schaar, 2009c), the reward of a peer is defined as a guaranteed rates (and thus, guaranteed media quality) that can be achieved from its associated peers.

Since each peer in a P2P network that consists of N total peers can individually deploy the MDP, the resource reciprocation game in the network can be described by a tuple $(\mathcal{I}, \mathcal{S}, \mathcal{A}, \mathcal{P}, \mathcal{R})$, where $\mathcal{I}$ is the set of N peers, $\mathcal{S}$ is the set of state profiles of all peers, i.e., $\mathcal{S} = \mathbf{S}_1 \times \cdots \times \mathbf{S}_N$, and $\mathcal{A} = \mathbf{A}_1 \times \cdots \times \mathbf{A}_N$ denotes the set of action profiles. $\mathcal{P} : \mathcal{S} \times \mathcal{A} \times \mathcal{S} \rightarrow [0,1]$ is a state transition probability function that maps from the current state profile $s \in \mathcal{S}$, corresponding joint action $a \in \mathcal{A}$ and the next state profile $s' \in \mathcal{S}$, into a real number between 0 and 1, and $\mathcal{R} : \mathcal{S} \times \mathcal{A} \rightarrow \mathbb{R}^N$ is a reward function that maps an action profile $a \in \mathcal{A}$ and a state profile $s \in \mathcal{S}$ into the derived reward. Thus, we can focus on the resource reciprocation game in a group, as this resource game can be extended to the resource reciprocation game in a P2P network.

5.3 Foresighted Resource Reciprocation Strategy

The solution to the MDP described in Section 5.2 is represented by peer i's optimal policy π_i^*, which is a mapping from the states to optimal actions. The optimal policy can be obtained using well-known methods such as value iteration and policy iteration (Bertsekas, 1976). Hence, peer i can decide its actions based on the optimal policy π_i^*, i.e., $\pi_i^*(s_i) = \mathbf{a}_i$ for all $s_i \in \mathbf{S}_i$. Note that policy π_i^* enables peer i to make *foresighted* decisions on its resource reciprocation.

A conventional approach is *myopic* decision making. Myopic peers only focus on maximizing the immediate expected rewards, i.e., a myopic peer i takes its action $\mathbf{a}_i^*$ (i.e., upload bandwidth allocation) such that the action leads to the maximum immediate expected reward, i.e.,

$$\mathbf{a}_i^* = \arg\max_{\mathbf{a}_i \in \mathbf{A}_i} \sum_{s_i^{(t+1)} \in S} P_{\mathbf{a}_i}\left(s_i^{(t)}, s_i^{(t+1)}\right) R\left(s_i^{(t+1)}\right)$$
$$\text{subject to } \sum_{k \in C_i} a_{ik} \leq L_i \qquad (7)$$

Unlike the myopic peers, the foresighted peers take their actions considering the immediate expected reward as well as the future rewards. Since future rewards are generally considered to be worth less than the rewards received now (Watkins & Dayan, 1992), the foresighted peers try to maximize the cumulative discounted expected rewards. Hence, a foresighted peer i in state s_i at time t_c given a discount factor γ_i tries to maximize its cumulative discounted expected rewards, i.e.,

$$\text{maximize} \quad \sum_{t=t_c+1}^{\infty} \gamma_i^{(t-(t_c+1))} \cdot E\left[R(s_i^{(t)})\right] \qquad (8)$$

where $R(s_i^{(t)}) = \sum_{l=1}^{N_{C_i}} r_i(s_{il})$ for $s_i^{(t)} = (s_{i1},\ldots,s_{iN_{C_i}})$. More precisely, the expression in (8) can be rewritten as (see Box 1.)

The discount factor γ_i in the considered P2P network can alternatively represent the validity of the expected future rewards, as the state transition probability can be affected by system dynamics such as peers' joining, switching, or leaving groups (Park & van der Schaar, 2009c). Hence, for example, if P2P network is in transient regime, a small value of discount factor is desirable, while a large value of discount factor can be used if the P2P network is in stationary regime (de Veciana & Yang, 2003). We note that the myopic decisions are a special case of the foresighted decisions when $\gamma_i = 0$.

Illustrative performances achieved based on different resource reciprocation strategies are shown in Figure 6. As discussed in this section, resource reciprocation based on the myopic strategy is aiming to maximize the immediate expected rewards (equation (8)). However, resource reciprocation based on the foresighted strategy targets on maximizing the cumulative (discounted) expected rewards (equation (9)). Figure 6 confirms this, as the rewards obtained by the actions of myopic policy are always higher (or equal) than the other policies for immediate rewards (left of Figure 6). However, a peer can achieve the highest cumulative discounted expected rewards based on the foresighted policy. Thus, the foresighted resource reciprocation strategy may be beneficial for peers, as they are generally interacting with each other in a long period of time. In (Lee et al., 2009), the foresighted resource reciprocation strategies in conjunction with scheduling algorithms have been deployed for media streaming over P2P, which shows improved performance.

5.4 Bounded Rationality on Resource Reciprocation

Conventional stochastic games have been developed based on the implicit assumptions on players' rationality, where players have the abili-

Figure 6. Expected rewards achieved by different resource reciprocation strategies

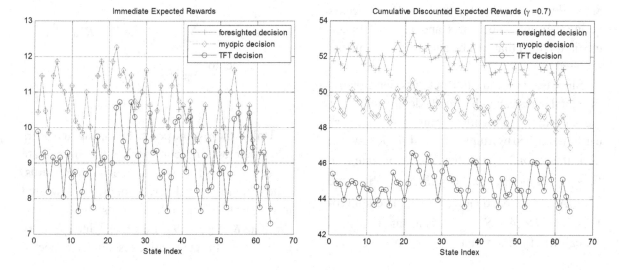

ties to collect and process relevant information, and select alternative actions among all possible actions. However, peers are often *boundedly rational* in practice (Simon, 1955., Haruvy, 1999). This is because perfectly rational decisions are often infeasible in practice due to memory and computational constraints. Due to the bounded rationality, peers may have incorrect beliefs on the other players' behavior and limited ability to analyze their environment. Therefore, it is essential to study the impact of the bounded rationality of peers on (1) the performance degradation of the proposed resource reciprocation strategy and (2) their repeated interactions (resource reciprocation) for practical implementations. We overview several studies, which investigate how the bounded rationality of peers can impact the peers' interactions and the corresponding performances.

5.4.1 Bounded Rationality: Attitude towards Resource Reciprocations

In (Park & van der Schaar, 2009), the bounded rationality is represented by the resource reciprocation *attitude* of peers, and its impact on resource reciprocation and the corresponding individual peers' performances is discussed.

Peers in the considered P2P networks are characterized based on their attitudes towards the resource reciprocation, which are pessimistic, neutral, or optimistic (Park & van der Schaar, 2009). These characteristics determine how peers can respond to their resource reciprocations. Let $\left(a_{ik}, s_{ik}\right)$ be recent resource reciprocation between peer i and peer k, which is a pair of peer i's action to peer k and peer k's response to peer i. Peer i is referred to as *neutral*, if it presumes that peer k linearly changes its response (i.e. resource allocation) corresponding to peer i's next action (a_{ik}'). Peer i is referred to as *pessimistic* if it presumes that peer k reduces its resource allocation to peer i fast for $a_{ik}' \leq a_{ik}$ but increases the resource allocation slowly for $a_{ik}' \geq a_{ik}$. Finally, peer i is

optimistic if it presumes that peer k reduces its resource allocation to peer i slowly for $a_{ik}' \leq a_{ik}$ but increases the resource allocation fast for $a_{ik}' \geq a_{ik}$. Illustrative examples of these characteristics of resource reciprocation are shown in Figure 7.

These types of peers discussed above obviously affect their resource reciprocation strategies. In (Park & van der Schaar, 2009), it has been analytically shown that if a peer has only one attitude for resource reciprocation and makes myopic decisions, it cannot efficiently reciprocate its resources. Thus, it has been concluded that peers can improve their performance by considering various reciprocation attitudes and multiple observations for past resource reciprocations and making foresighted decisions.

5.4.2 Bounded Rationality: Limited Memory and Computation Power

In (Park & van der Schaar, 2009b., Park & van der Schaar, 2009c), the bounded rationality of peers induced by their limited memory for storing the resource reciprocation history and limited computation power is discussed. Recall that a peer's received resources from its associated peers are

Figure 7. Attitudes for resource reciprocation of boundedly rational peers

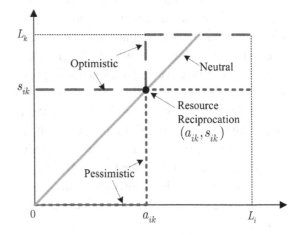

captured by its state. Boundedly rational peers can have limited ability to characterize their resource reciprocation with other peers (i.e. they can distinguish their received resources using only a limited number of states). This is due to the large complexity requirements associated with their decision making processes.

In (Park & van der Schaar, 2009b), it has been investigated how this bounded rationality of peers can impact the accuracy of the long-term expected rewards. It is obvious that using more states (i.e., finer states) enables each peer to compute the actual long-term rewards more accurately. However, increasing the number of states also leads to higher computational complexity to find the optimal resource reciprocation strategy. Therefore, it is important for each peer to find the minimum number of states, while achieving a tolerable accuracy of the actual long-term rewards. In this study, the impact of the number of states on the accuracy of the long-term rewards is analytically quantified, and shows how to determine an optimal number of states that achieves the tolerable accuracy.

Alternatively, (Park & van der Schaar, 2009c) has focused on how the heterogeneous peers having different abilities to refine their states can interact with each other, and the corresponding long-term rewards. This study analytically shows that a peer may have multiple actions that are optimal because these actions do not alter its associated peers' states, and thus, they do not alter the resource reciprocation of these peers. This is because peers cannot differentiate among all possible download rates from their associated peers due to the limited number of state descriptions. It is observed that peers can mutually improve their long-term rewards (i.e., download rates) only if they simultaneously refine their states. It also studies the impact of the heterogeneity of peers on their group formations, and concludes that peers prefer to form groups with other peers, which not only have similar or higher upload rates but also have similar abilities to refine their state descriptions.

5.4.3 Practical Implementation of Foresighted Strategies

The foresighted resource reciprocation strategy discussed in Section 5.3 has been actually implemented in BitTorrent-like system. The foresighted strategy replaces the TFT resource reciprocation strategy and the optimistic unchoke mechanism, which have been implemented in the BitTorrent protocol. By deploying the foresighted resource reciprocation strategy, the following advantages against the regular BitTorrent protocol:

- It improves the fairness - the peers that contribute more resources (i.e., higher upload capacities) can achieve higher download rates. However, the peers that contribute less resources may achieve limited download rates
- It promotes cooperation among high-capacity peers.
- It discourages free-riding by limiting the upload to non-cooperative peers.
- It improves the system robustness by minimizing the impact of free-riding on contributing peers' performance.

Several illustrative experiment results are shown in the following. The experiments host 54 Planet-Lab nodes, 50 leechers and 4 seeds with combined capacity of 128 KB/s serving a 100 MB file. All peers start the download process simultaneously, which emulate a flash crowd scenario. The initial seeds are stayed connected through the whole experiments. A leecher disconnects immediately after it completes its downloads, and reconnects immediately while requesting the entire file again. This enables our experiments to have the same upload bandwidth distribution during the entire experiment time.

Figure 8 shows the download completion time of leechers. The results show the clear performance difference among high-capacity leechers, which are the fastest 20% leechers, and

Figure 8. Download completion time for leechers

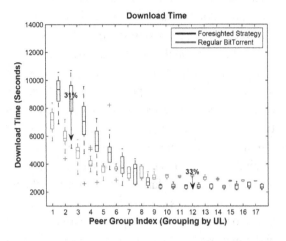

Figure 9. Percentage of free-riders' download from contributing leechers

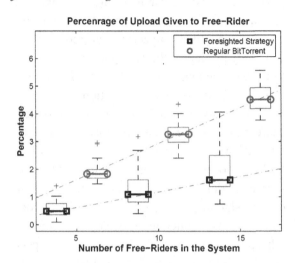

low-capacity leechers, which are the slowest 80% leechers. High-capacity leechers can significantly improve their download completion time. Unlike in the regular BitTorrent system, where leechers determine their choking decisions based on the TFT that uses only the last reciprocation history, the leechers adopting the foresighted strategy determine their choking decisions based on the long-term history. This enables the leechers to estimate the behaviors of their associated peers more accurately. Moreover, since part of the choking decisions is randomly determined in the regular BitTorrent, there is a high probability that high-capacity leechers need to reciprocate with the low-capacity leechers. However, the randomly determined choking decisions are significantly reduced in the proposed approach, as the random decisions are taken only in the initialization phase or in order to collect the reciprocation history of newly joined peers. As a result, the high-capacity leechers increase the probability to reciprocate resources with the other high-capacity leechers.

When leechers adopt the foresighted strategy, they can efficiently capture the selfish behavior of the free-riders. Thus, they can unchoke the free-riders with a significantly low probability. Hence, the free-riders can download their content mainly from seeds not from the leechers. The results shown in Figure 9 also confirm that the

leechers in the regular BitTorrent system upload approximately 2.8-3.7 times more data to the free-riders compared to the leechers in the system where foresighted strategy is adopted. This also shows that the P2P networks consist of leechers adopting the foresighted strategy are more robust against the selfish behaviors of peers than the networks operating using the regular BitTorrent protocol.

In summary, the experiment results confirm that the foresighted strategy provides more incentives for leechers to maximize their upload rate by improving fairness, enables the leechers to discourage non-cooperative behaviors such as free-riding, and enhances the robustness of the network.

6. NEW DIRECTIONS FOR GAME-THEORETIC APPROACHES TO INCENTIVE DESIGN IN P2P NETWORKS

P2P networks are widely used to share user-generated content such as photos, videos, news, and customer reviews. In the case of user-generated content, peers play the roles of producers, suppliers, and consumers at the same time. Most of existing work on incentives in P2P networks focuses on incentives for peers to share content that is already produced, thereby ignoring incentives to produce content. In (Park & van der Schaar, 2010), a game theoretic formulation is proposed to jointly analyze incentives for peers to produce, share, and consume content in P2P networks. The interaction among peers that are connected in a P2P network and interested in content on the same item is modeled as a three-stage game. In stage one (production stage), each peer produces content, while its production decision is not known to other peers. In stage two (sharing stage), each peer makes a portion of its produced content available in the P2P network. In stage three (transfer and consumption stage), peers transfer content available in the P2P network and consume content they have after transfer, which is the sum of produced and downloaded content.

In the one-shot non-cooperative outcome of the content production and sharing game, peers do not share any content at all while producing and consuming an autarkic optimal amount. As upload incurs costs to the uploader while it does not benefit the uploader in the absence of an incentive mechanism, peers do not have an incentive to share their content in the P2P network. On the contrary, social optimum requires full sharing of produced content, where the optimal amount of total production is chosen to equate the marginal benefit of production to peers under full sharing and the marginal cost of production and transfer. As content sharing in the P2P network reduces the overall cost of obtaining content, peers consume more content at social optimum than at one-shot non-cooperative equilibrium. An alternative scenario where the P2P network can enforce full sharing of produced content but cannot enforce the production decisions of peers is also considered. In such a scenario, each peer faces a higher effective marginal cost of production since it has to upload produced content to other peers. As a result, each

peer produces a smaller amount than the autarkic optimal amount, and the welfare implication of enforced full sharing is ambiguous.

In (Park & van der Schaar, 2010), two pricing schemes are proposed to achieve social optimum among non-cooperative peers. A marginal product (MP) pricing scheme determines payments to peers based on their sharing decisions in stage two. Using the main idea of the VCG mechanism, an MP pricing scheme provides incentives for users to maximize social welfare. A linear pricing scheme compensates peers for their upload and charges peers for their download at predetermined upload and download prices, respectively. Depending on the system objective, the upload and download prices can be chosen to obtain social optimum as a non-cooperative outcome or to maximize the profit of the P2P network. The model of (Park & van der Schaar, 2010) offers a basic framework which can be extended to analyze more complex situations. For example, a dynamic extension of the model can be formulated to address the incentives of peers interacting over time when each peer can share not only content it produced but also content it downloaded in the past.

7. CONCLUSION AND FUTURE CHALLENGES

In this chapter, we discussed P2P systems that have been deployed in file sharing and real-time media streaming. We overviewed various P2P system structures and discussed their advantages and disadvantages for different illustrative implementations. Then, we investigated existing P2P-based file sharing and media streaming applications in detail, and discussed the limitations of their implementations. One of the drawbacks of the existing implementation is induced by a lack of optimal resource reciprocation strategies among self-interested peers. While BitTorrent systems deploy incentive strategies based on TFT strategy, the myopic resource reciprocations based on this strategy provides only a suboptimal performance. More advanced resource reciprocation strategies are discussed, where the resource reciprocation among the interested peers as a stochastic game, and thus, peers can make foresighted decisions on their resource distribution in a way that maximizes their cumulative utilities. This is a desirable property of resource reciprocation strategy, as peers generally are involved in long-term and repeated interactions. Finally, we investigated the impact of the bounded rationality of peers on their resource reciprocation and the corresponding performance.

While preliminary results achieved by the foresighted resource reciprocation strategies show that they are promising for file sharing and media streaming, additional modules that can support robust and efficient media streaming should be designed and developed. Then, the foresighted resource reciprocation strategies in conjunction with the supporting modules can ultimately improve the media streaming over P2P networks. Moreover, novel algorithms that can reduce the computational complexity required for deploying the foresighted strategies are still to be developed for real-time media streaming.

ACKNOWLEDGMENT

The authors would like to thank Mr. Nicholas Mastronarde for his valuable comments and corrections, which helped us to clarify this chapter. We also would like to thank Dr. Jaeok Park for providing Section 6, which discussed new directions for game-theoretic approaches to incentive design in P2P networks. Finally, this work was done while the first author was with Ecole Polytechnique Fédérale de Lausanne (EPFL), Lausanne, Switzerland, and was supported by the Swiss National Science Foundation grants 200021-118230.

REFERENCES

Adar, E., & Huberman, B. A. (2000). Free Riding on Gnutella. *First Monday, 5*(10).

Ali, S. Mathur, A. & Zhang, H. (2006). Measurement of commercial peer-to-peer live video streaming. *Workshop on Recent Advances in P2P Streaming*, Waterloo, ON.

Anagnostakis, K. G., & Greenwald, M. B. (2004). Exchange-based Incentive Mechanisms for Peer-to-Peer File Sharing. In *Proceeding of International Conference on Distributed Computing Systems*, Philadelphia.

Banerjee, S., Bhattacharjee, B., & Kommareddy, C. (2002). Scalable application layer multicast. In *Proceeding of ACM Special Interest Group on Data Communication*, Pittsburgh, PA.

Bertsekas, D. P. (1976). *Dynamic Programming and Stochastic Control*. New York: Academic.

Bharambe, A. R., Herley, C., & Padmanabhan, V. N. (2006). Analyzing and Improving BitTorrent Performance. In *Proceedings of IEEE Conference on Computer Communications*, Barcelona.

Buchegger, S., & Le Boudec, J.-Y. (2004). A Robust Reputation System for P2P and Mobile Ad-hoc Networks. [*Systems*, Cambridge, MA.]. *De Economía*, ▪▪▪, 2P.

Buragohain, C., Agrawal, D., & Suri, S. (2003). A Game Theoretic Framework for Incentives in P2P Systems. In *Proceedings of IEEE International Conference on Peer-to-Peer Computing*. Linköpings, Sweden.

Castro, M., Druschel, P., Kermarrec, A.-M., Nandi, A., Rowstron, A., & Singh, A. (2003). SplitStream: High-bandwidth multicast in cooperative environments. In *Proceedings of ACM Symposium on Operating Systems Principles,* New York.

Chen, L., Low, S. H., & Doyle, J. C. (2007). Contention Control: A Game-Theoretic Approach. In In *Proceedings of IEEE Conference on Decision and Control,* New Orleans, LA.

Chow, A. L., Golubchik, L., & Misra, V. (2008). Improving BitTorrent: A Simple Approach. In *Proceedings of International Workshop on Peer-to-Peer Systems*, Tampa Bay, FL.

Chu, Y.-H., Chuang, J., & Zhang, H. (2004). A Case for Taxation in Peer-to-Peer Streaming Broadcast. In *Proceeding of ACM Special Interest Group on Data Communication,* Portland, OR.

Chu, Y.-H., Rao, S. G., & Zhang, H. (2000). A Case for End System Multicast. In *Proceedings of ACM International Conference on Measurement and Modeling of Computer Systems,* Santa Clara, CA.

Cohen, B. (2003). Incentives build robustness in BitTorrent. In *Proceedings of* (p. 2P). Berkeley, CA: Economics Workshop.

Deshpande, H., Bawa, M., & Garcia-Molina, H. (2001). Streaming live media over peers. Technical Report 2001-31, Computer Science Department, Stanford University.

Despotovic, Z., & Aberer, K. (2005). P2P reputation management: probabilistic estimation vs. social networks. *Computer Networks, 50* (2006).

Eugster, P., Guerraoui, R., Kermarrec, A.-M., & Massoulié, L. (2004). From epidemics to distributed computing. *IEEE Computer, 37*(5), 60–67.

Fan, B., Chiu, D.-M., & Lui, J. C. (2006). The Delicate Tradeoffs in BitTorrent like File Sharing Protocol Design. In *Proceedings of IEEE International Conference on Network Protocols*, Santa Barbara, CA.

Feldman, M., Lai, K., Stoica, I., & Chuang, J. (2004). Robust Incentive Techniques for Peer-to-Peer Networks. In *Proceedings of ACM Conference on Electronic Commerce,* New York.

Fudenberg, D., & Tirole, J. (1991). *Game Theory.* Cambridge, MA: MIT Press.

Gkantsidis, C., Mihail, M., & Saberi, S. (2004). Random Walks in Peer-to-Peer Networks. In *Proceedings of IEEE Conference on Computer Communications*, Hong Kong.

Gkantsidis, C., & Rodriguez, P. R. (2005). Network coding for large scale content distribution. *Proceedings*In *Proceedings of IEEE Conference on Computer Communications*, Miami, FL.

Golle, P., Leyton-Brown, L., Mironov, I., & Lillibridge, M. (2001). Incentives for Sharing in Peer-to-Peer Networks. *Lecture Notes in Computer Science, 2322*, 75–87. doi:10.1007/3-540-45598-1_9

Goyal, V. K. (2001). Multiple Description Coding: Compression meets the network. *IEEE Signal Processing Magazine*, 74–93. doi:10.1109/79.952806

Guo, L., Chen, S., Ren, S., Chen, X., & Jiang, S. (2004). PROP: a scalable and reliable P2P assisted proxy streaming system. *Proceedings*In *Proceedings of International Conference on Distributed Computing Systems*, Tokyo, Japan.

Guo, L., Chen, S., Xiao, Z., Tan, E., Ding, X., & Zhang, X. (2005). Measurements, Analysis, and Modeling of BitTorrent-like Systems. *Internet Measurement Conference*, Berkeley, CA.

Gupta, M., Judge, P., & Ammar, M. (2003). A Reputation System for Peer-to-Peer Networks. *Proceedings*In *Proceedings of International Workshop on Network and Operating System Support for Digital Audio and Video,* Monterey, CA.

Haruvy, E., Stahl, D. O., & Wilson, P. W. (1999). Evidence for optimistic and pessimistic behavior in normal-form games. *Economics Letters, 63*, 255–259. doi:10.1016/S0165-1765(99)00028-2

Hefeeda, M., Bhargava, B., & Yau, D. K.-Y. (2004). A hybrid architecture for cost-effective on-demand media streaming. *Computer Networks, 44*(3). doi:10.1016/j.comnet.2003.10.002

Heffeeda, M., Habib, A., Botev, B., Xu, D., & Bhargava, B. (2003). PROMISE: Peer-to-peer media streaming using CollectCast. *Proceedings*In *Proceedings of ACM Multimedia*, Berkeley, CA.

Izal, M., Urvoy-Keller, G., Biersack, E. W., Felber, P. A., Al Hamra, A., & Garc'es-Erice, L. (2004). *Dissecting BitTorrent: Five Months in a Torrent's Lifetime, " Passive and Active Measurement Workshop*. France: Antibes Juan-les-Pins.

Izhak-Ratzin, R. (2009). Collaboration in BitTorrent systems. *Networking, 5550/2009*, 338-351.

Izhak-Ratzin, R., Liogkas, N., & Majumdar, R. (2009). Team incentives in BitTorrent systems. *Proceedings*In *Proceedings of International Conference on Computer Communications and Networks*, San Francisco, CA.

Jain, K., Lovász, L., & Chou, P. A. (2007). Building scalable and robust peer-to-peer overlay networks for broadcasting using network coding. *Journal on Distributed Computing, 19*(4), 301–311. doi:10.1007/s00446-006-0014-9

Jaramillo, J. J., & Srikant, R. (2007). DARWIN: Distributed and Adaptive Reputation mechanism for WIreless ad-hoc Networks. *Proceedings*In *Proceedings of International Conference on Mobile Computing and Networking*, Montreal, Quebec, Canada.

Jun, S., & Ahamad, M. (2005). Incentives in BitTorrent Induce Free Riding. *Workshop on Economics of Peer-to-Peer Systems*, Philadelphia.

Kamvar, S. D., Schlosser, M. T., & Garcia-Molina, H. (2003). The EigenTrust Algorithm for Reputation Management in P2P Networks. In *Proceedings of International World Wide Web Conference*, Budapest.

Kostic, D., Rodriguez, A., Albrecht, J., & Vahdat, A. (2003). Bullet: High bandwidth data dissemination using an overlay mesh. *Proceedings*In *Proceedings of ACM Symposium on Operating Systems Principle*, Bolton Landin, NY.

Lai, K., Feldman, M., Stoica, I., & Chuang, J. (2003). Incentives for Cooperation in Peer-to-Peer Networks. *Workshop on Economics of Peer-to-Peer Systems*, Cambridge, MA.

Lee, S. I., Park, H., & van der Schaar, M. (2009). *Foresighted Joint Resource Reciprocation and Scheduling Strategies for Real-time Video Streaming over Peer-to-Peer Networks*. Seattle, WA: International Packet Video Workshop.

Legout, A., Liogkas, A., Kohler, E., & Zhang, L. (2007). Clustering and sharing incentives in BitTorrent systems. *SIGMETRICS Performance Evaluation Review, 35*(1), 301–312. doi:10.1145/1269899.1254919

Legout, A., Urvoy-Keller, G., & Michiardi, P. (2006). Rarest first and choke algorithms are enough. *Internet Measurement Conference*, Rio de Janeiro, Brazil.

Levin, D., LaCurts, K., Spring, N., & Bhattacharjee, B. (2008). BitTorrent is an Auction: Analyzing and Improving BitTorrent's Incentives. *Proceedings*In *Proceedings of ACM Special Interest Group on Data Communication*, Seattle, WA.

Li, J., Chou, P. A., & Zhang, C. (2004). Mutualcast: An Efficient Mechanism for One-To-Many Content Distribution. *Proceedings*In *Proceedings of ACM Special Interest Group on Data Communication*, Beijing, China.

Lian, Q. Peng, Y., Yang, M., Zhang, Z., Dai, Y. & Li, X. (2006). Robust incentives via multi-level tit-for-tat. *Proceedings*In *Proceedings of International Workshop on Peer-to-Peer Systems*, Santa Barbara, CA.

Liang, C., Guo, Y., & Liu, Y. (2009). Investigating the Scheduling Sensitivity of P2P Video Streaming: An Experimental Study. *IEEE Transactions on Multimedia, 11*(3), 348–360. doi:10.1109/TMM.2009.2012909

Lin, W. S., Zhao, H. V., & Liu, K. J. R. (2009). Incentive Cooperation Strategies for Peer-to-Peer Live Multimedia Streaming Social Networks. *IEEE Transactions on Multimedia, 11*(3), 396–412. doi:10.1109/TMM.2009.2012915

Liogkas, N. Nelson, R., Kohler, E. & Zhang, L. (2006). Exploiting BitTorrent For Fun (But Not Profit). In *Proceedings of International Workshop on Peer-to-Peer Systems*, Santa Barbara, CA.

Liogkas, N., Nelson, R., Kohler, E., & Zhang, E. (2007). In Exploring the Robustness of BitTorrent Peer-to-Peer Systems. *Concurrency and Computation, 10*(2), 179–189.

Liu, J., Li, B., & Zhang, Y.-Q. (2003). Adaptive video multicast over the Internet. *IEEE MultiMedia, 10*(1), 22–31. doi:10.1109/MMUL.2003.1167919

Locher, T. Moor, P., Schmid, S., & Wattenhofer, R. (2006). Free Riding in BitTorrent is Cheap. *Workshop on Hot Topics in Networks*, Irvine, CA.

Locher, T., Schmid, S., & Wattenhofer, R. (2007). Rescuing Tit-for-Tat with Source Coding. *International Peer-to-Peer conference*, Galway, Ireland.

Massoulié, L., & Vojnovi, Ć. M. (2005). Coupon replication systems. *Proceedings*In *Proceedings of the International Conference on Measurements and Modeling of Computer Systems*, Banff, Alberta, Canada.

Neglia, G., Presti, G. L., Zhang, H., & Towsley, D. (2007). A network formation game approach to study BitTorrent tit-for-tat. In *Proceedings of Network Control and Optimization*, Avignon, France.

Nguyen, K., Nguyen, T., & Cheung, S.-C. (2007). Peer-to-Peer streaming with hierarchical network coding. In *Proceedings of IEEE International Conference on Multimedia & Expo*. Beijing, China.

Padmanabhan, V. N. Wang H. J., Chou, P. A., & Sripanidkulchai, K. (2002b). Distributing streaming media content using cooperative networking. In *Proceedings of International Workshop on Network and Operating System Support for Digital Audio and Video*. Florida.

Padmanabhan, V. N., & Sripanidkulchai, K. (2002). The case for cooperative networking. *Proceedings*In *Proceedings of International Workshop on Peer-to-Peer Systems*, Cambridge, MA, USA.

Padmanabhan, V. N., Wang, H. J., & Chou, P. A. (2003). Resilient peer-to-peer streaming. In *Proceedings of IEEE International Conference on Network Protocols*, Atlanta, GA.

Pai, V. Kumar, K., Tamilmani, K., Sambamurthy, V & Mohr, A. E. (2005). Chainsaw: Eliminating trees from overlay multicast. *Proceedings*In *Proceedings of International Workshop on Peer-to-Peer Systems*, Ithaca, NY.

Park, H., & van der Schaar, M. (2007). Bargaining strategies for networked multimedia resource management. *IEEE Transactions on Signal Processing, 55*(7), 3496–3511. doi:10.1109/TSP.2007.893755

Park, H., & van der Schaar, M. (2009). A framework for foresighted resource reciprocation in P2P networks. *IEEE Transactions on Multimedia, 11*(1), 101–116. doi:10.1109/TMM.2008.2008925

Park, H., & van der Schaar, M. (2009b). On the impact of bounded rationality in peer-to-peer networks. *IEEE Signal Processing Letters, 16*(8), 675–678. doi:10.1109/LSP.2009.2022146

Park, H., & van der Schaar, M. (2009c). Evolution of resource reciprocation strategies in P2P networks. *IEEE Transactions on Signal Processing, 58*(3), 1205–1218.

Park, H., & van der Schaar, M. (2009d). Quality-based resource brokerage for autonomous networked multimedia applications. *IEEE Transactions on Circuits and Systems for Video Technology*, *19*(12), 1781–1792. doi:10.1109/TCSVT.2009.2026983

Park, J., & van der Schaar, M. (2010). Pricing and Incentives in Peer-to-Peer Networks. *ProceedingsIn Proceedings of IEEE Conference on Computer Communications*, San Diego.

Piatek, M., Isdal, T., Anderson, T., Krishnamurthy, A., & Venkataramani, A. (2007). Do incentives build robustness in BitTorrent? *Symposium on Networked Systems Design and Implementation*, Cambridge, MA.

Piatek, M., Isdal, T., Krishnamurthy, A., & Anderson, T. (2008). One hop reputations for peer to peer file sharing workloads. *Symposium on Networked Systems Design and Implementation*, San Francisco, CA.

Pouwelse, J. A. Garbacki, P., Epema, D. H. J. & Sips, H. J. (2005). The BitTorrent P2P file-sharing system: Measurements and Analysis. In *Proceedings of International Workshop on Peer-to-Peer Systems*, Ithaca, NY.

Qiu, D., & Srikant, R. (2004). Modeling and Performance Analysis of BitTorrent-Like Peer-to-Peer Networks. In *Proceedings of ACM Special Interest Group on Data Communication*, Portland, OR.

Ratnasamy, S., Francis, P., Handley, M., Karp, R., & Shenker, S. A. (2001). Scalable Content-Addressable Network. *ProceedingsIn Proceedings of ACM Special Interest Group on Data Communication*, San Diego, CA.

Rowstron, A., & Druschel, P. (2001). Pastry: Scalable, distributed object location and routing for large scale peer to peer systems. In *Proceedings of IFIP/ACM International Conference on Distributed Systems Platforms (Middleware 2001)*, Heidelberg, Germany.

Shi, S., & Turner, J. (2002). Routing in overlay multicast networks. In *Proceedings of IEEE Conference on Computer Communications*, New York, NY.

Shneidman, J., Parkes, D. C., & Massoulié, L. (2004). *Faithfulness in Internet Algorithms*. Portland, OR: Practice and Theory of Incentives and Game Theory in Networked Systems.

Simon, H. A. (1955). A behavioral model of rational choice. *The Quarterly Journal of Economics*, *59*, 99–118. doi:10.2307/1884852

Sirivianos, M. Park, J. H., Chen, R. & Yang, X. (2007). Free-riding in BitTorrent Networks with the Large View Exploit. *ProceedingsIn Proceedings of International Workshop on Peer-to-Peer Systems*, Bellevue, WA.

Stoica, I., Morris, R., & Karger, D. FransKaashoek, M., Dabek, M., & Balakrishnan, H. (2001). Chord: A Scalable Peer-To-Peer Lookup Service for Internet Applications. *ProceedingsIn Proceedings of ACM Special Interest Group on Data Communication*, San Diego.

Tian, R., Zhang, Q., Xiang, Z., Xiong, Y., Li, X., & Zhu, W. (2005). Robust and efficient path diversity in application-layer multicast for video streaming. *IEEE Transactions on Circuits and Systems for Video Technology*, *15*(8), 961–972. doi:10.1109/TCSVT.2005.852416

Tran, D. A., Hua, K. A., & Do, T. T. (2004). A Peer-to-Peer Architecture for Media Streaming. *IEEE Journal on Selected Areas in Communications*, *22*(1), 121–133. doi:10.1109/JSAC.2003.818803

van der Schaar, M., & Chou, P. A. (Eds.). (2007). *Multimedia over IP and Wireless Networks*. New York: Academic.

Venkataraman, V. Francis, P. & Calandrino, J. (2006). ChunkySpread: Multitree unstructured peer-to-peer multicast. In *Proceedings of International Workshop on Peer-to-Peer Systems*, Santa Barbara, CA.

Vlavianos, A., Iliofotou, M., & Faloutsos, M. (2006), "BiToS: Enhancing BitTorrent for supporting streaming applications. In *Proceedings of IEEE Conference on Computer Communications*, Barcelona, Catalunya, Spain.

Walsh, K., & Sirer, E. G. (2006) Experience with an Object Reputation System for Peer-to-Peer Filesharing. In *Proceedings of Symposium on Networked Systems Design and Implementation*, San Jose, CA.

Wang, M., & Li, B. (2007). R²: Random push with random network coding in live peer-to-peer streaming. *IEEE Journal on Selected Areas in Communications*, *25*(9), 1–12. doi:10.1109/JSAC.2007.071205

Wang, M., & Li, B. (2007b) "Lava: A reality check of network coding in peer-to-peer live streaming. *Proceedings*In *Proceedings of IEEE Conference on Computer Communications*, Anchorage, AK.

Watkins, C. J. C. H., & Dayan, P. (1992). Q-learning. *Machine Learning*, *8*(3-4), 279–292. doi:10.1007/BF00992698

Xiong, L., & Liu, L. (2004). PeerTrust: Supporting Reputation-Based Trust for Peer-to-Peer Electronic Communities. *IEEE Transactions on Knowledge and Data Engineering*, *16*(7), 843–857. doi:10.1109/TKDE.2004.1318566

Yang, M., Zhang, Z., Li, X., & Dai, Y. (2005) "An Empirical Study of Free-Riding Behavior in the Maze P2P File-Sharing System. In *Proceedings of International Workshop on Peer-to-Peer Systems*, Ithaca, NY.

Zhang, M., Luo, J.-G., Zhao, L., & Yang, S.-Q. (2005b). A peer-to-peer network for live media streaming using a push-pull approach. In *Proceedings of ACM Multimedia*, Hilton, Singapore.

Zhang, Q., Xue, H.-F., & Kou, X.-D. (2007). An Evolutionary Game Model of Resources-sharing Mechanism in P2P Networks. *Proceedings*In *Proceedings of the Workshop on Intelligent Information Technology Application*, Zhang Jiajie, China.

Zhang, X., Liu, J., Li, B., & Yum, T. S. P. (2005). CoolStreaming/DONet: A data-driven overlay network for efficient live media streaming. In *Proceedings of IEEE Conference on Computer Communications*, Miami, FL.

Zhao, B. Y., Huang, L., Stribling, J., Rhea, S. C., Joseph, A. D., & Kubiatowicz, J. D. (2004). Tapestry: A resilient global scale overlay for service deployment. *IEEE Journal on Selected Areas in Communications*, *22*(1), 41–53. doi:10.1109/JSAC.2003.818784

Zhuang, S. Q. Zhao, B. Y., & Joseph, A. D. (2001). Bayeux: An architecture for scalable and fault-tolerant wide-area data dissemination. In *Proceedings of International Workshop on Network and Operating System Support for Digital Audio and Video*, New York.

KEY TERMS AND DEFINITIONS

Torrent (or Swarm): A collection of end hosts (or peers) participating in the download of content, where content may refer to one or multiple files.

Tracker: A server that coordinates and assists the peers in the swarm.

Leecher and Seed: A peer in the leecher state is still downloading pieces of a content, while a peer in the seed state has a complete set of pieces and is sharing them with other peers.

Interested: Peer A is interested in peer B if peer B has pieces that peer A does not have and would like to have.

Choked: Peer A is choked by peer B if peer B decided to provide no pieces to peer A

Resource Reciprocation: Resource reciprocation among peers is a set of resources that they have exchanged.

Chapter 12
A Survey of P2P Data–Driven Live Streaming Systems

Fabio Pianese
Alcatel-Lucent Bell Labs, Belgium

ABSTRACT

Data-driven peer-to-peer live streaming systems challenge and extend the traditional concept of overlay for application-layer multicast data distribution. In such systems, software nodes propagate individually-named, ordered segments of the stream (called chunks) by independently conducting exchanges with their neighboring peers. Chunk exchanges are solely based on information that is available locally, such as the status of a node's receive buffer and an approximate knowledge of the buffer contents of its neighbors. In this Chapter, we motivate and retrace the emergence of P2P data-driven live streaming systems, describe their internal data structures and fundamental mechanisms, and provide references to a number of known analytical bounds on the rate and delay that can be achieved using many relevant chunk distribution strategies. We then conclude this survey by reviewing the deployment status of the most popular commercial systems, the results from large-scale Internet measurement studies, and the open research problems.

1 INTRODUCTION

Internet-based media streaming has been a long-standing subject in networking research. Only quite recently has it become a thriving and viable application, attracting widespread interest from both users and service providers. The rapid growth of the Internet during the last two decades,

DOI: 10.4018/978-1-61692-831-5.ch012

together with the development of cheap, powerful hardware, and the widespread deployment of broadband access technologies (such as cable and DSL), have contributed to the profound change in the way streaming is perceived today. The progression from the early days of do-it-yourself Internet radio (e.g. Shoutcast in the late nineties) to the development of huge on-demand media repositories has been so fast that, from a niche application used by few amateurs, streaming has

Copyright © 2011, IGI Global. Copying or distributing in print or electronic forms without written permission of IGI Global is prohibited.

now become ubiquitous and is having an ever-increasing impact on the way users perceive and approach the World Wide Web.

The main commercial focus of the major telecom operators today is video-on-demand (VoD) streaming, which consists of delivering videos (i.e. stored media files) upon a user's request from a server to the user's player application. The biggest challenge of VoD streaming is choosing an appropriate delay to start the playback such that buffer starvation shall not occur and the video will be played from beginning to end without interruptions. A technique which is often used in VoD involves quickly providing the users with the initial part of the media file, so that the delay between their request and the beginning of the video playout will be short. This feature requires the VoD application to transmit the data at a rate which is much greater than the stream's actual rate. For these reasons, videos are often stored in repositories that heavily rely on caching techniques and content distribution networks (CDNs) in order to alleviate the enormous bandwidth requirements that could not be sustained by the VoD storage servers alone (Yu et al., 2006).

Another popular application of VoD techniques is user-generated content distribution (UGC), mainly offered by large-scale Internet application providers (such as Google's YouTube). UGC differs from VoD by the fact that the users of the system are the main source of the content that is made available. This property results in the need for a huge data repository and complex heuristics to index, retrieve, and replicate a set of media objects extremely heterogeneous by size, quality, and popularity (Cha et al., 2007).

During the last few years, a third mode of media distribution has also become feasible and reached a considerable popularity: live media streaming. In live streaming, a source generates a video stream on-the-fly and transmits it immediately to the audience. Every user must then receive the data consistently at its full rate, being only able to rely on small buffers to mitigate the random disruptions introduced by the underlying network. Live streaming is an application that presents a different set of challenges compared to VoD. For instance, the usual caching techniques on which VoD broadly relies cannot be applied: live streaming requires at any point in time the availability of a sufficient upload capacity, which in turn depends linearly on the number of users connected to each source. On the other hand, live streams do not require long-term storage and durable indexing of the available content.

The linear scaling of bandwidth requirements, coupled with extremely variable and volatile user workloads, make live streaming a difficult application to implement using a client-server architecture. The bandwidth resources available to a server are rigidly allocated and cannot usually be extended on-the-fly. If the user population is smaller than the allocated system capacity, resources are wasted and efficiency suffers. However, when the capacity is exceeded, resources are fully used but the service quality perceived by the users degrades. This limitation becomes particularly penalizing when dealing with live streaming, as the difference in the required upload capacity between peak and average loads can span several orders of magnitude. A trade-off has to be reached between the cost of the provisioning and the ability to accommodate the occasional flash crowds.

In this context, peer-to-peer (P2P) architectures provide many advantages as they offer better scalability: while the total bandwidth demand increases, the users of the system are also able to provide their resources and help the content provider support the data distribution process.

This chapter provides a survey on the latest techniques for P2P live streaming, known as data-driven or mesh-based architectures. In the next Section, we will briefly summarize the earlier developments of live streaming technologies and enumerate their strengths and open issues. Section

3 presents the principles of data-driven systems and surveys the recent advances in the P2P live streaming field. Section 4 discusses the status of the deployment of real-world streaming systems and enumerates the main research topics which are still being investigated. Section 5 concludes our survey.

2 LIVE STREAMING AND THE INTERNET

The earliest research efforts toward network support for live media streaming were devoted to implement multicast functionality over IP networks. The first approach to be explored was native IP multicast, a technique introduced in the 1980s by S. Deering (Deering and Cheriton, 1990). Native multicast operates at the OSI layer 3 (network), and requires router support to construct minimal spanning trees over the Internet topology. Unfortunately, global inter-domain native multicast proved not viable as a solution because of few critical reasons, such as issues with group and membership management (Biersack, 2005) and scalability limits of flow control for reliable data delivery (Chaintreau et al., 2002). However, lately several major Internet service providers have been successfully using IP multicast in their networks as the main technology to support live IPTV distribution to their own clients.

Single-Tree Peer-to-Peer Overlays

The open, end-to-end architecture of the Internet became a powerful driving force in the development of new techniques to transmit bandwidth-intensive media streams. Subsequent research shifted the focus from the network layer toward the applicative layer, in the context of the emerging field of peer-to-peer (P2P) applications. The goal of the earliest systems for P2P live streaming was indeed an attempt to reproduce the benefits of native multicast support by creating and maintaining an overlay network[1] of unicast end-to-end connections, where the routing functionality would be provided by applications running on the end hosts (called nodes or peers). Among the most notable precursors, SpreadIt (Bawa et al., 2002) and NICE (Banerjee et al., 2002) had a major impact on the subsequent literature[2].

The early approaches, based on single-tree overlays, proved unsuitable to support large-scale deployments. In practical environments (Chu et al., 2004), single-tree based systems were found to suffer greatly from high node transience (also known as churn), scarcity and/or uneven distribution of host upload bandwidth, and deliberate *freeloading* (that is, exploitation of resources without a proper reciprocation) by the users of the system. A major weakness of single trees lies in the fact that they structurally limit the resource contribution by the peers, as the large numbers of leaf nodes in the system are, by definition, prevented from serving other nodes. Moreover, since tree overlays are directed acyclic graphs, a unique path connects every peer to the source. Thus, any disruption in the data flow, due to churn, upload shortage, or lack of cooperation at the internal nodes, is thus propagated to the entire sub-tree rooted at the affected node.

Single trees offered few opportunities for overlay optimizations, which could be introduced mainly as improved tree-building policies. It is for instance possible to perform measurements at join time and to only select resourceful peers to be non-leaf (i.e. internal) nodes in the tree, thus building trees that are optimized for minimal delay or maximum throughput. However, after the overlay is built, there is no way for the system to detect a node's uncooperative behavior or transient lack of resources, nor any "fair" incentive for a cooperative peer to contribute more upload capacity to the system than the rate of the stream it is receiving.

Multiple-Trees or "Structured Meshes"

In response to these issues, a number of multiple tree-based overlays such as Splitstream (Castro et al., 2003) and many others were developed and thoroughly evaluated. Multiple-tree approaches require the adoption of more advanced stream encodings, such as *multiple description coding* (*MDC*), in order to support live media streaming. MDC, which is frequently implemented as a special form of priority-based redundant packing of a layer-encoded stream (Chou et al., 2003), allows the creation of a number of sub-streams or descriptions from an original stream. Each description can be reproduced on its own (with the lowest, *base layer* quality), or combined with other descriptions in order to recover additional *enhancement layers*, up to the full quality on receipt of all of the descriptions.

Multiple-tree overlays address most of the shortcomings of single trees, as their forest of trees overlay mesh can be constructed to be interior-node-disjoint. Each tree is used to deliver a different description, and the disjointness property ensures that any event involving a single node in the system does not impact more than a single description, introducing only a slight loss in media quality. Another property of the disjoint tree construction is that every node can be required to provide as much bandwidth as it consumes (by serving exactly N copies of a stream description in exactly one of the N trees).

The multiple tree architecture has its drawbacks, however. In its basic form, it supposes a uniform distribution of resources in the system and a fixed-degree regular tree construction, which cannot be expected to hold in non-cooperative environments such as the Internet. Incentive-based approaches such as CROSSFLUX (Schiely and Felber, 2006) have been studied to adapt multiple trees to heterogeneous resource distributions, achieving their goal at the price of losing inte-

rior-node-disjointness. Moreover, multiple-tree systems incur a higher overhead for tree building and maintenance, and usually require the use of *distributed hash table* (DHT) substrates to efficiently cope with it. The use of DHTs for live media streaming has been shown in (Bharambe et al., 2005) to be sub-optimal under churn, and it also limits the exploitation of network locality information during the tree-building process, as overlay trees are in fact built based on DHT IDs that are randomly assigned using cryptographical hash functions. Finally, the MDC coding scheme introduces a decoding delay due to the fact that data has to be buffered until all the descriptions have been received (or until a timeout has expired). Thus, all nodes must wait for a time proportional to the worst-case tree depth before they can decode and reproduce the media.

The most recent generation of multiple tree-based systems have shown a significant degree of convergence toward unstructured solutions in order to mitigate the issues with link locality and tree maintenance. An outstanding example of this convergence is the approach to tree-building used by Chunkyspread (Venkataraman et al., 2006), where the data messages, exchanged by the nodes over an unstructured mesh of connections, are labeled with Bloom filters in order to dynamically set up loop-free paths that can be re-used for many subsequent pieces of data from the same sub-stream.

3 DATA-DRIVEN PEER-TO-PEER LIVE STREAMING

In the rest of this chapter, we focus our attention on P2P unstructured mesh-based systems for live streaming. We establish the terminology required to describe these systems, provide a brief reasoned bibliography, and draft a global classification of data-driven streaming architectures.

Definitions

In data-driven systems, the stream is split into an ordered sequence of data chunks, which represent the base unit of data exchange. The name data-driven refers to the fact that chunk exchanges in the system are negotiated independently by each node on the basis of local information about the state of the data exchange process in the network. As a consequence, the data exchange process is no longer strictly determined by the unstructured "overlay" of a data-driven system: rather, the overlay can now be understood as a graph representing the state of knowledge of each node about its surroundings (also known as nodes' local view on the system), a subset of which is the actual graph of active connections that can evolve over time. Nodes can maintain their local view either via direct information exchanges, through the use of distributed network primitives such as gossip protocols, or using centralized mechanisms, similar to BitTorrent "trackers" (Cohen, 2005).

Node Internals

The core elements of a live streaming node program are the buffer, an internal data structure that manages the data chunks so far received by a peer, and the algorithms used to select neighbors to perform data exchanges (peer selection) and to decide which pieces of the stream to receive or send next (chunk selection). These algorithms take as inputs the current state of the node's buffer and, when available, up-to-date information about the neighbors in the node's local view. While the amount of state information that needs to be known about the receiving or sending party is variable from system to system, every node is assumed to be at least aware of the chunk content of its own buffer and of the ordering of the chunk sequence in the media stream.

Moreover, as live streaming is strongly time-dependent, a certain amount of synchronization, both among the nodes and with respect to the source, may be required. For instance, it is often useful to be able to establish a loose relationship between the time a chunk was generated and its sequence number, e.g. in order to perform actions based on the chunk's age or the remaining time before its playback is scheduled.

Finally, live streaming systems can also differ by the type of encoding they apply to the stream of chunks. In several cases, as we will see, *layered coding*, *random network coding*, and *MDC* have been adopted in an unstructured context in order to introduce specific enhancements useful in real-world scenarios, such as improved resilience to churn, incentives, or graceful quality degradation.

Data Exchange Protocols

Nodes in a peer-to-peer live streaming system usually implement a protocol to exchange control information to support the data exchange. A fundamental distinction can be established between *two-sided* and *one-sided* protocols. Two-sided protocols require up-to-date deterministic knowledge of the remote node buffers in order to reconcile the differences between the sets of available chunks. Nodes therefore exchange control messages with all their neighbors at a rate roughly similar to the chunk rate of the stream. On the other hand, one-sided protocols are able to operate with a much lower communication footprint, for instance by exploiting the properties of randomized peer selection, a theoretical framework which allows to calculate probabilistic bounds for global chunk distribution.

Another factor that has a noticeable practical impact on protocol footprint is the order in which peer selection and chunk selection are performed. While performance greatly depends on the size of the nodes' partial views, in general selecting the peer first and then the chunk generates a lower overhead than doing the reverse. Despite having an inferior performance than choosing a chunk first and then the peer expected to provide it, most implemented protocols adopt the peer-then-chunk scheme.

The two elementary data exchange operations that peers are allowed to perform with respect to their neighbors are sending data (push) and requesting data (pull). Nodes may support either of these operations alone or even combinations of the two (hybrid). The way these operations are used defines the class to which a given system belongs. While there are differences in performance between systems that belong to a same class, e.g. due to implementation details, they may be seen as having similar strengths and weaknesses.

Classes and Global Properties

The class of an individual system and the type of stream encoding adopted determine in practice the type of data exchange protocol that can be supported by a peer-to-peer live streaming system. For instance, a push-based chunk selection is not suitable in the context of unencoded media, as such a scheme typically leads to a highly inefficient use of the system resources with bandwidth being wasted in redundant replication of chunks. Schemes which have been adopted with success are, for instance, "two-sided pull-based" and "one-sided push-based with network coding". We will discuss the performance of these and other schemes below.

The Evolution of Data-Driven Systems

The first instances of mesh-based systems appeared in the literature starting in 2004. Chainsaw (Pai et al., 2005) demonstrated for the first time a proof-of-concept mesh-based system that used randomized peer and chunk selection algorithms. A few months later, Coolstreaming/DONet (X. Zhang et al., 2005) introduced a smarter chunk scheduling algorithm that takes into account the expected play-out time of the individual chunks, gives higher priority to the locally-rarest chunks,

and distributes the chunks based on an estimate of the available upload capacity at the sender nodes.

One of the main issues with data-driven systems is the requirement for a *steady flow of information exchange* among the nodes in order to support the actual chunk replication. A significant advantage in this respect is achieved by multiple-tree based systems, where for low churn rates their structured mesh of connections is maintained with low expenses. Subsequent research thus strived to better understand the trade-offs of hybrid or push-pull algorithm design. GridMedia (M. Zhang et al., 2005) used a combination of pull (mesh) and push (trees) to improve the efficiency of chunk distribution. PRIME (Magharei and Rejaie, 2005) proposed a peculiar mesh-based design which is also similar to a multiple-tree system: it builds several separate tree structures to initially facilitate the distribution of new data chunks, while mesh-based "swarming" (obtained by making the leaves of each tree serve data toward random members of the other trees) is used to complete their distribution. The boundaries between structured and unstructured meshes have been shown to be indeed very thin, as in the unstructured tree building process used by Chunkyspread (Venkataraman et al., 2006) mentioned previously. All these systems demonstrate that an intermediate ground definitely exists where hybrid data-driven and tree-based architectures can strive for a trade-off between overhead and resilience to churn.

A few alternative solutions have been devised in order to reduce the communication overhead without reintroducing trees. Lava (Wang and Li, 2007a) implemented random network coding with a classic pull-based protocol in order to test its viability for live streaming. Network coding (Ahlswede et al., 2000) eliminates the need for node buffer reconciliation. Nodes exchange random linear combinations of the stream chunks without prior negotiation and are enabled to better exploit the available link capacity in resource-constrained scenarios. A positive finding in Lava was that the overhead of chunk encoding and decoding can be made low, and the delay introduced by the decoding process may be almost eliminated using the Gauss-Jordan elimination technique to solve the linear systems progressively as chunks are received. Unfortunately, the rather large number of parameters involved in this scheme and the lack of behavioral consistency across scenarios suggest that a network coding approach with pull-based policies suffers from scalability limits. The authors of Lava went on to improve on their previous design with R2 (Wang and Li, 2007b), which adopts a random push protocol and obtains much better results in playback stability and bandwidth efficiency.

More recently, a strong interest has grown about another family of algorithms for data distribution known as epidemic (Massoulié et al., 2007), closely related to gossip communication algorithms. Epidemic streaming systems leverage the theory of probabilistic random walks on a network graph. Among the main achievements of this approach there has been the definition of optimality bounds on the delay of chunk distribution for live streaming in symmetric networks with unitary link bandwidth, which were proved to be $log2\ N + 1$ in (Sanghavi et al., 2007). This seminal paper has provided the required theoretical framework that enabled the evaluation of a large set of peer and chunk selection policies. Under this framework, impressive results were obtained by simple two-step, one-sided pull-push systems such as INTERLEAVE. With the low communication footprint required for its operation, the distribution efficiency was analytically shown to be $O(log2\ N)$ in symmetric networks. A rather complex example of rate-optimal scheme achieving the $log2\ N + 1$ delay bound was studied in (Abeni et al., 2009).

A thorough analysis of several epidemic distribution techniques has been subsequently performed under both symmetric and asymmetric network settings (Bonald et al., 2008), covering a significant portion of the algorithm design space, including stateful (pull, push, and hybrid) and stateless (random) selection policies. This analysis

was later extended to evaluate the performance of epidemic algorithms under churn, limited view on the system, and delayed propagation of control information (Chatzidrossos et al., 2009). While a general closed form for optimal rate and delay has yet to be found under asymmetric scenarios, peer selection policies such as "most deprived peer / random useful chunk" (dp/ru) have been shown as having optimal rate bounds (but not optimal delay). Subsequent studies have observed that, in practical environments, optimal schemes become sometimes inefficient. Researchers also investigated similar policies such as "most deprived peer / latest useful" (dp/lu) (Picconi and Massoulié, 2008) and found that, despite the lack of analytical bounds, they show optimal results in realistic scenarios.

Classification and Notes on Performance Evaluation

Whereas theoretical bounds have been obtained for a few combinations of selection policies in simple, abstract scenarios, researchers need to resort to simulation and emulation techniques to evaluate the performance of data-driven streaming applications in realistic conditions.

Unfortunately, simulation-based approaches have limited descriptive power. Since data-driven systems are characterized by the lack of an overlay in its traditional sense, i.e. a graph of network connections linking all the nodes in the network and over whose edges data exchanges occur permanently, it is difficult to settle on a common set of metrics that are meaningful and generic enough to encompass an adequate range of peer and chunk selection algorithms. Moreover, the large possible choice of granularity and detail level in the simulation studies, together with the trade-off between "complexity and realism" versus "simplicity and control" in the emulated deployments, make a fair comparison among data-driven systems in similar conditions a very difficult task.

Table 1. Classification of data-driven P2P live streaming systems

Name	Class	Peer Selection	Chunk Selection	Protocol	Incentives	Coding
Chainsaw	pull	random	random	2-sided	no	none
Coolstreaming DONet	pull	random	rarity + priority	1-sided	no	none
GridMedia	hybrid	random	subscription + random	2-sided	no	none
PRIME	hybrid	trees + random	description + priority	1-sided	no	MDC
New Coolstreaming	hybrid	buffering delay	subscription + random	2-sided	no	none
Lava	pull	random	playback priority	2-sided	no	network coding
R2	push	random	random + priority	1-sided	no	network coding
Interleave	hybrid	random	pull oldest, push latest	1-sided	no	none
Epidemic DP/RU	push	most de-prived	random useful	2-sided	no	none
Epidemic DP/LU	push	most de-prived	latest useful	2-sided	no	none
PULSE	pull	incentive based	rarest useful	2-sided	TFT + delay	FEC
Substream Trading	pull	substream-based	substream + priority	2-sided	TFT	layered

While such an in-depth comparison is out of the scope of this survey, we provide the reader with a global outlook on the strengths and weaknesses of each approach in real-world environments. Table 1 contains a synthetic classification of the data-driven live streaming systems mentioned in this chapter. Its columns present the design parameters that we deem to be relevant for many practical aspects of the deployment of a streaming system on the Internet. These aspects include: amount of control overhead, support of heterogeneous nodes, response to variable network conditions, and operation under scarcity of resources. In the following, we discuss these parameters and their impact on the overall behavior of a live streaming system.

System Class vs. Protocol Type

Table 1 highlights a few dominant combinations of protocol and class which are adopted by many streaming systems. The most common type of live streaming protocols is the *two-sided* type. This scheme requires a double exchange of control information between the sender and receiver for each chunk to be transmitted. Simple optimizations, such as piggybacking one or more requests to an ongoing chunk transfer, can reduce the bandwidth overhead determined by control traffic. However, at least one RTT has to elapse for a data exchange to be initiated. This delay may limit the system throughput when a significant number of nodes are connected by high-latency links. Two-sided protocols can support virtually any class and combination of selection algorithms, the most relevant being the following:

- **Two-sided pull:** This is the most popular and flexible scheme. It enables the use of complex policies for both peer and chunk selection. For instance, *chunk rarity and playout deadlines* can be combined with random peer selection, such as in Coolstreaming/DONet. More advanced peer selection policies can also be used, such as the *most deprived* criterion. These have a strong theoretical appeal and have led to optimality proofs under simple chunk selection algorithms. Lack of chunks conveys implicit information on the long-term state of a remote node, but may in practice be exploited by greedy peers, resulting in freeloading and performance disruption. Incentive-based systems adopt more complex selection policies that are much harder (if at all possible) to analyze, but show a high resilience in non-cooperative environments.

- **Two-sided hybrid:** The use of *push-pull policies* was explored in order to improve on the simple pull-based design (M. Zhang et al., 2007). These hybrid architectures, while still using a two-sided protocol, introduce elements of structure in order to reduce the need for control exchanges.

On the other hand, *one-sided* protocols are more limited in scope. Their major advantage is that they do not require a bi-directional data exchange between sender and receiver, avoiding both the delay and part of the network overhead due to buffer reconciliation. However, the need to blindly decide about sending or requesting a chunk, without any information on the remote state, does limit significantly the range of peer-selection and chunk-selection policies that can be adopted. Without a return channel for remote feedback, one-sided protocols require external mechanisms to implement incentives or to become aware of the underlying network conditions. Few schemes of one-sided protocols have shown practical interest:

- **One-sided push:** While efficient when used over a loop-free overlay, randomized one-sided push schemes may never reach a complete chunk distribution and their performance is unsatisfactory[3]. However, the use of random network coding schemes on the stream data can solve most of these shortcomings, as shown in R2 (Wang and Li, 2007b).
- **One-sided hybrid:** Schemes such as INTERLEAVE combine push and pull. Push is most effective in the initial phases of data distribution and pull works best when chunks have already been spread throughout the system.

Peer and Chunk Selection

The use of a given combination of peer and chunk selection is mainly determined by the network environment in which the P2P live streaming system is expected to operate. In symmetric cooperative scenarios peer selection is not very relevant. Indeed, many earlier theoretical studies focused on this case because of its relative ease of analysis. Epidemic systems increased the relevance of peer selection in order to improve the rate and delay bounds of the data distribution. The most-deprived policy can exploit the number of buffered chunks as an additional source of information about the remote peer.

In non-cooperative and asymmetric scenarios, peer selection becomes much more important than in the previous case. The schemes with random peer selection are likely to suffer from uneven performance, as the chunk diffusion speed across the system heavily depends on the resources of the first few nodes. These environments thus benefit the most from bandwidth-aware and incentive-based selection policies. Interactions between complex peer selection policies and chunk selection are still not completely understood. In practice, it is common to use chunk selection policies that introduce randomness (e.g. random-useful) in order to maximize the opportunity for data exchange, and thus the exchange rate between nodes. Policies that exploit the chunk sequence number as an estimator of rarity (e.g. latest-useful), on the other hand, tend to minimize the delay of data distribution.

Stream Coding

The use of coding in live streaming has been popularized by structured mesh architectures, such as Splitstream, mainly because it was an easy and practical way to overcome the weaknesses of single tree designs: splitting the media with MDC allowed fault tolerance and graceful quality degradation to be achieved at the same time, with an acceptable cost in bandwidth and processing overhead.

Data-driven systems, on the other hand, show an intrinsic fault tolerance due to the largely random and volatile structure of their mesh of connections. While chunks can be lost due to transient network events, the presence of bursts of losses (such as those due to ancestors disconnecting from tree overlays) is highly unlikely. Standard forward error correction (FEC) techniques (such as Reed-Solomon) can also be successfully applied in these architectures, as well as MDC or other more advanced forms of encodings such as network coding or fountain coding. Layered coding has been proposed in an incentive-based context to provide adaptation between resources offered and received media quality (Z. Liu et al., 2008).

4 P2P LIVE STREAMING AND THE INTERNET

In this section, we survey the status of large-scale deployed applications, provide a synthetic excerpt of the main results gleaned by measurement studies, and describe the subjects of current research in peer-to-peer live streaming.

Large-Scale Deployed Systems

Several P2P live streaming systems have been deployed during the last few years, but just a few of them stemmed from research projects. Among these, ESM (Chu et al., 2004) was the first practical deployment of an instrumented tree-based overlay, a fundamental step toward understanding the issues of real-world Internet live streaming. Coolstreaming, which we believe to be the first data-driven system to be deployed on the Internet (2004), was in its subsequent developments transformed into a hybrid multiple-tree system, adopting a push-pull chunk exchange scheme (Xie et al., 2007). Another system from research, GridMedia, has become a commercial venture and enjoys popularity in China. Most of the other academic projects, except for trial deployments on Planetlab or other large-scale network testbeds, do not seem to have achieved a significant deployment, probably due to a lack of development efforts or a small initial user base.

It is more difficult to trace the earliest examples of commercial mesh-based streaming systems on the Internet. Scarce documentation was indeed available on the algorithms and infrastructures these systems employ. A common claim was the use of "swarming" technologies, a quite vague marketing term that probably tried to capitalize on the success of BitTorrent and other P2P content distribution applications. A number of self-proclaimed commercial mesh-based applications started to appear in 2005. Today, the most successful among them seem to be SOPCast, TVAnts, PPStream, and PPLive (Silverston & Fourmaux, 2007). Since the algorithms used by most commercial systems have not been fully disclosed, in many cases it is not officially known whether they are actually data-driven, what the extent of the server infrastructure involvement is, or whether their algorithms have been modified at some point (e.g. from server-assisted to tree- or mesh-based) in order to scale better.

Measurement Studies

Measurement studies have helped understand and quantify the performance of commercial live streaming systems, leading in several cases to the reverse-engineering of sizable portions of the streaming application protocol and algorithms. For an overview of the main techniques used by measurement studies to quantify both the quantitative and qualitative aspects of a streaming application, such as crawling, buffer map inference, and traffic analysis, we refer the reader to (Hei et al., 2008). Recent measurement studies on PPLive (Hei et al., 2007) have revealed the astonishing success and impressive deployment status of this system. During the observed period, it averaged 400,000 users daily and hosted simultaneous audiences in the order of 100,000 viewers for the most popular individual channels. Up-to-date inside information provided by PPLive staff (Huang 2007) accounted for peak simultaneous audiences in the order of more than 2 million individual peers, confirming an astonishing growth of the PPLive user base in little more than one year.

Another fundamental insight provided by measurements concerns user behavior in large-scale streaming applications. While the earliest system designs could rely only on a small number of vague assumptions about the type of workload imposed by the users on the network, today a large knowledge base of datasets describing the habits of real audiences using Internet-based streaming has become available and is being used to assist and guide the development of current streaming architectures. Among these insights is the fact that users of IPTV streaming services show similar behavior to TV audiences (Cha et al., 2008): high volatility (most streaming sessions are shorter than 10s) as the users "zap channels" while seeking an interesting program; linear zapping patterns; pareto-distributed channel popularity; churn rates which are strongly correlated with the time of the day; and presence of highly correlated departure events. Similar behaviors were also detected in live streaming systems (Hei et al., 2007), suggesting common patterns in the user consumption of online streaming media content.

Current Research

The research activity on data-driven streaming systems has become frantic between 2007 and 2009. Here we provide a non-exhaustive list of the main topics and issues that are still being investigated today.

Heterogeneous and Non-Cooperative Scenarios

Several techniques have been proposed in order to encourage cooperation and prevent free-riding in live streaming systems. In the structured live streaming literature, typical solutions to heterogeneity involve external mechanisms that prevent nodes with insufficient resources from being admitted to the system (e.g. Splitstream). While data-driven systems can provide the flexibility required to address resource heterogeneity and lack of cooperation among nodes, only a small number of works have focused on this aspect. The use of reputation (Pouwelse et al., 2004) has been suggested since early on as a possible way to prevent nodes from misrepresenting their contribution to the system. In order for this approach to operate correctly, either the presence of trusted third parties (to perform measurements or keep records of transactions) is required or a separate distributed watchdog system must exist, which would add a cumbersome new layer of complexity. Pairwise currency exchanges (Tamilmani et al., 2004) were also proposed as a way to keep track of user contributions and prevent freeloading in bulk data distribution applications.

Streaming-aware incentive mechanisms, whose potential in stimulating user contribution has been highlighted by the success of BitTorrent, have been implemented recently with promising results. PULSE (Pianese et al., 2007) introduced an incentive scheme that leveraged reception delay as a dynamic feedback information on the availability of upload capacity in the system. Such incentive mechanism mitigates free riding by inducing a loose proportional retribution between node upload and download, selects resourceful peers to perform the first few replications of fresh data chunks and thus reduces the overall delay of data distribution. Similar incentives have also been extended to layer-encoded streams (Z. Liu et al., 2008). A scheme called "substream trading" has been developed in order to more flexibly support non-cooperative scenarios where nodes of heterogeneous capabilities can receive a different level of media quality according to their upload contribution.

Another field of ongoing research is the performance bounds of epidemic systems in heterogeneous network scenarios (Massoulié 2008). A variety of deterministic peer-selection policies are also being investigated in order to increase the likelihood that resourceful peers become involved in the earliest phases of chunk distribution, thus leading to improved theoretical delay bounds for asymmetric systems (Mathieu and Perino, 2009).

Network Locality Support

A serious concern, shared by many Internet service providers, has been emerging during the last few years about the growth of P2P networks for large-scale content distribution. While the first commercial systems tended to use TCP as their transport protocol, more recent ones have adopted UDP for delivering both data and control information. These applications establish a large number of network connections and exchange a lot of traffic, sometimes even disregarding every notion of TCP friendliness.

The ongoing debate about network neutrality, though heavily influenced by business reasons such as the decreasing operational margins of Internet service providers, is also backed by sound technical reasons. Many P2P systems indeed use the network in a very inefficient way, partly by lack of care by the application writers and partly because applications can only approximately gauge the conditions of the underlying IP network without any explicit network support. Introducing

network support for overlay-based applications has been a leading area of research for some time with notable joint efforts between academic and industrial partners (Leonardi et al., 2008), leading to standardization attempts that are currently in progress (Kiesel et al., 2009).

Recent measurement studies about deployed commercial streaming systems have highlighted their lack of locality awareness (Ciullo et al., 2009). Except for some affinity between peers connected to the same IP subnet, observed in PPLive and TVAnts, high-bandwidth nodes from distant autonomous systems (AS) are always preferred as exchange partners regardless of path length. Early attempts to integrate on-line RTT measurements to improve the locality of peer selection are described in (Pianese & Perino, 2007). A centralized ISP-managed framework for providing network awareness to applications (called P4P) was first proposed in (Xie et al., 2008). Finally, a scheduling-agnostic mechanism for ISP-friendly peer selection was proposed in (Picconi & Massoulié, 2009). It relies on a randomized control overlay to dynamically bias the local peer selection towards low-cost nodes (i.e. within the boundaries of the same ISP), in order to avoid an excessive use of inter-ISP backbone and peering links.

User Dynamics and Streaming Experience

User behavior and activity patterns can heavily influence the overall performance of a P2P streaming system. Results from measurements confirm that churn occurs massively, chiefly determined by users sampling new channels and zapping among them. Resilience to node churn is the main strength of data-driven systems, compared to previous structured architectures. However, by modeling user behavior in a more accurate way, it might be possible to detect and harness the more stable peers in order to provide better support to the transient nodes (Wang et al., 2008).

Another area where current commercial systems could be especially improved is the initial delay between the decision of the user to join a video channel and the start of video playback. This delay depends on many factors, such as the number of peers in the streaming channel, their aggregate upload capacity, and the efficiency of chunk scheduling algorithms to retrieve a contiguous sequence of chunks. Additional servers could be introduced to transmit either a lower-quality version of the video to newcomers to the channel, providing a sort of "channel preview" as suggested by (Hei et al., 2008), or even an initial sequence of recent contiguous chunks, in order to rapidly bootstrap the newcomers' buffers.

Security

Security is a traditional weak spot of peer-to-peer systems, and mesh-based live streaming networks are not exempt from the usual security weaknesses of networked, unmanaged distributed systems. Apart from the inevitable denial-of-service (DoS) attacks on the source and Sybil scenarios, P2P streaming systems can also be easily subverted by less resource-intensive attacks such as stream data pollution (Yang et al., 2008) and Byzantine node behavior (or other system-specific information and protocol attacks). Pollution attacks have been studied in-depth, leading to the design of non-intrusive, lightweight measures to prevent nodes from spreading invalid data through the system (Dhungel et al., 2007). On the other hand, advanced fault-tolerance mechanisms to protect live streaming systems from more complex adversarial scenarios can quickly become too cumbersome and resource-intensive to be practical.

5 SUMMARY

This chapter contributes a comprehensive survey about data-driven (or mesh-based) live streaming systems. It discusses the reasons behind the emergence of systems designed without tree-based overlays, describes the strengths and the weaknesses of these architectures, and presents a coherent view of the current know-how on data-driven algorithm design. An overview of the current deployment status of Internet-based commercial streaming applications is provided, along with the latest results from large-scale measurement studies. Finally, it briefly illustrates the current directions of the research about data-driven live streaming systems.

REFERENCES

Abeni, L. Kiraly, C., & Lo Cigno, R. (2009, May). On the optimal scheduling of streaming applications in unstructured meshes. In *Proceedings of Networking 2009, 8th International IFIP-TC 6 Networking Conference*, Aachen, Germany.

Ahlswede, R., Cai, N., Li, S. R., & Yeung, R. W. (2000, July). Network information flow. *IEEE Transactions on Information Theory*, 46(4), 1204–1216. doi:10.1109/18.850663

Banerjee, S. Bhattacharjee, B., & Kommareddy, C. (2002, August). Scalable application layer multicast. In *Proceedings of the 2002 ACM SIG-COMM Conference*.

Bawa, M. Deshpande, H. & Garcia-Molina, H. (2002). Transience of peers and streaming media. *In HotNets-I*, Princeton, NJ, (pp. 107–112).

Bharambe, A. Rao, S. Padmanabhan, V. Seshan, S., & Zhang, H. (2005). The impact of heterogeneous bandwidth constraints on DHT-based multicast protocols. In *Proceedings of the 4th International Workshop on Peer-to-Peer Systems*.

Biersack, E. W. (2005). Where is multicast today? *SIGCOMM Comput. Commun. Rev.*, 35(5), 83–84. doi:10.1145/1096536.1096549

Bonald, T. Massoulié, L. Mathieu, F. Perino, D., & Twigg, A. (2008). Epidemic live streaming: optimal performance trade-offs. In *Proceedings of the 2008 ACM SIGMETRICS International Conference on Measurement and Modeling of Computer Systems*, Annapolis, MD, USA.

Castro, M., Druschel, P., Kermarrec, A. M., Nandi, A., Rowstron, A., & Singh, A. (2003, February). Splitstream: high-bandwidth multicast in cooperative environments. *Proceedings of IPTPS'03*.

Cha, M. Kwak, H. Rodriguez, P. Ahn, Y., & Moon, S. (2007, October). I tube, you tube, everybody tubes: analyzing the world's largest user generated content video system. In *Proceedings of the 7th ACM SIGCOMM Conference on Internet Measurement*, San Diego.

Cha, M. Rodriguez, P. Crowcroft, J. Moon, S., & Amatriain, X. (2008, October). Watching television over an IP network. In *Proc. of the 8th ACM SIGCOMM Conference on Internet Measurement*, Vouliagmeni, Greece.

Chaintreau, A. Baccelli, F., & Diot, C. (2002). Impact of network delay variation on multicast sessions performance with TCP-like congestion control. *IEEE Transactions on Networking*, pp. 500-512.

Chatzidrossos, I., Dán, G., & Fodor, V. (2009, May). Delay and playout probability trade-off in mesh-based peer-to-peer streaming with delayed buffer map updates. *Peer-to-Peer Networking and Applications*.

Chou, P. A., Wang, H. J., & Padmanabhan, V. N. (2003). *Layered multiple description coding*. Proceedings of Packet Video Workshop.

Chu, Y., Ganjam, A., Ng, T. S. E., Rao, S. G., Sripanidkulchai, K., Zhan, J., & Zhang, H. (2004). Early experience with an internet broadcast system based on overlay multicast. *USENIX Annual Technical Conference, General Track*, pp. 155–170.

Ciullo, D., Garcia, M. A., Horvat, A., Leonardi, E., Mellia, M., Rossi, D., et al. (2009, May). Network awareness of P2P live streaming applications. *In HotP2P'09*, Rome, Italy.

Cohen, B. (2003, June). Incentives build robustness in BitTorrent. In *Proceedings of the 1st Workshop on the Economics of Peer-to-Peer Systems*, Berkeley.

Deering, S. E., & Cheriton, D. R. (1990, May). Multicast routing in datagram internetworks and extended LANs. *ACM Transactions on Computer Systems*, *8*(2), 85–110. doi:10.1145/78952.78953

Dhungel, P., & Hei, X. W. Ross, K., & Saxena, N. (2007, August). The pollution attack in P2P live video streaming: measurement results and defenses. *In Sigcomm P2P-TV Workshop*.

Ganesh, A., Kermarrec, A. M., & Massoulié, L. (2003). Peer-to-peer membership management for gossip-based protocols. *IEEE Transactions on Computers*, *52*, 139–258. doi:10.1109/TC.2003.1176982

Hei, X., Liang, C., Liang, J., Liu, Y., & Ross, K. W. (2007, December). A measurement study of a large-scale P2P IPTV system. *IEEE Transactions on Multimedia*, *9*(8), 1672–1687. doi:10.1109/TMM.2007.907451

Hei, X., Liu, Y., & Ross, K. W. (2008, February). IPTV over P2P streaming networks: the mesh-pull approach. *IEEE Communications Magazine*, *46*(2), 86–92. doi:10.1109/MCOM.2008.4473088

Huang, G. (2007). *Experiences with PPLive. Keynote at ACM SIGCOMM* (p. 2P). TV Workshop.

Kiesel, S. Popkin, L. Previdi, S. Woundy, R., & Yang, Y. R. (2009, March). Application-Layer Traffic Optimization (ALTO) Requirements (draft-kiesel-alto-reqs-02.txt). *IETF-74, ALTO WG*, San Francisco.

Leonardi, E., Mellia, M., Horvart, A., Muscariello, L., Niccolini, S., & Rossi, D. (2008, April). Building a cooperative P2P-TV application over a wise network: the approach of the european FP-7 STREP NAPA-WINE. *IEEE Communications Magazine*, *46*(4), 20–22. doi:10.1109/MCOM.2008.4481334

Liu, J. Rao, S. G. Li, B. & Zhang, H. (2008, January). Opportunities and challenges of peer-to-peer Internet video broadcast. In *Proceedings of the IEEE, 96*(1), 11-24.

Liu, Z. Shen, Y. Ross, K. W. Panwar, S. & Wang, Y. (2008, October). Substream trading: towards an open P2P live streaming system. In *Proceedings of the International Conference on Network Protocols (ICNP)*, Orlando.

Lua, E. K., Crowcroft, J., Pias, M., Sharma, R., & Lim, S. (2005). A survey and comparison of peer-to-peer overlay network schemes. *IEEE Communications Surveys and Tutorials*, *7*(1-4), 72–93.

Magharei, N., & Rejaie, R. (2007). *PRIME: peer-to-peer receiver-driven mesh-based streaming. Proceedings of IEEE INFOCOM'07*. AK: Anchorage.

Massoulié, L. Twigg, A. Gkantsidis, C., & Rodriguez, P. R. (2007). Randomized decentralized broadcasting algorithms. In *Proceedings of IEEE INFOCOM'07*, Anchorage, AK.

Massoulié, L. (2008, March). Peer-to-peer live streaming: optimality results and open problems. In *Proceedings of the 42nd Annual Conference on Information Sciences and Systems*, pp. 313-315.

Mathieu, F., & Perino, D. (In Press). *On resource aware algorithms in epidemic live streaming*. Manuscript under submission.

Pai, V. Kumar, K. Tamilmani, K. Sambamurthy, V., & Mohr, A. (2005, February). Chainsaw: eliminating trees from overlay multicast. In *Proceedings of the 4th International Workshop on Peer-to-Peer System*s.

Pianese, F., & Perino, D. (2007, August). Resource and locality awareness in an incentive-based P2P live streaming system. *SIGCOMM P2P-TV Workshop*.

Pianese, F., Perino, D., Keller, J., & Biersack, E. W. (2007, December). PULSE: an adaptive, incentive-based, unstructured P2P live streaming system. *IEEE Transactions on Multimedia*, *9*(8), 1645–1660. doi:10.1109/TMM.2007.907466

Picconi, F., & Massoulié, L. (2008). Is there a future for mesh-based live video streaming? In *Proceedings of the Eighth International Conference on Peer-to-Peer Computing*, pp. 289-298.

Picconi, F., & Massoulié, L. (2009). ISP-friend or foe? Making P2P live streaming ISP-aware. In *Proceedings of the 29th IEEE International Conference on Distributed Computing Systems*.

Pouwelse, J. A., Taal, J. R., Lagendijk, R. L., Epema, D. H. J., & Sips, H. J. (2004, October). Real-time video delivery using peer-to-peer bartering networks and multiple description coding. *IEEE Int'l Conference on Systems, Man and Cybernetics*.

Sanghavi, S., Hayek, B., & Massoulié, L. (2007). Gossiping with multiple messages. *IEEE Transactions on Information Theory*, *53*(12), 4640–4654. doi:10.1109/TIT.2007.909171

Schiely, M., & Felber, P. (2006). CROSSFLUX: an architecture for peer-to-peer media streaming. *Global Data Management, Volume 8. Emerging Communication: Studies on New Technologies and Practices in Communication, IOSPress*, *8*, 342–358.

Silverston, T., & Fourmaux, O. (2007, June). Measuring P2P IPTV systems. In *Proceedings of ACM NOSSDAV'07*, Urbana-Champaign, IL.

Tamilmani, K. Pai, V., & Mohr, A. E. (2004, June). SWIFT: a system with incentives for trading. *Proceedings of the 2nd Workshop of Economics in Peer-to-Peer Systems (P2PECON)*.

Venkataraman, V., Yoshida, K., & Francis, P. (2006). Chunkyspread: heterogeneous unstructured end system multicast. In *Proceedings of the 14th IEEE International Conference on Network Protocols*.

Wang, F. Liu, J., & Xiong, Y. (2008, April). Stable peers: existence, importance, and application in peer-to-peer live video streaming. In *Proceedings of IEEE INFOCOM 2008*, Phoenix, AZ, USA.

Wang, M., & Li, B. (2007a). Network coding in live peer-to-peer streaming. *IEEE Transactions on Multimedia, 9*(8), 1554–1567. doi:10.1109/TMM.2007.907460

Wang, M., & Li, B. (2007b). R2: random push with random network coding in live peer-to-peer streaming. *IEEE Journal on Selected Areas in Communications, 25*(9), 1655–1666. doi:10.1109/JSAC.2007.071205

Xie, H., Yang, Y. R., & Krishnamurthy, A. Liu, Y., & Silberschatz, A. (2008, October). P4P: provider portal for applications. In *Proceedings of the 8th ACM SIGCOMM Conference on Internet Measurement*, Vouliagmeni, Greece.

Xie, S., Li, B., Keung, G. Y., & Zhang, X. (2007, December). Coolstreaming: Design, Theory and Practice. *IEEE Transactions on Multimedia, 9*(8), 1661–1671. doi:10.1109/TMM.2007.907469

Yang, S. Jin, H., Li, B., Liao, X., Yao, H., & Tu, X. (2008). The content pollution in peer-to-peer live streaming systems: analysis and implications. In *Proceedings of the 37th International Conference on Parallel Processing*, pp. 652-659.

Yu, H., Zheng, D., Zhao, B. Y., & Zheng, W. (2006, October). Understanding user behavior in large-scale video-on-demand systems. *SIGOPS Oper. Syst. Rev., 40*(4), 333–344. doi:10.1145/1218063.1217968

Zhang, M. Luo, J.-G. Zhao, L., & Yang, S.-Q. (2005). A peer-to-peer network for live media streaming using a push-pull approach. *MULTIMEDIA '05:* In *Proceedings of the 13th annual ACM international conference on Multimedia*, pp. 287–290, New York, NY, USA.

Zhang, M., Zhang, Q., Sun, L., & Yang, S. (2007, December). Understanding the power of pull-based streaming protocol: Can we do better? *IEEE Journal on Selected Areas in Communications, 25*(9).

Zhang, X. Liu, J. Li, B. & Yum, T.-S. P. (2005, March). CoolStreaming/DONet: a data-driven overlay network for peer-to-peer live media streaming. In *Proceedings of IEEE INFOCOM'05*, Miami, FL.

ENDNOTES

[1]   For a comprehensive background survey about structured and unstructured overlay networks in the context of generic p2p applications, we strongly recommend (Lua et al., 2005].

[2]   A global survey on overlay-based live streaming systems can be found in (J. Liu et al., 2008].

[3]   It has been shown in (Sanghavi et al., 2007] that one-sided randomized push-based protocols are especially slow in the final stages of dissemination.

Chapter 13
Epidemic Live Streaming

Diego Perino
Orange Labs, France

Fabien Mathieu
Orange Labs, France

ABSTRACT

Epidemic algorithms have emerged as a simple, yet effective solution for disseminating live streaming contents to a large audience. Typically, the use of epidemic algorithms is motivated by the fact that they do not rely on a specific underlying structure to work, so they are very robust against network dynamics and volatility. However, the performance of these algorithms is still little understood. This chapter is intended as an introduction to epidemic live streaming. We propose some simple metrics to understand the behavior of a diffusion algorithm, and we use elementary diffusion schemes to understand the basics of the diffusion process, for both homogeneous and heterogeneous systems. The approach that we propose mixes theoretical results, when available, with empirical observations in order to give the best possible insights.

INTRODUCTION

In the past few years several commercial live streaming systems have been proposed. Experimental analysis highlights that the most popular applications, like PPLive (http://www.pplive.com), SopCast (http://www.sopcast.com/), TVants (http://tvants.en.softonic.com/), and UUSee (http://www.uusee.com/), rely on a *mesh-based approach* for the stream distribution, and confirms

DOI: 10.4018/978-1-61692-831-5.ch013

the effectiveness of this solution for the deployment of large-scale live streaming systems over the Internet. In mesh-based P2P live streaming the stream is not forwarded as a continuous flow of data but is divided in a series of pieces (chunks), which are injected in the system by a source and exchanged among peers in order to retrieve the continuous sequence and play out the stream. Every chunk thus follows its own broadcast tree from source to peers. This approach contrasts with *structured systems* where the stream is forwarded over one or multiple static spanning

Copyright © 2011, IGI Global. Copying or distributing in print or electronic forms without written permission of IGI Global is prohibited.

trees. The inherit scalability and robustness of the *mesh-based* approach make it more suitable for the heterogeneous dynamic environment of the Internet, where peers have different bandwidth capacities and may join and leave the system in unpredictable ways (Magarei *et al.* 2007).

However, despite their popularity, the fundamental mechanisms of data dissemination in mesh-based systems have not been completely understood mainly because of the random hardly predictable behaviors for which an adequate analytical model has not been proposed yet. Moreover, it is not possible to fully understand this approach by means of experimental evaluation of commercial systems because the underlying allocation algorithms are not disclosed.

In this chapter we consider P2P live streaming from a theoretical perspective: in order to fully understand the stream dissemination process in mesh-based systems, we focus on the data exchange policies only, and we disregard the other issues. In particular, we consider epidemic-style distribution algorithms where data forwarding is the result of a chunk/peer selection (a chunk is a logical, atomic, unit of data) performed locally at one node.

The goal of the approach is to address questions like: is it possible to achieve optimal or near-optimal rate/delay performance in mesh-based live streaming systems? Which are the main performance trade-offs of such algorithms?

In the following, we first introduce the problem of peer-to-peer (P2P) live streaming, and the basics of epidemic dissemination. Then we give an overview of optimality results concerning diffusion performance of epidemic-style algorithms. After introducing some possibly interesting allocation schemes, their performance is studied for homogeneous bandwidth systems; we then propose an extension of the model that handles resource-aware allocation algorithms, and we analyze heterogeneous bandwidth scenarios. Finally, we highlight the important role that system parameters, like chunk size and neighborhood size, play in the algorithms performance.

MODEL

We consider a P2P system of n peers and a single source S. L is the set of peers so that $|L|=n$. The source receives a *live* streaming content from an entity external to the system. The purpose of the system is to use its resources (of both source and peers) to broadcast the stream to all peers in an efficient manner.

The Stream

We assume the stream has a constant bitrate SR. In most P2P systems, the stream is subdivided into smaller entities, in order to allow dissemination through multiple paths. This allows a greater flexibility and therefore a better use of the available resources.

Two families of stream subdivision are usually considered: spatial or temporal. Spatial subdivision splits the stream into a (finite) number of subtreams (*stripes*). The spatial approach is usually associated to *structured* diffusion, each stripe being associated to its own deterministic broadcast tree. On the other hand, the temporal approach splits the stream into small pieces of data called *chunks*, in a way similar to what happens for lower network layers (like the splitting of a network flow into IP packets). Under the *chunk-based* (or *data-driven*) approach, each single chunk may follow its own broadcast tree, so chunks are used in most non-deterministic (unstructured) algorithms.

As the epidemic approach is unstructured by nature, it relies on a chunk subdivision. In the following, we assume that all chunks have a common size value c. The stream is therefore characterized by a chunk generation rate $\lambda = \dfrac{SR}{c}$ (equivalently a new chunk is generated every $T_{SR}=c/SR$ time units).

System Resources

Many types of resources are involved in a *live* diffusion: storage (for managing a stream buffer), CPU, bandwidth... We assume here that the main resource bottleneck is the access upload bandwidth, which is a reasonable assumption if system is made of not too old computers with asymmetric DSL Internet connections. Other resources are considered to be provisioned enough. For instance, there is no constraint on the number of chunks that each peer can *receive* per time unit. Similarly, we suppose that there is no congestion outside the access network.

Let u_S denotes the source upload. Unless otherwise stated, we assume that a single copy of each chunk is transmitted by the source, so $u_S = SR$. The upload of a peer $l \in L$ is $u(l)$, or simply u if there is no ambiguity (for instance with homogeneous systems).

In a first time, latencies are not taken into account, so the time needed by a peer l to upload a chunk to a peer v is $c/u(l)$. The validity of this approximation will be discussed later in this chapter.

The Epidemic Approach

The epidemic approach considers the set of peers that possess a given chunk as an *infected* population, which *contaminates* the others. The idea is to mimic the efficient propagation mechanisms of biological and computer viruses (Bailey 1975).

Concretely, the chunk diffusion within the system is described by an atomic *contamination* process: the copy of a chunk from one peer to another. We suppose the copy is initiated by the owner of the chunk (*push* approach). In addition to mimicking the dynamics of epidemic diffusion, this model simplifies the description of the chunk exchanges. We assume that each peer has only a partial knowledge of the overall system. This is represented as a directed graph $G=(L,E)$ where $(l,v) \in E$ if and only if l knows v (we say that l

is a neighbor of v). We denote the set of neighbors of peer l as $N(l)$ and we suppose that a peer can only send chunks to one of its neighbors.

For any $l \in L$, let $B(l)$ be the collection of chunks that peer l has received. We denote by $\mathcal{B}$ the set of possible collections of chunks owned by a peer. An epidemic diffusion is formally described by a *push-based selection scheme*: a (possibly random) mapping that gives for any sender peer l, as a function of its state and the one of its neighborhood, the destination peer $v \in N(l)$ and the chunk $b \in B(l)$ to be sent.

Note that a selection scheme may fail in returning a (destination/chunk) pair, or return a chunk already possessed by the destination. Initially, we consider that such a failure results in the waste of the opportunity to send a chunk: the sender l has to wait another $c/u(l)$ before trying to send another chunk. A more accurate model will be proposed later in this chapter.

A convenient way to describe a diffusion scheme is by its two elementary selections: destination and chunk. As they are usually not commutative, a scheme is denoted by a *peer selection/chunk selection* or a *chunk selection/ peer selection* pair, according to the order in which they are performed. Concrete examples will be provided later.

Performance

The main goal of a live streaming application is to minimize the playout delay (the time elapsing between the happening of a live event and its display on the user device) while guaranteeing playback continuity and media quality at receiver nodes.

The most important metrics to evaluate the performance of allocation algorithms for such applications are therefore the *diffusion delay* and *diffusion rate*.

The rate/delay performance trade-off achieved by a given algorithm is evaluated through the diffusion function r, where $r(t)$ is the probability that

Figure 1. Performance metrics associated with the diffusion function: rate and delay

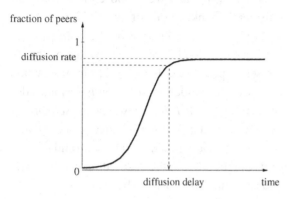

it takes no more than *t* time units for an arbitrary chunk created by the source to reach an arbitrary peer. Equivalently, *r(t)* is the fraction of peers that receive any given chunk no later than *t* time units after its creation, averaged over all chunk transmissions.

A diffusion function is typically S-curved, as illustrated by Figure 1. We refer to the asymptotic value of *r(t)* as *t* tends to infinity as the *diffusion rate*. This corresponds to the average fraction of chunks received by an arbitrary peer; equivalently, this is the average fraction of peers that eventually receive any given chunk.

It is also convenient to define the *chunk miss ratio* (or simply *miss ratio*) as the complementary value of the diffusion rate, i.e. the probability for an arbitrary peer to miss a chunk.

As concern the *diffusion delay* we should distinguish two main metrics: the *average diffusion delay* and the *maximal diffusion delay* (which we use by default). The former is defined as the time needed for a chunk to reach a peer on average. The latter is defined as the delay it takes for an arbitrary chunk to reach a fraction 1-ε of the peers that will eventually receive that chunk, where ε is an arbitrary, small constant.

Another important metric to take into account for the evaluation of diffusion schemes is the *overhead*, which is the difference between the bandwidth used by peers (throughput) and the

actual data received (the diffusion rate, or goodput). We can distinguish the overhead related to the maintenance of the knowledge overlay, the overhead needed to negotiate chunk exchanges, and the overhead created by unnecessary data transmission (for instance sending two copies of the same chunk to a given peer).

OPTIMAL DIFFUSION SCHEMES

In this section, we focus on diffusion schemes whose performance has been proven optimal in specific scenarios. In particular, we consider performance optimality in terms of diffusion rate and diffusion delay. We only consider effective data transfers, and we do not take directly into account other overheads like control messages, protocol overheads and so on.

In live streaming, as for all other fixed-rate applications, the maximal goodput *d* achieved by a node cannot be larger the content generation rate i.e. the stream rate *SR* (but the throughput can). If there are not enough resources available, the effective throughput is necessary lower for some nodes. We say that a diffusion scheme is *rate optimal* if it perfectly exploits the available bandwidth. In other words:

- the overhead is small, so goodput and throughput are almost the same;
- if there are enough resources available, then *d=SR* for all nodes of the system;
- if not, the sum of the throughputs is equal to the total available bandwidth.

Please refer to Benbadis *et al.* (2008) for more details. In particular, in a scenario where the bandwidth shared by every node is on average equal to the stream rate, a scheme achieving optimal diffusion rate is able to provide every chunk to every peer.

As concern delay optimality, it has been shown that in a homogeneous system, where all peers provide an amount of bandwidth equal to the stream rate, the minimal diffusion delay is $\log_2(i)+1$ time units, where i is the number of peers receiving a given chunk, and a time unit is the time needed by a peer to upload a chunk (all peers upload exactly one chunk per time unit). Therefore, we say a scheme is *delay optimal* if the last peer receiving a given chunk gets it in $\log_2(i)+1$ time units after it has been generated by the source. The minimal diffusion delay in heterogeneous system is more complex, but some bounds have been proposed (Liu, 2007; Mathieu, 2009).

There is a natural trade-off between diffusion rate and delay. The diffusion rate is typically maximized by a homogeneous dissemination of chunks among peers, irrespective of the age of these chunks. However, such age-agnostic dissemination may lead to high diffusion delays.

On the other hand, to minimize the diffusion delay, priority should be given to the transmission of the more recent chunks rather than to the homogeneous dissemination of chunks among peers. The price to pay is a sub-optimal diffusion rate because older chunks are not retransmitted anymore by a given peer once it has received fresher ones.

Zhang *et al.* (2007) focus on throughput optimization. They propose an optimization framework to model the chunk scheduling problem and they derive a min-cost flow formulation to solve it in polynomial time. This solution is centralized and therefore not directly applicable to peer-to-peer systems, but they derive a sub-optimal distributed heuristic based on a local optimal chunk scheduling performed at every node.

Zhang *et al.* (2007) prove that pull-based protocols can achieve near optimal capacity utilization and throughput. This optimality strongly depends on parameter settings, and an important trade-off between control overhead and diffusion delay emerges. To improve performance, they propose a hybrid push-pull protocol but they do not provide optimality results for it. In a nutshell, the protocol pushes packets along the near-optimal diffusion trees formed by the pull technique.

Massoulié *et al.* (2007) prove the rate optimality of the so-called *most deprived peer/random useful chunk* algorithm, and Sanghavi, Hajek and Massoulié (2007) prove the delay optimality of the *random peer/latest blind chunk* algorithm (these algorithms are detailed further in this chapter). It turns out, however, that the delay performance of the former is poor due to the random chunk selection, while the rate performance of the latter is poor due to the random peer selection.

Bonald *et al.* (2008) prove that the *random peer/latest useful chunk* algorithm can achieve optimal diffusion rate within a delay of $\log_2(n)+O(1)$, where the $O(1)$ additive term is a random variable bounded in probability uniformly in the number of peers n. However, as we are going to highlight later, when the system is close to a critical regime, this additive constant may be significant and other schemes can achieve optimal rate dissemination in shorter times. This has also been shown by Zhou et al. (2007), which derive recursive formulas to describe the diffusion functions of *latest useful* and *earliest useful* chunk selection policies, and of a *mixed latest/earliest strategy*. They show that latest useful is not optimal for any given delay and that the mixed strategy can achieve a better diffusion rate within the same delay.

Bonald *et al.* (2008) also show that the *random peer/latest blind chunk* algorithm can achieve optimal diffusion rate too, if coupled with source coding. Such a diffusion scheme is known to achieve a diffusion rate of only $1 - e^{-1}$ in the critical regime (Shangavi *et al.*, 2007). It is thus necessary to add some redundancy to the original signal to allow the peers to recover from chunk losses. They show that the additional delay due to the coding/decoding scheme can be controlled (that is, made be equal to $O(1)$) by bounding the correlation of successive missing chunks.

More recently, Abeni, Kiraly and Lo Cigno (2009) prove that there exists a diffusion scheme that can distribute a chunk to *n* peers in exactly $\log_2(n)+1$ time units. This scheme, first selects the chunk by means of a *deadline-based* chunk selection policy, and then the peer by means of an *earliest-latest* peer selection policy.

An interesting survey on optimality results and open questions about optimal diffusion schemes has been performed by Massoulié (2008).

HOMOGENEOUS BANDWIDTH SYSTEMS

We start our analysis by considering schemes that run on homogeneous systems, where all peers have the same upload capacity. For these scenarios, where there is no need to take into account the respective resources of the nodes, we consider some simple, yet practically interesting, diffusion schemes and we analyze the rate/delay trade-offs they achieve by means of simulations and recursive formulas. This part is mainly based on our contribution in *Epidemic Live Streaming: Optimal Performance Trade-Offs* (Bonald, Massoulié, Mathieu, Perino and Twigg, 2008).

Model and Algorithms

The time unit is defined as the time needed for any peer to upload one chunk; in other words, the time is normalized such that $c/u=1$. The source creates a sequence of chunks, numbered 1, 2, 3, ..., at rate λ (expressed in chunks per time unit), and sends each chunk to one of the *n* peers, chosen uniformly at random. We say that the system is in *underload* regime if $\lambda<1$, in *critical* regime if $\lambda=1$ and in *overload* regime if $\lambda>1$. The exact critical value is indeed $1+1/(n-1)$ (Benbadis *et al.*, 2008), but we use 1 as a valid approximation for *n* large enough.

In the overload regime, some peers can only receive a fraction of the chunks sent by the source: there is not enough available bandwidth to sustain the rate for all peers. Nevertheless, peers may

successfully decode the original audio or video streaming signal if some redundancy has been added to this signal and is included in the chunks sent by the source. Thus all three regimes are of practical interest.

In this section, we shall restrict the analysis to the following epidemic (push-based), peer/chunk, selection schemes:

- **Random peer:** The destination peer is chosen uniformly at random among the neighbors of *l*;
- **Random useful peer:** The destination peer is chosen uniformly at random among those neighbors *v* of *l* such that $B(l)\backslash B(v) \neq \emptyset$. When the chunk *b* is selected first, the choice of the destination peer is restricted to those neighbors *v* of *l* such that $b \in B(v)$;
- **Most deprived peer:** The destination peer is chosen uniformly at random among those neighbors *v* of *l* for which $|B(l)\backslash B(v)|$ is maximum. When the chunk *b* is selected first, the choice of the destination peer is restricted to those neighbors *v* of *l* such that $b \in B(v)$;
- **Latest blind chunk:** The sender peer *l* chooses the most *recent* chunk (that is, the chunk of highest index) in its collection $B(l)$;
- **Latest useful chunk:** The sender peer *l* chooses the most recent chunk *b* in its collection $B(l)$ such that $b \in B(v)$ for at least one of its neighbors *v*. When the destination peer *v* is selected first, *b* is the most recent chunk in the set $B(l)\backslash B(v)$.
- **Random useful chunk:** The sender peer *l* chooses uniformly at random a chunk *b* in its collection $B(l)$ such that $b \in B(v)$ for at least one of its neighbors *v*. When the destination peer *v* is selected first, *b* is chosen uniformly at random in the set $B(l)\backslash B(v)$.

A rich class of push-based schemes follows from the combination of these peer/chunk se-

Table 1. Some push-based diffusion schemes

Notation	Scheme
rp/lb	Random peer/latest blind chunk
rp/lu	Random peer/latest useful chunk
dp/lu	Most deprived peer/latest useful chunk
dp/ru	Most deprived peer/random useful chunk
lb/rp (= rp/lb)	Latest blind chunk/random peer
lb/up	Latest blind chunk/useful peer
lu/up	Latest useful chunk/useful peer
lu/dp	Latest useful chunk/most deprived peer

lection algorithms. When a given peer has the opportunity to send one chunk, each scheme can possibly propose a different chunk and destination for that peer. The schemes considered in this section are summarized in Table 1. A toy example for understanding the differences between them is proposed by Bonald *et al.* (2008).

We assume that the time is slotted, with one slot per time unit, so that the transfer of any chunk by any peer takes exactly one time slot. The source sends $\lfloor\lambda\rfloor$ chunks per time slot, plus one additional chunk with probability $\lambda-\lfloor\lambda\rfloor$, corresponding to an arrival rate λ. Note that for $\lambda<1$, the source sends chunks according to a Bernoulli process. In a first approach, we assume that at each slot, every peer can get a perfect knowledge of the state of its target peer, including the intended transmissions of other peers to the same target peer. In particular, all conflicts are solved at the beginning of each slot, prior to the chunk transmission. The impact of imperfect knowledge resulting in transmissions of the same chunk to the same target peer will be analyzed later in this chapter for the example of the *lb/ru* scheme.

Recursive Formulas

We propose here to derive recursive formulas for the diffusion function of the *latest blind chunk/ random peer* and the *latest blind chunk/random useful peer* schemes through mean-field approxi-

mations. Under the former, each peer simply sends the latest chunk it has to a randomly chosen peer; under the latter, it sends the latest chunk it has to a randomly chosen peer among those peers that have not yet received this chunk, if any.

We consider a reference scenario with complete graph knowledge. We assume first $\lambda=1$, before extending the results to the overload regime $\lambda>1$. The number of peers $n\,\square$ is assumed to be sufficiently large so that the system may be considered in a mean-field regime where peers are mutually independent. We further assume that, for any given peer l, the event that a chunk belongs to the collection $B(l)$ of chunks owned by l is independent of the event that any other chunk belongs to $B(l)$. The validity of the derived formulas will be assessed by comparison with simulations.

Besides from the work by Bonald, Massoulié, Mathieu, Perino and Twigg (2008), two other papers propose recursive formulas for the diffusion functions of allocation algorithms. The *latest useful*, the *earliest useful* and the mixed *latest/earliest* chunk selection policies are analyzed by Zhou *et al.* (2007). The diffusion functions of *random useful peer/random useful chunk*, *deprived peer* (every sender peer l selects a neighbor v with a probability proportional to the number of useful chunks it has for peer v; this is different from the most deprived peer scheme considered here, where peer l selects the neighbor v for which it has the highest number of useful chunks)/*random useful chunk*, *latest blind chunk/random useful peer*, and *latest useful chunk/random useful peer* are analyzed by Chatzidrossos *et al.* (2009) in case of a limited number of neighbors and in presence of delayed buffer map updates and overlay churning.

Latest Blind Chunk / Random Peer

We first consider the *lb/rp* scheme. Recall that $r(t)$ corresponds to the average fraction of peers that receive any given chunk no later than t time slots after its creation. Without any loss of generality, we assume that some tagged chunk is created at time $t=0$ and that the system is in steady state at that time. Since the source sends each new chunk to a randomly chosen peer, we have $r(1)=1/n$. Now at any time $t\geq 1$, the tagged chunk is the latest of the collection owned by an arbitrary peer i with probability:

$$p(t) = r(t)\prod_{k=1}^{t-1}(1 - \lambda r(k)) \qquad (1)$$

This follows from the independence assumption, noting that for all $k=1, 2,..., t$, $r(k)$ is the probability that a chunk created at time $t-k$ is in the collection $B(i)$ of chunks owned by peer i at time t.

Due to the random peer selection strategy, the number of copies of the tagged chunk that are received by an arbitrary peer at time $t+1$ is a binomial random variable with parameters $(n-1,p(t)/(n-1))$. For large n, this can be approximated by a Poisson random variable with mean $p(t)$. Thus the probability that an arbitrary peer receives at least one copy of the tagged chunk at time $t+1$ is approximately equal to $1-e^{-p(t)}$.

A fraction $1-r(t)$ of the peers that receive the chunk at time $t+1$ actually need it.

We deduce the recursive formula:

$$r(t+1) = r(t) + (1 - e^{-p(t)})(1 - r(t)), \quad t \geq 1, \qquad (2)$$

where $p(t)$ is given by (1).

Latest Blind Chunk / Random Useful Peer

We now consider the *lb/ru* scheme. The only difference with the *lb/rp* scheme is that all transfers are useful as long as some peers need the considered chunk. This gives the recursion:

$$r(t+1) = r(t) + \min(p(t), 1 - r(t)), \quad t \geq 1, \qquad (3)$$

where $p(t)$ is given by (1).

Delayed Updates

As explained earlier, some control messages are needed to maintain a fresh view of the collection of chunks owned by each peer. Delaying some control messages may reduce the overhead but may impact the performance of the system.

A possible way to model such delayed updates it to assume that peers know the state of system in the previous slot, but are not aware of the ongoing transfers of the current slot. Therefore, collisions can occur even under the *lb/ru* scheme when several peers send the same chunk to the same target peer.

Consider the diffusion of the chunk created at time $t=0$. A fraction $1-r(t)$ of the n peers has not yet received this chunk at time t. Thus the number of copies of this chunk that are received by one of these $n(1-r(t))$ peers at time $t+1$ is a binomial random variable with parameters $(n-1,p(t)/n(1-r(t)))$, where $p(t)$ is given by. For large n, this can be approximated by a Poisson random variable with mean $p(t)/(1-r(t))$. Thus the probability that a peer that has not yet received the considered chunk at time t receives at least one copy of this chunk at time $t+1$ is approximately equal to $1-e^{-p(t)/(1-r(t))}$. We deduce the recursive formula:

$$r(t+1) = r(t) + (1 - r(t))(1 - e^{\frac{-p(t)}{1-r(t)}}), \quad t \geq 1. \qquad (4)$$

Overload Regime

In the overload regime, $\lfloor\lambda\rfloor$ new chunks are created by the source at each slot, plus one additional chunk with probability $\lambda - \lfloor\lambda\rfloor$. The diffusion processes of these $\lfloor\lambda\rfloor$ or $\lfloor\lambda\rfloor + 1$ chunks will interfere in the diffusion process. We number these chunks as 1, 2, ..., $\lfloor\lambda\rfloor$ (or $\lfloor\lambda\rfloor + 1$), where chunk 1 corresponds to the last created chunk. Thus chunk 1 has priority over chunk 2, chunk 2 over chunk 3, and so on...

Now let r_i be the diffusion function associated with a chunk of index i. Again, we assume that some tagged chunk of index i is created at time $t=0$ and that the system is in steady state at that time.

At any time $t \geqq 1$, this chunk is the latest of the collection owned by an arbitrary peer u if u has got it and hasn't got any fresher chunk. This happens with probability:

$$p_i(t) = r_i(t)\prod_{j=1}^{i-1}(1-r_j(t)) \times \prod_{k=1}^{t-1}\left[(1-(\lambda - \lfloor\lambda\rfloor)r_{\lceil\lambda\rceil}(k))\prod_{j=1}^{\lfloor\lambda\rfloor}(1-r_j(k))\right].$$
(5)

There are now $\lceil\lambda\rceil$ recursive formulas, one per diffusion function r_i. These can be deduced from (2), (3) and (4) by replacing the functions r and p by r_i and p_i, respectively, for each considered diffusion scheme. The global diffusion function follows then by averaging:

$$r(t) = \frac{1}{\lambda}\left((\lambda - \lfloor\lambda\rfloor)r_{\lceil\lambda\rceil}(t) + \sum_{i=1}^{\lfloor\lambda\rfloor}r_i(t)\right).$$
(6)

Validation

Empirically, the proposed formulas are quite accurate for both rate and delay (Bonald *et al.*, 2008). The most significant difference concerns the *rp/lb* scheme, where the formula overestimates the delay for some underloaded regimes up to a 10% error. Regarding the *lb/up* scheme, the delay estimation is very good but the formula slightly overestimates the rate near the critical regime (λ close to 1), with an error less than 4%. Finally, the formula of the *lb/up* scheme with imperfect knowledge slightly overestimates both delay and rate for slightly underloaded regimes (error less than 6% for both metrics). Interestingly, the anomalies occur at the maximum source speed λ for which the diffusion rate is very close to 1; this is due to the fact that the formulas approximate the fraction of peers that need any given chunk

at time t by a deterministic value $1-r(t)$, which becomes a weak estimate for these specific regime.

Simulation Results

In this section, we present the evaluation of the rate/delay performance trade-offs achieved by the push-based diffusion schemes of Table 1 by means of simulations (Bonald *et al.*, 2008). Unless otherwise specified, results are derived for $n=600$ homogeneous peers with a complete graph, which corresponds to an optimal diffusion delay of $\log_2(n) + 1 \approx 10$ slots. Chunks that arrive more than 50 slots after their creation are not taken into account, which is representative of a real live streaming system with limited playback delay. In particular, the diffusion rate is approximated by the value of the diffusion function $r(t)$ at time $t=50$, and we consider as the delay the time needed to reach 95% of $r(t)$.

Reference Scenario

We first consider a reference scenario that consists of a complete graph in the critical regime $\lambda=1$. Figure 2 shows the corresponding diffusion functions. Recall that the time unit is the slot duration, which corresponds to the transmission time of a chunk by any peer.

In such a scenario, the simulations show that four of the considered schemed, namely *dp/lu*, *lu/dp*, *lu/up* and *lb/up*, clearly outperform the three others. The four of them but *lb/up* achieve an optimal diffusion rate, and all but *dp/lu* show a diffusion delay very close to 10 slots. The *dp/lu* tends to be slower than the other three as a consequence of the priority given to the peer selection over the chunk selection. Then the performance of *dp/ru* and *rp/lb* schemes is good regarding either rate or delay but not both, as predicted (Massoulié *et al.*, 2007; Sanghavi *et al.*, 2007). In fact, the delay performance of the former is poor due to the random chunk selection, while the rate performance of the latter is poor due to

Figure 2. Diffusion in the reference scenario (Bonald et al., 2008)

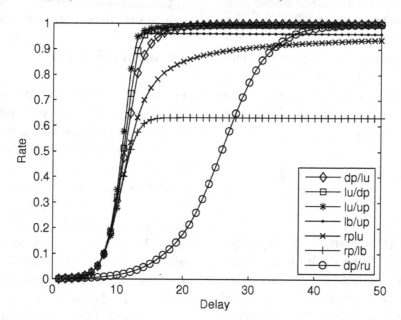

the random peer selection. Finally, the *rp/lu* scheme tends to take a non negligible delay to achieve an acceptable rate, which may be surprising in view of the delay optimality of this scheme stated by Bonald *et al.* (2008). This is because the optimality result is not valid in the considered critical regime. Moreover, we shall see later that the additional constant delay predicted is significant even in the underload and overload regimes, as soon as the source speed λ is close to 1.

To summarize, we observe that the latest chunk selection policy can achieve near optimal diffusion delays, and, if it is coupled with a useful chunk selection, it can also achieve optimal diffusion rate. To select the peer first may reduce diffusion rate because, when the selection is performed, the sender peer is not sure to have useful chunks for the target peer. Then again, this can be circumvented by selecting a peer for which there is useful chunks. However, useful peer/chunk selection first should require higher overhead because a fresher view of neighbor buffers is required with respect to a blind selection. A possible way to

lower overhead is to reduce the neighborhood size, which we investigate later.

Impact of the Number of Peers

If we vary the number of peers of the system, simulations show the following:

- All schemes but the *dp/ru* have an optimal diffusion delay of $\log_2(n)+O(1)$, which shows the good scalability of these schemes. The additional constant is significant for the *rp/lu* scheme (around 25 slots), moderate for the *dp/lu* scheme (between 5 and 10 slots), slight for the other schemes (less than 5 slots). Note that the poor delay performance of the *dp/ru* scheme may impact the rate, as a deadline exists for the transmission of a chunk.
- The diffusion rate is constant for all schemes but the *lb/up* for which it increases with *n*, suggesting the asymptotic rate optimality of this scheme. As expected, the diffusion rate of *rp/lb* stays equal to $1-e^{-1}$.

The *rp/lu* scheme, where the last useful chunk is selected, achieves a rate close to 0.93. All the other schemes but *dp/ru* (cf above) achieve an optimal diffusion rate for all values of *n*.

Impact of Bandwidth Provisioning

Remember that the chunk generation rate λ is an indication of the bandwidth provisioning of the system. For the *rp/lu* scheme, we observe a significant delay not only in the critical regime λ=1 but in all regimes close to critical. This means that the additional constant delay is far from negligible.

The *rp/lb* scheme achieves a diffusion rate close to $1-e^{-1/\lambda}$ with low delay, as expected (Sanghavi et al., 2007).

The performance of the other schemes is nearly optimal for both rate and delay, except for the *dp/ru* and *dp/lu* schemes that behave poorly in overload regime. Note that the *dp/ru* scheme doesn't reach any steady state, which is a consequence of the random chunk selection coupled with the fact that each peer receives at most a fraction 1/λ of the chunks. Intuitively, in an overloaded regime, there are always old chunks to send, and *dp/ru* tries to send them; therefore the average relative age of chunks sent will grow linearly with the age of the stream, while a steady state would require that age to remain bounded.

Restricted Neighborhoods

A complete overlay graph presents a lot of practical issues: each node must be aware of all participants of the system (and it must be updated in case of arrivals or departures). Moreover, when a chunk exchange requires to know the current status of neighbors (this is for instance mandatory for *most deprived peer* schemes), the overhead burden can become prohibitive. On the other hand, for schemes like the *rp/lu*, where the blind peer selection reduce the need of fresh information to only one selected peer, or for completely blind

schemes like the *rp/lb*, which do not require any information at all, the issue is lessened.

We propose to investigate three basic ways to bypass the overhead issue and make feasible the deployment of all the schemes presented here, and to analyze the impact of a limited knowledge on the performance. We consider:

- **Static graph**, with a limited number of neighbors for every node. Bonald *et al.* use an Erdös-Rényi graph with an average degree of 10, that ensures the graph is connected with high probability for the considered set of *n=600* peers. The graph remains the same during the whole diffusion process.

- **Random graph**: for each chunk transmission, the sender peer selects uniformly at random two peers among the *n-1* other peers; the diffusion scheme then applies to these two potential target peers. Note that the graph is now dynamic.

- **Adaptive graph** is an intermediate between the two solutions above. For each chunk transmission, the sender peer keeps track of the last target peer and selects uniformly at random another peer among the *n-2* other peers; again, the diffusion scheme then applies to these two potential target peers. Note that this technique is somewhat reminiscent of the ``optimistic unchoking'' used by BitTorrent (Cohen, 2003).

The impact of these techniques on scheme performance greatly depends on both the schemes and scenarios (Bonald *et al.*, 2008). However, some trends arise: for most diffusion schemes, the static restriction of the neighborhood strongly reduces the diffusion rate. This is particularly true for the *dp/lu* and *dp/ru* schemes in heterogeneous cases, where chaotic results are observed, which illustrates the sensitivity of the most deprived peer selection scheme to the network structure.

The adaptive neighborhood, on the other hand, increases the diffusion delay of most schemes.

Overall, it turns out that the basic random graph approach, where the sender peer selects two potential target peers at random, achieves the best trade-off. The performance degradation is slight in most cases compared to the complete graph. In particular, the top three schemes have very good performance, even in the worst case of heterogeneous networks in the critical regime. Moreover, the *rp/lu* behaves as in the complete graph case (and so do *rp/lb*). This is not surprising because the peer is randomly selected anyway so the reduction to a random set of potential recipients cannot affect the performance.

From that perspective, the best compromise for real deployment in homogeneous systems is provided by selection policies like *rp/lu*, where a useful chunk selection is performed over only one peer. The drawback is that sometimes the selection of a peer may not be useful because the sender peer has not useful chunk for it. A possible solution is to select more than one peer in order to increase the probability to find a useful chunk. We investigate the impact of the size of this probe set later in the chapter.

HETEROGENEOUS SYSTEMS AND RESOURCE-AWARE ALGORITHMS

The practically interesting case of heterogeneous upload capacities is much less well understood than the homogeneous case we just considered. Of all strategies above, the *dp/ru* scheme is the only one for which optimality results (rate-optimality) exist for heterogeneous upload capacities (Massoulié *et al.*, 2007). Moreover, the considered schemes do not take into account upload capacities when performing peer selection.

According to simulations, when introducing some heterogeneity in the system (other parameters, including the global bandwidth provisioning, being the same), the performance of the top three

schemes (*dp/lu, lu/dp, lu/up*) worsens for both rate and delay. In particular, the diffusion delay can double for scenarios where the ratio between the maximal and minimal upload bandwidths (the bandwidth condition number) is 4. The impact of heterogeneity is less significant for the *rp/lu* scheme; in particular the diffusion rate remains approximately unchanged. Regarding the *rp/lb* and *lb/up* schemes, the diffusion delay is almost insensitive to heterogeneity, but the diffusion rate is strongly impacted, especially for the latter.

Another key phenomenon that occurs with heterogeneity is the variability of the diffusion of distinct chunks: while for homogeneous systems all chunks' diffusions are pretty much similar (little variance), for heterogeneous systems, some chunks are quickly disseminated with a low miss ratio while others take a longer time to achieve a lower rate. This is illustrated by Figure 3 for the *rp/lu* scheme.

When looking in details at the reasons for this dispersion in the heterogeneous case, it appears that the quality of a given chunk's diffusion is mostly determined by its early dissemination (where and when the very first copies of the chunk are sent): as predicted by the intuition, having the first copies of a chunk located in rich peers (in term of bandwidth) is far better than the opposite. Because of the competition between chunks, this early differentiation can hardly be compensated after that, except if a *rarest chunk* policy is used, which is not considered here (the dispersion is reduced, but the overall performance can be impacted). For delay-aware schemes like the *latest useful* ones, the competition actually accentuates the difference (the dissemination of under-represented chunks tends to be jammed by the dissemination of fresher, over-represented, chunks). This highlights the interest of using resource awareness in peer selection. In particular, the resources of the first peers receiving a given chunk are crucial for the final diffusion performance.

We therefore consider diffusion algorithms that take into account the resources shared by

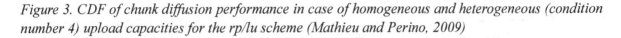

Figure 3. CDF of chunk diffusion performance in case of homogeneous and heterogeneous (condition number 4) upload capacities for the rp/lu scheme (Mathieu and Perino, 2009)

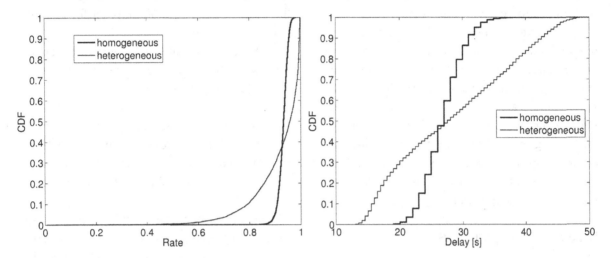

nodes when performing the selection. As the most important resource in live streaming systems is the network bandwidth, we consider diffusion schemes targeting to be aware of the bandwidth provided by peers. Nevertheless, we argue that a certain level of altruism (agnostic selection, like the one performed in the homogeneous case) is needed for the functioning of the system. In this section, we consider this awareness-agnostic trade-off and we derive a highly versatile model that explicitly takes this trade-off into account, and that can represent several existing resource-aware schemes, as well as new ones.

In particular, we focus on the peer selection process while for the chunk selection we just consider the two simple selection policies *latest blind (lb)* and *latest useful (lu)* of the previous section. We argue that to deal with heterogeneous peers, chunk selection is less crucial while it is very important to optimize peer selection. This is true only if chunks are all equal in size and if they all have the same importance. On the contrary, if some chunks have higher priority or are bigger than others, for example because they have been coded with layered techniques, the chunk selection policy plays an important role (Liu *et al.*, 2007).

For an easier understanding of the impact the awareness has on selection policies, we consider diffusion schemes where the peer is selected first, although our model can be extended to chunk selection first. We argue that, if the chunk is selected first, the peer selection is restricted to the peers missing the given chunk, so that resource awareness is potentially limited. Consider for example, a tit-for-tat peer selection policy. If only free-riders are missing the selected chunk, the Tit-for-Tat policy has no effect on the peer selection. Moreover, as said before, peer first schemes are more adapted to a practical implementation because they potentially generate low overhead while providing near-optimal rate/delay performance.

Mesh-based diffusion schemes designed to deal with heterogeneous upload capacities have mainly been studied by means of simulations (da Silva *et al.*, 2008; Liu *et al.*, 2007) or experimental evaluation (Pianese and Perino, 2007; Picconi and Massoulié, 2008). Analytical studies of resource-aware algorithms for P2P systems have mainly been performed for file-sharing (Qiu and Srikant, 2004; Gai *et al.*, 2007), or for generic applications by means of a game theory approach (Buragohain *et al.*, 2003; Ma *et al.*, 2006; Zhao *et al.*, 2008). As concern live streaming, Chu *et al.* (2004) propose a framework to evaluate the achievable download performance of receivers as a function of the altruism from the bandwidth budget perspective. They highlight that altruism has a strong impact on the performance bounds of receivers, and that a small degree of altruism brings significant benefit. The same authors also propose a taxation model in which peers with more upload capacity supply the missing bandwidth of poorer peers. Lin *et al.* (2008) propose a game-theoretic framework to model and evaluate incentive-based strategies to stimulate user cooperation.

Model and Algorithms

Differently from the previous section, here we consider a continuous model instead of a slotted one, in order to better represent the different resources shared by peers.

In particular, we express for each peer l its upload capacity $u(l)$ as the amount of data per time unit it can upload. For simplicity, we assume a discrete set of U possible upload speeds, and classify peers in U classes $C_1, ..., C_u$ according to their upload capacity. We denote as α_i the percentage of peers belonging to class C_i.

As stated before, we focus on diffusion schemes where the peer is selected first, and for the chunk selection, we just consider *latest blind* and *latest useful* policies. In both cases (blind or useful), the sending time of peer l of class i is defined by $T_i=c/u(l)$ if the selected chunk is indeed useful for the destination peer. If not, the destination peer can send back a notification so that the sender can select another peer.

Peer Selection Process

We now propose a general model for representing various non-uniform peer selection schemes. The non-uniform selection is represented by weight functions $\{H_l\}$. A peer l associates to every neighbor $v \in N(l)$ a weight $H_l(v)$. Typical weight func-

tions will be expressed later for some schemes. $H_l(v)$ can be time-dependent, although we make the possible time variable implicit for avoiding to clutter notation.

Whenever a given peer l can upload a chunk, we assume it can use one of the two following peer selection policies:

- **Aware**: peer l selects one of its neighbors $v \in N(l)$ proportionally to its weight $H_l(v)$.
- **Agnostic**: peer l selects one of its neighbors $v \in N(l)$ uniformly at random.

The choice between the two policies is performed at random: every time a chunk is sent by a peer, the aware policy is selected with a probability W, called the *awareness probability* ($0 \leq W \leq 1$). W expresses how much a peer takes resources into account when performing the selection, so that it represents the level of awareness of the diffusion scheme.

The H_l function and the W variable entirely define the peer selection scheme: when a peer l can upload a chunk, the probability $\beta(l,v)$ that it selects one of its neighbors v is given by

$$\beta(l, v) = \underbrace{\frac{H_l(v)}{\sum_{k \in N(l)} H_l(k)} W}_{\text{Aware}} + \underbrace{\frac{1-W}{N(l)}}_{\text{Agnostic}}. \quad (7)$$

In the following we express H and/or W for some peer selection schemes. Remember that in this section we focus on diffusion schemes where the peer is selected first. This means that, unless otherwise specified, a sender peer has no prior knowledge about the buffer state of its neighbors, so it is not guaranteed that it will have useful chunks for the peer it will select.

Random Peer Selection (*rp*)
The random peer selection is the limit case, where peers are completely unaware of their neighbors'

characteristics. It covers the *rp* schemes analyzed in the previous section for the homogeneous case. We then have $W=0$, and there is no need to define a weight function. This results in

$$\beta(l,v) = \frac{1}{N(l)} \qquad (8)$$

Bandwidth-Aware Selection (*ba*)

This is one of the simplest schemes taking into account the resources nodes devote to the system. A peer l selects one of its neighbors $v \in N(l)$ proportionally to its upload capacity, so we have $H_l(v)=u(v)$. Note that in the homogeneous case, the selection is equivalent to the random uniform selection.

This scheme has been introduced by da Silva *et al.* (2008). However there are two main differences between our model and the framework they propose, as in their work:

- the chunk is selected first, and the bandwidth-aware selection is performed among the neighbors that need the selected chunk from the sender.
- the selection scheme is fully-aware (corresponding to $W=1$ in our model), while we propose to discuss later the influence of the awareness probability W.

Although we focus on an edge-constraint scenario, the upload estimation may differ in practice depending on the measurement points. Our model could be easily generalized by setting $H_l(v)=u_l(v)$, where $u_l(v)$ is the available bandwidth capacity from v to l (although the usefulness of this value for peers other than l may be discussed).

Latency-Aware Selection (*la*)

As latencies matter in a distributed system, it is important to take them into account. The simplest way is to use $H_l(v)=1/RTT(l,v)$, which brings the following advantages:

- in absence of congestion, such function privileges local exchanges;
- overlay connections that use underlying congested links are avoided because the remaining capacity of a link is in inverse proportional to the latency of that link.

Tit-for-Tat Peer Selection (*tft*)

Tit-for-tat mechanisms have been introduced in P2P by the BitTorrent protocol (Cohen, 2003), and have been widely studied for file sharing systems. Such mechanisms can also be very effective in live streaming applications (Pianese & Perino, 2007).

In the original BitTorrent protocol, a subset of potential receivers is periodically selected (Cohen, 2003). Following Liu *et al.* (2007), we propose a simpler protocol where a receiver peer is selected every time a chunk is sent. We propose to drive the peer selection by using as weight function $H_l(v)$ an historic variable that is computed every *epoch* T_e; this historic value indicates the amount of data peer l downloaded from peer v during the last epoch. In this way, a peer v is selected by a peer l proportionally to the amount of data it provided to l during last epoch.

Data-Driven Peer Selection

The model we introduced so far is not only able to describe the behavior of resource-aware algorithms, but also to represent diffusion schemes that take into account the collection of chunks B when performing peer selection.

The *most deprived selection* presented for the homogeneous case, as well as the *proportional deprived selection* proposed by Chatzidrossos *et al.* (2009), can be represented by our model.

The former selects the destination peer uniformly at random among those neighbors v of l for which $|B(l)\backslash B(v)|$ is maximal. The weight function can be expressed as:

$$H_l(v) = \begin{cases} 1 \text{ if } |B(l) \setminus B(v)| = \max_{v \in N(l)} |B(l) \setminus B(v)|, \\ 0 \text{ otherwise} \end{cases}$$

$$(9)$$

The latter selects a destination peer v proportionally to the number of useful chunks the sender peer l has for it. The weight function can be expressed as $H_l(v) = |B(l) \backslash B(v)|$.

In the following we are not going to analyze these data-driven peer selection schemes because we focus on resource-aware policies.

Hybrid Selection

It is possible to mix several weighting functions in order to handle more than one parameter of the system. However, mixing different functions while preserving the importance of each individual weight is quite complex and we will not investigate it in this chapter. An example of hybrid selection schemes can be found in Christakidis *et al.* (2009).

Implementation Issues

The simplicity and strength of the bandwidth-aware selection comes from the fact that it directly uses the amount of bandwidth provided by a node as weight function. The upload capacity can be measured by means of bandwidth estimation tools, or can be provided by an external oracle/tracker. However, both approaches highlight several practical drawbacks.

In the case of measurements made by the peers themselves, known bandwidth estimation tools may be inaccurate, particularly when used in large-scale distributed systems (Croce *et al.*, 2009). Moreover, the measured value may vary over time according to network condition, so that the measurement should be frequently repeated generating high overhead and interference.

If some tracker or oracle is used, the upload capacity monitored by the central authority can be a nominal one, provided by the peers, or can be inferred from measurements made from different points. Apart from accuracy issues, the authority providing the information, as well as the measurement points, should be trusted and should not cheat on the values it provides.

In our model we do not take all these issues into account, but we argue that this scheme is currently hard to implement in real systems. However, some projects, like Napa-Wine (http://www.napa-wine.eu/), or standardization efforts, like ALTO (http://www.ietf.org/html.charters/alto-charter.html), are working in order to provide reliable resource-monitoring to peers by using both oracle and measurements at nodes.

On the other hand, with *tit-for-tat* mechanisms every peer can easily evaluate the amount of data provided by its neighbors. This information is trusted and very accurate while it requires no overhead at all. The issue is more to ensure that such mechanisms are efficient to improve the system performance, and are able to discriminate peer resources, giving advantages to nodes contributing the more to the system.

As concern data-driven peer selection, as stated in the previous section, it generates a lot of overhead and suffers of strong performance degradation if the neighborhood is restricted. Moreover, this selection scheme is very sensitive to *cheating* because it is based on information provided by neighbors. In fact, a peer can largely increase the probability of being selected by simply advertising altered chunk collections and pretending to possess less chunks than it actually does.

Recursive Formulas

As in the homogeneous bandwidth scenario, it is possible to derive recursive formulas to describe the diffusion function of some schemes. However, the heterogeneous case is more complex because of the different upload capacity of peers, the consequent different definition of time slot and the variability of the diffusion performance highlighted before.

Model and formulas for the heterogeneous scenario are not described here but are reported in Mathieu and Perino (2009). They are more complex and slightly less accurate than in the homogeneous case but allow a good approximation of scheme diffusion performance anyway. They allow analyzing a large number of scenarios faster than simulations, which are more accurate but take longer time to run.

Simulation Results

In this section, we evaluate the rate (or miss ratio)/delay trade-off achieved by resource aware selection schemes (we consider here the average delay, i.e. the time needed for a chunk to reach a peer on average). In particular, we focus on the performance of three representative peer selection policies: random peer (*rp*), bandwidth-aware (*ba*) and tit-for-tat (*tft*). We used a customized version of an event-based simulator developed by the Telecommunication Networks Group of Politecnico di Torino (http://www.napa-wine.eu/cgi-bin/twiki/view/Public/P2PTVSim) where we implement the aforementioned schemes.

Unless otherwise stated, we suppose there are *n=1000* peers and we set their uplink capacities according to the distribution reported in Table 2, which is derived from the measurement study presented by Ashwin *et al.* (2006), and has been used for the analysis by Guo *et al.* (2008). We suppose that every peer has about 50 neighbors: $N(l) \approx 50$ (we consider that G is an Erdös-Rényi graph with edge probability equal to 0.05). The source has about 50 neighbors as well, an upload capacity $u_s = 1.1 Mbps$ and uses a *rp* selection policy.

Table 2. Upload capacity distribution with mean 1.02 Mbps

Class	Uplink [Mbps]	Percentage of peers
C1	4	15%
C2	1	25%
C3	0.384	40%
C4	0.128	20%

In order to avoid critical regime effects, we suppose the stream rate *SR=0.9Mbps* that leads to a bandwidth balance of 1.13*SR*. We set the chunk size to *c=0.09Mb*, we suppose that peers have a buffer of 30 seconds and for the *tft* scheme the epoch length is set to $T_e=10s$.

The chunk selection policy considered here is *latest useful*.

Reference Scenario

Like for the homogeneous case, we first study a reference scenario in order to have a first idea of the whereabouts for heterogeneous systems whose diffusion rate/delay performance of the different schemes is pictorially represented in Figure 4 for the four classes. For *ba* and *tft* peer selection we consider two values of awareness probability: *W=1* and *W=0.128* corresponding to a fully-aware and a generous approach respectively. We observe that the schemes that take into account peer contributions/resources tend to decrease the diffusion delay, compared to the agnostic *rp* for all classes. *ba* gives priority to richer peers, so that the diffusion process is speeded up thanks to their high upload capacity placed at the top of chunk diffusion trees. On the other hand, *tft* clusters peer according to their resources (Gai *et al.*, 2007), leading to a similar effect.

Such resource aware schemes increase the diffusion rate of the richer classes C1-C2, while they reduce the one of poorer classes C3-C4. This rate decrease is particularly dramatic in case of a completely aware selection (W=1). On the other hand, if the selection is more generous (W=0.128), this drastic reduction is avoided, but the diffusion delay increases with respect to a fully-aware approach. Anyway, for this W=0.128 value, both *tft* and *ba* brings an overall improvement of the system without impacting the poorer peers too hard.

This clearly highlights a rate/delay/fairness trade-off as a function of the awareness probability *W*.

Figure 4. Chunk diffusion in the reference scenario for classes C_1 (top left), C_2 (top right), C_3 (bottom left), C_4 (bottom right)

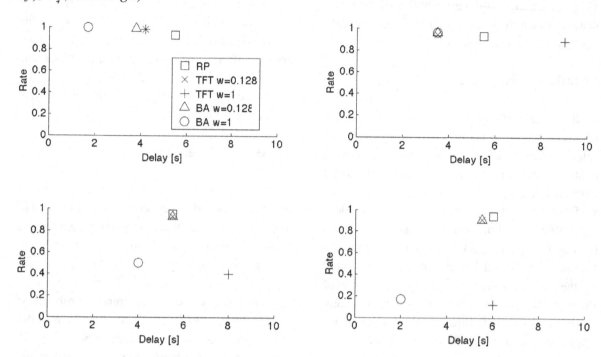

Awareness-Agnostic Peer Selection Trade-Off

Experiments under various bandwidth distributions show that the diffusion delay decreases as the awareness probability increases for all bandwidth classes (Mathieu and Perino, 2009). This indicates that the placement of the nodes with higher upload capacities at the top of the diffusion trees effectively speeds up the diffusion process. We also notice that, by increasing the awareness probability, the delay gap between different classes increases as well. In particular, for W close to 0, all classes achieve the same diffusion delay because the selection is equivalent to *rp*. On the other hand, when $W=1$, the discrimination is maximal because the selection is purely aware.

As concern miss ratio, richer classes take advantage of the increasing awareness. On the other hand, the miss ratio of the poorer classes stagnates until a certain awareness value (depending on the bandwidth distribution), after which peers start missing more and more chunks. The intuition is that richer peers are selected with increasing frequency decreasing their miss ratio and, as a consequence, poorer classes tend to be "forgotten".

We also observe that *ba* slightly outperforms *tft* in most cases. This is not surprising: *ba* weights peers according to their upload capacity, so that it perfectly discriminates them according to their resources. However, the performance gap is very small, making *tft* appealing for real deployment, as it is simpler and more reliable than *ba*. Notice that a pure *tft* approach $W=1$ performs poorly: without agnostic disseminations, the peer clustering generated by *tft* interferes with the chunk dissemination. This effect is less obvious under a *ba* scheme because every peer can be selected with low probability, even poorer ones, giving a minimal chance for a chunk to reach poorer peers.

In all scenarios, we observe the presence of a minimum suitable value of awareness probability.

Empirically, it does not seem interesting to select an awareness probability $W < 0.1$ because there is almost no gain with respect to a *rp* selection. From this value to $W=1$ a trade-off arises. The awareness improves the performance of the richer peers, but on the other hand, an awareness set too high can make the poorer classes loose lot of chunks, even if there is enough bandwidth. This can be seen as a good property of the system because it incentives peers to contribute more to the system in order to improve their performance. On the other hand, part of the bandwidth is lost. The best value for the awareness probability depends on the application environment and on the intended fairness, but in any case this value should be larger than 0.1 in order to initiate a discrimination of the peers according to their resources, to improve system performance and to recompense peers contributing the more.

Source Scheduling

The performance of a system is deeply impacted by the source capacity and selection policy (Mathieu and Perino, 2009). For instance, when considering a source capacity of *SR*, the source selection of a peer of the richest class can reduce up to an order of magnitude the delay, and generate lower miss ratios with respect to the selection of a peer of the poorest class, while the agnostic random selection stands in-between. However as explained earlier, it is very difficult to estimate the upload capacity of peers for performing a bandwidth-based selection, and the source cannot employ a *tft* mechanism because it is not supposed to download any data.

It is interesting to observe that, if the source has an upload capacity of a few *SR*, a simple *rp* selection performs almost like the richest class selection, the overall performance being greatly improved. This means that, if the source is "slightly" over-provisioned (remind that the system should handle thousands of peers, so a source bandwidth of a few *SR* can be considered negligible with respect to overall bandwidth involved), it does

not need to discriminate peers according to their resources. Note that increasing the source capacity beyond a few *SR* does not seem to be particularly significant for the performance. Regarding the chunk detailed distribution, the variance of both delay and miss ratio decreases by increasing the source upload capacity. Again, the first additional copies highlight the larger variance decrease. This indicates that the chunk diffusion is more stable, and schemes can provide steady performance for a sequence of chunks, by increasing the source upload capacity.

Convergence Time and Epoch Length

We have highlighted that *tft* behaves similarly to *ba* peer selection while being more appealing for real deployment. Such a scheme is driven by the evaluation of peer contributions performed every epoch T_e. As a consequence, algorithms based on *tft* may need a certain period of time, called *convergence time*, before they reach a steady-state where their performance (diffusion delay and miss ratio) is stable.

This leads to another trade-off: having a large epoch time T_e allows a more precise evaluation of the resources, leading to a more accurate peer selection, and therefore to better results like a lower diffusion delay for all bandwidth classes, and a lower miss ratio for richer classes (Mathieu and Perino, 2009). The price to pay is that longer epoch times require longer convergence times, the behavior of the scheme until convergence being close to the one of a *rp* scheme.

OPTIMIZING PARAMETERS

So far we have focused on the design and the analysis of chunk exchange algorithms and we have highlighted a good scheme is essential to mesh-based live streaming systems. For a given scheme however, an optimization at a detailed level of parameters not related to the scheme itself is also important. This involves the fine tuning of dissemination parameters, such as the chunk size, receiver buffer size, number of peers to probe, etc... Intuitively, the chunk size has a significant impact on performance, since smaller chunk sizes may be more efficient but incur relatively higher overhead, and larger chunk sizes have lower overhead but may result in higher delay. The receiver buffer size (relative to chunk size) impacts the diversity in choice available to a peer for transmission. In schemes where random peer choices can be made, probing more than one peer for the decision of chunk exchange may help (power of choices), but it also increases overhead. These are some of the finer details of any dissemination scheme that must be closely examined.

There has been some study on parameter sizing for peer-to-peer file sharing systems. Marciniak *et al.* (2008) have shown that small chunk sizes are not always best for file transfer; Laoutaris *et al.* (2008) propose uplink allocation strategies designed to improve uplink utilization of BitTorrent-like systems. However, results obtained for file sharing systems are not directly applicable to live streaming applications. First, a newly created chunk should be disseminated as fast as possible in live streaming, so there is a strong delay component, naturally limiting the chunk size. Secondly, missing chunks may be acceptable if a resilient codec is used, so optimal values are not always comparable to those in the file transfer case. Then, the buffer size, which is a parameter specific to streaming, can impact the performance (Zhou *et al.*, 2007).

In this section, we investigate dissemination parameters in mesh-based peer-to-peer live streaming through extensive simulations. In particular, we focus on the chunk size, on the probe set size and on the number of parallel upload connections of dissemination algorithms where the peer is selected first.

Methodology

For our analysis we use the event-based simulator already used in the previous section that we customized to take network latencies, control overhead and parallel upload connections into account. With respect to the model used in the previous section, we assume here that every link connecting a pair of peers $\{l, v\}$ is characterized by a constant round trip delay RTT_{lv} and is lossless. We further assume that there are no queuing nor processing delays, so the *transfer delay* (the time for a chunk or a control packet to travel from peer *l* to peer *v*) is equal to *transmission delay*$+RTT_{lv}/2$. The choice of such a network model allows us to discuss schemes results that are not related to transport network congestion or losses.

We consider three representative diffusion schemes where the peer is selected first: *rp/lb*, *rp/lu*, and *ba/lu*. Every peer periodically selects a subset *m'* of its neighbors (the probe set), according to one of the aforementioned algorithms, and probes them in order to discover their missing chunks (except for the case of the *latest blind* scheme). We refer to the set of neighbors probed as the probe set. Based on the responses possibly received, the peer then transmits corresponding chunks.

A peer can upload a chunk to at maximum *m* peers in parallel by fairly sharing its upload bandwidth. It may happen that a peer cannot serve *m* recipients because it does not have enough useful chunks. In that case it uploads the chunks faster (since there are less than *m* active connections), but it may stay idle for the subsequent period of time (because it needs to acquire new chunk maps from newly selected peers). An additional overhead is taken into account at every peer to reply to control messages coming from potential sender peers.

The reference parameters are similar to the one used before: unless otherwise stated we consider a network of 1000 peers, all with the same upload bandwidth u_i=1.03*Mbps*, an unlimited download

Figure 5. Performance as a function of the chunk size: miss ratio (left), average diffusion delay (middle), goodput/throughput/overhead (right) (Hegde et al., 2009)

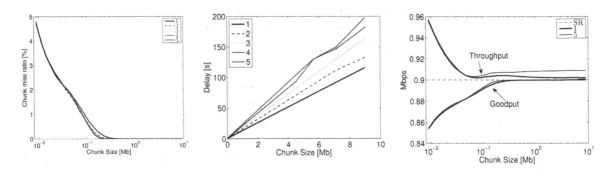

bandwidth and about 50 neighbors, the overlay being an Erdös-Rényi graph. We set the stream rate to *SR=0.9Mbps*.

The latencies between nodes are taken from the data set of the Meridian project (http://www.cs.cornell.edu/People/egs/meridian/). A buffer of size up to 300 chunks is available at all peers, in order to avoid possible missing chunks due to buffer shortage (this implies a buffer size proportional to the chunk size).

Chunk Size and Performance

As a first experiment, we analyze the impact of the chunk size c. The results are shown in Figure 5 for the *rp/lu* scheme with $m=m'$ varying from 1 to 5.

Chunk Miss Ratio

We observe two cases:

- For large chunks (in our experiment, c greater than a few hundred kilobits, the exact value depends on the number of simultaneous connections m), there are no missing chunks.
- As the chunk size goes below a certain critical value, chunks start to miss, roughly proportional to the logarithm of the chunk size.

This phenomenon can be explained as follows: the time between two consecutive chunks is c/SR, and is therefore proportional to the chunk size c. When c is big enough (all other parameters being the same), we can assume that more and more control messages per chunk can be exchanged between peers. This should achieve a proper diffusion, provided enough bandwidth is available, since a sender peer will have enough time to find a neighbor needing a given chunk. On the contrary, when c/SR is too small, peers do not have enough time to exchange control messages, resulting in missing chunks. Note that increasing m slightly improves the performance.

Delay

The main result regarding the average diffusion delay is that it is proportional to the chunk size, and grows with m. In fact, the chunk is the unit of data exchange and a peer can re-transmit a chunk only if it has fully received it. To increase the chunk size increases the time needed to exchange a chunk, and as a consequence the diffusion delay increases. To increase the number of parallel upload connections, leads to a similar effect: the time needed to exchange a chunk increases with the number of connections because the upload bandwidth is shared with more nodes, and as a consequence the diffusion delay increases.

This result is consistent with theoretical results obtained by Picconi and Massoulié (2008), where RTT is neglected and the chunk transmission time is simply considered inversely proportional to the sender's bandwidth. Under that framework, the minimal diffusion delay is given by:

$$d_{\min} = \frac{mc\ln(n)}{\ln(1+m)SR}.$$ (10)

Overhead

The performance with respect to overhead, i.e. the difference between the throughput and goodput, is shown in the right part of Figure 5 (only the curves for $m=1$ and $m=5$ are displayed for readability). For very small chunks, we have a non-intuitive trend, where as c grows, the goodput increases and the throughput decreases (or equivalently, the overhead decreases faster than the goodput increases). This process slows down so that at some point the throughput increases again. For big enough chunks, the overhead becomes roughly constant (for a given m), while the goodput becomes equal to the stream rate (meaning no missing chunks).

For very small chunks, chunk miss ratio is high, which, as mentioned earlier, comes from the fact that not enough control messages can be sent. Asymptotically, we may imagine that only one control message per sent chunk is produced, resulting in an overhead/goodput ratio of c_c/c, where c_c is the size of a control message.

On the other hand, in the limit as the chunk size is increased, we may expect that a peer can send a number of messages per sent chunk that is proportional to the chunk characteristic time c/SR. This would result in an overhead ratio proportional to c_c/SR, and thus independent of c (but not of other parameters like the median RTT or m).

Suitable Range for c

In light of the study above, there is a good order of magnitude for suitable chunk size. For the parameters considered here, c should be greater than $0.06 Mbps$ (which corresponds to about 15 chunks per second) and smaller than $0.3 Mbps$ (3 chunks per second):

- to send the stream at more than 15 chunks per second is good for the delay (which stays roughly proportional to c), but results in both an increase in throughput and a decrease in goodput;
- goodput and throughput are stationary for c greater than $0.3 Mbps$: using bigger chunks only means longer delay;
- between these values, the choice of c results in a chunk miss ratio/delay trade-off: smaller delay with some missing chunks or greater delay with no missing chunks. Choosing a precise value for c depends then on factors that will not be discussed here, such as the coding techniques used, the required QoS, etc...

One should retain that there is a suitable range for the chunk size, which begins when the chunk characteristic time (c/SR) has the same order of magnitude than the median RTT, and ends an order of magnitude later. This is confirmed by experiments where the RTT distribution is scaled so its average value can vary. Also note that this suitable range does not seem to be directly impacted by the scheme actually used: the performance is obviously impacted by the scheme, but the qualitative behavior with respect to the chunk size is not (Hegde *et al.*, 2009). However, the range may be shifted by a fine tuning of the diffusion parameters, leading to better delays (see below).

Size of Probe Set

In the results presented so far, we have assumed that the number of simultaneous upload connections, m, is identical to the size of the probe set m'. We now consider the impact of probing more peers than the number of simultaneous chunks

Figure 6. m/m' miss ratio/delay trade-offs for two values of c: c=0.15Mb (left) and c=0.035Mb (right)

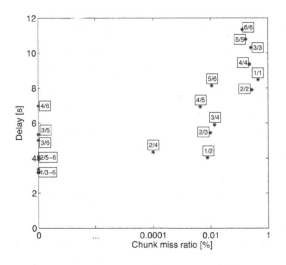
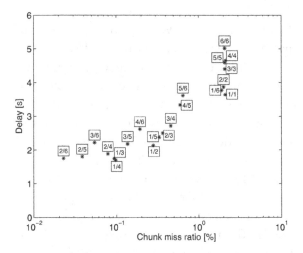

actually sent. A larger probe set affords a sender peer a higher chance to find a recipient peer for whom it has useful chunks (power of choices principle). However, it also increases the overhead, and possibly the delay.

The left part of Figure 6 plots the chunk miss ratio/delay trade-off for various *m/m'* pairs (each point indicates the miss ratio and delay obtained if one uses the corresponding *m/m'* pair). The scheme is *rp/lu*, the bandwidth is homogeneous and the chunk size is set to *c=0.15Mb* (middle of the suitable range for the system). The figure shows that using *m'=m* is not optimal, and some pairs with *m'>m* significantly reduce both delay and missing chunks.

The delay decreases from about 10s for the *m=m'* case, to less than 4s for the 1/3,...,6 cases (meaning *m=1* and *m'=3,...,6*). As for the chunk miss ratio, there are some (*m/m'*) pairs for which no missing chunks could be observed in our experiment: 1/3-6, 2/5-6, 3/5-6, 4/6. This suggests that a consequence of using *m<m'* is a shift of the suitable range for *c*.

In order to verify this interpretation, we now set *c=0.035Mb*, which is clearly below the suitable range *m=m'*. The results are shown in the right part of Figure 6. We observe that no pair

(*m'/m*) can achieve diffusion without missing chunks for such a small value of *c*, however the trade-offs are still worthwhile with respect to the *m=m'* case: using *m/m'=2/6*, we get a delay of 1.7s with a chunk miss ratio of about 0.02%, which represents an excellent trade-off, far better than the one observed for *c=0.15Mb* and *m=m'*. This indicates that *c=0.035Mb* is definitively within the suitable range for *m/m'=2/6*. Also note how the relative efficiency of the various *m/m'* values is impacted by the choice of *c*: for instance, 1/6, which is optimal for *c=0.15Mb*, performs rather poorly for *c=0.035Mb*.

Although the results presented here refer to the *rp/lu* scheme, we performed experiments with other schemes and we observed similar trends, confirming that using a proper *m<m'* can significantly improve the delay. On the other hand, there is a price for going below the suitable range: for a given scheme, the overhead still depends on *m'* and *c*. For instance, *rp/lu*'s overhead stays close to the one displayed in the right part of Figure 5 even for *m<m'*. So using small *c* with a carefully chosen (*m/m'*) pair can reduce the delay, but it requires more throughput.

CONCLUSION

In this chapter, we have considered the diffusion process in mesh-based peer-to-peer live streaming systems from a more theoretical perspective. First, we have proposed an overview of schemes whose performance have been proven optimal in term of diffusion delay, rate or both. We have then identified a large set of practically interesting chunk distribution schemes, and provided explicit formulas to describe the diffusion functions of some of them. We have highlighted the existence of a rate/delay/overhead trade-off, and the significant impact a limited neighborhood and peer heterogeneity may have on the performance of the system.

We have shown that, in heterogeneous systems, the resources of the peers receiving the first copies of a given chunk strongly influence the final diffusion performance. In such scenarios chunk distribution schemes should therefore take into account the resources shared by nodes when performing the peer selection. Nevertheless, a certain level of agnostic selection is needed for the functioning of the system: a kind of equilibrium between aware and agnostic selection should be found that ensures a good utilization of the powerful nodes, while guaranteeing that weaker nodes are not excluded from the diffusion process.

We have proposed a model that explicitly takes this trade-off into account: such model is highly versatile and can encompass several existing resource aware algorithms. We highlighted the critical role the source peer selection policy plays on the performance of heterogeneous systems.

We have also analyzed the importance of crucial parameters, like the chunk size and the probe set size. We have shown the existence of a suitable range of chunk size that is mostly related to RTTs between nodes, and that a probe set larger than the maximum number of parallel upload connections may improve the performance a given scheme can achieve.

REFERENCES

Abeni, L., Kiraly, C., & Lo Cigno, R. (2009). On the optimal scheduling of streaming applications in unstructured meshes. In *networking*.

Ashwin, C. H., Bharambe, R., & Padmanabhan, V. N. (2006). Analyzing and Improving a BitTorrent Network Performance Mechanisms. In *Proceedings of INFOCOM*.

Bailey, N. T. (1975). *The Mathematical Theory of Infectious diseases* (2nd ed.). Halfner Press.

Benbadis, F., Mathieu, F., Hegde, N., & Perino, D. (2008). Playing with the bandwidth conservation law. In *Proceedings of the 2008 Eighth International Conference on Peer-to-Peer Computing* (pp. 140-149).

Bonald, T., Massoulié, L., & Mathieu, F. Perino, & D., Twigg, A. (2008). Epidemic live streaming: optimal performance trade-offs. In *Proceedings of ACM International Conference on Measurement and Modeling of Computer Systems (SIGMETRICS)*.

Buragohain, C., Agrawal, D., & Suri, S. (2003). A Game Theoretic Framework for Incentives in P2P Systems. In Proceedings of the 3rd International Conference on Peer-to-Peer Computing (P2P).

Chatzidrossos, I., Dán, G., & Fodor, V. (2009). Delay and playout probability trade-off in mesh-based peer-to-peer streaming with delayed buffer map updates. *Peer-to-peer Networking and Applications*.

Christakidis, A., Efthymiopoulos, N., Denazis, S., & Koufopavlou, O. (2009). On the architecture and the design of P2P live streaming system schedulers, In *Proceedings of ICUMT.*

Chu, Y. H., Chuang, J., & Zhang, H. (2004). *A Case for Taxation in Peer-to-Peer Streaming Broadcast*. PINS.

Chu, Y. H., & Zhang, H. (2004). Considering Altruism in Peer-to-Peer Internet Streaming Broadcast. In *IEEE NOSSDAV*.

Ciullo, D., Mellia, M., Meo, M., & Leonardi, E. (2008). TV Systems Through Real Measurements. In *Proceedings of Globecom* (p. 2P). Understanding.

Cohen, B. (2003). Incentives Build Robustness in BitTorrent. In *Proceedings of* (p. 2P). ECON.

Croce, D., Mellia, M., & Leonardi, E. (2009). The Quest for Bandwidth Estimation Techniques for large-scale Distributed Systems. In *Proceedings of Hotmetrics*.

da Silva, A. P. C., Leonardi, E., Mellia, M., & Meo, M. (2008). A Bandwidth-Aware Scheduling Strategy for P2P-TV Systems. In *Proceedings of the Eighth International Conference on Peer-to-Peer Computing*.

Gai, A. T., Mathieu, F., de Montgolfier, F., & Reynier, J. (2007). Stratification in P2P Networks: Application to BitTorrent. In *Proceedings of the International Conference on Distributed Computing Systems (ICDCS)*.

Guo, Y., Liang, C., & Liu, Y. (2008). Adaptive Queue-based Chunk Scheduling for P2P Live Streaming. In *Proceedings of IFIP Networking*.

Hegde, N., Mathieu, F., & Perino, D. (2009). Size Does Matter (in Epidemic Live Streaming). *INRIA Research Report RR-7032*.

Laoutaris, N., Carra, D., & Michiardi, P. (2008). Uplink allocation beyond choke/unchoke or how to divide and conquer best. In *Proceedings of CoNEXT 2008, 4th ACM International Conference on emerging Networking Experiments and Technologies*.

Lin, W. S., Zhao, H. V., & Liu, K. J. R. (2008). *A game theoretic framework for incentive-based peer-to-peer live-streaming social networks*. ACASSP.

Liu, Y. (2007). On the minimum delay peer-to-peer video streaming: how realtime can it be? In *Proceedings of the 15th international conference on multimedia* (pp. 127-136).

Liu, Z., Shen, Y., Panwar, S., Ross, K. W., & Wang, Y. (2007). Using Layered Video to Provide Incentives in P2P Streaming. In *Proceedings of the Sigcomm P2P-TV Workshop*.

Ma, R. T. B., Lee, S. C. M., Lui, J. C. S., & Yau, D. K. Y. (2006). Incentive and Service Differentiation in P2P Networks: A Game Theoretic Approach. In *IEEE/ACM Transactions on Networking*.

Magharei, N., Rejaie, R., & Guo, Y. (2007). Mesh or multiple-tree: A comparative study of live p2p streaming approaches. In *Proceedings of the 2007 IEEE Infocom conference*.

Marciniak, P., Liogkas, N., Legout, A., & Kohler, E. (2008). Small Is Not Always Beautiful. In *Proceedings of the Seventh International Workshop on Peer-to-Peer Systems (IPTPS)*.

Massoulié, L. (2008). Optimality Results and Open Problems. In *IEEE CISS*. Peer-to-Peer Live Streaming.

Massoulié, L., Twigg, A., Gkantsidis, C., & Rodriguez, P. (2007). Randomized decentralized broadcasting algorithms. In *Proceedings of the 2007 IEEE Infocom conference*.

Mathieu, F. (2009). Heterogeneity in Distributed Live Streaming: Blessing or Curse? *Orange Labs Research Report RR-OL-2009-09-001*.

Mathieu, F., & Perino, D. (2009). On Resource Aware Algorithms in Epidemic Live Streaming. *INRIA Research Report RR-7031*.

Pianese, F., & Perino, D. (2007). Resource and Locality Awareness in an Incentive-Based P2P Live Streaming System. In *Proceedings of Peer-to-Peer Streaming and IPTV Sigcomm Workshop (P2P-TV)*.

Picconi, F., & Massoulié, L. (2008). Is There a Future for Mesh-Based live Video Streaming? In *Proceedings of the Eighth International Conference on Peer-to-Peer Computing.*

Qiu, D., & Srikant, R. (2004). Modeling and Performance Analysis of BitTorrent-like Peer-to-Peer networks. In *Proceedings of Sigcomm* (pp. 367-378).

Sanghavi, S., Hajek, B., & Massoulié, L. (2007). Gossiping with multiple messages. In *Proceedings of the 2007 IEEE Infocom conference.*

Saroiu, S., Gummadi, P., & Gribble, S. (2002). *A Measurement Study of Peer-to-Peer File Sharing Systems.* Multimedia Computing and Networking.

Zhang, M., Xiong, Y., Zhang, Q., & Yang, Q. (2007). Optimizing the throughput of data-driven peer-to-peer streaming. *Lecture Notes in Computer Science*, 4351.

Zhang, M., Zhang, Q., Sun, L., & Yang, S. (2007). Understanding the power of pull-based streaming protocol: Can we do better? *IEEE JSAC, special issue on advances in peer-to-peer streaming systems.*

Zhao, B. Q., Lui, J. C. S., & Chiu, D. M. (2008). Mathematical modeling of incentive policies in P2P systems. In *Proceedings of NetEcon.*

Zhou, Y. P., Chiu, D. M., & Lui, J. C. S. (2007). A simple model for analysis and design of P2P streaming protocols. In *Proceedings of the IEEE ICNP Conference.*

Chapter 14
A Chunkless Peer-to-Peer Transport Protocol for Multimedia Streaming

Roberto Cesco
Università di Udine (DIEGM), Italy

Riccardo Bernardini
Università di Udine (DIEGM), Italy

Roberto Rinaldo
Università di Udine (DIEGM), Italy

ABSTRACT

Video transmission over IP is currently a hot topic both in entertainment and research communities. A problem that threatens the development of video over IP services is the bandwidth required to serve a potentially very large number of users. In this context, Peer-to-peer (P2P) technologies are considered a possible solution for the distribution of video content to many users. This chapter describes a novel P2P transport protocol suited for live multimedia streaming. The described protocol has low start-up time, it is robust with respect to data losses (due to congestion or node departure) and it can help counteracting the malicious injection of "bogus packets" in the media stream. The proposed protocol can be used with any type of data and, from the application point of view, it appears as a protocol similar to TCP or UDP, making the reuse of existing software and protocols easier.

1. INTRODUCTION

Because of its potentially large user base, Internet is currently considered to be an interesting platform for implementation and deployment of innovative video services. Although a large audience is clearly what a video service provider desires, serving a large number of users requires powerful bandwidth resources[1] to be allocated, on a worst-case basis, to the server(s). Moreover, the bandwidth problem, already a serious issue with video media, will get even worse with new emerging type of multimedia such as 3D data. A possible solution to the bandwidth problem could be the use of IP multicast. Unfortunately, IP multicast is not a universally feasible solution

DOI: 10.4018/978-1-61692-831-5.ch014

Copyright © 2011, IGI Global. Copying or distributing in print or electronic forms without written permission of IGI Global is prohibited.

since it requires multicast-enabled routers which are not widely deployed.

Peer-to-peer (P2P) systems are considered a promising solution for video streaming to a large number of users (Alstrup & Rauhe, 2005, Kozamernik, 2000, Fodor & Dán, 2007, Padmanabhan, Wang, Chou, & Sripanidkulchai, 2002). The reason for this interest is that each new node contributes with its own resources by forwarding the received data to other nodes. This means that although the download bandwidth increases linearly with the number of users, also the available upload bandwidth increases with the number of users. Ideally, if each user were able to provide an upload bandwidth equal to the download one, the server would need only to "seed" few nodes of the network, and the network would take care of the distribution by itself.

What makes media streaming over P2P networks an active field of research is that multimedia streaming (and, in particular, live event streaming) has requirements that are quite different from the requirements of the more common P2P file-sharing applications (e.g., Napster, Gnutella, KaZaA, BitTorrent). Maybe the most important difference is that while in a file-sharing system there is no time constraint, in a streaming context, packets have an *expiration date* and if a node misses a few packets, the user can experience an unacceptable drop in quality. This problem, together with other problems related to P2P streaming (such as the *asymmetric bandwidth* problem or the possibility of *stream poisoning*, analyzed in detail in Section 2.3) makes multimedia streaming a peculiar applicative context for P2P solutions.

This chapter has the following structure. First, in Section 2 we review the main P2P structures, both for file sharing and multimedia streaming, and the requirements that a P2P system for media streaming must satisfy. Successively, in Section 3 we describe a new P2P transport protocol, suited for live multimedia streaming, based on the *chunkless* approach described in (Bernardini,

Rinaldo, & Vitali, 2008) and currently developed as part of the *SourceForge* project corallo[2]. The described protocol does not require buffering and is robust with respect to data losses (due to congestion or node departure) and stream poisoning attacks. Although the protocol was developed for streaming applications, it makes no assumption on the format of transported data, so it can be used with any type of data (audio, video, documents...).

2. BACKGROUND

2.1 Taxonomy of P2P Systems

The goal of this section is to give a brief overview of some of the current P2P systems, with emphasis on systems for live multimedia streaming.

2.1.1 Taxonomy Based on the Application

Most of the current P2P solutions can be classified as P2P software for *content retrieval* (or *file sharing*) or as P2P software for *media streaming*.

Content retrieval refers to those applications where a user uses a P2P network to access some shared content. This is maybe the most popular application for P2P systems. Actually, it is so popular that most of the general public consider P2P as a synonymous of file sharing (and, also, of software piracy).

Media streaming refers to those applications where the P2P network is used to distributed some multimedia content (typically video) among the users. Within the class of systems for media streaming, one can distinguish systems for streaming stored content (video on demand) and systems for streaming live content.

A major difference between the two applicative classes of P2P systems is that media streaming has more stringent time constraints than content retrieval. Indeed, the download of a large (and rare) file can take several hours and still the user can consider it acceptable; with media streaming, instead, packets must arrive at a minimum rate or the user will perceive an unacceptable reproduction quality (e.g., video "freezes"). Time constraints can get especially severe in the case of live streaming where one would like a minimum delay between the event and what the user sees.

2.1.2 Taxonomy Based on the Control/Overlay Structure

The two classes of P2P applications considered here (content retrieval and media streaming) have different requirements for what concerns the creation of the overlay network.

P2P System for Content Retrieval

Since content retrieval is maybe the most popular application of P2P technologies, the number of known solutions is quite large and it is not possible to describe them completely here. We will limit ourselves to recall briefly the main control/overlay structures used in content retrieval and refer the reader to (Lua et al., 2005) for a more complete survey.

In content retrieval applications the user typically wants to access some resource (e.g., a file) available somewhere on the network. Therefore, the most important problem in content retrieval is to *locate* the node(s) with the required resource.

A first solution to the location problem is the centralized approach where a central server is used to index the available resources and keep track of which nodes are currently present. The main drawback of centralized systems (such as *Napster*) is that they have a single point of failure represented by the central server.

In order to avoid the weakness of a single point of failure, distributed P2P systems have been developed. In a distributed system indexing and peer discovery is not carried out by a central server, but by the network nodes (or by a subset of special nodes, as it happens in semi-distributed systems such as KaZaA or BitTorrent). Distributed systems can be further classified in *structured* and *unstructured* systems depending on the technique used to index the network.

- Structured P2P networks typically use Distributed Hash Tables (DHT) to localize a desired content. A DHT is a distributed structure that, as a normal hash table, maps *keys* in *values*. In the context of content retrieval systems, the *value* is the desired content or a pointer to where the content is actually stored, while the *key* is typically a binary word obtained by hashing the content "identifier" (e.g., a file name). Every node of a DHT is "in charge" of a set of keys and it holds the values associated with its key set. The set of keys is assigned to the node when it joins the DHT and it can change when other nodes join or leave the network. There are many possible ways to implement a DHT; for the sake of brevity we do not recall them here but refer the reader to (Lua et al., 2005). Since in a DHT the content is indexed, the time required to locate an uncommon item can be expected to be equal to the time required to locate a very popular one. A drawback that DHTs share with other types of hash tables is that complex queries (e.g., *"find files whose name matches gcc-*.exe"*) are difficult to support.

- Unstructured P2P networks do not use an indexing system, but organize peers in a graph (which can be hierarchical or flat) and employ *flooding* or various graph walk techniques to locate the content stored on the network. Typically, every time a node receives a query it replies with a list of contents that match the query and/or forwards the query to other nodes. This type of approach is quite efficient in locating popular content and it supports complex queries, but it is not suited to find rare items. Several popular P2P file sharing systems (e.g., Gnutella, KaZaA, BitTorrent, and so on) belong to this category. As with structured networks, we refer the reader to (Lua et al., 2005) for a more complete survey.

P2P Systems for Media Streaming

The problem of data access in media streaming application is quite different from the case of file sharing. While in file sharing a user is interested in downloading a specific file that maybe no other user wants, in media streaming there is a community of users, all interested in the same content which is, typically, a stream of data (e.g., a video relative to a live event) and not a file. Therefore, while in content access the main problem is to locate who has the requested file, in media streaming is important to organize a structure that allows for a continuous data flow across the peer community and this reflects itself on the type of P2P structures used for media streaming.

P2P structures for media streaming can be partitioned into tree-based (*rigid*) structures, where data flows along the edges of an oriented graph that remains stable as long as no node joins or leaves the network, and mesh-based (*flexible*) structures, where there is no fixed relationship among the nodes.

Tree-Based Networks

Tree-based systems can be further classified in systems based on a *single or multiple tree.*

In a single tree network, the nodes are connected according to a tree structure. The data source is the root of the tree and each node forwards the received data to its children. Since each node transmits autonomously (i.e., without receiving an explicit request), tree-based networks are typically called *push* networks. The advantage of a tree-based network is its simplicity and its low overhead, since the only control messages that the nodes exchange are those necessary to the initial

handshaking between nodes. The main drawback with a single-tree network is that if an intermediate node suddenly leaves, all the descending nodes will stop receiving data. This problem is especially serious in a media streaming context since data loss can cause problems such as video freezes.

Another important problem in a tree-based network is that most of the nodes are leaves of the tree. Since a leaf has no children, those nodes do not retransmit the received data and do not contribute to the overall upload bandwidth. In order to mitigate the drawbacks of single-tree networks, multiple tree-based networks have been proposed.

In a multiple tree network (e.g., SplitStream, CoopNet, ChunkySpread) the nodes are connected in several "parallel" trees and every tree carries a *sub-stream* obtained from the original stream. A critical property of the sub-streams is that a node must be able to recover the multimedia content (maybe with a lower, but still acceptable quality) even if some sub-streams are not received. Sub-streams can be created, for example, by using Multiple Description Coding (MDC) or Forward Error Correction (FEC) (Fodor & Dán, 2007, Padmanabhan et al.., 2002),

An advantage of a multiple tree network is that, since for every node there is more than one path that goes from the root to the node itself, the node will continue to receive data even when other nodes leave. Another advantage of a multiple tree network is that it can be more efficient than a single tree network since it is possible to build the trees in a way such that every node is an intermediate node in at least one tree.

Mesh-Based Network

A drawback of both types of tree based networks is that they are relatively complex to build. In a high-churn environment, where nodes can leave or join the network at a fast rate, the overhead due to the control messages required to rebuild the network can be non-negligible. Because of this concern, mesh-based networks (such as CoolStreaming (Zhang, Liuy, Liz, & Yum, 2005), AnySee (Liao,

Jin, Liu, Ni, & Deng, 2006), PRIME (Magharei & Rejaie, 2007), PRO (Rejaie & Stafford, 2004), DagStream (Liang & Nahrstedt, 2006)) have been proposed. In a mesh-based network, the stream is partitioned in segments called *chunks* and each node *requires* missing *chunks* to other peers. In order to know which peer has the required chunks, nodes in a mesh-based network exchange *buffer maps* that are descriptions of the set of chunks owned by a node. Mesh based network are often *pull* networks, although this is not universally true and there is lot of discussion about what is better between *push, pull* or hybrid solutions

Mesh networks can further be divided into unstructured and structured mesh networks. In an unstructured mesh network (e.g., PRIME, CoolStreaming) each node connects with a large number of randomly chosen peers, in order to have more neighbors and path diversity. In a structured mesh network nodes are grouped on the basis of their geographical position, in order to lower the propagation delay from the source to the node.

The advantages of mesh-based networks are their intrinsic robustness (since there is no rigid parent-child relationship), their efficiency (every node retransmits to other nodes) and their low building cost (there is no need to check for loop avoidance and no messages are sent to reorganize the network). Their main drawback is the overhead due to the exchange of buffer maps.

It is also worth observing that while a tree-structured network can be naturally used in a streaming context without the need of an explicit division in chunks (as soon as a packet is produced, it is propagated along the tree), mesh structured networks are necessarily chunk-based and this makes their application in a live streaming context more difficult. The solution typically employed for using mesh networks in media streaming requires the use of a *chunk buffer* that is written by the P2P software and read by the media player. This, however, introduces a start-up delay (due to buffer filling) that can be unacceptable to the user. This problem can be mitigated by means of

some "tricks" (e.g., showing the initial part at a lower speed, showing some commercial and/or a signature tune, pre-loading the most popular contents).

2.2 Existing P2P Systems

2.2.1 P2P Systems for File Sharing

The first P2P system for file sharing was the centralized system Napster. Since Napster was centralized, it had a single *point of failure* and this allowed the RIAA (Recording Industry Association of America) to shutdown it. However, Napster caught the attention of the public and stimulated the development of new file sharing systems, but this time based on a distributed approach. Maybe one of the most extreme examples of distributed P2P systems is Gnutella that is *totally server-less* and distributes both the content and the search among the nodes. However, Gnutella suffers from a lack of scalability since queries are *flooded* among the peers and this makes the load on each node grow linearly with the network size.

In order to overcome the loss of scalability of Gnutella, while avoiding the weakness of having a single point of failure, people developed solutions which can be considered intermediate between the server-less structure of Gnutella and the centralized structure of Napster. For example, in BitTorrent (a very popular P2P file sharing system) a user that wants to download a file must first get, via suitable search engines, a metadata *.torrent* file that contains several informations about the required file (e.g., the number of chunks the file has been split into and hash values used to check for the integrity of the chunks). In the *.torrent* file, the user finds also the address of a *tracker* which is a node that keeps track of who is currently downloading the file and who has which chunks (but it is worth noting that also nodes have statistics about the download state). Another example of a partially centralized system (where the query is directed to suitable super-nodes) is KaZaA.

2.2.2 P2P Systems for Media Streaming

Here we briefly review some of the most popular P2P systems for media streaming. It should be said that there are many IPTV services that use the P2P paradigm (e.g., TVants, TVUPlayer, QQLive, PPStream, SopCast, Joost, Octoshape, LiveStation). However, since the details of the implementation of many of these systems are proprietary and generally not available, we will not describe them here.

CoolStreaming (Zhang et al.., 2005) is a mesh system developed in Python. CoolStreaming has a structure similar to *BitTorrent* in the sense that a node, which wants to join a session, first contacts the origin of the program which acts like a BitTorrent *tracker*. A main problem with CoolStreaming is that it may require a large amount of time before a node can receive a stable data stream. This can be a nuisance in a live streaming context.

PPLive is maybe the most popular video streaming system. Since the protocol is proprietary, many details about its structure are not known. However, it seems that it can be classified as a mesh-based system. In order to meet the time constraints, PPLive has two buffers: one is managed by PPLive itself and the other by the media player. A main drawback of this buffered structure is the long start-up delay (approximately between 20 and 30 seconds).

AnySee (Liao et al., 2006) is a P2P live streaming system that adopts a multiple overlay mesh based architecture. The mesh is built with a location based algorithm, in order to match the physical topology. AnySee employs two level of optimization: an *intra-overlay* optimization that processes the join/leave operations of the peers and an *inter-overlay* optimization that builds backup links and cuts off paths with low quality of service.

Vanilla is an implementation of a pull-based P2P live streaming protocol that has been proposed also in combination with network coding.

In (Wang & Li, 2007), an experimental test-bed referred to as Lava has been designed to access the performance of network coding within Vanilla.

VidTorrent is an MIT project of a P2P protocol for real-time streaming, whose source code is publicly available under the GNU GPL.

2.3 Requirements of P2P Networks for Streaming

The goal of this section is to review, in some detail, the features that a good P2P system for media streaming should have.

Robustness to data losses. An important cause of data loss in streaming P2P systems is the sudden departure of nodes. Indeed, if a peer suddenly leaves, the nodes that were receiving data from it must search for another peer. Since the time required to find another peer can be "long" when compared with the video data rate, the overall effect seen by the final user will be a noticeable loss of quality. Therefore, a first requirement is that a P2P streaming system must be robust with respect to data losses, especially the long ones due to node departure.

Adaptability. A second issue with streaming over P2P networks is due to the *band asymmetry*, i.e., the difference between the upload and the download bandwidths available to residential users. Indeed, the upload bandwidth of a residential user can be 8-10 times smaller than the download bandwidth and this means that although a node can have enough download bandwidth to receive multimedia data, it has not enough upload bandwidth to retransmit it. Since in any P2P network the overall upload bandwidth (including the upload bandwidth due to the *servers*) must be equal to the overall download bandwidth, we are interested in exploiting as much as possible the upload bandwidth available at a given node. A good P2P streaming system should be adaptable to the available upload bandwidth, allowing nodes with small bandwidth to contribute, while allowing the efficient exploitation of the nodes with large upload bandwidth (e.g., *supernodes*).

Short startup times. As said above, some P2P streaming solutions store the data received from the network in an internal *buffer*. Although data buffering gives resiliency with respect to node departure and it allows the use of chunk-based approaches with live stream data, data buffering requires the user to wait for the buffer to fill, causing long start-up times. This can be annoying, especially in an IPTV context where a user wants to change "channel" frequently. A good P2P streaming solution should allow short start-up times.

Security. Several attacks in P2P streaming networks are possible, but here we will consider only two attacks specific to P2P streaming. In the *stream poisoning attack* a node "injects" corrupted data in the network. Such data will not decode correctly and, even worse, will be propagated to the whole network by the P2P mechanism. Therefore a good P2P streaming solution should be robust to stream poisoning.

The second type of attack is the *unauthorized* access to the multimedia content (e.g., without paying a subscription). An example of this type of attack is the following: one user subscribes to the service and authenticates itself with the server and receives a list of peers. The user shares this list with one or more friends which can access the content for free. To avoid this, some form of inter-peer authentication must be provided.

NAT friendly. An important problem with any type of P2P application is the fact that most residential users are behind *Network Address Translators* (NAT) and/or firewalls that allow only for the connections that go from the user to the network. Several solutions to the NAT problem are available (Srisuresh et al., 2008). Although the simplest and most reliable solution is to use a node with a publicly visible IP as a "bridge" between NAT-ed nodes, in a live streaming context, this solution would require to the intermediate server to provide the same bandwidth provided by the

user, nullifying the advantage of a P2P system. Because of this, suitable procedures (known as *hole punching procedures*) must be employed in order to allow for the communication among peers. Therefore, a good P2P streaming protocol must contain procedures to deal with the presence of NATs.

2.4 Network Coding

The cornerstone of the protocol proposed here is a *reduction procedure* that allows one to create from the original content stream a number of smaller, independent sub-streams to be exchanged between peers. Since the procedure used to create the sub-stream can be interpreted as a type of *network coding*, it is worth to summarize briefly here the main ideas about this technique.

Network coding has been suggested as a way to distribute in an efficient way some content among several nodes (Ahlswede R. et al., 2000, Li et al., 2003, Koetter & Medard, 2003, Ho et al., 2003, Chou et al., 2003). The basic idea in network coding is to let the nodes exchange linear combinations of the information bytes (in some finite field) instead of the bytes themselves. By a suitable design of the coding scheme one can grant that (1) the destination nodes will be able to recover the original bytes from the received data and (2) the overall throughput will be larger than the throughput that one could obtain by the standard approach. We refer the reader to (Ahlswede R. et al., 2000, Li et al., 2003, Wang & Li, 2007) and the references therein for more details.

About the application of network coding to practical scenarios, it can be said that it has been proved that network coding can increase the throughput in P2P networks for content retrieval (Gkantsidis & Rodriguez, 2005, Gkantsidis et al., 2006) and in wireless networks (Katti et al., 2006). An example of application of network coding in the context of P2P streaming is the experimental test-bed Lava described in (Wang & Li, 2007).

3 THE PPETP PROTOCOL

3.1 Introductory Remarks

In this section we introduce PPETP (Peer-to-Peer Epi-Transport Protocol), a P2P *transport* protocol which addresses most of the desired features outlined above (i.e., robustness to data loss, adaptability to different bandwidths, short start-up times, robustness to stream poisoning and inter-peer authentication). This name was chosen because, from the application point of view (better, from the point of view of the programmer who writes the application), the protocol will be seen as a transport protocol similar to TCP or UDP. We added the prefix *epi-* to emphasize that this is not a true transport protocol but it relies on (it "lies over") a true transport protocol. The transport protocol will be typically UDP (and we will talk of PPETP/UDP), but other choices (such as the *Data Congestion Control Protocol* (Floyd, Handley, & Kohler, 2006)) are possible.

The fact that PPETP is at the transport level has several interesting practical consequences

- PPETP does not dictate a specific network structure, nor the procedures used by the peers to find each other[3]. In other words, PPETP is *transparent to the network structure* and this allows its use with any network topology and peer discovery procedure (centralized or not). See Section 3.1.1 for some examples of possible network topologies and Section 3.3.4 for two examples of peer discovery procedures compatible with PPETP.
- In PPETP the data to be transmitted are just binary packets and no knowledge of the multimedia format is built-in in the PPETP specifications. This means that PPETP is transparent to the data format and it can be used with any type of data and any type of encoding (scalable, multiple description, encrypted, …).

- Finally, the fact of being a transport protocol will allow to reuse existing software and protocols (e.g., the Real Time Streaming Protocol (RTSP) (Arkko, Lindholm, Naslund, Norrman, & Carrara, 2006), the Session Description Protocol (SDP) (Handley, Jacobson, & Perkins, 2006)) by simply extending them to include PPETP as a possible transport protocol. For example, a video stream that in a unicast context would have been sent in RTP (Schulzrinne, Casner, Frederick, & Jacobson, 2003) packets over UDP, can be sent over a P2P network by simply sending the same RTP packets using PPETP as a transport protocol.

From the point of view of the application, PPETP looks like a datagram unreliable protocol (like UDP), but with a connection phase (like TCP). That is, the application receives and sends data organized in *packets* and there is no guarantee that the packets arrive. However, before receiving the data, the node must join the P2P network and the joining step will appear to the application as a connection phase.

3.1.1 Overview of a PPETP Session

In order to ease the description of the protocol, it is worth to introduce some nomenclature used in the following.

Our goal is to broadcast a *content stream*, which is a sequence of *content packets*. Each packet in the content stream is identified by a progressive *sequence number*.[4] The data stream originates from one or more *root servers*. In the P2P network, each *node* receives data from its *upper peers* and sends data to its *lower peers*[5]. Each node has typically several upper peers and several lower peers. The data stream between peers will be called *peer stream* or (for reasons that will be clear in the following) *reduced stream*. These definitions are pictorially summarized in Figure 1.

Table 1. Comparison between the steps carried out to open a PPETP session and a TCP session

Step	PPETP session	TCP session
1	The application opens a new session	The application creates a new socket with socket()
2	The application associates a port to the session	The application binds an address to the socket with bind()
3	The application configures the session (e.g., by setting authentication credentials)	The application configures the socket with setsockopt()
4	The application finds out the addresses of the upper peers (e.g., by querying the root server)	The application finds out the address of the server (e.g., by a DNS query)
5	The application contacts the upper peers	The application contacts the server with connect()
6	The application reads data from the session	The application reads data from the connected socket

Figure 1. Pictorial description of some of the nomenclature used in the paper

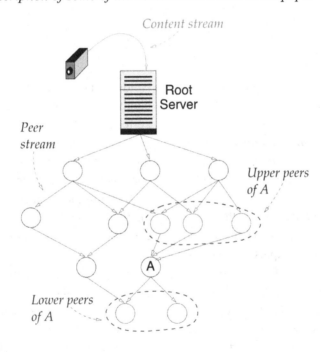

Since some nodes can have an upload bandwidth which is not large enough for transmitting the original content, we allow each node to send to its lower peers a data stream whose bandwidth is R times smaller than the bandwidth of the content stream. The node creates the reduced stream by processing each content packet with a *reduction function*, chosen by the node from a *function pool* that is fixed by the PPETP specifications. The result of the *reduction function* will be called *reduced packet*. Each reduced packet inherits the

sequence number of the original content packet. Reduction functions are the cornerstone of PPETP and are discussed in more detail in Section 3.2; here it suffices to say that reduction functions are designed in a way that (i) the size of the result of the function is approximately R times smaller than the size of the original content packet and (ii) a content packet can be recovered as soon as R different reduced packets are received.

From the point of view of an application, a node joins a P2P network by *opening a PPETP*

Figure 2. Three network structures compatible with PPETP: (a) multiple tree (b) cube-structured network (c) network with nodes with different upload bandwidths; larger circles denote nodes with more upload bandwidth. In all the three schemes the reduction factor is supposed to be equal to 2. Different arrows exiting from the same node denotes different channels

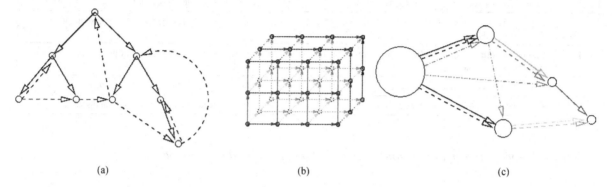

(a)   (b)   (c)

session. From the point of view of the node, the session is uniquely identified by its local *PPETP port number*. Each node provides a maximum number C of *PPETP channels* numbered from 1 to C. Each channel carries a *different* reduced stream and it can be connected to any number of lower peers.

The fact that a node can have more than one channel allows for the construction of many types of network overlays. Few examples of network overlays compatible with PPETP can be seen in Figure 2. Common conventions used in all the structures of Figure 2 are: (1) the reduction factor R is always supposed to be equal to 2, (2) different channels of the same node are depicted as different arrows exiting from the node and (3) if a node has less than two entering arrows, it is supposed to receive the missing data from a source not shown in the figure (for example, the root server).

Figure 2a shows a typical two-tree network. Figure 2b shows a network organized like a cube where each node receives three input streams. Node that even if a node of Figure 2b suddenly leaves, the other nodes still continue receiving data. Figure 2c is interesting since it shows a network with nodes having different upload

bandwidth (a larger circle means a larger upload bandwidth). Note that the largest node in Figure 2c feeds all its three channels to a node. This is possible because each channel carries a different reduced stream, so that the node can recover the content stream from the received data.

Streaming session example It is worth concluding this overview by describing the steps of what could be a typical streaming session over PPETP.

1. At the beginning, the user, using a browser, contacts the server of a program provider. Supposing we are using the SDP format, the server replies with an SDP description of the desired content. The *media description* field (m=) of the reply specifies PPETP as the transport protocol (e.g., RTP/AVP/PPETP/UDP for audio-video data enveloped in RTP packets transmitted via PPETP/UDP), the a=control: attribute gives the address of an RTSP server used for streaming control.

2. The user's browser, on the basis of the Content-Type field, starts an *helper application* (e.g., an external player or a browser plug-in) and gives to it the received data (i.e., the SDP description).

3. The player interprets the description, finds that the streaming will be done over PPETP and opens a PPETP local port. In order to setup the streaming session, the player sends to the RTSP server a SETUP request which includes the PPETP port number. If necessary, server and client authenticate one another by using RTSP or some other mean.

4. The server replies by sending all the informations that are necessary to join the network. For example, the server could send a list of upper peers (giving for each of them the IP address, the PPETP port and the channel number) or maybe the address of few *bootstrap peers* if a distributed peer discovery procedure is employed (see Section 3.3.4). The reply will also include every information that is necessary to configure the PPETP session, for example, the number of output channels the node is expected to open or authentication details such as the size of the packet signature or the server public key (see in the following for details).

Technically, the steps described so far are outside the scope of PPETP, so they could be organized differently, depending on the specific applicative context. What is important is that now the user node knows everything is needed to join the network. At this point, the node chooses its own reduction function(s) and contacts its upper nodes. After completing the handshaking procedure (see Section 3.3.2), the node begins listening for reduced packets. As soon as enough reduced packets with the same sequence number are received, the node

1. reconstructs the corresponding content packet;

2. moves the reconstructed packet toward the application level where will be read by application (i.e., the player) via the PPETP programming interface (see Section 3.4);

3. reduces the content packet and sends it to its lower peers (if any).

3.2 Mathematical Description

As anticipated, the key idea in PPETP is to reduce the upload bandwidth required by a node by applying a *reduction function* (chosen from a suitable *function pool* fixed in the PPETP specifications) to the packets of the content stream. The functions in the function pool are indexed by the elements of a finite set F of *reduction parameters*. We will denote with $S \triangleq card(F)$ the number of elements of F.

Informally, a reduction function is a function which maps a bit-string (i.e., a packet) into a bit-string that is R times shorter. The only constraint we put on the reduction functions is that one must be able to recover the original bit-string when at least R *different* reduced versions (i.e., reduced packets obtained by the application of R different reduction functions) are known.

For the sake of flexibility, the description of the set of reduction functions is not done in the PPETP main specifications, but it is demanded to some side documents called *reduction profiles*. This will allow for future addition of new reduction techniques by simply defining a new profile[6]. Since many of the properties of PPETP described in the following (e.g., robustness to packet loss and stream poisoning) do not depend on the actual reduction functions, but on the fact that the original packet can be recovered as soon as R reduced versions are known, we can deduce that the same properties will hold for every future reduction profile.

Currently only two reduction profiles are defined. One profile is the basic profile where no reduction is done. One could say that in the basic profile the pool of reduction functions contains only the identity function. The basic profile is to be used in some very special cases, for example, for testing purposes or for content streams with a very small bandwidth (fore example, to the sever-to-clients RTPC stream). The other profile is the Vandermonde profile based on the approach described in (Bernardini et al.., 2008) and briefly recalled here.

Let $d > 0$ be an integer and let $GF(2^{8d})$ denote the Galois field with 2^{8d} elements (Jacobson, 1985). At start-up, the node chooses $c \in GF(2^{8d})$ and constructs the *reduction vector*

$$\mathbf{r}_c \triangleq \begin{bmatrix} 1 & c & c^2 & \cdots & c^{R-1} \end{bmatrix} \tag{1}$$

The packet to be reduced is mapped into an R-row matrix C with entries in $GF(2^{8d})$ by considering every d-ple of bytes as an element of $GF(2^{8d})$. Matrix C is multiplied by $\mathbf{r}_c$ to obtain

$$\mathbf{u}_c = \mathbf{r}_c \mathbf{C} \tag{2}$$

which represents the reduced packet to be sent to the lower peers. Note that $\mathbf{u}_c$ is R times smaller than C. Note also that the pair (c, R) plays the role of the reduction parameter.

From the knowledge of $\mathbf{u}_{c_1}, \ldots, \mathbf{u}_{c_R}$ one can recover C by solving the linear system

$$\begin{bmatrix} \mathbf{u}_{c_1} \\ \mathbf{u}_{c_2} \\ \vdots \\ \mathbf{u}_{c_R} \end{bmatrix} = \begin{bmatrix} \mathbf{r}_{c_1} \\ \mathbf{r}_{c_2} \\ \vdots \\ \mathbf{r}_{c_R} \end{bmatrix} \mathbf{C} = \begin{bmatrix} 1 & c_1 & \cdots & c_1^{R-1} \\ 1 & c_2 & \cdots & c_2^{R-1} \\ \vdots & \vdots & & \vdots \\ 1 & c_R & \cdots & c_R^{R-1} \end{bmatrix} \mathbf{C} \triangleq \mathbf{RC} \tag{3}$$

Since matrix R in (3) is a Vandermonde matrix (with entries in $GF(2^{8d})$), it is invertible as soon as all the c_k are different.

3.2.1 Properties

In this section we discuss few interesting properties of the proposed scheme.

Distributed assignment of the reduction function A first interesting property is that if the set of reduction parameters F is large enough, each node can choose its parameter at random, since the probability of having two nodes with the same reduction parameter is negligible. This simplifies the assignation of the reduction parameters to the nodes, since no central authority is required.

In order to be more quantitative, let N_{up} be the number of upper peers of a given node and let c_k be the reduction parameter of the k-th upper peer, $k = 1, \ldots, N_{up}$. The node is able to recover the content stream if and only if there are least R different values of c_k. Figure 3 shows the probability P_{fail} that this does not happen as a function of S, the reduction factor R and the ratio $\alpha = N_{up}/R$ (interpretable as a redundancy factor). It is clear from Figure 3 that one can achieve negligible P_{fail} by using F of reasonable size and small redundancy factors. It is possible to show that P_{fail} goes to zero with N_{up} as $[(R-1)/S]^{N_{up}}$.

Robustness with respect to packet loss The scheme is inherently robust with respect to packet losses. Actually, a node that contacts more than $N_{up} > R$ upper peers will be able to recover the transmitted data as long as not more than $N_{up} - R$ packets are lost.

Robustness to churn A major problem with streaming over P2P network is the *churn* due to node frequent joining and leaving. In this section we want to show that the PPETP structure is robust with respect to churn.

Let us denote with Π_t the set of the upper peers of the current node at time t, and let $H(t) = \text{card}(\Pi_t) \in \{0, \ldots, N_{up}\}$. Note that if $H(t) < R$ (*underflow event*), the node will not receive enough data to recover the content packets and the user will experience a drop in quality. In order to estimate the probability P_{under} of the underflow event, we will suppose that (i) the search of a new peer requires a time that can be described by an exponential random variable, with appropriate parameter λ and that (ii) the time a peer remains connected can

Figure 3. Probability P_{fail} of having less than R different reduction parameters out of N_{up} vs. redundancy ratio $\alpha = N_{up}/R$ for different values of S and R

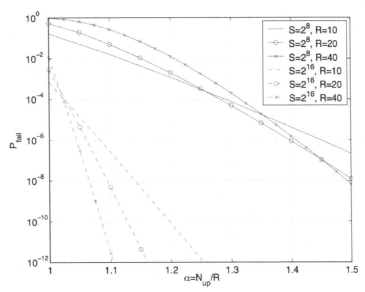

be described by an appropriate distribution[7] with average $1/\mu$. The average $1/\lambda$ can be expected to be typically in the order of a few seconds, while typical values of $1/\mu$ can be expected to be in the order of at least several minutes.

Within these hypotheses, the process $H(t)$ can be described as a continuous time random process corresponding to an $M/G/N_{up}/N_{up}$ queue (Gross & Harris, 1998), i.e., with intensity-λ Poisson arrivals, and generic time of service with average $1/\mu$, N_{up} servers and capacity N_{up}. Specifically, a new customer "arrives" when a new peer for the current node is found and a customer is "served" as soon as one peer leaves the network.

The steady state probability $P_Q(n)$ that n peers are in Π_t is $P_Q(n) = p_0 \rho^n / n!$, $n \in \{0,...,N_{up}\}$, (where p_0 is a suitable normalization constant which represents the probability that the system is empty) and depends on the parameter $\rho = \lambda/\mu$, and not on the specific service time distribution (Gross & Harris, 1998). Figure 4 shows

$$P_{under} = P[H(t) < R] = \sum_{n=0}^{R-1} P_Q(n) \quad \text{versus the}$$

normalized reduction factor R/ρ. It is clear that small values of P_{under} can be obtained by employing a limited redundancy ($\alpha \approx 1.1$).

Robustness to stream poisoning To counteract stream poisoning attacks the node contacts $N_{up} > R$ upper peers, uses R reduced versions to recover the original data and checks that the result is coherent with the remaining reduced packets. This procedure can be considered as a generalization of the use of error correcting codes with the important difference that in this case, data are not corrupted by a noisy channel, but by a malicious attacker which could, in principle, send carefully crafted data which cause the node to recover garbage data that nevertheless pass the just described test. However, it is possible to show that this is impossible, or, in other words, that the test will fail if the data sent by the malicious peer will cause the recovery of a wrong packet. Moreover, it is easy to show that if $N_{up} \geq R + A$, then the system is immune from a coordinated attack by A peers.

Figure 4. Logarithmic plots of the underflow probability P_{under} as function of ρ, the normalized reduction factor R/ρ and redundancy factor $\alpha = N_{up}/R$. (a) P_{under} for different values of ρ and $\alpha=1.1$ (b) P_{under} for different values of α and $\rho=400$

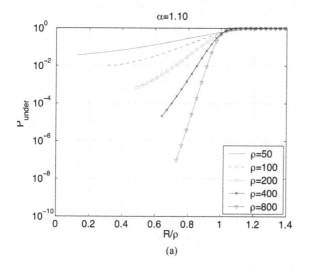

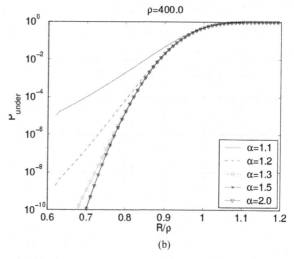

(a)　　　　　　　　　　　　　(b)

3.3 Protocol Description

The goal of this section is to describe the structure of PPETP. Since space constraints do not allow us to give all the protocol details, we will content ourselves with an overview of the most important aspects of the protocol.

Underlining transport protocol As said above, the *epi-* prefix in *Peer-to-Peer Epi-Transport Protocol* is due to the fact that PPETP is not a true transport protocol, but relies on a lower transport layer. It is not required that the transport layer used by PPETP grants for packet delivery or for packet order preserving. The most commonly used transport protocol compatible with PPETP is of course UDP, but other choices (e.g., the *Data Congestion Control Protocol*, Floyd et al.., 2006) are possible.

PPETP port number A PPETP session on a single node is uniquely identified by its *PPETP port number* which is mapped to one or more port numbers of the underling transport protocol. In the case of PPETP/UDP the PPETP port p is mapped to UDP ports p and $p+1$. Port p is used by the node to send packets, while port $p+1$ is used to receive packets.[8]

3.3.1 Packet Types

PPETP defines two types of packets: data packets and control packets (see Figure 5). Every PPETP packet has a progressive sequence number. The spaces of sequence numbers for data and control packets are independent, i.e., it is possible to have a data packet and a control packet with the same sequence number.

Data packets are obtained by the reduction of content packets. They inherit their sequence number from the corresponding content packet. For example, in the case of RTP packets, the PPETP sequence number can coincide with the RTP sequence number (Schulzrinne et al.., 2003). In Figure 5 it is possible to see the format of a data packet. A brief explanation of the fields follows.

• The first field (bits 0 and 1) is the version number (currently equal to 0).

Figure 5. PPETP data and control packet header

```
PPETP Data packet:

0                   1                   2                   3
0 1 2 3 4 5 6 7 8 9 0 1 2 3 4 5 6 7 8 9 0 1 2 3 4 5 6 7 8 9 0 1
+-+-+-+-+-+-+-+-+-+-+-+-+-+-+-+-+-+-+-+-+-+-+-+-+-+-+-+-+-+-+-+-+
|V=0|0|I|P|Flags|Profile|            Sequence number            |
+-+-+-+-+-+-+-+-+-+-+-+-+-+-+-+-+-+-+-+-+-+-+-+-+-+-+-+-+-+-+-+-+
:                                                               :
:               Signature (0, 32, 64 or 128 bit)               :
:                                                               :
+=+=+=+=+=+=+=+=+=+=+=+=+=+=+=+=+=+=+=+=+=+=+=+=+=+=+=+=+=+=+=+=+
:               Optional Profile-specific data ...             :
+-+-+-+-+-+-+-+-+-+-+-+-+-+-+-+-+-+-+-+-+-+-+-+-+-+-+-+-+-+-+-+-+
:               Payload   (reduced data)                       :
+-+-+-+-+-+-+-+-+-+-+-+-+-+-+-+-+-+-+-+-+-+-+-+-+-+-+-+-+-+-+-+-+


PPETP Control packet:

0                   1                   2                   3
0 1 2 3 4 5 6 7 8 9 0 1 2 3 4 5 6 7 8 9 0 1 2 3 4 5 6 7 8 9 0 1
+-+-+-+-+-+-+-+-+-+-+-+-+-+-+-+-+-+-+-+-+-+-+-+-+-+-+-+-+-+-+-+-+
|V=0|1| Request |Profile|            Sequence number            |
+-+-+-+-+-+-+-+-+-+-+-+-+-+-+-+-+-+-+-+-+-+-+-+-+-+-+-+-+-+-+-+-+
:                                                               :
:               Signature (0, 32, 64 or 128 bit)               :
:                                                               :
+=+=+=+=+=+=+=+=+=+=+=+=+=+=+=+=+=+=+=+=+=+=+=+=+=+=+=+=+=+=+=+=+
:                     Optional Payload                         :
+-+-+-+-+-+-+-+-+-+-+-+-+-+-+-+-+-+-+-+-+-+-+-+-+-+-+-+-+-+-+-+-+
```

- The second field (bit 2) is used to distinguish between data and control packets. It is always zero in a data packet.
- The third field (bit 3) is the Inline bit. If the Inline bit is one, it means that the reduction parameter used for the packet is included in the packet itself in the section Optional profile-specific data (see Figure 4); if Inline is zero, the default reduction parameter (declared with the Reduction_Param command, see in the following) was used.

In order to understand the use of the Inline bit, observe that a node that receives a reduced packet must know the reduction parameter that was used to create it, in order to build matrix R in (3).

Since each node chooses its reduction parameter at the beginning of the section, the reduction parameter is typically transmitted with the Reduc-tion_Param command, right after the handshake phase.

However, sometimes it could be necessary to send packets obtained with a different reduction parameter. For example, it could happen that a node does not receive enough packets to recover the content packet in time. Although the content packet is lost for the node, the information can be nevertheless propagated by sending to the lower peers one of the received reduced packets, almost certainly obtained with a different reduction parameter. In this case the node will set Inline to 1 and insert the reduction parameter just before the payload.

- The fourth field (bit 4) is the Padding bit and it has a meaning similar to the corresponding bit in RTP (Schulzrinne et al.., 2003).

- The fifth field (bits 5 to 7) is the Flags field. Similarly to the marker bit in RTP, the interpretation of this field is defined by the profile.
- Bits from 8 to 11 are the Profile field and represent the profile number. Currently, only profiles 0 (*basic profile*) and 1 (*Vandermonde profile*) are defined.
- Bits from 12 to 31 are the packet Sequence number.
- The field following the *sequence number* is the packet Signature. It can be 0, 32, 64 or 128 bits long (depending on the security and bandwidth requirements) and it is computed as follows: the packet with the signature field forced to zero is hashed with MD5 (to obtain a 128-bit string) and the result is encrypted with AES using a key agreed between the nodes at the hand-shaking time (see in the following for further details about the key exchange procedure). The first 1, 2 or 4 quadwords (32-bit words) of the encrypted hash are inserted in the Signature field.
- Data following the Signature field contains the optional reduction parameter and the reduced data. Note that since the meaning of these fields depends on the used profile, their definition is demanded to the reduction profile document.

Control packets are used to exchange control information and are mainly used during the hand-shaking phase. Since PPETP does not require a reliable protocol and no guarantee of delivering is supposed, each control packet requires an acknowledge. (Data packet are never acknowledged.) A node that sends a control packet will not assume that the packet achieved its effect until an acknowledgement is received. A node that receives a control packet will always acknowledge it, even if it is a duplicate of previously acknowledged packets. The format of a generic control packet can be seen in Figure 5. A brief explanation of the fields follows.

- The first field (bits 0 and 1) is the version number (currently equal to 0).
- The second field (bit 2) is used to distinguish between data and control packets. It is always 1 in a control packet.
- Bits from 3 to 7 are the Request field which represents the actual command. Request values greater than 16 and lower than 31 can be defined by the reduction profile. Other request values are reserved.
- Bits from 8 to 11 are the Flags field. Its meaning depends on the actual request. If the request is one of the profile-reserved requests, this field contains the profile index. If a request does not use this field, this field should be equal to 0.
- Bits from 12 to 31 are the packet Sequence number.
- The 128 bits following the *sequence number* are the packet Signature. This field is computed as in the data packet case.
- The meaning of the packet Payload (i.e., the bytes following the Signature field) depends on the specific request.

The request values currently defined are

- Nul (Request=0) This packet is a no-op, but it requires an acknowledge. It is used in hole punching procedures and it can be used to "keep alive" a connection (see below).
- Reduction_Param (Request=1) Used to transmit the default reduction parameter. The Flags field contains the profile index.
- Acknowledge (Request=2) Used to acknowledge the receipt of other control packets. The payload contains the sequence number of the acknowledged packet. This request does not require an acknowledge. The meaning of Flags depends on the com-

Figure 6. Payload of the Data_Control request

```
Data_Control payload:
 0                   1                   2                   3
 0 1 2 3 4 5 6 7 8 9 0 1 2 3 4 5 6 7 8 9 0 1 2 3 4 5 6 7 8 9 0 1
+-+-+-+-+-+-+-+-+-+-+-+-+-+-+-+-+-+-+-+-+-+-+-+-+-+-+-+-+-+-+-+-+
|V| SC|        Channel        |              Port               |
+-+-+-+-+-+-+-+-+-+-+-+-+-+-+-+-+-+-+-+-+-+-+-+-+-+-+-+-+-+-+-+-+
:              :             :                 :               :
:              :     IP address (32 or 128 bits) :            :
:              :             :                 :               :
+=+=+=+=+=+=+=+=+=+=+=+=+=+=+=+=+=+=+=+=+=+=+=+=+=+=+=+=+=+=+=+=+
|                  Optional Diffie-Hellman public key          :
+-+-+-+-+-+-+-+-+-+-+-+-+-+-+-+-+-+-+-+-+-+-+-+-+-+-+-+-+-+-+-+-+
```

mand acknowledged, but the zero value has always the meaning of "positive acknowledge" (i.e., no error occurred).

- Data_Control (Request=3) This command is used to request a node to send data to another node, to stop the data transmission to another node or to start the hole punching procedure. The payload (see Figure 6) contains the following fields:
  ◦ Bit 0 (flag V) is set to 1 if the IP_address field stores an IPV6 address.
  ◦ Bit 1 and 2 (SC field) specify the actual "sub-command." It is equal to 0 for a "*start*", to 1 for a "*stop*" and to 2 for a "*punch*." Value 3 is reserved.
  ◦ Bits from 3 to 15 are the Channel field and represent the output channel number of the source peer to be used.
  ◦ Bits from 16 to 31 are the Port field and represent the PPETP port of the destination node
  ◦ Field IP Address can be 32 or 128 bits long and contains the IP address of the destination node. If flag V is 0, this field contains a 32 bits long IPv4 address; if flag V is 1, this field contains a 128 bits long IPv6 address.
  ◦ The last field (Diffie-Hellman public key) has variable size, it is present only with the *start* sub-command and

it contains the public key of the new lower peer.

Note that the Data_Control command is not signed by the lower peer, but by the server. If the signature is correct, the node replies with an Acknowledge packet with Flags equal to zero and carries out the requested action; otherwise, it replies with a packet with Flags equal to 1.

3.3.2 Peer Handshaking Details

Hole punching procedure The goal of a hole punching procedure (HPP) is to open a connection between two peers that are behind a NAT. A good survey of procedures for P2P communication across NATs can be found in the recent RFC 5128 (Srisuresh et al., 2008). The handshaking procedure of PPETP is a specific instance of the HPP described in section 3.3 of RFC 5128. We chose to include this HPP because it requires an external host only in the initial phase and because it fails only in the presence of Endpoint-Dependent Mapping NATs (EDM-NAT) (Srisuresh et al., 2008). EDM-NATs are quite difficult to "punch" and if one user is behind one EDM-NAT the best solution is to use a host with a public IP as a bridge.

The HPP can be initiated both by the application (by calling a suitable method of the programming interface, see Section 3.4) or by the reception of a Data_Control/Punch request. In the HPP each node sends *two* Nul packets: one packet from its output port to the input port of the remote node and one packet *from* its *input* port *to* the *output* port of the remote node. The node will then wait for the first packet to be acknowledged (no acknowledge is expected for the second packet). If no acknowledge is received after a fair amount of time, the procedure is repeated. This "crossed" exchange of packets it is necessary in order to open NAT channels in both directions.

Key exchange Two nodes agree on a common key by carrying out a Diffie-Hellman (DH) key exchange procedure (Rescorla, 1999). The DH public key of a node can be transmitted both in a Data_Control/Start packet or by some means external to PPETP. For example, the client could include its DH public key in an header of the SETUP request sent to the RTSP server and the server could send in the reply the DH public keys of the peers (see also the session example in Section 3.1.1).

Handshaking procedure The following is a brief summary of the typical handshaking procedure between two peers.

- The server sends a Data_Control/Punch command to both nodes, causing them to start the HPP.
- When the HPP is concluded, the *lower* peer sends a Data_Control/Start request (signed by the server) to the upper peer.
- If the Data_Control/Start request is correctly signed, the *upper* peer sends a Set_Default request to the lower one.
- As soon as the Set_Default command is acknowledged, the upper peer begins streaming reduced packets to the lower peer until a Data_Control/Stop command is received. The upper peer will send also at regular intervals Nul requests to check if the lower peer is still alive.

3.3.3 Peer Departure

There are two possible cases of peer departure: *graceful* departure (when the user closes the program) and *ungraceful* departure (due, for example, to a program crash). In the case of graceful departure, the node, before leaving the networks, contacts the server which will use suitable Data_Control commands to "repair" the network. In the case of ungraceful departure the departure will be noticed by the lower peers that will observe an absence of data from the departed node. The lower peers will inform the server which will "repair" the network as in the case of graceful departure. If the node has no lower peer, its departure will be noticed by upper peers because of the missing replies to the Nul commands.

3.3.4 Overlay Network Structure

As explained above, PPETP does not mandate a specific overlay structure, nor a specific peer discovery procedure since those details, although fundamental for any P2P application, are *outside the scope* of PPETP. Actually, the relationship between PPETP and the overlay structure is similar to the relationship between TCP and DNS. TCP is a transport protocol and it describes how two hosts communicate, but it does not specify how the address of the remote host is discovered. The address of the host is found by some means *external* to TCP, for example by querying a DNS server. Similarly, PPETP describes the how two peers communicate, but not how peers find each other. The peer discovery procedure will be carried out by some means *external* to PPETP.

Although peer discovery and overlay management are not in the scope of PPETP, in this section, for the sake of completeness, we briefly *outline* two possible different procedures: the first one uses a central host that manages the overlay network, the second approach is a distributed approach that uses a DHT (Lua et al., 2005).

- **Centralized approach.** The new node, after being authenticated, receives from the server the address of a *overlay manager*. The node registers itself with the overlay manager, receives a list with the address of its upper peers and sends a Data_Control/ Send command to those peers (note that only this last step requires the interaction with the PPETP API). *Vid Torrent* uses a centralized approach similar to this one. (In *Vid Torrent* the overlay manager is called *rewire*.)

- **Distributed approach.** This approach requires the use of a DHT. In the literature one can find several possible techniques for implementing a DHT (Lua et al. 2005). For the purposes of this example, it does not matter which technique is actually employed, as long as it complies with the following general model:

  ○ A DHT is a structure composed of several nodes and it is indexed by *keys* represented by *m*-bit numbers. Typically a DHT is queried to retrieve an object associated with a given key, but in our context the usage is slightly different.

  ○ Each node is in charge of a subset of the keys; the key subset is assigned to the node when the node joins the DHT and it can change when other nodes join or leave the DHT.

  ○ The DHT can be queried to find the node that is in charge of a given key.

  ○ A DHT has a set of *bootstrap peers* (BP) to be contacted to join the network.

The distributed approach to overlay construction works as follows: the node, after authentication, receives from the address of a BP. The node contacts the BP and joins the DHT. In order to find an upper peer, the node generates a random key k and uses the DHT to find the node in charge of k.

A distributed approach based on DHT is used, for example, in *SplitStream*.

3.4 API Description

In this section we briefly summarize the Application Programming Interface (API) that an application programmer would use to access the PPETP library. Since the details of the API will clearly depend on the environment and the programming language used, we simply give an "abstract" view of the API, specifying the main methods that a programmer can expect from an actual implementation of the PPETP API.

PPETP sessions are created with New_Session, destroyed with Close_Session and *configured* with Configure_Session. Examples of configurable values are the size of the signature and the server public key used to sign the Data_Control command.

New reduction functions can be created with the New_Reducer method which will require as input data the reduction profile and the reduction parameters. New PPETP channels can be created with New_Channel and destroyed with Close_Channel. Method New_Channel requires in input the reduction function to be used. Note that the act of *creating* a channel does not *connect* the channel to a lower peer. Such a connection will be done by the PPETP layer itself as the result of receiving a Data_Control/Start command. Alternatively, the connection/disconnection can be forced by the application level by calling methods Connect_Channel and Disconnect_Channel. The HPP toward another node can be initiated by the reception of a Data_Control/Punch command or by calling method Punch. Data can be read/ sent from/over the PPETP session with methods Receive_Packet and Send_Packet.

Packets in PPETP session can have an "expiration time." In order to declare a packet *expired*, the PPETP API provides two methods: by calling Expired the application can declare that the packet with a given sequence number is expired;

alternatively, by calling Expiration_Time the application says to the PPETP library that the packet with sequence number S_q will expire at time $aS_q + t_0$, where a and t_0 are given as parameters to Expiration_Time.

4 FUTURE RESEARCH DIRECTIONS

The *Vandermonde profile* requires the use of arithmetic in $GF(2^{8d})$ which, in some architecture, could be expensive, especially for $d=2$ or $d=4$. However, large values of d are required if one wants to exploit the possibility of doing a reduction functions distributed assignment, since too small values for d could make the probability of having duplicate reduction vectors non negligible. Future research directions are aimed to finding other reduction profiles with low computational cost that nevertheless grant for a negligible probability of duplicated reduction parameters.

Another future research direction is about a stronger protection against stream poisoning. With the current solution the detection of a stream poisoning attack requires the reconstruction of the content packet that will be checked by using redundant reduced packets. It would be better if the packet could be "signed" by the server with a signature that can be "inherited" by the reduced packet.[9] This would allow the node to check the correctness of the packets without the need of carrying out the recovering procedure.

5 CONCLUSION

We described a P2P transport protocol suited for multimedia streaming. The proposed protocol has low start-up time, it is robust with respect to data losses and it counteracts stream poisoning attacks. The proposed protocol can be used with any type of data and, from the application point of view, appears as a protocol similar to TCP or UDP, making easier to reuse existing software and protocols.

REFERENCES

Ahlswede, R., Cai, N., Li, S. Y. R., & Yeung, R. W. (2000). Network information flow. *Information Theory, IEEE Transactions on, 46*(4), 1204–1216. Retrieved December 22, 2009 from http://dx.doi.org/10.1109/18.850663

Alstrup, S., & Rauhe, T. (2005, July). Introducing Octoshape – a new technology for large-scale streaming over the Internet. *EBU Technical Review,* (303), 1-10.

Arkko, J., Lindholm, F., Naslund, M., Norrman, K., & Carrara, E. (2006, July). Key Management Extensions for Session Description Protocol (SDP) and Real Time Streaming Protocol (RTSP) (No. 4567). *RFC 4567 (Proposed Standard). IETF.* Retrieved December 22, 2009 from http://www.ietf.org/rfc/rfc4567.txt

Bernardini, R., Rinaldo, R., & Vitali, A. (2008, March). A reliable chunkless peer-to-peer architecture for multimedia streaming. In *Proc. Data Compression Conference* (pp. 242–251). Snowbird, Utah: IEEE Computer Society.

Chou, P., Wu, Y., & Jain, K. (2003), Practical Network Coding. In *Proc. of the 41st Allerton Conference on Communication, Control and Computing.* Retrieved November 20, 2009 from http://flipflop.usc.edu/~mvieira/NetworkCoding/google/chou03practical.pdf

Floyd, S., Handley, M., & Kohler, E. (2006, March). Problem Statement for the Datagram Congestion Control Protocol (DCCP) (No. 4336). *RFC 4336 (Informational). IETF.* Retrieved December 22, 2009 from http://www.ietf.org/rfc/rfc4336.txt

Fodor, V., & D´an, G. (2007, June). Resilience in live peer-to-peer streaming. *IEEE Communications Magazine*, *45*(6), 116–123. doi:10.1109/MCOM.2007.374428

Gkatsidis, C., Miller, J., & Rodrigues, P. (2006) Anatomy of a P2P Content Distribution System with Network Coding, in *Proc. of the 5th International Workshop on Peer-to-Peer Systems (IPTPS 2006)*, (pp. 1-6).

Gkatsidis, C., & Rodrigues, P. (2005), Network Coding for Large Scale Content Distribution. In *Proc. INFOCOM 2005. 24th IE EE International Conference on Computer Communications*, (pp. 2235-2245).

Gross, D., & Harris, C. (1998). *Fundamentals of queueing theory*. New York: Wiley-Interscience.

Handley, M., Jacobson, V., & Perkins, C. (2006, July). SDP: Session Description Protocol (No. 4566). *RFC 4566 (Proposed Standard). IETF*. Retrieved December 22, 2009 from http://www.ietf.org/rfc/rfc4566.txt

Ho, T., Medard, M., Koetter, R., Karger, D., Effros, M., & Shi, J. (2006, Oct.). A random linear network coding approach to multicast. *Information Theory. IEEE Transactions on, 52*(10), 4413–4430.

Jacobson, N. (1985). *Basic algebra I*. New York, NY: W.H. Freeman.

Kozamernik, F. (2000, March). Webcasting – the webcasters' perspective. *EBU Technical Review* (282), 1-28.

Li, S.-Y., Yeung, R., & Cai, N. (2003, Feb.). Linear network coding. *Information Theory. IEEE Transactions on, 49*(2), 371–381.

Liang, J., & Nahrstedt, K. (2006, January). Dagstream: locality aware and failure resilient peer-to-peer streaming. In *Proc. Multimedia Computing and Networking 2006*, Vol. 6071, No. 1. Retrieved November 20, 2009 from http://citeseerx.ist.psu.edu/viewdoc/download?doi=10.1.1.94.6130&rep=rep1&type=pdf

Liao, X., Jin, H., Liu, Y., Ni, L., & Deng, D. (2006, April). AnySee: Peer-to-Peer live streaming. In *Proc. INFOCOM 2006. 25th IEEE International Conference on Computer Communications* (pp. 1-10).

Lua E. K., Crowcroft J., Pias M., Sharva R. & Lim S. (2005). A Survey and Comparison of Peer-to-Peer Overlay Network Schemes. *IEEE Communications Surveys*, 72-93.

Magharei, N., & Rejaie, R. (2007, May). Prime: peer-to-peer receiver-driven mesh-based streaming. In *Proc. INFOCOM 2007. 26th IEEE International Conference on Computer Communications* (pp. 1415-1423).

Padmanabhan, V., Wang, H., Chou, P., & Sripanidkulchai, K. (2002, May). Distributing streaming media content using cooperative networking. In *Proceedings of the 12th international workshop on Network and operating systems support for digital audio and video* (pp. 177-186). Miami, Florida.

Rejaie, R., & Stafford, S. (2004, June). A framework for architecting peer-to-peer receiver-driven overlays. In *Proceedings of the 14th international workshop on Network and operating systems support for digital audio and video* (pp. 177-186). Cork, Ireland.

Rescorla, E. (1999, June). Diffie-Hellman Key Agreement Method (No. 2631*). RFC 2631 (Proposed Standard). IETF*. Retrieved December 22, 2009 from http://www.ietf.org/rfc/rfc2631.txt

Schulzrinne, H., Casner, S., Frederick, R., & Jacobson, V. (2003, July). RTP: A Transport Protocol for Real-Time Applications (No. 3550). *RFC 3550 (Standard). IETF*. Retrieved December 22, 2009 from http://www.ietf.org/rfc/rfc3550.txt

Srisuresh, P., Ford, B., & Kegel, D. (2008, March). State of Peer-to-Peer (P2P) Communication across Network Address Translators (NATs). *RFC 5128. IETF*. Retrieved December 22, 2009 from http://www.ietf.org/rfc/rfc5128.txt

Stutzbach, D., & Rejaie, R. (2006). Understanding churn in peer-to-peer networks. In *Proceedings of the 6th acm sigcomm conference on internet measurement* (pp. 189-202). Rio de Janeiro, Brazil: SIGCOMM.

Wang, M., & Li, B. (2007, Dec.). Network coding in live peer-to-peer streaming. *Multimedia. IEEE Transactions on, 9*(8), 1554–1567.

Yang, M., & Yang, Y. (2008, June). Peer-to-peer file sharing based on network coding. In *Distributed computing systems, 2008. icdcs '08. the 28th international conference on* (pp. 168–175). Beijing, China: IEEE Computer Society.

Zhang, X., Liuy, J., Liz, B., & Yum, P. (2005, March). CoolStreaming/DONet: a data-driven overlay network for efficient live media streaming. In *Proc. INFOCOM 2005. 24th IEEE International Conference on Computer Communications* (pp. 2102-2111).

ADDITIONAL READING

Castro, M., Druschel, P., Kermarrec, A. M., Nandi, A., Rowstron, A., & Singh, A. (2003). Splitstream: high-bandwidth multicast in cooperative environments. In *Sosp '03: Proceedings of the nineteenth ACM symposium on operating systems principles* (pp. 298–313). New York. Retrieved December 22, 2009 from http://dx.doi.org/10.1145/945445.945474

Comer, D. E. (2000). Internetworking with TCP/IP: *Vol. 1. Principles, protocols, and architecture* (4th ed.). Prentice Hall.

Cover, T. M., & Thomas, J. A. (1991). *Information theory*. New York: Wiley.

Dhungel, P., Hei, X., Ross, K. W., & Saxena, N. (2007). The pollution attack in P2P live video streaming: measurement results and defenses. In *P2P-TV '07: Proceedings of the 2007 workshop on peer-to-peer streaming and IP-TV* (pp. 323–328). New York, NY, USA: ACM. Retrieved December 22, 2009 from http://dx.doi.org/10.1145/1326320.1326324

Fodor, V., & Dan, G. (2007). Resilience in live peer-to-peer streaming. *Communications Magazine, IEEE, 45*(6), 116–123. Retrieved December 22, 2009 from http://dx.doi.org/10.1109/MCOM.2007.374428

Hain, T. (2000, November). Architectural Implications of NAT (No. 2993*). RFC 2993 (Informational). IETF.* Retrieved December 22, 2009 from http://www.ietf.org/rfc/rfc2993.txt

Hei, X., Liu, Y., & Ross, K. W. (2008). IPTV over P2P streaming networks: the mesh-pull approach. *Communications Magazine, IEEE, 46*(2), 86–92. Retrieved December 22, 2009 from http://dx.doi.org/10.1109/MCOM.2008.4473088

Hsieh, H.-Y., & Sivakumar, R. (2005). On transport layer support for peer-to-peer networks. In *Peer-to-peer system III.* Berlin, Springer (pp. 44–53). Retrieved December 22, 2009 from http://www.springerlink.com/content/xn0695d7gbn8ny45

Li, B., & Yin, H. (2007). Peer-to-peer live video streaming on the internet: issues, existing approaches, and challenges. *Communications Magazine, IEEE, 45*(6), 94–99. Retrieved December 22, 2009 from http://dx.doi.org/10.1109/MCOM.2007.374425

Li, J. (2008, March). On peer-to-peer (P2P) content delivery. *Peer-to-Peer Networking and Applications, 1*(1), 45–63. Retrieved December 22, 2009 from http://dx.doi.org/10.1007/s12083-007-0003-1

Liu, Y., Guo, Y., & Liang, C. (2008, March). A survey on peer-to-peer video streaming systems. *Peer-to-Peer Networking and Applications, 1*(1), 18–28. Retrieved December 22, 2009 from http://dx.doi.org/10.1007/s12083-007-0006-y

Oram, A. (2001). *Peer-to-peer: Harnessing the power of disruptive technologies. O'Reilly*. Hardcover.

R. Koetter & M. Medard. (2003) An algebraic Approach to Network Coding, *IEEE/ACM Transactions on Networking, 11*(5), 782-795

Rosenberg, J., Weinberger, J., Huitema, C., & Mahy, R. (2003, March). STUN - Simple Traversal of User Datagram Protocol (UDP) Through Network Address Translators (NATs) (No. 3489*). RFC 3489 (Proposed Standard). IETF.* Retrieved December 22, 2009 from http://www.ietf.org/rfc/rfc3489.txt

Senie, D. (2002, January). Network Address Translator (NAT)-Friendly Application Design Guidelines *(No. 3235). RFC 3235 (Informational). IETF.* Retrieved December 22, 2009 from http://www.ietf.org/rfc/rfc3235.txt

Sentinelli, A., Marfia, G., Gerla, M., Kleinrock, L., & Tewari, S. (2007). Will IPTV ride the peer-to-peer stream? *Communications Magazine, IEEE, 45*(6), 86–92. Retrieved December 22, 2009 from http://dx.doi.org/10.1109/MCOM.2007.374424

Shah, P., & Paris, J. F. (2007). Peer-to-peer multimedia streaming using BitTorrent. In *Performance, computing, and communications conference, 2007. IPCCC 2007.* (pp. 340–347). Retrieved December 22, 2009 from http://dx.doi.org/10.1109/PCCC.2007.358912

Srisuresh, P., & Holdrege, M. (1999, August). IP Network Address Translator (NAT) Terminology and Considerations *(No. 2663). RFC 2663 (Informational). IETF.*). Retrieved December 22, 2009 from http://www.ietf.org/rfc/rfc2663.txt

Stevens, R. W. (1990). *Unix network programming.* Upper Saddle River, NJ: Prentice Hall PTR. Paperback.

KEY TERMS AND DEFINITIONS

Peer-to-Peer (P2P): A network communication paradigm, where every single user can act as a client as well as a server for other peer nodes. In this way, each user can contribute with its own resources to the network functioning.

Multimedia Streaming: An application where the desired multimedia content is not downloaded first, and then played, but it is played during transmission, as soon as enough data are available. Streaming can be used for stored as well as for live multimedia distribution.

Network Topology: The nodes in the network are logically organized according to a desired geometry or topology, reflecting the direction of the information flow. The most common topologies are tree-based and mesh-based.

Network Coding: In network coding, each intermediate node does not simply forward the data packets, but computes a linear combination, in an appropriate finite field, of the data blocks. As in error coding, the algebraic properties of this combination can be exploited to gain robustness to data losses and also for other purposes.

Churn: This term refers to the fact that, in a Peer-to-Peer network, the nodes can leave or join the network at a fast and dynamic rate.

Asymmetric Bandwidth: Most residential users use ADSL links, and have an upload bandwidth which is much smaller than the download bandwidth. This means that a node cannot in general forward its multimedia content directly, and that some form of reduction has to be employed.

Poisoning Attacks: This term refers to the fact that a malicious node can inject corrupted data into the network. A good P2P streaming solution should be robust to stream poisoning, to avoid the propagation of corrupted information among peers.

Network Address Translation (NAT): Most Internet node IP addresses are not directly accessible. A device, called NAT, can be used to hide the structure of a local network by making visible the NAT's IP address only, and managing appropriate translation tables to access individual hidden nodes. In a P2P system, peers need to communicate, so there must be procedures to deal with the presence of NATs.

ENDNOTES

[1] For example, serving video with DVD-like quality to millions of users requires a bandwidth of the order of Terabits per second.

[2] http://sourceforge.net/projects/corallo/

[3] This is similar to what happens, for example, with TCP, which specifies details like the node handshaking and data format, but not how the client finds the server address.

[4] In the case of RTP packets, the PPETP sequence number can coincide with the RTP sequence number (Schulzrinne et al., 2003), but this is not necessary.

[5] This nomenclature is inspired by the typical picture of a tree-structured network where data flow from top to bottom.

[6] A similar profile-based approach is used by other protocols such as RTP (Schulzrinne et al., 2003) and RTSP (Arkko et al., 2006).

[7] Even if not directly related to the streaming application, the results of (Stutzbach & Rejaie, 2006) show that distributions other than the simple exponential model can be more appropriate.

[8] The necessity to fix both the output and the input ports is due to the necessity of knowing the output port of a node to carry out the NAT hole punching procedure.

[9] An example of "inheritable signature" is the use of a linear redundancy check appended to the packet. Unfortunately, this type of signature is too easy to forge, so it is of no use in this context.

Section 4
Applications of Streaming Media

Chapter 15
Low Latency Audio Streaming for Internet–Based Musical Interaction

Alexander Carôt
Anhalt University of Applied Sciences, Germany

ABSTRACT

With the current Internet bandwidth capacities and machine processing performance the personal computer has become an affordable and flexible multimedia platform for high quality audio and video content. Besides the delivery of services such as TV, telephone and radio, the Internet can also be used for the instantaneous bidirectional exchange of musical information. Due to the variety and complexity of already existing remote music and communication approaches, an elaboration on this topic is mandatory, which covers any relevant musical, technical or interdisciplinary aspect of remote musical interaction. Therefore, this chapter gives an overview of currently applied technologies and possibilities with their theoretical background.

1 INTRODUCTION

Due to the conventional "best-effort" manner without any guarantee of packet delivery, the Internet was not originally developed for the purpose of sending real time traffic as it is the case with audio data: Packet loss and delay variations typically lead to dropouts in the received audio stream which result in signal errors, and correspondingly, disturbing clicks and noise cracks. Recent Voice-over-IP (VoIP) and video

conferencing services overcome these problems by applying large audio frames, large network buffers, and the principle of packet retransmissions. Consequently this results in additional latencies of several hundred milliseconds. Such delays do not represent a problematic figure in the context of voice communication.

As part of the evolving globalization process and its distributed work processes telecommunication on the Internet has become a widely accepted and commonly used service. Based on these facts it is the author's intend to show in how far distributed communication on the Internet can be applied

DOI: 10.4018/978-1-61692-831-5.ch015

Copyright © 2011, IGI Global. Copying or distributing in print or electronic forms without written permission of IGI Global is prohibited.

in terms of artistic music performances: Such a scenario exhibits signal delay boundaries below 30 ms as though musicians were to perform in the same room. In this context the author aims to determine the primary problematic aspects related to delay and quality in order to achieve adequate realistic performance conditions.

Hence, as a first step, the author will present the precise cognitive restrictions for a delayed musical interplay and determine the relating technical requirements: Based on these cognitive restrictions, each technical aspect of latency will be examined in terms of its inherent signal delivery speed and the corresponding latency. The corresponding technical approach sends UDP packets as quick as possible across a network. It uses a minimal audio frame size and small network buffers and avoids packet retransmissions in order to eliminate any source of additional delay. Audio dropouts due to jitter and packet loss are consciously taken into account up to an individually adjustable level.

This chapter is based on the author's doctoral thesis. In order to provide a descriptive overview of remote music interaction the author extracted the main significant aspects and expressed them in a compressed way. The interested reader can find the full comprehensive analysis and further technical approaches in [Carôt, 2009].

2 FUNDAMENTALS IN MUSIC COGNITION

The speed of sound of about 340 m/s [Everest, 2001] results in signal delays depending on the physical distance between rehearsing musicians. Hence, two musicians' beats can never occur in precise synchrony. In a number of cognitive experiments the author simulated this effect up to any desired dimension with an artificial delay [Carôt/Werner, 2009]. Based on the experiment's results the author introduced a model, which is illustrated in figure 1. It shows the time shift between a local and an external pulse. In the following

this is defined as the "inter pulse delay" (IPD). According to the outcome of the experiment's trials, the maximal IPD, music can be performed with, depends on the musician's personality and style. However, it decreases with an increasing rhythmical resolution and the speed of a tune: Depending on style and personal rhythmical attitude, musicians consider the time of a musical piece more or less as a fixed and precise beat reference. As a result a musician's motivation to play precisely on the beat can vary significantly and – depending on the skill – one might even consciously play in advance or behind the beat or in a changing manner. Depending on the value of this stylistic device it is possible to define a time spread around the theoretical beat reference, within a played pulse can be perceived and considered as correct. The so-called personal beat shift range (PBSR) describes a musician's temporal range of acceptance, which can be divided into the left range before the theoretical beat and the right range after the beat [Carôt/Werner, 2009].

In case of a musical interaction it is the PBSR of a musician, which determines, in how far an external pulse is considered as correct or as out of time, however, the closer the external pulse resides at the range's edges, the more difficult and inconvenient the interaction will be. Figure 1 illustrates the closeness of an external pulse to a theoretical beat, which could have been generated with a precise metronome, by a continuous transition from white to black. The darker the color is, the larger the distance from the theoretical main pulse and the harder it is to interpret external pulses within this area as correct. As shorter notes result in a larger number of pulses in a fixed time frame, it is also clear that an increase of speed and a higher note resolution both correspond to a smaller PBSR. The first row of figure 1 shows a sequence of eighth note pulses. The incoming external pulses range twice as much in the darker area as they do in the lower quarter note sequence below. Any musician unconsciously accepts and copes with this phenomenon de-

Figure 1. Visualization of human musical interaction

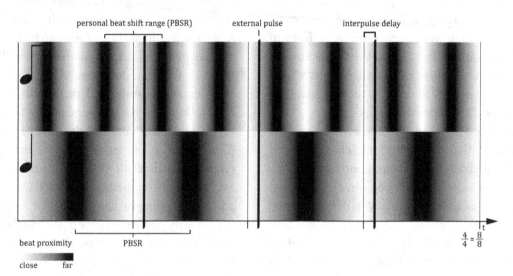

pending on the personal taste and favor. In order to compensate these effects of latency, musical gear such as stage or "Inear"-Monitors, rhythm devices and special band setups can be applied according to this personal rhythmical attitude and style.

Due to the described aspects numerous musicians generally do not exhibit the same PBSR, which is why it is not possible to define a common valid latency threshold, under which musical interaction is feasible or not. However, since a musical interaction involves at least two musicians, respectively two PBSR and the corresponding playing styles have to be taken into account. Hence, it is rather a collective latency-acceptance-limit, which determines the latency threshold and defines the ideal conditions musicians can perform under. As a result in [Carôt/Werner, 2009] the author introduced the term "ensemble delay acceptance limit" EDAL, which is typically not a known number and must be figured in a dedicated test setup. In the past the author assumed a common valid maximal delay threshold of 25 ms for any musician under any musical condition [Carôt, 2004]. However, according to this experiment and its findings this number can only be used as

rough guide value since the maximal playable latency depends on a number of variable factors and therefore cannot be stated by a fixed number [Carôt & Werner, 2009].

In the following the author will outline any aspect related to latency introduced by technical equipment, network architectures and transmission media. The final section will combine the cognitive aspects of this section with the technical outcome of the following section. In that context further alternative interaction styles will be introduced, which overcome the issue of delay by a change of the musical and rhythmical attitude.

3 PHYSICAL AND TECHNICAL FUNDAMENTALS

The process of hearing implies air waves of changing pressure to trigger a person's ear drum membrane in order to finally convert the signal to electric impulses in the brain [Levine, 2001]. If musicians are rehearsing in the same room they are separated by a certain distance and since the average transmission speed of air lines at 340 m/s, this introduces delays of about 3 ms/m. With

Figure 2. Total signal path

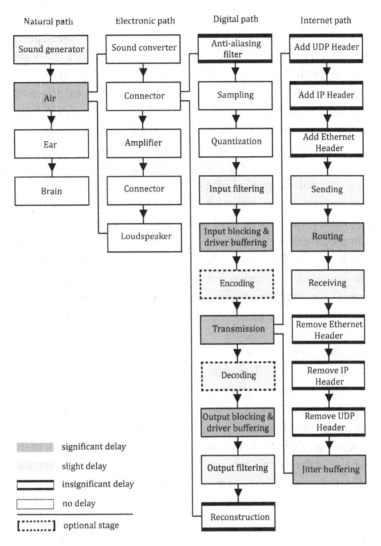

respect to an EDAL of 25 ms this corresponds to a physical distance of 8.5 m. The stages are part of the natural signal path. Considering the idea of placing two musicians abroad, technology would need to convert sound waves to electronic signals and transmit them on an existing network. This process is realized in the electronic path. Since nowadays audio technology and transmission systems process data digitally, the signal additionally requires a conversion from analogue to digital representation and back. The respective stages are part of the digital path. Regarding the

applied network one can choose between numerous technologies, which have either a synchronous, an asynchronous or isochronous characteristics. Since this work aims at using the asynchronous Internet, the total signal chain consists of the natural path, the electronic path, the digital path and an additional Internet path as illustrated in Figure 2. Each of the stages is marked in either white, light grey or dark grey as an indicator of latency.

In the following the author describes each signal chain regarding its functionality and the introduced delay. In spite of a relatively large set the majority of signal stages does not or just slightly introduce a delay. Within the natural signal chain it is just the physical distance which has to be kept as low as possible due to the air's transmission speed. In the electronic signal path the analogue processing is virtually not associated with a delay. Excluding the analogue anti aliasing, reconstruction filter and the quantization process it is mainly the digital signal path, which introduces most of the delay: After passing the anti aliasing low pass, a signal is sampled at a certain sample rate and quantized in a certain bit resolution. Generally sound cards also apply digital filters to the sampled signal in their input- and output sections. What these filter precisely do is a vendor and device specific criterion but in any case filters require a number of input samples to work properly – the so-called filter length. After the retrieval of this x amount of samples the filter generates output samples according to its actual filter architecture. Typically the input and out filters apply an oversampling in order to reduce the effect of aliasing and quantization noise [Pohlmann, 2005]. Digital filters introduce delay depending on their filter length in samples. Hence, the higher the sample rate the lower this delay of a filter. According to the professional RME Fireface 400 sound card's datasheet the input filter requires 43.2 samples and the output filter requires 28 samples, which add to 71.2 samples in total and leads to a corresponding delay of 1.48 ms at a sample rate of 48 kHz – 0.74 ms at 96 kHz respectively [RME, 2007]. However, the major latency appears due to the stages related to the audio blocking and the transmission, which will be outlined in the following subsections.

3.1 Device Blocking and Driver Buffering

Sound cards can provide each generated sample to the next processing stage, however, current PC-based sound systems are not able to process data with that processing speed due to internal scheduling and general architecture: On an abstract level, the time to process n samples must be constant in order to provide a solid audio stream. This is described in equation 1, where $t(n)_{processing}$ represents the total processing time for n samples. $t(n)_{functioncall}$ is associated with the execution time for n samples with the respective system call. The problem occurs due to the implied function overhead, which increases the execution time with a constant value $t_{overhead}$. Hence, the lower the number of samples n, the more function calls the system has to perform within a given time frame, and in turn the stronger the impact of the overhead. Respectively, the higher the number of samples to be processed, the less often the function is called in a given time frame and in turn the overhead decreases.

$$t(n)_{processing} = t(n)_{functioncall} + t_{overhead} \qquad (1)$$

Furthermore, another source of delay occurs due to the fact that a personal computer is not designed in terms of explicit audio processing. In that context – rather than immediately executing the respective processes – the system's scheduler serves them at a certain moment in time. As a result, it takes an amount of time to transfer an audio sample to the user space of a system. The precise value varies from system to system, however, in any case it resides significantly beyond the interval between two subsequent audio samples. As a result the system has to collect an amount of samples before actually processing them. Hence – rather than sample by sample – sound cards generate audio in blocks of a fixed number of samples. Once the sound card has collected this fixed number of samples, it generates an interrupt and addresses the block of samples via DMA (direct memory access) [Carôt, 2006] to the machine. A sample block also corresponds to the term "sample frame" or "audio buffer". The size of each processed block depends on the actual system's performance and is limited to a number of 32 samples as the lowest adjustable value. If we assume audio data to have a 16 Bit resolution – that is one sample consists of 2 bytes – the currently lowest possible block size equals 64 bytes. Without performance optimization of a device's operating system in the form of a special low latency kernel or further technical improvements such as the use of a realtime operating system, current personal computers can handle block sizes of 512 samples/block. More recently – with increasing CPU speeds – devices can work with 128, 64 or even 32 samples/block. In any case, blocking implies a tradeoff between stability and delay: On one hand larger blocks require less computational power so that a more stable system behavior can be achieved – on the other hand the delay increases with larger block sizes since it needs more time to generate an appropriate number of samples. Given a fixed sample rate, the blocking delay is directly related to the block size. Assuming a fixed block size and increasing the sample rate, higher frequencies can be captured, which leads to a higher audio quality. Additionally – due to smaller sampling intervals – it as well leads to proportionally smaller delay times so that altogether the blocking delay depends on the block size and the sample rate. According to this the blocking delay can be calculated with the following equation 2.

$$\text{blocking delay} = \text{block size} / \text{sample rate} \tag{2}$$

After the sound card has blocked for a certain amount of samples, a filled block or buffer is available to be processed by a digital device or computer application. Practically this means, that the buffer values can now be modified in any way a user desires to. As an example the signal's data could be scaled, distorted, muted, etc. In any case of modification, the existing sample values of the current block need to be changed according to the rules of digital signal processing: In case of a muting all values need to be set to zero, scaling requires all values to be multiplied by a fixed

desired factor, while distortion assumes a varying multiplication factor over the appropriate block values. In common computer operating systems (Windows, Mac OS X, Linux), so-called "callback functions" [Bencina, 2003] are used by the audio device as a programmer's interface for the retrieval and modification of such audio blocks. Their execution corresponds to a sound card's interrupt and according to the previous equation, this interval depends on the actual sound card settings. As a standard case a sampling rate of 48 kHz with a frame size of 128 samples results in callback events every 2.7 ms. E.g. a block size of 512 samples corresponds to a blocking delay of 10.8 ms at a sample rate of 48 kHz. The digital application processes the filled buffer's n samples, while at the same time another buffer is filled with the next n samples. This principle is illustrated in Figure 3. Once the buffer is full, both buffers are swapped and the next period starts in the same way. At the moment t the callback event occurs after all sample values had been captured and made available to the application. The interval T represents the blocking delay. At that state the sound card has just captured audio data, which is now ready to be processed and actually ready to be sent to a desired destination. However, the system has not created any audible feedback yet. The direct playback of a captured signal block also refers to the term "loopback" [RME, 2007] and would require the buffer to pass the sound card's output process as the next step.

Nevertheless, one has to be aware that on top of the input filter- and blocking delay, there can be additional audio driver latencies depending on the actual hardware technology and operating system. E.g. in contradiction to PCI bus data transfer with the corresponding fast direct memory access, the Firewire [IEEE, 2008] audio driver introduces an additional so-called "safety buffer" [RME, 2007] of at least 64 samples in order to provide a stable audio capture. Furthermore, the "Core Audio" of the Apple Macintosh operating system OS X e.g. requires the so-called

Figure 3. Audio playout process

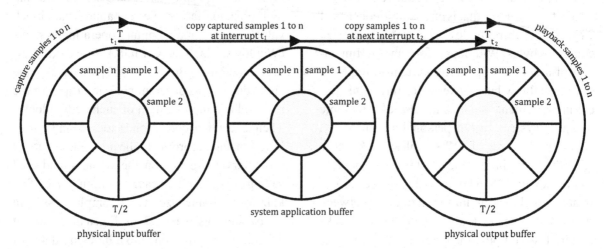

"safety offset" of at least 64 samples up to even 292 samples due to its general architecture, which is described in [Apple, 2001]. In any case, additional driver latencies approach an improvement of the sound card's stability and performance but as this conflicts with the low delay requirements of network music performances it eventually is the user's responsibility to figure the best combination of sound card, operating system and driver.

Equally to the problem described at the audio input stage data cannot be processed sample by sample and hence the sound card's output architecture is as well designed as a double buffer system. While the second playout buffer offers its samples to the physical output, the application buffer holds the samples previously captured by the system's physical input, which also introduces a delay of one audio block. As a result the blocking delay of a sound card appears twice – first by the input double buffer and secondly by the output double buffer [Carôt, 2006]. The total audio capture and playout process is illustrated in figure 3, while figure 4 shows the total sound card delay: Without taking potential network delays into account, the illustration marks the acceptable sound card configurations. In that context the author used an EDAL of 25 ms as a guide value. Configura-

tions, which result in a total delay below 25 ms, are illustrated on a white, close to 25 ms delay on a light grey and beyond 25 ms on a dark grey background. As the user is supposed to figure the lowest possible latency a sound system can achieve, this graph helps to verify the system's ability to suit the requirements of distributed music performances. However, equal to the capture process, users must again be aware of additional driver delays possibly caused by the applied interface technology and operating system and have to add them to the graph's delay values respectively.

3.2 Coding (Optional)

After the retrieval of an audio block it could theoretically be sent directly across a network. The following section 3.3 will outline the requirements of an uncompressed audio stream regarding a network connection. However, if these requirements cannot be met, the audio stream data must be reduced. Hence, signal compression can be applied optionally before transmitting the actual audio block on the network. In that context we have to distinguish between "lossless" and "lossy" compression techniques: Lossless data compression allows the exact original data to be reconstructed from the compressed data. Depend-

Figure 4. Total audio latencies

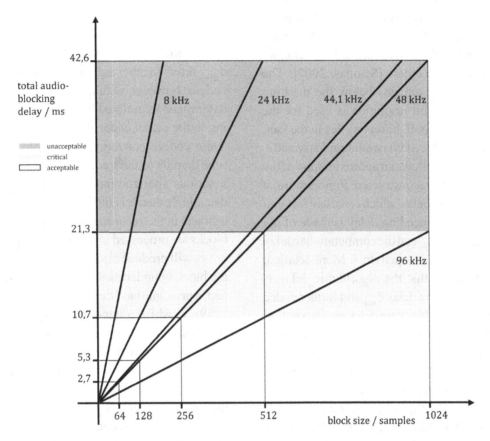

ing on the mathematical algorithm and the actual content, lossless compression achieves a compression rate of approximately 2 by either generating a statistical model for the input data or mapping the input data to probability bit sequences [Spanias, 2007]. This happens in such way that more frequently encountered data will produce shorter output than less frequently encountered data. The latency, introduced by the lossless encoding of an audio block, can be considered as relatively low with values less than 200 μs depending on the machine's processing performance. Hence, in the case of lossless audio compression the final encoding delay $d_{encoding(lossless)}$ is only made of the encoding computational delay $d_{encodeComp}$, which a machine requires to encode the current audio block as shown in equation 3.

$$d_{encoding(lossless)} = d_{encodeComp} \qquad (3)$$

Despite the possibility of perfectly reconstructing the original signal with a minimal amount of delay, lossless compression suffers from a low compression rate and hence does not necessarily meet the bandwidth requirements of narrow band consumer network connections. An alternative are the so-called lossy data compression techniques, which achieve comparably higher compression rates. The principle of lossy audio compression is based on the phenomenon of psychoacoustics that under certain circumstances related to signal frequency and amplitude, frequencies of a signal are masked by others: Specific signal parts must exhibit a certain intensity in order not to be masked by other signal parts. The required intensity refers to the term "masking threshold" [Spanias, 2007].

In order to achieve compression rates of 4 up to 16, lossless coding forms the quantization noise of the signal according to the masking threshold. Thus certain signal parts are encoded with a higher bit resolution than others [Spanias, 2007]: The lower a frequency remains below the masking threshold the less bit resolution is used for the encoding. The tradeoff, however, lies in the fact, that due to the reduced bit resolution lossy audio compression only allows an approximation of the original data to be reconstructed. Furthermore, it introduces a higher delay, which consists of several factors: The final encoding delay is made of the algorithmic delay d_{alg} and the computational delay $d_{encodeComp}$ as shown in equation 4. More detailed, equation 5 shows that the algorithmic delay is made of the blocking delay d_{blck} and further codec related delays. The blocking delay corresponds to a block of a fixed number of samples, that a codec requires in order to calculate an encoded output block according to its technical architecture. The blocking delays of conventional and often applied codecs such as AAC [Spanias, 2007] or Ogg Vorbis [Goncalves, 2008] already reside at 1024 samples and a corresponding delay of more than 20 ms at a sample rate of 48 kHz.

$$d_{encoding(lossy)} = d_{alg} + d_{encodeComp} \qquad (4)$$

$$d_{alg} = d_{blck} + d_{others} \qquad (5)$$

However, with respect to the actual stage in the digital signal path, an audio block has already been captured and in turn the codec blocking delay has no impact on the overall application encoding latency anymore. Therefore, the codec blocking delay can be subtracted from the sum of coding latencies in this specific application. Finally, it is the computational delay and the codec specific delay, which remain in order to calculate the final lossy application encoding delay $d_{appEncoding(lossy)}$. This context is described in equation 6.

$$d_{appEncoding(lossy)} = d_{encoding(lossy)} - d_{blck} = d_{encodeComp} + d_{others} \qquad (6)$$

According to the name of its index, the delay d_{others} refers to other aspects in context with audio codecs, however, with most codecs this delay is determined as outlined in the following: According to the actual coder structure, the majority of audio codecs convert an audio block from the time domain to the frequency domain. However, a serious shortcoming of the block transform decoding scheme is the introduction of blocking artifacts in the reconstructed signal. Because the blocks are processed independently, quantization errors will produce discontinuities in the signal at the block boundaries. In order to prevent this effect, a principle has been investigated by [Malvar, 1989], in which a window of samples from two consecutive blocks undergoes the transformation. The window is then shifted by samples and the next set of transform coefficients is computed. Thus, each window overlaps the last samples of the previous window. The overlap ensures the continuity of the reconstructed samples despite the alteration of transform coefficients due to quantization. The corresponding calculations take a certain amount of time, which represents a part of the computational delay. The drawback of the described overlap processing principle is an increased latency of n overlapping samples, which corresponds to the term "lookahead". In fact, a number of transformation principles in context with various window types exist as stated in [Shlien, 1997] and [Spanias, 2007]. As an example, figure 5 shows a transformation as described in [Valin, 2009]. The audio block size equals 128 samples and the lookahead consists of 64 samples. If – with respect to figure 5 – a distributed system was configured with a sample rate of 48 kHz and a block size of 128 samples, the only additional coder delay would be introduced by the lookahead of 64 samples, which would result in 1.35 ms. Nevertheless, – as mentioned previously – audio codecs are generally designed

Figure 5. Example of a coder working with a frame size of 128 samples and a lookahead of 64 samples [Valin, 2009]

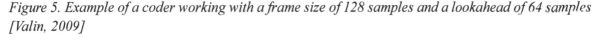
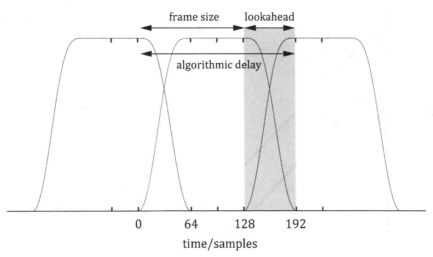

for larger block sizes, which involves a larger lookahead respectively. Furthermore, one would not want to configure a low delay music system depending on compression codecs with large block sizes such as 1024 samples. Hence, the described unproblematic relation between sound processing and codec blocking is only valid for respective small audio block sizes. In turn, an ideal lossy audio codec exhibits a minimal block size in order to match the low delay restrictions of the distributed music domain. However, since most codecs are either designed for the purpose of offline audio encoding or for VoIP applications, block sizes below 1024 samples are a rather uncommon number. Nevertheless, two compression codecs exist, which were designed for low audio block sizes:

The CELT codec – developed by Jean-Marc Valin – is distributed under an opensource license. CELT stands for "Constrained Energy Lapped Transform". It features full audio bandwidth of 44.1 kHz and 48 kHz at a constant bit rate from 32 kbps to 512 kbps and is meant to support applications where both high quality audio and low delay are desired. CELT is able to work with audio blocks of 256 samples and a lookahead of

128 samples, which in total results in 384 samples and the corresponding algorithmic delay [Valin, 2009]. However, the lowest adjustable delay can be achieved with a block configuration of 64 samples with the respective lookahead of 32 samples. This leads to a total algorithmic delay of 96 samples corresponding to 2 ms of delay for a sample rate of 48 kHz. The subtraction of the blocking delay of 64 samples leads to an encoding delay of only 0.67 ms for the lookahead.

The ULD compression codec ("ultra low delay"), developed by Gerald Schuller at Fraunhofer IDMT Ilmenau (Institute for Digital Media Technologies), supports sampling frequencies from 32 kHz to 48 kHz and is designed to process audio blocksizes of 128 samples with an adjustable constant bit rate (CBR) down to 96 kbps [Krämer, 2007]. Due to a lookahead of 128 samples the total algorithmic delay is made of 256 samples. After the subtraction of the blocking delay the additional ULD encoder delay results in 2.7 ms delay for a sample rate of 48 kHz.

In fact data compression implies an advantage in terms of the audio transmission time: With respect to the compression ratio a compressed audio block is proportionally faster transmitted

Figure 6. Network device transmission latencies

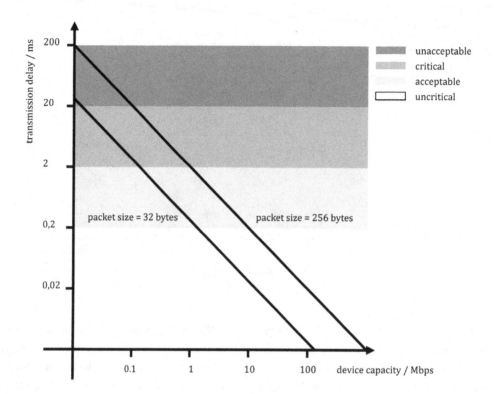

by the involved network gear as described in the following subsection and illustrated in figure 6.

If a sender has sent an encoded audio block the receiver must decode it in order to retrieve a usable audio signal. In that context the decoder must know the compression scheme the received block was encoded with. E.g. if the encoder transformed the audio to the frequency domain the decoder has to transform it back to the time domain in order to reconstruct an audible signal. Alternatively – if the encoder has decimated the signal – the decoder has to apply an upsampling by artificially inserting sample values into the received audio block. In fact, numerous encoding schemes exist, however, the decoding latency is only determined by the computational delay the decoder requires to complete the process. Hence – unlike the encoding – the decoding is not associated with additional algorithmic delays as shown in equation 7. However, according to the

actual codec, the final computational decoder delay might still introduce latencies beyond 1 ms, which is why the author marks the decoding stage as well with a slight delay.

$$d_{decoding} = d_{decodeComp} \qquad (7)$$

3.3 Signal Propagation and Transmission

Like analogue signals, digital signals can be transmitted on any kind of cable or radio wave but especially for long distance digital connections, fiber optic lines are used, which transmit the binary data via light impulses. Due to a reduction factor of 0.67 their maximum speed lies 10% below the speed of copper [Eberlein, 2007]. In case two musicians were connected with a fiber optic link and if we deny the existence of the previously mentioned sound card delays or additional sources of delay, the propagation delay would only depend on the propagation speed of the fiber optic medium. For an EDAL of 25 ms this would allow a fiber length of 5,025 km as calculated in equation 8.

$$(300,000 \text{ km} / 1,000 \text{ ms}) * 25 \text{ ms} * 0.67 = 5,025 \text{ km} \qquad (8)$$

Apart from the fact that sound data can be transmitted via fiber optic or copper lines with their appropriate signal speeds of $0.67 * c$ or $0.77 * c$, a further transmission speed limitation has to be taken into account: Digital networks are equipped with network gear such as switches or routers [Larisch, 2004], which basically guide each light impulse through a network in order to make it reach its correct and final destination. These network devices typically expect an input signal to be assigned to an output signal but in contradiction to the pure cable transmission this assignment suffers from further latencies: It is rather the capacity of a network device, which determines the delay for a signal to be mapped from one input port of a network device to an output port and this capacity is typically stated with the amount of bits per second (bps). The core of current networks consists of devices with capacities of several gigabits per second (Gbps). These so-called "backbone connections" [Douglas, 2002] are able to serve several millions of users directly or indirectly by linking traffic to or from interconnected sub networks. Device and network capacities depend on the amount of users a network has to serve. The lower the amount of users, the lower the bandwidth capacity a network is generally administrated with. Nowadays current backbone links provide capacities from 10 Gbps to 5 Gbps down to 2.5 Gbps or 1 Gbps, in contradiction a user's endpoint connection is able to achieve about 20 Mbps down to 128 kbps or even 56 kbps in worst case of modem usage [Tanenbaum, 2003]. Within these two extremes further links typically range from 10, 34 or 100 Mbps up to 622 Mbps as common figures. In

that context the term "wire speed" refers to this hypothetical maximum data transmission rate and in turn determines the theoretical best throughput and performance of a network device. We typically expect an optimized hardware device to operate at wire speed, rather than a software implementation, which might possibly suffer from CPU limitations.

With respect to the sound data the total required bandwidth b_{total} equals the product of the sample rate, the bitdepth and the number of channels, which equals 768 kbps for one audio stream with the standard settings of sample rate = 48 kHz, bitdepth = 16 Bit and a channel number of 1 as calculated in equation 9. This pure amount of audio data also refers to the term "payload". As a precondition for a successful data delivery any involved network component has to be able to handle at least this amount of payload data.

$$b_{total} = 48 \text{ kHz} * 16 \text{ Bit} * 1 = 768 \text{ kbps} \qquad (9)$$

In terms of latency it is important to distinguish between the propagation delay and the transmission delay: As illustrated in figure 6 an audio block of 256 bytes (128 samples * 16 Bit) already requires 16 ms to be fully transmitted on a 128 kbps link – in contradiction to just 25.6 ns on a 10 Gbps backbone connection. This delay, however, does not take the previously introduced signal propagation on the link into account: Nowadays networks exhibit a complex structure with a huge amount of interconnected sub networks. According to the network provider's capabilities and interests the treatment of a signal can vary significantly: Rather than providing a direct link between two peers the signal delivery mainly depends on the interconnected sub networks. In that context it could pass various paths from a sender to a receiver. These paths refer to the term "route", which is determined by the specific network providers. The longer the route the longer the propagation delay. As a consequence also the routing has a significant impact on the overall latency.

Hence, when estimating an audio block's total network transfer latency $d_{transfer}$, it is firstly the sum M of propagation delays $d_{propagation}$ caused by the total conductor length of each specific propagation medium divided by the respective medium propagation speed and secondly the sum N of packet transmission delays caused by the involved network components [Kurose, 2004]. This relationship is described by equation 10.

$$d_{transfer} = \sum_{M} d_{propagation} + \sum_{N} d_{transmission} \qquad (10)$$

Considering an audio block decimation or compression (c.f. section 3.2) the stated transmission delay values can be reduced by a fixed factor according to the actual compression rate. Figure 6 additionally illustrates the transmission delays of a 32 bytes packet, which corresponds to this decimation or compression factor of 8 compared to the original 256 bytes packet.

3.4 Principle of Internet-Based Low-Delay Audio Networking

The Internet as an asynchronous network is based on the asynchronous time division multiplex principle (ATDM), which implies that signal transmission happens randomly depending on stochastic host transmission activities. Furthermore, any network host is allowed to send a desired amount of data in a blockwise restricted manner, that is, if a sequence of bytes exceeds a certain upper size limit, this sequence will be split into chunks of that maximal size. Such chunks of data are also considered as packets, blocks or frames and their maximal size is called the maximum transfer unit (MTU) [Tanenbaum, 2003]. This uncomplicated approach, however, has a significant drawback, which refers to the terms "network jitter" [Tanenbaum, 2003] and describes a delay variation of the delivered data blocks. This effect occurs due to the fact that certain data blocks cannot be transmitted

before a network component has completed the transmission of a previous data block. This results in additional waiting times, which increase with the amount of so-called "cross traffic" of additional network hosts. The less transmission capacity a network component has the higher the amount of network jitter. Especially in context with the small subsequent data blocks of low-delayed audio streams this leads to significant problems: The larger a cross traffic data packet is the longer it blocks the transmission medium. According to this waiting time the subsequent audio block will be delivered later [Douglas, 2002]. However, as the playout buffer of a sound card expects data in constant time intervals depending on the actual settings (c.f. section 3.1), sudden increases of the network delay would violate this precondition of constant and errorfree audio stream playback. This leads to a so-called "drop out" in the received audio stream. Due to this problem the Internet was mainly designed as a non-real-time-communication system, which does not make strong demands on the network in terms of delay or jitter. However, since the Internet has such an impact on our daily life and since modern personal computers can already provide high quality multimedia content, the idea of the Internet as a network for supporting any desired service, has become attractive to users and the industry as well. Hence, despite the drawbacks of asynchrony, realtime services such as Internet radio, video conferencing and Internet telephony (VoIP) [Black, 2000] [ITU, 1998] have evolved quickly. These services have been improved constantly and almost 20 years later they have become extremely reliable and a generally accepted form of realtime communication [ITU, 2007].

The common approach to compensate the effect of network jitter is the application of a jitter buffer at a receiver's end: By storing up an amount of audio packets in the network queue, the audio process can still provide a solid playback in case of late arriving packets. The drawback of this principle is a higher latency as packets are not processed right after the reception [Kos,

2002]. Nevertheless, with increasing bandwidth capacities in the backbone and the endpoints the network jitter looses significance over time. In that context the domain of distributed music with the respective low audio- and network buffer sizes can be considered as the next evolutionary step.

4 ALTERNATIVE INTERACTION APPROACHES

In the first section the author described the cognitive aspects of delay-influenced musical interaction and defined the EDAL (ensemble delay acceptance limit) as an individual and speed-dependent measure, below which musical interaction is possible. As the next step, the author explained any technical aspect in terms of latency in the previous section and concluded with the total signal path, an audio signal has to undergo when being transmitted on the Internet. This chapter will bring together the cognitive and the technical results by creating a descriptive categorization of various interaction approaches depending on the expected signal latencies. In this context it examines further situations, in which the EDAL requirements cannot be met. Such a situation can appear when either the physical route length between two peers is too large, strong jitter requires a high amount of audio buffering or various network gear results in additional undesired delays.

Generally, in rhythmical music we have to distinguish between a solo instrument and a rhythm instrument. Apart from that the placement of the so-called "rhythm section" is of significant importance. As an example with drums, bass and saxophone, a simple case is present in which drums and bass form the "rhythm section" while the saxophone player represents the "solo section". Though of course the solo section and any musician must have a sense of rhythm, it is basically the interplay of bass and drums which forms the essential fundamental groove of an

ensemble which allows other solo instruments to play upon. In this scenario the saxophone player relies on and plays on the groove that is produced by the rhythm section. Due to the fact that rhythm and synchrony are the main fundament of groove-based music, the following subsections put emphasis on rhythm based instruments and the groove building process.

The rhythm section will consist of drums and bass, the solo section is represented by a saxophone player as a simple example scenario. Based on the actual delay between two players, the author will divide the possibilities of a musical interplay into three main categories A to C. Category A represents the ideal scenario with delays up to the EDAL. Category B approaches to maintain a rhythmical interplay despite latencies beyond the EDAL by applying three different artistic compromises. Category C introduces a further form of remote musical interaction. In this context the currently existing related work is embedded into the appropriate categories.

4.1 Category A: Realistic Interaction Approach (RIA)

A realistic musical interaction, as if in the same room, assumes a stable one-way latency below the EDAL between two rhythm-based instruments such as drums and bass. In this scenario both instruments' grooves merge and the real musical interplay can happen [Chafe, 2004]. From the perceptual point of view the delay appears to be not existent, which is similar to musicians playing with a physical distance of numerous meters in a rehearsing space, where the speed of sound is the limiting time delay factor. The realistic interaction approach (RIA) is the only approach professional musicians accept without any compromise since it is the only scenario, which exactly represents the conventional process of creating music in groups or bands. Beyond the EDAL, the groove-building-process cannot be realized by musicians and thus different compromises are required [Carôt, 2007].

Figure 7 shows that below the EDAL both players are able to play at the same instant and receive each other's signals as if no delay was existent.

Due to technical difficulties in applying the required RIA conditions, RIA has so far not turned into a commercial entity but has mainly been examined in research projects, such as Sound-WIRE [Caceres, 2008] and the author's "Soundjack" system [Carôt, 2008][Soundjack, 2010].

4.2 Category B1: Master Slave Approach (MSA)

Assuming an attendance to compromise and to step back from musical perfection and ideals, it really is feasible to perform with two rhythm-based instruments such as drums and bass, even when exceeding the EDAL – simply if one of the musicians keeps track of his rhythm and does not listen to the incoming high delayed signal anymore. In that situation the remote side can perfectly play to the incoming signal since the other no longer cares about the response anymore – a change in the musical interaction is happening, which the author terms the master slave approach (MSA). The first musician takes the master role since he is producing the basic groove, while the remote musician simply relies on it and hence takes the slave role [Schuett, 2002]. Of course, the higher the delay, the more difficult the ignorance of the delayed input can be realized by the master, since shorter delays will easier establish a musical connection to the previously played notes. In terms of delay MSA generates no latency and perfect synchronization on the slaves side but on the other hand it delays the slave with the roundtrip delay on the master's side. The slave has a perfect synchronization but musically depends on the master, while the master has musical independency but an unsatisfying sync [Carôt, 2007]. Figure 8 shows a situation with a delay beyond the EDAL between two players. Due to the high delay the slave has to abstain from playing until the master's signal has arrived, which finally leads to a roundtrip delay on the master's end.

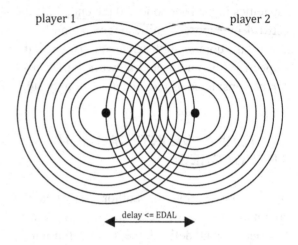

Figure 7. Realistic interaction approach

player 1   player 2

delay <= EDAL

In general the master role is taken by a rhythmic instrument in order to let solo instruments play on its groove in slave mode. An exception can occur when a rhythmic instrument suddenly starts with a solo part. In this case it will require the other instrument to take over the leading rhythmic role, which in turn leads to a switch of roles. MSA can be applied with any system that allows the transmission of realtime data on the Internet. This could be a tool for IP telephony or videoconferencing, which does not put emphasis on low delay signal transmission, but also high speed audio transmitters in an intercontinental setup. In the latter case the main source of latency is the long physical distance. Nevertheless MSA has more to be considered as a theoretical model, which does not provide a real musical interaction. Due to an artistically inconvenient situation it is not likely that musicians would ever use it as a serious musical approach, however, it represents the base for the following two approaches.

4.3 Category B2: Laid Back Approach (LBA)

The laid back approach (LBA) is based on the "laid back" playing manner, which is a common and accepted solo style in jazz music. The Laid

Figure 8. Master slave approach

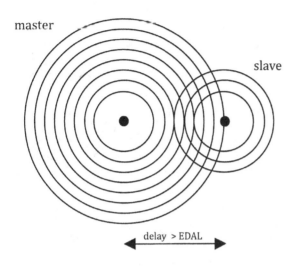

Back Approach is similar to the principle of the Master/Slave Approach and is mainly determined by the number of participating instruments and their role. As previously mentioned, two rhythm-based instruments separated by delays beyond the EDAL have to play with MSA but in case of one of the instruments being a solo instrument, the situation changes. Exchanging the drums with a saxophone in the example scenario results in a remote rhythm/solo-constellation in which the bass represents the rhythm instrument and the saxophone the solo instrument. Since the bass no longer has a rhythmic counterpart, it alone takes the responsibility for the groove while the saxophone plays its solo part on it. Equally to MSA the saxophone has a perfect sync on its side and is transmitted back with the roundtrip time but in comparison to MSA this has no disturbing effect on the rhythm instrument in LBA. The saxophone is delayed by the roundtrip delay time, which adds an artificial laid back style on it and hence this playing constellation is no longer considered as problematic. LBA of course does not work for unison music parts, in which both parties have to play exactly on the same beat and at the same time.

The additional delay on the master's end can range between 20 ms up to a maximum of 150 ms

[Carôt, 2009]. The precise value mainly depends on the bpm of the actual song and the musician's subjective perception [Carôt, 2007]. Figure 9 is similar to the MSA principle but due to the according lower maximal one-way delay and the determination of a rhythm and a solo section this situation leads to an artificial "laid back" effect. LBA can be used when the delay ranges in areas slightly beyond the EDAL threshold up to latencies at which the signal's "laid back" character starts shifting to an "out of time" character and in turn MSA has to be used. Musicians typically do not know of LBA as a serious form of musical interaction and hence it does not represent a popular or commonly applied approach for musical interaction. Nevertheless, the author already performed numerous LBA sessions with his Soundjack software.

4.4 Category B3: Delayed Feedback Approach (DFA)

In case the EDAL is exceeded, the delayed feedback approach (DFA) tries to make musicians feel like playing with the RIA by delaying the player's own signal artificially: By principle delays beyond the EDAL lead to either LBA or MSA, in which the master hears the slave with a delay equal to the roundtrip time while the slave plays in perfect sync. When delaying the playback of the master's signal, both sounds finally have a closer proximity at the master's ear, which improves the problematic delay gap in MSA or reduces the laid back effect in LBA and finally terminates the master/slave separation. Details in context with the DFA can be found in [Carôt, 2009].

The larger the self-delay, the better the synchronization of both signals. The best synchronization can be reached with a self-delay equal to the roundtrip-time. More descriptively this particular situation is present if one player listens to his own signal via a feedback loop on the remote side. As this setup guarantees the elimination of a delay gap between the two sides, rhythmical RIA conditions

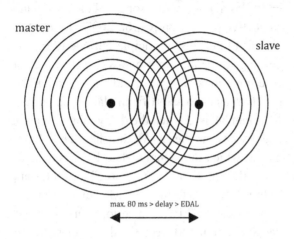

Figure 9. Laid back approach

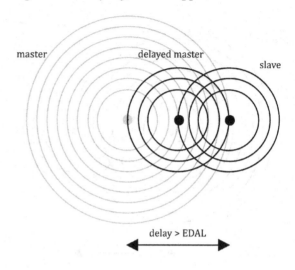

Figure 10. Delayed feedback approach with SDF

can be achieved this way if the master consciously plays ahead of time in order to compensate its self-delay. This principle is illustrated in figure 10. Since only one player suffers from the artificial self delay, this principle refers to the term SDF (single delayed feedback). A second variation of DFA is present when both instruments play with an artificial self-delay as illustrated in figure 11. In this so-called DDF (dual delayed feedback) setup the previously applied roundtrip delay can be provided either symmetrically or asymmetrically to the two players. In either DFA principle the amount of self-delay can be reduced up to a certain limit. This offset value can be calculated according to [Carôt, 2009]. Nevertheless, although DFA improves the delay situation between two musicians, it is no doubt that a delay of one's own signal typically can be considered as inconvenient and not natural. The larger the delay gets and the louder the instrument's direct noise, the worse the realistic instrument feel and playing conditions. A system based on DFA is the NcMP project of a research group lead by Prof. Dr. Lars Wolf at the University of Braunschweig, Germany [Xiaoyuan, 2004]. It uses a central server between two players, which receives either stream, mixes them and sends this mix back to the original sender. This way an asymmetric DDF is applied to the

players, however, the route to the additional server results in additional delays, furthermore this principle determines the amount of self delay to the theoretical maximum without the possibility of adjusting a self delay offset. Moreover, an SDF-based audio transmitter has been presented in [Carôt & Hohn, 2009].

4.5 Category C1: Latency Accepting Approach (LAA)

While previous approaches have attempted to uncover alternative ways to achieve realistic network music performances, the latency accepting approach (LAA) steps back from latency-optimized or compromised solutions and simply accepts delays beyond the EDAL. In principle LAA has no motivation to create conventional music and thus can allow any delay, which is consciously taken it into account. In this scenario musicians play with the delay and use it as an artistic way of expression. LAA is the most avantgardistic approach resulting in a total dissociation of musical conventions and functions with the Internet as the core technology. The latency between the players in figure 12 has such a strong dimension that their rhythmical interaction is no longer related.

Figure 11. Delayed feedback approach with DDF

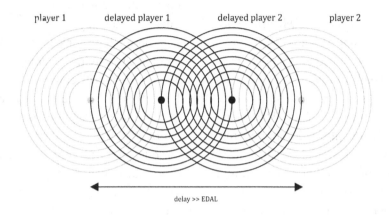

In terms of new avantgardistic music in LAA, the Quintet.net framework by Georg Hajdu [Hajdu, 2003] fulfills relevant requirements and can be applied under any kind of network condition. Quintet.net transmits MIDI control data and does not necessarily require the user to play a musical instrument, rather the user can play with an electronic input device for the sound generation. Apart from that, various worldwide network sessions with the Jacktrip software [Caceres, 2008] as part of the SoundWIRE project have taken place, in which contemporary music is the dominating style of performance [Carôt, 2007].

5 CONCLUSION AND FUTURE WORK

The area of distributed music represents an extremely complex field of interdisciplinary research and development, which embraces aspects of music cognition, sound engineering and computer science. Special aspects of audio engineering, related to the strong cognitive restrictions in terms of latency and quality, make strong demands on a successful network music performance in order to provide musicians with a convenient and playable situation as if in the same room. Although the Internet constantly evolves regarding the delivery of high qualitative realtime traffic, the main is-

Figure 12. Rhythmically unrelated sound sources in LAA mode

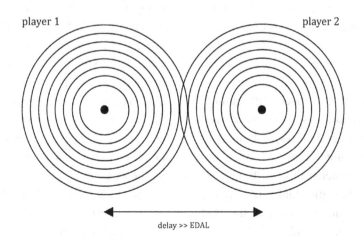

sue is still the transmission latency between two music peers.

A convenient latency condition, which matches a situation as in the same room, is difficult to obtain due to a variety of factors. The conductor's propagation speed, the total cable length and transmission capacities of routers and switches determine the total transfer delay. The sound processing and network jitter buffers generate significant additional delays and finally restrict the radius of a playable situation to a maximum of approximately 1,000 km. In that context one must no longer consider the Internet as a location-independent medium as is the case for conventional web services such as web browsing, email and even VoIP. Although the latter can currently be considered as the most representative realtime traffic application, its feasibility is – in contradiction to the domain of distributed music – not determined by the physical distance between two peers. The precise maximal delay and in turn the precise maximal distance musicians can perform with, however, cannot be stated by a precise number: As the result of numerous experiments with professional musicians, this value primarily depends on the speed of a rhythm in bpm and also on the musicians individual delay acceptance limit. This so-called "ensemble delay acceptance limit" (EDAL) corresponds to an individual rhythmical attitude and has the same significance in conventional music scenarios played in the same room as it has on a network. Practically observed values range between 5 ms for fast rhythms up to 65 ms for slow rhythms.

In order to give a musician the possibility to precisely figure the best possible latency to a remote host, the author developed a distributed music system, which is able to stream low delayed audio data on the Internet and allows for the manual adjustment of any relevant stream parameter. Depending on the current network condition users can individually set the audio frame size and the jitter buffer sizes in order to approach the best compromise between latency and audio dropouts.

Hence, unlike in VoIP, dropouts are consciously taken into account as the main goal lies in the reduction of latency. Generally it can be stated that the approach of consciously accepting a certain amount of individually tolerable audio dropouts also conflicts with conventional disciplines in the field of audio engineering, where the achievement of maximal audio quality is the dominating motivation. Nevertheless, disrupted audio signals can be concealed with conventional audio restoration techniques such as audio extrapolation: Based on the signal's past it is possible to calculate its future, which in turn allows to fill noise gaps with such artificially calculated signal parts. However, investigations in context with low delayed audio streams lead to the conclusion that on current PC hardware and respective operating systems the existing algorithms are unable to generate such extrapolated audio blocks with the desired quality at the the required speed. Hence, with respect to future work, a major goal lies in achieving a high-quality-extrapolation speed, which remains below the critical minimal audio block duration of 1 ms.

In case a network does not offer enough bandwidth for the delivery of uncompressed audio streams, it is also possible to apply either decimation or lossless compression techniques with corresponding delays below 500 µs but with a low compression factor of 2. Alternatively the developed distributed music system hosts two lossy low delay audio codecs with compression rates of factor 8: The Fraunhofer ULD codec achieves an additional latency of approximately 2.7 ms, while the open-source CELT codec provides approximately 0.65 ms at a sampling rate of 48 kHz. The CELT codec additionally implies a conventional packet loss concealment (PLC), but also in this context numerous practical tests again confirmed, that current PLC techniques are insufficient in terms of low delayed audio streams on the Internet.

However, even if either insufficient sound card latencies, long network routes, or large jitter buffers, result in latencies beyond the ensemble-delay-acceptance-limit (EDAL). The author defined a number of musical interaction categories, which allow a compromized interplay, which either work with the effect of an artificially laid back, avantgardistic music styles without a rythmic reference or with artificial self delays. In any case – even if alternative interaction categories are being applied – latency improvement is appreciated in order to either approach a realistic musical interaction or reduce the effects of compromised interplay such as the amount of self delay or the artificial laid back effect. Consequently the author's streaming solution takes both aspects into account: On one hand it offers minimal latency by directly accessing the sound card driver and processing data as described above, on the other hand it supports both the single-delayed-feedback approach (SDF) and the dual-delayedfeedback approach (DDF) by applying an adjustable self delay, an automatic high quality feedback loop and a customizable metronome without the need for additional sound engineering setups or devices. In terms of the master/slave approach (MSA), laid-back-approach (LBA) and the latency-appecting approach (LAA), no additional functionality is required as such approaches address the players ability to adapt their musical interaction styles. Hence, the current distributed music system supports each of the proposed categories.

With respect to more than 5 years of experience with the proposed concept of low delay audio transmission on the Internet, the author comes to the conclusion, that – apart from audio engineering, network and music skills – the awareness of delay dimensions and their musical consequences is the main basic requirement for a successful network music performance. Depending on the actual network connection and the respective delays, the user has to consciously apply the suitable category of musical interplay, which finally allows him to perform under any given network situation.In turn this allows him awareness of actual possibilities and limitations in his current situation. However, due to the high amount of

interdisciplinary knowledge, distributed music has thus far been used in a limited capacity by a small community of experts in IT as well as in music, so that it cannot be considered as an established technology for musical interaction. Despite the existence of first commercial products, musicians and sound engineers remain passive in terms of accepting and applying this new approach. As the technical facts clearly prove the feasibility of network music performances, with this elaboration, the author hopes to motivate musicians and engineers to take advantage of the musical possibilities distributed music can offer. In the future the author will further investigate in the realistic interaction approach for the Internet in order to increase the radius, in which realistic interaction approach (RIA) can be applied.

REFERENCES

Apple Computer Inc. (2001). *Audio and MIDI on Mac OS X*, Technical report.

Bencina, R. (2003). Portaudio and media synchronisation – it's all in the timing. In *Proceedings of the ACMC Conference*, Perth, Australia.

Black, U. (2000). *Voice Over IP* (1st ed.). Upper Saddle River, NJ: Prentice Hall.

Caceres, J. P., Hamilton, R., Iyer, D., Chafe, C., & Wang, G. (2008, November). To the edge with china: Explorations in network performance. In *Proceedings of the 4th International Conference on Digital Arts*, Porto, Portugal.

Carôt, A. (2004). *Livemusic on the Internet*. Diploma thesis, Fachhochschule Lübeck, Germany.

Carôt, A. (2009). *Musical Telepresence – A Comprehensive Analysis Towards New Cognitive and Technical Approaches*. (PhD Thesis), Institute of Telematics – University of Lübeck, Germany.

Carôt, A., Hohn, T., & Werner, C. (2009). Netjack – remote music collaboration with electronic sequencers on the internet. In *Proceedings of the Linux audio conference*, Parma, Italy.

Carôt, A., Krämer, U., & Schuller, G. (2006, May). Network music performance in narrow band networks. In *Proceedings of the 120th AES convention*, Paris, France.

Carôt, A., & Werner, C. (2007, September). Network music performance – problems, approaches and perspectives. In *Proceedings of the Music in the Global Village – Conference*, Budapest, Hungary.

Carôt, A., & Werner, C. (2008). Distributed network music workshop with soundjack. In *Proceedings of the 25th Tonmeistertagung*, Leipzig, Germany.

Carôt, A., Werner, C., & Fischinger, C. (2009, August). Towards a comprehensive cognitive analysis of delay-influenced rhythmical interaction. In *Proceedings of the International Computer Music Conference (ICMC)*, Montreal, Canada.

Chafe, C., Gurevich, M., Leslie, G., & Tyan, S. (2004, March). Effect of time delay on ensemble accuracy. In *Proceedings of the International Symposium on Musical Acoustics*, Nara, Japan.

Comer, D. E. (2002). *Computernetzwerke und Internets mit Internet-Anwendungen* (3rd ed.). Pearson Studium.

Eberlein, D. (2007). *Lichtwellenleiter-Technik: Grundlagen, Verbindungs- und Messtechnik, Systeme, Trends* (7th ed.). Berlin, Germany: Verlag.

Everest, F. A. (2001). *The Master Handbook of Acoustics* (2nd ed.). New York: McGraw-Hill.

Goncalves I., Pfeiffer, S., & Montgomery, C. (2008, September). RFC 5334: *Ogg media types*.

Hajdu, G. (2003). Quintet.net – a quintet on the internet. In *Proceedings of the International Computer Music Conference*, Singapore.

Institute of Electrical and Inc. Electronics Engineers (2008). *1394-2008 IEEE Standard for a High-Performance Serial Bus*.

International Telecommunication Union (ITU). Recommendation H.323 (1998). Audiovisual *and multimedia systems – Infrastructure of audiovisual services* – Systems and terminal equipment for audiovisual services – Packet-based multimedia communications systems.

International Telecommunication Union (ITU) (2007). Document: FoV/04: *Future of Voice - Status of VoIP*.

Kos, A., Klepec, B., & Tomazic, S. (2002). Techniques for performance improvement of voip applications. In *Proceedings of the 11th Electrotechnical Conference MELECON*, Cairo, Egypt.

Krämer, U., Hirschfeld, J., Schuller, G., Wabnik, S., Carôt, A., & Werner, C. (2007, October). Network music performance with ultra-low-delay audio coding under unreliable network conditions. In *Proceedings of the 123rd AES-Convention*, New York, USA.

Kurose, J., & Ross, K. (2004). *Computer Networking: A Top-Down Approach Featuring the Internet* (3rd ed.). Reading, MA: Addison Wesley.

Larisch, D. (2004). *TCP/IP* (2nd ed.). New York: Moderne Industrie Buch AG.

Levine, M. W., & Shefner, J. M. (2001). *Fundamentals of Sensation and Perception* (3rd ed.). Oxford University Press.

Malvar, H., & Staelin, D. (1989). The lot transform coding without blocking effects. *IEEE Transactions on Speech and Audio Processing*, (37): 553–559.

Pohlmann, K. C. (2005). *Principles of Digital Audio* (5th ed.). New York: The Mcgraw-Hill Companies.

Schuett, N. (2002). *The effect of latency on ensemble performance*, (Bachelor thesis), Stanford University.

Shlien, S. (1997). The modulated lapped transform, its time-varying forms, and its applications to audio coding standards. *IEEE Transactions on Speech and Audio Processing*, (5): 359–366. doi:10.1109/89.593311

Soundjack website (2010, February). *Soundjack*. Retrieved February 5, 2010, from http://www.soundjack.eu.

Spanias, A., Painter, T., & Atti, V. (2007). *Audio Signal Processing and Coding* (1st ed.). New York: Wiley-Interscience. doi:10.1002/0470041978

Tanenbaum, A. S. (2003). *Computer Networks* (4th ed.). Upper Saddle River, NJ: Pearson Studium.

Valin, J. M., Terriberry, T., Montgomery, C., & Maxwell, G. (2009). A high-quality speech and audio codec with less than 10 ms delay. In *Proceedings of IEEE Transactions on Audio, Speech and Language Processing*.

Xiaoyuan, G., Dick, M., Noyer, U., & Wolf, L. (2004, June). NMP – A new networked music performance system. In *Proceedings of the 4th NIME Conference*.

ADDITIONAL READING

The domain of distributed music on the Internet must be considered a relatively new research track, which has been existing since the late 1990s. As a consequence the amount of existing publications still exhibits a limited number. In addition to the references of this chapter the author suggests to further examine work carried out by the following persons (in alphabetical order): Alain Renaud, Alvaro Barbosa, Chris Chafe, Elaine Chew, Franziska Schröder, Georg Hajdu, Jeremy Cooperstock, Pedro Rebello.

KEY TERMS AND DEFINITIONS

Internet: An asynchronous network of internationally connected devices using the IP protocol.

Latency: The time duration between two events.

Low Delay: A relatively low time duration between two events. In audio streaming "low-delay" generally corresponds to latencies below 30 ms.

Cognition: Aspects related to the human perception and their physical and/or psychological consequences.

Musical Interaction: The ability to artistically correspond with another person in an individual, meaningful way.

Digital Signal Processing: Principles and mathematical terms related to the description of digital signals and systems.

Audio Processing: A special form of signal processing related to audible signals — nowadays mainly digital rather than analogue.

Sound Cards: Electronic circuits boards, which operate in personal computers in order to capture and playback sound data.

Audio Streaming: The process of transmitting chunks of digital audio data across an IP network.

Synchronisation: Linking or controlling two or more processes in order to achieve equal execution intervals.

Chapter 16
The 3rd Generation Partnership Project Packet-Switched Streaming (3GPP-PSS):
Fundamentals and Applications

Sasan Adibi
Research in Motion (RIM), Canada

Nayef Mendahawi
Research in Motion (RIM), Canada

Maiyuran Wijayanathan
Research in Motion (RIM), Canada

ABSTRACT

Streaming is a service by which real-time data traffic is transferred between the streaming server and the wireless/wired device. Streaming was initially designed for broadband Internet audio and video transmissions, which soon expanded to cover mobile networks as well. The third Generation Partnership Project (3GPP) was created in 1998, which embodied collaboration agreements of numerous telecommunication standardization organizations and bodies, initially targeted for evolved GSM and UMTS (WCDMA) networks. The 3GPP Packet Switched Streaming (3GPP-PSS) specifications define the framework for streaming capabilities for 3GPP mobile devices and networks, including the functionality, interoperability, media types and compatibility specifications. This chapter embodies the chronological advances of 3GPP-PSS and discussions on the general specifications of different releases, including Release 4, 5, 6, 7, and 8 with a focus on the Quality of Service (QoS) support.

INTRODUCTION

Streaming is the capability of an application running on a wired or wireless device to play synchronized media streams, such as audio and video data in a continuous or batch method while the streaming data contents are delivered to the client over a data network.

Applications being built on top of streaming services, can be classified into live information and on-demand delivery applications. An example

DOI: 10.4018/978-1-61692-831-5.ch016

Copyright © 2011, IGI Global. Copying or distributing in print or electronic forms without written permission of IGI Global is prohibited.

of the first category is live delivery of radio and television programs. News-on-demand and music applications are examples of the second category.

One of very important applications is streaming over fixed-IP networks. While IETF has developed a set of protocols based on fixed-IP streaming services, there is no complete standardized framework defined for streaming framework. In 3G systems, the gap between 3G MMS has been filled with the 3G packet-switched streaming service (PSS), which includes conversational and downloading services. PSS runs on top of mobile systems using streaming applications. Compared to conversational services, PSS requires lower protocol and terminal complexity, which is in contract with streaming terminals that require media encoders, media input devices, and more complex protocols.

This chapter describes an application level transparent 3G packet-switched streaming services (3G PSS) based on the 3GPP PSS evolution, across different releases; Releases 4 (2001) and 5 (2002) for general concept and architectures and later Releases; Release 6 (2004), 7 (2006), and 8 (2008), for more advanced features (i.e., QoS support, etc).

BACKGROUND

The third generation partnership project (3GPP), established in 1998, is a collaboration agreement between several telecommunication standardization bodies. The original scope was to produce globally applicable technical specification and reports for a third generation mobile system on evolved GSM networks on top of UMTS.

Transparent end-to-end packet switch streaming service is a specification that defines a framework for an interoperable streaming service in 3GPP mobile networks. PSS is an application level service that mostly deals with the client and server streaming.

Table 1 (H. Schulzrinne et al (1996), H. Schulzrinne (1996), H. Schulzrinne et al (2003), C. Huitema (2003), D. Wing (2007), J. Ott et al (2006), H. Schulzrinne et al (1998), M. Handley (1998), S. Casner (2003), M. Handley et al (2006)) contains a summary of PSS streaming related protocols, namely; RTP (Real-Time Protocol), RTCP (Real-Time Control Protocol), RTSP (Real-time Streaming Protocol), and SDP (Session Description Protocol). These protocols are introduced and their updates are provided in a series of Request For Comments (RFCs). The related RFCs are also mentioned in Table 1, including the initial RFC and the subsequent updated RFCs.

The PSS session/transport-related protocols are further explained:

RTP: RTP provides end-to-end network functions suitable for applications transmitting real-time data, such as audio or simulation data, over multicast or unicast network services. RTP does not address resource reservation and does not guarantee any Quality of Service (QoS) for real-time services. It should be noted that in PSS, RTP is carried over UDP only.

Furthermore RTP is a dominant transport-independent streaming media transport protocol, which is mostly run on top of UDP and usually accompanied by RTCP. RTP provides end-to-end delivery services for real-time traffic, including: interactive audio and video. It also provides sequence numbering, time-stamping and delivery monitoring. RTP is fast and ideal for multicasting.

RTCP: The primary function of RTCP is to provide feedback on the quality of data distribution. This is achieved by periodic "receiver report" packets sent on the receiver to the sender (reports contain items such as: inter-arrival jitter measured by the receiver and number of packet lost).

Furthermore RTCP is used to synchronize across different media streams and to provide feedback on the quality of data using lost packet counts. It identifies and keeps track of participants and accommodates retransmission requests. Unlike what mentioned in some literatures, RTCP

Table 1. Summary of PSS session/transport-related protocols

RTP	RFC 1889 - RTP: A Transport Protocol for Real-Time Applications RFC 1890 - RTP Profile for Audio and Video Conferences with Mini RFC 3550 - RTP: A Transport Protocol for Real-Time Applications
RTCP	RFC 3605 - Real Time Control Protocol (RTCP) attribute in Session Description Protocol (SDP) RFC 4961 - Symmetric RTP / RTP Control Protocol (RTCP) RFC 4585 - Extended RTP Profile for Real-time Transport Control Protocol (RTCP)-Based Feedback (RTP/AVPF)
RTSP	RFC 2326 - Real Time Streaming Protocol (RTSP)
SDP	RFC 2327 - SDP: Session Description Protocol RFC 3556 - Session Description Protocol (SDP) Bandwidth Modifiers for RTP Control Protocol (RTCP) Bandwidth RFC 4566 - SDP: Session Description Protocol

is not a signaling protocol and is merely used to collect end-to-end information about the quality of the session to each participant. Some of RTCP packet fields include: SR (sender report), RR (receiver report), SDES (Source DEScription), BYE (Hangs up from a session), and ASP (Application-Specific packet).

RTSP: RTSP is used to establish and control time-synchronized streams of continuous media. It acts as a "network remote control" for multimedia services. The protocol itself is textual and resembles HTTP, the main differences being that RTP is stateful and the media data is (usually) delivered out-of-band using a separate transport protocol (normally RTP). RTSP is a Client-server protocol, which provides functionality to establish and control a streaming session. RTSP is a transaction-oriented, request-response protocol similar to HTTP.

Furthermore RTSP is a text-based, transaction-oriented and request-response protocol, and can handle rough synchronization (fine-grained) with virtual presentations capability having synchronized playback from several servers. During stream, RTSP can accommodate load balancing using redirection at connect and supports any session description, including SDP. Examples of RTSP methods include: OPTIONS, SETUP, ANNOUNCE, DESCRIBE, PLAY, RECORD, REDIRECT, PAUSE, SET, PARAMETER, and

TEARDOWN. Figure 1 (adapted from Anshuman Mishra et al (2004)) shows the RTSP protocol state machines which are comprised of 4 states: Initiate, Ready, Play, and Recording. This figure shows RTSP's minimum architectural requirements.

It's vital to differentiate between RTSP and RTP. RTSP allows a two-way communication and is particularly used when users communicate with a unicast server and with the streaming server and perform functions dealing with the movie/music contents (i.e., rewind, fast forward, etc). RTP, by contrast, is a one-way protocol conveying stored or live streams between client-server pairs.

RTSP comes in two versions of RTSP; namely RTSP v1.0 and v2.0. RTSP 1.0 is merely based on RFC 2326. RTSP 2.0 (H. Schulzrinne et al (2009)) is an updated version, which is not backwards compatible with RTSP 1.0, except for the basic version negotiation mechanism part. The differences between these two versions include changes in the syntaxes, media play behaviors, explicit IPv6 supports, variations in negotiation capabilities, and feature tags.

SDP: The purpose of SDP is to convey information about media streams in multimedia sessions to allow the recipients of a session description to participate in the session. It is a text based protocol with relatively simple and extendable syntax.

Furthermore SDP is also text-based and is widely deployed in VoIP protocols (i.e., SIP,

Figure 1. RTSP protocol state machine

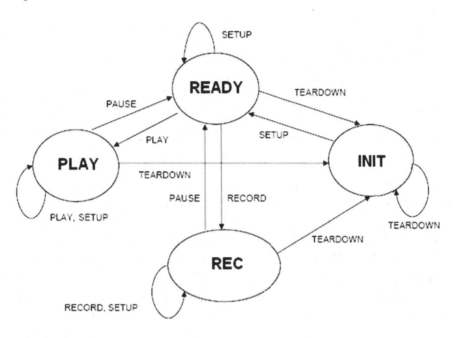

Table 2. PSS audio and video codecs

Type	Codec (Decoder)	Support	Average Bitrate Range
Speech	AMR-NB	Required	8 kbps – 12.2 kbps
Speech	AMR-WB	Required	16 kbps – 23.85 kbps
Audio	MPEG-4 AAC-LC	Recommended	8 kbps – 48 kbps
Audio	MPEG-4 AAC-LTP	Optional	8 kbps – 48 kbps
Video	H.263	Recommended	64 kbps
Video	MPEG-4 VSP	Optional	64 kbps
Video	H.264 Full Baseline	Optional	64 kbps

MGCP, etc) and can be carried as a payload of session control protocol. SDP is can engage in negotiation (offer/answer model), exchange of encryption keys, SDPng, etc. It should be noted that SDP is not really a protocol, but a format or description, which was originally used with SAP (Session Announcement Protocol) to announce Mbone sessions. SDP uses the following three parts: (1) Session description (version, owner, session name, etc), (2). Timing information, and (3) Media description: Which controls the following areas: (a). Media type (i.e., video, audio,

etc), (b) Transport protocol (RTP/UDP/IP), and (c) Media format (i.e., MPEG4 video, H.261). Other optional Session Control Protocols include WSP (Wireless Session Protocol) and SIP (Session Initiation Protocol).

The PSS-related protocols are responsible for the delivery of multimedia traffic, including: Speech, Audio, and Video information. Table 2 contains the most popular multimedia codecs covered under PSS-related protocols, mainly maintained in 3GPP-PSS Releases 4, 5, and 6 (C. Huitema (2003), 3GPP Rel6 V650 (2008),

Table 3. PSS functional-related protocols

Session Setup	RTSP	General Control and Setup
Session Control	SDP	Media Description
Transport	RTP/UDP (incl. RTCP)	For Continuous Media
	HTTP/TCP	For Discontinuous Media
Presentation Layout	SMIL 2.0 Basic Profile	Spatio-Temporal Layout of Presentation
Capability Exchange	UAProf	XML Based Description of Capabilities/Properties

3GPP TS 22.233 V6.3.0 (2003), 3GPP TS 22.173 V7.3.0 (2007), 3GPP TS 32.313 V6.4.0 (2007), 3GPP TS 26.244 V6.7.0 (2007), 3GPP TS 26.245 V6.1.0 (2004), ARIB STD-T63-26.246 V6.1.0 (2006), TSGS#19(03)0169 (2003), Emre B. Aksu (2004), Odd Inge Hillestad (2007), Packet Switched Streaming Service (2003), 3GPP TS 26.233 Release 8.0 V8.0.0 (2008), ARIB STD-T63-26.233 V8.0.0 (2008)).

THE 3RD GENERATION PARTNERSHIP PROJECT PACKET-SWITCHED STREAMING (3GPP-PSS) PROTOCOL

PSS: Functional Protocols

So far we have described the session/transport-related protocols. In this section we will describe the functional-related protocols, which are described in Table 3 (adapted from J. Hautakorpi, et al (2005)). The session setup and control is done using RTSP and SDP. The transport-related protocols including RTP, UDP, TSCP, and HTTP (based on TCP). The presentation layout is based on SMIL (Synchronized Multimedia Integration Language) specifications. SMIL is a description XML-based language similar to HTML. It combines media elements (video, audio, image, and text) to create interactive multimedia presentation. At the client application level it is also used for media rendering.

The capabilities exchange in wireless devices is performed through User Agent Profile (UAProf) specification. UAProf can be used by content providers to produce content in an appropriate format for the specific device. Composite Capabilities / Preferences Profile (CC/PP) provides capabilities and profiles of a device or a user agent and is XML compatible. It allows server to customize presentation and media with client capabilities. Whenever a client establishes a link with a server, the list of capabilities (i.e., screen size, 3GPP PSS version, etc) will be sent to the other side and both parties will agree on the best possible matches. This is done through the UAProfile file exchange. In general, a UAProf file describes the capabilities of a mobile handset, including Vendor, Model, Screen size, Multimedia Capabilities, Character Set support, and more.

Other types of Media Transport Protocols (MTPs) include: HTTP, which can be used for capability exchange and static media transport, RTSP Tunneling, which is used specifically when firewalls block RTP/UDP, and Plain UDP.

PSS: Protocol Stack

Table 4 (adapted from J. Hautakorpi, et al (2005)) summarizes the protocol stack for 3GPP PSS and Figure 2 (adapted from J. Hautakorpi, et al (2005)) shows the protocol stack of 3GG-PSS architecture, including the scope of PSS, Layer 2 3GPP packet based network interface and other standard interfaces (i.e., user, graphical, sound, and terminal).

Table 4. PSS protocol stack

Real-time media transport (audio, video, speech, etc)	Capability Exchange SMIL files, Static media transport	Capability Exchange Presentation description Session setup and control	
RTP	HTTP	RTSP, SDP	
UDP	TCP		UDP
IP			

Figure 2. PSS: Protocol tack

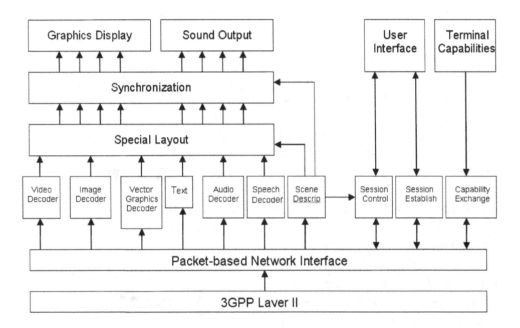

PSS: Domain Architecture

The 3GPP-PSS domain architecture includes streaming related agents (client/server), Proxy server, user and profile servers, portals, SGSN and GGSN.

PDP Context Activation Procedure

To create a PDP context, a PDP context activation procedure is used. This procedure is usually initiated by the MS or it can also be initiated by the network. The PDP context activation may automatically or manually be performed. To remove a PDP context, a PDP context deactiva-

tion procedure is used. Figure 3 (adapted from J. Hautakorpi, et al (2005)) shows the context activation procedure.

PSS: Streaming Multimedia Session Establishment

Figure 4 shows the PSS streaming multimedia session establishment procedure. There are two PDP Context activations involved; primary and secondary. The primary PDP Context is used to accommodate RTSP control signaling (i.e., DE-SCRIBE, SETUP, etc) and once the channel is setup, the secondary PDP Context is activated to initiate the transmission of the actual payloads.

Figure 3. PDP context activation procedure

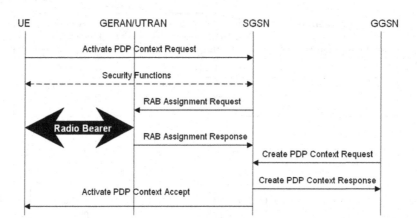

Quality of Service can be critical after the secondary PDP Context initiation. The fact that two PDP Context sessions are used is to have two separated QoS settings applied to control signaling and data individually.

General Service Architecture

Figure 5 (adapted from 3GPP TS 22.233 V7.0.0 (2006)) depicts major service-specific entities of a 3G packet-switched streaming system. For a streaming service, there are at least two requirements: a streaming client and a content server. A download or streaming or server is situated behind the G_i interface. The other components behind the G_i interface may include: profile servers, portals, proxies, and caching servers may be involved to improve the overall service quality or to provide additional services.

Convenient access to streamed media content is allowed through servers called; portals. A portal, for instance, may offer search facilities and content browsing and in the simplest form, it may include a WAP or HTTP-based page featuring a list of links and associated downloadable or streaming contents. The media contents are usually stored on content servers, located anywhere on the network.

Figure 4. PSS streaming multimedia session establishment procedure

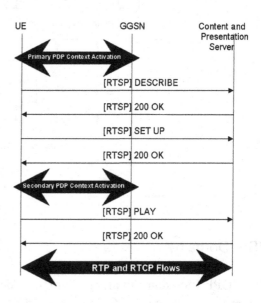

Device profile servers and user are used to store device capabilities and user preferences. This information is used to control the streamed media content presentation available to the mobile user. Such a high-level capability exchange framework illustration is shown in Figure 4.

Figure 5. Network elements involved in a 3G packet switched streaming service

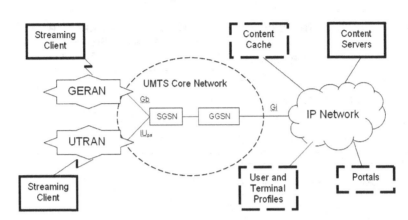

Interworking with Other Core Network Services

Interworking with WAP

Internetworking with WAP is not required and as presented in Figures 6 (adapted from 3GPP TS 26.233 Release 8.0 V8.0.0 (2008)), a WAP server may send a SDF file or initiate a service through an URI.

Interworking with MMS

A new optional feature for the MMS is (TS 23.140), where the message recipient enables the MMS message streaming. According to TS 26.234, the MMS streaming option utilizes the specific protocols and codecs.

According to TS 23.140 and TS 26.244, the usage of the interchange format recommendation is mandated for the MMS purposes (ARIB STD-T63-26.233 V8.0.0 (2008)).

PSS Releases

Release 4: Simple Streaming

Release 4 includes a basic set of streaming control protocols, media codecs, transport and scene

description protocols. In this release, there is no explicit capability exchange, nor digital rights management or any encryption capabilities.

A URI related to specific content, suitable for the user terminal is provided to the mobile user, which may come from a WAP-based or WWW-based browser. This may also come from a manual address entry by the user. In any case, the URI specifies the server content address or a streaming server address. A 3GPP-PSS-based application that establishes the multimedia-based session is expected to understand the SDP file format. A SDP file is not required in the session establishment is the sessions contain only non-streamable content such as a still images, SMIL file, and text, which form a time synchronized presentation. Instead a SDP file, HTTP protocol is used for receiving the presentation files. The URIs to streamable contents may be included in PSS SMIL, requiring a SDP file and/or RTSP signaling parsing.

There are numerous methods to obtain a SDP file, including through a link within a downloadable HTML page, through a typed URI, or via the DESCRIBE method and through RTSP signaling. In case of MMS service streaming delivery option, the SDP file may be received through the MMS user agent via a modified MMS message through a MMS server or relay. The session description (session name, author, etc) is part of the SDP file

Figure 6. Schematic view of a basic streaming session

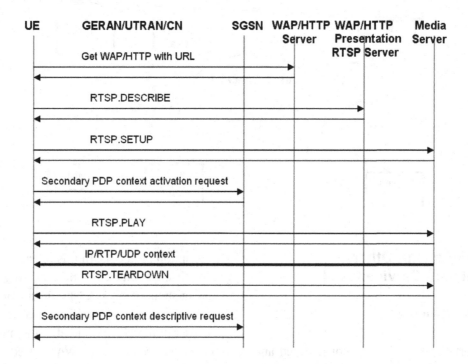

contents along with the type of presented media, and the media bitrate.

It is worthy to mention that the session establishment is a process in which the mobile user's browser invokes a streaming client in which a session is set up against the server. At the start of session establishment signaling, the UE is expected to have an active PDP context based on the type of radio bearer that enables IP packet transmission. The client should be allowed to request more information regarding the content and initiate the bearer provisioning with appropriate streaming media QoS settings.

The streaming service set up is performed via a client-selected RTSP.SETUP message transmission for each media stream, returning the TCP and/or UDP port information being used for the respective media stream. The client transmits a RTSP.PLAY message to the server, which initiates transmitting one or more streams over the IP network.

Such a scenario is depicted in Figure 6. Figure 7 (adapted from 3GPP TS 26.233 Release 8.0 V8.0.0 (2008)) presents the service use-case in a scenario where MMS provides the SDP file.

Release 5: Enhanced Streaming Service

All of the features defined in Release 4 streaming cases are supported in the streaming services defined in Release 5, as the PSS supports are fully backwards compatible. In addition to Release 4 functionalities, other functions such as capability exchange (UAProf) and advances in media file format and data transport mechanism, and other optional features are covered under Release 5. These comparisons are summarized among three Releases; 4 and 5 in Table 5 (adapted from Emre B. Aksu (2004)) in section 5.3.8.

Figure 7. Schematic view for streaming session originated via MMS

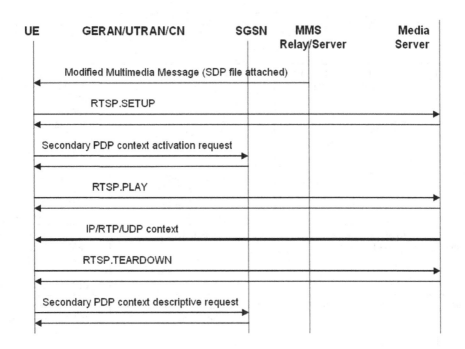

Release 6: Some Extensions

The PSS Release 6 specification includes a few advancements compared to the Releases 4 and 5, which are mentioned in this section (summarized in Table 5).

End-to-End Bit-Rate Adaptation

The streaming session is enabled via an end-to-end bit-rate adaptation enables, which adapts to varying network conditions. 3GPP-PSS could be deployed in networks with various capabilities, based on EDGE, GPRS, WCDMA, and best-effort or QoS with guaranteed bit-rate. The bit-rate adaptation can potentially help intra and especially inter-system handovers to function smoothly and seamlessly. In the current mechanism, the streaming server is responsible for stream sampling bit-rate and transmission rate adaptation and the client is responsible for providing required feedback to the server. The goal of this mechanism is to keep the client pre-decoder buffer full in order to prevent audio or video playback gaps from occurring.

Adaptation of Continuous Media

3GPP-PSS Rel. 6 features a number of functions and protocols that can be used to allow PSS sessions adapt to the transmission and the content rates based on the available network resources. The goal is to maintain interrupt-free playback of the media and achieve the end-user's highest possible Quality of Experience (QoE) with the available resources, simultaneously. For this, the available network resources should be estimated and transmission rates should be adapted to the available network link rates. This can prevent packet losses through overflowing network buffer prevention. In order to avoid late media content arrival, the real-time transmitted media properties must be considered to maintain usefulness. For this, the media content rate is adapted to the transmission rate.

Table 5. Compatibility and supported medias/mechanisms between Releases 4, 5, and 6

	Release 4	Release 5	Release 6
Capability Exchange	None	UAProf	UAProf
Video Codecs	H.263 P0L10 (Mandatory) P3L10, MPEG4 VSP L0 (Optional)	Same as in Release 4	Same as in Release 4 H.263 P0 L45 (Optional) MPEG-4 VSP L 0b (Optional) H.264 Full Baseline (Optional)
Audio & Speech Codecs	AMRNB & WB (M) MPEG4 AAC LC, LTP (Optional)	Same as in Release 4	Same as in Release 4 AMR-WB+ or AACPlus (Optional)
Media File Format	3GPP File Format (.3gp) .amr	Same as in Release 4 ISO Base Format Conformance (M) Timed-text (O)	Same as in Release 5 Various 3GP file profiles (MMS, server, downloadable, generic), DRM (Optional)
Session Establishment	RTSP, SDP (Mandatory) HTTP (Optional)	Same as in Release 4	Same as in Release 4 Media Alternatives in SDP Metadata signalling in SDP (Optional) MBMS - FLUTE (Mandatory)
Data Transport	RTP, RTCP (Mandatory)	Same as in Release 4Progressive Download (O)	Same as in Release 5 MBMS Download (Mandatory) DRM and SRTP(Optional) Progressive Download (Mandatory)
QoS	None	Same as in Release 4	Additional RTSP/SDPsignalling QoE Protocol, and RTCP extentions (all three Optional)
Rate Control	None	Video only	Same as in Release 5 3GPP Rate Adaptation (Optional)

Buffer overflows while still allowing the server to deliver maximum amount of data into the client buffer will result in the client's useful data being discarded and to avoid that, a function for client buffer feedback needs to be in place. This allows the buffering situation on the client side to be monitored closely by the server to avoid client buffer underflow and keep the performance up to its capabilities.

The client specifies the desired target protection level with the aid of new RTSP signaling and the amount of buffer space the server is capable of utilizing. The server may utilize all the resources beyond the needed limit to maintain the protection level to increase the quality of the media when the desired level of protection is achieved. To decide if the media quality needs to be lowered, the server can utilize the buffer feedback information in order to avoid a buffer underflow and the resulting play-back interruption.

Quality Metrics

The purpose of quality metrics is to enable the 3GPP-PSS servers to obtain client generated quality metrics. These metrics are used to determine the client's subjective quality of experience and monitor the service improvements. The quality metrics may not be used for billing purposes and may include information such as the number of lost packets, the number of corruptions, gaps in reception and other information.

Reliable Streaming

Streaming with reliable transport (reliable streaming) means having all the media delivered to the receiver, which can be in an intermediate form between download supporting and streaming of the following modes: (1) A client starting to view the presentation before the entire contents is transmitted (streaming), (2) A lossless delivery of all the media contents (download).

These two modes are achieved by compromising uninterrupted playback, real-time, and favoring lossless reception even if they causes more interruptions. Therefore for live streams, reliable streaming is not particularly suitable.

The following mechanisms have been proposed for reliable streaming: HTTP-based progressive download, RTSP tunneling (RTSP over TCP and RTP interleaved) and a retransmission mechanism.

New Codecs

In the design of PSS Release 6, the H.264 (MPEG-4 AVC) video codec has been considerd, in addition to Releases 4 and 5 supported codecs and a few mandatory codecs including: extended AMR-WB in the lower bit-rate (12-32 kbps) range, aacPlus (MPEG-4 HE-AAC) in the higher bit-rate range (> 32 kbps).

PSS Release 6 while remains backward compatible to earlier PSS releases, however it completes the PSS feature set with a comprehensive content delivery framework by updating the list of recommended codecs and media types to achieve higher service quality within the 3GPP environments.

PSS Rel.6 consists of a predefined streaming and download framework appended with progressive downloading alternative in an end-to-end delivery context, enabling optional integrity protection and strong content encryption capabilities, as well as cryptographic key management interoperability systems. A standardized container

file exchange is possible between PSS providers as a specific server file format.

PSS Rel. 6 allows selection of alternative SDP streaming session alternatives and dynamic, link-aware bandwidth adaptation to adapt the session bandwidth to the potentially time-varying cellular network bandwidth, which is particularly useful in cellular networks in which QoS-enabled bearers are unavailable. There is also a defined mechanism at the PSS service provider's premises to gather streaming session Quality of Experience metrics.

PSS Rel.6 features strengthened and upgraded capability exchange mechanisms available in Release 5 to enable service filtering better for both static media contents and streaming.

Digital Rights Management (DRM)

Other features of PSS Rel.6 include key management systems centered around playback access to cryptographic keys. All file format profiles support encryption and key management system specific parameters carry required additional meta-information.

Protected payloads are supported by streaming supports and SDP attributes for signaling DRM information. OMA has worked with 3GPP to support the OMA DRM Release 2.0 in PSS Rel. 6 and file format, while keeping open formats for other key management systems usage in a later phase (Figure 8, adapted from 3GPP TS 26.233 Release 8.0 V8.0.0 (2008)). The OMA DRM Release 2.0 is an open standard, enjoying a substantial support from the mobile and content industries and 3GPP Rel. 6 is relying on this momentum.

The OMA DRM version supported by PSS Rel. 6 (Release 2.0) supports strong cryptographic algorithms and Public Key Infrastructure (PKI) to provide commercial content a with high level of security, supporting an end-to-end system architecture with trust relationships and roles providing robust and flexible components. The main features of OMA DRM include subscription, preview, content super-distribution, export and

Figure 8. OMA DRM system architecture

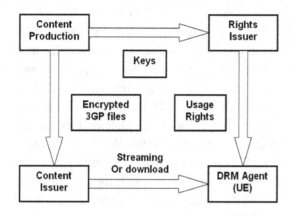

user domains support, enabling a good user experience and many different business models.

OMA DRM 2.0 architecture includes a Content Issuer, a Rights Issuer, and a DRM Agent, usually one per each device. A Content Issuer is typically a download or streaming service, a Rights Issuer is responsible for setting usage permissions and authorizing devices with keys, and DRM Agent is responsible for applying a set of Rights provided for a piece of content. When this is combined with PSS Release 6, content in 3GP files is pre-encrypted at a production facility delivered through streaming service to a device or a download session, and during delivery or playback, the the device OMA DRM Agent handles authorization through acquiring Rights from a Rights Issuer (ARIB STD-T63-26.233 V8.0.0 (2008)).

Progressive Downloading

The term progressive downloading is the ability to start media playback while the media data or file is still being downloaded.

Such a functionality operates using a HTTP download over TCP/IP connection. This service option is available for specific media types having a container format suitable for progressive download and other types of media contents,

including: audio, video, timed text, which use vector graphics and progressive download profile.

One or more HTTP GET requests issued by the client to the server establish a progressive-download session and a valid HTTP URL point to the media resource (i.e., a progressively downloadable 3GP file). Figure 9 (adapted from 3GPP TS 26.233 Release 8.0 V8.0.0 (2008)) shows signaling in progressive downloading session and the data flow.

SUMMARY

PSS Release 6 offers major advances compared to the Release 5. It offers end-to-end bit-rate adaptation and adaptation of continuous media. QoS is being considered as a subjective quality of experience (QoE) for the client, for which, at the end of the session, end user experience is reported back to the server and uses several QoS-related metrics, such as: rebuffering duration, initial buffering duration, and successive loss of RTP packets.

Release 6 also offers reliable streaming ensuring that all the deliverable streaming data is transported to the client. Release 6 supports new codecs, including H.264. Digital Rights Management (DRM) is also considered for Rel. 6 based on OMA DRM 2.0. Another nice feature added is the progressive downloading capability.

Adaptive streaming is also available under Release 6 with rate adaptation that transmits the content to the available network resources. It also avoid network and client buffer overflows.

Release 7

The Release 7 of 3GPP-PSS includes more functionality compared to the previous releases (3GPP TS 22.233 V7.0.0 (2006), 3GPP TS 22.233 V7.1.0 (2009)). In Release 7, the PSS provides the capability that allows clients of different capabilities to maximize the user experience. The

Figure 9. Schematic view of progressive downloading use case

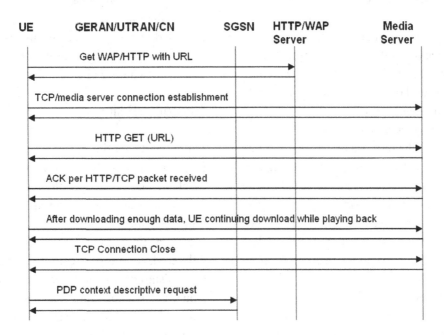

PSS also support the transfer to the terminal of information on the accessed content in addition to the filename (e.g. song title, artist).

Transport

The PS Domain offers PSS transport with Quality of Service (e.g. time delay) supports in accordance with requirements in 22.105. Such a QoS support should work over different QoS bearers. The PSS provides a mechanism in which the client is sent a list of media encoding bit rates and the client determines which one to use based on the user preferences and the offered network service bearers. The PSS client is capable of requesting an appropriate session QoS level and the QoS supplied may be limited by the local operator's access policy or network functionality. The PSS provides mechanisms for streaming clients and servers to adapt to the network conditions to achieve significant improvement in the quality of streaming, such as using information on network end-to-end transport quality. The PSS provides

a reliable delivery mechanism enabling the user to receive the content without any errors, such as a delivery mechanism without packet loss or bit errors. Such mechanism supports the following features: (a) The rendering of video content without any transport degradation, in which case the content is downloaded without any errors, it assures that the subscribers see the content that has been designed by the content creators, (b) The capability of the PSS client to detect what content is missing and to ask the server to send this content, therefore enabling a broken session to restart efficiently without going back to the beginning:

Note that reliable delivery mechanism is not considered for live video content rendering, where under poor conditions it may be difficult to achieve. Therefore the content rendering should start before the transfer is complete.

The user has the ability to play the content while the file is being downloaded, providing a similar situation similar to the regular PSS transport mechanism.

Service Personalization

The PSS supports the client ability to have specific preferences described in the user profile. For instance, if the user desires watching a news channel, the preferred language (subtitles or speech) is presented in the user profile.

The PSS supports a basic set of terminal capabilities and for the purpose of media streaming optimized presentation, PSS includes negotiation mechanisms and capability exchange on client/server capabilities and session set up user preferences. The server receives user preferences (i.e., toggling between stereo and mono sound selection) from the client during a streaming session.

Service Management

User service control includes user full control over the initiation, pause, resume, and ending of a streaming session contents. The simultaneous functions of both streaming and cellular activities are also maintained in this release.

Service Provider's management of the service include end-user notification when PSS services are unavailable and other types of streaming management (i.e., initiation, discontinuation, etc).

Security

Security has been fundamentally enhanced in PSS Rel. 6. Encryption is available to both streamed and downloaded transport contents for protection and integrity. Release 6 supports content-level and transport-level integrity encryption and protection, which may be applied at the time of content creation, ensuring protected content and end-to-end confidentiality. Digital Rights Management framework offers a high level of security for the purpose of protecting commercial content can. Maximum flexibility can be provided by the component-based design for building security features into services.

The security mechanisms function in a way to ensure that the media objects are only sent to and accessed by the intended end-user(s) by supporting end-to-end security (e.g. between the server and the Streaming client).

Charging/Billing

Billing and charging for PSS services are a challenging issue. PSS supports various charging mechanisms, including, volume-based, time-base, event-based, and content-based charging schemes. Other schemes may be based on: Streaming type (i.e.,. real-time or non real-time), volume of data delivered, volume of streaming content delivered, time of start of delivery, QoS, including transmission rate, packet, duration, loss ratio, transfer delay (jitter, latency), streaming service sender-recipient pair, number of streaming events sent, number of Streaming events received, content ID (the particular content stream being accessed), and media type.

Release 8

The Release 8 features various updates, including the 3GPP Multimedia Broadcast and Multicast Service (MBMS), which provides broadcasting and multicasting streaming framework for download applications in 3GPP networks supporting the MBMS bearer service (3GPP TS 26.234 V8.3.0 Rel 8 (2009)). The MBMS user services support a set of specified media codecs, formats and application/transport protocols and are built on top of the MBMS bearer service. There are two delivery methods for the MBMS user services: streaming and download.

Broadcast and multicast services are used extensively for streaming and multimedia data delivery and the scheme's efficiency is particularly crucial in wireless systems (3GPP TS 24.008 V8.6.0 (2009)).

Integrated Mobile Broadcast (IMB) is a part of 3GPP's Rel. 8 Standard, which provides broadcast services capabilities, similar to the 3G TDD bands MBMS broadcast element.

The Evolved Multimedia Broadcast Multicast Service (eMBMS), which is an evolution of MBMS supported by LTE, offers a smooth migration of IMB services towards LTE-based deployments, which is expected to provide operators and end users with confidence in the longevity of mobile broadcast and multicast services.

In addition to time-domain separation of the channels within the frame structure, services within a carrier are mapped to channels as used in MBMS that are separated using standard FDD WCDMA spreading codes. IMB will provide around 20 broadcast channels in 5 MHz of unpaired spectrum at 256 Kbps for each channel.

The Implementation of IMB on devices is expected to be cheaper compared to other broadcast technologies due to the fact that it utilizes device-ready WCDMA technology.

In conjunction with TD-SCDMA and where TD-SCDMA is deployed, MBMS could provide an alternative approach for implementing Broadcast services in markets.

Since IMB is mostly based on MBMS FDD technology, therefore many subsystems are common and the architecture of both devices and Node-Bs should enable both common subsystems to reuse unicast and broadcast and avoid duplication. Examples of this are MBMS protocol stack in both the device and the network based elements, device media players, some of the baseband components in the devices and in the BM-SC and Node-B.

Every RNC receives the same broadcast data one by one from a conventional MBMS. As IMB constantly takes 5Mbps of data traffic, same broadcast data transmission duplication from BM-SC to RNC becomes significant and impacts the core network unless efficient data transmission is implemented.

The 3GPP Rel. 10 is expected to specify LTE deployments sharing a single carrier of up to 20MHz between eMBMS broadcast and unicast and services for both TDD and FDD variants.

The specification of LTE and LTE-based IMB deployments is likely to follow in a later 3GPP release. It is essentially possible to offer all the same services supported by IMB, including EPG and ESG, over LTE unicast and eMBMS with LTE eMBMS or shared or dedicated carrier with equal or even better user experience.

Through the LTE eMBMS standardization progression and LTE-capable user device penetration, network operators will need a smooth migration path from IMB to LTE eMBMS with an operational IMB network. It is desirable to promote interworking of 3G/LTE unicast technologies, IMB, LTE eMBMS with shared carrier, and LTE eMBMS with dedicated carrier offering transparency to the user to extend the longevity of the network operators' returns from investing in the IMB network idea.

The 3GPP IP Multimedia Subsystem (IMS) supports the IP multimedia applications deployment. Both MBMS User Services and are IP multimedia services available before the introduction of IMS. IMS brings features and enablers to subscribers and operators that can enhance the experience of MBMS User Services and PSS. Note that the present specification uses components of the 3GPP MBMS, 3GPP PSS, Open IPTV Forum standards specifications, and ETSI TISPAN IPTV.

The MBMS User Services (MUS) may use more than one Multimedia Broadcast/Multicast Service (bearer service) (based on 3GPP TS 22.246) and more than one Multicast/Broadcast sessions.

IMS BASED PSS AND MBMS USER SERVICE ARCHITECTURE

Figure 10 (adapted from ARIB STD-T63-26.237 V8.0.0 (2008)) describes the MBMS User Service and IMS based PSS functional architecture. In addition to MBMS User Service and PSS functions, the IMS core and other related functions have also been added.

Figure 10. IMS based PSS and MBMS functional architecture

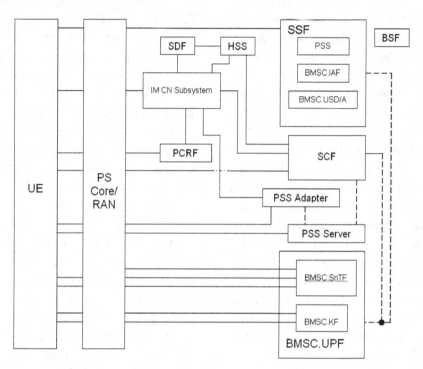

Standardized QoS Characteristics

General

Release 8 features a comprehensive QoS scheme based on QoS Class Identifier (QCI) and each Service Data Flow (SDF) is associated with one and only one QCI. The QCI is scalar used as a reference to node specific parameters controlling packet forwarding treatment (i.e., admission thresholds, scheduling weights, link layer protocol configuration, queue management thresholds, etc.) and that have been pre-configured by the operator owned node (i.e., eNodeB). Multiple SDFs with the same QCI and ARP can be treated as a single traffic aggregate for the same IP-CAN session which is referred to as an SDF aggregate. The service level (i.e., per SDF aggregate or per SDF) QoS parameters are QCI, GBR, MBR, and ARP.

Standardized QCI Characteristics

The standardized QCI characteristics define the packet forwarding treatment that an SDF aggregate receives edge-to-edge between the UE and the PCEF (see Figure 11, adapted from 3GPP TS 23.203 V9.1.0 (2009)) in terms of the following performance characteristics: *Priority, Resource Type (GBR or Non-GBR), Packet Error Loss Rate,* and *Packet Delay Budget.*

The standardized characteristics are guidelines for the pre-configuration of node specific parameters for each QCI and not signaled on any interface. The goal of standardizing a QCI with corresponding characteristics is to ensure that applications and services mapped to that QCI receive the same level of QoS in multi-vendor network deployments. A standardized QCI and corresponding characteristics are independent of the UE's current access. Table 6 (adapted from 3GPP TS 23.203 V9.1.0 (2009)) captures the

Figure 11. Scope of the standardized QCI characteristics for client/server (upper figure) and peer/peer (lower figure) communication

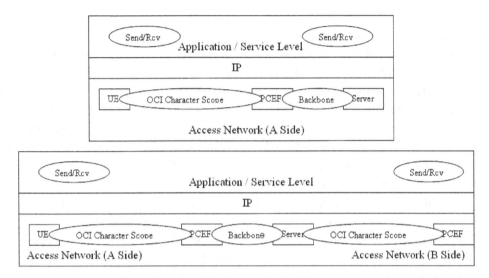

Table 6. Standardized QCI characteristics

QCI	Resource Type	Priority	Packet Delay Budget	Packet Error Loss Rate	Example Services
1		2	100 ms	10-2	Conversational Voice
2	GBR	4	150 ms	10-3	Live Streaming and Conversational Video
3		3	50 ms	10-3	Real Time Gaming
4		5	300 ms	10-6	Buffered Streaming and Non-Conversational Video
5		1	100 ms	10-6	IMS Signaling
6		6	300 ms	10-6	Buffered Streaming Video, TCP-based progressive video
7	Non-GBR	7	100 ms	10-3	Live Streaming, Voice, Video, Interactive Gaming
8		8	300 ms	10-6	Buffered Streaming Video, TCP-based progressive video
9		9			

one-to-one mapping of standardized QCI values to standardized characteristics.

The Resource Type determines if resources related to the dedicated network, bearer level Guaranteed Bit Rate (GBR) value, or a service is permanently allocated, using an admission control function in a radio base station. The GBR SDF aggregates are thus typically authorized "on demand" which requires charging control and dynamic policy. Through static policy and charging control, a non GBR SDF aggregate may be pre-authorized.

An upper bound can be defined for the Packet Delay Budget (PDB) for the time that a packet may be delayed between the PCEF and the UE. The value of the PDB is the same in uplink and downlink for a certain QCI. The purpose of the PDB is to support link layer functions (i.e., HARQ target operating points and the setting of scheduling priority weights) and the configuration of scheduling. The PDB is interpreted as a maximum delay with a confidence level of 98%.

The PDB specifies a soft upper bound in the sense that an expired packet, such as a link layer SDU, which has been exceeded the PDB, does not have to be discarded by RLC in E-UTRAN. The dropping of packets (discarding) is expected to be controlled by a queue management function, based on pre-configured dropping thresholds and limits.

Congestion related packet drops are expected to happen for services using a Non-GBR QCI and 98% of the packets, which are not dropped because of congestion should not experience exceeding the QCI's PDB delay limit, which might occur when the UE becomes coverage limited or during traffic load peaks.

Services based on GBR QCI and transmissions at rates lower than or equal to GBR can generally assume that congestion related packet drops will not occur, and 98% of the packets shall not experience a delay exceeding the QCI's PDB. Exceptions, such as transient link outages, may occur in a radio access system, leading to congestion related packet drops, even for GBR QCI-related services and transmission rates lower than or equal to GBR. Packets that have not been dropped due to congestion may still be subject to non congestion related packet losses.

Each QCI value (GBR and Non-GBR) is associated with a Priority level, where the priority level of 1 is the highest Priority level. The Priority levels are used to differentiate between the same UE's SDF aggregates and it is also used to differentiate between SDF aggregates between various UEs. An SDF aggregate is associated with a Priority level and a PDB via its QCI value. Scheduling among various SDF aggregates is based on the PDB and when the target set by the PDB can no longer be met for any number of SDF aggregates across all UEs with sufficient radio channel quality, then Priority is used in a case where a scheduler meets the PDB of SDF aggregates on Priority level N in preference to meeting the PDB of SDF aggregates on Priority level $N+1$.

The Packet Error Loss Rate (PELR) is defined ass an upper bound for the rate of SDUs (e.g. IP packets) processed by the link layer protocol of the sender, such as that in RLC for E-UTRAN, which are not successfully delivered by the corresponding receiver to the upper layer, such as in PDCP for E-UTRAN. Therefore the PELR is defined by an upper bound for a non congestion related packet loss rate of. The purpose of the PELR is to allow appropriate link layer protocol configurations, such as in HARQ and RLC for E-UTRAN. The PELR is the same in uplink and downlink for a certain QCI the value.

The characteristics PELR and PDB are specified only based on service- or application-level requirements, such as in those characteristics, which should be regarded as being access agnostic, independent from operator policies, and independent from the roaming scenario (roaming or non-roaming).

Allocation and Retention Priority characteristics

The ARP QoS parameter contains information about the priority level, the pre-emption vulnerability, and the pre-emption capability. The priority level defines the relative importance of a resource request (3GPP TS 23.203 V9.1.0 (2009)), allowing to decide whether modification request or a bearer establishment can be accepted or rejected in case of resource limitations, usually for admission control of GBR traffic. It can also be used to decide the existing bearers pre-emption during resource limitations.

The range of the ARP priority level is from 1 to 15 where 1 being the highest level of priority. The pre-empting capability information defines if a service data flow can get resources that were already assigned to another service data flow having a lower priority level. The pre-empting vulnerability information defines whether a service data flow should lose the resources assigned to it in order to admit a service data flow marked with higher priority level. The vulnerability and pre-emption capability can both be either set to yes or no.

The ARP priority levels from 1 to 8 are only assigned to resources for services that are authorized to receive prioritized treatment within an authorized serving network operator domain. The ARP priority levels from 9 to 15 are assigned to resources authorized by the home network and therefore applicable for a roaming UE.

This ensures that future releases may use ARP priority levels from 1 to 8 to indicate backward compatible emergency and other priority services within an operator domain. This is not preventing the use of ARP priority levels from 1 to 8 in roaming situations where appropriate roaming agreements exist to ensure a compatible use of these priority levels.

QoS Information Elements among Various Releases

The purpose of the QoS Information Element (IE) is to specify the QoS-related parameters for a PDP context (3GPP TS 23.203 V9.1.0 (2009)). The QoS IE is defined to offer backward compatibility to earlier version of Session Management Protocol (SMP).

Releases 4 to 7 follow the same guidelines (3GPP TS 24.008 V8.6.0 (2009)), where the QoS metric is a type 4 information element with a maximum length of 18 octets and a minimum length of 14 octets. The MS requests the QoS to be encoded both in the QoS attributes specified in octets 6-14 and in the QoS attributes specified in octets 3-5.

In the MS-to-network and the network-to-MS directions, the following applies:

- Octets 15-18 are optional and if octet 15 is included, then octet 16 is also included, and octets 17 and 18 may also be included.
- If octet 17 is included, then octet 18 is also included.

- A QoS IE received without octets 6-18, 14-18, 15-18, or 17-18, will be accepted by the receiving entity.

The QoS-IE is coded as shown in Table 7 (adapted from 3GPP TS 24.008 V8.6.0 (2009)).

QoS Information Elements Releases 8 and After

Release 8 and after, follows the EPS (Evolved Packet System) QoS guidelines (3GPP TS 24.301 V8.2.1 (2009)). The purpose of the EPS quality of service information element is to specify the QoS parameters for an EPS bearer context. The EPS QoS-IE is coded as shown Table 8 (adapted from 3GPP TS 24.301 V8.2.1 (2009)).

The EPS-QoS is a type 4 IE with a maximum length of 11 octets and a minimum length of 3 octets. Octets 4-11 are optional and if octet 4 is included, then octets are also included. The length of the EPS QoS IE can be either 3, 7 or 11 octets. 3GPP TS 23.203 includes more information on the QoS Class Identifier (QCI) topic.

Industrial and Research-Based Advances

We have so far considered the past and current standards regarding 3GPP-PSS. In this section we will discuss the applications of 3GPP-PSS in the research and application arenas. Reference (Odd Inge Hillestad (2007)) consider mobile multimedia for creating, discovering, sharing, and consuming multimedia content on anytime and anywhere bases in a secure way. The core elements of mobile multimedia includes: contents, services, applications, devices, and underlying networks architecture. The role of mentioned standards is to provide a natural technological evolution path supporting backward compatibility and interoperability.

Table 7. QoS-IE format

8	7	6	5	4	3	2	1	Octet
Quality of service (QoS – IE)								1
Length of quality of service (QoS – IE)								2
0 0 spare		Delay class			Reliability class			3
Peak throughput			0 spare		Precedence class			4
0 0 0 spare			Mean throughput					5
Traffic Class (TC)			Delivery order		Delivery of erroneous SDU			6
Maximum SDU size								7
Maximum bit rate for uplink								8
Maximum bit rate for downlink								9
Residual BER				SDU error ratio				10
Transfer delay					Traffic Handling priority			11
Guaranteed bit rate for uplink								12
Guaranteed bit rate for downlink								13
0 0 0 spare			Signaling Indication	Source Statistics Descriptor				14
Extended maximum bit rate for downlink								15
Extended guaranteed bit rate for downlink								16
Extended maximum bit rate for uplink								17
Extended guaranteed bit rate for uplink								18

The 3GPP-PSS signal quality-related optional metrics are specified as followed (Packet Switched Streaming Service (2003)):

- **Duration of Jitter:** The period during which the amount of error in playback time is larger than 100 ms.
- **Initial Duration Buffering:** The time delay until playback starts.
- **Duration of Rebuffering:** The duration of interruption in continuous playback.
- **Duration of Corruption:** The duration period in which the received media is corrupted.
- **Successive Loss:** The number of succession RTP packets loss.
- **Deviation of Frame Rate:** The difference between correct and actual frame rate.

The 3GPP-PPS includes recommendations and specifications for IP-based streaming applications in 3G mobile networks (Odd Inge Hillestad (2007)) and it decides which media codecs and signaling control protocols to use and apply capability negotiation and media protection used in a 3GPP compliant system. Aspects of these specifications are related to adaptive media delivery, where RTP is used for media transport, while reporting and media-specific signaling are performed using RTCP and SDP Extended Reports.

A RTCP application specific report block is defined in addition to loss statistics based on Loss RLE reports (RTP packets are lost/received), which provides information related to the client receiver buffer operation, such as: available buffer space, current playout delay, and next RTP sequence number (NSN) and decoded application data unit (ADU). There is no explicit specifica-

Table 8. EPS QoS-IE Format

8	7	6	5	4	3	2	1	Octet
EPS QoS-IEI								1
EPS-QoS contents length								2
QCI								3
Maximum uplink bit rate								4
Maximum downlink bit rate								5
Guaranteed uplink bit rate								6
Guaranteed downlink bit rate								7
Extended maximum uplink bit rate								8
Extended maximum downlink bit rate								9
Extended guaranteed uplink bit rate								10
Extended guaranteed downlink bit rate								11

tion for transmission rate adaptation mechanism, however, the feedback reports are facilitated by the design and implementation of rate-adaptive systems.

The PSS specifications include a signaling mechanism from the client to the server, allowing the server to acquire the information it requires to choose both the best transmission and media encoding rates at any given time period (Y. Falik et al (2007)).

As mentioned earlier, the PSS facilitates rate adaptation (aka curve control). The playout curve shows the data the decoder cumulative amount which is processed by the client buffer in any given time. If the media encoder runs in a real-time mode, the encoding curve will indicate the data generation progress.

The transmission and reception curves show the cumulative amount of data being sent and received by the client/server at any given time and the distance between the transmission and reception curves corresponds to the amount of data in the buffer. The distance between the playout and reception curves corresponds to the amount of data in the client buffer and curve control in here indicate constrains of some limits the distance between the two curves, corresponding to a maximum amount of data or a maximum delay figure.

Reference (Y. Falik et al (2007)) proposed Adaptive streaming algorithm (ASA), which controls these buffers' occupancy levels by controlling the encoding rates and the transmission of the streaming server to achieve high QoS streaming. ASA overcomes the inherent bandwidth fluctuations, which due to: Radio network conditions, available bandwidth, and network load. The algorithm was tested on GPRS, EDGE, UMTS and CDMA networks and the results showed substantial improvements over other conventional standard streaming methods.

The ASA uses standard protocols such as RTP and RTSP can work with any 3GPP standard client. The algorithm satisfies the Buffer Occupancy Condition (BOC) condition that enables optimal network resources utilization without video quality degradation. BOC is a state of a buffer in which each buffer stays in any of the partially full state, never empty, or never full condition.

Therefore ASA is able to generate a more steady encoding rate by putting some limitation on the streaming and by filtering the data from the RTCP receiver reports and encoding rate change.

CONCLUSION

This chapter was concerned about 3GPP Packet Switch Streaming services with a special focus on 3GPP chronological developments through various releases, specifying the general functionality, and protocol specifications. The session and transport protocols include: RTP, RTCP, RTSP, and SDP and the first release; Release 4 (2001) provided simple and basic streaming functionality. Release 5 (2002) provided more enhanced streaming services, including capability exchange (UA-Prof). Release 6 (2004) offered major advances compared to the Release 5, including end-to-end bit-rate adaptation and adaptation of continuous media. It featured QoS in the form of client-based subjective quality of experience (QoE). Release 6 also offered reliable streaming ensuring that all the deliverable streaming data is transported to the client. Release 6 also supported new codecs, including H.264. Digital Rights Management (DRM) was also considered for Rel. 6 based on OMA DRM 2.0. Another nice feature added was the progressive downloading capability. Adaptive streaming was also available under Release 6 with rate adaptation that transmitted the content to the available network resources, avoiding network and client buffer overflows. Release 7 (2006) featured advancement on transport domain, service management and personalization and security.

The current release; Release 8 (2008), features MBMS User Service functional architecture and QoS characteristic standardization. Release 9 is still under consideration and has not been officially a standard.

Finally we considered a few fine-tuned research outcomes based on 3GPP-PSS, one of which was the Adaptive streaming algorithm (ASA) proposal, which discussed a method to control buffers' occupancy levels by controlling the encoding rates and the transmission of the streaming server to achieve high QoS streaming.

REFERENCES

ARIB STD-T63-26.233 V8.0.0 (2008). Transparent end-to-end packet switched streaming service (PSS);

ARIB STD-T63-26.237 V8.0.0 (2008). *IMS based PSS and MBMS User Service; Protocols (Release 8), ARIB STD-T63-26.237 V8.0.0*. Retrieved from http://www.arib.or.jp/IMT-2000/V720Mar09/2_T63/ARIB-STD-T63/Rel8/26/A26237-800.pdf

ARIB STD-T63-26.246 V6.1.0 (2006). Technical Specification 3rd Generation Partnership Project; Technical Specification Group Services and System Aspects; Transparent end-to-end packet switched streaming service (PSS); 3GPP SMIL Language Profile (Release 6), 3GPP TS 26.246 V6.1.0, Sep 2006, http://www.arib.or.jp/IMT-2000/V720Mar09/2_T63/ARIB-STD-T63/Rel6/26/A26246-610.pdf

Casner, S. (2003). *Request For Comments (RFC) 3556 - Session Description Protocol (SDP) Bandwidth Modifiers for RTP Control Protocol (RTCP)*. Bandwidth.

Emre, B. Aksu (2004). Mobile Multimedia and Evolution of 3GPP Packet Switched Streaming Service (PSS), Nokia Corporation, IMTC Forum, May 2004, San Jose, CA, USA, http://www.imtc.org/events/forum%20events/forum_2004/presentations/day_2/d2eaksu18.ppt

Falik, Y., Averbuch, A., Yechiali, U. (2007, February). Transmission algorithm for video streaming over cellular networks. *Wireless Networks*.

General description (Release 8), http://www.arib.or.jp/IMT-2000/V740Dec09/2_T63/ARIB-STD-T63/Rel8/26/A26233-800.pdf

3GPP Rel6 V650 (2008). *3rd Generation Partnership Project; SPEC Cross Reference*, Retrieved from http://www.arib.or.jp/IMT-2000/V650Mar08/4_Cross_Reference/3GPP_SPEC_Cross_ReferenceV650_Rel6.pdf

3GPP TS 22.173 V7.3.0 (2007). 3rd Generation Partnership Project; Technical Specification Group Services and System Aspects; IP Multimedia Core Network Subsystem (IMS) Multimedia, Telephony Service and supplementary services Stage 1; (Release 7), Retrieved March 2007, from http://www.arib.or.jp/IMT-2000/V620May07/5_Appendix/Rel7/22/22173-730.pdf

3GPP TS 22.233 V6.3.0 (2003). *3rd Generation Partnership Project; Technical Specification Group Services and System Aspects; Transparent end-to-end packet-switched streaming service; Stage 1* (Release 6), Retrieved Sept. 2003, from http://www.arib.or.jp/IMT-2000/V650Mar08/5_Appendix/Rel6/22/22233-630.pdf

3GPP TS 22.233 V7.0.0 (2006). *Technical Specification, 3rd Generation Partnership Project; Technical Specification Group Services and System Aspects*; Transparent end-to-end packet-switched streaming service; Stage 1, (Release 7)

3GPP TS 22.233 V7.1.0 (2009). *Technical Specification, 3rd Generation Partnership Project; Technical Specification Group Services and System Aspects; Transparent end-to-end packet-switched streaming service*; Stage 1, (Release 7), Retrieved from http://www.arib.or.jp/IMT-2000/V730Jul09/2_T63/ARIB-STD-T63/Rel7/22/A22233-710.pdf

3GPP TS 23.203 V9.1.0 (2009). *3rd Generation Partnership Project; Technical Specification Group Services and System Aspects; Policy and charging control architecture*, (Release 9), Retrieved from http://www.quintillion.co.jp/3GPP/Specs/23203-910.pdf

3GPP TS 24.008 V8.6.0 (2009). Technical Specification, 3rd Generation Partnership Project; Technical Specification Group Core Network and Terminals; Mobile radio interface Layer 3 specification; Core network protocols; Stage 3, (Release 8)

3GPP TS 24.301 V8.2.1 (2009). *Technical Specification. 3rd Generation Partnership Project; Technical Specification Group Core Network and Terminals*; Non-Access-Stratum (NAS), protocol for Evolved Packet System (EPS); Stage 3, (Release 8)

3GPP TS 26.233 Release 8.0 V8.0.0 (2008). Technical Specification, 3rd Generation Partnership Project; Technical Specification Group Services and System Aspects; Transparent end-to-end packet switched streaming service (PSS); General description, 3GPP TS 26.233 Release 8.0 (V8.0.0), Retrieved December 2008, from http://www.ofdm.jp/3GPP/Specs/26233-800.pdf

3GPP TS 26.234 V8.3.0 Rel. 8 (2009). 3rd Generation Partnership Project; Technical Specification Group Services and System Aspects; Transparent end-to-end Packet-switched Streaming Service (PSS); Protocols and codecs

3GPP TS 26.244 V6.7.0 (2007). Technical Specification, 3rd Generation Partnership Project; Technical Specification Group Services and System Aspects, Transparent end-to-end packet switched streaming service (PSS); 3GPP file format (3GP), (Release 6), 3GPP TS 26.244 V6.7.0, Retrieved Jun 2007, from http://www.arib.or.jp/IMT-2000/V650Mar08/5_Appendix/Rel6/26/26244-670.pdf

3GPP TS 26.245 V6.1.0 (2004). *Technical Specification, 3rd Generation Partnership Project; Technical Specification Group Services and System Aspects, Transparent end-to-end Packet switched Streaming Service* (PSS); Timed text format, (Release 6), 3GPP TS 26.245 V6.1.0. Retrieved Dec 2004, from http://www.arib.or.jp/IMT-2000/V650Mar08/5_Appendix/Rel6/26/26245-610.pdf

3GPP TS 32.313 V6.4.0 (2007). *3rd Generation Partnership Project; Technical Specification Group Services and System Aspects, Telecommunication management; Generic Integration Reference Point (IRP) management; Common Object Request Broker Architecture* (CORBA), Solution Set (SS), (Release 6), Retrieved Mar 2007, from http://www.arib.or.jp/IMT-2000/V650Mar08/5_Appendix/Rel6/32/32313-640.pdf

GSMA IMB WP. (2009). Integrated Mobile Broadcast (IMB) Service Scenarios and System Requirements, GSMA TM, Retrieved on September 25th, 2009 from http://www.gsmworld.com//press-releases//3858.htm

GSMA IMB WP. (2009). GSMA Endorses Integrated Mobile Broadcast (IMB), a New 3GPP Standard That Will Accelerate the Global Adoption of Mobile Data and Broadcast Services. Retrieved from http://www.gsmworld.com//GSMA_IMB_WP_final.doc

Handley, M., Jacobson, V. (1998). *Request for Comments* (RFC) 2327 - SDP: Session Description Protocol

Handley, M., Jacobson, V., & Perkins, C. (2006). *Request for Comments* (RFC) 4566 - SDP: Session Description Protocol

Hautakorpi, J., & Pohan, H. (2005). *Streaming Media Protocols, T-110.456.* Retrieved from http://www.tml.tkk.fi/Studies/T-110.456/2005/slides/Streaming_Media_Protocols_lastVersion.pdf

Huitema, C. (2003). *Request For Comments (RFC) 3605 - Real Time Control Protocol (RTCP) attribute in Session Description Protocol.* SDP.

Mishra, A., & Saudagar, M. G. (2004). *Streaming Multimedia: RTSP.* Retrieved from http://www.facweb.iitkgp.ernet.in/~rkumar/media/resource/RTSP.pdf

Odd Inge Hillestad. (2007). Evaluating and Enhancing the Performance of IP-based Streaming Media Services and Applications, Ph.D. Thesis, Norwegian University of Science and Technology, May 2007 http://www.q2s.ntnu.no/~hillesta/thesis/Hillestad_PhD_thesis_08.06.2007.pdf

Odd Inge Hillestad. (2007). *Evaluating and Enhancing the Performance of IP-based Streaming Media Services and Applications*, (Ph.D. Thesis), Norwegian University of Science and Technology. Retrived May 2007, from http://www.q2s.ntnu.no/~hillesta/thesis/Hillestad_PhD_thesis_08.06.2007.pdf

Ott, J., Wenger, S., Sato, N., Burmeister, C., & Rey, J. (2006). *Request for Comments (RFC) 4585 – Extended RTP Profile for Real-time Transport Control Protocol (RTCP)-Based Feedback.* RTP/AVPF.

Packet Switched Streaming Service. (2003). *TeliaSonera Finland, MediaLab.* Retrieved Nov 19, 2003, from http://www.medialab.sonera.fi/workspace/PacketSwitchedStreamingWP.pdf

Packet Switched Streaming Service. (2003). *TeliaSonera Finland, MediaLab.* Retrieved Nov 19, 2003, from http://www.medialab.sonera.fi/workspace/PacketSwitchedStreamingWP.pdf

Schulzrinne, H. (1996). Request For Comments (RFC) 1890 - RTP Profile for Audio and Video Conferences with Mini

Schulzrinne, H., Casner, S., Frederick, R., & Jacobson, V. (1996). *Request For Comments* (RFC) 1889 - RTP: A Transport Protocol for Real-Time Applications

Schulzrinne, H., Casner, S., Frederick, R., & Jacobson, V. (2003). *Request For Comments* (RFC) 3550 - RTP: A Transport Protocol for Real-Time Applications

Schulzrinne, H., Rao, A., & Lanphier, R. (1998). *Request For Comments (RFC) 2326 - Real Time Streaming Protocol*. RTSP.

Schulzrinne, H., Rao, A., Lanphier, R., Westerlund, M., & Stiemerling, M. (2009). *Real Time Streaming Protocol 2.0 (RTSP), draft-ietf-mmusic-rfc2326bis-22*. Retrieved July 13, 2009, from http://www.h-online.com/nettools/rfc/drafts/draft-ietf-mmusic-rfc2326bis-22.shtml

TSGS#19(03)0169 (2003). WID for Higher Bitrate Audio Codec, Dolby Laboratories, Apple Computer, AT&T Wireless Services, RealNetworks, Technical Specification Group Services and System Aspects, Meeting #19, Birmingham, UK, 17-20 March 2003, http://www.3gpp.org/ftp/tsg_sa/tsg_sa/TSGS_19/Docs/PDF/SP-030169.pdf

Wing, D. (2007). *Request For Comments (RFC) RFC 4961 - Symmetric RTP / RTP Control Protocol*. RTCP.

KEY TERMS AND DEFINITIONS

3GP: 3GPP file format

3GPP: The Third Generation Partnership Project

AAC: Advanced Audio Coding

AAC-LC: AAC-Low Complexity

ADU: Application Data Unit

AMR: Adaptive Multi-Rate

AMR-NB: AMR-Narrow Band

AMR-WB: AMR-Wide Band

APR: Allocation and Retention Priority

ASP: Application-Specific packet

AVC: Advanced Video Coding

B2BUA SIP: Back-to-Back User Agent

BMSC: Broadcast/Multicast Service Centre

BMSC.UPF: BMSC User Plane

BOC: Buffer Occupancy Condition

BSF: Bootstrapping Server Function

CC/PP: Composite Capability / Preference Profiles

DCT: Discrete Cosine Transform

DLS: Downloadable Sounds

DRM: Digital Rights Management

EDGE: Enhanced Data for GSM Evolution

eMBMS: Evolved Multimedia Broadcast Multicast Service

Enhanced aacPlus: MPEG-4 High Efficiency AAC plus MPEG-4 Parametric Stereo

ETSI: European Telecommunications Standards Institute

EUTRAN: Evolved UMTS Terrestrial Radio Access Network

FDD: Frequency Division Duplex

FLUTE: File Delivery over Unidirectional Transport

GBA: Generic Bootstrapping Architecture

GBR: Guaranteed Bit Rate

GGSN: GPRS Core Network

GIF: Graphics Interchange Format

GPRS: General Packet Radio Service

HE-AAC: High-Efficiency Advanced Audio Coding

HSS: Home Subscriber Server

HTML: Hyper Text Markup Language

HTTP: Hypertext Transfer Protocol

IETF: Internet Engineering Task Force

IM CN: IP Multimedia Core Network

IMB: Integrated Mobile Broadcast

IMS: IP Multimedia Subsystem

IP: Internet Protocol

IPTV: Internet Protocol-based Television

ITU-T: International Telecommunications Union – Telecommunications

JFIF: JPEG File Interchange Format

LTE: Long Term Evolution

LTP: Long Term Predictor

MBMS: Multimedia Broadcast Multicast Service

MBR: Maximum Bit Rate

MGCP: Media Gateway Control Protocol

MIDI: Musical Instrument Digital Interface

MIME: Multipurpose Internet Mail Extensions

MMS: Multimedia Messaging Service

MS: Mobile Station
MUS: MBMS User Services
NADU: Next Application Data Unit
OMA: Open Mobile Alliance
PCEF: Policy and Charging Enforcement Function
PCRF: Policy and Charging Rules Function
PDB: Packet Delay Budget
PDCP: Packet Data Convergence Protocol
PDP: Packet Data Protocol
PELR: Packet Error Loss Rate
PNG: Portable Networks Graphics
PSS: Packet-Switched Streaming Service
QCI: QoS Class Identifier
QCIF: Quarter Common Intermediate Format
QoE: Quality of Experience
QoS: Quality of Service
RAB: Reverse link Activity Bit
RAN: Radio Access Networks
RDF: Resource Description Framework
RLC: Radio Link Control
RNC: Radio Network Controller
RR: Receiver Report
RTCP: RTP Control Protocol
RTP: Real-time Transport Protocol
RTSP: Real-Time Streaming Protocol
SAP: Session Announcement Protocol
SBR: Spectral Band Replication
SCF: Service Control Function
SDES: Source DEScription
SDF: Service Discovery Function
SDP: Session Description Protocol
SDU: Service Data Unit
SGSN: GPRS Core Network
SIP: Session Initiation Protocol

SMIL: Synchronized Multimedia Integration Language
SP-MIDI: Scalable Polyphony MIDI
SR: Sender Report
SRTP: The Secure Real-Time Transport Protocol
SSF: Service Selection Function
SVG: Scalable Vector Graphics
TCP: Transmission Control Protocol
TD-SCDMA: Time Division-Synchronous CDMA
TDD: Time Division Duplex
TISPAN: Telecoms and Internet converged Services & Protocols for Advanced Networks
UAProf: User Agent Profile
UCS-2: Universal Character Set (the two octet form)
UDP: User Datagram Protocol
UE: User Equipment
UMTS: Universal Mobile Telecommunications System
URI: Uniform Resource Identifier
USD: User Service Description
UTF-8: Unicode Transformation Format (the 8-bit form)
VSP: VideoStudio Project
W3C: WWW Consortium
WAP: Wireless Application Protocol
WCDMA: Wideband Code Division Multiple Access
WML: Wireless Markup Language
WSP: Wireless Session Protocol
XHTML: Extensible Hyper Text Markup Language
XMF: Extensible Music Format
XML: Extensible Markup Language

Chapter 17
Perspectives of the Application of Video Streaming to Education

Marco Ronchetti
Università Degli Studi di Trento, Italy

ABSTRACT

The field of e-learning has been a precursor in using the video streaming over the Internet. Both the synchronous and the asynchronous options have been explored over the last decade, with the asynchronous one becoming the dominant paradigm in recent years. Pedagogical research lecture reported evidence that video-streaming is an effective way of teaching, provided certain conditions are met. Technological research has attempted to investigate various ways to better produce or deploy video lectures: video segmentation, summarization, multimodal extraction of text and metadata, semantic search and gesture analysis are among the research areas that were involved. The present paper reviews the main technological research achievements and trends, and suggests directions in which we may be seeing the streaming of lectures to venture in near future.

INTRODUCTION

The field of e-learning has been a precursor in using the video streaming over the Internet. To our knowledge, the first proposal of an architecture for recording and distributing lectures in the form of video streaming over the Internet dates back to 1995 (Tobagi). Tobagi also implemented and demonstrated a first prototype: however apparently the system was never brought into routine

production. The first systematic application of video streaming to teaching followed three years later (Hayes 1998). At that time, a VHS based system for delivering lectures to a geographically remote place (from USA to France) was substituted first with an audio stream with synchronized power point images, and shortly thereafter it evolved into a video transmission that included both the teacher and the slides with a technique called chroma key[1]. In recent years several custom systems were developed, some were commercialized, some were put in the public domain and others

DOI: 10.4018/978-1-61692-831-5.ch017

Copyright © 2011, IGI Global. Copying or distributing in print or electronic forms without written permission of IGI Global is prohibited.

were used locally as prototypes. A review of the desirable features for such systems can be found in (Ronchetti 2008). After a short time in which pioneers opened the way showing a possible but uncertain future, big players are coming onto the scene today, such as in the case of the Massachusetts Institute of Technology on-line video collection[2] and the one of University of California at Berkeley who, according to U.S. Government news[3] of January 2008, was the first University with a plan to offer full courses on You Tube.

Research has shown that, from a pedagogical point of view, the video streaming of lectures is an effective practice (for a review see Ronchetti 2009). Moreover its production costs are already quite low. Systems like Lode[4] and OpenEya[5] are available at no cost since they are either open-source or free, and their hardware requirements are rather basic for today's computers. Hence, although there are still some problems, like the unwillingness of some teachers of being recorded, we believe that there are little doubts that the use of video streaming applied to education is here to stay, and will continue to expand. Already today, the list of websites dedicated to offer on-line video-lectures is impressive (see e.g. the partial catalog[6] compiled by University of Wisconsin at Milwaukee).

Although some of the early applications of video streaming to teaching were focusing on synchronous usage, in recent years most of the cases are concerned with asynchronous consumption. These two modalities present very different implications: in synchronous lectures it is desirable to allow remote users to interact with the speaker/teacher, while for the asynchronous ones the focus is shifted to other issues such as intelligent information extraction, ability to search, interconnect, navigate and annotate lectures. This second area has been very active, and has elicited several research streams.

In this chapter we shall review the research directions and results that matured over the last decade. Our coverage will reflect what has been happening in the last years, in which not much emphasis has been paid to the synchronous aspects, and many efforts have gone towards the view of a flexible, searchable collections of multimedia material built around video streaming, available on demand, in which the content allows random access and the user can easily find information about the content and locate interesting spots: a perspective that goes under the name of next generation digital library.

Synchronous Videolectures

Synchronous video streaming breaks spatial constraints and allows users to participate in real time to remote events. Students' physical presence in the teacher's location is not required any more. This solution allows for distributed classes (e.g. two classrooms on the same campus to accommodate a very large audience) and/or distributed individuals (e.g. students following a lecture in real time from their home). However, by simply using traditional video streaming solutions, an important obstacle arises: the lack of interaction. How can students in the remote classroom, or in their home, request teacher attention for asking a clarification? Ron Baecker (2003) has addressed this issue when designing the e-Presence system. e-Presence is a web-casting tool that was originally designed with the scientific seminar model in mind. It is based on unidirectional synchronous video streaming, with synchronized slides that accompany the speaker's video. The interaction problem is attacked by integrating a textual chat into the system, and introducing the role of the "mediator": a person that is located in the physical place where the event takes place, and monitors the chat (Schick et al. 2005). S/he acts as a proxy for the remote user: when a question comes into the chat, s/he calls the attention of the speaker and poses the question. A small problem came from the fact that the streaming of the "synchronous" flow was always 10-15 seconds late (because of the delay induced by the real-time compression that is performed on the flight). As an evolution of the textual chat model, Baecker et al. (2006, 2007) also investigated the possibility of introducing a VOIP channel for allowing direct interaction between student and teacher, and/or among students.

Bidirectional video streaming among multiple points is actually fairly common in many videoconferencing systems. Obviously, we cannot review here the whole vast world of videoconferencing, as this chapter focuses on specific applications on teaching and learning. We shall hence limit the discussion to the use of videoconference in the didactic framework. As we shall see, however, even though marrying videoconference and distance education seems to be a quite natural idea, it never really caught up in a significant way. In 2004 Raymond et al. noticed that, in spite of the diffusion of videoconferencing tools, it was difficult to find examples of successful application to the educational field. This is in striking contrast with the vast success that asynchronous video lecture systems started having in those years. Five years later, the situation has not changed much. Raymond et al. argued that the problem is connected with the lack of friendliness on multi-user videoconference systems. Even today, systems like Skype are widely used for point-to-point interaction, but their support for multipoint conferences is not as simple and intuitive as for the point-to-point case. Even systems that were designed with videoconference in mind are typically limited to a relatively small number of participants. In contrast, a lecture is a traditional academic setting involves a large number of actors (of the order of one hundred) with strongly asymmetric responsibilities, so that the flow of information is mostly unidirectional. Typical videoconference tool are aimed at much smaller communities, with more symmetric roles. They have been used in teaching for various activities, such as tutoring, or allowing faculty members to participate in a thesis defense at a remote institution, but their impact and diffusion is orders of magnitude less than their asynchronous counterpart.

In part this is due to a relatively complex technical set-up. Certainly the scenario of a synchronous, interactive tele-lecture suffers from the extra managerial burden imposed to the teacher. In an asynchronous scenario the teacher can almost forget that s/he's being recorded, and can run "business as usual", while in a mixed setting (in which s/he is teaching to a traditional classroom and at the same time s/he is involved in a videoconference) there is a cognitive overload, unless a mediator is used, as in the above-quoted Baecker's approach.

Our feeling is that an implicit cost/benefit analysis has severely limited the use of synchronous video streaming as opposed to the asynchronous version: the users' perception is that the extra effort required to apply synchronous video streaming to teaching largely outperforms the obtainable benefits.

Synchronous video streaming still has interesting uses in educational setting in more restricted and specific application areas. It is used in point-to-point versions for involving a remote expert in a traditional lecture: in such case the teacher becomes the natural mediator between the class and the expert. It can be used for inclusion in class of a remote child in hospitals (see e.g. the TelecomItalia Smart Inclusion project[7]), or for inclusion of a few children living on remote places (e.g. in the "Isole in rete" project[8] in which children living on a small island are virtually included in a larger remote classroom). In all these cases a simple point-to-point paradigm is used, and additional tools, such as e.g. interactive whiteboards, augment the interactivity palette.

Asynchronous Applications

In the previous section we concluded that asynchronous video streaming of lectures has been perceived by teachers, institutions and students as a higher value, simpler activity than the synchronous one. We should not overlook an obvious but essential advantage of the asynchronous mode: while synchronous streaming only allows breaking spatial constraints, the asynchronous one also breaks temporal constraints, and hence it supports e.g. students who have full time jobs, or who need catching up on missed classes. Moreover, asynchronous mode allows for more freedom in using the material: like in books, it is not necessary to take the entire content, or to consume it sequentially. In fact, the analysis of usage patterns has shown that students tend not to watch an entire video-lecture, but rather to jump to video-fragments that are interesting for them for checking their notes, or re-hearing an explanation. Evidence in this sense was provided by the work by Zupancic & Horz (2002), and reinforced by the report by Ronchetti (2003). Moreover, Soong et al. (2006) reported that students accessed mostly those parts of lectures, which they did not understand, implicitly confirming that they watch fragments rather than full lectures. Zhang et al. (2006) stated that students using video-lectures with the possibility of random access performed better than those in other settings, and showed better learner satisfaction. The possibility to quickly navigate the lectures is therefore essential (and this is probably the main aspect that makes digital recording deeply different from more traditional VHS-based videos). Watching an entire video is in fact a time consuming experience, and we need ways to quickly identify and access the information of our interest. Moreover, the focus is shifted from a single lecture to the whole collection of available material: the notion of a digital library becomes central, and the "library" is not any more (digital) text only, but a vast collection of multimedia. Video streaming becomes one component in the new, broader scenario.

This brought research to focus on a set of topics that include the ability to:

- automatically summarize video-lectures;
- segment videos into semantically homogeneous chunks;

- generate indexes that enable effective search;
- mine audio and video to extract explicit information that can be used for post-processing the videos and/or be passed to the users;
- extract metadata;
- produce personal annotations (which might be textual or multimedia-based), and share them with peers.

In the rest of this chapter we shall discuss these issues, because even though they are not directly related to video streaming, their impact on video streaming usage is fundamental. In fact the success of these research streams will enable a new generation of on-demand video streaming, in which random access to information tokens in a large collection of videos, and within the videos themselves, will be made possible.

Summarizing Videolectures

When we try to find some information from traditional sources (e.g. books) we have tools that help us. For instance, we search for books on a given topic through an OPAC (On-line Public Access Catalogue[9]) service and we identify a set of candidates. To actually understand if one of the candidate books is relevant to us, we have a wealth of techniques to gather information. On the back or inner cover of the book, we can read a short summary and get some information on the author. We can look at the index and read the titles of the chapters. We can read the introduction (of the book or of a specific chapter). We also browse the book, and skim the text. In a few minutes we are able to get a pretty good understanding of the utility of the book for us, and we are able to do a random access to the part that is most relevant for us.

When it comes to multimedia, we do not have (yet) anything similar. Digital libraries start to offer services for searching a multimedia resource, but then it is difficult to gain perspectives of a document without watching the video (or listening an audio recording) in its entirety. The research area called "video abstracting" deals with this issue. The review article by Truong and Venkatesh (2007) describes this area in general, without specific reference to the case of video-lectures. Unfortunately many of the techniques described there are not very useful in the case of video-lectures, especially when these are recording of events that took place in a classroom. Both key-frame sampling and video skimming are not very useful when the images are rather homogeneous, even though they can be helpful e.g. in detecting slide transitions. Most e-lecture systems however already deal in a special way with slides (keeping track of the time at which slide change occur, and maintaining snapshots of each individual slide).

He et al. (1999) proposed an ad hoc technique for summarizing video-lectures. It is interesting to follow their line of thinking, since they envisioned several ways top mine information although they followed only a subset of them. We'll follow their paper, but for sake of completeness we'll also integrate some additional information not present in their work. Their top taxonomy comprises:

- Video channel;
- Audio channel;
- Speaker action;
- End users' actions.

The former can in principle be used for several means, such as detecting slide transitions (if such information does not come from other sources), identifying sections in which the speaker writes on the blackboard, and identifying the use of multimedia within the lecture (such as when the speaker gives a live demonstration through a computer simulation or shows a video in class). Also, speaker gesture can be extracted and analyzed. In their paper they apply none of these techniques because the video consisted only of a "talking head", and hence not much could be inferred from video analysis.

Audio could be used by attempting to extract meaning from the spoken works. While several other authors followed this line of research (as we shall discuss later), He et al. (1999) focused on the audio channel examining pitch, pause, intonation and other prosody information. For instance, it is known form previous research that the introduction of a new topic often corresponds with an increased pitch range. Pauses were used to detect the beginning of phrases. In such way it was possible to avoid including in the generated summary segments that start in the middle of a phrase. In fact, He's et al. report that users found segments starting in the middle of a phrase to be very annoying.

Speaker actions could be deducted from the video or captured through other means. For instance, many video-lecture capturing software applications offer the possibility to record both the time at which slide changes occur, and the slide itself. As we mentioned, gesture analysis could be a valuable source of information. Also facial expressions could be helpful.

End user actions are a very valuable source of information. If videos are watched on-line, the server can record users' activity – such as jumps to different parts of the lecture, logs of which parts of lectures were watched the most etc. He et al. actually deployed such information. Some systems however rely on local watching (after downloading the whole video). Sometimes this is done because watching on-line suffers from network congestion, so that users find it more convenient to obtain (in batch) a local copy and then use it on their own machine. In such case it is much more difficult to gather information about behavioral patterns.

He et al also defined the desirable attributes of a good summary:

- Each segment should be concise;
- The set of selected segments should cover all key points;
- Earlier segments should establish the right context for the following ones;
- The flow in the summary should be natural and fluid, so as to provide overall coherence.

They proposed three summarization algorithms: the first one was one only on slide transitions points, the second one used only the pitch information while the third one used all the available information (slide transition points, pitch and user-access patterns). They did not find any significant difference among the three approaches, and concluded that the simplest one is therefore preferable.

Yokoi and Fujiyoshi (2007) proposed a technique that, although is not a summarization technique, reduces the time needed to watch the video of a lecture. Their idea is that there are portion of lectures that are not significant, and hence they cut or compress them. They identified content-free segments (those characterized by pauses and silence) and cut them out. Also, they spotted the chalkboard writing segments and apply a fast-forwarding increasing the video speed by 3 times during these segments. The identification of chalkboard writing phases was based on image analysis. The final result was that the processed lecture is 20% to 30% shorter than the original one. The whole process was automatic and the final result was comparable with what can be obtained by manual editing of the videos. At the time of their report they were not able to produce a lecture index, but they mentioned it as a future activity. Of course, since most of their compression comes from chalkboard writing identification, this approach is best suited to traditional lectures (not the ones mostly based on electronic presentations).

Extracting Text from the Audio Track

The idea of deploying Automated Speech Recognition (ASR) techniques to the audio tracks of video-lectures to generate a transcript is very natural. The transcripts can then be used in a variety of ways. Wald (2005) suggested that they could be used to create captions (e.g. for deaf learners), and to assist those who, for cognitive, physical or sensory reasons, find note taking difficult. Also the possibility to allow searching multimedia material by using the transcripts is mentioned in his work.

However, using an ASR to extract text from a video-lecture in not trivial, as a good quality of the sound is not always guaranteed. Poor acoustic conditions, differences in speakers' style and accent, and the use of generic vocabularies are the main obstacles. In ideal conditions (i.e. anechoic room, slow speaking rate, and limited vocabulary) a previously trained state-of-the-art ASR system can achieve a Word Error Rate (WER) of less than 3%. In general conditions however the error ranges from 20% to about 45%.

The performance of ASR systems can be improved by creating ad-hoc acoustic model training the system on the speaker's voice. Typically, this requires the teacher to run a training session in which s/he reads a predefined text, so that the system can adjust itself comparing its prediction and the known (exact) expected result. Although such operation takes only a relatively short time (such as half a hour) it might be considered annoying by the teachers, with the result of increasing their unwillingness to use lecture recording systems. Many teachers are in fact nervous about the idea of being recorded, as such operation exposes their performance outside the classroom, and possible mistakes or imprecise wording cannot be hidden behind a "you did misunderstand what I said". Adding an additional nuisance is certainly not needed. Hence a "speaker independent" ASR (i.e. one that does not need specific training) is a better choice, even if performances are lower.

Another way to improve the ASR performance is to have a specific language model. The likelihood of the used words is not flat across all domains: by changing domain certain words become more common and other more rare. Some words are domain-specific, and sometimes – especially in languages other than English – words in a different language are used. Hence, by knowing in advance the domain and the corresponding word distribution, one can greatly improve the results of the ASR system. Textbooks relative to the specific domain of the lecture can be used as a baseline to create the language model, by calculating word frequencies and correlations between words. Often such sources can be found in electronic form, which makes the process of building an ad-hoc language model relatively easy. However, often lecture language resembles conversational language (Glass et al. 2007): the effect is that, in spite of the coincidence of the semantic domain, textbook material has been found to be a rather poor predictor of the spoken language (Park et al. 2007) and was not helpful in reducing the WER. In contrast, it was found to improve the results in terms of retrieval performance (i.e. when the transcripts are used to respond to user queries to identify a relevant portion of the associated video). Park et al. consider this artifact to be caused by the spontaneous nature of the language used in class, as opposed to the more formal one employed by books. Although we could not find decisive evidence in literature, one could deduce that probably, by using textbooks as sources of the vocabulary, the word error rate is decreased on the most relevant words (i.e. the domain specific ones) and increased on more generic and common ones. Hence although the overall WER does not improve, terms that are most likely to be used in queries are better identified.

Munteanu et al. (2007) demonstrated that the language model can be improved also by taking into account the set of slides that often accompany the video-lecture. Their result seems to be in agreement with the above hypothesis, since slides are likely to contain almost only domain specific words.

Choudary et al. (2007) used textbook indexes, as they are manually created by experts, contain no trivial words and hence are very effective in representing the instructional videos.

Including the user in the loop can improve the results. Munteanu et al. (2006) suggested using a wiki-like system to allow users to manually intervene and correct errors in transcripts. Problems connected with conflicts, spam and history of the text can be solved in the traditional wiki way that has been popularized by Wikipedia. Munteanu's work shows an implementation of such technology, but as far as we know the results of their pilot study aimed at measuring the effectiveness of such approach were never published.

Lecture Segmentation

Once the text transcripts are available, further mining becomes possible. A useful task is to segment a lecture into smaller chunks. In fact a lecture typically includes several topics, but finding the boundaries among different subjects is not easy. Generic video segmentation in many cases relies on image analysis, but as we already discussed, in the case of video-lectures this not a very useful option. Rarely the video carries semantic meaning, and its usefulness relies mostly on psychological reasons: learners show a better concentration in front of a video than on audio + slide version (Glowalla 2004), and viewing the speaker gives a sense of familiarity that helps getting emotionally more involved. A limited extraction of information from the video has however been attemped by some authors. For instance, Liao and Syu (2008) identify three classes of scenes: *Teacher-Blackboard* (when the teacher is writing something on the blackboard or is explaining something), *Teacher-Student* (when the teacher is talking with students) and *Students* (when the scene shows the audience). Such information is reinforced by a classification of audio features (background noise, uniqueness of the speaking voice). This knowledge is then used to provide a first level of segmentation of the lecture.

In most cases however detecting lecture segments relies on the availability of audio transcripts. Text segmentation is an active research area. For a short review of the general principle and techniques used, see section 2.1 in Lin et al. (2004). Here we shall focus on the specific applications of text segmentation to lecture transcripts.

Yamamoto et al. (2003) associated ASR transcripts with the textbook used in the lecture. They considered a window (called "Analysis section") in the ASR text and compared its content with the textbook content. They used term frequency–inverse document frequency (TF-IDF[10]) measure to associate the window content with the books sections represented by a vector-space model. They moved the analysis section along the speech transcript and obtain a map of the speech on the textbook sections. Some post-processing allowed cleaning the results by removing the noise generated by analysis sections that are wrongly associated and fall in the middle of otherwise homogeneous sections. Evaluation of their results reports a correct chapter association of 98%. Smaller grain (book) section association turned out to be correct in 89% of the cases.

This approach can be traced back to Hallyday and Hasan (1976) lexical cohesion theory, according to which text segments with a similar vocabulary are likely to belong to the same coherent topic segment.

Lin et al (2004) used a similar technique. They used a text window of fixed length (120 words) and slided the window through the text moving by 20 words at the time. They calculated the similarity between adjacent windows by taking into account seven language features (noun phrases, verb classes, word stems, topic words, combined features, pronouns, and cue phrases) and for each of them calculating a derivation of TF-IDF, which they named TF*ISF, here ISF stands for "Inversed Segment Frequency". The TF*ISF values is used

to detect boundaries of sections. The best results were obtained for values obtained from noun phrases. This approach has the advantage of being universal, since it does not need a domain reference as in Yamamoto's case. However, Yamamoto's approach has the advantage that the reference provides a baseline for extracting semantic clues and understanding the section topic, while Lin's approach only identifies the section without providing any semantic indication.

Repp and Meinel (2008) poposed a hybrid approach that uses slides, transcripts and raw audio to extract various indicators: pauses in the audio track (the longest silences being used as segment boundaries), slides transition markers (they were assumed as boundaries in the transcripts), sliding window (with the same parameters used by Lin), clusters of adjacent similar words in the transcript, similarity between the text contained in sliding windows and adjacent slides, correlation between relevant keywords extracted from the slides and the text in the sliding window. Their results show that imperfect ASR transcripts severely harm the effectiveness of their approach, and that reasonable results can be obtained based on slide transition markers and on pauses. Their results are partially bases on the work reported in another paper (Repp et al. 2007) where they devise an algorithm to find slide transition times based on slide content and transcript in the case that the acquisition software did not already provide slide transition markers.

Search, Semantic Indexing and Multimodal Access

The ability to perform indexing and search on a video stream is another important feature that can be added when once the text transcripts are available. Search involves mainly two kind of queries:

1. given a collection of lectures, identify which lecture is dealing with a given search target;
2. given a lecture, identify the time locations where the search target is present.

Although the two queries can be combined, it is better to keep them conceptually separated. The first one can rely on additional metadata that may be present (e.g. if lectures are stored in a learning management system), while the second one depends on the availability of a temporally annotated transcription. Many ASR provide temporal annotation of the transcribed words, i.e. for every identified word they provide the time at with it was uttered. In such case, it is easy to create an inverted index of all the words contained in the speech. Using the index to search a given word, one can retrieve the portion of phrase that contains the searched word, and the time at which the word occurred during the speech.

Zhang & Nunamaker (2004) manually segmented lectures into semantically homogeneous fragments, provided metadata for each fragment and then allowed user to express queries in natural language. In response to the queries, the system used the metadata to identify the relevant segments and proposed them to the user. Such approach, that addresses the first type of query, strongly relies on human intervention (both for the segmentation and for the generation of metadata), and hence it is difficult and costly to use it on a large scale.

Yoshida et al. (2003) created a system that requires teachers to define a set of keywords for every lecture. These keywords are then matched again a text transcribed by an ASR, and the user is shown a trackbar where the location of any chosen keyword is highlighted.

Fuji et al. (2006) built a system, which searches a lecture video for specific segments in response to a text query. Their results showed that by using specific acoustic and language models (i.e. adapting speech recognition to the lecturer and the topic of the target lecture), the recognition accuracy was increased and consequently the retrieval accuracy was comparable with that obtained by human transcription. This result is partially in contrast with Hürst's finding (Hürst 2005): an investigation of the impact of the ASR errors turned out not to be dramatic, and showed that the imperfect transcripts of recorded lectures are anyway useful for further standard indexing processes.

Hürst and Deutschmann (2006) and Fogarolli et al. (2007) implemented systems that allow searching for arbitrary words in a video-lecture. In both cases the search was multimodal, as it also allowed searching in the slides accompanying the lectures. An excellent review of multimodal video indexing has been published by Snoek and Worring (2005).

Akiba et al. (2009) used a collection of (spoken) lecture documents and evaluate effectiveness of retrieval of searched targets. They concluded that correct retrieval from lectures is much more difficult that for broadcast news. They do not offer an explanation for this fact, but it could be argued that while news span over vastly different topics, a lecture generally has a precise semantic focus – hence the set of terms used throughout a lecture is probably less heterogeneous than in news and this causes more difficulties.

An interesting alternative approach to search has been reported by Iwatsuki et al. (2007). They used a (patented) technique called Fast-Talk Phonetic-Based Searching designed to build search databases from phonemes. The process hence does not need to go through the step of extracting text by using an ASR, and does not search keywords. The authors claim speaker independence and recognition rates of 98%. The main drawback of this method is that adding a semantic layer is impossible, since the concept of "word" does not play any role in the system.

Indexing and searching is an interesting option, but an important step forward would be being able to provide a semantic layer. Such a layer could be useful for both the type of queries we mentioned, and would allow automatic generation of metadata. Although most research on extracting semantics is performed in the framework of the Semantic Web vision (Berners-Lee et al. 2001) where ontologies and logic reasoning play a important role, there are alternative approaches that attempt to extract semantic information such as the latent semantic indexing technique (Deerwester et al. 1990) and explicit semantic analysis (Gabrilovich & Markovitch 2007, Jambunathan et al. 2008), or that use lighter forms of ontologies (Giunchiglia et al. 2006). There have been several papers and projects on approaching e-learning under the umbrella of the Semantic Web, but to our knowledge most of them were not dealing with the specific theme of video-lectures. Repp, Linckels and Meinel (2008) built a system based on the use of ontologies, description logics and natural language processing. The system generated automatically semantic annotation and used it to provide a Query/Answer system. Repp and Meinel (2006) also showed that a smart semantic indexing can be done even with partially incorrect transcripts.

One of the main problems when working in the Semantic Web perspective is the need to use ontologies: getting a good ontology for a generic application domain is not (at least, yet) a trivial task. Hence approaches to semantics with a vision alternative to the Semantic Web are interesting, and a few papers concerned with extraction of semantic information from video-lectures using alternative approaches have been published. For instance, Choudary et al. (2007) have dealt with semantic retrieval from instructional videos. They dealt with the lack on an ontology by using textbook indexes to define the semantic concept space, represented each video in such space, and performed semantic retrieval. Fogarolli & Ronchetti (2008b) used Wikipedia as a reference for additional information, trying to extract semantics from the ASR text by relating it with Wikipedia's content. They have combined the terms extracted from the corpus (a set of lectures) with lexicographic relationships from Wikipedia. Wikipedia has been used as an alternative to ontologies and as a basis for cross-language references (Fogarolli et al. 2008a). They also used relations extracted

from Wikipedia pages to graphically represent the main concepts and their relations within one video lecture (Fogarolli, Seppi & Ronchetti 2009).

Gesture Analysis

Early work on gesture analysis applied to video-lectures was done by Ju et al. (1998). They analyzed the speaker movements and defined three temporal gesture models. Their aim was to be able to identify the portion of a projected slide that the speaker wants to attract students' attention to. The first gesture is characterized by the hand entering over the projected slide, pausing for at least 1/3 of a second and then exiting. The second gesture is more complex: a hand enters, pauses, then moves and pauses an arbitrary number of times before exiting. The last is a waving gestures in which the hand enters and never comes to rest, but rather moves continuously within a small spatial neighbourhood: in such case they to determine the location of a waving gesture by selecting the centre by the pointing positions.

Wang, Ngo and Pong focused in 2004 on three basic gestures: circling (draw a circle around something), lining (draw a line along something) and pointing (point to somewhere for emphasis). Gesture detection was then used to automatic editing the videos, performing close-up of a particular slide region. In 2006 they (Wang et al. 2006) introduced a feature to predict the completion of these gestures: prediction is relevant for real time processing. They also included a study of the relations among gestures, ASR text and slide content. These correlations were used to improve accuracy and responsiveness of gesture detection. In a following work (Wang et al. 2007) automatic video editing was improved by including an analysis of poses, gestures and texts in lectures. They defined a Finite State Machine that, based on the information obtained by this analysis, can generate a simulated camera motion from the existing video.

It is interesting to mention that recent development of work done on real-time gesture detection brought Pong's group (Wang et al. 2008) to develop a system that can be used during the lecture (and not "*a-posteriori*" on the video-lecture) that can simulate an interactive whiteboard: the lecturer can draw on the slides simply by performing gestures in front of the projected slide.

Videolectures Annotation

The idea of allowing users to annotate generic web documents and possibly share these annotations with others has been around for quite a long time (see e.g. the Annotea project (Kahan et al. 2001). Somehow related ideas include tools like Google Notebook[11] and bookmark sharing systems like Delicious[12]. The original ideas about annotation were more ambitious, in that they aimed at being able to attach annotation not just to a page, but to a particular position in that page (hence allowing also multiple annotation of the same page). Similarly, annotation of streaming video has been a subject able to spawn a whole research branch that was also applied to video-lectures (see e.g. Bargeron et al 1999, Correia and Cabral 2005). For example, anchoring discussions to specific (video-lecture) resources rather than collecting them in bulletin boards or forums sounds like a reasonable thing to do, since it would provide a context for the discussion. There have been proposals in this sense (Abowd et al 1998, Haga 2002, Lauer et al. 2005). Another idea, a precursor of the Web 2.0 fashion, was to have students taking lecture notes, attaching them to the video or to a slide-cast and sharing them (e.g. Truong 1999, Kam et al 2005). Curiously, although the needed technology seems to be ripe and these approaches seem to be interesting and useful, none of these initiatives appears to have yet gathered much success. It is possible that the new emphasis given by the Web 2.0 will revitalize this area, allowing the creation and growth of social communities around multimedia resources in the learning domain.

OTHER TOPICS

We already discussed how gesture analysis could be used to post-process videos, e.g. zooming in the region of interest. Other researchers have attempted to implement a "virtual cameraman". In fact, capturing visual details – such as following the teacher to better capture his/her expressions and body language, or zooming on the blackboard when needed is one of the advantages offered by a (costly) human operator. In principle, a virtual cameraman (either in the acquisition phase or during post-processing) could achieve the same goal at a fraction of the cost. We shall not review here what can be done during the acquisition phase, and we'll rather focus on the operations that can be performed as post-processing of an existing video. A possible approach is to use just one camera with panoramic video capturing, and then to extract the portion of image of interest (Sun et al. 2005). A somehow similar idea is implemented in the EYA system (Canessa et al. 2008). They used a wide-angle photo camera to record high resolution pictures every 10 seconds. At present they leave to the user the possibility to focus on the details of interest: the browser shows the video and a large thumbnail of the current picture. When the user moves the mouse over the thumbnail, a high-resolution subset of the image is shown where other systems put the slide. In this way, the user can focus on the detail s/he wants (be it the blackboard, the projected screen or other). They are presently working to enrich the system by automatically extracting some feature, like detecting the slide transitions that occur during the lecture.

The problem of automatically detect slide transitions has been faced by many authors during the last decade, since slide transitions carry a semantic meaning and can help segmenting a lecture. A first system was proposed by Mukhopadhyay (1999), but it required a special synchronization tone to be emitted during the lecture recording. Later approaches were based on computer vision-based, statistical techniques: reviews can be found in the papers by Gigonzac et al (2007) and De Lucia et al. (2008).

Chen & Heng (2003) used the ASR transcripts to match in the slide to identify transitions. Other techniques include detecting slide changes through an http proxy – but this approach only works for HTML-based presentations (Tanaka et al. 2004).

Since in many lectures the blackboard still plays an important role, it is important to be able to effectively capture what happens there. Again, this operation can be done in the recording phase (e.g. using an interactive whiteboard[13]), or an ad-hoc digital desk (see e.g. Joukov & Chiueh 2003) Early work (since 1996 till 2001) on the capture of several experiences in the classroom, including whiteboard traces, was performed in the frame-work of the Classroom2000/eClass project (see eClass 2001). The other possibility is to act during post-processing of the video. The E-chalk project (Friedland & Rojas 2006) extracts handwriting from a traditional blackboard via image analysis.

Finally, we mention that a careful and comprehensive study of a user interface that would offer the possibility of getting the most out of recorded video-lectures is, to our knowledge, still missing.

Steps in this direction have been taken by Mertens et al. (2004, 2006). Such a study should take into consideration also mobile and ubiquitous devices, and analyze also their pedagogical effectiveness. There is in fact little doubt that new generation devices like the Apple iPhone, that has a reasonably high-resolution screen and that already delivers you-tube videos can open new frontiers also in the field of video-lectures, and in fact Apple recently started the iTunes U[14] initiative dedicated to the diffusion of video-lectures coded ad-hoc for the iPhone. Other work that pays attention to mobile devices has been reported by Friedland & Rojas (2006), who used mobile phones and iPods to show the videos of their E-chalk videos.

CONCLUSION

Given the growing needs for continuous education requested by today's society, video streaming applied to education is become more and more popular, and we expect this trend to continue.

To summarize the state of art, it is interesting to refer to the tele-education space as defined by Pullen (2000) and shown in Figure 1. Up to now,

Figure 1. The Tele-education space

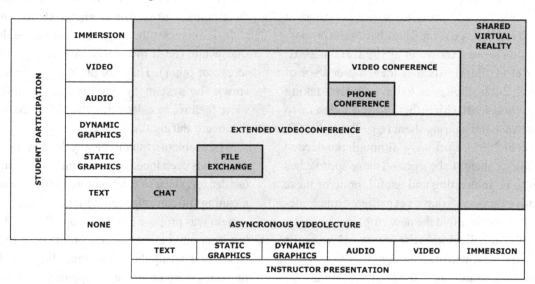

most efforts (both on research and deployment) have been concentrated on a tiny portion of the whole space in the bottom part, where the interaction level between teacher and learner is null. Attempts to deploy the part that seems to be the most interesting one (the extended videoconference/video-lecture region) are either limited to point-to-point interactions, or failed to become a standard model. The main challenges seem to be mainly on finding a convincing, natural and efficient user interface model, and probably on modifying and evolving the teaching paradigm, that is still too much teacher-centered. At present, extensions that will allow the participants to live an immersive learning experience are only at the beginning. In the meantime, we can enjoy the growing wealth of asynchronous video lectures that can support institutional and continuous education. We expect that within a few years they will be enriched by harvesting the research lines discussed here, which will ultimately allow a more efficient use of our time while learning.

REFERENCES

Abowd, G. D., Atkeson, C. G., Brotherton, J., Enqvist, T., Gulley, P., & LeMon, J. (1998) Investigating the capture, integration and access problem of ubiquitous computing in an educational setting, *Proc. of the SIGCHI Conf. on Human factors in computing systems*, (pp. 440-447)

Akiba T., Aikawa K., Ithoh Y., Kawahara T. & Nanjo H. (2009) Construction of a Test Collection for Spoken Document Retrieval from Lecture Audio Data. *Journal of Information Processing (17)* 82-94

Baecker, R. M. (2003). A Principled Design for Scalable Internet Visual Communications with Rich Media, Interactivity, and Structured Archives. *Proceedings of CASCON, 2003*, 83–96.

Baecker R. M., Baran M., Birnholtz J., Laszlo J., Rankin K., Schick R. and Wolff P. (2006) Enhancing interactivity in webcasts with VoIP. *CHI '06: CHI '06 extended abstracts on Human factors in computing systems*

Baecker R.M., Birnholtz J., Causey R., Laughton S.,Kelly Rankin K., Mak C.,Weir A., Wolff P. (2007) Webcasting Made Interactive: Integrating Real-Time Videoconferencing in Distributed Learning Spaces, *Human Interface and the Management of Information. Interacting in Information Environments, LNCS (4558)* 269-278

Bargeron, G. A. Grudin J, & Sanocki E. (1999) Annotations for streaming video on the web. *CHI '99 Extended Abstracts on Human factors in computing systems* pp. 278-279

Berners-Lee, T., Hendler, J., & Lassila, O. (2001). The Semantic Web. *Scientific American*, (May): 2001.

Canessa, E., Fonda, C., & Zennaro, M. (2008) Academic Webcasting using the Automated EyA Recording System *INTED-International Technology, Education and Development*, Valencia/Spain, March 2008.

Chen, Y., & Heng, W. J. (2003) Automatic synchronization of speech transcript and slides in presentation. *Proc. of the Int. Symp. on Circuits and Systems, ISCAS '03.* vol. 2 pp. II-568-571

Choudary, C., Liu, T., & Huang, C. (2007) Semantic Retrieval of Instructional Videos. *Ninth IEEE International Symposium on Multimedia Workshops* (2007)

Correia, N., & Cabral, D. (2005). *VideoStore: A system to store, annotate and share video based content. Recent Research Developments in Learning Technologies 2005* (pp. 1299–1303). FORMATEX.

De Lucia, A., Francese, R., Passero, I., & Tortora, G. (2008). Migrating legacy video lectures to multimedia learning objects. *Software, Practice & Experience*, (38): 1499–1530. doi:10.1002/spe.877

Deerwester, S., Dumais, S. T., Furnas, G. W., & Landauer, T. K. (1990). Indexing by latent semantic analysis. *Journal of the American Society for Information Science American Society for Information Science*, *41*(6), 391–497. doi:10.1002/(SICI)1097-4571(199009)41:6<391::AID-ASI1>3.0.CO;2-9

eClass (2001) for various references on the eClass project, see http://www.cc.gatech.edu/fce/eclass/pubs/index.html Retrieved Sept. 16, 2009

Fogarolli, A., Riccardi, G., & Ronchetti, M. (2007) Searching information in a collection of video-lectures. *Proceedings of World Conference on Educational Multimedia, Hypermedia and Telecommunications ED-MEDIA 2007*, p. 1450-1459

Fogarolli, A., & Ronchetti, M. (2008a). Intelligent Mining and Indexing of Multi-Language e-Learning Material. In Virvou, M., Howlett, R. J., & Jain, L. C. (Eds.), *New Directions in Intelligent Interactive Multimedia George* (pp. 395–404). Springer. doi:10.1007/978-3-540-68127-4_41

Fogarolli A., Ronchetti M., (2008b) Extracting Semantics from Multimedia Content. *Special Issue of Scalable Computing: Practice and Experience (9)* 1895-1767

Fogarolli, A., Seppi, G., & Ronchetti, M. (2009) RDF Graph Representation for Digital Content Visualization Summrization and Navigation. *International Conferences on Digital Libraries and the Semantic Web (ICSD2009)* pp 165-177

Friedland, G., & Rojas, R. (2006). Human-centered Webcasting of Interactive-Whiteboard *Proc. of the Eight IEEE Int. Symposium on Multimedia*

Fujii, A., Itou, K., & Ishikawa, T. (2006). LODEM: A system for on-demand video lectures. *Speech Communication*, (48): 516–531. doi:10.1016/j.specom.2005.08.006

Gabrilovich, E. and S. Markovitch S. (2007) Computing Semantic Relatedness is using Wikipedia-based Explicit Semantic Analysis. *Proceedings of the 20th International Joint Conference on Artificial Intelligence*, pp.1606--1611

Gigonzac, G., Pitie, F., & Kokaram, A. (2007) Electronic slide matching and enhancement of a lecture video. *4th European Conference on Visual Media Production, IETCVMP 2007*, pp. 1 – 7

Giunchiglia, F., Marchese, M., & Zaihrayeu, I. (2006) Encoding classifications into lightweight ontologies. *Proceedings of ESWC'06*

Glass, J., Hazen, T. J., Cyphers, S., & Malioutov, I. (2007). Recent progress in the MIT spoken lecture processing project. Proc. *Interspeech, 2007*, 2553–2556.

Glowalla U. (2004) Utility and Usability von E-Learning am Beispiel von Lecture-on-demand Anwendungen. *Entwerfen und Gestalten*, 2004 (in German)

Haga. (2002) Combining video and bulletin board systems in distance education systems. *The Internet and Higher Education (5)*, 119-129

Halliday, M., & Hasan, R. (1976). *Cohesion in English*. London, UK: Longman.

Hayes, M. H. (1998) Some approaches to Internet distance learning with streaming media, *Second IEEE Workshop on Multimedia Signal Processing* pp. 514-519

He, L., Sanocki, E., Gupta, A., & Grudin, J. (1999). Auto-Summarization of audio-video presentations. *Proceedings of the ACM Multimedia Conference (ACMMM)* pp.489–498.

Hürst, W. (2005) *Multimediale Informationssuche in Vortrags- und Vorlesungsaufzeichnungen*. Doctoral dissertation Universitaet Freiburg, Fakultaet fuer Angewandte Wissenschaften. (in German)

Hürst, W., & Deutschmann, N. (2006) Searching in recorded lectures. *Proc. of World Conf. on Educational Multimedia, Hypermedia and Telecommunications ED-MEDIA 2006* pp. 2859-2866

Iwatsuki, M., Takeuchi, N., Kobayashi, H., & Yana, K. (2007). Automatic Digital Content Generation System for Real-Time Distance Lectures. *International Journal of Distance Education Technologies*, (5): 7–18.

Jambunathan, A., & Ronchetti, M. (2008). Exploiting the collective intelligence contained in Wikipedia to automatically describe the content of a document. In Ronchetti, M. (Ed.), *The Semantic Web: a view on data integration, reasoning, human factors, collective intelligence and technology adoption* (pp. 209–216). Bangkok, Thailand: AIT e-Press.

Joukov, J., & Chiueh, T. (2003). Lectern II: a multimedia lecture capturing and editing system. *Proc. of Int. Conf. on Multimedia and Expo, 2003. ICME '03.* vol. 2 pp. II - 681-684

Ju S.X., Black M., Minneman S. & Kimber D. (1998) Summarization of videotaped presentations: Automatic analysis of motion and gesture. *IEEE Transactions on Circuits and Systems for Video (8)* no. 5, 686-696

Kahan, J., & Koivunen, M.-R. Prud'Hommeaux, E. and Swick R.R., (2001) Annotea: An Open RDF Infrastructure for Shared Web Annotations, *Proc. of the WWW10 International Conference*

Kam, M., Wang, J., Iles, A., Tse, E., Chiu, J., Glaser, D., et al. (2005) Livenotes: a system for cooperative and augmented note-taking in lectures. *CHI '05: Proceedings of the SIGCHI conference on Human factors in computing systems* pp.531-540

Lauer, T., Trahasch, S., & Zupancic, B. (2005) Anchored Discussions of Multimedia Lecture Recordings. *Proceedings 35th Annual Conference - Frontiers in Education - FIE'05* pp. 12-17

Liao, Y.-C., & Syu, M.-H. (2008) An Actor-Based Video Segmentation System Using Visual and Audio Information in E-Learnin". *Eighth International Conference on Intelligent Systems Design and Applications. ISDA '08.* vol. 3 pp. 575 - 580

Lin, M., Nunamaker, J., Chau, M., & Chen, H. (2004) Segmentation of lecture videos based on text: a method combining multiple linguistic features. *Proc. of the 37th Annual Hawaii Int. Conf. on System Sciences, 2004*. pp. 1-9

Mertens, R., Ketterl, M., & Vornberger, O. (2006) Interactive Content Overviews for Lecture Recordings. *Eighth IEEE International Symposium on Multimedia* pp. 933-937

Mertens, R., Schneider, H., Muller, O., & Vornberger, O. (2004) Hypermedia navigation concepts for lecture recordings. *E-Learn: World Conference on E-Learning in Corporate*, pp. 2480–2847

Mukhopadhyay, S., & Smith, B. (1999) Passive capture and structuring of lectures. *MULTIMEDIA '99: Proceedings of the seventh ACM international conference on Multimedia* Part 1 pp.477-477

Munteanu, C., Penn, G., & Baecker, R. (2007) Web-Based Language Modelling for Automatic Lecture Transcription *Proceedings of the Tenth ISCA European Conference on Speech Communication and Technology – EuroSpeech / Eighth International INTERSPEECH Conference*, pp. 2353–2356

Munteanu, C., Zhang, Y., Baecker, R., & Penn, G. (2006) Wiki-like editing for imperfect computer generated webcast transcripts, *Proc. Demo track of ACM Conf. on Computer Supported Cooperative Work – CSCW*, pp. 83–84

Park, A., Hazen, T. J., & Glass, J. R. (2005) Automatic processing of audio lectures for information retrieval: Vocabulary selection and language modeling. *IEEE International Conference on Acoustics*

Pullen, J. M. (2000) The Internet-based lecture: converging teaching and technology. ITiCSE '00: *Proceedings of the 5th annual SIGCSE/SIGCUE ITiCSEconference on Innovation and technology in computer science education* pp. 101-104

Raymond, D., Kanenishi, K., Matsuura, K., & Yano, Y. (2004). IP Videoconferencing in Distance Education: Ideas for a Successful Integration. *Proceedings of World Conference on Educational Multimedia, Hypermedia and Telecommunications 2004* pp. 4179-4184

Repp, S., Linckels, S., & Meinel, C. (2008) Question answering from lecture videos based on an automatic semantic annotation. *Proc. of the 13th annual conf. on Innovation and technology in computer science education ITiCSE '08* pp.17-21

Repp, S., & Meinel, C. (2006) Semantic indexing for recorded educational lecture videos. *Proceedings of the 4th IEEE Conference on Pervasive Computing and Communications Workshops (PerCom)*, pp 240–245

Repp, S., & Meinel, C. (2008) Segmentation of Lecture Videos Based on Spontaneous Speech Recognition. *Tenth IEEE Int. Symp. on Multimedia ISM 2008* pp. 692 – 697

Repp, S., Waitelonis, J., Sack, H., & Meinel, C. (2007) Segmentation and annotation of audio-visual recordings based on automated speech recognition. *Proceedings of the 8th International Conference on Intelligent Data Engineering and Automated Learning (IDEAL)* pp. 620–629

Ronchetti, M. (2003) Has the time come for using video-based lectures over the Internet? A Test-case report *CATE - Web Based Education Conference 2003*

Ronchetti, M. (2008) Requirements for videolectures: which system is the best for you? *World Conference on Educational Multimedia, Hypermedia and Telecommunications (EDMEDIA) 2008*. pp. 2192-2199.

Ronchetti, M. (2010 in press). The impact of Internet-carried video-lectures on education. In Magoulas, G. (Ed.), *E-Infrastructures and Technologies for Lifelong Learning*. IGI Global.

Schick, R., Baecker, R. M., & Scheffel-Dunand, D. (2005). Bimodal Text and Speech Conversation During On-line Lectures, *Proceedings of ED-MEDIA 2005*

Snoek, C., & Worring, M. (2005). Multimodal video indexing: A review of the state-of-the-art. *Multimedia Tools and Applications*, (25): 5–35. doi:10.1023/B:MTAP.0000046380.27575.a5

Soong, S. K. A., Chan, L. K., & Cheers, C. (2006) Impact of video recorded lectures among students. *Proceedings of the 23rd annual ascilite conf.: Who's learning? Whose technology?* Pp.789-792

Sun X., Foote L, Kimber D. & Manjunath B.S., (2005) Region of interest extraction and virtual camera control based on panoramic video capturing. *IEEE Transactions on Multimedia, (7)* n.5 981 - 990

Tanaka, Y., & Itamiya, T. Hagino. T., & Chiyokura, H. (2004) HTTP-proxy-assisted automatic video indexing for e-learning. *International Symposium on Applications and the Internet Workshops. SAINT 2004*. pp. 502 - 507

Tobagi, F. (1995) Distance learning with digital video. *Multimedia IEEE (2)* n.1 90 - 93

Truong, B. T. and Venkatesh, S. (2007). Video abstraction: A systematic review and classification. *ACM Trans. Multimedia Comput. Commun. Appl. (3)*, n.1, 1-37

Truong, K., & Abowd, G. (1999) StuPad: integrating student notes with class lectures. *CHI '99 extended abstracts on Human factors in computing systems* pp. 208 – 209

Wald, M. (2005) 'SpeechText': Enhancing Learning and Teaching by Using Automatic Speech Recognition to Create Accessible, Synchronized Multimedia *World Conf. on Educational Multimedia, Hypermedia and Telecommunications EDMEDIA-2005*

Wang, F., Ngo, C.-W., & Pong, T.-C. (2004) Gesture tracking and recognition for lecture video editing. *Proceedings of the 17th International Conference on Pattern Recognition ICPR 2004. vol. 3* pp. 934 - 937

Wang, F., Ngo, C.-W., & Pong, T.-C. (2006) Prediction-Based Gesture Detection in Lecture Videos by Combining Visual, Speech and Electronic Slides. *IEEE International Conference on Multimedia and Expo, 2006* pp. 653 - 656

Wang F., Ngo C-W., Pong T-C. (2007) Lecture Video Enhancement and Editing by Integrating Posture, Gesture, and Text. *IEEE Transactions on Multimedia (9)* n.2. 397–409

Wang F., Ngo C-W., Pong T-C. (2008) "Simulating a Smartboard by Real-Time Gesture Detection in Lecture Videos". *IEEE Transactions on Multimedia (10)* n.5 926 - 935

Yamamoto, N., Ogata, J., & Ariki, Y. (2003) Topic segmentation and retrieval system for lecture videos based on spontaneous speech recognition, *European Conference on Speech Communication and Technology.* pp. 961–964

Yokoi and Fujiyoshi. (2006) Generating a Time Shrunk Lecture Video by Event Detection. *2006 IEEE International Conference on Multimedia and Expo*, pp. 641 – 644

Yoshida, T., Tada, K., & Hangai, S. (2003). A keyword accessible lecture video player and its evaluation. *Proceedings of the International Conference on Information Technology: Research and Education, ITRE2003*, 610–614.

Zhang D. & Nunamaker, J.F.Jr. (2004) A natural language approach to content-based video indexing and retrieval for interactive e-learning. *IEEE Transactions on Multimedia (6)* n.3 450 - 458

Zhang, D., Zhu, L., Briggs, L. O., & Nunamaker, J. F. Jr. (2006). Instructional video in e-learning: Assessing the impact of interactive video on learning effectiveness. *Information & Management*, (43): 15–27. doi:10.1016/j.im.2005.01.004

Zupancic, B., & Horz, H. 2002. Lecture recording and its use in a traditional university course. *Proc. of the 7th Annual Conf. on Innovation and Technology in Computer Science Education IT-iCSE '02.* pp.24-28

KEY TERM AND DEFINITIONS

Automated Speech Recognition: A computational technique that converts spoken words to text.

Continuous Education: An all-encompassing term within a broad spectrum of post-secondary learning activities and programs.

Digital Library: A library in which collections are stored in digital formats (as opposed to print, microform, or other media) and accessible by computers.

Distance Education: A field of education that focuses on the pedagogy and andragogy, technology, and instructional systems design that aim to deliver education to students who are not physically "on site".

E-Learning: A term that encompasses all forms of Technology-Enhanced Learning, i.e. support of any pedagogical approach that utilizes technology.

Gesture: A form of non-verbal communication in which visible bodily actions communicate conventionalized particular messages, either in place of speech or together and in parallel with spoken words.

Multimodality, Multimodal (Interaction): A form of man-machine interaction using multiple modes of input/output.

Semantic Web: An evolving development of the World Wide Web in which the meaning (semantics) of information and services on the web is defined, making it possible for the web to "understand" and satisfy the requests of people and machines to use the web content.

Text Segmentation: The identification of lexical units in writing systems.

Video Abstracting: A research area that deals with gaining perspectives of a video document without watching it entirely.

Video Conference: A set of interactive telecommunication technologies which allow two or more locations to interact via two-way video and audio transmissions simultaneously.

Video-Lecture: lecture recorded in a video and delivered through a variety of media.

Video Segmentation: The identification of boundaries among regions that differ for content or aspect in a video.

ENDNOTES

[1] http://it.wikipedia.org/wiki/Chroma_key
[2] http://watch.mit.edu/
[3] http://www.america.gov/st/educ-english/2008/January/200801221815081CJsamohT0.1036035.html
[4] http://latemar.science.unitn.it/LODE
[5] http://www.openeya.org
[6] http://www4.uwm.edu/libraries/media/streaming.cfm
[7] http://www.telecomitalia.it/cgi-bin/ti-portale/TIPortale/ep/contentView.do?channelId=-9793&LANG=IT&contentId=33796&programId=9596&programPage=%2Fep%2FTImedia%2FTICSList.jsp%3Ffonte%3DTelecom%2BItalia&tabId=6&pageTypeId=-8663&contentType=EDITORIAL
[8] http://www.scuola-digitale.it/isoleinrete/content/index.php?action=read_pag1&id_cnt=6679
[9] http://en.wikipedia.org/wiki/Online_public_access_catalog
[10] http://en.wikipedia.org/wiki/Tf%E2%80%93idf
[11] http://www.google.com/notebook/
[12] http://delicious.com/
[13] http://en.wikipedia.org/wiki/Interactive_whiteboard
[14] http://www.apple.com/education/mobile-learning/

Compilation of References

Abanoz, T. B., & Tekalp, A. M. (2009). SVC-based scalable multiple description video coding and optimization of encoding configuration. *Signal Processing Image Communication*, 24, 691–701. doi:10.1016/j.image.2009.07.003

Abeni, L. Kiraly, C., & Lo Cigno, R. (2009, May). On the optimal scheduling of streaming applications in unstructured meshes. In *Proceedings of Networking 2009, 8th International IFIP-TC 6 Networking Conference*, Aachen, Germany.

Abowd, G. D., Atkeson, C. G., Brotherton, J., Enqvist, T., Gulley, P., & LeMon, J. (1998) Investigating the capture, integration and access problem of ubiquitous computing in an educational setting, *Proc. of the SIGCHI Conf. on Human factors in computing systems*, (pp. 440-447)

Adar, E., & Huberman, B. A. (2000). Free Riding on Gnutella. *First Monday*, 5(10).

Adlakha, S., Zhu, X., Girod, B., & Goldsmith, A. J. (2007, September). Joint capacity, flow and rate adaptation for multiuser video streaming over wireless networks. *IEEE International Conference on Communications*, (pp. 69-72).

Ahlswede, R., Cai, N., Li, S. Y. R., & Yeung, R. W. (2000). Network information flow. *Information Theory, IEEE Transactions on, 46*(4), 1204–1216. Retrieved December 22, 2009 from http://dx.doi.org/10.1109/18.850663

Ahn, J. H., Kim, C. S., & Ho, Y. S. (2006). Predictive Compression of Geometry, Color and Normal Data of 3-D Mesh Models. *IEEE Trans. on Circuits and Systems for Video Technology*, 16(2), 291–299. doi:10.1109/TCSVT.2005.861945

Ajib, W., & Haccoun, D. (2005). An overview of scheduling algorithms in MIMO-based fourth-generation wireless systems. *IEEE Network*, 19(5), 43–48. doi:10.1109/MNET.2005.1509951

Akiba T., Aikawa K., Ithoh Y., Kawahara T. & Nanjo H. (2009) Construction of a Test Collection for Spoken Document Retrieval from Lecture Audio Data. *Journal of Information Processing (17)* 82-94

Akkaya, K., & Younis, M. (2005). A Survey of Routing Protocols in Wireless Sensor Networks. *Elsevier Ad Hoc Network Journal*, 1(3), 325–349.

Akkaya, K., & Younis, M. (2003, May). *An energy-aware QoS routing protocol for wireless sensor networks*. Paper presented at the IEEE Workshop on Mobile and Wireless Networks, Providence, RI.

Albanese, A., Blomer, J., Edmonds, J., Luby, M., & Sudan, M. (1996). Priority encoding transmission. *IEEE Transactions on Information Theory*, 42(6), 1737–1744. doi:10.1109/18.556670

Ali, S. Mathur, A. & Zhang, H. (2006). Measurement of commercial peer-to-peer live video streaming. *Workshop on Recent Advances in P2P Streaming*, Waterloo, ON.

Alliez, P., & Desbrun, M. (2001). Valence-driven connectivity encoding of 3D meshes. *Computer Graphics Forum*, 20, 480–489. doi:10.1111/1467-8659.00541

Alstrup, S., & Rauhe, T. (2005, July). Introducing Octoshape – a new technology for large-scale streaming over the Internet. *EBU Technical Review*, (303), 1-10.

Copyright © 2011, IGI Global. Copying or distributing in print or electronic forms without written permission of IGI Global is prohibited.

Ameigeiras, P. (2003). *Packet Scheduling And Quality of Service in HSDPA*. (PhD thesis), Institute of Electronic Systems, Aalborg University.

Amon, P., Rathgen, T., & Singer, D. (2007). File Format for Scalable Video Coding. *IEEE Transactions on Circuits and Systems for Video Technology*, *17*(9), 1174–1185. doi:10.1109/TCSVT.2007.905521

Amonou, I., Cammas, N., Kervadec, S., & Pateux, S. (2007). Optimized rate-distortion extraction with quality layers in the scalable extension of H.264/AVC. *IEEE Transactions on Circuits and Systems for Video Technology*, *17*(9), 1186–1193. doi:10.1109/TCSVT.2007.906870

Anagnostakis, K. G., & Greenwald, M. B. (2004). Exchange-based Incentive Mechanisms for Peer-to-Peer File Sharing. In *Proceeding of International Conference on Distributed Computing Systems,* Philadelphia.

Apostolopoulos, A. G. (1999). Error-resilient video compression via multiple state streams, *Proc. International Workshop on Very Low Bit rate Video Coding (VLBV '99)*, Kyoto, Japan.

Apostolopoulos, J. G. (2001, January). Reliable video communication over lossy packet networks using multiple state encoding and path diversity. *Visual Communications and Image Processing*, (pp. 392-409).

Apple Computer Inc. (2001). *Audio and MIDI on Mac OS X*, Technical report.

Arce, P., Guerri, J. C., Pajares, A., & Lázaro, O. (2008). Performance evaluation of video streaming over ad hoc networks using flat and hierarchical routing protocols. *Mobile Networks and Applications*, *30*, 324–336.

ARIB STD-T63-26.233 V8.0.0 (2008). Transparent end-to-end packet switched streaming service (PSS);

ARIB STD-T63-26.237 V8.0.0 (2008). *IMS based PSS and MBMS User Service; Protocols (Release 8), ARIB STD-T63-26.237 V8.0.0*. Retrieved from http://www.arib.or.jp/IMT-2000/V720Mar09/2_T63/ARIB-STD-T63/Rel8/26/A26237-800.pdf

ARIB STD-T63-26.246 V6.1.0 (2006). Technical Specification 3rd Generation Partnership Project; Technical Specification Group Services and System Aspects; Transparent end-to-end packet switched streaming service (PSS); 3GPP SMIL Language Profile (Release 6), 3GPP TS 26.246 V6.1.0, Sep 2006, http://www.arib.or.jp/IMT-2000/V720Mar09/2_T63/ARIB-STD-T63/Rel6/26/A26246-610.pdf

Arkko, J., Lindholm, F., Naslund, M., Norrman, K., & Carrara, E. (2006, July). Key Management Extensions for Session Description Protocol (SDP) and Real Time Streaming Protocol (RTSP) (No. 4567). *RFC 4567 (Proposed Standard). IETF.* Retrieved December 22, 2009 from http://www.ietf.org/rfc/rfc4567.txt

Ashwin, C. H., Bharambe, R., & Padmanabhan, V. N. (2006). Analyzing and Improving a BitTorrent Network Performance Mechanisms. In *Proceedings of INFOCOM*.

Aspert, N., Santa-Cruz, D., & Ebrahimi, T. (2002). MESH: Measuring Error between Surfaces using the Hausdorff Distance. In. *Proceedings of the IEEE International Conference on Multimedia and Expo*, *I*, 705–708.

Baccichet, P., Rane, S., & Girod, B. (2006, May). Systematic lossy error protection based on H.264/AVC redundant slices and Flexible Macroblock Ordering. *Journal of Zhejiang University. Scientific American*, *7*(5), 727–736.

Baecker, R. M. (2003). A Principled Design for Scalable Internet Visual Communications with Rich Media, Interactivity, and Structured Archives. *Proceedings of CASCON, 2003*, 83–96.

Baecker R. M., Baran M., Birnholts J., Laszlo J., Rankin K., Schick R. and Wolff P. (2006) Enhancing interactivity in webcasts with VoIP. *CHI '06: CHI '06 extended abstracts on Human factors in computing systems*

Baecker R.M., Birnholtz J., Causey R., Laughton S., Kelly Rankin K., Mak C., Weir A., Wolff P. (2007) Webcasting Made Interactive: Integrating Real-Time Videoconferencing in Distributed Learning Spaces, *Human Interface and the Management of Information. Interacting in Information Environments, LNCS (4558)* 269-278

Bai, F., Adagopan, N., & Helmy, A. (2003, April). IMPORTANT: A framework to systematically analyze the Impact of Mobility on Performance of routing protocols over Adhoc NeTworks. *IEEE INFOCOM*, 825-835.

Bailey, N. T. (1975). *The Mathematical Theory of Infectious diseases* (2nd ed.). Halfner Press.

Bajaj, C. L., Pascucci, V., & Zhuang, G. (1999). Single resolution compression of arbitrary triangular meshes with properties. *Computational Geometry Theory and Application, 14*, 167–186.

Bakker, D., Comboom, D., Dams, T., & Munteanu, A. (2008). Priority-based error protection for the scalable extension of H.264/AVC. *In Proc. SPIE, Optical and Digital Image Processing. Vol. 7000.*

Baldo, N., Horn, U., Kampmann, M., & Hartung, F. (2004). RTCP feedback based transmission rate control for 3G wireless multimedia streaming. *IEEE Int. Symp. Personal, Indoor and Mobile Radio Com., 3*, 1817–1821.

Banerjee, S., Bhattacharjee, B., & Kommareddy, C. (2002). Scalable application layer multicast. In *Proceeding of ACM Special Interest Group on Data Communication*, Pittsburgh, PA.

Bargeron, G. A. Grudin J, & Sanocki E. (1999) Annotations for streaming video on the web. *CHI '99 Extended Abstracts on Human factors in computing systems* pp. 278-279

Barmada, B., Ghandi, M. M., Jones, E., & Ghanbari, M. (2005, Aug.). Prioritized transmission of data partitioned H.264 video with hierarchical QAM. *IEEE Signal Processing Letters, 12*(8), 577–580. doi:10.1109/LSP.2005.851261

Bawa, M. Deshpande, H. & Garcia-Molina, H. (2002). Transience of peers and streaming media. *In HotNets-I*, Princeton, NJ, (pp. 107–112).

BBC-a. (2010). *The technology behind Dirac*. Retrieved February 2010, from http://www.bbc.co.uk/rd/projects/dirac/technology.shtml

BBC-b. (2010). *Dirac Video Codec Referencing Software*. Retrieved February 2010, from http://sourceforge.net/projects/dirac/

BBC-c. (2010). *Dirac algorithm*. Retrieved February 2010, from http://dirac.sourceforge.net/documentation/algorithm/algorithm/index.htm

BBC-d. (2010). *Dirac specification*. Retrieved February 2010, from http://diracvideo.org/download/specification/dirac-spec-latest.pdf

BBC-e. (2010). *Dirac Transcoder*. Retrieved February 2010, from http://diracvideo.org/download/ffmpeg2dirac/

Benbadis, F., Mathieu, F., Hegde, N., & Perino, D. (2008). Playing with the bandwidth conservation law. In *Proceedings of the 2008 Eighth International Conference on Peer-to-Peer Computing* (pp. 140-149).

Bencina, R. (2003). Portaudio and media synchronisation – it's all in the timing. In *Proceedings of the ACMC Conference*, Perth, Australia.

Bernardini, R., Rinaldo, R., & Vitali, A. (2008, March). A reliable chunkless peer-to-peer architecture for multimedia streaming. In *Proc. Data Compression Conference* (pp. 242–251). Snowbird, Utah: IEEE Computer Society.

Berners-Lee, T., Hendler, J., & Lassila, O. (2001). The Semantic Web. *Scientific American*, (May): 2001.

Bertsekas, D. P. (1976). *Dynamic Programming and Stochastic Control*. New York: Academic.

Bharambe, A. R., Herley, C., & Padmanabhan, V. N. (2006). Analyzing and Improving BitTorrent Performance. In *Proceedings of IEEE Conference on Computer Communications*, Barcelona.

Bharambe, A. Rao, S. Padmanabhan, V. Seshan, S., & Zhang, H. (2005). The impact of heterogeneous bandwidth constraints on DHT-based multicast protocols. In *Proceedings of the 4th International Workshop on Peer-to-Peer Systems*.

Biersack, E. W. (2005). Where is multicast today? *SIGCOMM Comput. Commun. Rev., 35*(5), 83–84. doi:10.1145/1096536.1096549

Black, U. (2000). *Voice Over IP* (1st ed.). Upper Saddle River, NJ: Prentice Hall.

Blake, S., Black, D., Carlson, M., Davies, E., Wang, Z., & Weiss, W. (1998). *An architecture for differentiated services, RFC-2475. Internet Engineering Task Force*. IETF.

Bogomjakov, A., & Gotsman, C. (2002). Universal Rendering Sequences for Transparent Vertex Caching of Progressive Meshes. *Computer Graphics Forum, 21*(2), 137–148. doi:10.1111/1467-8659.00573

Bolot, J., Fosse-Parisis, S., & Towsley, D. (1999). Adaptive FEC-based error control for interactive audio in the internet. *Proceedings - IEEE INFOCOM*, (March): 1999.

Bolot, J., & Garcia, A. (1996, November). Control mechanisms for packet audio in the internet. *Proceedings - IEEE INFOCOM, 1*, 232–239.

Bolot, J., & Turletti, T. (1994, November). A rate control mechanism for packet video in the internet. *Proceedings - IEEE INFOCOM, 3*, 1216–1223.

Bolot, J., & Turletti, T. (1998). Experience with rate control mechanisms for packet video in the Internet. *Computer Communication Review, 28*(1), 4–15. doi:10.1145/280549.280551

Bonald, T. Massoulié, L. Mathieu, F. Perino, D., & Twigg, A. (2008). Epidemic live streaming: optimal performance trade-offs. In *Proceedings of the 2008 ACM SIGMETRICS International Conference on Measurement and Modeling of Computer Systems*, Annapolis, MD, USA.

Borer, T., & Davies, T. (2005). Dirac - video compression using open technology. *BBC R&D White Paper*. Retrieved February 2010, from http://downloads.bbc.co.uk/rd/pubs/whp/whp-pdf-files/WHP117.pdf

Braden, R., Clark, D., & Shenker, S. (1994). *Integrated services in the Internet architecture: An overview, RFC-1633. Internet Engineering Task Force*. IETF.

Broch, J., Maltz, D. A., Johnson, D. B., et al. (1998). A performance comparison of multi-hop wireless ad hoc network routing protocols. *ACM Mobicom Conference*, 85-97.

Bucciol, P., Ridolfo, F., & de Martin, J. C. (2008, April). Multicast voice transmission over vehicular ad hoc networks: Issues and challenges", *7th International Conference. on Networking*, (pp. 746-751).

Buchegger, S., & Le Boudec, J.-Y. (2004). A Robust Reputation System for P2P and Mobile Ad-hoc Networks. [*Systems*, Cambridge, MA.]. *De Economía*, ▪▪▪, 2P.

Buragohain, C., Agrawal, D., & Suri, S. (2003). A Game Theoretic Framework for Incentives in P2P Systems. In *Proceedings of IEEE International Conference on Peer-to-Peer Computing*. Linköpings, Sweden.

Caccamo, M., & Zhang, Y. L., & Sha, L., & Buttazzo, G. (2002). An Implicit Prioritized Access Protocol for Wireless Sensor Networks. In *Proceedings of 23rd IEEE Real-Time Systems Symposium,* 39–48.

Caceres, J. P., Hamilton, R., Iyer, D., Chafe, C., & Wang, G. (2008, November). To the edge with china: Explorations in network performance. In *Proceedings of the 4th International Conference on Digital Arts*, Porto, Portugal.

Canessa, E., Fonda, C., & Zennaro, M. (2008) Academic Webcasting using the Automated EyA Recording System *INTED-International Technology, Education and Development*, Valencia/Spain, March 2008.

Carôt, A. (2004). *Livemusic on the Internet.* Diploma thesis, Fachhochschule Lübeck, Germany.

Carôt, A. (2009). *Musical Telepresence – A Comprehensive Analysis Towards New Cognitive and Technical Approaches*. (PhD Thesis), Institute of Telematics – University of Lübeck, Germany.

Carôt, A., & Werner, C. (2007, September). Network music performance – problems, approaches and perspectives. In *Proceedings of the Music in the Global Village – Conference*, Budapest, Hungary.

Carôt, A., & Werner, C. (2008). Distributed network music workshop with soundjack. In *Proceedings of the 25th Tonmeistertagung*, Leipzig, Germany.

Carôt, A., Hohn, T., & Werner, C. (2009). Netjack – remote music collaboration with electronic sequencers on the internet. In *Proceedings of the Linux audio conference*, Parma, Italy.

Carôt, A., Krämer, U., & Schuller, G. (2006, May). Network music performance in narrow band networks. In *Proceedings of the 120th AES convention*, Paris, France.

Carôt, A., Werner, C., & Fischinger, C. (2009, August). Towards a comprehensive cognitive analysis of delay-influenced rhythmical interaction. In *Proceedings of the International Computer Music Conference (ICMC)*, Montreal, Canada.

Carzaniga, A., Rutherford, M., & Wolf, A. (2004). A Routing Scheme for Content-Based Networking. *Proceedings of IEEE 2004 International Conference on Computer Communications, HK, 2,*918-928.

Casner, S. (2003). *Request For Comments (RFC) 3556 - Session Description Protocol (SDP) Bandwidth Modifiers for RTP Control Protocol (RTCP)*. Bandwidth.

Castro, M., Druschel, P., Kermarrec, A.-M., Nandi, A., Rowstron, A., & Singh, A. (2003). SplitStream: High-bandwidth multicast in cooperative environments. In *Proceedings of ACM Symposium on Operating Systems Principles,* New York.

Cavers, J. K. (2000). *Mobile Channel Characteristics*. Hingham, MA: Kluwer Academic Publishers.

Cha, H., Kim, J., & Ha, R. (2003). Bandwidth constrained smoothing for multimedia streaming with scheduling support. *Journal of Systems Architecture, 48*(11-12), 353–366. doi:10.1016/S1383-7621(03)00022-5

Cha, M. Kwak, H. Rodriguez, P. Ahn, Y., & Moon, S. (2007, October). I tube, you tube, everybody tubes: analyzing the world's largest user generated content video system. In *Proceedings of the 7th ACM SIGCOMM Conference on Internet Measurement*, San Diego.

Cha, M. Rodriguez, P. Crowcroft, J. Moon, S., & Amatriain, X. (2008, October). Watching television over an IP network. In *Proc. of the 8th ACM SIGCOMM Conference on Internet Measurement*, Vouliagmeni, Greece.

Chafe, C., Gurevich, M., Leslie, G., & Tyan, S. (2004, March). Effect of time delay on ensemble accuracy. In *Proceedings of the International Symposium on Musical Acoustics*, Nara, Japan.

Chai, Y., & Ye, D. (2007). The Design and Implementation of a Scalable Wireless Video Streaming System Adopting TCP Transmission Mode. In *Proceedings of the 7th IEEE International Conference on Computer and Information Technology, Fukushima,* 534-538.

Chaintreau, A. Baccelli, F., & Diot, C. (2002). Impact of network delay variation on multicast sessions performance with TCP-like congestion control. *IEEE Transactions on Networking*, pp. 500-512.

Chakareski, J., Han, S., & Girod, B. (2005). Layered coding vs. multiple descriptions for video streaming over multiple paths. *Multimedia Systems, 10*(4), 275–285. doi:10.1007/s00530-004-0162-3

Chakareski, J., Apostolopoulos, J. G., Wee, S., Tan, W., & Girod, B. (2005). Rate-distortion hint tracks for adaptive video streaming. *IEEE Transactions on Circuits and Systems for Video Technology, 15*(10), 1257–1269. doi:10.1109/TCSVT.2005.854227

Chakareski, J., & Frossard, P. (2006). Rate-distortion optimized distributed packet scheduling of multiple video streams over shared communication resources. *IEEE Transactions on Multimedia, 8*(2), 207–218. doi:10.1109/ TMM.2005.864284

Chakareski, J., & Chou, P.A. (2006). Radio edge: Rate-distortion optimized proxy-driven streaming from the network edge. *IEEE/ACM Transactions on Networking, 14*(6), 1302–1312.

Chakereseki, J., Han, S. & Girod, B. (2005). Layered coding vs. multiple descriptions for video streaming over multiple paths. *Multimedia Systems*, online journal.

Chang, S.-F., & Vetro, A. (2005). Video Adaptation: Concepts, Technologies, and Open Issues. *Proceedings of the IEEE, 93*(1), 148–158. doi:10.1109/JPROC.2004.839600

Chang, E. Y., Hur, N., & Jang, E. S. (2008). 3D model compression in MPEG, *International Conference on Image Processing*. (pp. 2692-2695).

Chatzidrossos, I., Dán, G., & Fodor, V. (2009). Delay and playout probability trade-off in mesh-based peer-to-peer streaming with delayed buffer map updates. *Peer-to-peer Networking and Applications*.

Chen, J., Chan, S., & Li, V. (2004). Multipath routing for video delivery over bandwidth-limited networks. *IEEE Journal on Selected Areas in Communications*, 22(10), 1920–1932. doi:10.1109/JSAC.2004.836000

Chen, M., Leung, V., Mao, S., & Yuan, Y. (2007). Directional Geographical Routing for Real-Time Video Communications in Wireless Sensor Networks. *Elsevier Computer Communications*, 30(17), 3368–3383.

Chen, K. M. Sivalingam, Agrawal, P., & Kishore, S. (1998). A comparison of MAC protocols for wireless local networks based on battery power consumption. *IEEE INFOCOM*, (pp. 150-157).

Chen, L., Low, S. H., & Doyle, J. C. (2007). Contention Control: A Game-Theoretic Approach. In In *Proceedings of IEEE Conference on Decision and Control*, New Orleans, LA.

Chen, Y., & Heng, W. J. (2003) Automatic synchronization of speech transcript and slides in presentation. *Proc. of the Int. Symp. on Circuits and Systems, ISCAS '03*. vol. 2 pp. II-568-571

Cheng, P., Li, J., & Kuo, C.-C. J. (1997). Rate control for an embedded wavelet video coder. *IEEE Transactions on Circuits and Systems for Video Technology*, 7(4), 696–702. doi:10.1109/76.611180

Cho, S., & Pearlman, W. A. (2002). A Full-Featured, Error-Resilient, Scalable Wavelet Video Codec Based on the Set Partitioning in Hierarchical Trees (SPIHT) Algorithm. *IEEE Transaction Circuits System Video Technology*, 12, 157–171. doi:10.1109/76.993437

Chou, P. A., & Miao, Z. (2006, April). Rate-distortion optimized streaming of packetized media. *IEEE Transactions on Multimedia*, 8(2), 390–404. doi:10.1109/TMM.2005.864313

Chou, P. H., & Meng, T. H. (2002). Vertex Data Compression through Vector Quantization. *IEEE Transactions on Visualization and Computer Graphics*, 8(4), 373–382. doi:10.1109/TVCG.2002.1044522

Chou, P. A., Wang, H. J., & Padmanabhan, V. N. (2003). *Layered multiple description coding*. Proceedings of Packet Video Workshop.

Chou, P., Wu, Y., & Jain, K. (2003), Practical Network Coding. In *Proc. of the 41st Allerton Conference on Communication, Control and Computing*. Retrieved November 20, 2009 from http://flipflop.usc.edu/~mvieira/Network-Coding/google/chou03practical.pdf

Choudary, C., Liu, T., & Huang, C. (2007) Semantic Retrieval of Instructional Videos. *Ninth IEEE International Symposium on Multimedia Workshops* (2007)

Chow, M. M. (1997). *Optimized geometry compression for real-time rendering* (pp. 346–354). IEEE Visualization.

Chow, C.-O., & Ishii, H., H. (2007). Enhancing real-time video streaming over mobile ad hoc networks using multipoint-to-point communication. *Computer Communications*, 30, 1754–1764. doi:10.1016/j.comcom.2007.02.004

Chow, A. L., Golubchik, L., & Misra, V. (2008). Improving BitTorrent: A Simple Approach. In *Proceedings of International Workshop on Peer-to-Peer Systems*, Tampa Bay, FL.

Christakidis, A., Efthymiopoulos, N., Denazis, S., & Koufopavlou, O. (2009). On the architecture and the design of P2P live streaming system schedulers, In *Proceedings of ICUMT*.

Chu, M., Reich, J., & Zhao, F. (2004). Distributed Attention in Large Scale Video Sensor Networks. In *Proceedings of IEEE Intelligent Distributed Surveilliance Systems*, 61-65.

Chu, Y. H., & Zhang, H. (2004). Considering Altruism in Peer-to-Peer Internet Streaming Broadcast. In *IEEE NOSSDAV*.

Chu, Y., Ganjam, A., Ng, T. S. E., Rao, S. G., Sripanidkulchai, K., Zhan, J., & Zhang, H. (2004). Early experience with an internet broadcast system based on overlay multicast. *USENIX Annual Technical Conference, General Track*, pp. 155–170.

Chu, Y.-H., Chuang, J., & Zhang, H. (2004). A Case for Taxation in Peer-to-Peer Streaming Broadcast. In *Proceeding of ACM Special Interest Group on Data Communication,* Portland, OR.

Chu, Y.-H., Rao, S. G., & Zhang, H. (2000). A Case for End System Multicast. In *Proceedings of ACM International Conference on Measurement and Modeling of Computer Systems,* Santa Clara, CA.

Cisco (Sept. 2009). Reshaping Cisco: The world according to Chambers. *The Economist*, 54-56.

Ciullo, D., Mellia, M., Meo, M., & Leonardi, E. (2008). TV Systems Through Real Measurements. In *Proceedings of Globecom* (p. 2P). Understanding.

Ciullo, D., Garcia, M. A., Horvat, A., Leonardi, E., Mellia, M., Rossi, D., et al. (2009, May). Network awareness of P2P live streaming applications. *In HotP2P '09*, Rome, Italy.

Cohen, R., Cohen-Or, D., & Ironi, T. (2002). *Multi-way geometry encoding, (Technical report)*. Tel-Aviv University.

Cohen, B. (2003). Incentives build robustness in BitTorrent. In *Proceedings of* (p. 2P). Berkeley, CA: Economics Workshop.

Cohen-Or, D., Levin, D., & Remez, O. (1999). Progressive compression of arbitrary triangular meshes, *Proc. IEEE Visualization* (pp. 67-72).

Comer, D. E. (2002). *Computernetzwerke und Internets mit Internet-Anwendungen* (3rd ed.). Pearson Studium.

Correia, N., & Cabral, D. (2005). *VideoStore: A system to store, annotate and share video based content. Recent Research Developments in Learning Technologies 2005* (pp. 1299–1303). FORMATEX.

Cosma, M., Pescaru, D., Ciubotaru, B., & Todinca, D. (2006, May). *Routing and Topology Extraction Protocol for a Wireless Sensor Network using Video Information.* Paper presented at 3rd Romanian-Hungarian Joint Symposium on Applied Computational Intelligence, Timisoara, Romania.

Coulson, G., Campbell, A., Rodin, P., Blair, G., Papathomas, M., & Shepherd, D. (1995). The design of a QoS-controlled ATM-based communications system in Chorus. *IEEE Journal on Selected Areas in Communications, 13*(4), 686–699. doi:10.1109/49.382159

Creusere, C. D. (1997). A new method of robust image compression based on the embedded zerotree wavelet algorithm. *IEEE Transactions on Image Processing, 6*, 1436–1442. doi:10.1109/83.624967

Croce, D., Mellia, M., & Leonardi, E. (2009). The Quest for Bandwidth Estimation Techniques for large-scale Distributed Systems. In *Proceedings of Hotmetrics*.

da Silva, A. P. C., Leonardi, E., Mellia, M., & Meo, M. (2008). A Bandwidth-Aware Scheduling Strategy for P2P-TV Systems. In *Proceedings of the Eighth International Conference on Peer-to-Peer Computing*.

De Lucia, A., Francese, R., Passero, I., & Tortora, G. (2008). Migrating legacy video lectures to multimedia learning objects. *Software, Practice & Experience*, (38): 1499–1530. doi:10.1002/spe.877

Deering, S. E., & Cheriton, D. R. (1990, May). Multicast routing in datagram internetworks and extended LANs. *ACM Transactions on Computer Systems, 8*(2), 85–110. doi:10.1145/78952.78953

Deering, M. F. (1995). Geometry compression, *Proc. ACM SIGGRAPH.* (pp. 13-20).

Deerwester, S., Dumais, S. T., Furnas, G. W., & Landauer, T. K. (1990). Indexing by latent semantic analysis. *Journal of the American Society for Information Science American Society for Information Science, 41*(6), 391–497. doi:10.1002/(SICI)1097-4571(199009)41:6<391::AID-ASI1>3.0.CO;2-9

Deshpande, H., Bawa, M., & Garcia-Molina, H. (2001). Streaming live media over peers. Technical Report 2001-31, Computer Science Department, Stanford University.

Despotovic, Z., & Aberer, K. (2005). P2P reputation management: probabilistic estimation vs. social networks. *Computer Networks, 50* (2006).

Dhungel, P., & Hei, X. W. Ross, K., & Saxena, N. (2007, August). The pollution attack in P2P live video streaming: measurement results and defenses. *In Sigcomm P2P-TV Workshop.*

Dilmaghani, R. B., & Rao, R. R. (2007, June). Future wireless communication infrastructure with application to emergency services. *IEEE International Symposium on the World of Wireless, Mobile and Multimedia Networks,* (pp. 1-7).

Duffield, N.G., Ramakrishnan, K.K. & Reibman, A.R. (1998). SAVE: An algorithm for smoothed adaptive video over explicit rate networks. *IEEE/ACM Transactions on Networking, 6*(6), 717-728.

Eberhard, M., Celetto, L., Timmerer, C., Quacchio, E., Hellwagner, H., & Rovati, F. (2008). An Interoperable Streaming Framework for Scalable Video Coding based on MPEG-21. In *Proc. 5th IET Visual Information Engineering Conference (VIE'08),* (pp. 723-728). Xi'an, China.

Eberlein, D. (2007). *Lichtwellenleiter-Technik: Grundlagen, Verbindungs- und Messtechnik, Systeme, Trends* (7th ed.). Berlin, Germany: Verlag.

eClass (2001) for various references on the eClass project, see http://www.cc.gatech.edu/fce/eclass/pubs/index.html Retrieved Sept. 16, 2009

Eleftheriadis, A., & Batra, P. (2004). Optimal data partitioning of MPEG-2 coded video. *IEEE Transactions on Circuits and Systems for Video Technology, 14*(10), 1195–1209. doi:10.1109/TCSVT.2004.835149

Emre, B. Aksu (2004). Mobile Multimedia and Evolution of 3GPP Packet Switched Streaming Service (PSS), Nokia Corporation, IMTC Forum, May 2004, San Jose, CA, USA, http://www.imtc.org/events/forum%20events/forum_2004/presentations/day_2/d2eaksu18.ppt

Eugster, P., Guerraoui, R., Kermarrec, A.-M., & Massoulié, L. (2004). From epidemics to distributed computing. *IEEE Computer, 37*(5), 60–67.

Evans, F., Skiena, S., & Varshney, A. (1996). *Optimizing triangle strips for fast rendering* (pp. 319–326). IEEE Visualization.

Everest, F. A. (2001). *The Master Handbook of Acoustics* (2nd ed.). New York: McGraw-Hill.

Everett, H. (1963). Generalized Lagrange multiplier method for problems of optimum allocation of resources. *Operations Research, 11,* 399–417. doi:10.1287/opre.11.3.399

Falik, Y., Averbuch, A., Yechiali, U. (2007, February). Transmission algorithm for video streaming over cellular networks. *Wireless Networks.*

Fan, B., Chiu, D.-M., & Lui, J. C. (2006). The Delicate Tradeoffs in BitTorrent like File Sharing Protocol Design. In *Proceedings of IEEE International Conference on Network Protocols,* Santa Barbara, CA.

Fang, Q., Gao, J., & Guibas, L. (2004). Locating and bypassing routing holes in sensor networks. In *Proceedings of the 23rd Conference of the IEEE Communications Society, China, 4,* 2458-2468.

Fattah, H., & Leung, C. (2002). An overview of scheduling algorithms in wireless multimedia networks. *IEEE Wireless Communications, 9*(5), 76–83. doi:10.1109/MWC.2002.1043857

Feldman, M., Lai, K., Stoica, I., & Chuang, J. (2004). Robust Incentive Techniques for Peer-to-Peer Networks. In *Proceedings of ACM Conference on Electronic Commerce,* New York.

Feng, W., & Rexford, J. (1997). A comparison of bandwidth smoothing techniques for the transmission of prerecorded compressed video. *Proceedings - IEEE INFOCOM,* (April): 58–66.

Feng, W., & Sechrest, S. (1995). Critical bandwidth allocation for delivery of compressed video. *Computer Communications, 18*(10), 709–717. doi:10.1016/0140-3664(95)98484-M

Feng, W., Jahanian, F. & Sechrest, S. (1997) An optimal bandwidth allocation strategy for the delivery of compressed prerecorded video. *ACM/Springer-Verlag Multimedia Systems Journal, 5*(5), 297 – 309.

FFmpeg. (2010). *FFmpeg Project.* Retrieved February 2010, from http://ffmpeg.org/

Fiandrotti, A., Gallucci, D., Masala, E., & De Martin, J. C. (2008, December). High-performance H.264/SVC video communications in 80211e ad hoc networks. *International Workshop on Traffic Management and Engineering for the Future Internet.*

Fiore, M., Härri, J., Filali, F., & Bonnet, C. (2007, March). Vehicular mobility simulation for VANETs. *40th Annual Simulation Symposium,* (pp. 301-307).

Floyd, S., Handley, M., & Kohler, E. (2006, March). Problem Statement for the Datagram Congestion Control Protocol (DCCP) (No. 4336). *RFC 4336 (Informational). IETF.* Retrieved December 22, 2009 from http://www.ietf.org/rfc/rfc4336.txt

Fodor, V., & D'an, G. (2007, June). Resilience in live peer-to-peer streaming. *IEEE Communications Magazine, 45*(6), 116–123. doi:10.1109/MCOM.2007.374428

Fogarolli, A., Riccardi, G., & Ronchetti, M. (2007) Searching information in a collection of video-lectures. *Proceedings of World Conference on Educational Multimedia, Hypermedia and Telecommunications ED-MEDIA 2007,* p. 1450-1459

Fogarolli, A., Seppi, G., & Ronchetti, M. (2009) RDF Graph Representation for Digital Content Visualization Summrization and Navigation. *International Conferences on Digital Libraries and the Semantic Web (ICSD2009)* pp 165-177

Folli, M., & Favalli, L. (2008). Scalable multiple description coding of video sequences. In *Proc. of the 2008 GTTI Annual Meeting,* Florence, Italy.

Franchi, N., Fumagalli, M., Lancini, R., & Tubaro, S. (2004). Multiple description video coding for scalable and robust transmission over IP. *IEEE Transactions on Circuits and Systems for Video Technology, 15*(3), 321–334. doi:10.1109/TCSVT.2004.842606

Friedland, G., & Rojas, R. (2006). Human-centered Webcasting of Interactive-Whiteboard *Proc. of the Eight IEEE Int. Symposium on Multimedia*

Fu, X., Lei, J., & Shi, L. (2007). *An experimental analysis of Joost peer-to-peer VoD service.* Germany: Technical Report, Institute of Computer Science, University of Göttingen.

Fudenberg, D., & Tirole, J. (1991). *Game Theory.* Cambridge, MA: MIT Press.

Fujii, A., Itou, K., & Ishikawa, T. (2006). LODEM: A system for on-demand video lectures. *Speech Communication,* (48): 516–531. doi:10.1016/j.specom.2005.08.006

Gabrilovich, E. and S. Markovitch S. (2007) Computing Semantic Relatedness is using Wikipedia-based Explicit Semantic Analysis. *Proceedings of the 20th International Joint Conference on Artificial Intelligence,* pp.1606--1611

Gai, A. T., Mathieu, F., de Montgolfier, F., & Reynier, J. (2007). Stratification in P2P Networks: Application to BitTorrent. In *Proceedings of the International Conference on Distributed Computing Systems (ICDCS).*

Gamal, A. E., & Cover, T. (1982, November). Achievable rates for multiple descriptions. *IEEE Transactions on Information Theory, 28,* 851–857. doi:10.1109/TIT.1982.1056588

Gandoin, P. M., & Devillers, O. (2002). Progressive Lossless Compression of Arbitrary Simplicial Complexes. *ACM Transactions on Graphics, 21*(3), 372–379.

Ganesh, A., Kermarrec, A. M., & Massoulié, L. (2003). Peer-to-peer membership management for gossip-based protocols. *IEEE Transactions on Computers, 52,* 139–258. doi:10.1109/TC.2003.1176982

Gao, K., Gao, W., He, S., & Zhang, Y. (2005). Real-time smoothing for network adaptive video streaming. *Journal of Visual Communication and Image Representation, 16*(4-5), 512–526. doi:10.1016/j.jvcir.2004.12.001

General description (Release 8), http://www.arib.or.jp/IMT-2000/V740Dec09/2_T63/ARIB-STD-T63/Rel8/26/A26233-800.pdf

Ghanbari, M. (1999). *Video Coding an introduction to standard codecs*. The Institute of Electrical Engineers.

Gigonzac, G., Pitie, F., & Kokaram, A. (2007) Electronic slide matching and enhancement of a lecture video. *4th European Conference on Visual Media Production, IETCVMP 2007*, pp. 1 – 7

Girod, B., Kalman, M., Liang, Y., & Zhang, R. (2002). Advances in channel adaptive video streaming. *Wireless Communications and Mobile Computing, 2,* 549–552. doi:10.1002/wcm.87

Girod, B., & Fäber, N. (2001). Wireless Video. In Sun, M.-T., & Reibman, A. R. (Eds.), *Compressed Video over Networks* (pp. 465–511). New York: Marcel Dekker.

Giunchiglia, F., Marchese, M., & Zaihrayeu, I. (2006) Encoding classifications into lightweight ontologies. *Proceedings of ESWC '06*

Gkantsidis, C., & Rodriguez, P. R. (2005). Network coding for large scale content distribution. *Proceedings*In *Proceedings of IEEE Conference on Computer Communications*, Miami, FL.

Gkantsidis, C., Mihail, M., & Saberi, S. (2004). Random Walks in Peer-to-Peer Networks. In *Proceedings of IEEE Conference on Computer Communications*, Hong Kong.

Gkatsidis, C., & Rodrigues, P. (2005), Network Coding for Large Scale Content Distribution. In *Proc. INFOCOM 2005. 24th IE EE International Conference on Computer Communications*, (pp. 2235-2245).

Gkatsidis, C., Miller, J., & Rodrigues, P. (2006) Anatomy of a P2P Content Distribution System with Network Coding, in *Proc. of the 5th International Workshop on Peer-to-Peer Systems (IPTPS 2006)*, (pp. 1-6).

Glass, J., Hazen, T. J., Cyphers, S., & Malioutov, I. (2007). Recent progress in the MIT spoken lecture processing project. Proc. *Interspeech, 2007*, 2553–2556.

Glowalla U. (2004) Utility and Usability von E-Learning am Beispiel von Lecture-on-demand Anwendungen. *Entwerfen und Gestalten*, 2004 (in German)

Golle, P., Leyton-Brown, L., Mironov, I., & Lillibridge, M. (2001). Incentives for Sharing in Peer-to-Peer Networks. *Lecture Notes in Computer Science, 2322,* 75–87. doi:10.1007/3-540-45598-1_9

Goncalves I., Pfeiffer, S., & Montgomery, C. (2008, September). RFC 5334: *Ogg media types*.

Gorkemli, B., & Civanlar, M. R. (2006). SVC Coded Video Streaming over DCCP. In *Proc. 8th IEEE International Symposium on Multimedia (ISM '06)*, (pp. 437-441). San Diego, CA.

Goyal, V. K. (2001). Multiple description coding: compression meets the network. *IEEE Signal Processing Magazine, 18,* 74–93. doi:10.1109/79.952806

Goyal, V. K., & Kovacevic, J. (2001, September). Generalized multiple description coding with correlating transforms. *IEEE Transactions on Information Theory, 47*(6), 2199–2224. doi:10.1109/18.945243

Goyal, V. K. (2001). Multiple Description Coding: Compression meets the network. *IEEE Signal Processing Magazine,* 74–93. doi:10.1109/79.952806

GPP & BenQmobile. (2006). *Components for* TR *on video minimum performance requirements. Doc. for decision.* TSG Services and System Aspects.

GPP & Siemens. (2005). *Software simulator for* MBMS *streaming over* UTRAN *and* GERAN. *Doc. for proposal.* TSG Services and System Aspects.

GPP (2009). Radio Link Control (RLC) protocol specification. *Technical Specification TS 25.222.*

GPP (2009). Technical High Speed Downlink Packet Access (HSDPA); Overall description; Stage 2. *Technical Specification TS 25.308.*

GPP Rel6 V650 (2008). *3rd Generation Partnership Project; SPEC Cross Reference*, Retrieved from http://www.arib.or.jp/IMT-2000/V650Mar08/4_Cross_Reference/3GPP_SPEC_Cross_ReferenceV650_Rel6.pdf

GPP TS 22.233 V6.3.0 (2003). *3rd Generation Partnership Project; Technical Specification Group Services and System Aspects; Transparent end-to-end packet-switched streaming service; Stage 1* (Release 6), Retrieved Sept. 2003, from http://www.arib.or.jp/IMT-2000/V650Mar08/5_Appendix/Rel6/22/22233-630.pdf

GPP TS 22.233 V7.1.0 (2009). *Technical Specification, 3rd Generation Partnership Project; Technical Specification Group Services and System Aspects; Transparent end-to-end packet-switched streaming service*; Stage 1, (Release 7), Retreived from http://www.arib.or.jp/IMT-2000/V730Jul09/2_T63/ARIB-STD-T63/Rel7/22/A22233-710.pdf

GPP TS 23.203 V9.1.0 (2009). *3rd Generation Partnership Project; Technical Specification Group Services and System Aspects; Policy and charging control architecture*, (Release 9), Retrieved from http://www.quintillion.co.jp/3GPP/Specs/23203-910.pdf

GPP TS 26.233 Release 8.0 V8.0.0 (2008). Technical Specification, 3rd Generation Partnership Project; Technical Specification Group Services and System Aspects; Transparent end-to-end packet switched streaming service (PSS); General description, 3GPP TS 26.233 Release 8.0 (V8.0.0), Retrieved December 2008, from http://www.ofdm.jp/3GPP/Specs/26233-800.pdf

GPP TS 26.234 V8.3.0 Rel. 8 (2009).3rd Generation Partnership Project; Technical Specification Group Services and System Aspects; Transparent end-to-end Packet-switched Streaming Service (PSS); Protocols and codecs

GPP. Transparent end-to-end Packet-switched Streaming Service (PSS); Protocols and codecs. *Technical Specification TS 26.234.*

Gross, D., & Harris, C. (1998). *Fundamentals of queueing theory*. New York: Wiley-Interscience.

GSMA IMB WP. (2009). Integrated Mobile Broadcast (IMB) Service Scenarios and System Requirements, GSMA TM, Retrieved on September 25th, 2009 from http://www.gsmworld.com/newsroom/press-releases/2009/3858.htm (GSMA Endorses Integrated Mobile Broadcast (IMB), a New 3GPP Standard That Will Accelerate the Global Adoption of Mobile Data and Broadcast Services, 09, September 2009), http://www.gsmworld.com/documents/GSMA_IMB_WP_final.doc

Gumhold, S. (2000). *New bounds on the encoding of planar triangulations*, (Technical Report WSI-2000-1), Univ. of Tubingen.

Gumhold, S., & Straßer, W. (1998, July). Real time compression of triangle mesh connectivity, *Proc. ACM SIGGRAPH.* (pp. 133-140).

Guo, L., Chen, S., Ren, S., Chen, X., & Jiang, S. (2004). PROP: a scalable and reliable P2P assisted proxy streaming system. *Proceedings*In *Proceedings of International Conference on Distributed Computing Systems*, Tokyo, Japan.

Guo, L., Chen, S., Xiao, Z., Tan, E., Ding, X., & Zhang, X. (2005). Measurements, Analysis, and Modeling of BitTorrent-like Systems. *Internet Measurement Conference*, Berkeley, CA.

Guo, S., Fan, C., & Little, T. (2008, July). Supporting Concurrent Task Deployment in Wireless Sensor Networks. *Symposium on Network Computing and Applications* (pp. 111-118). Los Alamitos, CA: IEEE Computer Society.

Guo, Y., Liang, C., & Liu, Y. (2008). Adaptive Queue-based Chunk Scheduling for P2P Live Streaming. In *Proceedings of IFIP Networking.*

Gupta, M., Judge, P., & Ammar, M. (2003). A Reputation System for Peer-to-Peer Networks. *Proceedings*In *Proceedings of International Workshop on Network and Operating System Support for Digital Audio and Video*, Monterey, CA.

H.264 (2010). *H.264 video codec referencing software.* Retrieved February 2010, from http://iphome.hhi.de/suehring/

Hafarkhani, J., & Tarokh, V. (1999). Multiple description trellis-coded quantization. *IEEE Transactions on Communications, 47*(6), 799–803. doi:10.1109/26.771331

Haga. (2002) Combining video and bulletin board systems in distance education systems. *The Internet and Higher Education (5)*, 119-129

Hajdu, G. (2003). Quintet.net – a quintet on the internet. In *Proceedings of the International Computer Music Conference*, Singapore.

Halbach, T. (2010). *A performance assessment of the royalty-free and open video compression specifications Dirac, Dirac Pro, and Theora and their open-source implementations.* Retrieved February 2010, from http://etill.net/projects/dirac_theora_evaluation/#intro

Halliday, M., & Hasan, R. (1976). *Cohesion in English.* London, UK: Longman.

Handley, M., Jacobson, V., & Perkins, C. (2006). SDP: Session Description Protocol. *RFC 4566.*

Handley, M., Jacobson, V. (1998). *Request for Comments* (RFC) 2327 - SDP: Session Description Protocol

Haruvy, E., Stahl, D. O., & Wilson, P. W. (1999). Evidence for optimistic and pessimistic behavior in normal-form games. *Economics Letters, 63*, 255–259. doi:10.1016/S0165-1765(99)00028-2

Hautakorpi, J., & Pohan, H. (2005). *Streaming Media Protocols, T-110.456.* Retrieved from http://www.tml.tkk.fi/Studies/T-110.456/2005/slides/Streaming_Media_Protocols_lastVersion.pdf

Hayes, M. H. (1998) Some approaches to Internet distance learning with streaming media, *Second IEEE Workshop on Multimedia Signal Processing* pp. 514-519

He, L., Sanocki, E., Gupta, A., & Grudin, J. (1999). Auto-Summarization of audio-video presentations. *Proceedings of the ACM Multimedia Conference (ACMMM)* pp.489–498.

Hefeeda, M., Bhargava, B., & Yau, D. K.-Y. (2004). A hybrid architecture for cost-effective on-demand media streaming. *Computer Networks, 44*(3). doi:10.1016/j.comnet.2003.10.002

Heffeeda, M., Habib, A., Botev, B., Xu, D., & Bhargava, B. (2003). PROMISE: Peer-to-peer media streaming using CollectCast. *Proceedings*In *Proceedings of ACM Multimedia*, Berkeley, CA.

Hegde, N., Mathieu, F., & Perino, D. (2009). Size Does Matter (in Epidemic Live Streaming). *INRIA Research Report RR-7032.*

Hei, X., Liang, C., Liang, J., Liu, Y., & Ross, K. W. (2007, December). A measurement study of a large-scale P2P IPTV system. *IEEE Transactions on Multimedia, 9*(8), 1672–1687. doi:10.1109/TMM.2007.907451

Hei, X., Liu, Y., & Ross, K. W. (2008, February). IPTV over P2P streaming networks: the mesh-pull approach. *IEEE Communications Magazine, 46*(2), 86–92. doi:10.1109/MCOM.2008.4473088

Heinzelman, W., Chandrakasan, A., & Balakrishnan, H. (2002). An application-specific protocol architecture for wireless microsensor networks. *IEEE Transactions on Wireless Communications, 1*(4), 660–670. doi:10.1109/TWC.2002.804190

Heinzelman, W., Chandrakasan, A., & Balakrishnan, H. (2000). Energy-efficient Communication Protocol for Wireless Microsensor Networks. In *Proceedings of Hawaii International Conference System Sciences.*

Hellge, C., Mirta, S., Schierl, T., & Wiegand, T. (2009). Mobile TV with SVC and hierarchical modulation for DVB-H broadcast. In *Proc. IEEE International Symposium on Broadband Multimedia Systems and Broadcasting (BMSB'09)*, (pp. 1-5). Bilbao, Spain.

Hellwagner, H., Kuschnig, R., Stütz, T., & Uhl, A. (2009). Efficient in-network adaptation of encrypted H.264/SVC content. *Signal Processing Image Communication, 24,* 740–758. doi:10.1016/j.image.2009.07.002

Ho, T., Medard, M., Koetter, R., Karger, D., Effros, M., & Shi, J. (2006, Oct.). A random linear network coding approach to multicast. *Information Theory. IEEE Transactions on, 52*(10), 4413–4430.

Ho, J., Lee, K. C., & Kriegman, D. (2001). Compressing Large Polygonal Models. *IEEE Visualization Conference Proceedings.* (pp. 357–362).

Holma, H., & Toskala, A. (2004). *WCDMA for UMTS, Radio Access for Third Generation Mobile Communications.* New York: Wiley.

Holman, R., Stanley, J., & Ozkan-Haller, T. (2003). Applying Video Sensor Networks to Nearshore Enviroment Monitoring. *IEEE Persave computing,* 14-21.

Hoppe, H. (1999). *Optimization of mesh locality for transparent vertex caching* (pp. 269–276). ACM SIGGRAPH.

Horowitz, M., Joch, A., Kossentini, F., & Hallapuro, A. (2003). H264/AVC Baseline Profile Decoder Complexity Analysis. *IEEE Transactions on Circuits and Systems for Video Technology, 13*(7), 704–716. doi:10.1109/TCSVT.2003.814967

Huang, C., Juan, H.-H., Lin, M.-S., & Chang, C.-J. (2007). Radio resource management of heterogeneous services in Mobile WiMax systems. *IEEE Wireless Communications, 14*(1), 20–26. doi:10.1109/MWC.2007.314547

Huang, G. (2007). *Experiences with PPLive. Keynote at ACM SIGCOMM* (p. 2P). TV Workshop.

Huitema, C. (2003). *Request For Comments (RFC) 3605 - Real Time Control Protocol (RTCP) attribute in Session Description Protocol.* SDP.

Hürst, W. (2005) *Multimediale Informationssuche in Vortrags- und Vorlesungsaufzeichnungen.* Doctoral dissertation Universitaet Freiburg, Fakultaet fuer Angewandte Wissenschaften. (in German)

Hürst, W., & Deutschmann, N. (2006) Searching in recorded lectures. *Proc. of World Conf. on Educational Multimedia, Hypermedia and Telecommunications ED-MEDIA 2006* pp. 2859-2866

Ibarria, L., & Rossignac, J. (2003). Dynapack: Space-time compression of the 3d animations of triangle meshes with fixed connectivity. *Proceedings of the ACM SIGGRAPH/Eurographics Symposium on Computer Animation.* (pp. 126-135).

Institute of Electrical and Inc. Electronics Engineers (2008). *1394-2008 IEEE Standard for a High-Performance Serial Bus.*

Intanagonwiwat, C., Govindan, R., & Estrin, D. (2000, August). *Directed diffusion: a scalable and robust communication paradigm for sensor networks.* Paper presented at the 6th Annual ACM/IEEE International Conference on Mobile Computing and Networking, Boston, MA.

International Telecommunication Union (ITU). Recommendation H.323 (1998). Audiovisual *and multimedia systems – Infrastructure of audiovisual services –* Systems and terminal equipment for audiovisual services – Packet-based multimedia communications systems.

International Telecommunication Union (ITU) (2007). Document: FoV/04: *Future of Voice - Status of VoIP.*

Isenburg, M. (2002). Compressing polygon mesh connectivity with degree duality prediction, *Graphics Interface Conference Proceedings.* (pp. 161-170).

Isenburg, M., & Alliez, P. (2002). Compressing polygon mesh geometry with parallelogram prediction, *IEEE Visualization Conference Proceedings.* (pp. 141-146).

Isenburg, M., & Gumhold, S. (2003, July). Out-of-Core Compression for Gigantic Polygon Meshes, *Proceedings of SIGGRAPH.* (pp. 935-942).

Isenburg, M., & Snoeyink, J. (1999). Mesh collapse compression, *Proceedings of SIBGRAPI*, (pp. 27-28). Campinas, Brazil.

Isenburg, M., & Snoeyink, J. (2000). Spirale reversi: reverse decoding of the edgebreaker encoding, In *Proceedings of 12th Canadian Conference on Computational Geometry*. (pp. 247-256).

ISO/IEC & ITU-T Rec. (2003). *H.264: Advanced Video Coding for Generic Audio-visual Services. Technical report, Joint Video Team (JVT) of ISO-IEC MPEG&ITU-T VCEG, Int*. Standard.

ISO/IEC 13818-1:2000 (2000). *Generic coding of moving pictures and associated audio information: Systems.* Geneva, Switzerland: International Organization for Standardization.

ISO/IEC 13818-1:2006/FPDAM 3.2 (2008). *Transport of SVC Video (ISO/IEC 14496-10 Amd.3) over ISO/IEC 13818-1 Streams.* Geneva, Switzerland: International Organization for Standardization.

ISO/IEC 13818-2 (1994). *Generic coding of moving pictures and associated audio information.* Technical report, MPEG (Moving Pictures Expert Group), International Organization for Standardization, 1994.

ISO/IEC 14496-12:2005 Part 12 (2005). *ISO Base Media File Format.* Geneva, Switzerland: International Organization for Standardization.

ISO/IEC 14496-15:2004/Amd2 (2008). *SVC File Format.* Geneva, Switzerland: International Organization for Standardization.

ITU-T Rec. H.264 (2005). *ISO/IEC 14496-10 Advanced Video Coding (Version 4).* Geneva, Switzerland: International Organization for Standardization.

ITU-T Rec. H.264 (2007). *ISO/IEC 14496-10 Advanced Video Coding / Amd. 3.* Geneva, Switzerland: International Organization for Standardization.

Iwatsuki, M., Takeuchi, N., Kobayashi, H., & Yana, K. (2007). Automatic Digital Content Generation System for Real-Time Distance Lectures. *International Journal of Distance Education Technologies*, (5): 7–18.

Izal, M., Urvoy-Keller, G., Biersack, E. W., Felber, P. A., Al Hamra, A., & Garc'es-Erice, L. (2004). *Dissecting BitTorrent: Five Months in a Torrent's Lifetime,"* Passive and Active Measurement Workshop. France: Antibes Juan-les-Pins.

Izhak-Ratzin, R. (2009). Collaboration in BitTorrent systems. *Networking, 5550/2009*, 338-351.

Izhak-Ratzin, R., Liogkas, N., & Majumdar, R. (2009). Team incentives in BitTorrent systems. *Proceedings*In *Proceedings of International Conference on Computer Communications and Networks*, San Francisco, CA.

Jacobson, N. (1985). *Basic algebra I.* New York, NY: W.H. Freeman.

Jain, K., Lovász, L., & Chou, P. A. (2007). Building scalable and robust peer-to-peer overlay networks for broadcasting using network coding. *Journal on Distributed Computing, 19*(4), 301–311. doi:10.1007/s00446-006-0014-9

Jambunathan, A., & Ronchetti, M. (2008). Exploiting the collective intelligence contained in Wikipedia to automatically describe the content of a document. In Ronchetti, M. (Ed.), *The Semantic Web: a view on data integration, reasoning, human factors, collective intelligence and technology adoption* (pp. 209–216). Bangkok, Thailand: AIT e-Press.

Jaramillo, J. J., & Srikant, R. (2007). DARWIN: Distributed and Adaptive Reputation mechanism for WIreless ad-hoc Networks. *Proceedings*In *Proceedings of International Conference on Mobile Computing and Networking*, Montreal, Quebec, Canada.

Jia, W., Wang, T., Wang, G., & Guo, M. (2007). Hole avoiding in advance routing in wireless sensor networks. In *Proceedings of the IEEE Wireless Communication & Networking Conference, USA,* 3519-3523.

Joukov, J., & Chiueh, T. (2003). Lectern II: a multimedia lecture capturing and editing system. *Proc. of Int. Conf. on Multimedia and Expo, 2003. ICME '03.* vol. 2 pp. II - 681-684

Ju S.X., Black M., Minneman S. & Kimber D. (1998) Summarization of videotaped presentations: Automatic analysis of motion and gesture. *IEEE Transactions on Circuits and Systems for Video (8)* no. 5, 686-696

Jun, S., & Ahamad, M. (2005). Incentives in BitTorrent Induce Free Riding. *Workshop on Economics of Peer-to-Peer Systems*, Philadelphia.

Jurca, D., Chakareski, J., Wagner, J., & Frossard, P. (2007). Enabling adaptive video streaming in P2P systems. *IEEE Communications Magazine*, *45*(6), 108–114. doi:10.1109/MCOM.2007.374427

Jurdak, R. (2007). *Wireless ad hoc and sensor networks: A cross-layer design perspective*. New York: Springer-Verlag.

Kahan, J., & Koivunen, M.-R. Prud'Hommeaux, E. and Swick R.R., (2001) Annotea: An Open RDF Infrastructure for Shared Web Annotations, *Proc. of the WWW10 International Conference*

Kalman, M., Ramanathan, P., & Girod, B. (September 2003). Rate-Distortion optimized video streaming with multiple deadlines. *International Conference on Image Processing*, (pp. 662-664).

Kalva, H., Vetro, A., & Sun, H. (2003). Performance optimization of the MPEG-2 to MPEG-4 video transcoder. In proceeding, *SPIE Conference on VLSI Circuits and Systems* (pp. 341–350).

Kam, M., Wang, J., Iles, A., Tse, E., Chiu, J., Glaser, D., et al. (2005) Livenotes: a system for cooperative and augmented note-taking in lectures. *CHI '05: Proceedings of the SIGCHI conference on Human factors in computing systems* pp.531-540

Kamvar, S. D., Schlosser, M. T., & Garcia-Molina, H. (2003). The EigenTrust Algorithm for Reputation Management in P2P Networks. In *Proceedings of International World Wide Web Conference,* Budapest.

Kanellopoulos, D., & Kotsiantis, S. (2006). C_MACSE: A novel ACSE protocol for hard real-time multimedia communications. *Int. J. of Computer Science and Network Security*, *6*(3), 57–72.

Kanellopoulos, D., Pintelas, P., & Giannoulis, S. (2006). QoS in wireless multimedia networks. *Annals of Mathematics. Computing & TeleInformatics*, *1*(4), 66–75.

Kanellopoulos, D. (2009). High-speed multimedia networks: Critical issues and trends. In Lee (Ed.) *Handbook of Research on Telecommunications Planning and Management for Business*. (pp.775-787). Western Illinois University, USA, PA: Information Science Reference.

Kanellopoulos, D., Kotsiantis, S., & Pintelas, P. (2008). Internet and multimedia communications. In Mehdi Khosrow-Pour (Ed.) *Encyclopedia of Information Science and Technology.* Second Edition (pp.2176-2182), Idea Group Inc (IGI).

Karim, H. A., Hewage, C., Worrall, S., & Kondoz, A. M. (2008). Scalable multiple description video coding for stereoscopic 3D. *IEEE Transactions on Consumer Electronics*, *54*(2), 745–752. doi:10.1109/TCE.2008.4560156

Karlsson, J., Li, H., & Erikson, J. (October 2005). Real-time video over wireless ad-hoc networks. *14th International Conference on Computer Communications and Networks*, (pp. 596-607).

Karni, Z., & Gotsman, C. (2000). Spectral Compression of Mesh Geometry. *ACM SIGGRAPH Conference Proceedings*. (pp. 279-286).

Karni, Z., & Gotsman, C. (2001, June). 3D Mesh Compression Using Fixed Spectral Bases, *Proceedings of Graphics Interface*. (pp. 1-8). Ottawa.

Karp, B., & Kung, H. (2000, August). *GPSR: Greedy Perimeter Stateless Routing for Wireless Networks.* Paper presented at the 6th Annual International Conference on Mobile Computing and Networking, Boston, MA.

Katsaggelos, A. K., Zhai, F., Eisenberg, Y., & Berry, R. (2005). Energy efficient wireless video coding and delivery. *IEEE Wireless Communications*, *12*(4), 24–30. doi:10.1109/MWC.2005.1497855

Kawadia, V., & Kumar, P. R. (2005). A cautionary perspective of cross-layer design. *IEEE Wireless Communications*, *12*(1), 3–11. doi:10.1109/MWC.2005.1404568

Khodakovsky, A., Alliez, P., Desbrun, M., & Schroder, P. (2002). Near-optimal connectivity encoding of 2-manifold polygon meshes, *Graphical Models*, special issue, *64*(3-4), 147-168.

Khodakovsky, A., Schroder, P., & Sweldens, W. (2000). Progressive Geometry Compression. *Proc. SIGGRAPH*. (pp. 271-278).

Kiesel, S. Popkin, L. Previdi, S. Woundy, R., & Yang, Y. R. (2009, March). Application-Layer Traffic Optimization (ALTO) Requirements (draft-kiesel-alto-reqs-02.txt). *IETF-74, ALTO WG*, San Francisco.

Kim, S., Kim, S., & Kim, C. (2002). *Discrete differential error metric for surface simplification* (pp. 276–283). Pacific Graphics.

King, D., & Rossignac, J. (1999). Guaranteed 3.67V bit encoding of planar triangle graphs, *11th Canadian Conference on Computational Geometry*. (pp. 146-149).

Kofler, I., Kuschnig, R., & Hellwagner, H. (2009). Improving IPTV Services by H.264/SVC Adaptation and Traffic Control. In *Proc. IEEE International Symposium on Broadband Multimedia Systems and Broadcasting (BMSB'09)*, (pp. 1-6). Bilbao, Spain.

Kofler, I., Prangl, M., Kuschnig, R., & Hellwagner, H. (2008). An H.264/SVC-based adaptation proxy on a WiFi router. In *Proc. 18th International Workshop on Network and Operating Systems Support for Digital Audio and Video (NOSSDAV'08)*, (pp. 63-68). Braunschweig, Germany.

Kofler, I., Timmerer, C., Hellwagner, H., Hutter, A., & Sanahuja, F. (2007). Efficient MPEG-21-based Adaptation Decision-Taking for Scalable Multimedia Content. In *Proc. 14th SPIE Annual Electronic Imaging Conference - Multimedia Computing and Networking (MMCN 2007)*, (pp. 65040J-1 - 65040J-8). San Jose, CA.

Kondi, L. P. (2004). A rate-distortion optimal hybrid scalable/multiple-description video codec," in *Proc. IEEE Int. Conf. Acoustics, Speech, and Signal Processing (ICASSP'04)*, Montreal, Canada, May 2004, pp. 269–272.

Kos, A., Klepec, B., & Tomazic, S. (2002). Techniques for performance improvement of voip applications. In *Proceedings of the 11th Electrotechnical Conference MELECON*, Cairo, Egypt.

Kosch, T., Kulp, I., Bechler, M., Strassberger, M., Weyl, B., & Laswoski, R. (2009, May). Communication architecture for cooperative systems in Europe. *IEEE Communications Magazine*, *47*(5), 116–125. doi:10.1109/MCOM.2009.4939287

Kostic, D., Rodriguez, A., Albrecht, J., & Vahdat, A. (2003). Bullet: High bandwidth data dissemination using an overlay mesh. *Proceedings* In *Proceedings of ACM Symposium on Operating Systems Principle,* Bolton Landin, NY.

Kozamernik, F. (2000, March). Webcasting – the webcasters' perspective. *EBU Technical Review* (282), 1-28.

Krämer, U., Hirschfeld, J., Schuller, G., Wabnik, S., Carôt, A., & Werner, C. (2007, October). Network music performance with ultra-low-delay audio coding under unreliable network conditions. In *Proceedings of the 123rd AES-Convention*, New York, USA.

Kronrod, B., & Gotsman, C. (2002). Optimized compression of triangle mesh geometry using prediction trees, *Proceedings of 1st International Symposium on 3D Data Processing, Visualization and Transmission*. (pp. 602-608).

Kulkarni, P., Ganesan, D., Shenoy, P., & Lu, Q. (2005). SensEye: A Multi-tier Camera Sensor Network. In *Proceedings of the 13th annual ACM international conference on Multimedia*, 229-238.

Kumwilaisak, W., Hou, Y. T., Zhang, Q., Zhu, W., Kuo, C.-C. J., & Zhang, Y.-Q. (2003). A cross-layer Quality-of-Service mapping architecture for video delivery in wireless networks. *IEEE Journal on Selected Areas in Communications, 21*(10), 1685–1698. doi:10.1109/JSAC.2003.816445

Kurose, J., & Ross, K. (2004). *Computer Networking: A Top-Down Approach Featuring the Internet* (3rd ed.). Reading, MA: Addison Wesley.

Kuschnig, R., Kofler, I., Ransburg, M., & Hellwagner, H. (2008). Design options and comparison of in-network H.264/SVC adaptation. *Journal of Visual Communication and Image Representation, 19*, 529–542. doi:10.1016/j.jvcir.2008.07.004

Lai, K., Feldman, M., Stoica, I., & Chuang, J. (2003). Incentives for Cooperation in Peer-to-Peer Networks. *Workshop on Economics of Peer-to-Peer Systems*, Cambridge, MA.

Lakshman, K., Yavatkar, R., & Finkel, R. (1998). Integrated CPU and network-I/O QoS management in an end system. *Computer Communications, 21*(4), 325–333. doi:10.1016/S0140-3664(97)00166-7

Lambert, P., de Neve, W., Dhondt, Y., & van de Walle, R. (2006). Flexible macroblock ordering in H.264/AVC. *Journal of Visual Communication, 17*, 358–375.

Laoutaris, N., Carra, D., & Michiardi, P. (2008). Uplink allocation beyond choke/unchoke or how to divide and conquer best. In *Proceedings of CoNEXT 2008, 4th ACM International Conference on emerging Networking Experiments and Technologies*.

Larisch, D. (2004). *TCP/IP* (2nd ed.). New York: Moderne Industrie Buch AG.

Lauer, T., Trahasch, S., & Zupancic, B. (2005) Anchored Discussions of Multimedia Lecture Recordings. *Proceedings 35th Annual Conference - Frontiers in Education - FIE'05* pp. 12-17

Lavoue, G., Gelasca, E. D., Dupont, F., Baskurt, A., & Ebrahimi, T. (2006). Perceptually driven 3D distance metrics with application to watermarking, *Proc. of the SPIE Electronic Imaging: Vol. 6312.* (pp. 63120L.1–63120L.12).

Lee, Y.-C., Kim, J., Altunbasak, Y., & Mersereau, R. M. (2003). Layered coding vs. multiple description coded video over error-prone networks. *Signal Processing Image Communication, 18*, 337–356. doi:10.1016/S0923-5965(02)00138-8

Lee, S. I., Park, H., & van der Schaar, M. (2009). *Foresighted Joint Resource Reciprocation and Scheduling Strategies for Real-time Video Streaming over Peer-to-Peer Networks*. Seattle, WA: International Packet Video Workshop.

Lee, E., & Ko, H. (2000). Vertex data compression for triangular meshes. In *Proceedings of Pacific Graphics*. (pp. 225-234).

Lee, Y.-C., Kim, J., Altunbasak, Y., & Mersereau, R. M. (2003). Performance comparisons of layered and multiple description coded video streaming over error-prone networks. In *Proc. International Conference on Communications*, Anchorage, AK, pp. 35–39.

Legout, A., Liogkas, A., Kohler, E., & Zhang, L. (2007). Clustering and sharing incentives in BitTorrent systems. *SIGMETRICS Performance Evaluation Review, 35*(1), 301–312. doi:10.1145/1269899.1254919

Legout, A., Urvoy-Keller, G., & Michiardi, P. (2006). Rarest first and choke algorithms are enough. *Internet Measurement Conference,* Rio de Janeiro, Brazil.

Leonardi, E., Mellia, M., Horvart, A., Muscariello, L., Niccolini, S., & Rossi, D. (2008, April). Building a cooperative P2P-TV application over a wise network: the approach of the european FP-7 STREP NAPA-WINE. *IEEE Communications Magazine, 46*(4), 20–22. doi:10.1109/MCOM.2008.4481334

Levin, D., LaCurts, K., Spring, N., & Bhattacharjee, B. (2008). BitTorrent is an Auction: Analyzing and Improving BitTorrent's Incentives. *Proceedings*In *Proceedings of ACM Special Interest Group on Data Communication*, Seattle, WA.

Levine, M. W., & Shefner, J. M. (2001). *Fundamentals of Sensation and Perception* (3rd ed.). Oxford University Press.

Li, B., & Yin, H. (2007). Peer-to-peer live streaming on the internet: issues, existing approaches, and challenges [peer-to-peer multimedia streaming]. *IEEE Communications Magazine*, *45*(6), 94–99. doi:10.1109/MCOM.2007.374425

Li, W. (2001). Overview of fine granularity scalability in MPEG-4 video standard. *IEEE Transactions on Circuits and Systems for Video Technology*, *11*(3), 301–317. doi:10.1109/76.911157

Li, X., Ammar, M., & Paul, S. (1999). Video multicast over the internet. *IEEE Network*, *13*(2), 46–60. doi:10.1109/65.768488

Li, H., Li, M., & Prabhakaran, B. (2006). Middleware for streaming 3D progressive meshes over lossy networks. *ACM Transactions on Multimedia Computing, Communications, and Applications*, *2*(4), 282–317. doi:10.1145/1201730.1201733

Li, S.-Y., Yeung, R., & Cai, N. (2003, Feb.). Linear network coding. *Information Theory. IEEE Transactions on*, *49*(2), 371–381.

Li, J., Chou, P. A., & Zhang, C. (2004). Mutualcast: An Efficient Mechanism for One-To-Many Content Distribution. *Proceedings*In *Proceedings of ACM Special Interest Group on Data Communication*, Beijing, China.

Li, P., Gu, Y., & Zhao, B. (2007, December). *A Global-Energy-Balancing Real-time Routing in Wireless Sensor Networks*. Paper presented at the 2nd IEEE Asia-Pacific Service Computing Conference, Tsukuba Science City, Japan.

Li, S., Neelisetti, R., Liu, C., & Lim, A. (2008, June). Delay-Constrained High Throughput Protocol for Multi-Path Transmission over Wireless Multimedia Sensor Networks. *IEEE 2008 International Symposium on a World of Wireless, Mobile and Multimedia Networks* (PP.1-8). Los Alamitos, CA: IEEE Computer Society.

Lian, Q. Peng, Y., Yang, M., Zhang, Z., Dai, Y. & Li, X. (2006). Robust incentives via multi-level tit-for-tat. *Proceedings*In *Proceedings of International Workshop on Peer-to-Peer Systems,* Santa Barbara, CA.

Liang, C., Guo, Y., & Liu, Y. (2009). Investigating the Scheduling Sensitivity of P2P Video Streaming: An Experimental Study. *IEEE Transactions on Multimedia*, *11*(3), 348–360. doi:10.1109/TMM.2009.2012909

Liang, J., & Nahrstedt, K. (2006, January). Dagstream: locality aware and failure resilient peer-to-peer streaming. In *Proc. Multimedia Computing and Networking 2006*, Vol. 6071, No. 1. Retrieved November 20, 2009 from http://citeseerx.ist.psu.edu/viewdoc/download?doi=10.1.1.94.6130&rep=rep1&type=pdf

Liao, X., Jin, H., Liu, Y., Ni, L., & Deng, D. (2006, April). AnySee: Peer-to-Peer live streaming. In *Proc. INFOCOM 2006. 25th IEEE International Conference on Computer Communications* (pp. 1-10).

Liao, Y.-C., & Syu, M.-H. (2008) An Actor-Based Video Segmentation System Using Visual and Audio Information in E-Learnin". *Eighth International Conference on Intelligent Systems Design and Applications. ISDA '08.* vol. 3 pp. 575 - 580

License (2010). *Summary of AVC/H.264 License Terms*. Retrieved February 2010, from http://www.mpegla.com/main/programs/avc/Documents/AVC_TermsSummary.pdf

Liebl, G., Jenkac, H., Stockhammer, T., & Buchner, C. (2005). *Radio Link Buffer Management and Scheduling for Wireless Video Streaming*. New York: Springer Science & Business Media.

Liebl, G., Schierl, T., Wiegand, T., & Stockhammer, T. (2006). Advanced Wireless Multiuser Video Streaming using the Scalable Video. In *Proc. IEEE International Conference on Multimedia and Expo (ICME'2006)*, (pp. 625-628). Toronto, Ontario.

Lin, S., & Costello, D. J. (1995). *Error Control Coding: Fundamentals and Applications*. Englewood Cliffs, NJ: Prentice Hall.

Lin, W. S., Zhao, H. V., & Liu, K. J. R. (2009). Incentive Cooperation Strategies for Peer-to-Peer Live Multimedia Streaming Social Networks. *IEEE Transactions on Multimedia, 11*(3), 396–412. doi:10.1109/TMM.2009.2012915

Lin, W. S., Zhao, H. V., & Liu, K. J. R. (2008). *A game theoretic framework for incentive-based peer-to-peer live-streaming social networks*. ACASSP.

Lin, M., Nunamaker, J., Chau, M., & Chen, H. (2004) Segmentation of lecture videos based on text: a method combining multiple linguistic features. *Proc. of the 37th Annual Hawaii Int. Conf. on System Sciences, 2004*. pp. 1-9

Liogkas, N., Nelson, R., Kohler, E., & Zhang, E. (2007). In Exploring the Robustness of BitTorrent Peer-to-Peer Systems. *Concurrency and Computation, 10*(2), 179–189.

Liogkas, N. Nelson, R., Kohler, E. & Zhang, L. (2006). Exploiting BitTorrent For Fun (But Not Profit). In *Proceedings of International Workshop on Peer-to-Peer Systems*, Santa Barbara, CA.

Little, T., Dib, P., Shah, K., Barraford, N., & Gallagher, B. (2008). Using LED Lighting for Ubiquitous Indoor Wireless Networking. In *Proceedings of the 4ᵗʰ IEEE Intl. Conf. on Wirless and Mobile Computing, Networking and Communications, Avignon, France*

Little, T., Ishwar, P., & Konrad, J. (2007). A Wireless Video Sensor Network for Autonomous Coastal Sensing. In *Proceedings of Conference on Coastal Environmental Sensing Networks*.

Liu, C., Xie, Y., Lee, M. J., & Saadawi, T. N. (1998). Multipoint multimedia teleconference system with adaptive synchronization. *IEEE Journal on Selected Areas in Communications, 14*(7), 1422–1435.

Liu, J., Li, B., & Zhang, Y.-Q. (2004). An end-to-end adaptation protocol for layered video multicast using optimal rate allocation. *IEEE Transactions on Multimedia, 6*(1), 87–102. doi:10.1109/TMM.2003.819753

Liu, B., Khorashadi, B., Du, H., Ghosal, D., Chuah, C.-N., & Zhang, M. (2009, May). VGSim: An integrated networking and microscopic vehicular mobility simulation platform. *IEEE Communications Magazine, 47*(5), 134–141. doi:10.1109/MCOM.2009.5277467

Liu, Y., & Das, S. (2006, November). Information-Intensive Wireless Sensor Networks: Potential and Challenges. *IEEE Communications Magazine, 44*(11), 142–147. doi:10.1109/MCOM.2006.248177

Liu, J., Li, B., & Zhang, Y.-Q. (2003). Adaptive video multicast over the Internet. *IEEE MultiMedia, 10*(1), 22–31. doi:10.1109/MMUL.2003.1167919

Liu, J. Rao, S. G. Li, B. & Zhang, H. (2008, January). Opportunities and challenges of peer-to-peer Internet video broadcast. In *Proceedings of the IEEE, 96*(1), 11-24.

Liu, M., & Ce, Z. (2007). Multiple description video coding using hierarchical B pictures, *Proc. IEEE Conference on Multimedia and Expo*, Beijing, China, (pp. 1367-1370).

Liu, X., Wang, Q., Sha, L., & He, W. (2003). Optimal QoS Sampling Frequency Assignment for Real-Time Wireless Sensor Networks. In *Proceedings of 24th IEEE Real-Time Systems Symposium*, 308–319.

Liu, Y. (2007). On the minimum delay peer-to-peer video streaming: how realtime can it be? In *Proceedings of the 15ᵗʰ international conference on multimedia* (pp. 127-136).

Liu, Y., Guo, Y., & Liang, C. (2008). A survey on peer-to-peer video streaming systems. *Journal of P2P Networking and Applications, 1*(1), 18-28.

Liu, Z. Shen, Y. Ross, K. W. Panwar, S. & Wang, Y. (2008, October). Substream trading: towards an open P2P live streaming system. In *Proceedings of the International Conference on Network Protocols (ICNP)*, Orlando.

Liu, Z., Shen, Y., Panwar, S., Ross, K. W., & Wang, Y. (2007). Using Layered Video to Provide Incentives in P2P Streaming. In *Proceedings of the Sigcomm P2P-TV Workshop*.

Locher, T. Moor, P., Schmid, S., & Wattenhofer, R. (2006). Free Riding in BitTorrent is Cheap. *Workshop on Hot Topics in Networks*, Irvine, CA.

Locher, T., Schmid, S., & Wattenhofer, R. (2007). Rescuing Tit-for-Tat with Source Coding. *International Peer-to-Peer conference*, Galway, Ireland.

Lotfallah, O., Reisslein, M., & Panchanathan, S. (2006). Adaptive video transmission schemes using MPEG-7 motion intensity descriptor. *IEEE Transactions on Circuits and Systems for Video Technology*, 16(8), 929–946. doi:10.1109/TCSVT.2006.877387

Lu, Z. M., & Li, Z. (2007). Dynamically Restricted Codebook Based Vector Quantisation Scheme for Mesh Geometry Compression. *Springer Journal of Signal. Image and Video Processing*, 2(3), 251–260. doi:10.1007/s11760-008-0053-8

Lu, W.-F., & Wu, M. (2002). MADF: Mobile-Assisted data forwarding for wireless data networks. *Journal of Communications and Networks*, 6(3), 216–233.

Lua, E. K., Crowcroft, J., Pias, M., Sharma, R., & Lim, S. (2005). A survey and comparison of peer-to-peer overlay network schemes. *IEEE Communications Surveys and Tutorials*, 7(1-4), 72–93.

Luby, M., Gasiba, T., Stockhammer, T., & Watson, M. (2007). Reliable multimedia download delivery in cellular broadcast networks. *IEEE Transactions on Broadcasting*, 53(1), 235–246. doi:10.1109/TBC.2007.891703

Ma, R. T. B., Lee, S. C. M., Lui, J. C. S., & Yau, D. K. Y. (2006). Incentive and Service Differentiation in P2P Networks: A Game Theoretic Approach. In *IEEE/ACM Transactions on Networking*.

Magharei, N., & Rejaie, R. (2007). *PRIME: peer-to-peer receiver-driven mesh-based streaming. Proceedings of IEEE INFOCOM'07*. AK: Anchorage.

Magharei, N., Rejaie, R., & Guo, Y. (2007). Mesh or multiple-tree: A comparative study of live p2p streaming approaches. In *Proceedings of the 2007 IEEE Infocom conference*.

Malvar, H., & Staelin, D. (1989). The lot transform coding without blocking effects. *IEEE Transactions on Speech and Audio Processing*, (37): 553–559.

Manoj, B. S., & Siva Ram Murthy, C. (2004). *Ad Hoc Wireless Networks*. New Jersey: Prentice Hall.

Mantyla, M. (Ed.). (1988). *An Introduction to Solid Modeling*. New York: Computer Science Press.

Mao, S., Lin, S., Panwar, S. S., Wang, Y., & Celebi, E. (2003). Video transport over ad hoc networks: multistream coding with multipath transport. *IEEE Journal on Selected Areas in Communications*, 21(4), 1721–1737.

Mao, S., Lin, S. S. S., Panwar, S. S., & Wang, Y. (2001). Reliable transmission of video over ad-hoc networks using automatic repeat request and multi-path transport. *IEEE Vehicular Technology Conference*, (pp. 615-619).

Marciniak, P., Liogkas, N., Legout, A., & Kohler, E. (2008). Small Is Not Always Beautiful. In *Proceedings of the Seventh International Workshop on Peer-to-Peer Systems (IPTPS)*.

Marpe, D., Schwarz, H., & Wiegand, T. (2003). Context-based adaptive binary arithmetic coding in the H.264/AVC video compression standard. *IEEE Transactions on Circuits and Systems for Video Technology*, 13(7), 620–636. doi:10.1109/TCSVT.2003.815173

Massoulié, L. (2008). Optimality Results and Open Problems. In *IEEE CISS*. Peer-to-Peer Live Streaming.

Massoulié, L. (2008, March). Peer-to-peer live streaming: optimality results and open problems. In *Proceedings of the 42nd Annual Conference on Information Sciences and Systems*, pp. 313-315.

Massoulié, L. Twigg, A. Gkantsidis, C., & Rodriguez, P. R. (2007). Randomized decentralized broadcasting algorithms. In *Proceedings of IEEE INFOCOM'07*, Anchorage, AK.

Massoulié, L., & Vojnovi, Ć. M. (2005). Coupon replication systems. *Proceedings*In *Proceedings of the International Conference on Measurements and Modeling of Computer Systems*, Banff, Alberta, Canada.

Massoulié, L., Twigg, A., Gkantsidis, C., & Rodriguez, P. (2007). Randomized decentralized broadcasting algorithms. In *Proceedings of the 2007 IEEE Infocom conference*.

Mathieu, F. (2009). Heterogeneity in Distributed Live Streaming: Blessing or Curse? *Orange Labs Research Report RR-OL-2009-09-001*.

Mathieu, F., & Perino, D. (In Press). *On resource aware algorithms in epidemic live streaming*. Manuscript under submission.

Mathieu, F., & Perino, D. (2009). On Resource Aware Algorithms in Epidemic Live Streaming. *INRIA Research Report RR-7031*.

Matolak, D. W. (2008, May). Channel modeling for vehicle-to-vehicle communications. *IEEE Communications Magazine*, 46(5), 76–83. doi:10.1109/MCOM.2008.4511653

Maugey, T., André, T., Pesquet-Popescu, B., & Farah, J. (2008). *Analysis of error propagation due to frame losses in a distributed video coding system*. Paper presented at the conference EUSIPCO2008, Lausanne, Switzerland.

McCanne, S., Jacobson, V., & Vetterli, M. (1996). Receiver-driven layered multicast. In *Conference Proceedings on Applications, Technologies, Architectures, and Protocols for Computer Communications (SIGCOMM'96)*, (pp. 117-130). Palo Alto, CA.

Mertens, R., Ketterl, M., & Vornberger, O. (2006) Interactive Content Overviews for Lecture Recordings. *Eighth IEEE International Symposium on Multimedia* pp. 933-937

Mertens, R., Schneider, H., Muller, O., & Vornberger, O. (2004) Hypermedia navigation concepts for lecture recordings. *E-Learn: World Conference on E-Learning in Corporate*, pp. 2480–2847

Mishra, A., & Saudagar, M. G. (2004). *Streaming Multimedia: RTSP*. Retrieved from http://www.facweb.iitkgp.ernet.in/~rkumar/media/resource/RTSP.pdf

Mohr, A. E., Riskin, E. A., & Ladner, R. E. (2000). Unequal loss protection: Graceful degradation of image quality over packet erasure channels through forward error correction. *IEEE Journal on Selected Areas in Communications*, 18, 819–828. doi:10.1109/49.848236

MPEG-4 (2004). *Coding of Audio-Visual Objects, Part-2 Visual, Amendment 4: Streaming Video Profile*, ISO/IEC 14496-2/FPDAM4, July 2000.

MSU. (2010). *MSU Video Quality Measurement Tool*. Retrieved February 2010, from http://compression.ru/video/quality_measure/video_measurement_tool_en.html

Mukhopadhyay, S., & Smith, B. (1999) Passive capture and structuring of lectures. *MULTIMEDIA '99: Proceedings of the seventh ACM international conference on Multimedia* Part 1 pp.477-477

Munteanu, C., Penn, G., & Baecker, R. (2007) Web-Based Language Modelling for Automatic Lecture Transcription *Proceedings of the Tenth ISCA European Conference on Speech Communication and Technology – EuroSpeech / Eighth International INTERSPEECH Conference*, pp. 2353–2356

Munteanu, C., Zhang, Y., Baecker, R., & Penn, G. (2006) Wiki-like editing for imperfect computer generated webcast transcripts, *Proc. Demo track of ACM Conf. on Computer Supported Cooperative Work – CSCW, pp. 83–84*

Mushtaq, M., & Ahmed, T. (2008). Smooth Video Delivery for SVC Based Media Streaming Over P2P Networks. In *Proc. 5th IEEE Conference on Consumer Communications and Networking (CCNC'08)*, (pp. 447-451). Las Vegas, NV.

Navda, V., Kashyap, A., & Ganguly, S. (2006). Real-time video stream aggregation in wireless mesh network. In *Proceedings of 17th International Symposium on Personal, Indoor and Mobile Radio Communications, Finland*, 1-7

Neglia, G., Presti, G. L., Zhang, H., & Towsley, D. (2007). A network formation game approach to study BitTorrent tit-for-tat. In *Proceedings of Network Control and Optimization*, Avignon, France.

Newsome, J., & Song, D. (2003). GEM: Graph Embedding for Routing and Data-Centric Storage in Sensor Networks without Geographic Information. *Proceedings of the First ACM Conf.: Embedded Networked Sensor Systems, USA*, 76-88.

Nguyen, K., Nguyen, T., & Cheung, S.-C. (2007). Peer-to-Peer streaming with hierarchical network coding. In *Proceedings of IEEE International Conference on Multimedia & Expo*. Beijing, China.

Nguyen, V., Chang, E., & Ooi, W. (2004). Layered coding with good allocation outperforms multiple description coding over multiple paths. In *Proc. International Conference on Multimedia and Exhibition*, Taipei, Taiwan.

Oda, Y., Tasunekawa, K., & Hata, M. (2000, November). Advanced LOS path-loss model in microcellular mobile communications. *IEEE Transactions on Vehicular Technology, 49*(6), 2121–2125. doi:10.1109/25.901884

Odd Inge Hillestad. (2007). *Evaluating and Enhancing the Performance of IP-based Streaming Media Services and Applications*, (Ph.D. Thesis), Norwegian University of Science and Technology. Retrived May 2007, from http://www.q2s.ntnu.no/~hillesta/thesis/Hillestad_PhD_thesis_08.06.2007.pdf

Onthriar, K., Loo, K. K., & Xue, Z. (2006). *Performance Comparison of Emerging Dirac Video Codec with H.264/AVC*. In proceedings, *International Conference on Digital Telecommunications ICDT06* (pp. 22-26).

Ortega, A., & Wang, H. (2007). Mechanisms for Adapting Compressed Multimedia to Varying Bandwidth Conditions. In van der Schaar, M., & Chou, P. (Eds.), *Multimedia over IP and Wireless Networks* (pp. 81–116). New York: Academic Press. doi:10.1016/B978-012088480-3/50005-9

Ott, J., Wenger, S., Sato, N., Burmeister, C., & Rey, J. (2006). *Request for Comments (RFC) 4585 – Extended RTP Profile for Real-time Transport Control Protocol (RTCP)-Based Feedback*. RTP/AVPF.

Ould-Ahmed-Vall, E., Blough, D., Heck, B., & Riley, G. (2005). Distributed global identification for sensor networks. In *Proceedings of 2nd IEEE International Conference on Mobile Ad-hoc and Sensor Systems, Washington, DC*.

P2P-Next (2009). *P2P-Next Project*. Retrieved August, 14, 2009 from http://www.p2p-next.org

Packet Switched Streaming Service. (2003). *TeliaSonera Finland, MediaLab*. Retrieved Nov 19, 2003, from http://www.medialab.sonera.fi/workspace/PacketSwitchedStreamingWP.pdf

Padmanabhan, V. N., & Sripanidkulchai, K. (2002). The case for cooperative networking. *Proceedings In Proceedings of International Workshop on Peer-to-Peer Systems*, Cambridge, MA, USA.

Padmanabhan, V. N., Wang, H. J., & Chou, P. A. (2003). Resilient Peer-to-Peer streaming. *IEEE International Conference on Network Protocols*, (pp. 16-27).

Padmanabhan, V., Wang, H., Chou, P., & Sripanidkulchai, K. (2002, May). Distributing streaming media content using cooperative networking. In *Proceedings of the 12th international workshop on Network and operating systems support for digital audio and video* (pp. 177-186). Miami, Florida.

Pai, V. Kumar, K., Tamilmani, K., Sambamurthy, V & Mohr, A. E. (2005). Chainsaw: Eliminating trees from overlay multicast. *Proceedings In Proceedings of International Workshop on Peer-to-Peer Systems*, Ithaca, NY.

Paila, T., Luby, M., Lehtonen, R., Roca, V., & Walsh, R. (2004). FLUTE - File Delivery over Unidirectional Transport. *RFC 3926*.

Pancha, P., & Zarki, M. (1993). Bandwidth-allocation schemes for variable-bit-rate MPEG sources in ATM networks. *IEEE Transactions on Circuits and Systems for Video Technology, 3*(3), 190–198. doi:10.1109/76.224229

Panis, G., Hutter, A., Heuer, J., Hellwagner, H., Kosch, H., Timmerer, C., et al. (2003). Bitstream Syntax Description: A Tool for Multimedia Resource Adaptation within MPEG-21. *Signal Processing: Image Communication Journal - Special Issue on Multimedia Adaptation, 18*(8), 721-747.

Park, H., & van der Schaar, M. (2007). Bargaining strategies for networked multimedia resource management. *IEEE Transactions on Signal Processing, 55*(7), 3496–3511. doi:10.1109/TSP.2007.893755

Park, H., & van der Schaar, M. (2009). A framework for foresighted resource reciprocation in P2P networks. *IEEE Transactions on Multimedia, 11*(1), 101–116. doi:10.1109/TMM.2008.2008925

Park, A., Hazen, T. J., & Glass, J. R. (2005) Automatic processing of audio lectures for information retrieval: Vocabulary selection and language modeling. *IEEE International Conference on Acoustics*

Park, J., & van der Schaar, M. (2010). Pricing and Incentives in Peer-to-Peer Networks. *Proceedings*In *Proceedings of IEEE Conference on Computer Communications,* San Diego.

Park, J.-S., Lee, U., Oh, S. Y., Gerla, M., & Lun, D. (2006). Emergency related video streaming in VANETs using network coding. UCLA CSD Technical Report, TR-070016.

Pearlman, M., Haas, Z., Sholander, P., & Tabrizi, S. (2000). On the Impact of Alternate Path Routing for Load Balancing in Mobile Ad Hoc Networks. In *Proceedings of the 1ˢᵗ ACM International Symposium on Mobile Ad hoc Networking and Computing, Boston, MA,* 3-10.

Perkins, C. E., & Royer, E. M. (1999). Ad hoc on-demand distance vector routing (AODV). 2ⁿᵈ*IEEE Workshop on Mobile Computing Systems and Applications*, (pp. 90-100).

Pesquet-Popescu, B., Li, S., & van der Schaar, M. (2007). Scalable Video Coding for Adaptive Streaming. In van der Schaar, M., & Chou, P. (Eds.), *Multimedia over IP and Wireless Networks* (pp. 117–158). New York: Academic Press. doi:10.1016/B978-012088480-3/50006-0

Pianese, F., Perino, D., Keller, J., & Biersack, E. W. (2007, December). PULSE: an adaptive, incentive-based, unstructured P2P live streaming system. *IEEE Transactions on Multimedia, 9*(8), 1645–1660. doi:10.1109/TMM.2007.907466

Pianese, F., & Perino, D. (2007). Resource and Locality Awareness in an Incentive-Based P2P Live Streaming System. In *Proceedings of Peer-to-Peer Streaming and IPTV Sigcomm Workshop (P2P-TV)*.

Piatek, M., Isdal, T., Anderson, T., Krishnamurthy, A., & Venkataramani, A. (2007). Do incentives build robustness in BitTorrent? *Symposium on Networked Systems Design and Implementation,* Cambridge, MA.

Piatek, M., Isdal, T., Krishnamurthy, A., & Anderson, T. (2008). One hop reputations for peer to peer file sharing workloads. *Symposium on Networked Systems Design and Implementation,* San Francisco, CA.

Picconi, F., & Massoulié, L. (2008). Is there a future for mesh-based live video streaming? In *Proceedings of the Eighth International Conference on Peer-to-Peer Computing,* pp. 289-298.

Picconi, F., & Massoulié, L. (2009). ISP-friend or foe? Making P2P live streaming ISP-aware. In *Proceedings of the 29th IEEE International Conference on Distributed Computing Systems*.

Pinson, M., & Wolf, S. (2004). A New Standardized Method for Objectively Measuring Video Quality. *IEEE Transactions on Broadcasting, 50*(3), 312–322. doi:10.1109/TBC.2004.834028

Podilchuk, C. I., Jayant, N. S., & Farvardin, N. (1995). Three-dimensional sub-band coding of video. *IEEE Transactions on Image Processing, 4*, 125–139. doi:10.1109/83.342187

Pohlmann, K. C. (2005). *Principles of Digital Audio* (5th ed.). New York: The Mcgraw-Hill Companies.

Politis, I., Tsagkaropoulos, M., Dagiuklas, T., & Kotsopoulos, S. (2008). Power Efficient Video Multipath Transmission over Wireless Multimedia Sensor Networks. *Mobile Networks and Applications, 13*(3-4), 274–284.

Politis, I., Tsagkaropoulos, M., Dagiuklas, T., & Kotso-poulos, S. (2007). Intelligent Packet Scheduling for Optimized Video Transmission over Wireless Networks. In *Proceedings of the 3rd International Mobile Multimedia Communications Conference, Nafpaktos, Greece, 329*

Pouwelse, J. A. Garbacki, P., Epema, D. H. J. & Sips, H. J. (2005). The BitTorrent P2P file-sharing system: Measurements and Analysis. In *Proceedings of International Workshop on Peer-to-Peer Systems*, Ithaca, NY.

Pouwelse, J. A., Taal, J. R., Lagendijk, R. L., Epema, D. H. J., & Sips, H. J. (2004, October). Real-time video delivery using peer-to-peer bartering networks and multiple description coding. *IEEE Int'l Conference on Systems, Man and Cybernetics*.

Proakis, J. G. (2001). *Digital Communications* (4th ed.). New York: McGraw Hill.

Pullen, J. M. (2000) The Internet-based lecture: converging teaching and technology. ITiCSE '00: *Proceedings of the 5th annual SIGCSE/SIGCUE ITiCSEconference on Innovation and technology in computer science education* pp. 101-104

Qiu, D., & Srikant, R. (2004). Modeling and Performance Analysis of BitTorrent-Like Peer-to-Peer Networks. In *Proceedings of ACM Special Interest Group on Data Communication*, Portland, OR.

Radha, H., van der Schaar, M., & Chen, Y. (2001). The MPEG-4 fine-grained scalable video coding method for multimedia streaming over IP. *IEEE Transactions on Multimedia, 3*(1), 53–68. doi:10.1109/6046.909594

Radulovic, I., Wang, Y.-K., Wenger, S., Hallapuro, A., Hannuksela, M. N., & Frossard, P. (September 2007). Multiple description H.264 video coding with redundant pictures", *International. Workshop on Mobile Video*, (pp. 37-42).

Ramakrishnan, K., Floyd, S., & Black, D. (2001). *The addition of Explicit Congestion Notification (ECN) to IP, RFC-3168, Internet Engineering Task Force*. IETF.

Ramchandran, K., & Vetterli, M. (1993). Best wavelet packet bases in a ratedistortion sense. *IEEE Transactions on Image Processing, 2*, 160–175. doi:10.1109/83.217221

Ransburg, M., Devillers, S., Timmerer, C., & Hellwagner, H. (2007). Processing and Delivery of Multimedia Metadata for Multimedia Content Streaming. In *Proc. Datenbanksysteme in Business, Technologie und Web (BTW 2007)*, (pp. 117-138). Aachen, Germany.

Rao, A., Ratnasamy, S., Papadimitriou, C., Shenker, S., & Stoica, I. (2003). Geographic Routing without Location Information. In *Proceedings of the 9th Annual International Conference on Mobile Computing and Networking, San Diego, CA*.

Ratnasamy, S., Francis, P., Handley, M., Karp, R., & Shenker, S. A. (2001). Scalable Content-Addressable Network. *Proceedings*In *Proceedings of ACM Special Interest Group on Data Communication*, San Diego, CA.

Raymond, D., Kanenishi, K., Matsuura, K., & Yano, Y. (2004). IP Videoconferencing in Distance Education: Ideas for a Successful Integration. *Proceedings of World Conference on Educational Multimedia, Hypermedia and Telecommunications 2004* pp. 4179-4184

Reibman, A. R., Jafarkhani, H., Orchard, M., & Wang, Y. (1999). Performance of multiple description coders on a real channel. In *Proc. International Conference on Acoustics, Speech, and Signal Processing*, Phoenix, AZ, (pp. 2415–2418).

Reibman, A. R., Jafarkhani, H., Orchard, M. T., & Wang, Y. (October 2001). Multiple description video using rate-distortion splitting. *IEEE International Conference on Image Processing*, (pp. 971-981).

Reibman, A. R., Wang, Y., Qiu, X., Jiang, Z., & Chawla, K. (2000). Transmission of multiple description and layered video over an EGPRS wireless network, *Proc. IEEE International Conference on Image Processing (ICIP '00)*, Vancouver, Canada, pp. 136–139.

Reichel, J. Schwarz, H., & Wien, M. (2005). Joint Scalable Video Model JSVM-4. ISO/IEC JTC1/SC29/WG11, Doc. JVT-Q202.

Reichel, J., Schwarz, H., & Wien, M. (2007). Joint Scalable Video Model JSVM-12 text. *JVT_Y202, Output document of the 25th JVT meeting.*

Rejaie, R. (2006). Anyone can broadcast video over the Internet. *Communications of the ACM, 49,* 55–57. doi:10.1145/1167838.1167863

Rejaie, R., & Stafford, S. (2004, June). A framework for architecting peer-to-peer receiver-driven overlays. In *Proceedings of the 14th international workshop on Network and operating systems support for digital audio and video* (pp. 177-186). Cork, Ireland.

Repp, S., & Meinel, C. (2006) Semantic indexing for recorded educational lecture videos. *Proceedings of the 4th IEEE Conference on Pervasive Computing and Communications Workshops (PerCom),* pp 240–245

Repp, S., & Meinel, C. (2008) Segmentation of Lecture Videos Based on Spontaneous Speech Recognition. *Tenth IEEE Int. Symp. on Multimedia ISM 2008* pp. 692 – 697

Repp, S., Linckels, S., & Meinel, C. (2008) Question answering from lecture videos based on an automatic semantic annotation. *Proc. of the 13th annual conf. on Innovation and technology in computer science education ITiCSE '08* pp.17-21

Repp, S., Waitelonis, J., Sack, H., & Meinel, C. (2007) Segmentation and annotation of audiovisual recordings based on automated speech recognition. *Proceedings of the 8th International Conference on Intelligent Data Engineering and Automated Learning (IDEAL)* pp. 620–629

Rescorla, E. (1999, June). Diffie-Hellman Key Agreement Method (No. 2631*). RFC 2631 (Proposed Standard). IETF.* Retrieved December 22, 2009 from http://www.ietf.org/rfc/rfc2631.txt

Richardson, I. E. (2003). *H.264 and MPEG-4 video compression.* New York: John Wiley & Sons. doi:10.1002/0470869615

Ronchetti, M. (2003) Has the time come for using video-based lectures over the Internet? A Test-case report *CATE - Web Based Education Conference 2003*

Ronchetti, M. (2008) Requirements for videolectures: which system is the best for you? *World Conference on Educational Multimedia, Hypermedia and Telecommunications (EDMEDIA) 2008.* pp. 2192-2199.

Rossignac, J. (1999). Edgebreaker: Connectivity compression for triangle meshes. *IEEE Transactions on Visualization and Computer Graphics, 5*(1), 47–61. doi:10.1109/2945.764870

Rowe, A., Goel, D., & Rajkumar, R. (2007). FireFly Mosaic: A Vision-Enabled Wireless Sensor Networking System. In *Proceedings of the 28th IEEE International Real-Time Systems Symposium,* 459-468.

Rowstron, A., & Druschel, P. (2001). Pastry: Scalable, distributed object location and routing for large scale peer to peer systems. In *Proceedings of IFIP/ACM International Conference on Distributed Systems Platforms (Middleware 2001),* Heidelberg, Germany.

Salehi, J. D., Zhang, Z.-L., Kurose, J. F., & Towsley, D. (1996). Supporting stored video: Reducing rate variability and end-to-end resource requirements through optimal smoothing. In *ACM SIGMETRICS,* May 1996, (pp. 221-231).

Sanghavi, S., Hayek, B., & Massoulié, L. (2007). Gossiping with multiple messages. *IEEE Transactions on Information Theory, 53*(12), 4640–4654. doi:10.1109/TIT.2007.909171

Saroiu, S., Gummadi, P., & Gribble, S. (2002). *A Measurement Study of Peer-to-Peer File Sharing Systems.* Multimedia Computing and Networking.

SCALNET Project. (2009). Retrieved August 27, 2009, from http://www.scalnet.info

Schick, R., Baecker, R. M., & Scheffel-Dunand, D. (2005). Bimodal Text and Speech Conversation During On-line Lectures, *Proceedings of ED-MEDIA 2005*

Schiely, M., & Felber, P. (2006). CROSSFLUX: an architecture for peer-to-peer media streaming. *Global Data Management, Volume 8. Emerging Communication: Studies on New Technologies and Practices in Communication, IOSPress, 8,* 342–358.

Schierl, T., Stockhammer, T., & Wiegand, T. (2007). Mobile Video Transmission Using Scalable Video Coding. *IEEE Transactions on Circuits and Systems for Video Technology*, *17*(9), 1204–1217. doi:10.1109/TCSVT.2007.905528

Schierl, T., Jhansen, S., Perkis, A., & Wiegand, T. (2008). Rateless scalable video coding for overlay multisource streaming in MANETs. *Journal of Visual Communication and Image Representation*, *19*, 500–507. doi:10.1016/j.jvcir.2008.06.004

Schierl, T., & Wenger, S. (2009). Signaling Media Decoding Dependency in the Session Description Protocol (SDP). *RFC 5583*.

Schierl, T., Johansen, S., Hellge, C., & Stockhammer, T. (2007). Distributed Rate-Distortion Optimization for Rateless Coded Scalable Scalable Video in Mobile Ad Hoc Networks. In *Proc. IEEE International Conference on Image Processing (ICIP 2007)*, *6*, pp. VI-497-VI-500. San Antonio, TX.

Schuett, N. (2002). *The effect of latency on ensemble performance*, (Bachelor thesis), Stanford University.

Schulzrinne, H., Rao, A., & Lanphier, R. (1998). *Request For Comments (RFC) 2326 - Real Time Streaming Protocol*. RTSP.

Schulzrinne, H. (1996). Request For Comments (RFC) 1890 - RTP Profile for Audio and Video Conferences with Mini

Schulzrinne, H., Casner, S., Frederick, R., & Jacobson, V. (1987). *RTP: A Transport Protocol for real-time applications*. Audio-video transport working group. RFC 1889, Sept.1987.

Schulzrinne, H., Casner, S., Frederick, R., & Jacobson, V. (2003). RTP: A Transport Protocol for Real-Time Application. *RFC3550*.

Schulzrinne, H., Rao, A., & Lanphier, R. (1998). *Real Time Streaming Protocol (RTSP)*. RFC 2326, April 1998.

Schulzrinne, H., Rao, A., Lanphier, R., Westerlund, M., & Stiemerling, M. (2009). *Real Time Streaming Protocol 2.0 (RTSP), draft-ietf-mmusic-rfc2326bis-22*. Retrieved July 13, 2009, from http://www.h-online.com/nettools/rfc/drafts/draft-ietf-mmusic-rfc2326bis-22.shtml

Schwarz, H., Marpe, D., & Wiegand, T. (2007). Overview of the Scalable Video Coding Extension of the H.264/AVC Standard. *IEEE Transactions on Circuits and Systems for Video Technology*, *17*(9), 1103–1107. doi:10.1109/TCSVT.2007.905532

Schwarz, H., Marpe, D., & Wiegand, T. (2006). Analysis of hierarchical B pictures and MCTF, in *Proc. IEEE International Conference on Multimedia & Expo (ICME'06)*, Toronto, Canada, pp. 1929–1932.

Schwarz, H., Marpe, D., & Wiegand, T. (2006). Overview of the scalable H.264/MPEG4-AVC extension. *IEEE Int. Conf. on Image Proc.*, 161–164.

Seeling, R., & Reisslein, M. (2005). Video coding with multiple descriptors and spatial scalability for device diversity in wireless multi-hop networks, in *Proc. IEEE Conference on Consumer Communications and Networking*, Las Vegas, Nevada, USA, Jan. 2005, pp. 278–283.

Segall, A., & Zhao, J. (2008). Bit stream rewriting for SVC-to-AVC conversion. In *Proc. 15th IEEE International Conference on Image Processing (ICIP 2008)*, (pp. 2776-2779). San Diego, CA.

Sentinelli, L., Marfia, G., Gerla, M., Kleinrock, L., & Tewari, L. (2007, June). Will IPTV ride the P2P storm? *IEEE Communications Magazine*, *45*(6), 86–92. doi:10.1109/MCOM.2007.374424

Setton, E. (2003). *Congestion-aware video streaming over peer-to-peer networks*. (PhD thesis), Information Systems Laboratory, Department of Electrical Engineering, Stanford University, Stanford, USA, 2003.

Shakkottai, S., Rappaport, T. S., & Karlsson, P. S. (2003). Cross-layer design for wireless networks. *IEEE Communications Magazine*, *41*(10), 74–80. doi:10.1109/MCOM.2003.1235598

Shan, Y. (2005). Cross-layer techniques for adaptive video streaming over wireless networks. *EURASIP Journal on Applied Signal Processing*, (2): 220–228. doi:10.1155/ASP.2005.220

Sheltami, T. R. (2008). Performance evaluation of H.264 protocol in ad hoc networks. *Journal of Mobile Multimedia*, *4*(1), 59–70.

Shi, S., & Turner, J. (2002). Routing in overlay multicast networks. In *Proceedings of IEEE Conference on Computer Communications*, New York, NY.

Shin, J., Chin, M., & Kim, C. (2006). Optimal Transmission Range for Topology Management Wireless Sensor Networks. In *Proceedings of International Conference on Information Networking, Japan, 3961,* 177-185.

Shlien, S. (1997). The modulated lapped transform, its time-varying forms, and its applications to audio coding standards. *IEEE Transactions on Speech and Audio Processing*, (5): 359–366. doi:10.1109/89.593311

Shneidman, J., Parkes, D. C., & Massoulié, L. (2004). *Faithfulness in Internet Algorithms*. Portland, OR: Practice and Theory of Incentives and Game Theory in Networked Systems.

Shu, L., Zhang, Y., Zhou, Z., Hauswirth, M., Yu, Z., & Hyns, G. (2008). Transmitting and Gathering Streaming Data in Wireless Multimedia Sensor Networks within Expected Network Lifetime. *Mobile Networks and Applications*, *13*(3-4), 306–323.

Silverston, T., & Fourmaux, O. (2007, June). Measuring P2P IPTV systems. In *Proceedings of ACM NOSSDAV '07*, Urbana-Champaign, IL.

Simon, H. A. (1955). A behavioral model of rational choice. *The Quarterly Journal of Economics*, *59*, 99–118. doi:10.2307/1884852

Singh, R., Ortega, A., Perret, L., & Jiang, W. (2000). Comparison of multiple description coding and layered coding based on network simulations, *Proc. SPIE Conference on Visual Communication Image Processing*.

Sirivianos, M. Park, J. H., Chen, R. & Yang, X. (2007). Free-riding in BitTorrent Networks with the Large View Exploit. *Proceedings*In *Proceedings of International Workshop on Peer-to-Peer Systems*, Bellevue, WA.

Snoek, C., & Worring, M. (2005). Multimodal video indexing: A review of the state-of-the-art. *Multimedia Tools and Applications*, (25): 5–35. doi:10.1023/B:MTAP.0000046380.27575.a5

Sohrabi, K., Gao, J., Allawadhi, V., & Pottie, G. (2000). Protocols for Self-organization of a Wireless Sensor Network. *IEEE Personal Communications*, *7*(5), 16–27. doi:10.1109/98.878532

Soldani, C., Leduc, G., Verdicchio, F., & Munteanu, A. (2006). Multiple description coding versus transport layer FEC for resilient video transmission. In *Proc. IEEE International Conference on Digital* Telecommunications, Cap Esterel, France, pp. 20-27.

Soldani, D. Man, Li., & Renaud, C. (2004). *QoS and QoE Management in UMTS Cellular Systems*. New York: Wiley.

Soong, S. K. A., Chan, L. K., & Cheers, C. (2006) Impact of video recorded lectures among students. *Proceedings of the 23rd annual ascilite conf.: Who's learning? Whose technology?* Pp.789-792

Sorkine, O., Cohen-Or, D., & Toldeo, S. (2003). High-pass quantization for mesh encoding. In *Proceedings of Eurographics Symposium on Geometry Processing.* (pp. 42-51).

Spanias, A., Painter, T., & Atti, V. (2007). *Audio Signal Processing and Coding* (1st ed.). New York: Wiley-Interscience. doi:10.1002/0470041978

Srisuresh, P., Ford, B., & Kegel, D. (2008, March). State of Peer-to-Peer (P2P) Communication across Network Address Translators (NATs). *RFC 5128. IETF.* Retrieved December 22, 2009 from http://www.ietf.org/rfc/rfc5128.txt

Srivastava, V., & Motani, M. (2005). Cross-layer design: A survey and the road ahead. *IEEE Communications Magazine*, *43*(12), 112–119. doi:10.1109/MCOM.2005.1561928

Stankovic, V., Hamzaoui, R., & Xiong, Z. (2005). Robust layered multiple description coding of scalable media data for multicast. *IEEE Signal Processing Letters*, *12*(2), 154–157. doi:10.1109/LSP.2004.840895

Stibor, L., Zhang, Y., & Reumann, H.-J. (2007, March). Evaluation of communication distance in a vehicular ad hoc network using IEEE 802.11p. *Wireless Communication and Networking Conference*, (pp. 254-257).

Stockhammer, T., Gasiba, T., Samad, W. A., Schierl, T., Jenkac, H., & Wiegand, T. (2007). Nested harmonic broadcasting for scalable video over mobile datacast channels. *Wireless Communications and Mobile Computing*, *7*(2), 235–256. doi:10.1002/wcm.476

Stockhammer, T., & Hannuksela, M. M. (2005). H.264/AVC video for wireless transmission. *IEEE Wireless Communication*, *12*(4), 6–13. doi:10.1109/MWC.2005.1497853

Stockhammer, T., Hannuksela, M. M., & Wiegand, T. (2003). H.264/AVC in wireless environments. *IEEE Transactions on Circuits and Systems for Video Technology*, *13*(7), 657–673. doi:10.1109/TCSVT.2003.815167

Stockhammer, T. (2006). *Robust System and Cross-Layer Design for H.264/AVC-Based Wireless Video Applications.* EURASIP Journal on Applied Signal Processing.

Stockhammer, T., & Zia, W. (2007). Error-resilient coding and decoding strategies for video communication. In Chou, P. A., & van der Schaar, M. (Eds.), *Multimedia in IP and Wireless Networks* (pp. 13–58). Burlington, MA: Academic Press. doi:10.1016/B978-012088480-3/50003-5

Stoica, I., Morris, R., & Karger, D. FransKaashoek, M., Dabek, M., & Balakrishnan, H. (2001). Chord: A Scalable Peer-To-Peer Lookup Service for Internet Applications. *Proceedings*In *Proceedings of ACM Special Interest Group on Data Communication*, San Diego.

Stoufs, M. R., Munteanu, A., Barbarien, J., Cornelis, J., & Schelkens, P. (2009), Optimized scalable multiple-description coding and FEC-based joint source-channel coding: a performance comparison, *Proc. 10th Workshop on Image Analysis for Multimedia Interactive Services (WIAMIS'09)*, London, UK, pp. 73-76.

Stütz, T., & Uhl, A. (2008). Format-Compliant Encryption of H.264/AVC and SVC. In *Proc. 10th IEEE International Symposium on Multimedia (ISM 2008)*, (pp. 446-451). Berkeley, CA.

Stutzbach, D., & Rejaie, R. (2006). Understanding churn in peer-to-peer networks. In *Proceedings of the 6th acm sigcomm conference on internet measurement* (pp. 189-202). Rio de Janeiro, Brazil: SIGCOMM.

Sullivan, G. J., & Wiegand, T. (2005). Video compression – from concepts to the H.264/AVC standard. *Proceedings of the IEEE*, *93*(1), 18–31. doi:10.1109/JPROC.2004.839617

Sun, H., Vetro, A., & Xin, J. (2007). An overview of scalable video streaming. *Wireless Communications and Mobile Computing*, *7*(2), 159–172. doi:10.1002/wcm.471

Sun, Q., Tan, S. Y., & Tan, K. C. (2005, July). Analytical formulae for path loss prediction in urban street grid microcellular environments. *IEEE Transactions on Vehicular Technology*, *54*(4), 1251–1258. doi:10.1109/TVT.2005.851298

Sun Microsystems. (1999), *The Java3D API Specification*. Retrieved November 30, 2009, from http://java.sun.com/javase/technologies/desktop/java3d/forDevelopers/j3dguide/j3dTOC.doc.html

Sun X., Foote L, Kimber D. & Manjunath B.S., (2005) Region of interest extraction and virtual camera control based on panoramic video capturing. *IEEE Transactions on Multimedia, (7)* n.5 981 - 990

Szymczak, A., King, D., & Rossignac, J. (2001). An edgebreaker-based efficient compression scheme for regular meshes. *Computational Geometry*, *20*(1-2), 53–68. doi:10.1016/S0925-7721(01)00035-9

Tamilmani, K. Pai, V., & Mohr, A. E. (2004, June). SWIFT: a system with incentives for trading. *Proceedings of the 2nd Workshop of Economics in Peer-to-Peer Systems (P2PECON).*

Tanaka, Y., & Itamiya, T. Hagino. T., & Chiyokura, H. (2004) HTTP-proxy-assisted automatic video indexing for e-learning. *International Symposium on Applications and the Internet Workshops. SAINT 2004.* pp. 502 - 507

Tanenbaum, A. S. (2003). *Computer Networks* (4th ed.). Upper Saddle River, NJ: Pearson Studium.

Taubin, G., Horn, W., Rossignac, J., & Lazarus, F. (1998). Geometry coding and VRML. *Proceedings of the IEEE, 86*(6), 1228–1243. doi:10.1109/5.687837

Taubin, G., & Rossignac, J. (1998). Geometric compression through topological surgery. *ACM Transactions on Graphics, 17*(2), 84–115. doi:10.1145/274363.274365

Taubman, D., & Zakhor, A. (1996). A common framework for rate and distortion based scaling of highly scalable compressed video. *IEEE Transactions on Circuits and Systems for Video Technology, 6*(4), 329–354. doi:10.1109/76.510928

Teixeira, T., & Savvides, A. (2007). Lightweight People Counting and Localizing in Indoor Spaces Using Camera Sensor Nodes. In *Proceedings of the first ACM/IEEE International Conference,* 36-43.

Teixeira, T., Lymberopoulos, D., Culurciello, E., Aloimonos, Y., & Savvides, A. (2006). A Lightweight Camera Sensor Network Operating on Symbolic Information. In *Proceedings of the first Workshop on Distributed Smart Cameras, Boulder, CO, USA.*

Tham, J., Ranganath, S., & Kassim, A. (1998). Highly scalable wavelet-based video codec for very low bit-rate environment. *IEEE Journal on Selected Areas in Communications, 16*(1), 12–27. doi:10.1109/49.650917

Thang, T. C., Kim, J.-G., Kang, J. W., & Yoo, J.-J. (2009). SVC adaptation: Standard tools and supporting methods. *Signal Processing Image Communication, 24,* 214–228. doi:10.1016/j.image.2008.12.006

Tian, R., Zhang, Q., Xiang, Z., Xiong, Y., Li, X., & Zhu, W. (2005). Robust and efficient path diversity in application-layer multicast for video streaming. *IEEE Transactions on Circuits and Systems for Video Technology, 15*(8), 961–972. doi:10.1109/TCSVT.2005.852416

Tizon, N., & Pesquet-Popescu, B. (2008). *Scalable and media aware adaptive video streaming over wireless networks.* EURASIP Journal on Advances in Signal Processing.

Tizon, N., & Pesquet-Popescu, B. (2007). *Content based QoS differentiation for video streaming in a wireless environment.* Paper presented at the conference EUSIPCO 2007, Poznan, Poland.

Tobagi, F. (1995) Distance learning with digital video. *Multimedia IEEE (2)* n.1 90 - 93

Tonguz, O. K., Viriyasitavat, W., & Bai, F. (2009, May). Modeling urban traffic: a cellular automata approach. *IEEE Communications Magazine, 47*(5), 142–150. doi:10.1109/MCOM.2009.4939290

Touman, C., & Gotsman, C. (1998). Triangle mesh compression. In *Proceedings of Graphics Interface 98 Conference* (pp. 26-34).

Tourapis, A., Leontaris, A., Sühring, K., & Sullivan, G. (2009). H.264/MPEG-4 AVC Reference Software Manual. *JVT_AD010, Output document of the 30th JVT meeting.*

Tran, D. A., Hua, K. A., & Do, T. T. (2004). A Peer-to-Peer Architecture for Media Streaming. *IEEE Journal on Selected Areas in Communications, 22*(1), 121–133. doi:10.1109/JSAC.2003.818803

Treiber, M., Henneke, A., & Helbing, D. (2000, August). Congested traffic states in empirical observations and microscopic simulations. *Physical Review E: Statistical Physics, Plasmas, Fluids, and Related Interdisciplinary Topics, 62*(2), 1805–1824. doi:10.1103/PhysRevE.62.1805

Truong, B. T. and Venkatesh, S. (2007). Video abstraction: A systematic review and classification. *ACM Trans. Multimedia Comput. Commun. Appl. (3)*, n.1, 1-37

Truong, K., & Abowd, G. (1999) StuPad: integrating student notes with class lectures. *CHI '99 extended abstracts on Human factors in computing systems* pp. 208 – 209

Tun, M., Loo, K. K., & Cosmas, J. (2007, Sept.). Error-Resilient Performance of Dirac Video Codec over Packet-Erasure Channel. *IEEE Transactions on Broadcasting, 53*(3), 649–659. doi:10.1109/LPT.2007.903636

Tun, M., Loo, K. K., & Cosmas, J. (2008). Rate Control Algorithm Based on Quality Factor Optimization for DIRAC Video Codec. *Elsevier Image Communication, 23*(9), 649–664.

Vaishampayan, V. (1993). Design of multiple description scalar quantizers. *IEEE Transactions on Information Theory, 39*, 821–834. doi:10.1109/18.256491

Vaishampayan, V., Sloane, N. J. A., & Servetto, S. D. (2001). Multipledescription vector quantization with lattice codebooks: Design and anaysis. *IEEE Transactions on Information Theory, 47*(5), 1718–1734. doi:10.1109/18.930913

Valette, S., & Prost, R. (2004). Wavelet-Based Progressive Compression Scheme for Triangle Meshes: Wavemesh. *IEEE Transactions on Visualization and Computer Graphics, 10*(2), 123–129. doi:10.1109/TVCG.2004.1260764

Valin, J. M., Terriberry, T., Montgomery, C., & Maxwell, G. (2009). A high-quality speech and audio codec with less than 10 ms delay. In *Proceedings of IEEE Transactions on Audio, Speech and Language Processing.*

van der Schaar, M., & Chou, P. A. (Eds.). (2007). *Multimedia over IP and Wireless Networks.* New York: Academic.

Van der Schaar, M., & Sai Shanker, N. (2005). Cross-layer wireless multimedia transmission: Challenges, principles, and new paradigms. *IEEE Wireless Communications, 12*(4), 50–58. doi:10.1109/MWC.2005.1497858

van der Schaar, M., & Shankar N, S. (2005). Cross-layer wireless multimedia transmission: challenges, principles, and new paradigms. *IEEE Wireless Communications Magazine, 12*(4), 50-58.

Vandalore, B., Feng, W.-C., Jain, R., & Fahmy, S. (2001). A survey of application layer techniques for adaptive streaming of multimedia. *Real-Time Imaging, 7*(3), 221–235. doi:10.1006/rtim.2001.0224

Venkataraman, V. Francis, P. & Calandrino, J. (2006). ChunkySpread: Multitree unstructured peer-to-peer multicast. In *Proceedings of International Workshop on Peer-to-Peer Systems*, Santa Barbara, CA.

Venkataraman, V., Yoshida, K., & Francis, P. (2006). Chunkyspread: heterogeneous unstructured end system multicast. In *Proceedings of the 14th IEEE International Conference on Network Protocols.*

Verdicchio, F., Munteanu, A., Gavrilescu, A. I., Cornelis, J., & Schelkens, P. (2006). Embedded multiple description coding of video. *IEEE Transactions on Image Processing, 15*(10), 3114–3130. doi:10.1109/TIP.2006.877495

Vetro, A. (2004). MPEG-21 Digital Item Adaptation: Enabling Universal Multimedia Access. *IEEE MultiMedia, 11*(1), 84–87. doi:10.1109/MMUL.2004.1261111

Vetro, A., Christopoulos, C., & Sun, H. (2003). Video transcoding architectures and techniques: An overview. *IEEE Signal Processing Magazine, 20*(2), 18–29. doi:10.1109/MSP.2003.1184336

Vickers, B., Albuquerque, C., & Suda, T. (1998). Adaptive multicast of multi-layered video: rate-based and credit-based approaches. *In Proc. of IEEE INFOCOM*, San Francisco, Vol. 3, (pp. 1073–1083).

Vitali, A., Rovati, F., Rinaldo, R., Bernardini, R., & Durigon, M. (2005). Low-complexity standard-compatible robust and scalable video streaming over lossy/variable bandwidth networks, *IEEE International Conference on Consumer Electronics*, Las Vegas.

Vlavianos, A., Iliofotou, M., & Faloutsos, M. (2006), "BiToS: Enhancing BitTorrent for supporting streaming applications. In *Proceedings of IEEE Conference on Computer Communications*, Barcelona, Catalunya, Spain.

Wald, M. (2005) 'SpeechText': Enhancing Learning and Teaching by Using Automatic Speech Recognition to Create Accessible, Synchronized Multimedia *World Conf. on Educational Multimedia, Hypermedia and Telecommunications EDMEDIA-2005*

Walsh, A. E., & Bourges-Sevenier, M. (Eds.), *(n.d.). MPEG-4 Jump Start.* Upper Saddle River, NJ: Prentice-Hall.

Walsh, K., & Sirer, E. G. (2006) "Experience with an Object Reputation System for Peer-to-Peer Filesharing". In *Proceedings of Symposium on Networked Systems Design and Implementation*, San Jose, CA.

Wang, Y., Hannuksela, M., Pateaux, S., Eleftheriadis, A., & Wenger, S. (2007). System and Transport Interface of SVC. *IEEE Transactions on Circuits and Systems for Video Technology*, *17*(9), 1149–1163. doi:10.1109/TCSVT.2007.906827

Wang, H., & Ortega, A. (2003). *Robust video communication by combining scalability and multiple description coding techniques*. Proc. Image and Video Communications and Processing.

Wang, Y., Reibman, A. R., & Lin, S. (2005). Multiple description coding for video delivery. *Proceedings of the IEEE*, *93*(1), 57–70. doi:10.1109/JPROC.2004.839618

Wang, Y., Wenger, S., Wen, J., & Katsaggelos, K. (2000). Error resilient video coding tecnniques. *IEEE Signal Processing Magazine*, 61–82. doi:10.1109/79.855913

Wang, Y., & Zhu, Q.-F. (2005). Error control and concealment for video communication: A review. *Proceedings of the IEEE*, *86*(5), 974–997. doi:10.1109/5.664283

Wang, Y.-K., Hannuksela, M. M., Pateux, S., Eleftheriadis, A., & Wenger, S. (2007). System and transport interface of SVC. *IEEE Trans. on Circuits and Systems for Video Technology*, *17*(9), 1149–1163. doi:10.1109/TCSVT.2007.906827

Wang, Y., Reibman, A. R., & Lee, S. (2005). Multiple description coding for video delivery. *Proceedings of the IEEE*, *93*(1), 57–70. doi:10.1109/JPROC.2004.839618

Wang, M., & Li, B. (2007). R^2: Random push with random network coding in live peer-to-peer streaming. *IEEE Journal on Selected Areas in Communications*, *25*(9), 1–12. doi:10.1109/JSAC.2007.071205

Wang, M., & Li, B. (2007, Dec.). Network coding in live peer-to-peer streaming. *Multimedia. IEEE Transactions on*, *9*(8), 1554–1567.

Wang F., Ngo C-W., Pong T-C. (2007) Lecture Video Enhancement and Editing by Integrating Posture, Gesture, and Text. *IEEE Transactions on Multimedia (9)* n.2. 397–409

Wang F., Ngo C-W., Pong T-C. (2008) "Simulating a Smartboard by Real-Time Gesture Detection in Lecture Videos". *IEEE Transactions on Multimedia (10)* n.5 926 - 935

Wang, F. Liu, J., & Xiong, Y. (2008, April). Stable peers: existence, importance, and application in peer-to-peer live video streaming. In *Proceedings of IEEE INFOCOM 2008*, Phoenix, AZ, USA.

Wang, F., Ngo, C.-W., & Pong, T.-C. (2004) Gesture tracking and recognition for lecture video editing. *Proceedings of the 17th International Conference on Pattern Recognition ICPR 2004. vol. 3* pp. 934 - 937

Wang, F., Ngo, C.-W., & Pong, T.-C. (2006) Prediction-Based Gesture Detection in Lecture Videos by Combining Visual, Speech and Electronic Slides. *IEEE International Conference on Multimedia and Expo, 2006* pp. 653 - 656

Wang, H., & Ortega, A. (2003). Robust video communication by combining scalability and multiple description coding techniques. In *Proceedings of the SPIE*, 111-124.

Wang, J., Masilela, M., & Liu, J. (2007, December). Supporting Video Data in Wireless Sensor Networks. In *Proceedings of the 9th IEEE International Symposium on Multimedia* (pp. 310-317). Los Alamitos, CA

Wang, Y., Panwar, S., Lin, S., & Mao, S. (2002, September). Wireless video transport using path diversity: multiple description vs. layered coding. In *Proc. IEEE International Conference on Image Processing (ICIP '02)*, New York (pp. 21-24).

Wang, Z., Lu, L., & Bovic, A.C. (2004). Video quality assessment using structural distortion measurement. *Signal Processing: Image Communication special issue on Objective video quality metrics. 19*(2), 121-132.

Watkins, C. J. C. H., & Dayan, P. (1992). Q-learning. *Machine Learning*, *8*(3-4), 279–292. doi:10.1007/BF00992698

Wei, W., & Zakhor, A. (2009). Interference aware multipath selection for video streaming in wireless ad hoc networks. *IEEE Transactions on Circuits and Systems for Video Technology*, *19*(2), 165–178. doi:10.1109/TCSVT.2008.2009242

Wei, W., & Zakhor, A. (2004, October). Multipath unicast and multicast video communication over wireless ad hoc networks. *International Conference on Broadband Networks*, (pp. 494-505).

Wei, W., & Zakhor, A. (2006, October). Path selection for multi-path streaming in wireless ad hoc networks. *International Conference on Image Processing*, (pp. 3045-3048).

Wenger, S., Wang, Y.-K., & Schierl, T. (2007). Transport and Signaling of SVC in IP Networks. *IEEE Transactions on Circuits and Systems for Video Technology, 17*(9), 1164–1173. doi:10.1109/TCSVT.2007.905523

Wenger, S. (2003). H.264/AVC over IP. *IEEE Transactions on Circuits and Systems for Video Technology, 13*(7), 645–656. doi:10.1109/TCSVT.2003.814966

Wenger, S., Hannuksela, M., Stockhammer, T., Westerlund, M., & Singer, D. (2004). *RTP payload format for H.264 Video, RFC-3984, Internet Engineering Task Force*. IETF.

Wenger, S., Knorr, G. D., Ou, J., & Kossentini, F. (1998). Error resilience support in H.263+. *IEEE Transactions on Circuits and Systems for Video Technology, 8*(7), 867–877. doi:10.1109/76.735382

Wenger, S., Sato, N., Burmeister, C., & Rey, J. (2006). Extended RTP profile for real-time transport control protocol (RTCP)-based feedback. *RFC4585*.

Wenger, S., Wang, Y.-K, & Schierl, T. (2009). RTP payload format for SVC video. *IETF draft*.

Wenger, S., Wang, Y., Schierl, T., & Eleftheriadis, A. (2009). RTP Payload Format for SVC Video. *Internet Draft (draft-ietf-avt-rtp-svc-18.txt)*.

Wiegand, T., Sullivan, G., Bjøntegaard, G., & Luthra, A. (2003). Overview of the H.264/AVC Video Coding Standard. *IEEE Transactions on Circuits and Systems for Video Technology, 13*(7), 560–576. doi:10.1109/TCSVT.2003.815165

Wiegand, T., Schwarz, H., Joch, A., Kossentini, F., & Sullivan, G. J. (2003). Rate-constrained coder control and comparison of video coding standards. *IEEE Transactions on Circuits and Systems for Video Technology, 13*(7), 688–703. doi:10.1109/TCSVT.2003.815168

Wiegand, T., Sullivan, G., Reichel, J., Schwarz, H., & Wien, M. (2007). Joint Draft ITU-T Rec. H.264 | ISO/IEC 14496-10/Amd.3 Scalable video coding. *JVT_X201, Output document of the 24th JVT* meeting.

Wien, M., Cazoulat, R., Graffunder, A., Hutter, A., & Amon, P. (2007). Real-Time System for Adaptive Video Streaming Based on SVC. *IEEE Transactions on Circuits and Systems for Video Technology, 17*(9), 1227–1237. doi:10.1109/TCSVT.2007.905519

Wing, D. (2007). *Request For Comments (RFC) RFC 4961 - Symmetric RTP / RTP Control Protocol*. RTCP.

Wu, D., Hou, Y. T., Zhu, W., & Zhang, Y.-Q. (2001). Streaming video over the Internet: approaches and directions. *IEEE Transactions on Circuits and Systems for Video Technology, 11*(3), 282–300. doi:10.1109/76.911156

Wu, F., Li, S., & Zhang, Y.-Q. (2001). A framework for efficient progressive fine granularity scalable video coding. *IEEE Transactions on Circuits and Systems for Video Technology, 11*(3), 332–344. doi:10.1109/76.911159

Wu, D., & Negi, R. (2003). Effective capacity: A wireless link model for support of Quality of Service. *IEEE Transactions on Wireless Communications, 2*(4), 630–643.

Wu, H., Qiao, C., De, S., & Tonguz, O. (2001). Integrated cellular and ad hoc relaying service: iCAR. *IEEE Journal on Selected Areas in Communications, 19*(10), 2105–2113. doi:10.1109/49.957326

Wu, H. R., Fujimoto, R. M., & Riley, G. (2004, September). Analytical models for information propagation in vehicle-to-vehicle networks. *Vehicular Technology Conference*, (pp. 4548-4552).

Wu, X., Cho, J., d'Auriol, B., & Lee, S. (2007). Energy-aware routing for wireless sensor networks by AHP. In *Proceedings of IFIP Workshop on Software Technologies for Future Embedded & Ubiquitous Systems, Greece*, 446-455.

Xiang, W., Zhu, C., Xu, Y., Siew, C. K., & Liu, M. (2009). Forward error correction-based 2-D layered multiple description coding for error-resilient H.264 SVC video transmission. *IEEE Transactions on Circuits and Systems for Video Technology, 19*(12), 1730–1738. doi:10.1109/TCSVT.2009.2022787

Xiao, X., & Ni, M. L. (1999). Internet QoS: A Big Picture. *IEEE Network, 13*(2), 8–18. doi:10.1109/65.768484

Xiaogang, Y., & Lei, L. (2007). End-to-End Congestion Control for H.264/SVC. In *Proc. 6th International Conference on Networking (ICN'07)*, (pp. 84-89). Sainte-Luce, Martinique.

Xiaoyuan, G., Dick, M., Noyer, U., & Wolf, L. (2004, June). NMP – A new networked music performance system. In *Proceedings of the 4th NIME Conference*.

Xie, S., Li, B., Keung, G. Y., & Zhang, X. (2007, December). Coolstreaming: Design, Theory and Practice. *IEEE Transactions on Multimedia, 9*(8), 1661–1671. doi:10.1109/TMM.2007.907469

Xie, F., Hua, K. A., Wang, W., & Ho, Y. H. (2007, October). Performance study of live video streaming over highway vehicular ad hoc networks. *Vehicular Technology Conference*, (pp. 2121-2125).

Xie, H., Yang, Y. R., & Krishnamurthy, A. Liu, Y., & Silberschatz, A. (2008, October). P4P: provider portal for applications. In *Proceedings of the 8th ACM SIGCOMM Conference on Internet Measurement*, Vouliagmeni, Greece.

Xiong, L., & Liu, L. (2004). PeerTrust: Supporting Reputation-Based Trust for Peer-to-Peer Electronic Communities. *IEEE Transactions on Knowledge and Data Engineering, 16*(7), 843–857. doi:10.1109/TKDE.2004.1318566

Yamamoto, N., Ogata, J., & Ariki, Y. (2003) Topic segmentation and retrieval system for lecture videos based on spontaneous speech recognition, *European Conference on Speech Communication and Technology*. pp. 961–964

Yang, M., & Yang, Y. (2008, June). Peer-to-peer file sharing based on network coding. In *Distributed computing systems, 2008. icdcs '08. the 28th international conference on* (pp. 168–175). Beijing, China: IEEE Computer Society.

Yang, M., Zhang, Z., Li, X., & Dai, Y. (2005) "An Empirical Study of Free-Riding Behavior in the Maze P2P File-Sharing System. In *Proceedings of International Workshop on Peer-to-Peer Systems*, Ithaca, NY.

Yang, S. Jin, H., Li, B., Liao, X., Yao, H., & Tu, X. (2008). The content pollution in peer-to-peer live streaming systems: analysis and implications. In *Proceedings of the 37th International Conference on Parallel Processing*, pp. 652-659.

Yau, D. K. Y., & Lam, S. S. (1997). Adaptive rate-controlled scheduling for multimedia applications. *IEEE/ACM Transactions on Networking, 5*(4), 475-488.

Yokoi and Fujiyoshi. (2006) Generating a Time Shrunk Lecture Video by Event Detection. *2006 IEEE International Conference on Multimedia and Expo*, pp. 641–644

Yoshida, T., Tada, K., & Hangai, S. (2003). A keyword accessible lecture video player and its evaluation. *Proceedings of the International Conference on Information Technology: Research and Education, ITRE2003*, 610–614.

Yu, H., Zheng, D., Zhao, B. Y., & Zheng, W. (2006, October). Understanding user behavior in large-scale video-on-demand systems. *SIGOPS Oper. Syst. Rev., 40*(4), 333–344. doi:10.1145/1218063.1217968

Yu, F., Lee, E., Choi, Y., Park, S., Lee, D., & Tian, Y. (2007). A modeling for hole problem in wireless sensor networks. In *Proceedings of the International Wireless Communications and Mobile Computing Conference, USA*, 370-375.

Yu, M., Ye, X., Jiang, G., Wang, R., Xiao, F., & Kim, Y. (2005). New multiple description layered coding method for video communication, *Proc. 6th International Conference on Parallel and Distributed Computing, Applications and Technologies (PDCAT'05)*, Dalian, China, pp. 694-697.

Yu, Y., Govindan, R., & Estrin, D. (2001, May). *Geographical and energy aware routing: a recursive data dissemination protocol for wireless sensor networks.* Unpublished UCLA Computer Science Department Technical Report UCLA/CSD-TR-01-0023, UCLA, CA.

Zeng, X., Bagrodia, R., & Gerla, M. (1998, May). GloMoSim: A library for parallel simulation of large-scale wireless networks. 12th *Workshop on Parallel and Distributed Simulations*, (pp. 154-161).

Zhang, Q., Zhu, W., & Zhang, Y. (2005). End-to-end QoS for video delivery over wireless Internet. *Proceedings of the IEEE*, *93*(1), 123–134. doi:10.1109/JPROC.2004.839603

Zhang, D., Zhu, L., Briggs, L. O., & Nunamaker, J. F. Jr. (2006). Instructional video in e-learning: Assessing the impact of interactive video on learning effectiveness. *Information & Management*, (43): 15–27. doi:10.1016/j.im.2005.01.004

Zhang D. & Nunamaker, J.F.Jr. (2004) A natural language approach to content-based video indexing and retrieval for interactive e-learning. *IEEE Transactions on Multimedia (6)* n.3 450 - 458

Zhang, L., Hauswirth, M., Shu, L., Zhou, Z., Reynolds, V., & Han, G. (2008, June). *Multi-priority Multi-Path Selection for Video Streaming in Wireless Multimedia Sensor Networks.* Paper presented at the fifth International conference on Ubiquitous Intelligence and Computing, Oslo, Norway.

Zhang, M., Zhang, Q., Sun, L., & Yang, S. (2007). Understanding the power of pull-based streaming protocol: Can we do better? *IEEE JSAC, special issue on advances in peer-to-peer streaming systems.*

Zhang, Q., Xue, H.-F., & Kou, X.-D. (2007). An Evolutionary Game Model of Resources-sharing Mechanism in P2P Networks. *Proceedings*In *Proceedings of the Workshop on Intelligent Information Technology Application*, Zhang Jiajie, China.

Zhang, X., Liu, J., Li, B., & Yum, T. S. P. (2005). CoolStreaming/DONet: A data-driven overlay network for efficient live media streaming. In *Proceedings of IEEE Conference on Computer Communications*, Miami, FL.

Zhao, A., Wang, W., Chi, H., & Tang, K. (2007). Efficient multiple description scalable video coding scheme based on weighted signal combinations. *Journal of Tsinghua Science and Technology*, *12*(1), 86–90. doi:10.1016/S1007-0214(07)70013-5

Zhao, Y., Chen, Y., Li, B., & Zhang, Q. (2007). Hop ID: A Virtual Coordinate-Based Routing for Sparse Mobile Ad Hoc Networks. *IEEE Transactions on Mobile Computing*, *6*(9), 1075–1089. doi:10.1109/TMC.2007.1042

Zhao, B. Y., Huang, L., Stribling, J., Rhea, S. C., Joseph, A. D., & Kubiatowicz, J. D. (2004). Tapestry: A resilient global scale overlay for service deployment. *IEEE Journal on Selected Areas in Communications*, *22*(1), 41–53. doi:10.1109/JSAC.2003.818784

Zhao, B. Q., Lui, J. C. S., & Chiu, D. M. (2008). Mathematical modeling of incentive policies in P2P systems. In *Proceedings of NetEcon.*

Zheng, R., Zhuang, W., & Jiang, H. (2005). Scalable multiple description coding and distributed video streaming in 3G mobile communications. *Wireless Communications and Mobile Computing*, *5*, 95–111. doi:10.1002/wcm.279

Zhou, Y. P., Chiu, D. M., & Lui, J. C. S. (2007). A simple model for analysis and design of P2P streaming protocols. In *Proceedings of the IEEE ICNP Conference.*

Zhuang, S. Q. Zhao, B. Y., & Joseph, A. D. (2001). Bayeux: An architecture for scalable and fault-tolerant wide-area data dissemination. In *Proceedings of International Workshop on Network and Operating System Support for Digital Audio and Video*, New York.

Zupancic, B., & Horz, H. 2002. Lecture recording and its use in a traditional university course. *Proc. of the 7th Annual Conf. on Innovation and Technology in Computer Science Education ITiCSE '02*. pp.24-28

About the Contributors

Ce Zhu received the BS degree from Sichuan University, Chengdu, China, and the M.Eng and PhD degrees from Southeast University, Nanjing, China, in 1989, 1992, and 1994, respectively, all in electronic and information engineering. He is currently an Associate Professor at the School of Electrical & Electronic Engineering, Nanyang Technological University, Singapore. His research interests include image/video coding, streaming and processing, joint source-channel coding, 3D video, multimedia systems and applications. He has authored or co-authored over 80 papers and holds two granted patents. Dr. Zhu currently serves as an Associate Editor of *IEEE Transactions on Broadcasting* and *IEEE Signal Processing Letters*. He has served on technical/program committees, organizing committees and as track/session chairs for over 40 international conferences.

Yuenan Li received the B.Eng. degree and M.Eng. degree in Automatic Test and Control, and the PhD degree in Information and Communication Engineering, all from Harbin Institute of Technology (HIT), P. R. China, in 2004, 2006 and 2010, respectively. He is currently a lecturer at the School of Electronic and Information Engineering, Tianjin University, P. R. China. His research interests include video indexing and retrieval, multimedia signal processing, and multimedia security.

Xiamu Niu received the B.Eng. degree and M.Eng. degree in Communication and Electronic Engineering, the PhD degree in Instrument Science and Technology, all from Harbin Institute of Technology (HIT), P. R. China, in 1982, 1989 and 2000, respectively. From 2000 to 2002, he was an invited scientist and staff member in Department of Security Technology for Graphics and Communication System, Fruanhofer Institute for Computer Graphics, Germany. He was awarded the Excellent PhD Dissertation of China in 2002. He is currently a Professor at the School of Computer Science, HIT. He is also the head of the Information Countermeasure Institute (ICT) at HIT. He had served as the executive chair of IIHMSP08 and the organizing chair of CIS07.

* * *

Sasan Adibi is currently a Technical Staff Member of Advanced Research at Research in Motion (RIM). He is also expected to graduate from University of Waterloo in 2010 with a PhD degree from Electrical and Computer Engineering Department. He has an extensive research background mostly in the areas of wireless Quality of Service (QoS) and security, including; Wi-Fi (IEEE 802.11 a/b/g/n), Cellular (HSPA and LTE), and applications in eHealth (Electronic Health Systems). He is the first author of +25 journal/conference/book chapter/white paper publications. He has also worked in other high-tech companies, including Nortel Networks and Siemens Canada.

Copyright © 2011, IGI Global. Copying or distributing in print or electronic forms without written permission of IGI Global is prohibited.

Muhammad Altaf received his BSc degree from the University of Engineering and Technology, Peshawar, Pakistan in 2001 and his MSc degree in computer system engineering from the National University of Science and Technology, Rawalpindi, Pakistan in 2004. He is currently working towards his PhD at the University of Essex, UK. His research interests are video compression and video streaming over wired and wireless networks.

Riccardo Bernardini was born in Genova (Italy) in 1964. He received the "Laurea in Ingegneria Elettronica" degree from the University of Padova in 1990. Since then he has been with the Dipartimento di Elettronica e Informatica of the University of Padova with a scholarship of the Consorzio Padova Ricerche, and, from November 1992 to November 1995, as a PhD student. He spent the last year of his PhD at formerly AT&T Bell Labs (Murray Hill). From April 1996 to April 1997 he was in EPFL (Lausanne) as a Postdoctoral Fellow. Now he is working as researcher in the Dipartimento di Ingegneria Elettrica, Gestionale e Meccanica of the University of Unide. His main interests are in the area of multidimensional signal processing, wavelets, filter banks, video coding, coding for reliable transmission and streaming over peer-to-peer. He is reviewer for international scientific journals.

Alexander Carôt, Besides a practical training in programming and electrical engineering, Dr. Alexander Carôt has actively been playing bass and the NS-chapman-stick in several rock, pop and jazz ensembles. In 2004 he received a german engineering diploma within an interdisciplinary study program in order to combine the arts and technology. Motivated by the passion for remote music performances with musicians in different places, he completed his PhD in computer science in 2004 at the University of Lübeck/Germany. In this context he developed the "Soundjack" software (http://www.soundjack.eu) which has been used in numerous network music performances all over the world. Apart from valuable collaborations with CCRMA/Stanford, SARC/Belfast and IRCAM/Paris he is continuously improving "Soundjack" in terms of signal latency, quality and user friendliness. Currently he´s playing in an avant-garde-jazz project "Triologue" (http:/www.triologue.de), and in his recent research activities he´s focusing on novel delay-optimized transmission approaches for network music performances.

Yoong-Choon Chang obtained his B.Eng. (First Class Honours) degree in Electrical & Electronic Engineering from University of Northumbria at Newcastle (Northumbria University), UK, the M.Eng. Sc and the PhD (Engineering) degrees from Multimedia University, Malaysia. He is currently a Senior Lecturer in the Faculty of Engineering, Multimedia University in which he is the program coordinator for B.Eng. (Hons) Electronics majoring in Multimedia program. He has been teaching multimedia engineering subjects at Multimedia University since 2003. Besides academic teaching, he is an active researcher where he is currently the project director of digital home project funded by Malaysian Communications and Multimedia Commission. He is currently supervising six postgraduate research students in the area of multimedia communications. His main research interests are multimedia communications and video compression.

Zhen Zhong Chen received the B.Eng. degree from Huazhong University of Science and Technology (HUST) and the PhD degree from Chinese University of Hong Kong (CUHK), both in electrical engineering. His current research interests include visual signal processing and compression, visual perception, and multimedia communications. He is currently a Lee Kuan Yew research fellow at Nanyang Technological University (NTU), Singapore. Before joining NTU, he was an ERCIM fellow at National

Institute for Research in Computer Science and Control (INRIA), France. He held visiting positions at Universite Catholique de Louvain (UCL), Belgium, and Microsoft Research Asia, Beijing. He received CUHK Faculty Outstanding PhD Thesis Award, Microsoft Fellowship, and ERCIM Alain Bensoussan Fellowship. He serves as voting member of IEEE Multimedia Communications Technical Committee, technical program committee member of IEEE Global Communications Conference (GLOBECOM), and IEEE Consumer Communications and Networking Conference (CCNC). He is a member of IEEE and SPIE.

Yongjin Cho received the BS degree in electronic engineering from Yonsei University, Seoul, Korea in 2001, and MS degree in computer science from University of Southern California, Los Angeles, USA in 2003. He is currently a PhD candidate in electrical engineering at USC. His research interests include the analysis and modeling of digital image/video characteristics, rate and distortion optimal multimedia data compression and efficient communication of multimedia data.

Seong-Ping Chuah received the B.Eng from Universiti Teknologi Malaysia, Malaysia and MS from National Taiwan University, Taiwan, R.O.C. in 2003 and 2007 respectively, both in electrical engineering. He was with Intel Penang Design Center, Malaysia in 2004. He joined the School of Electrical and Electronic Engineering, Nanyang Tech. Univ., Singapore as a Research Associate in 2008. He is currently working toward the PhD degree in the same university. His research interest includes wireless communication, multimedia networking and video signal processing.

Michael Eberhard received his MSc (Dipl.-Ing.) degree from Klagenfurt University in March 2008. In his master thesis, he evaluated approaches to perform adaptation of scalable bitstreams in streaming environments utilizing the MPEG-21 multimedia framework. In January 2008 he started to work as a research assistant in the Multimedia Communications group of the Institute of Information Technology (ITEC) at Klagenfurt University in the scope of the P2P-Next project. Since 2008 he has published several papers on multimedia adaptation in streaming environments and Peer-to-Peer systems. The current focus of his work is the integration of adaptation mechanism for scalable bitstreams into Peer-to-Peer systems.

Roberto Cesco Fabbro obtained the laurea degree in Electronic Engineering in 2008 from the University of Udine, Udine, Italy. He is currently a PhD candidate at the Electrical, Mechanical and Management Department of the University of Udine. His research interests include peer-to-peer live video transmissions.

Martin Fleury has a degree in Modern History (Oxford University, UK) and a Maths/Physics based degree from the Open University, Milton Keynes, UK. He obtained an MSc in Astrophysics from QMW College, University of London, UK in 1990 and an MSc from the University of South-West England, Bristol in Parallel Computing Systems in 1991. He holds a PhD in Parallel Image Processing Systems from the University of Essex, Colchester, UK. He is currently employed as a Senior Lecturer at the University of Essex and is Director of Graduate Research. Martin has authored over one hundred and fifty articles and a book on high-performance computing for low-level image- and signal-processing algorithms (including document and image compression algorithms), performance prediction of parallel systems, software engineering, and vision systems. His current research interests are video communication over MANS, WLANs, PANs, BANs, MANETs, and VANETs.

Mohammed Ghanbari is best known for his pioneering work on two-layer video coding for ATM networks (which earned him an IEEE Fellowship in 2001), now known as SNR scalability in the standard video codecs. He has served as an Associate Editor for IEEE Trans. on Multimedia. He has registered for eleven international patents on various aspects of video networking and was the co-recipient of A.H. Reeves prize for the best paper published in the 1995 Proc. of IEE on the theme of digital coding. He is the co-author of "Principles of Performance Engineering", a book published by IET press in 1997, the author of "Video Coding: An Introduction to Standard Codecs", a book also published by IET press in 1999, which received the year 2000 best book award by the IET, and the author of "Standard Codecs: Image Compression to Advanced Video Coding" also published by the IET press in 2003. Prof. Ghanbari has authored or co-authored about 450 journal and conference papers, many of which have had a fundamental influence in this field.

Song Guo is a PhD Candidate in the Department of Electrical and Computer Engineering at Boston University. He received BS degree from University of Electronic Science and Technology of China and his MS degree from Boston University in 2005 and 2007 respectively. His research interests include efficient wireless sensor network reprogramming design and efficient network routing protocol design. He is currently working with Professor Little to conduct research in the field of mathematical modeling of data sending interference and data path throughput estimation over the wireless video sensor networks with the intention of proposing an innovative video streaming routing protocol for wireless sensor network which would be optimized in energy consumption and quality of service.

Hermann Hellwagner received the MSc (Dipl.-Ing.) and PhD (Dr. techn.) degrees in Informatics from the University of Linz, Austria, in 1983 and 1988, respectively. He has been a full professor of Informatics in the Institute of Information Technology (ITEC), Klagenfurt University, Austria, for eleven years, leading the Multimedia Communications group. His current research areas are distributed multimedia systems, multimedia communications, and quality of service. He has received many research grants from national (Austria, Germany) and European funding agencies as well as from industry. Dr. Hellwagner is the editor of several books and has published more than 100 scientific papers on parallel computer architecture, parallel programming, and multimedia communications and adaptation. He has organized several international conferences and workshops. He is a member of the IEEE, ACM, GI (German Informatics Society) and OCG (Austrian Computer Society), and a member of the Scientific Board of the Austrian Science Fund (FWF).

Dimitris N. Kanellopoulos holds a PhD in multimedia communications from the Department of Electrical and Computer Engineering of the University of Patras, Greece. He is a member of the Educational Software Development Laboratory (ESDLab) in the Department of Mathematics at the University of Patras. His research interests include multimedia communications, intelligent information systems, knowledge representation and web-based education. He has authored many papers in international journals and conferences at these areas. He serves as an Editor in ten scientific journals.

Ingo Kofler studied Computer Science at Klagenfurt University and received his M.Sc. (Dipl.-Ing.) degree in 2006. In his master thesis he investigated the use of binary encoded metadata for adaptation decision-taking. From 2006 to 2008 he was involved in two EC-funded research projects (DANAE, ENTHRONE II) in the context of multimedia streaming and metadata. Since 2008 he holds the position of a research and teaching assistant in the Multimedia Communications group of the Institute of Information Technology (ITEC) at Klagenfurt University. His research interests cover multimedia streaming and adaptation with a focus on scalable video coding and wireless networks.

C.-C. Jay Kuo received the PhD degrees from the Massachusetts Institute of Technology, Cambridge, in 1987. He is presently Director of the Signal and Image Processing Institute (SIPI) and Professor of Electrical Engineering and Computer Science at the University of Southern California (USC). His research interests are in the areas of digital image/video analysis and modeling, multimedia data compression, communication and networking, and biological signal/image processing. Dr. Kuo has guided about 100 students to their Ph.D. degrees and supervised 20 postdoctoral research fellows. Currently, his research group at USC has around 30 Ph.D. students (please visit website http://viola.usc.edu), which is one of the largest academic research groups in multimedia technologies. He is co-author of about 170 journal papers, 800 conference papers and 10 books. Dr. Kuo is a Fellow of IEEE and SPIE. He is Editor-in-Chief for the *Journal of Visual Communication and Image Representation* (an Elsevier journal).

Robert Kuschnig received his MSc (Dipl.-Ing.) degree from Klagenfurt University in 2006 for his master thesis on a lightweight configuration management platform for IT infrastructures. From 2000 to 2002 he was working as digital designer at Infineon along the way with his studies of Computer Science at Klagenfurt University. From 2006 to 2007 he worked as a software developer and architect for a web-based supply chain solution at appliLog. Since 2007 he is working towards the PhD degree as a research assistant in the Multimedia Communications group of the Institute of Information Technology (ITEC) at Klagenfurt University. His research interest is focused on congestion-aware adaptive streaming of scalable video, in particular H.264/SVC.

Maodong Li received the BSc degree in 2007 in Electronic and Information Science and Technology from University of Science and Technology of China, Hefei, China. He is currently working toward the Ph.D degree with the School of Electrical and Electronic Engineering, Nanyang Technological University, Singapore. His current research interests focus on resource allocation for video delivery over wireless broadband systems.

Zhen Li received the BS degree and M. S. degree in Measurement Technology and Instrumentation from Harbin University of Science and Technology, and Automatic Control and Test from Harbin Institute of Technology in China in 2004 and 2006, respectively. He spent 2 years as a post-master's research associate in Communication Technology in both Harbin Institute of Technology Shenzhen Graduate School and Sun Yat-sen University in China. From 2008, he is working toward a PhD degree in School of Electrical and Electronic Engineering, Nanyang Technological University, Singapore. He has published more than 20 international journal and conference papers including 3D model coding and content & context based image/video understanding and processing.

Thomas D.C. Little is a professor in the Department of Electrical and Computer Engineering at Boston University. He is Associate Chair for Graduate Studies for the department and is director of the Multimedia Communications Lab where he is involved in the development of enabling technologies and applications for networked and distributed systems. Dr. Little is Associate Director of the Smart Lighting Engineering Research Center—a collaboration of Rensselaer Polytechnic Institute, the University of New Mexico, and Boston University. His recent efforts include research in video sensor networks and streaming in wireless settings, ubiquitous optical networking with visible light, vehicle-to-vehicle/infrastructure (V2X) communications, and the application of wireless sensors in health monitoring. Dr. Little received his BS degree in biomedical engineering from RPI in 1983, and his MS degree in electrical engineering and PhD degree in computer engineering from Syracuse University in 1989 and 1991.

Minglei Liu received the B.Eng. degree and M.Eng. degree from Harbin Institute of Technology, Harbin, China, and the PhD degree from Nanyang Technological University, Singapore in 2001, 2003 and 2010, respectively. Dr. Liu is now a research associate at Nanyang Technological University, Singapore. His research interests include lossless image compression, lossless data embedding, multiple description image/video coding and multiple description quantization.

Kok-Keong (Jonathan) Loo received his MSc degree in Electronics (with Distinction) from University of Hertfordshire, UK in 1998 and the PhD degree in Electronics and Communications from the same university in 2003. Between August 2003 and May 2010, he was a Lecturer in Multimedia Communications at the School of Engineering and Design, Brunel University, UK. Currently, he is a Reader (Associate Professor) at the School of Engineering and Information Sciences, Middlesex University, UK. At Brunel, he was a Course Director for the MSc in Digital Signal Processing programme. He also involved in several research projects where he was a Principle Investigator for a joint research project between BBC and Brunel University on Dirac video codec research and development, and a co-investigator for several European funded projects namely IST FP6 PLUTO IST FP6 ENABLE, and recently the IST FP7 3D-Vivant. He is currently supervising 14 PhD candidates as a Director of Studies. His research interests are in the general area of multimedia communications include visual media processing, video coding and transmission, wireless communications, digital signal processing, embedded systems and wireless network, protocols and security. In the past 7 years, he published in total of 119 publications (book chapters, journals, conferences) in the aforementioned areas.

Fabien Mathieu is a researcher in the Traffic and Resource Allocation group at Orange Labs. He was a student at the École Normale Supérieure, rue d'Ulm from 1998 to 2002. He completed a PhD in Computer Science in 2004, on Web Graphs and PageRank-like measurements. He received the 2007 best paper award of the IEEE International Conference on Peer-to-Peer Computing. In 2009, he passed the Habilitation à Diriger des Recherches (official agreement for supervising PhD students) on the topic of P2P and acyclic preference-based systems. His current topics of interest are distributed content distribution, preference-based systems and green networking.

Nayef Mendahawi holds a MSc in Electrical and Computer Engineering (with specialization in wireless technology). He has over 14 years of experience as a Senior Technical Consultant, including over 6 years of R&D experience in various wireless technologies. He has an extensive research background in the areas of VoIP, WLAN-Cellular integration architecture for cellular operators, Quality of Service (QoS), IEEE 802.11 a/b/g/n, WiMAX handover, UMA and IPv6. He is currently working at Research In Motion (RIM) as R&D engineer in wireless technology. He is an author for patents (some pending) in the area of wireless technology and has different professional certifications.

Hyunggon Park received the BS degree in electronics and electrical engineering from Pohang University of Science and Technology (POSTECH), Pohang, Korea, in 2004 and the M.S. and PhD degrees in electrical engineering from the University of California, Los Angeles, in 2006 and 2008, respectively. In 2008, he was an Intern at the IBM T. J. Watson Research Center, Hawthorne, NY, and he was a senior researcher in the Signal Processing Laboratory (LTS4), Swiss Federal Institute of Technology, Lausanne, Switzerland in 2009-2010. Currently, he is a tenure-track Assistant Professor at the Ewha Womans University, Seoul, Korea. His research interests include game theoretic approaches for distributed resource management (resource reciprocation and resource allocation) strategies for multiuser systems and multiuser transmission over wireless/wired/peer-to-peer (P2P) networks. Dr. Park received the Graduate Study Abroad Scholarship from the Korea Science and Engineering Foundation during 2004–2006, and the Electrical Engineering Department Fellowship from the University of California, in 2008.

Diego Perino is a researcher in the "Networking and Networks" domain at Bell Labs, Alcatel-Lucent France. He received his PhD in Computer Science and Networking from the Paris Diderot-Paris 7 University in 2009. The Ph.D. thesis has been carried out at Orange Labs in collaboration with INRIA, and focus on algorithms for peer-to-peer multimedia streaming. He received his MS in Networking engineering from Politecnico di Torino and Eurecom Institute of Sophia Antipolis in 2006. He also obtained a Research Master in Networking and Distributed Systems from Université de Nice-Sophia Antipolis. He received his BS in Telecommunication engineering from Politecnico di Torino in 2004. His previous works are about content distribution networks, P2P and distributed systems, multimedia streaming and multi-path routing. His current main research interests are Content Centric Networking and Green Networking.

Beatrice Pesquet-Popescu received the engineering degree in telecommunications from the "Politehnica" Institute in Bucharest in 1995 (highest honours) and the PhD thesis from the Ecole Normale Supérieure de Cachan in 1998. In 1998 she was a Research and Teaching Assistant at Université Paris XI and in 1999 she joined Philips Research France, where she worked during two years as a research scientist, then project leader, in scalable video coding. Since Oct. 2000 she is with Ecole Nationale Supérieure des Télécommunications (Télécom ParisTech), first as an Associate Professor, and since 2007 as a Professor, Head of the Multimedia Group. Beatrice Pesquet-Popescu is an EURASIP Administrative Committee member, a member of the Administrative Committee of the French GRETSI Society and an IEEE Signal Processing Society MMSP and IMDSP Technical Committees member. She is also a member of the Conference Board Executive Subcommittee of the IEEE SPS and serves as an Associate Editor for IEEE Trans. on Multimedia and for Elsevier Signal Processing journals. Beatrice Pesquet-Popescu is a recipient of the "Best Student Paper Award" in the IEEE Signal Processing Workshop on Higher-Order Statistics in 1997, of the Bronze Inventor Medal from Philips Research and in 1998 she received a "Young Investigator Award" granted by the French Physical Society. She holds 23 patents in wavelet-based video coding and has authored more than 160 book chapters, journal and conference papers in the field. In 2006, she is the recipient, together with D. Turaga and M. van der Schaar, of the IEEE Trans. on Circuits and Systems for Video Technology "Best Paper Award". Her current research interests are in source coding, scalable and robust video compression and adaptive wavelets.

Fabio Pianese obtained his BS in 2003 from Politecnico di Torino (Turin, Italy) and his MS in 2004 from University of Nice - Sophia Antipolis (France), where he was also awarded his PhD degree for work on media streaming systems under the guidance of Prof. E. W. Biersack. He is currently employed by Alcatel-Lucent Bell Labs (Antwerp, Belgium) in the "Service Infrastructure" Research Department. His main research interests are large-scale content distribution, distributed algorithms, practical peer-to-peer systems and applications, and network security.

Nadia N. Qadri is currently a PhD student at School of Computer Science and Electronics Engineering, University of Essex, UK. She received her Masters of Engineering (Communication Systems and Networks) and Bachelors of Engineering (Computer Systems), from Mehran University of Engineering and Technology, Jamshoro, Pakistan in 2004 and 2002 respectively. She has more than four years of teaching and research experience at renowned universities of Pakistan viz. Mehran University of Engineering & Technology, Fatima Jinnah Womens University and COMSATS Institute of Information Technology. Her research interests include video streaming for mobile ad hoc networks and vehicular ad hoc networks, along with P2P streaming.

Michael Ransburg received his MSc (Dipl.-Ing.) degree from Klagenfurt University in 2003 for his master thesis on MPEG-21 Digital Item Adaptation and his Dr. techn. degree in 2008 for his PhD thesis on "Codec-agnostic Dynamic and Distributed Adaptation of Scalable Multimedia Content". He joined Klagenfurt University in 2004 to work as a research assistant in the Multimedia Communications group of the Institute of Information Technology (ITEC) in the scope of the DANAE EU project. Subsequently he continued his work in the scope of the ENTHRONE II EU project. Since 2008 he has been working at Klagenfurt University as a Postdoctoral Researcher where he coordinates the Celtic SCALNET and FFG SCALIPTV projects. He published 12 papers, 2 book chapters and participated in the work of ISO/MPEG as an editor of 4 international standards in the scope of MPEG-21 DIA and the ISO Base Media File Format.

Rafit Izhak Ratzin is a PhD candidate in the Computer Science department at the University of California, Los Angeles (UCLA). She received her MS degree in Computer Science from UCLA in 2005 and her M.S. degree in Electrical Engineering from Tel-Aviv University, Israel in 2003. Her research focuses on improving different aspects of network protocols using game theoretic methods. Her recent research deals with improving the BitTorrent protocol in particular.

Roberto Rinaldo obtained the "Laurea in Ingegneria Elettronica" degree in 1987 from the University of Padova, Padova, Italy. From 1990 to 1992, he was with the University of California at Berkeley, where he received the MS degree in 1992. He received the Doctorate degree in "Ingegneria Elettronica e dell'Informazione" from the University of Padova in 1992. In 1992 he joined the Dipartimento di Elettronica eInformatica of the University of Padova as a "ricercatore". Starting from November 1st 1998, he was associate professor in Communications and Signal Processing in the same Department. Since November 2001, he has been an associate professor in the "Dipartimento di Ingegneria Elettrica, Gestionale e Meccanica" of the University of Udine. Starting December 2003, he is now a professor in the same department. His interests are in the field of multidimensional signal processing, video signal coding, fractal theory and image coding.

Marco Ronchetti is associate professor in Computer Science at the Università di Trento, Italy. After some years spent in Physics dealing with computer simulation of liquid, amorphous and quasicrystalline many body systems, his interests drifted to Computer Science. He has been working in the web and software engineering areas, and in the most recent years on e-learning, videos and on extraction of semantic information from text. In these areas he has approximately 70 international publications. He has been coordinator of the EASTWEB EU project. Presently he is director of the Master in technologies for e-Government at the Università di Trento.

Michael Sablatschan studied Computer Science at Klagenfurt University and received his M.Sc. (Dipl.-Ing.) degree for his master thesis on end-to-end quality of service management in the context of the EC-founded research project ENTHRONE II. He initially joined the Multimedia Communications group of the Institute of Information Technology (ITEC) at Klagenfurt University as a student in 2007 when he started with his master thesis. Since September 2008 Michael Sablatschan has been employed as a research assistant at the ITEC where he works in the Celtic SCALNET and FFG SCALIPTV projects. His field of research is multimedia adaptation with the focus on H.264/SVC to H.264/AVC rewriting.

C. K. Siew obtained his B. Eng, MSc. and PhD from Univ. of Singapore, Imperial College, U.K. and NTU, Singapore, respectively. He joined School of Electrical and Electronic Engineering, NTU in 1986 as a lecturer and is currently an Associate Professor. From 1995 to 2005, he was the Head of Information Communication Institute of Singapore. Dr. Siew has published about 100 refereed papers that comprise more than 40 journal papers. He had served as technical program committee member in conferences such as ASIA SIGCOMM Workshop 2005, INFOCOM 2006 and BROADNETS 2006. He also served as member of National Infocomm Competency Centre Steering Committee, Singapore from year 2000 to 2001. His research interests span three areas: (1) Quality of Service Provisioning; (2) Congestion Control; and (3) Application of intelligent control to networking problems.

Yap-Peng Tan (M'97-SM'04) received the B.S. degree from National Taiwan University, Taipei, Taiwan, R.O.C., in 1993, and the M.A. and Ph.D. degrees from Princeton University, Princeton, NJ, in 1995 and 1997, respectively, all in electrical engineering. He was the recipient of an IBM Graduate Fellowship from IBM T. J. Watson Research Center, Yorktown Heights, NY, from 1995 to 1997 and was with Intel and Sharp Labs of America from 1997 to 1999. In November 1999, he joined the School of Electrical and Electronic Engineering, Nanyang Technological University, Singapore, where he is presently an Associate Professor and Head of the Division of Information Engineering. His current research interests include image and video processing, content-based multimedia analysis, computer vision, and pattern recognition. He is the principal inventor/co-inventor of 15 U.S. patents in the areas of image and video processing. Dr. Tan is a member of the IEEE Circuits and Systems Society's Technical Committee on Visual Signal Processing and Communications, an editorial board member of the EURASIP Journal on Advances in Signal Processing and EURASIP Journal on Image and Video Processing, and an associate editor of the Journal of Signal Processing Systems.

Nicolas Tizon received the engineering degree in telecommunications from the Ecole Nationale Supérieure des Télécommunications de Bretagne (Télécom Bretagne) in 2005. In 2003-2004 he completed an internship in Texas Instruments (Villeneuve-Loubet, France) where he worked on the emerging H.264/AVC video coding standard. He received a PhD degree in signal and image processing from

Ecole Nationale Supérieure des Télécommunications (Télécom ParisTech) in 2009. During four years (2006-2009) he has worked on "Scalable video coding for wireless transmission" in collaboration with the French mobile phone company SFR. His current research activity focuses on video compression optimizations for wireless transmissions and multimedia oriented applications.

Myo Tun received his B.Eng. degree in Electronics from Yangon Institute of Technology, Myanmar, the MEng. Degree in Telecommunication from Asian Institute of Technology (AIT), Thailand, in 1996 and the PhD degree from Brunel University, UK, in 2008. He is currently a video coding engineer at Dialogic Corporation in Montreal, Canada. He was research assistant working on Dirac video codec research and development at Brunel University in collaboration with BBC. Prior to that, he was as a laboratory supervisor and research associate in the field of wireless and multimedia communication at AIT from 2001 to 2005.

Mihaela van der Schaar is currently an Associate Professor in the Electrical Engineering Department at the University of California, Los Angeles. She received in 2004 the NSF Career Award, in 2005 the Best Paper Award from IEEE Transactions on Circuits and Systems for Video Technology, in 2006 the Okawa Foundation Award, in 2005, 2007 and 2008 the IBM Faculty Award, and in 2006 the Most Cited Paper Award from EURASIP: Image Communications journal. She was an associate editor for IEEE Transactions on Multimedia, Signal Processing Letters, Circuits and Systems for Video Technology, Signal Processing Magazine etc. She holds 33 granted US patents and three ISO awards for her contributions to the MPEG video compression and streaming international standardization activities. Her research interests are in multimedia communications, networking, processing and systems and, more recently, on learning and games in engineering systems. She is a Fellow of IEEE since 2010.

Maiyuran Wijayanathan is a Senior Systems Designer at Research In Motion (RIM), Waterloo, Canada. He works as part of the Blackberry radio protocol stack development team, where he is responsible for requirements definition, functional analysis, performance evaluation and standardization of wireless communication systems (GSM/(E)GPRS, WCDMA/HSPA, GAN and WLAN 802.11a/b/g/n). He has extensive experience within the wireless and semi-conductor industry, both with start-up and established organizations, with research and design experience in the areas of Cellular/WLAN radio protocols, IP Mobility and SoC (System-on-a-Chip) architectures for multi-mode wireless base-band chips. Maiyuran has been recognized with many prestigious awards during his academic and professional carrier, including the Governor General of Canada's award for highest academic standing. He holds an Electrical Engineering degree (with specialization in Communications) and has authored more than 25 patents (some pending) in the area of wireless communications.

Yuanyuan Xu received the B.Eng. degree in biomedical engineering and the M.Eng. degree in signal and information processing from Beijing Jiaotong University, Beijing, China, in 2005 and 2007, respectively. She is currently pursuing the PhD degree in information engineering at the School of Electrical and Electronic Engineering, Nanyang Technological University, Singapore. Her research interests include joint source network coding and multiple description coding.

Wei Xiang received the B.Eng. and M.Eng. degrees, both in electronic engineering, from the University of Electronic Science and Technology of China, Chengdu, China, in 1997 and 2000, respectively, and the PhD. degree in telecommunications engineering from the University of South Australia, Adelaide, Australia, in 2004. Since January 2004, he has been with the Faculty of Engineering and Surveying, University of Southern Queensland, Toowoomba, Australia, where he was first an Associate Lecturer in Computer Systems Engineering from 2004 to 2006, then a Lecturer from 2007 to 2008, and currently holds a faculty post of Senior Lecturer. From January to June 2008, he was a visiting scholar at the School of Electrical and Electronic Engineering, Nanyang Technological University, Singapore. He has also been a visiting scholar at Tianjin University and Beijing University of Posts and Telecommunications. His research interests are in the broad area of communications and information theory, particularly coding and signal processing for multimedia communications systems.

Index

Copyright © 2011, IGI Global. Copying or distributing in print or electronic forms without written permission of IGI Global is prohibited.